Understanding the Economy

Understanding the Economy

Mark Brownrigg
Napier Polytechnic of Edinburgh

 ADDISON-WESLEY PUBLISHING COMPANY

Wokingham, England · Reading, Massachusetts · Menlo Park, California
New York · Don Mills, Ontario · Amsterdam · Bonn
Sydney · Singapore · Tokyo · Madrid · San Juan

© 1990 Addison-Wesley Publishers Ltd.
© 1990 Addison-Wesley Publishing Company, Inc.

All rights reserved. No part of this publication may be reproduced, stored in a retrieval system, or transmitted in any form or by any means, electronic, mechanical, photocopying, recording or otherwise, without prior written permission of the publisher.

Many of the designations used by manufacturers and sellers to distinguish their products are claimed as trademarks. Addison-Wesley has made every attempt to supply trademark information about manufacturers and their products mentioned in this book.

Cover designed by Hybert Design and Type, Maidenhead
and printed by The Riverside Printing Co. (Reading) Ltd.
Text designed by Lesley Stewart.
Typeset by Columns, Reading.
Printed in Great Britain by Mackays of Chatham plc, Chatham, Kent.

First printed 1990.

British Library Cataloguing in Publication Data
Brownrigg, Mark
   Understanding the economy.
   1. Macroeconomics
   I. Title
   339

ISBN 0–201–41690–5

Library of Congress Cataloging in Publication Data
Brownrigg, Mark, date.
   Understanding the economy / Mark Brownrigg.
     p. cm.
   ISBN 0–201–41690–5
   1. Macroeconomics.   I. Title.
HB172.5.B77   1990
339—dc20   90–292
                                                                                                       CIP

To Pat, Mark, Jenny and Ben —
who probably feels that his name should come first...

Preface

There comes a time in an author's life, usually after saying 'absolutely no . . . under no circumstances', when it becomes important to write a text. It has always been my argument that introductory economics can be made more interesting and accessible if it is taught in a more interactive way, where theory is blended with and emerges from the practical issues and problems of the real world. Not only does this approach convince the student of the need for theory; it underlines theory's role in providing both the rigour and the depth of understanding which are essential if real-world policy is ever to rise above the level of the political slogan, or the most loudly shouted argument in a public brawl. At the same time, there is no reason why such a marvellous and powerful subject should not be taught with a little compassion and humour; we were all students once, and more than one lofty professor has struggled with and stumbled in the initial stages of his or her own apprenticeship.

Objectives

The over-riding objective of this textbook is to help you to build up your own understanding of how the economy works. Whether you are a formal student, or a person operating in the business world, it is essential that you should know what is happening in the economic environment within which you live and function. It is impossible to turn you into a professional economist from a single, introductory text. But we can work together with you to make sure that you can read and understand the professional commentators in the financial press, in specialist papers such as *The Economist*, or the *Financial Times*, or in the business pages of any reputable newspaper. After all, these will be your main sources of information on current events and will provide you with the data upon which you will judge the likely implications for your own activities, and the actions which you should take.

Audience

This does not mean that this text skimps on the normal syllabus of theory; it simply approaches the syllabus from a different direction. The book is designed for use in a wide variety of courses, at University, or Polytechnic, or broader technical college level. It covers the normal syllabus for introductory macroeconomics, and is suitable for use in any Business Studies or Business Economics course for undergraduate, or postgraduate, or post experience students.

Structure

It is also, quite deliberately, designed to be 'user friendly'. The author is not so old that he has forgotten his own feelings of isolation, and of dismayed incomprehension when he opened his first student book on the subject. To try to minimize these, the text is designed as a loose partnership between author and student: you will not be treated as Superman, or Wonderwoman in terms of your ability to absorb technical material but, rather, will be helped sympathetically to master the different building blocks of the subject. There will be a lot of cross references between the various building blocks, with plenty of time taken to remind you of essential elements from earlier material. Extensive use will be made of current newspaper and journal material on the topic, both to supplement and extend the coverage of the text. Each chapter is structured to provide systematic stages in your learning path, and finishes with a series of Self-Assessment Questions against which you can check your grasp of the material.

Acknowledgements

In writing this book, I am indebted to a small but important group of contacts. My thanks must go to my original commissioning editor, Allison King, late of Addison-Wesley, my publishers: her advice and encouragement, together with her belief that there was a need for a textbook of this type, helped me immeasurably in the early stages of planning and writing the text; she has also played an important part in keeping my writing output on course with a well-judged blend of timely praise and ruthless nagging! Her successor, Maggie Pickering, has proved herself to be equally adept in both arts. Professor Neil Kay, from my previous Department of Economics in the University of Strathclyde, has had an equally vital influence: not only did he share my enthusiasm for the concept of a problem-orientated text; his unselfish support and willingness to discuss his own ideas on extract/text interaction provided a vital boost at a late and critical stage of the book. His reassurance and co-operation saved Glasgow from the environmental pollution problem of a rather large bonfire. Come on, Neil, there has to be a sequel, if only 'The Economy Strikes Back' . . . . To Dr Mike Greig, of Strathclyde Regional Council, I am indebted for (yet another) tutorial on international trade and its more advanced ramifications; I am convinced that the number of these tutorials over the years is due more to his incompetence as a tutor than to mine as a student, but he may well dispute this balanced view.

Last but not least I owe a great debt to Irene Love and Morag Pryce, my Departmental Secretaries at the University during the writing of the text, for the times without number when they rescued me from the defeats and humiliations inflicted upon me by the superior intelligence of my indispensable (but malignant) wordprocessor. I hope that the final result justifies the hours of university time which we spent trying to tame the brute. What are they going to do with their spare time, now that I'm finished?

It has been my choice to approach introductory macroeconomics in this manner; any errors which remain in content or approach are my responsibility and no one else's.

Mark Brownrigg

May 1990

Contents

Preface		vii
1	**Introduction**	1
2	**Economic Activity and the National Accounts**	5
	Introduction	5
	The measurement of economic activity	8
	The national accounts	17
	What do the measures really cover?	25
	Conclusions	29
	Self-assessment questions	30
	Exercises	32
3	**Development of the Basic Macroeconomic Model**	34
	Introduction	34
	The first stage in model building	36
	The equilibrium level of income	41
	Building international trade into the model	45
	Building the government sector into the model	48
	Equilibrium income and changes	51
	Testing the model	52
	Macroeconomic forecasting	54
	Conclusions	65
	Self-assessment questions	66
	Exercise	68
4	**Consumption**	69
	Introduction	69
	The national accounts data on consumption spending	71
	Consumption and income	76
	Consumption and savings	82
	Factors affecting the position of the consumption function	85

Consumption and which year's income . . .?	93
The consumption function and the multiplier	95
Conclusions	101
Self-assessment questions	102

5 Investment Expenditure 104

Introduction	104
Investment in the national accounts	107
A theory for investment behaviour	115
Investment appraisal	119
Other influences on investment behaviour	127
A final reminder	131
Conclusions	133
Appendix 5A: The discounting technique	134
Appendix 5B: The acceleration principle	138
Self-assessment questions	140
Exercise	141

6 Long-term Growth and Short-term Cycles 142

Introduction	142
The measurement of economic growth	146
The UK business cycle	149
The business cycle from 1970 to date	152
Causes of the business cycle	156
Comparison of economic growth rates	165
A theory of economic growth	170
Conclusions	181
Self-assessment questions	182

7 Fiscal Policy 185

Introduction	185
The national accounts data on expenditure and taxation	187
Fiscal policy: the Keynesian context	201
The basic fiscal model	204
The fiscal multipliers	209
Fiscal policy: the lessons of experience	216
Conclusions	228
Self-assessment questions	231

8 Money and Monetary Policy 233

Introduction	233
The nature of money	237
The demand for money	241

	The supply of money	246
	The banking sector and money creation	255
	Monetary policy	263
	Problem areas in monetary policy	276
	The rate of interest	280
	Conclusions	282
	Self-assessment questions	285

9 Inflation — 287

Introduction — 287
The measurement of inflation — 289
The need for policy correction — 296
The Keynesian view of inflation — 300
The role of expectations — 311
The Keynesian view of the role of money in inflation — 323
The monetarist view of inflation — 325
The monetarists' cure for inflation — 332
Conclusions — 337
Appendix 9A: Monetarism and the quantity theory — 339
Self-assessment questions — 340

10 Supply-side Economics — 343

Introduction — 343
The root of the problem — 347
The enhancement of competition — 352
The role for tax cuts — 357
Supply-side theory: a broad assessment — 360
Conclusions — 371
Self-assessment questions — 374

11 International Trade and the Balance of Payments — 376

Introduction — 376
The rationale for trade — 380
The UK trade flows — 383
The balance of payments — 392
The exchange rate — 401
'To be (a member of the EMS) or not to be . . .?' — 410
Some complications of the open economy — 417
Conclusions — 424
Self-assessment question — 427

Solutions — 437

Index — 453

Chapter 1

Introduction

You may have been told that economics is a difficult, abstract subject which has little to say about the real world in which we live. You may have picked up a textbook on the subject, and winced at the profusion of diagrams and equations which littered its pages. Indeed, you may only be taking the subject because there is no option which would let you avoid it. As such you must be facing the prospect with grim pessimism – hair shirts may well be character-building, but they don't half itch. . . .

If so, then you can relax a little – there is no reason at all why it should be as bad as you fear.

Few subjects are as relevant to everyday living as economics. Every individual person and business operates within an economic environment and is subject to the constantly changing influences of this environment. For example, we all spend money on food, clothing, holidays, even on textbooks. How much can we plan to spend at any moment in time? Are our consumption plans determined by our current, or our past income? Can we increase our level of consumption if we borrow against our anticipated future income? What is likely to happen to our income if there is a recession? Do we think systematically when we balance consumption against a number of years' income, or do we borrow first and worry second? How are we influenced by interest rates, as represented by the cost of credit? What do we spend our money on? How do we react to cuts – or increases – in our personal taxation burden? Do we consume more of our income than people in other countries; if so, does it matter? We are all consumers: consciously or subconsciously, we must all deal with these questions.

What happens if we spend our income increasingly on imported goods and services, on Spanish holidays, or German cars, or Japanese stereo systems? Will this affect employment levels and prosperity at home? Should we block off all international trade flows, to isolate ourselves from any unfair competition from other, lower-cost countries? How can we export more? What is the part played by the UK exchange rate – and has the discovery of the oil reserves in the North Sea been a blessing, or a curse? What do we mean when we talk about flows of international capital? Do they matter? How worried should we be if some ownership of UK business share capital passes to Arab, or German, or Japanese, or American hands? What is the European Monetary System and why is there such an argument over whether or not the UK should become a full member of the EMS? How would membership affect us, as consumers, or producers, or employees? We are all employed, or seeking some form of employment; perhaps we should know something about these matters . . . for every question above carries some implications for our present and our future prospects.

What causes the prices of goods and services to rise from year to year? Should wages be allowed to increase to protect peoples' standard of living when this happens? Why has the UK government taken such an obsessive stand against inflation – and has still been unable to prevent the rate of inflation rising over 1988 and 1989? Does it really matter – after all the UK's 8% or 9% inflation rate is as nothing compared to 40%, or 70% or even 100% (and greater) rates of inflation which are regularly experienced in some countries. We all pay prices for our purchases, and we all grumble when our money buys less, or when credit charges rise. And, if we wind up unemployed because of the government's anti-inflation policy, then we are likely to doubt that the benefits which others might gain will outweigh the costs which we must bear. Once again, we are all involved, either directly or morally. Maybe we should know a little more about the process of inflation and the problems and dilemmas posed by the search for its cure.

What do we mean when we talk about economic growth? Why is it important? How does it affect us as businesses and individuals? How do we measure it? How do we separate it from the effects of the business cycle? What are the consequences if we have a low rate of growth in the UK? How justified are the claims that we have enjoyed an unprecedented surge of growth since 1981/2? How much of the current prosperity, and of the fall in the still historically high (despite statistical revisions) level of unemployment is due to this growth? How much more growth do we need or, if we accept the arguments of some environmentalists, should we be trying to reduce growth and its resource depletion and pollution consequences? Whether your concern reflects a preoccupation with your own career prospects as a student, or whether it reflects your concern with our beleaguered environment, shouldn't you know a little more about growth?

These are only a selection of some of the macroeconomic issues which are explored in this text. From this small sample, does economics still seem to be abstract and unrealistic?

Given that the subject is relevant, the next problem is how to take the boredom – or even the terror – out of the textbook's presentation. It *is* possible to present the subject in a way in which you can grasp its essential message, even if you are not particularly mathematical. The best way to deal with boredom is to replace it with interest. The best way to deal with terror is to replace it with understanding.

Too many conventional textbooks focus on the *principles* of economics; in other words, their preoccupation is with the theoretical aspects of the subject. In effect they say: 'these are the technicalities of the relationships under analysis and this is how they operate collectively'. The elements of theory are defined and explained, then gradually built together into a coherent system. Some of the more sympathetic modern texts will then search for real-world case studies to which this theory can be applied; to others, the challenge of the theory is enough in itself. To all intents and purposes, you are treated as an apprentice concert pianist: first there is the drudgery of mechanical practice on scales, arpeggios, and other instruments of torture needed to develop manual dexterity; next there is the grind through the theory of music and composition, to enable you to read the output and to judge the intentions of the composer. Only after total mastery has been achieved over all aspects will you be turned loose on an unsuspecting public.

But what if you do not want to become a virtuoso performer? What if the height of your ambition is to lead a sing-song in your village pub? Or, equally, what if it is not your immediate intention to become a professional economist, but simply to gain a better understanding of the workings of the economy? Is the traditional textbook the appropriate means of education?

You will find that this text starts from the opposite end of the spectrum to most other books on economics. Its treatment is problem orientated, in the sense that it focuses on the real-world problems and decisions of the UK and other international economies. The theory which is used has been selected because it is appropriate for the analysis and the understanding of these real-world issues. One of the key elements in the textbook is its use of extracts, taken from professional economists' comments on current and emergent problems in a number of countries. These extracts serve two purposes: they not only underline the content and relevance of the topic under consideration; they also provide you with the chance to apply the theory insights gained from the text to these commentaries. The textook theory and the extracts are designed to interact to help you to build up a greater understanding of the subject.

Make no mistake; there is plenty economic theory in this textbook, and some of it will be difficult to grasp at first. But, once you know why you are looking for a theory, once you can appreciate the insight and the understanding which it can give you of complex real-world issues, then it is far more likely that you will make the commitment needed to master the technique, and have the determination to use it. Too few of the other texts take time to explain *why* you need the theory. Like some foul-tasting medicine of childhood, you are expected to accept that 'it is good for you' and get on with it.

Learning is never painless – but there is no reason why it should not also be exciting and enjoyable. If this text, despite its best efforts, is still a hair shirt then it is designed to tickle and stimulate, rather than to scratch and annoy.

Why not read a little more, to find out if it works for you?

Chapter 2

Economic Activity and the National Accounts

> Introduction
>
> The measurement of economic activity
>
> The national accounts
>
> What do the measures really cover?
>
> Conclusions
>
> Self-assessment questions
>
> Exercises

INTRODUCTION

Macroeconomics is concerned with the measurement and the analysis of **economic activity**. What does this term mean? How does it affect us? How should it be measured? What factors influence whether the level of economic activity will rise or decline over time? Can we influence the level of economic activity? What are the current trends in economic activity in the UK? Does the fact that we have such a high level of unemployment compared to the past imply that our level of economic activity has declined? How does our performance in the UK compare to that of our competitors, such as West Germany, or France, or the Netherlands, or the USA, or Japan?

Clearly, the very nature of macroeconomics takes us quickly into important and emotive issues. Therefore, it is essential that we take time to understand the key terms with which we shall be dealing, and to build up even a broad awareness of the influences involved. Without any real grasp of these issues, the scope for confusion – and embarassment – is unlimited!

You find this difficult to believe? Take a little time to read through Extract 2.1 and, in particular, try to understand what Ronald Reagan was trying to say when asked, as President of the USA, if he should be thinking about increasing taxes. How about that for confusion . . .? If you need a little motivation to encourage you to study this chapter, then why risk being quoted in such a fashion by a future textbook in economics, when you have become rich and famous?

Macroeconomics deals with the study of the broad aggregates within the national economy, such as the total consumption spending of all its households, or the total investment spending of all its firms, or with the government's own spending and taxation activities (both at national and at local authority level), or the exports of goods and services from the UK to world markets, or with the counterflow of imported goods and services to the UK to meet the demands of UK households, and firms – and even the government itself.

All of these elements interact to set the level of economic activity for the UK and to determine the trends of growth or decline which are experienced. Equally, some of these elements are themselves influenced by the level, or changes in the level, of economic activity.

An important first step will therefore be to set up a simple, introductory model, which shows at least conceptually how the various elements influence and reflect the level of economic activity in any country. Next, it will be essential to see how closely the analysis provided by this model fits with the official government statistics on the level of economic activity. It is our intention that, after reading this chapter, you should be able to understand and discuss the following key concepts:

- What is meant by the term 'economic activity';
- The alternative ways in which it might be measured;
- The factors which influence both the rise and fall of economic activity;
- What is meant by the term 'Gross Domestic Product' (GDP), in the context of the national accounts;
- The distinction between GDP and 'Gross National Product' (GNP);
- The distinction between GNP and 'national income';
- Some of the main problem areas in the use of GDP or GNP as a measure of national prosperity and welfare.

Extract 2.1 THE OBSERVER 25 OCTOBER 1987.

DOWN AND DOWN GOES REAGAN— FASTER THAN WALL ST

Simon Hoggart   Washington

DONALD REGAN used to be White House Chief of Staff and Ronald Reagan's closest professional friend until he was, in effect, sacked by Nancy Reagan earlier this year.

Last Friday he was tempted into a TV studio in Washington to talk about the progress of the Administration since his departure. He made it clear, privately, that he was delighted to be away from all the chaos.

During the recording, he roundly announced that his old pal Ronald Reagan had been 'snookered.' That may prove to be an understatement.

Last week was undoubtedly the worst for the Reagan presidency, unless you count the time that he was shot. The difference is that in 1981 he appeared to know what had happened. Now he doesn't know what has hit him.

That night before, Mr Reagan gave a Press conference at the White House, his first there for seven months. Here, verbatim, is one of his replies. It is worth reading with care.

The President was asked whether he would be prepared to raise taxes:

> 'But the problem is the—the deficit is—or should I say—wait a minute, the spending, I should say, of gross national product, forgive me—the spending is roughly 23 to 24 per cent. So that it is in—it

what is increasing, while the revenues are staying proportionately the same and what would be the proper amount they should, that we should be taking from the private sector.'

A month ago, Reagan's presidency also looked a sorry mess, but at least he had three consolations: the economy continued to prosper, at least on the surface. There was an excellent chance of a summit meeting with Mikhail Gorbachov, to be concluded with a treaty of the type known as 'historic,' (which generally means that Congress won't ratify it). And his 'social agenda' — stern views on abortion, welfare recipients, whingeing minorities and so forth — would be preserved after his death by the appointment of Judge Bork to the Supreme Court. Now all that is gone, possibly forever.

Take last week's Press conference. After a confident two-minute opening statement — read from an autocue — he had to adlib answers to questions for half an hour. In the impenetrable reply quoted above, he seemed to be saying that tax cuts increase production, so public spending should be reduced. But that's not evident from the sentence or its context, only from our past knowledge of the President's convictions.

Otherwise Reagan appeared to be groping through a clinging fog, guided only by the blurry outlines of his own most cherished beliefs.

He took credit for the last '59 months of expansion' in the US economy. When, however, he was asked what had gone wrong, he blamed the fact that Congress had been run by the Democrats for 'more than half a century.'

He even got on to the subject of John Maynard Keynes, the British economist, who he said had dominated the beliefs of the Democratic Party. In the middle of the worst economic crisis the West has faced for more than a decade, Reagan thought it necessary to say: 'I'd like to point out to them that Maynard Keynes didn't even have a degree in economics.'

It's hardly surprising that the next day the Stock Exchange refused to respond to the President's message, which could be summarised as 'clap hands if you believe in prosperity.'

The suggestion that nothing could go wrong as long as we believed nothing would go wrong clearly failed to buoy the market which rose a derisory one-third of one point on Friday. Experts were divided between those who thought it had avoided a fall because at last the President realised there was a crisis, and those who thought it had failed to rise because he didn't yet see what the crisis was.

Reprinted with permission from *The Observer* 25 October 1987 © *The Observer*.

Hopefully, by the time you finish, you should be able to tidy up the President's statement into something which makes a little more sense!

THE MEASUREMENT OF ECONOMIC ACTIVITY

Clearly, the term implies some overall level of output, or sales, or income, or employment, or even a combination of all four of these. Equally, there is an implication that the level of activity can ebb or flow over time.

The purpose of any conceptual model in economics is to simplify the more complex conditions of reality, and allow you to see in principle how the different elements fit together. As a starting point, let us take the simplest possible version of the national economy: for the moment, we will assume that there is no government, or public sector; at the same time, we will assume that there are no international trade flows of any kind. Once the model has been established, it will be a relatively simple task to build these two important sectors back into the economic system.

Our starting point, therefore, leaves us with an economic system in which only two broad sectors remain and interact. These are the **household** sector, which is concerned with the decisions and actions of all consumers in all markets for goods and services within the economy as a whole, and the **firms** sector, which deals with the decisions and actions of all business organizations involved in producing goods, or services within the national economy. The interactions which take place between the two sectors all involve flows, or series of transactions. The main transaction flows are indentified in Figure 2.1. From this you will see that:

(1) Households sell their productive services to firms as inputs for the production process, in the form of labour, land, capital: this appears as the outer lefthand side flow;

(2) In return, households receive payments from firms for the use of these services in the form of income from employment, or self-employment, interest, rent, profit: this appears as the inner lefthand side flow in the model;

(3) At the same time, firms sell their collective output of goods and services, produced from the inputs which they have hired: this is shown as the outer righthand side flow;

(4) In turn, these goods and services are purchased by households, using the income received from firms: this is represented by the inner righthand side flow, and completes the model.

Despite its simplicity, the model reveals the broad interrelationships which exist between the two main sectors in the national economy. On its

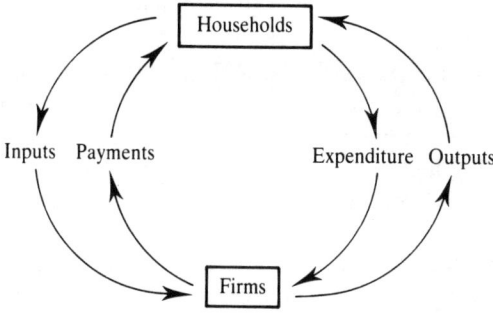

Figure 2.1 The measurement of economic activity

lefthand side, it shows the balancing flows of input purchases and input payments. On its righthand side, there are the balancing flows of output sales and expenditure receipts. The outer loop of the model shows that the whole range of input services are needed to produce the final output, which is the source of the income and prosperity of any economy. The inner loop shows the **circular flow of income** between the two sectors, where one sector's expenditure becomes the other sector's income. Overall, it contains the important message that employment, or the purchase of labour inputs, depends upon the level of output needed, which depends upon the level of expenditure or sales which, in this simple closed economy (that is, where there is no international trade transaction flows), depends upon the level of household income available.

But which of these flows represents economic activity? In fact, each flow represents a different aspect of economic activity. The absolute level of economic activity can therefore be measured by valuing or quantifying the flow of transactions in any one of the income, the expenditure, or the output loops. Conceptually at least, all should yield the same measure.

Our next task is to look at what is meant by the term **flow of transactions**. For the sake of accuracy in measurement, it is vital that a distinction must be drawn between transactions involving 'final' or completed goods and transactions involving 'intermediate' goods, which are simply part-completed goods which must be processed still further to produce a final good. To illustrate, assume that there is a completed or finished good which sells for £300. Before the final sale, there are two previous stages; the original raw materials were purchased for £100, and the good was also sold in a semi-finished state for £200. What is the true measure of the economic activity? Should all the transactions be added together to yield a total of £100 + £200 + £300 = £600?

The traditional illustration is provided by the humble loaf of bread (but would be equally applicable to a car, or a dishwasher, or a pair of wellington boots – obviously with differences in the description of the production process and the costs in each case). How should we value its production, from its genesis as the farmer's grain, through transportation to the miller to be converted into flour, through transportation to the baker to be converted into bread, through transportation to the shelves of your local store or supermarket, to be purchased as a final good by you, the consumer? Which is the true measure of economic activity, the price of the final loaf of bread on the shop's shelves, or the sum total of all the activities of farmer, miller, baker, lorry driver and sales assistant?

For consistency and accuracy, economic activity within the model (and in the subsequent national accounts, for we are now dealing with an international convention in measurement) will only value transactions either as:

(1) the sale price of the final good, that is £300 in the earlier illustration, since this is what the whole productive process has been geared towards or, alternatively, as;

(2) the sum of the **value added** at each stage in the production process, that is, £100 at the raw materials stage, plus £100 at the semi-finished stage (£200 sale price less £100 raw material cost), plus £100 at the finished stage (£300 sale price less £200 cost of semi-finished good), totalling £300. Note how the two approaches yield the same figure.

To simply add the total value of the various transactions would be to double-count the value of earlier outputs in the production process, thereby overstating the true level of economic activity.

Therefore, the level of economic activity reflects the flow of final transactions through the economy within a given time period, normally a year.

Having dealt with this important issue in measurement, we can now begin to make the simplified model of Figure 2.1 more realistic. If we concentrate on the inner loop, or the circular flow of income and expenditure between households and firms, this can be developed to show that, even within the simplified world of a two-sector economy, some adjustments must be made to the continuing flow of transactions. (See Figure 2.2.)

Firstly, households do not spend entirely the income they receive from firms: normally, they will save part of this. These **savings** represent a leakage, or withdrawal from the circular flow. In the figure, this is shown to take place between the receipt of income from firms, and the resultant outflow of expenditure from the household sector,[1] implying that

---

1. We do not imply by this that such withdrawals are kept under the mattress or the floorboards! Normally, they will be placed on deposit with some financial institution, for

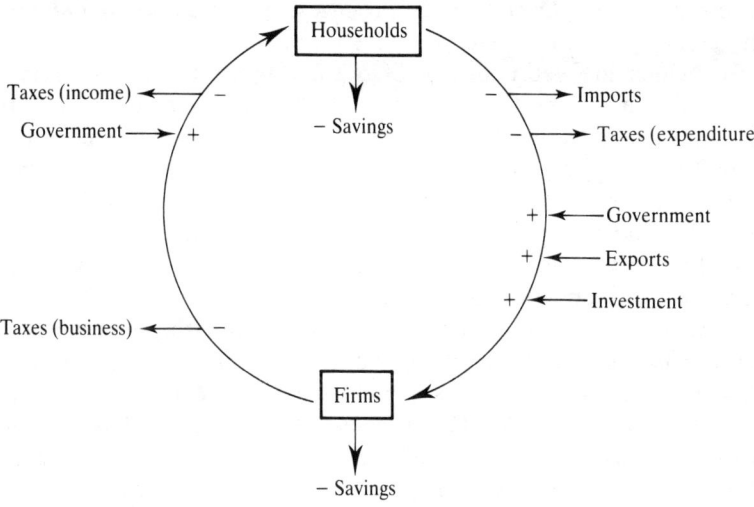

Figure 2.2 The circular flow of income

consumers' expenditure will be less than income received by the amount retained as savings. At the same time, the firms' sector need not pay out all of the income received from its sales of output; they too may decide to retain or withdraw as savings part of their expenditure receipts, for example, for contingency reserves, or to build up funds for investment purposes. Firms' savings are therefore shown as a leakage from the system between the receipt of income from sales, and the point where payments are made for the inputs which were used to produce that output which was sold, leaving income payments and distributions less that the flow of expenditure received.

So far, these amendments both involve withdrawals from, or reductions to the volume of the circular flow of income; to set against these, the next adjustment brings the injection, or addition, of **investment** spending into the model. In the initial version of the model (Figure 2.1), firms' receipts were shown to come solely from consumers' expenditure, that is, for goods and services sold for consumption purchases. But in the real world, not all firms produce goods which are directly used for consumption. Many will produce goods which are for sale in industrial

---

example, commercial bank or building society – and could very possibly be re-issued or injected by the latter into the economic system, for example, as funds borrowed by the firms' sector for investment expenditure. In fact these money flows will all involve a whole new dimension of transactions which exists on a different plane from that which is illustrated by the model, and which has not been shown, to keep the initial model as simple as possible. These will be dealt with in Chapter 8 on money and banking.

markets, for example, as factory premises, or offices, or equipment, or commercial computer systems and so on. These sales of 'producers' goods', which are subsequently used to produce goods or services for consumption purposes, are built into the model by showing an additional source of income from sale of output to other firms, as an injection to the expenditure loop of the circular flow. In other words, firms receive income from selling their output of consumption goods to households, and further income from selling their output of producer goods to other firms. This new source of sales receipts, or injection to the flow is described as **investment expenditure**.

At this point, it is important to underline that the term 'investment' has a precise and careful meaning within economics, which can be quite different to its normal conversational usage. To economists, investment spending will involve either the purchase of physical, fixed assets (such as factory premises, equipment, machinery, tools and so on) or the retention of unsold stock to act as inventories. In a sense, it involves either the expansion or the maintenance of the stock of productive capacity within the economy. When your maiden aunt decides to 'invest' some of her savings (or winnings from the horses, depending on the type of aunt . . .) in the purchase of shares in ICI, or British Telecom, to our mind this simply involves the transfer of paper ownership of existing physical assets, and is not in any way *true* investment. Yes, if it was a new share issue, which was designed to raise funds for real investment expenditure, then she would be involved in providing the funding for investment; but it is much more accurate to interpret the term in its proper, technical sense, which is the *expenditure by the firms' sector on new physical assets*, or retained output.

This more or less tidies up the model for the simple two-sector economic system. The next stage in our model building must be to bring into our model the flows of transactions which are involved in both the government and the international trade sectors; you will remember that we eliminated these temporarily, to simplify the task of initial model building.

As it stands, the model shows only UK households' income and expenditure, and UK firms' expenditure receipts and input payments. To build in the international trade sector, we need to make two new adjustments to the circular flow model. Firstly, the availability of international goods and services on our domestic market will mean that at least a proportion of consumers' expenditure will never reach UK firms, but will be directed towards the purchase of this foreign output, for example, Volkswagen cars, or Panasonic music systems, or holidays in Greece. These **import** purchases represent a further leakage, or withdrawal of expenditure from the UK circular flow; the model must show that the expenditure is made by UK households, but does not involve UK firms in the production and sale of output. The withdrawal is shown on the expenditure loop of Figure 2.2. At the same time, UK firms will sell goods and services to foreign customers, for example, whisky to

America, turbines to Russia, holidays for Swedish and Japanese tourists to the UK, or banking and insurance services to customers throughout the world. Thus UK firms' receipts from output sales will be augmented by these **export** sales; this additional source of income, or injection from international trade transaction flows, is added to the expenditure loop of Figure 2.2.

As a result of these amendments to the basic model, we have now built in the broad transaction flows which are associated with international trade, and which will influence the level of economic activity within the UK.

To complete our introductory model, we must build in the final component of the transaction flows which involve the government or public sector. Once again, this simply involves breaking down the government's activities into their broad withdrawal and injection components and incorporating these into the circular flow of income.

Taking the bad news first, there are various forms of government **taxation**, which take income from households and firms and can be shown as leakages or withdrawals from their respective flows. Direct taxation, or income tax, is deducted from household earnings (which includes not only income from employment, but also from other sources such as rent, or dividends received, or interest earned on savings balances) so that the net of tax income received is less than the gross of tax payment made for input services by firms; this is shown at the top of the income loop. Firms too pay direct taxation, for example, corporation tax, levied broadly on the amount of profit earned; this withdrawal is shown at the foot of the income loop, to indicate that it reduces the income available for distribution to households. Finally, part of consumers' expenditure on the market prices of goods and services is taken off in the form of indirect taxation, for example VAT, or Customs and Excise duties, or the various specialist taxes involved in car or house purchase; since the customer has to pay the full amount, but only part of this expenditure passes through to the firms' sector, these expenditure taxes are shown as a withdrawal from the expenditure loop of Figure 2.2.

However, even the government can make a positive contribution to the economic system; both the income and the expenditure loops are augmented by various forms of **government expenditure**. The government is a major employer; much of household income will be derived from the government, as distinct from the private sector, to reflect the input services provided by the police, the armed forces, teachers, local authority dustbin collectors, even university lecturers (on a good day . . .). These wages and salary payments are shown as an injection into the income loop of the model.[2] At the same time, the government is a major

---

2. Conventionally, people employed in nationalized industries (where these have not already been privatized) are included in the firms' sector although they are, technically, government employees.

purchaser of goods and services from the private sector, for example, from the construction industry for hospital extensions, or housing rehabilitation, from civil engineering firms for new bridges, or motorway work, from electronics firms, as part of the input to defence systems. Thus the firms' sector, as well as the households' sector, receives additional revenue from the government; this additional income from the sale of output to the government is shown on the expenditure loop of Figure 2.2.

At the end of it all, we are still left with a highly simplified model; but simplified or not, it does identify the main elements at work in the macroeconomy. It shows that the output from UK firms will be sold to UK consumers, to other UK firms for investment goods, to the UK government and, finally, as exports to international trade markets. At the same time, not all UK consumption expenditure will be received by UK firms, due to leakages in the form of imports and indirect taxation. Equally, not all of the expenditure receipts of firms will be passed through the households as payment for input services; part will be diverted via business taxation, and part retained as savings. In turn, household income receipts will also be depleted by various forms of taxation, but will also receive payment for input services from the government.

How useful is the final version of the model? What sort of insight does it give us into the influences which might affect the level of economic activity?

As an illustration, read Extract 2.2. Do not worry at this stage about all the technicalities of the exchange rate, and the government's and the Bank of England's responsibilities towards this; these topics will be covered in depth in later chapters. Concentrate rather on thinking through the consequences of possible variations in the international valuation of the pound.

During April and May 1988, there was a bitter debate on whether or not the international value of the pound sterling should be allowed to rise unchecked against other major world currencies, notably the American dollar and the German D-mark. What was at stake? Consider some of the possible implications of an ever stronger pound. One major consequence would be that greater amounts of foreign currency would be needed to pay for any transaction with a fixed sterling price; in effect, the price of British exports to world markets would rise against the price range of world competitors, with a real possibility that export sales would decline, reducing the positive influence of that injection into the expenditure loop of the model shown in Figure 2.2, and therefore reducing income received from output sales by UK firms. Simultaneously, fewer pounds would be needed to pay for any transaction with its price fixed in foreign currency, so that goods and services imported to our domestic market would become relatively cheaper; our experience has been that this would result in a switch of UK expenditure from domestic

Extract 2.2 THE SCOTSMAN 17 MAY 1988.

BANK SELLS POUNDS TO BUY TIME

Time for clear policy getting near as speculators heft sterling higher

Clifford German, City Editor

SPECULATORS kept up the pressure on the pound, the Prime Minister and the Chancellor yesterday, sending sterling to its highest level since 1985.

They forced the Bank of England to sell still more sterling to try and ease the upward pressure on the exchange rate.

After a tense morning, there was a sudden surge in demand for sterling in mid afternoon. The pound reached 3.1940 Deutschemarks and $1.8940 before the Bank intervened, buying dollars for sterling and forcing the pound down to $1.8895, marginally below last week's levels.

But at the close of business in London sterling stood at Dm 3.1893, up 0.75 pfennigs from Friday.

In the London money markets, short-term interest rates began to drift lower, and fixed-interest stocks were showing gains, but the prospect of an overvalued pound pricing British goods out of world markets depressed trading volume and sent share prices lower. The FT-SE 100-Share Index lost its initial gains and ended the day 5.2 points down at 1,776.6.

Supplying sterling only bought time for the authorities yesterday. If the demand for pounds continues, the Government will have to decide whether to go on supplying sterling to try and hold the exchange rate down, or to cut base rates to make the return on sterling less attractive.

Base rates are already at 8 per cent however, a ten-year low and perhaps 2 per cent below the level the Treasury and the Bank of England think is prudent for domestic reasons. A further cut to 7.5 per cent would increase the conflict between market forces and the Government's twin domestic objectives of a higher interest rate and a lower exchange rate.

But this may prove to be the only way of preventing further upward pressure on the pound.

Speculators now have a target of Dm3.20 in their sights, and several leading investment houses are talking of sterling going to Dm3.25 or even Dm3.50 if nothing happens, or is deliberately done to try and break the trend.

Today, the market will look first for the latest US trade figures for the month of March to give a clue to the strength of the dollar, and then to Parliament in the hope of getting a statement by the Prime Minister at Question Time to clear up the confusion over the Government's policy priorities.

On Thursday, the figures for UK bank lending and the money supply in April will be published. Analysts are expecting further evidence of boom conditions in the UK economy, including a further increase of at least £3 billion in bank lending, and a rise of between 1 per cent and 1.7 per cent in the money supply measure M4.

High figures, increasing the need for dearer money for domestic reasons, might even intensify the policy conflict and accentuate the short term demand for sterling.

The Government is now in the farcical situation of needing bad news to cool demand for sterling and provide good news for the embattled Chancellor, currency dealers admitted last night.

Reprinted with permission from *The Scotsman* 17 May 1988 © *The Scotsman*.

---

to imported output, so that the level of imports would rise, increasing the level of withdrawals from the system, and therefore reducing the flow of income receipts from output sales by UK firms. With output sales falling, the probability would be that UK firms would reduce their demand for labour, so that our already high level of unemployment would begin to rise again, thwarting government policy attempts to improve the position within the national and regional labour markets.

While the model does not attempt to quantify the effect, it does permit you to follow through the implications of events, in terms of the circular flow of income. As such, it cannot simply be dismissed as abstract academic nonsense; it is an important device which can be used to help to build your understanding of the workings of the economy.

How serious a threat was posed by the rising international value of the pound? Many economists would argue that an over-valued pound contributed to the very severe downturn and depression of 1979–82, and several senior commentators on economic issues supported Nigel Lawson's, then Chancellor of the Exchequer, argument that some form of intervention was needed to hold down the rise of the pound. Against this view, Margaret Thatcher, the Prime Minister of the day, took an initially firm stance which argued that it was wrong to try to 'buck market forces', with intervention likely to be both expensive and doomed to failure. Yet, ultimately, she reversed her view and conceded to the Treasury argument, allowing both interest rates to be cut and some strong selling of the pound against the dollar and the D-mark to take place.[3] This, it was felt, should defuse the situation a little – but nothing is truly simple in economics, as Extract 2.2 discusses; a breathing space might well have been bought against the rise in the exchange rate, but at a price. What if the lower interest rates, and the resultant cheaper credit triggered a new inflationary spiral, with a further loss of UK price competitiveness against the goods and services on offer in world and domestic markets? Might the short-term solution not just result in another series of problems to be faced in the longer term?

What do you think would be the likely consequences, in terms of Figure 2.2, if the policy decision of 18 May 1988 did have inflationary consequences?[4]

---

3. See Chapter 11 on international trade and the balance of payments for a more detailed discussion of this disagreement on strategy between the UK Chancellor and Prime Minister. Also, watch how the topic of the exchange rate appears again and again through the extracts in later chapters, as the problem escalated over 1988 and 1989.

4. If domestic inflation causes costs to rise, forcing up the price both of domestic UK goods and UK exports, then export sales could fall and import purchases could rise, so that the demand for UK firms' output will also fall, reducing the demand for labour, and therefore causing unemployment to rise . . . but was this not the argument for intervention in the first place? If so, might intervention, in the form of reducing interest rates in this case (to discourage the inflow of international capital, and so reduce this source of upward pressure on the exchange rate) not simply create the same problem which the Chancellor feared from the rising exchange rate? We raise the point not to discredit intervention, but merely to caution against simple minded intervention which does not think clearly through the possible consequences of the action about to be taken. It is a rough and painful rule of thumb in economics that most benefits can only be achieved at the expense of some form of costs – and that it is only a fool who focuses on the first and disregards the possibility of the second.

THE NATIONAL ACCOUNTS

In Chapter 1 we laid great stress on the need to apply theory to real-world problems, to use it and to learn from its use, rather than simply to master its abstract technicalities. The model which we have developed, and illustrated in Figure 2.2, can give some insights into the real-world economy and its problems. But how realistic is it? Can its various elements be quantified, to give at least a flavour of their relative size and importance?

The data on economic activity is provided by the official government statistics as set out in the national accounts and in the various specialist publications which stem from these. Tables 2.1 and 2.2 have abstracted the statistics on UK national income and expenditure for 1986, the most recently available full year, at the time of writing.

Before we turn to analyse this data, it is worthwhile to draw your attention to two important qualifications, right at the outset. Firstly it is tempting to assume that, given their status as official government statistics and their extensive usage within government economic planning and monitoring, the figures should be taken as accurate measures of fact. But a second's thought should be enough to make you realize that it would be impossible to register and record every single final transaction in goods and services throughout an economic system over an entire year. As a result, the official statistical data is no more than a series of estimates, based on a variety of recording and sampling techniques. Practice does tend to make perfect, so that the margin of error is generally fairly small[5] – with an error range of under 3% for most items – but some substantial corrections can still have to be made from year to year. Even government statistics are still a little short of a complete defence to the allegation that 'there are lies, damned lies, and there are statistics' and should therefore be treated with caution, as a careful blend of fiction and fact! If you take time to read Extract 2.3 (see p. 20) at this point, you will see that there can be major problems both in reconciling and in interpreting these official statistics.

Secondly, the measurement and procedures used in the national accounts are extremely complex.[5] While the nature of the measurement is conceptually similar to that implied by the text above, the practice of definition and measurement can result in differences in content between items in our simple model and their real-world counterparts. You will notice this, in particular, in the context of investment. Try not to become confused by these differences, or to feel that the introductory model has been discredited. The purpose of the model was to simplify the more complex details of reality; likewise, you are not expected to become a

---

5. For detailed discussion of the technical issues involved see publications such as Maurice R. ed. (1968) *National Accounts Statistics: sources and methods* Chapters 1–4, 1968, or *National Accounts – a short guide*, Studies in Official Statistics, No 36, HMSO, 1981.

Table 2.1 Gross National Product by category of expenditure.

		1986 (£ billions)
Consumers' expenditure		234.2
General government final consumption		79.4
Gross domestic fixed capital formation	64.2	
Value of increase in stocks and work in progress	0.6	64.8
Total domestic expenditure		378.4
Exports of goods and services	97.8	
Imports of goods and services	(101.3)[1]	(3.5)
Gross domestic product at market prices		374.9
Taxes on expenditure	(62.3)	
Subsidies	6.5	(55.8)
Gross domestic product at factor cost		319.1
Net property income from abroad		4.7
Gross national product at factor cost		323.8
Capital consumption		(46.0)
National income		277.8

(1. Figures in brackets should be subtracted. Sub-totals may not add due to rounding.)
(Source: *Annual Abstract of Statistics*, 1988, Table 14.1. Reprinted by permission of the Controller, HMSO.)

specialist in the technicalities of accounting, but simply to grasp how the various broad flows of transactions all influence the level of economic activity.

The previous section argued that the level of economic activity could be measured by metering either the income, or the expenditure loops of the circular flow model. However, it is easier to identify the elements of the conceptual model's expenditure loop in the national accounts measurement of real-world data. This will therefore be examined first.

The national accounts data, as shown in Table 2.1 break into the model at the point where UK households make their consumption expenditure, that is, at the top of the expenditure loop of Figure 2.2; in

Table 2.2 Gross Domestic Product by category of income.

	1986 (£ billions)
Income from employment	209.4
Income from self-employment	34.3
Gross trading profits of companies	48.5
Gross trading surplus of public corporations	8.1
Rent	22.5
Others	3.2
GDP (income-based)	326.0
Residual error	(6.9)
GDP (expenditure-based)	319.1

(Source: *Annual Abstract of Statistics*, 1988, Table 14.1. Reprinted by permission of the Controller, HMSO.)

1986, this expenditure totalled £234.2 billion (or thousand million), or 61.9% of total domestic expenditure at market prices. This covers expenditure on items such as food, clothing, entertainments, and consumer durables such as cars – but it excludes consumers' expenditure on dwellings.[6] Next, the injection of government expenditure is valued at £79.4 billion, or 21% of total domestic expenditure; this figure includes central and local government 'final consumption' expenditure, but excludes expenditure by this sector on fixed assets.

One of the main dissimilarities between reality and the model shown in Figure 2.2 is found in the definition of the items included under the heading of investment expenditure. In the conceptual model, this was treated solely as private sector investment in producer goods; in the national accounts, this is extended to cover consumers' expenditure on dwellings, and government expenditure on fixed assets such as premises, roads and so on. These items are aggregated under the term of gross domestic fixed capital formation which, in 1986, amounted to £64.2 billion (of which OECD *national accounts* estimates suggest that about 11% represented government expenditure, and residential buildings construction a further 17%). When the additional item of increase in stocks and work in progress (which amounted to a positive figure of £0.6 billion for

---

6. Houses are treated as productive assets; the owner-occupier is regarded as a producer, who sells the services of his house to himself at an imputed rent. This imputed rent is included in consumers' expenditure, whereas the initial house purchase would have been included in gross domestic fixed capital formation – see Maurice (1968) (note 5, p. 17).

Extract 2.3 THE ECONOMIST 4 JUNE 1988.

GARBAGE IN, GARBAGE OUT

WEATHERMEN can be wrong But when they make their forecasts for tomorrow they at least know whether it is raining or sunny today. How can economists hope to predict the path of the economy over the coming year when they can't even be sure where it has been in the past one?

Yet they cannot. Figures are regularly revised, "balancing items" run into billions. Now, after criticism from a Commons committee, the government's Central Statistical Office is considering an inquiry into how to make its numbers more reliable. Not before time: the discrepancies in Britain's national accounts seem to be getting bigger.

The figures for 1987 give a very blurred picture. In theory the income and expenditure measures of GDP should be the same. They are not. In 1987 the income measure showed GDP growing, in the 12 months to the fourth quarter, at a real 4.8% to £356 billion; the expenditure measure showed it growing at 2.9% to £347 billion.

That missing £9 billion shows up (by definition) in another discrepancy. In theory the current-account balance should equal the gap between domestic savings and total investment: if Britons invest more than they save, the extra money must come from abroad. In fact, last year a balancing item of £9 billion had to be included. One, two or all three of the measures must be wrong. Economists at Warburg Securities have been doing a spot of detective work to discover which.

The popular culprit is the external balance, which many think is better than the figures say. In 1986 there was a balancing item of £13 billion in the balance of payments, but this fell to only £1 billion last year. In contrast, there were huge discrepancies in the personal and company sectors. The personal sector's savings minus its investment should equal its identified acquisition of financial assets in building societies, banks and so on. In fact the gap between the two measures rose last year to £20 billion. The real savings are probably much higher than reported in the national accounts. So perhaps that explains the discrepancy between the expenditure and income measures of GDP? Alas, no: it would make it even wider.

The real villain may be the corporate sector. Last year, its reported financial surplus (the difference between retained profits and investment) was £27 billion higher than its identified net acquisition of financial assets. Warburg's economists conclude that the black hole in the national accounts masks a significant under-recording of business investment. This would explain why the recorded growth in investment in 1987 turned out to be much lower than investment intentions as reported by the CBI.

Higher investment is of more than statistical interest. If the reportedly widening current-account deficit has been matched by stronger domestic investment (not just consumption), then the deficit will be more easily financed without the pound needing to fall. It also implies that fears about capacity shortages may be exaggerated.

Why have government statistics apparently become less reliable? First, say some official number-crunchers, the government is trying to run its statistical services on the cheap. Second, its abolition of exchange controls in 1979 made flows of money in and out of Britain harder to measure. Third, the government has cut the burden of statistical paperwork on businessmen. The official statisticians are then dropping more bricks because they have less straw.

Reprinted with permission from *The Economist* 4 June 1988 © *The Economist*.

1985/86) is added to this, the final figure of £64.8 billion represents about 17.1% of total domestic expenditure.

These first three items summed together give the **total domestic expenditure** figure of £378.4 billion for 1986.

The next stage is to broaden this measure to include foreign trade; from the model, we know that this involves adding the injection of exports to and deducting the withdrawal of imports from the above total. In 1986, exports of goods and services amounted to £97.8 billion, against an imports figure of £101.3 billion, leaving a net deficit of £3.5 billion to be deducted from the expenditure flow. The resultant sub-total of £374.9 billion is known as the **GDP at market prices**. It measures the money value of all goods and services produced and sold by economic agents in the UK for that year.

However, it does not represent the expenditure received by UK firms, in terms of the circular flow model. Market prices include various expenditure taxes and subsidies; the taxes represent a withdrawal from the expenditure flow and must be deducted, whereas subsidies – ignored in the conceptual model – represent an additional source of income and must be added to the flow. For 1986, the net withdrawal figure (given the relative magnitudes, there will always be a net taxation withdrawal, as shown in the model) amounted to £55.8 billion. This adjusted sub-total was £319.1 billion; these receipts from the sale of output represent, in effect, the funds which are available to cover the cost of the various inputs, or factors of production, which were used to produce that output. The traditional term for this sub-total is **GDP at factor cost**, and it indicates that the taxation adjustment has been made to market prices, and that this final total represents the revenue received by UK firms from their sales of output for the year.

It is worth pausing here for a second to draw a breath. Given the definitional differences between real-world measurement and the conceptual model, we have in fact shown that the expenditure flow of Figure 2.2 can be measured, just at the point before it enters the firms' sector. It is worth realizing also that each of the withdrawals and injections showed exactly why various items were added to or deducted from the ongoing national accounts total for expenditure. In short, the model is a useful summary version of reality and its conceptual measure of the flow of economic activity corresponds to the value recorded for GDP at factor cost for the year.

At the same time, the national accounts are not simply an annual ritual which is confined to the UK. Table 2.3 shows the equivalent sets of national accounts (at current market prices, that is, without the additional adjustment for local expenditure taxation and subsidies), grouped under the same expenditure flow headings, for the USA, Japan, West Germany and the Netherlands. Whatever the local variations in measurement technicalities, the national accounts for any country can be broken down

22 Understanding the Economy

Table 2.3 Gross Domestic Product: selected international data (1986).

	USA ($bn)	Japan (yen bn)	West Germany (D-M bn)	Netherlands (glds bn)
Private consumption expenditure	2799.8	190,533	1081.4	244.8
Government consumption expenditure	869.7	32,670	381.7	67.5
Gross fixed capital formation	655.2	91,494	376.8	77.4
Increase in stocks	15.7	1,506	(2.9)	5.1
Exports	376.2	43,390	639.8	266.3
Imports	(481.7)	(28,841)	(529.2)	(246.0)
Gross domestic product	4235.0	330,752	1948.0	415.1

(Note: The Netherlands figure is not available in Quarterly Accounts; it has had to be taken for 1985, from Annual Accounts.)

(Reprinted by the permission of *Quarterly National Accounts*, No. 4, 1987, OECD, Department of Economics and Statistics; also, OECD *National Accounts*, 1973–85.)

into the same generic expenditure classes, as we have set up for the theory model; there will be consumption expenditure, government expenditure, investment expenditure (or gross domestic fixed capital formation), exports and imports expenditure. While care must be taken not to read too much into the comparison of a single year's figures, it is fascinating to observe both the similarities and the differences in the pattern provided by the various expenditure items. Note how both the UK and the USA show deficits on their balance of trade (the difference between export earnings and import payments) while all the others show clear surplus figures. Or again, while UK exports accounted for 26.1% of GDP at market prices (from Table 2.1), notice how West Germany with 32.8% and the Netherlands with 64.2% have far surpassed us in terms of international trading involvement, and can therefore carry their higher import percentages with relative ease (remembering also that some of these imports will be of raw materials or energy, to be used in the production of output for domestic and foreign sales). Or compare our UK figure of 21.2% for government expenditure with the 19.6% figure for West Germany, or the 16.3% figure for the Netherlands, or the 9.9% figure for this item in Japan, to provide a crude measure of the degree of involvement of the government in its economic system. Finally, compare our figure of 17.1% for gross domestic capital formation (ignoring the adjustment for changes in stock and work in progress) with the 18.6% for the Netherlands, or the 19.3% for West Germany, or the 27.7% for Japan, remembering that investment is the main transmission mechanism by which new technology is built into the economic system in question . . .

Moving on from this superficial exercise in international comparison, it is important to understand two further terms in the national accounts, namely GNP and national income; both involve simple adjustments to the final value which we showed for GDP at factor cost.

Remember that our basic objective is to measure the level of economic activity, or broadly the earnings from output of UK firms. But the real world insists on imposing some complications on this simple intent. What about the Nissan Datsun car assembly plant in the North East of England? It employs UK workers, and produces output for the UK and European markets from its UK location – but can it be counted as 'British' for the purpose of measurement? We can deal with its purchases of Japanese components under the heading of imports, but what about its payments to key Japanese management and labour personnel – or what about the profits which it will transfer back to Japan? Surely it is more truly a Japanese firm which is operating within the UK as part of its own domestic, or even global strategy? Equally, what about all the UK firms which work on civil engineering or development planning ventures in Egypt, or Saudi Arabia, or Nigeria, or wherever – and what about all the UK residents who work abroad under contract, but transmit whole or part of their wages back to their families in the UK? Should these UK activities throughout the world be added to our measure of UK economic activity?

GNP provides the broader measure of economic activity for which we are searching. To estimate GNP the analysis of purely domestic (that is, essentially UK production based) economic activity above must be broadened to include income from rent, interest, profit and dividends received by UK residents and firms from their overseas activities, less the corresponding income paid to overseas residents for their activities within the UK. This net adjustment figure is shown under the traditional term of 'net property income from abroad' and varies substantially from year to year; for 1986, it was a relatively minor positive figure of £4.7 billion (against £3.0 billion for 1985, or £4.2 billion for 1984 – or even a net figure of minus £0.2 billion for 1980). The effect of this adjustment is to raise the GDP at factor cost figure of £319.1 billion to the GNP at factor cost figure of £323.8 billion in Table 2.1.

Finally, where does the term **national income** fit in? To estimate national income from the figure for GNP, one further adjustment must be made. This can be explained via the 'matching principle' of accountancy. At the level of the individual firm, profit (or net earnings) is calculated by matching against the sales revenue for the year a figure for all the costs incurred in achieving these sales. These costs include, apart from the obvious items such as direct labour and materials, service items such as administration and distribution expenses; they must also include a charge for usage of *fixed assets*, such as equipment, or premises. At single firm level, this involves setting a charge for depreciation against revenue, to avoid overstating profits at the expense of consuming the firm's capital. The figure for national income corresponds to the wealth or income generated from all forms of economic activity during the year. To avoid overstating this, a charge is set against GNP to cover capital consumed through wear and tear, or obsolescence. This amounted to £46.0 billion for 1986, leaving a figure for net national product, or national income of £277.8 billion.[7]

So, in summary (for the multiplicity of final measures can be confusing), GDP at factor cost measures the earnings from output sales of UK firms operating from UK locations; it meters the flow of expenditure at the foot of that loop in Figure 2.2. In the more complex real world, the national accounts recognize that there will be an additional dimension of earnings gained from operating elsewhere in the world apart from the domestic location, and makes a net adjustment (to reflect both UK firms' activities in the rest of the world and the rest of the world's firms' activities in the UK) under net property income from abroad, to calculate GNP. When this figure, in turn, is adjusted downwards to reflect capital consumption or depreciation during the year, the resultant total is described as national income.

In rather less detail, the level of economic activity can also be measured from the income flow identified in the Figure 2.2 model. You will remember that this deals with all aspects of income payments for the input services provided by the households' sector, for example, wages, salaries, rent, dividends and so on. Further, since these input payments are made from the earnings received from the sales of output, this new income measure should equal the figure for GDP at factor cost, that is, the receipts available for distribution to the factors of production.

The income data is contained in Table 2.2. This table shows that income from employment, covering wages and salaries in cash and kind from both private sector (including, by convention the nationalized industries) and government employment, amounted to £209.4 billion in 1986. Income from self-employment, covering earnings from unincorporated businesses, for example, farmers, professional people, shopkeepers and so on, amounted to £34.3 billion. The gross trading profits of companies (£48.5 billion) include the separate streams of interest payments distributed, undistributed profits (that is, firms' savings in terms of the model), and an adjustment for stock appreciation. The gross trading surplus of public corporations (£8.1 billion) covers the net earnings of nationalized industries, and public utility boards, for example,

---

7. While the imputed charge is based on firms' estimates of depreciation, it has always been adjusted to conform to current cost accounting procedures, rather than the traditional historic cost accounting procedures used by firms in the past, in an attempt to ensure that productive capital was kept intact, and income not overstated, through the effects of inflation.

electricity, gas.[8] The rent figure of £22.5 billion represents the net receipts (that is, after repairs, maintenance and insurance charges are met) from ownership of land and buildings; additionally, this contains an imputed income figure for owner-occupied dwellings, rent-free farm houses, and houses owned by local authorities. 'Other' sources of income amount to £3.2 billion, covering trading surpluses of certain departments within central and local government (for example, harbours, docks, transport), together with an estimate of imputed income enjoyed by government and non-profit-making private sector bodies from ownership of non-trading fixed assets.

It will be noticed that the income based estimate for GDP at factor cost of £326.0 billion does not coincide with the expenditure based estimate of £319.1 billion. This merely reflects the different sources and samples used in each approach. While neither approach is completely accurate, the convention is that the two separate measures of economic activity are reconciled by including a residual error item in the income estimates; this can be positive or negative, and amounted to −£6.9 billion in 1986.

WHAT DO THE MEASURES REALLY COVER?

We have tried to show, firstly in terms of a simplified model, the different flows of transactions which all combine to set the level of economic activity. Next, the section which we have just completed shows how these flows can be quantified in the real world. But, if we focus simply on one single measure, such as GDP at factor cost (hereafter simply referred to as GDP), what does it really tell us? How much faith can we put in it? How accurate a measure of our welfare as a nation does it really provide?

We already know that it is simply not possible to trap and record every transaction which takes place within an economic system over the year; let us accept that our GDP figure is as good a guess as we can make from the measures and samples which we use. This will result in an inevitable but, hopefully, minor range of error.

But apart from this, there are several other major areas of weakness, common to all countries, which we must bear in mind when we are using the official national accounts data.

Firstly, there is the problem of GDP measurement over time. A few seconds' thought will show you what this problem is. GDP measures

---

8. These figures are stated gross of depreciation charges, as is some income from the self-employment category; the depreciation charge would be included in the charge for capital consumption which would convert GNP to national income, as in Table 2.1; remember also that some of the 'nationalized industries' have been taken formally into the private sector since these accounts were struck in 1986.

Table 2.4 UK GDP and the effect of price changes (£ billion).

	GDP at current prices	Index	GDP at 1980 prices	Index
1976	126.6	100	220.3	100
1980	230.6	182	230.6	105
1986	374.9	296	259.9	118

(Source: *Annual Abstract of Statistics*, 1988, Tables 14.1 and 14.8. Reprinted by permission of the Controller, HMSO.)

the money value of the output of goods and services produced in a single year: this money value figure will have two components:

- there will be a list of the physical outputs produced by all firms in all industries, but also
- there will be a list of the *prices* at which these various goods and services were sold.

What would happen if the physical output totals were to remain constant over a period of time, while the prices at which the various items were sold rose steadily as they would, for example, during a period of price inflation. The GDP total would also rise in response to this – yet there would have been no change in real output. Despite the rising GDP figure, has there really been any change in the level of economic activity?

How serious is this problem? Let us look back at some of the data we have already used. Table 2.4 shows how GDP at current market prices has risen steadily from £126.6 billion in 1976, to £230.6 billion in 1980, and to £374.9 billion by 1986. Not bad, you might think; this is a growth of 196% over the period – what's all this about the UK having a relatively low rate of economic growth? Yet look at what happens if you freeze the list of prices at constant values for a single year, so that the amended figure represents only movements in real, that is, physical output. Using 1980 prices, the 1976 figure rises to £220.3 billion (obviously it rises because 1980 prices were higher than the original prices at which output was sold in 1976); the 1980 figure for GDP is unchanged at £230.6 billion (because we are using the actual list of prices from that year, so that there is no change); and GDP for 1986 is now only £259.9 billion. Our apparent increase of 196% over the 10 year period has reduced to a mere 18% . . .

In other words, if you are analysing the behaviour of GDP over time, you must first adjust this to eliminate the effect of price changes, otherwise you are playing about with numbers which have little real meaning in the measurement of trends in economic activity. Because

GDP is a money value figure, it can be badly distorted by periods of rapidly changing prices.

The second major problem area is that not all final good transactions are included in the measurement of GDP; only those transactions which involved trading in formal open markets are included.

This creates all sorts of problems – because not all goods and services are formally marketed. Take, for example, the case of the married woman who remains at home to look after her helpless husband and the rest of the family. She provides a wide range of services, from acting as an alarm clock (with built-in escalating crises decibels), to cooking, shopping, house cleaning, dish washing, clothes washing, ironing, dog walking, mucking out the kids' bedrooms and the budgie's cage, to simply being around to be shouted at, or asked for advice, or expected to marvel at some family member's achievements. In short, she will probably work a longer day and produce a greater service output than her husband, yet she is valued as zero in the national accounts . . . unless she goes out to work and cooks and irons and housecleans for someone else *and* for formal payment. Yet her own domestic output is being produced without formal valuation and payment.

What would happen if she decided to run off with the milkman? What would happen if her deserted husband had to employ someone to clean and cook, or had to send his clothes to the local laundry services for washing and ironing, or had to eat pub meals every night in the local . . .? The original unpaid services would have entered the world of formal market trading and the GDP figure would rise in response – without any real change in the level of economic activity in terms of final output. But the fact remains that, unless there is a mass desertion of such wives, their output is quite excluded from the formal measurement of the national accounts. Similarly, if you happen to be useful in repairs around the house (which automatically excludes all academics, who are not really designed for the real world), all that do-it-yourself work is left unregistered (apart from materials purchases) in the GDP; yet, if you bring in a plumber to fit on that new toilet seat, or a joiner to replace that cupboard door, or a painter to do the outside of your house, or to decorate a couple of rooms for you then, once again, the transfer from your own untraded services into the formal market for these services, results in their inclusion for the first time in GDP – without any change in the final output or end result.

GDP does not measure every final transaction, only those which are traded in formal markets. This leads us to a further problem of exclusion: what about all those transactions which are carried out 'for cash' and which take great care *not* to be registered formally in any economic system? What about the plumber who fitted in your new shower 'in his own time'? The painter who came in one evening 'for a back-hander' to paint those high spots in the eaves, which would otherwise have left you clinging to and shivering on your ladder? The electrician who fitted in your new lighting system as 'a homer'? The slightly dubious building contractor who offers to concrete your garage base, or lay even more dubious tarmac on your drive 'for a bargain cash price' . . .?

In short, what about the whole underground or **informal economy**, the 'black economy', the 'moonlighting', the 'travail au noir', the 'lavorno nero'? In any economic system, many transactions will deliberately evade formal registration and measurement, so that they will also avoid taxation liability. These are still final good transactions, in the sense that some output is produced in exchange for payment. They are part of the total of transactions which flow through the expenditure and income loops of the conceptual model in Figure 2.2, but are simply not picked up[9] in the formal measurement of GDP. How serious an omission might this be, in terms of accuracy of measurement? Obviously no one can know for sure, but a series of research estimates on the extent of the informal economy would place it at anything between 6% and 25% of GDP . . . and that is serious enough in anyone's definition of accuracy!

Therefore, the second major problem in interpretation of the GDP estimates is that you must always bear in mind that they exclude any transaction which takes place outside formal market trading and, in doing so, will therefore underestimate substantially the real volume of economic activity for the year.

The third major problem area is really a further dimension of the theme of exclusion from the formal measurement of the national accounts. Many economists are uneasy when GDP – or GNP – is used to provide a simplistic measure of wealth creation or welfare for the economy in question. For a start, if GDP represents a formal measure of the 'goods' produced by the economic system, should it not also contain a countermeasure, or downwards adjustment for the 'bads' which have also been produced by the production process which generated these goods? After all, in most countries, illegal transactions in 'bads', for example, sales of heroin, cocaine, prostitution and so on, are excluded from the measure of the national accounts. Why should a similar reduction not be made to recognize the damage created by the production of goods, for example in the form of environmental pollution, an important nuisance good, or 'bad'? After all, there has been substantial damage from acid rain to Scottish lochs and forests, as well as the more publicized damage to Scandinavia (one export which we should be trying a little harder to

---

9. Some might argue that this illegal income should resurface as expenditure, sooner or later and, provided that this expenditure is on formally traded transactions, for example, purchases of food, drink, clothing, holidays and so on, it will reappear in the expenditure loop of our model. This is one of the reasons why the expenditure measure of GDP is felt to be a little more accurate, hence the residual error correction which adjusts the income flow measure towards it.

cut down ...). Equally, nuclear waste effusion from both energy production and waste treatment has created a lot of unease if not outright hostility in Ireland and the Isle of Man to conditions in the Irish Sea – although, once again, this has received less publicity than the plight of the UK hill farmers following the fall-out from the Chernobyl nuclear accident. If we want a more accurate measure of wealth created in the year, should we not include an allowance for the environmental or even human resource damage (for example, for occupational disease) which has been caused by our economic activity – if only as a logical development of the 'matching principle', which we already recognize in adjusting GNP to national income?

A further extension of this line of argument is that some 'goods' are not recognized in the measurement of the national accounts. For example, people might choose to consume leisure time rather than to work overtime: in accounting terms, GDP will be reduced by such a decision, since it would involve some loss of output – yet welfare would remain unchanged (or could even rise) with additional leisure replacing the input payments for labour.

Some extremely interesting work has been carried out by economists such as Nordhaus and Tobin to develop a more accurate measure of **net economic welfare**. In this, they have argued the case for adjusting GNP by deducting an allowance for bads, then by adding a further allowance for both non-marketed activities and leisure consumption.

However, rather than pursue this more complex piece of analysis, it is sufficient at this stage to be aware of the issues involved. Our national accounts seek to measure economic activity in the form of GDP (or GNP in a wider context) as accurately as available raw data permits. But be aware that there are potential errors inherent in the sample nature of much of the data, and that most certainly there are omissions of some goods and bads. Our accounting system is far from perfect – but the search for perfection would be elusive, and we could not be sure that it would not impose more costs in data collection and processing than would be justified by the benefits derived from the additional knowledge.

CONCLUSIONS

1. The nation's level of economic activity can be measured by estimating the flow of final goods transactions over the period of a year through either the income or expenditures loops of the circular flow of income model. The data provided for the various items in the national accounts is estimated – but subsequent adjustments of provisional, or inaccurate data are unlikely to involve substantial changes to the stated figures for GDP, GNP, or national income.

2. This data provides crucial information from the viewpoint of government policy formulation:
   (a) It shows the state of the economy at any moment;
   (b) Over time, it indicates trends in performance within the country, or in comparison with other countries, which might suggest the need for some form of policy response;
   (c) Over time, it allows the government to monitor the out-turn of previous policies, as these impact on the national economy.
3. If the figures are being used to assess the performance of the economy over a period of years, they must be interpreted with care. When the data given is in current prices (that is, the flows are valued in the prices of the years of their estimation), the monetary value of the transactions over time will be distorted by the effects of price inflation, to the point where it is difficult to identify changes in the real volumes underlying the flow. Clearly, the higher the rate of inflation, the greater the degree of distortion. To be more certain of identifying real, as opposed to monetary, trends, performance over time should be assessed in terms of constant rather than current prices.
4. Finally, in interpreting the data on GDP or GNP, it is important to remember that it does not pretend to be all-inclusive in its measurement of final goods transactions. It excludes transactions which involve informal services, whether these are freely provided, or whether they are part of the informal market of the 'black economy'. It omits the measurement of some goods, such as leisure, which yield a great deal of value to consumers. It excludes some 'bads', such as criminal activities - but makes no allowance for other bads such as environmental damage, or pollution, or damage to human resources from participating in the production process. In short, it provides the best working database that we can assemble – but should never be treated as being perfectly accurate in what it portrays.

SELF-ASSESSMENT QUESTIONS

TRUE/FALSE QUESTIONS

2.1. GDP at market prices can be computed by aggregating the net value added from intermediate as well as final goods.

2.2. House purchases by consumers should not be included in consumers' expenditure.

2.3. The sale of secondhand goods (for example, used cars) should be excluded from the computation of GDP, since this would involve the double counting of items which have already been included for the same or earlier period.

MULTIPLE CHOICE QUESTIONS

It is possible that more than one answer may be correct in some questions, to force you to think through the options a little more carefully . . . !

2.1. The gross domestic product at factor cost equals:

(a) The sum of all factor incomes (except profits) generated by production of final output;
(b) The sum of all expenditure on final output, excluding foreign trade;
(c) The market value of all intermediate and final goods and services produced in the economy;
(d) The sum of all expenditure on goods and services, net of indirect taxation and subsidies;
(e) The sum of all expenditure on final output, excluding replacement investment.

2.2. Double-counting would be involved in calculating GDP at factor cost if these items were added together:

(a) Indirect taxations and subsidies;
(b) The value of output in flour milling and the value of output in bakeries;
(c) Net value added in the steel industry and net value added in the car industry;
(d) Consumers' expenditure on goods and consumers' expenditure on services.

2.3. In calculating GDP at market prices how many – if any – of the following count as investment?

(a) Purchase of existing shares on the Stock Exchange;
(b) Purchase of a fixed asset, for example, a roadway by the government sector;
(c) Purchase of government securities on the Stock Exchange;
(d) Sale of gas turbines to Russia;
(e) Purchase of a new issue of shares on the Stock Exchange;
(f) Purchase of new machinery and premises.

2.4. Assume GDP at market prices was £68.4 billion in 1975 and had risen to £195.0 billion by 1980. If prices have risen by 160% over the period, what would be the approximate real value of 1980 GDP in terms of 1975 prices? Would it imply an increase or decrease in real output?

(a) £75.0 billion; increase
(b) £121.9 billion; increase
(c) £234.0 billion; increase

(d) £98.5 billion; increase
(e) £67.8 billion; decrease

EXERCISES

2.1. Check out your knowledge of how to measure the level of economic activity. The following are some of the national aggregates for the kingdom of Dalriada in 1989 (in millions of crowns):

Wages and salaries	75
Consumers' expenditure	90
Gross fixed investment	32
Rent income	3
Exports of goods and services	21
Imports of goods and services	18
Net property income received from abroad	−2
General government consumption	29
Stockbuilding	−5

There were no indirect taxes or subsidies.

What is the figure for GDP for Dalriada in 1989 (in millions of crowns)?

(a) 159
(b) 149
(c) 147
(d) 143

2.2. You have just been appointed as economic adviser to a beautiful tropical island. For your own protection, it has a very simple economy. Its only products are breadfruit, which is used for food; timber, half of which is used domestically and the other half exported; logs, which are entirely converted into timber; and houses, which use as materials all of the timber that is not exported. The value of total output of each of these items (without deduction of depreciation of capital goods) over 1989 was (in doubloons):

Breadfruit	20,000
Timber	30,000
Logs	12,000
Houses	23,000

You are asked to estimate the GDP of the island in 1989; while you have tried to remember how to deal with the problem of double-counting, you have calculated several possible results. Which is the correct one?

(a) 85,000
(b) 73,000
(c) 58,000
(d) 43,000

2.3. Can you make any sense yet out of that fabulous quotation from the President of the USA (see Extract 2.1)? What *would* probably happen to the level of economic activity (or GNP in his terms) if taxes (let us assume income tax rates, for simplicity of analysis) were raised?

FINAL OPTIONAL EXERCISE

Two factors have combined to leave the national accounts data in the text of the chapter a little out of date by the time you come to read it. Firstly, there will normally be a two-year lag between the publication of the data and the final year's figures (for example, the 1988 *Annual Abstract* will show a final year of 1986 national accounts figures – although other specialist sources are available for more up-to-date, if provisional, figures). Secondly, it takes time to write and publish a book of this length, so that a 1990 *Annual Abstract* may well be available before you open the pages (as against the 1988 edition which was available to the author at the time of writing). Why not go to your library and take the most recent copy of the *Annual Abstract*; select the corresponding data to that shown in Tables 2.1, 2.2 and 2.3 – and see if there have been any marked changes from the pattern which was discussed in the text.

Note: Solutions can be found at the end of the text.

Chapter 3

Development of the Basic Macroeconomic Model

> Introduction
> The first stage in model building
> The equilibrium level of income
> Building international trade into the model
> Building the government sector into the model
> Equilibrium income and changes
> Testing the model
> Macroeconomic forecasting
> Conclusions
> Self-assessment questions
> Exercise

INTRODUCTION

The previous chapter discussed how economic activity could be defined and measured, and examined how the different components of consumption, investment, government expenditure, exports and imports interacted within the national accounts to set the level of GDP. The main purpose of this chapter is to formalize and develop the circular flow model, to allow us to analyse and predict movements in the level of economic activity in response to specific events. For example, what would happen to the level of GDP in the UK if the exchange rate for the pound sterling rose (as was discussed in Extract 2.3)? Or if consumption expenditure increased in response to cheaper credit charges and lower interest rates? Or if businessmen (and women) became more optimistic and decided to increase their planned level of investment expenditure?

It is not only the professional economist who must be able to answer these questions. Anyone who is seriously involved in business must be able to form his or her own judgement about the likely outcome of events, then plan accordingly to counter or to use these future changes in the business environment. And to predict, we must have a model or systematic framework of analysis.

Much ill-informed criticism has been levelled at the use of abstract theory models in economics; it is often alleged that the subject is so locked into its various theories that it has little to offer the real world, in terms of genuine and practical advice.

This is complete and utter nonsense. The whole thrust and purpose of economics has always been to provide a method of analysis which interprets and provides an understanding of real-world events. It is not enough simply to *describe* what appears to be happening: in all probability, several things will be happening at once, and there could well be some conflict between their different influences. Simple description may only pick up the confusion, without being able to understand it or to provide a balanced view of the final result.

The main strength of economics has always been that it poses the vital question 'Why?' It seeks to probe beneath the surface of superficial observation and description; to provide a clearer understanding of why particular events appear to have followed particular actions; to be able to distinguish between cause and effect; to think through the consequences of a particular action; to identify and compare alternatives; to caution and warn against mindless sloganizing; to give unpopular advice and to draw attention to difficult choices if these do in fact exist behind the rhetoric of politics.

The use of formal theory models is an integral part of economic analysis and has three main purposes:

(1) To simplify complex real-world situations,
(2) To identify the main influences at work,
(3) To build up a systematic understanding of these influences so that past trends can be explained, and future behaviour can be predicted.

The value of any economic model lies in its explanatory and predictive power, relative to the real-world situation on which it is based. While it is essentially a simplification of reality, its analytical performance must still provide a meaningful insight into real-world events. It is this which is the ultimate and acid test of all modelling.

By the end of this chapter therefore, we would hope that you have developed:

- A clearer understanding of the behaviour of the different expenditure elements of consumption, investment, government, exports and imports;
- A better awareness of the process by which the level of GDP is established by these elements;
- An understanding of the concept of 'equilibrium income', and what is implied by this;
- An improved ability to analyse and explain why past actions and events have influenced the level of GDP;
- An ability to use the basic model to predict the possible future consequences of current events and policy actions;
- An understanding in principle of the process and problems of macroeconomic forecasting.

THE FIRST STAGE IN MODEL BUILDING

To allow the model to concentrate on the essential features of its given situation, a set of strict operational assumptions will normally be defined and used to simplify and strip away some of the complexities of the real world. Once the model has been established, it is normal for at least some of the assumptions to be relaxed, and the model modified to deal with the greater complexity which results. But, while the assumptions are operational, they define the conditions within which the model functions in its stated form. This must always be remembered since, if the model's conclusion and predictions are applied blindly to the real world, they could well contain dangerous naivities and inaccuracies.

Basic assumptions

To set up our basic macroeconomic model, it is normal to make two key, simplifying assumptions. These are that:

(1) *The price level remains constant throughout the analysis*.
    The purpose of this assumption is to postpone discussion of the

phenomenon of price inflation until a later stage of the book. An important consequence of this assumption is that changes in expenditure will always imply that there have been genuine changes in real output levels.

(2) *The stock of capital and labour resources within the economy remains constant but adequate, and the state of technology within which they are combined also remains constant.*

This assumption has two main purposes. Firstly, it excludes the complexities which would be introduced by economic growth. Secondly, it ensures that output adjustments will not be thwarted by input constraints and input price increases; the existing stocks of capital and labour can be used more or less intensively. An important consequence of the assumption is that any change in the level of output can only be made by changing the level of employment, that is, the variable input of labour combined with the fixed input or stock of capital.

These two assumptions strip away for the moment many of the complexities of the real world, and help us to build up a model capable of analysing the remaining real-world influences in a simple, stylized form. But, before we start to do so, it is necessary to make a third assumption, to build in a device which allows our model to adjust towards a solution for whatever set of events it seeks to analyse. This assumption is that:

(3) *Investment expenditure includes unsold stock or inventories, and firms will have a pre-planned, or target, level of inventories which they will try to achieve.*

There are two consequences of this assumption: firstly, it eliminates the real-world problem of passive investment, or disinvestment in output (that is, where sales diverge by more than is expected from planned levels of output); and, secondly, as we will shortly see, it provides us with a simple adjustment mechanism for the model.

We are now ready to start model building but, before we do so in earnest, think back to one of our main findings in Chapter 2, when we set up our circular flow model of the national accounts. We showed there that the total expenditure (E) received by UK firms, as measured at the foot of the expenditure loop in Figure 2.2, was the sum of consumption expenditure of households (C), investment expenditure, or the sale of production goods to other firms (I), government expenditure (G), and exports (X) – with negative adjustments for the leakages of imports (M) and net expenditure taxation (T_e). In summary form then:

$$E = C + I + G + X - M - T_e$$

38   Understanding the Economy

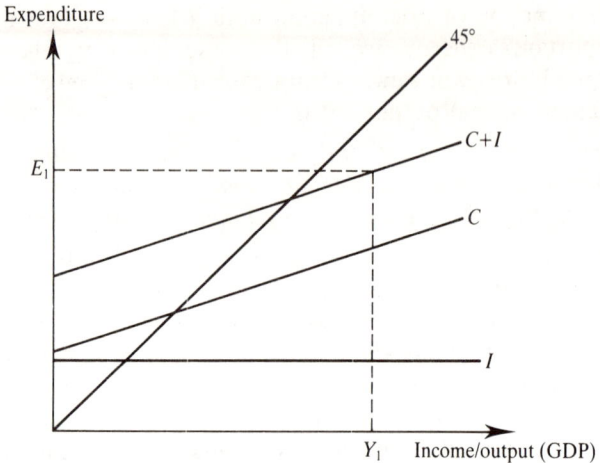

Figure 3.1   Consumption and investment expenditure.

When our model has been completed, it must, therefore, show what these various elements look like in diagram form, and how they interact to set the resultant level of GDP.

In constructing the model, the same stages will be used as in Chapter 2: only households' and firms' expenditure will be shown initially; then international trade will be added; finally, the government sector will be drawn into the analysis, to complete the model.

The first stage of the model is shown in Figure 3.1. The vertical axis measures expenditure (in the form of consumption from households and investment from firms). The horizontal axis measures GDP, which is given the symbol Y; it will be remembered from Chapter 2 that this is the money value of all goods and services produced in the country over the period of a year, and that it is simultaneously a measure of output, and of the income generated by that output.

The first element to be examined and then built into the model is household expenditure, or consumption (C). For the community as a whole, it is probable that total consumption spending will be related to the level of income which is available. As an opening argument it is likely that, as the level of income rises, then the absolute level of consumption expenditure will also rise. In short, against the range of incomes represented by the horizontal axis of Figure 3.1, the consumption expenditure function (that is, the graph showing consumption spending for each possible level of income) is likely to slope upwards from left to right.

But what sort of slope? If all income was consumed, then the consumption function would rise at 45° from the origin. If you can

Development of the Basic Macroeconomic Model

remember your basic geometry (it has nothing at all to do with economics; we get blamed for enough on our own account!), the 45° line links the coordinates of all points of equal distance along the two axes.

However, we can do a little better than this to set up a plausible pattern of consumption behaviour.

(1) At very low income levels, it is probable that the current level of income is not enough to cover expenditure needs for truly basic goods and services, such as food, clothing, shelter, and purchases of economics textbooks. (OK – but you can still suffer from insomnia, even if you are poor!) Therefore, consumption spending may exceed current income, being funded either from running down past savings, or from borrowing against future income; let us call both **dis-saving**. If we accept this argument, then we have decided that consumption will be some positive figure – even at zero income. But does this mean that the consumption function will start from some positive intercept (that is, positive consumption value above zero income) and lie parallel above the 45° line? Not necessarily.

(2) At the same time, households (with the possible exception of the author's own household) are unlikely to consume *all* of the income available, once this is enough to cover essential consumption needs. Normally, as additional income becomes available, a proportion of this will be saved; remember the leakage of savings from the model in Figure 2.2. If this is so, then the slope of the consumption function will be less than 45°.

The end result of our simple theorizing is that the consumption function is likely to have the form illustrated in Figure 3.1:

- It will have a positive intercept,
- It will have a slope of less than 45°,
- For simplicity in model building, it will take the form of a linear (or straight line) function.

In summary, we have argued that:

$$C = a + cY$$

where

C = the absolute level of consumption spending

a = the value of the intercept (that is, of consumption spending at zero income)

c = the proportion of new income which is consumed, (which is defined technically as 'the marginal propensity to consume')

For example, if

$a = 20$

$c = 0.8$

then, at an income level of, say 200

$C = a + cY$

$= 20 + 0.8(200)$

$= 180$

Or, where the income level is zero

$C = a + cY$

$= 20 + 0.8(0)$

$= 20$

In other words, having set up the equation for the consumption function, it is then possible to calculate the total amount of consumption spending for any given level of income. Chapter 4 will look at the behaviour of consumer spending in more detail.

The next step is to bring investment expenditure (I) into the model, recognizing that part of the firms sector's output will take the form of producer goods (including inventories). A similar intuitive approach can be taken, to define the behavioural nature of investment within the model. This time, the problem is that investment is likely to be more strongly influenced by factors other than the level of current incomes. After all, investment is essentially a long-term decision; it is a foolish firm which would increase or decrease its productive capacity on the basis of a temporary surge, or lapse of sales.

For modelling purposes, therefore, investment expenditure will be treated as being influenced by factors other than the absolute level of income in the UK for the period in question. For example, investment decisions might reflect factors such as the cost of capital, or the state of business expectations, or the size of the stock of productive capital available in the economy. Realistically, these factors may very well be influenced at least indirectly by the income level of the period. However, in terms of our basic model[1] we shall simply treat planned investment

---

1. If preferred, the investment function can be given a positive slope, that is, take the nature of $I = b + iY$ to show the influence of income, without disturbing the logic of the analysis.

expenditure as being *constant and autonomous*, that is, as being set by factors outside our model, so that it holds the same constant value over the range of possible incomes, for example, amounting to, say, 40 for any level of income.

This does not mean that investment expenditure will *always* have this value. If, for example, there is an upsurge in business optimism, or a reduction in the cost of capital borrowed for investment purposes, then it is quite likely that the figure for investment in our model will rise, say from the original value of 40 to a new higher value of 45. The key point to grasp is that the absolute level of investment, in our basic model, is completely insensitive to the level of current income, and is set by (and responsive to) influences which are not contained within that model. Chapter 5 will look at the factors influencing investment expenditure in more detail.

The model now contains both the expenditure elements from our simple households' and firms' two-sector economic system. We can now calculate the total level of expenditure (E) which will result from any given level of income, if the C and I functions in Figure 3.1 are added together, to give a $C + I$, or aggregate expenditure function. This will lie above the consumption function, with the vertical distance between the two functions representing the constant level of investment expenditure.

Total expenditure can now be read off any level of income, for example, at Y_1 total expenditure will be E_1. Alternatively, given the earlier values for the consumption function, and assuming a value, of say, 40 for the investment expenditure, then at an income level of 200, total expenditure (E) will be:

$$E = C + I$$
$$= 20 + 0.8(200) + 40$$
$$= 220$$

Or again, for an income level of 400

$$E = C + I$$
$$= 20 + 0.8(400) + 40$$
$$= 380$$

THE EQUILIBRIUM LEVEL OF INCOME

Up till now we have been content simply to say that the different elements of expenditure interact to set the level of GDP for the economic system in question. It is now time to take a more careful look at this process of interaction, and at the way in which the final level of economic activity emerges.

This involves us in a new concept of **equilibrium income**. The term 'equilibrium' is a vital concept within economics. In economics, an equilibrium situation is one from which there is no need for change, because a solution has been found which holds in balance the forces and flows at work in the model. In price theory, the equilibrium price is the price level at which the demand and supply flows are in balance; there is no excess demand (causing price to rise), or excess supply (causing price to fall) to disrupt the market price.

The same is true for the equilibrium level of income. This time we are dealing with the flow of output onto the macroeconomic market, and the flow of planned expenditure from households and firms which will take up these goods and services.

The equilibrium condition for our basic model (or the conditions which will bring the flows into balance) is that:

available output is taken up by planned expenditure

so that neither a surplus nor a deficit results.

In terms of the basic model, available output is simply the GDP which has been produced during the year; we have already given this the symbol Y. Planned expenditure, in turn, is simply the sum of the total expenditure from households and firms, which will result from that GDP; we have already given this total expenditure the symbol E, households' expenditure the symbol C for consumption, and firms' expenditure the symbol I for investment.

Therefore, in equilibrium:

$$Y = E$$

and, since

$$E = C + I$$

then

$$Y = C + I$$

becomes the condition for equilibrium.

How does this work, in terms of Figure 3.2? You will see from your first glance that this diagram simply repeats the information which we have already built up for the model in Figure 3.1. You know that we can read off total expenditure (or E) for any given level of GDP, from the aggregate expenditure function $C + I$; we can also read off the output

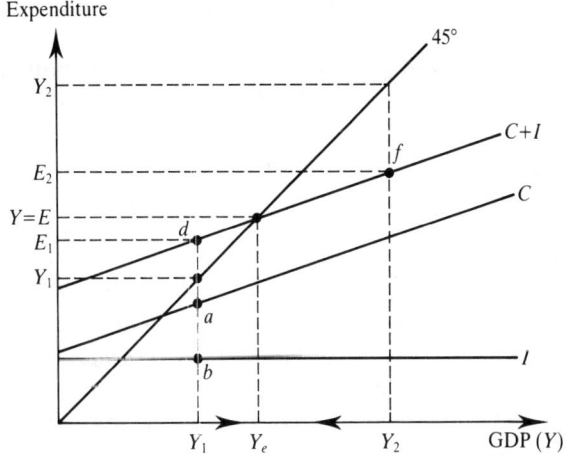

Figure 3.2 Equilibrium in the model.

available, or GDP from the horizontal axis. For convenience, we can use the 45° line to transfer this value from the horizontal to the vertical axis (remember, the 45° line links the co-ordinates of equal distance points along the two axes, which allows us to rotate values from one axis to the other).

To see how equilibrium income is established, select the level of economic activity measured by Y_1 on the horizontal axis.

At this level of economic activity, consumption expenditure will be aY_1 and investment expenditure bY_1; total expenditure will be the sum of these values, which is shown on the $C + I$ function as dY_1, or E_1, on the vertical axis. This is the level of expenditure which will be generated from the level of economic activity corresponding to Y_1. But does it represent an equilibrium? It does not. When the GDP level is rotated to the vertical axis, this shows that the level of expenditure (E_1) will exceed the level of output available, as measured by the GDP level of (Y_1).

Clearly this is not an equilibrium, but how then does the model move towards its equilibrium? We can show this adjustment process by returning to the various assumptions which we set up at the start of our model building exercise. If expenditure exceeds available output, then this must mean that, in the short term, expenditure (or demand), can only be met by running down the level of inventories available. But this means that firms will then hold *less* than their planned, or target level of inventories. To meet this higher than anticipated level of demand and also to restore inventories to their target level, the firms' sector will have to increase its level of output. Given our assumptions about fixed capital stock and constant technology, output can only be increased by increasing the labour input, that is, by raising the number of persons employed. This, will raise income from employment (and, in turn, expenditure), so that the economy will move to the right along the horizontal axis.

This will happen for all levels of GDP which lie to the left of Y_e; because, over this range of GDP, planned expenditure will *always* exceed available output, so that the expansion process which we have described will always be activated.

In contrast, if Y_2 had been taken as the starting point, the total level of expenditure at this income level could have been read from the $C + I$ function as fY_2, or E_2 on the vertical axis. When this was matched against the level of output implied by the GDP level of Y_2 income, then it would have been seen that expenditure (E_2) was less than the output available (Y_2). In this instance, unsold output would raise inventories beyond their target level. Firms would, therefore, cut their level of output to match the lower levels of demand, and to reduce inventories to their planned level. Output, employment, and income would fall; in terms of the model, Y would move to the left. This would hold for all levels of GDP to the right of Y_e, since available output would exceed planned expenditure over this range of GDP, triggering an adjustment process of contraction.

By a process of elimination, we have identified the equilibrium level of economic activity for the model. Clearly, the only level of income at which the flows of ouput and expenditure are in balance is at Y_e. Only at Y_e, below the intersection of the $C + I$ function and the 45° line does

$$Y = E$$

or

$$Y = C + I$$

so that the output available is taken up by the combined expenditures of households and firms, and the planned level of inventories (that is, unsold output) is achieved.

In short, within the artificial limits created by our set of assumptions we can see that the basic model will adjust naturally towards equilibrium, which represents a solution to the flows of information which are contained within the model. Having achieved this, there would then be no incentive for further change; the macroeconomy would remain at this equilibrium level of income, so long as there were no further changes in the information contained in the model.

BUILDING INTERNATIONAL TRADE INTO THE MODEL

As in the previous chapter, it is now time to broaden the simple two-sector model, by building into it the influences associated with the transaction flows of international trade. You will remember that these flows were split into the sale of output abroad in the form of exports, and the purchase of output from abroad in the form of imports.

The inclusion of exports is a simple matter, and follows the same type of logic which characterized our treatment of investment expenditure by UK firms. As with the latter, it is argued that export sales are influenced by factors other than the level of income in the UK; our exports are the sum of other countries' imports from us, and these imports, in turn, will reflect consumption levels and income levels in these overseas countries. This argument is plausible enough, but it ignores the uncomfortable relationship between UK exports and the UK's level of GDP; frequently, at high income levels, it would appear that goods destined for export have been diverted to the easier UK domestic market, to satisfy demand there – with the converse that export sales appear to have been pursued more earnestly when domestic demand levels were depressed. In short, to argue that the level of GDP in the UK does not influence the level of exports from the UK is very much a simplification of reality.[2]

Nevertheless, for the purposes of this present model, exports will be treated as constant and autonomous, or independent of the UK level of income, holding a constant value over the range of GDP on the horizontal axis, for example at, say, 25 for any level of income.

Given the similarity of behaviour between the two injections of investment and export expenditure, it is normal to gather them together into a single **injections function** and given the symbol $J = I + X$.

The inclusion of imports into the model is a little more complicated. In the real world, both consumption expenditure and investment expenditure will contain a significant element of imported goods and services. Since these imports represent a leakage of expenditure from the UK economic system, it is clear that they must be built into our basic model as a deduction from these other elements of expenditure. However, since our intention is to set up only a simple basic model, we will treat imports as affecting *only* consumption expenditure.[3]

---

2. There is also a price influence involved here, in that the higher levels of UK demand tend to result in higher rates of price inflation, and therefore higher export prices – which could help to explain why export sales tend to contract at higher levels of domestic economic activity. Apart from this, if you wish to build in this more realistic relationship then, as we did for investment, you can use the revised function of $X = d - xY$, without disturbing the logic of the analysis.

3. It would be an equally simple matter to treat I as I^*, that is, I net of import content ($I^* = I - M$); this would drop the horizontal level of the J function in Figure 3.4 to $J = I - M + X$.

46 Understanding the Economy

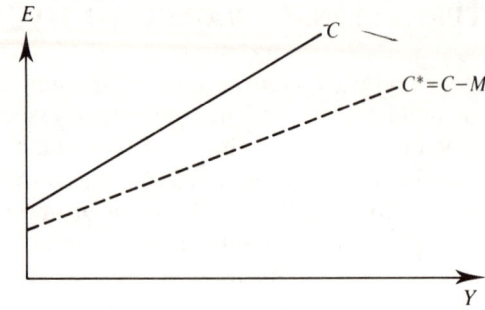

Figure 3.3 The effect of deducting imports from consumption.

If imports (M) are taken to be a proportion (m) of consumption expenditure (C), then:

$$M = mC$$

and consumption expenditure takes the revised form of:

$$C^* = C - M$$

or

$$C^* = C - mC$$
$$= C(1 - m)$$

How does this affect the consumption function of the basic model? Figure 3.3 shows both the original consumption function C, and the adjusted consumption function of C^*. The vertical distance between the two functions at any level of income represents the absolute level of expenditure on imported goods and services for this level of GDP.

Does this in any way affect the concept of equilibrium income?

There is absolutely no reason why it should. Figure 3.4 shows our amended model for income determination. The only changes from the model depicted in Figure 3.2 are that the consumption function C^* is now stated net of expenditure on imports, and exports are added to the original investment function to create a new injections function J. The logic of equilibrium income is unchanged; there will only be an equilibrium when available output (Y) is taken up exactly by planned expenditure (E), that is, where

$$Y = E$$

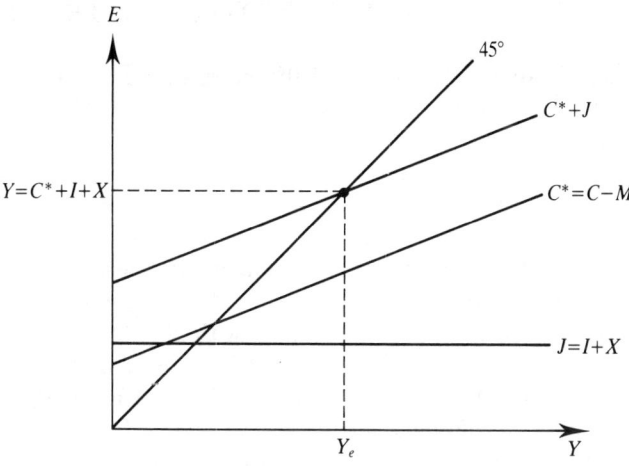

Figure 3.4 Imports and exports built into the model.

and, since

$$E = C^* + I + X$$

in our revised model, then there will only be an equilibrium when

$$Y = C^* + I + X$$

From Figure 3.4, you will see that this will only occur at Y_e, that is, the level of GDP immediately below the point where the aggregate expenditure function of $C^* + J$ cuts the 45° line. Think through what would happen at any other level of GDP. If it lies to the left of Y_e, then planned expenditure would exceed available output, so that the expansion adjustment process would be triggered, to nudge the economy back to Y_e; conversely, at any level of GDP to the right of Y_e, available output would exceed planned expenditure, so that inventories would exceed their target level, and the contraction adjustment process would be triggered, to nudge the economy back to the left, to Y_e.

In other words, despite the inclusion of the transaction flows associated with international trade, the economy would tend to adjust naturally, as before, towards its equilibrium level of income, which would still be the level of GDP where available output was just sufficient to satisfy the planned level of expenditure from all sectors within the model.

BUILDING THE GOVERNMENT SECTOR INTO THE MODEL

The final stage in our construction of the basic model is to modify it to include the transaction flows associated with the public or government sector. You will remember from the previous chapter that the government's activities were divided into the injection effect of government expenditure (through purchases of input services from households, or outputs of goods and services from firms), and the withdrawal effect of taxation (whether via taxes on household income, or firms' business profits, or as taxes on expenditure).

Government expenditure is dealt with in the same way as investment and export expenditure (and is discussed in more detail in Chapter 7). Once again it is argued that the element is influenced more by factors outside the model than by the level of GDP, at least in the context of the current year; in effect, external socio-political considerations will determine both decisions and budgets, which will be implemented as a separate issue from the level of economic activity in any single time period. Once again this is a simplification, in the sense that the level of income will have at least an indirect influence on government expenditure decisions. For instance, if a relatively low level of income, or economic activity is expected, with all the attendant problems of rising unemployment levels, the government might decide to increase its level of expenditure in a deliberate attempt to boost the economy. Conversely, if there is a fear that the macroeconomy is 'overheating' (that is, in response to excessive demand pressure) the government might choose to reduce its expenditure, in an attempt to take some demand pressure out of the economy.[4] But, on the other hand, the changes witnessed in government expenditure plans may reflect policy decisions taken against a longer-term context than that of current events; for example, the 'privatization' programme which has reduced the government's share of total domestic expenditure so dramatically over the 1980s has probably reflected a mixture of policy motives. The government has been keen to reduce the scale of the public sector within the UK economy for a variety of reasons (which will be discussed in Chapter 10); it has also helped to cut back on expenditure demands, and therefore to reduce the size of the **public sector borrowing requirement** (broadly the sums which have to be borrowed by government to make up any shortfall between expenditure plans and receipts from taxation); it is even possible that part of its enthusiasm for privatization is based on its contribution of revenue, which has helped to permit cuts to be made in income tax rates. None of these would come as a direct response to the current level of GDP.

Where we were left with this type of situation before, we simply

---

4. Such actions would imply a downwards sloping government expenditure function, of the form $G = e - gY$; again, this would not disturb the logic of the analysis.

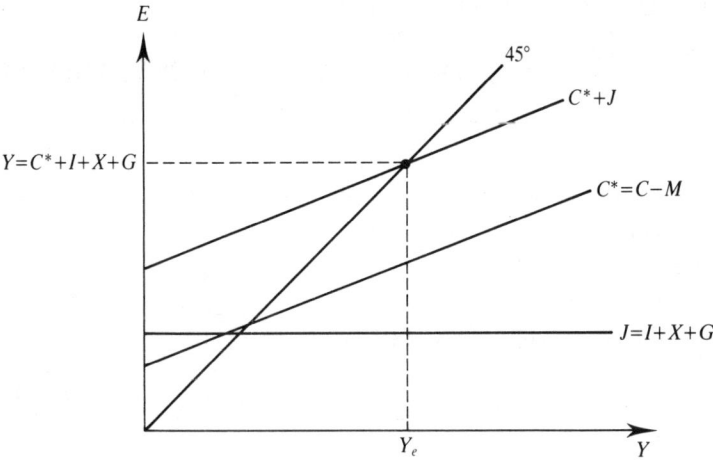

Figure 3.5 The completed model, with international trade flows and the public sector.

built the term into our model by taking it to be constant and autonomous, that is, indicating that it was primarily affected by influences from outside the model. The same approach is taken in relation to government expenditure; this element is assumed to have the same constant value, irrespective of the level of income; for the purpose of subsequent illustration, let us take this as, say, 30 for all levels of GDP.

In Figure 3.5 we show how the revised injection function now brings together the total expenditure figure from the three constant and autonomous elements of investment, exports and government expenditure, that is:

$$J = I + X + G$$

At first sight, the inclusion of the leakage effects of taxation would seem to be a rather more formidable task, but this is not the case. Remember that we are dealing, in effect, with the expenditure loop of the model depicted in Figure 2.2; expenditure taxes are the only leakage from this particular flow of transactions. If you think back to the detail of the national accounts, you will remember that the various expenditure elements were shown at their market price values, that is, inclusive of expenditure tax. But, although we deducted expenditure taxes as a total to convert our measurement of GDP from market prices to factor cost, it is also possible to do this item by item. Look at Table 3.1, and you will see that there is an alternative table in the national accounts which states consumption, investment and all the other elements at their factor cost values, that is, net of expenditure tax. The end figure for GDP at factor cost is the same in both cases.

Table 3.1 UK – GDP, 1986 (£ billion).

	At market prices	At factor cost
Consumption	234.2	192.2
Government final consumption	79.4	74.5
Gross domestic fixed capital formation	64.2	59.9
Stocks/wip	0.6	–
Total domestic expenditure	378.4	326.5
Exports	97.8	93.9
Imports	(55.8)	(101.3)
GDP	319.1	319.1

(Source: *National Income and Expenditure Accounts*, 1987, Table 1.2. Reprinted by permission of the Controller, HMSO.)

Therefore, to build expenditure taxes into our model, we need do no more that state each of the other elements at their factor cost values. No further adjustment is needed to build in the leakage from expenditure taxes.

The basic model has now been fully completed and is shown in Figure 3.5. Once again, there has been no change in the condition for equilibrium. The economic system will adjust until available output is just sufficient to satisfy the planned expenditure from all sectors at factor cost values or, in the now familiar form:

$$Y = E$$

and, since

$$E = C^* + I + X + G$$

then

$$Y = C^* + I + X + G$$

This will clearly only happen at the level of GDP immediately below the intersection of the aggregate expenditure function and the 45° line, that is, at Y_e level of GDP. At any level of GDP to the left of this, aggregate expenditure will exceed available output, triggering the expansion adjustment towards Y_e; conversely, at any level of GDP to the right of this, available output will exceed planned expenditure, triggering the contraction adjustment towards Y_e. Once again, the economy will tend to adjust naturally towards its equilibrium level of income and will then remain there, provided that there is no change to the information contained in the model.

EQUILIBRIUM INCOME AND CHANGES

This equilibrium will only hold if the behavioural patterns summarized in the model are unchanged. So long as the values for C, I, G, X, M and expenditure taxes remain as shown, then the economy will normally adjust back towards Y_e, following any short-term disturbance.

But if one or more of these elements changes in its behavioural pattern, then its new value must be built into the model in the form of a revision; this, in turn, will normally result in a new aggregate expenditure function (unless there are two changes in opposite directions, which cancel each other out, for example, if G rises by 10, and I falls by the same figure). If this happens, then the old equilibrium value for GDP will no longer bring the flows into balance, so that the model must search out a new solution, or equilibrium.

For example, let us assume that there is a rise in business optimism, as a result of which investment plans are revised upwards (say from the illustrated value of 40 to a new value of 45). Figure 3.6 illustrates the consequences of the change in information. The original information fed into the model was that the total of expenditure (E_1) would be made up from:

$$E_1 = C^*_1 + I_1 + G_1 + X_1$$

where all are stated at their factor cost adjusted values (that is, net of expenditure taxation). Given this information, the equilibrium level of income would be at the GDP level of Y_1, immediately below the intersection of the aggregate expenditure function (or $C^*_1 + J_1$) and the 45° line. If the level of investment expenditure rises from 40 to 45, or from I_1 to I_2 in terms of the diagram, then this will also raise the injection function to J_2 (where $J_2 = I_2 + G_1 + X_1$) and, as a result, aggregate expenditure function to $C^*_1 + J_2$. Note from the model that only investment of the various expenditure elements has been changed; all other elements still hold their original levels.

At the old equilibrium level of GDP Y_1, it can be seen that the higher level of total expenditure E' now exceeds available output; these values are shown on the vertical axis of the model. Inventories will fall below their planned, or target level. As before, firms will raise their level of output to compensate – and there will be the familiar upwards revision

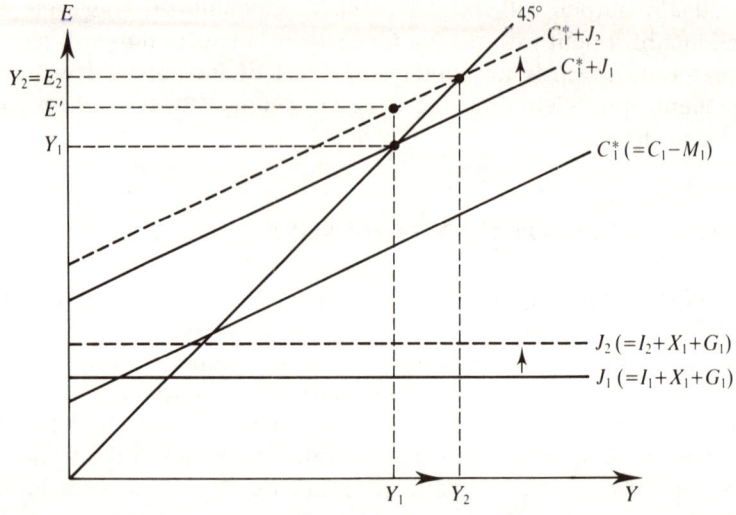

Figure 3.6 The effect on equilibrium GDP of an increase in investment.

of income and expenditure, as the economy adjusts to the right along the horizontal axis. This adjustment will continue until our equilibrium condition is once again satisfied; this will occur at the new equilibrium GDP level of Y_2, which lies below the intersection of the new aggregate expenditure function and the 45° line.

In other words, if there is a change of information within the model, here taking the form of a revised level of investment expenditure, then there is likely to be an adjustment towards a new equilibrium level of income. The equilibrium is only a position from which there is no incentive to change while it remains the solution for the original set of information within the model. If there is a change, there will be a search for a new solution, or revised equilibrium.

TESTING THE MODEL

Earlier in the unit, it was argued that the real worth of any model lies in its ability to explain, or predict in the real world. The model performs well here, despite its simplicity and the variety of assumptions upon which it is based. Over 1979–81, rising and then sustained high UK exchange rates embarrassed domestic manufacturing industries; the effects of the high exchange valuation of sterling were that UK exports were made substantially more expensive in terms of customer countries' currencies,

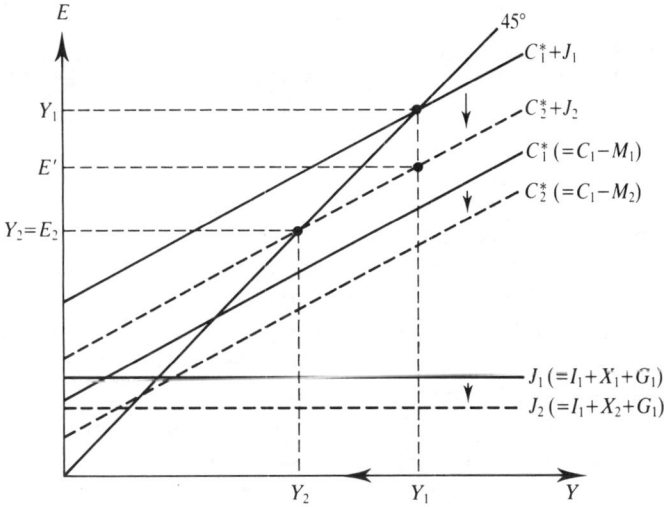

Figure 3.7 The effect on equilibrium GDP of an increase in the UK exchange rate.

while imports to the UK became relatively cheaper in terms of their pound sterling prices. The effect of this type of movement in exchange rates is analysed in Figure 3.7.

Higher imports, as a proportion of UK consumption expenditure would cause the consumption function to be revised downwards from C^*_1 to C^*_2, where M_2 represents the new higher expenditure figure on imports.[5] At the same time, the fall in exports would reduce these from X_1 to X_2, pulling the injection function downwards from J_1 to J_2. The overall effect of the increase in UK exchange rates would be to reduce the aggregate expenditure function from $C^*_1 + J_1$ to the lower level of $C^*_2 + J_2$. In terms of our basic model, at the old equilibrium level of income, output (Y_1) would exceed expenditure (now E'), so that inventory levels would rise above their planned, or target levels. UK firms would therefore cut back their output levels, because of the shortfall in demand, and the need to reduce inventories. As a result of this,

---

5. In the diagram, the shift has left the two C^* functions still parallel; but this is unlikely to be the case in reality. It is probable that the substitution towards greater import purchases would be greater at higher levels of income and, therefore, consumption expenditure – which would imply that the vertical distance between the functions would increase with income. This in turn would be reflected in the relative positions of the two aggregate expenditure, or $C^* + J$ functions (which would pick up the different slopes to the C^* functions). This effect has been ignored, for simplicity, in both the analysis given in the text of the chapter and in Figure 3.7.

employment would fall, reducing UK income levels. The new equilibrium would be established at the GDP level Y_2, where the aggregate expenditure function of $C^*_2 + J_2$ intersects the 45° line, and output is again taken up by the various expenditure elements and desired inventory holdings.

In fact, as you will no doubt remember, the UK economy did respond along these lines over 1979–81. It is very probable that exchange rate movement did exacerbate the drift into an already severe recession and depression. You will also remember from the previous chapter that fears of a similar adverse effect lay behind the bitter dispute between the Prime Minister and the Chancellor during April and May 1988. The basic model, for all its artificial simplicity, does provide a useful insight into the workings of the real world and more complex economy.

Equally, the model is capable of predictive analysis. For example, it can be run in the reverse to show what would happen if the UK succeeded in reducing its production costs to the point where it achieved a real competitive advantage in price terms, at home and abroad. If export prices were to be reduced, then exports would rise from X_2 to X_1; if UK goods could undercut import prices, then consumers would switch from the latter to domestically produced items, raising consumption net of imports from C^*_2 to C^*_1. Aggregate expenditure would therefore rise from $C^*_2 + J_2$ to $C^*_1 + J_1$. The initial excess of expenditure over current output levels, and the resultant fall in inventory levels, would make UK firms increase their output and employment levels, raising the income level ultimately to its new equilibrium of Y_1. To some extent, this explains the current government's insistence that the UK firms' sector *must* become more competitive – not least because of the implications of the completely free market conditions within the European Community by 1992.

Again it would seem that the model, despite its simplicity, can be used to provide insight and understanding. Its ability to do so will allow us to run it repeatedly in the chapters which follow.

MACROECONOMIC FORECASTING

We said above that the basic model can be used for prediction purposes, then illustrated how this might be done in simple, diagrammatic form. But in the real world, more sophisticated variants of our model are in regular use, by a wide variety of institutions, to provide a series of macroeconomic forecasts for the UK and other world economies. This allows both the government of the economic system, and also the managers of businesses operating within that economic system, to peer into the future and to plan how to exploit or counter the likely events which appear to be about to emerge and engulf them.

Over recent years there has been a proliferation of economic forecasting agencies, dealing with world, or national, or regional, or even industry wide forecasts. Given that forecasting, however sophisticated the model, remains little more than educated guessing, the output of these forecasters might well cause some confusion as they deluge us with a mass of figures. While there may be some broad consensus, there will always be some differences in the magnitude, or the timing of the events forecast – or even in the direction of movement to, or caused by these events. After all, for every two economists you will get three opinions – so why should the results from their models be any different?

To form some judgement on the basis of these forecasts, you must have some idea of how they are developed, and what they are trying to do. Only then can you pick your way through the jungle of forecast information.

Stripped of its mathematical detail, economic forecasting is a simple enough process. From our basic model we know that the economic system will tend towards equilibrium, when:

$$Y = C + I + G + X - M$$

This, in turn can be rearranged (by moving imports across the equals sign) to show that:

$$C + I + G + X = Y + M$$

In this form, the equation lists all the demand elements on its lefthand side (demand from UK households, firms, government, and exports), and lists the available supplies from which this demand will be satisfied on its righthand side (domestic GDP and imported goods and services). In passing, it is worth noting how this arrangement of the equilibrium equation shows very clearly why rapid increases in demand can spill over all too quickly into rising imports, since it is generally easier to obtain these than to increase domestic output at short notice.

Macroeconomic forecasting is simply the process of trying to establish values for these six elements over a given period ahead, usually six to 18 months. Obviously, professional forecasters use a more sophisticated version of our own basic model and normally work from a computerized system of equations – which, nevertheless, performs in the same broad way as is indicated by the diagrammatic model.

To give some idea of the problems involved, let us simply look at the single demand element of consumption expenditure. Without concerning ourselves too much with the modelling implications, what are likely to be the main economic influences on the absolute level of consumption? Commonsense tells us that it is likely to be related to available personal income. But this, in turn, is likely to have at least two separate sources: firstly, there will be income from current earnings – adjusted for savings decisions; secondly, there is the option of borrowing against future income, from banks, building societies, and other financial institutions. Our model must now move back down the chain; current earnings for the household sector will reflect influences such as the level of employment, productivity levels, and rates of pay. These in turn will depend upon the relationship between the level of demand for final output, and the consequences of this on the demand and supply position of the labour market. Additionally, productivity will reflect possible changes in technology, or in working practices, while pay rates will also be influenced by institutional factors such as the degree of militancy among workers. Then, realistically, we must build in current income from other sources apart from earnings, which brings in income from rent, interest payments received, dividends, pensions, unemployment and the whole range of other social security payments. Next, we must recognize that some of these income sources will be subject to taxation before becoming available for personal expenditure; are any changes in taxation policy likely for the period ahead – or will any recent major changes, such as those following the Spring 1988 budget, affect available income and therefore consumption? If we now go back to consider the borrowing element in consumption expenditure, this will start us on a new chain of relationships. It will reflect influences such as the cost and availability of credit – or even the sheer persuasion and aggression of the competition for credit from among the various financial institutions which are now operating directly within each other's markets. Nor are we finished yet: realistically, spending will reflect price levels, both in absolute terms and in terms of consumers' expectations about future prices. (Will it be cheaper, or more expensive if we postpone buying for a year?)

It is not our intention to confuse; the previous paragraph simply lists some of the influences which forecasters will have to systematize, then build into modelling relationships. The degree of sophistication will vary from model to model – and from element to element within each model. Most forecasters depend heavily on systems of equations – indeed new generations of forecasters have tended to make models ever more complex in the interests of 'making forecasting more scientific as an exercise'. Older sceptics may be forgiven for suspecting that part of the increasing complexity reflects the desire of young forecasters to 'personalize' the model. We will give them the benefit of the doubt; forecasting has become so important a part of our strategic planning, at both government and individual business level, that we need to achieve ever more accurate series of figures.

Finally, however impressive the model, there will always be a need for raw data beyond that which is available in the official statistics, and for assumptions to be made about possible future events. It is not enough simply to extrapolate past trends to extract future figures. In the immortal words of Sir Alex Cairncross,[6] written ruefully after years of involvement in preparing economic forecasts for a variety of governments:

> '... a trend is a trend is a trend
> but the question is, will it bend?
> Will it alter its course
> through some unforeseen force
> and come to a premature end ... ?'

Hence, buried within every model there will be some nasty and awkward little corners, where model builders have had to abandon their maths, or even their surveys of intent, and 'take a view'; lesser mortals would describe this exercise as 'guessing' – in fairness, informed and educated guessing, but guessing nevertheless. Scientists do not like guessing, hence, this provides another reason for the trend towards ever more complex models, which can do the guessing for you!

However, to repeat our initial statement, whatever the model, whatever its degree of complexity, its basic objective will be to produce a series of figures which will fill in values (or show percentage increases for future over current values) for each of the six elements in the equilibrium equation. See Table 3.2. This shows, as at June 1988, the most recent (at the time of writing) OECD forecast for the UK rates of change in demand and supply elements over the period 1987 to 1989, on a half yearly basis. Take time to study the table.

But what is this? 1988 forecasts of December and June 1987? Yes, it is quite true. The first job in any forecast if to forecast the recent past and the present. The reason for this is that the statistical data which is fed into the forecasting models is, in some cases, quite badly out of date. Some items we know on a day-to-day basis, such as movements in gold and currency reserves. Other data has to be collected, collated, processed, which imposes a whole series of lags in our basic information; the further removed the forecaster is from internal government data sources, the longer are these lags, since only published final data will be available. It is impossible to give an average lag but, even within government, where there can be an access to at least provisional figures, three to six months' delays might be experienced for some key data. Great efforts have been made to reduce these lags but, to borrow a vivid image from F.W. Paish (another senior government adviser of some 20 years ago), we are still very much in the position of driving a car, with our only area of vision (data availability) being through the rear view mirror; we

---

6. 'Economic forecasting', *Economic Journal* **LXXIX**, No. 316, December 1969.

Table 3.2 *UK demand, output and prices*. Percentage change from previous period, seasonally adjusted at annual rates, volume (1980 prices).

	1982 Current prices billion £	1985	1986	1987	1988	1989	1987 I	1987 II	1988 I	1988 II	1989 I	1989 II
Private consumption	168.2	3.9	6.0	5.2	5	3¼	3.7	8.3	4¼	3¼	3¼	3¼
Government consumption	60.4	0	1.2	1.2	1¼	1½	−0.2	3.7	0	1½	1½	1½
Gross fixed investment	44.8	3.0	−0.3	3.5	6¾	4	−0.4	8.2	7¼	5	4	3½
Public[a]	11.4	−14.3	0.7	−9.0	−¾	0	−13.1	−2.7	0	0	0	0
Private residential	6.8	−5.2	9.6	6.7	11¼	4	−11.8	27.2	7¾	4½	4	4
Private non-residential	26.6	12.7	−2.6	7.2	8	5¼	7.0	7.6	9¼	6½	5	4¼
Final domestic demand	273.3	2.9	3.9	4.1	4½	3	2.2	7.4	4	3¼	3	3
* change in stockbuilding	−1.2[b]	0.1	0	0.1	½	0	−0.5	1.8	¼	−¼	¼	0
Total domestic demand	272.1	3.0	3.8	4.2	5	3	1.6	9.2	4¼	3	3¼	3
Exports of goods and services	73.0	5.9	3.2	5.6	2	2	2.9	7.5	−½	2	2	1¾
Imports of goods and services	68.0	2.7	6.3	7.5	7¾	4¼	−2.4	20.6	3½	4½	4½	3¾
* change in foreign balance	5.0[b]	0.9	−0.8	−0.5	−1¾	−¾	1.5	−3.5	−1¼	−¾	−¾	−¾
* compromise adjustment	0.8[b]	−0.3	0.3	0.9	¼	0	1.0	0.5	0	0	0	0
GDP at market prices[c]	277.9	3.6	3.3	4.5	3½	2¼	4.2	6.0	3	2¼	2¼	2¼
GDP implicit price deflator	–	5.9	3.7	4.4	4¾	4½	4.3	5.3	4¾	4½	4½	4¼
Memorandum items												
Consumer prices[d]	–	5.2	3.7	3.3	3¼	3¼	3.2	3.4	3	3¼	3½	3
Industrial production	–	2.9	0.4	5.5	5	2½	3.7	8.6	4½	2½	2½	2½
Unemployment rate	–	11.7	11.8	10.4	9½	9¾	10.9	9.9	9¼	9½	9½	9¾

* As a percentage of GDP in the previous period.
[a] Including nationalized industries and public corporations.
[b] Actual amount of stockbuilding, foreign balance and compromise adjustment.
[c] Data for GDP in the past are based on a compromise estimate which is the average of the expenditure, output and income estimates of GDP. The compromise adjustment is the difference between compromise GDP and the expenditure estimate of GDP.
[d] National accounts implicit private consumption deflator.

(Reprinted by permission of the *OECD Economic Outlook*, No. 43, June 1988.)

Table 3.3 *Growth of real GNP/GDP in the OECD area.* Percentage changes from previous period, seasonally adjusted at annual rates.

	1982 Share in total OECD	1985	1986	1987	1988	1989	1987 I	1987 II	1988 I	1988 II	1989 I	1989 II
United States	40.6	3.0	2.9	2.9	2¾	2½	3.2	4.0	2¾	2	2¾	2¾
Japan	13.9	4.9	2.4	4.2	4¼	3¾	3.8	5.9	4	3¼	4	3¾
Germany	8.4	2.0	2.5	1.7	2¼	1¾	−0.4	4.3	1¾	1½	1¾	1¾
France	7.1	1.7	2.1	1.9	2	1¾	1.0	3.4	1½	1¾	1¾	2
United Kingdom	6.2	3.6	3.3	4.5	3½	2¼	4.2	6.0	3	2¼	2¼	2¼
Italy	5.2	2.9	2.9	3.1	2½	2¼	2.5	3.3	2	2¼	2¼	2
Canada	3.9	4.3	3.3	3.9	4	3¼	4.3	5.6	3¼	3¼	3	3¼
Total of above countries	35.2	3.2	2.8	3.1	3	2½	2.9	4.5	2¾	2¼	2¾	2¾
Other OECD countries	14.8	3.3	2.7	3.1	2½	2¼	3.5	2.4	2¾	2	2¼	2¼
Total OECD	100.0	3.2	2.8	3.1	3	2½	3.0	4.2	2¾	2¼	2¾	2¾
Four major European countries	26.9	2.5	2.6	2.7	2½	2	1.6	4.3	2	2	2	2
OECD Europe	39.3	2.6	2.7	2.8	2½	2	2.1	3.6	2¼	2	2	2
EEC	33.8	2.4	2.6	2.7	2½	2	2.0	3.7	2¼	2	2	2
Total OECD *less* the United States	59.4	3.4	2.6	3.3	3	2½	2.8	4.3	2¾	2¼	2½	2½
Industrial Production:												
Major seven countries	—	2.6	1.0	3.4	5¾	4	3.0	7.0	5½	4½	3¾	3¾
Total OECD	—	2.8	1.2	3.3	5¼	3¾	2.9	6.3	5¼	4¼	3¾	3½

(Reprinted by permission of the *OECD Economic Outlook*, No. 43, June 1988.)

can see where we have been, but not necesarily where we are at present — or where we are going in the immediate future.

Despite all these problems, international bodies such as the OECD will produce regular macroeconomic forecasts over a period of about 18 months ahead for member countries, using their own model (and their own interpretation and assumptions) to process the official statistics available for each member economy. See Table 3.3. At its simplest, this will allow both government and the individual business to compare the projected performance of their own domestic economy with that of the other member nations. While this summary table covers only the total level of GDP/GNP, the detailed breakdown of demand and supply elements for each country is also available in the *OECD Economic Outlook*, produced on a June and December basis each year; for businesses operating in a series of international markets, this is a valuable single source of reference.

What sort of agencies or institutions are involved in the provision of regular forecasts? Within the UK alone, there has been a remarkable mushroom growth of active macroeconomic forecasters. Starting from the original exclusive club of the Treasury forecasting team (the government's own forecasting model), and the National Institute of Economic and Social Research, originally set up in 1959 to produce an alternative series of forecasts and, therefore, an independent check on the government's own results,[7] we have witnessed a whole new wave of models and results. See Extract 3.1 — which is by no means an all inclusive list. There is a wide range of university models, for example, London, Liverpool, Cambridge (even regional models such as the Fraser of Allander forecasts for the Scottish economy, from the University of Strathclyde), business school models, plus a massive undergrowth of models from banking and other private sector financial institutions — and from the Confederation of British Industry itself. Some might argue that the growth of forecasting has provided one of the main career opportunities for the modern economist. (But perhaps Ronald Reagan had better not apply, even if he is equally as well qualified as John Maynard Keynes, as was suggested by Extract 2.1 . . .)

Do the models all agree? What a silly question: how could that number of economists ever agree? See Extracts 3.1 and 3.2, for a useful and interesting series of comments on the main areas of divergence between current forecasts, and on some of the reasons for these divergences.

---

7. In fact, there were so few forecasters initially, that career movement between the Treasury and the National Institute teams was commonplace; some economists moved back and forth as regularly as a tennis ball in a ladies' singles rally at Wimbledon, it has been claimed. As a result, there is a disturbingly incestuous flavour about the two models over these early years — which was far from the objective of independence!

Extract 3.1 FINANCIAL TIMES 6 APRIL 1988.

BUOYANT ECONOMIC ACTIVITY PREDICTED BY FT AVERAGE OF FORECASTS

Ralph Atkins

BUOYANT ACTIVITY but a decelerating rate of growth in 1988 and 1989 are predicted for the British economy in an average of economic forecasts compiled by the FT, and published today.[See table overleaf.]

Economic growth is expected to be slower this year than in 1987 but it will remain strong. A further deceleration is expected in 1989. The trade position will worsen with the balance on the current account rising to a record £6.1bn in 1989.

The FT survey shows that recent exchange rate and interest rate movements may have clouded the vision of forecasting groups. There are wide variations in forecasts for those variables – which have knock-on effects for other indicators.

Estimates for three-month interbank interest rates vary by 3 percentage points in 1989. Forecasts for the deficit next year on the balance of payments current account vary between about £4bn and £10bn.

The division reflects uncertainty among economists about the consequences of a rapid rate of economic expansion. While some forecasting groups fear excessive consumer spending will suck in overseas goods and push up inflation, others are more confident that British industry will be able to respond adequately to increased demand.

The worries of some forecasters about "overheating" have increased since last month's Budget. Several City economists revised upwards their projections for consumer spending and imports to take account of the extra demand resulting from the larger than expected tax give-away.

The variation between forecasting groups is shown in forecasts for the growth of export and import volumes. According to the forecasts, export volumes may grow by 2 per cent this year, or by almost 5 per cent.

The overall FT average shows exports rising by 3.3 per cent this year and by 2.5 per cent in 1989. Imports are predicted to rise by 6.9 per cent and 4.3 per cent respectively.

Similarly, there is disagreement about the path unemployment will take. The forecasts predict both falls and rises. The FT average suggests unemployment will remain constant at the present level of about 2.5m.

The survey sample is split evenly between City economists and groups based in universities and other research centres.

The overall results of the survey, which is intended to be published at regular intervals, should be taken with a fair-sized pinch of salt. The FT average is a simple unweighted average that takes no account of differences in measurement of the different variables.

Nor has any account been taken of different assumptions underlying economic models used by forecasting groups. Some forecasts were compiled before the Budget.

Future surveys will illustrate how economists' expectations vary as circumstances change, and how accurate the survey is as a forecaster. The wide variations between groups' predictions mean, however, that the FT average cannot pretend to represent a consensus. After all, as the saying goes, if you placed all economists end to end they would never reach a conclusion. [Author's italics]

Reprinted with permission from *Financial Times* 6 April 1988 © *Financial Times*.

Even in normal conditions, it is very unlikely that models will ever be in total agreement. Apart from differences in modelling, there will be differences in assumptions, or 'views taken'. Equally, the different models will publish at different times, and each model will have to be updated regularly, to adjust for corrections to provisional raw data used, and to modify assumptions or data for real events which were not anticipated by original forecasts (the economists' equivalent of the seaside

Extract 3.1 (*cont.*) Forecasts for the UK economy (Unemployment, sterling index and interest rates are average over period. Balance of payments in £bn. Retail price inflation is year to fourth quarter. Others are percentage change over 12 months. Dash indicates information not available.)

	Date	Gross Domestic Product 1988	1989	Consumer spending 1988	1989	Manufacturing output 1988	1989	Fixed investment 1988	1989	Retail price inflation 1988	1989	Unemployment Millions 1988	1989	Balance of payments current account 1988	1989	Sterling Index (1975=100) 1988	1989	Interest rates (3 month interbank) 1988	1989	Exports volume 1988	1989	Imports volume 1988	1989
Treasury	Mar	3	2.5	4	3	5	3.5	6.5	5	4	4	–	–	–4	–4	–	–	–	–	3	2	6.5	4
Confederation of British Industry	Mar	3.3	2.3	4.3	3.9	5.5	4.0	10.8	5.0	3.8	3.6	2.5	2.7	–5.3	–10.0	–	–	–	–	3.1	3.2	7.4	6.5
DRI Europe	Mar	3.1	2.5	4.4	2.8	4.7	4.2	6.0	3.8	4.8	5.2	2.6	2.4	–6.0	–10.0	71.0	65.0	9.5	9.0	4.9	3.4	9.6	5.3
European Commission	Feb	2.8	–	4.1	–	–	–	4.2	–	4.1	–	–	–	–	–	–	–	–	–	2.4	–	5.6	–
Henley Centre	Mar	2.6	1.5	3.9	2.6	4.1	1.8	5.3	3.2	4.3	5.3	2.4	2.23	–4.2	–6.2	75.2	74	9	9.7	1.8	1.6	5.8	3.5
ITEM	Mar	3.5	2.1	4.8	3.5	4.3	3.6	4.9	3.9	4.2	4.3	2.7	2.85	–5.8	–8.6	75	73	8.6	9.2	2.4	1.9	5.0	4.8
Liverpool University	Apr	3.3	3.6	–	–	–	–	–	–	2.7	1.5	2.2	1.9	–4.9	–4.1	73.1	70.9	8.8	7.0	–	–	–	–
London Business School	Mar	3.3	2.5	4.1	3.5	4.4	3.2	6.7	4.5	3.7	4.0	2.6	2.5	–4.2	–6.1	75	74	8.8	9	4.7	2.4	7.9	4.0
National Institute	Feb	2.9	1.9	4.3	2.3	3.8	3.2	5.2	2.7	4.5	5.5	2.3	2.2	–4.2	–6.4	75.2	73.4	9.0	9.5	4.2	2.2	7.6	3.0
OECD	Dec	2.75	1.75	3.25	2.25	–	–	5.75	3.5	4.5	4.25	–	–	–	–	–	–	9.1	9.5	2	1.25	4.75	3.5
Oxford Economic Forecasting	Mar	2.9	1.6	4.4	2.8	4.5	1.5	7.0	3.3	3.6	4.5	2.5	2.4	–4.5	–5.5	76.0	73.0	8.9	9.5	4.5	2.1	9.7	4.1
Credit Suisse First Boston	Mar	3.25	2.75	3.75	2.75	4.25	3	5.75	4.25	4	3.75	2.5	2.5	–5	–5	–	–	8.5	8	4	3.5	7.0	5
Goldman Sachs	Mar	3.6	2.3	4.4	3.3	6.2	2.9	5.5	3.1	3.6	4.3	2.4	2.3	–4.7	–6.1	75.0	69.0	9.0	9.0	3.8	2.9	8.6	4.2
Greenwell Montagu	Mar	3.5	3	5	3.5	4.5	3.5	5	4.5	3.75	4	2.25	2.25	–4	–5	75	72	8.25	8	3.5	3.5	5.5	4
Hoare Govett	Mar	3.5	2.5	4.5	3.5	4.5	3.5	5.0	3.6	4.7	4.5	2.35	2.3	–4.5	–5	77	75	10	9.75	4.5	2.6	5.6	4.0
James Capel	Mar	3.0	2.0	4.0	3.0	3.8	2.6	6.5	5.1	4.0	4.2	2.45	2.28	–4.3	–5.0	76.6	77.0	9.0	9.0	9.0	4.2	1.6	6.6
Lloyds Bank	Feb	2.5	1.5	4.1	2.7	–	–	5.2	2.8	4.3	5.4	2.6	2.6	–4	–5.3	72.5	70.0	9.4	10.8	3.4	1.7	7.3	4.1
Morgan Grenfell	Mar	3.4	2.5	5.9	2.8	4.2	3.2	5.4	3.0	3.9	4.5	2.4	2.2	–8.0	–7.7	77.0	75.2	9.5	10.3	1.9	2.7	6.9	1.8
National Westminster	Mar	2.4	2.3	3.5	3.0	–	–	4.8	3.3	4.6	5.3	2.5	2.35	–4.0	–3.5	–	–	9.45	9.55	3.4	4.0	5.7	5.0
Phillips & Drew	Apr	3.1	2.7	5.1	4.0	3.6	3.1	5.7	3.3	3.9	4.7	2.5	2.6	–5.3	–5.2	76.3	74.5	8.2	8.3	2.0	2.9	7.8	4.6
Shearson Lehman	Mar	4.0	1.5	4.8	1.3	–	–	–	–	6.8	8.6	2.44	2.34	–7.6	–10.4	70.0	67.0	9.9	12	2.0	1.9	6.7	4.3
Warburg Securities	Apr	3.4	2.3	4.5	3.8	4.3	1.7	5.7	3.8	3.8	4.3	2.5	2.5	–5.3	–7.3	77	77	8.6	9.2	2.9	1.8	7.0	4.7
FT average		3.1	2.3	4.3	3.0	4.5	3.0	5.9	3.9	4.2	4.6	2.5	2.4	–5.0	–6.1	74.8	72.5	9.0	9.3	3.3	2.5	6.9	4.3
Average of City forecasts		3.2	2.3	4.5	3.1	4.4	2.9	5.7	3.9	4.3	4.9	2.4	2.3	–5.2	–6.0	75.2	73.0	9.1	9.4	3.2	2.6	6.8	4.2

Reprinted with permission from *Financial Times* 6 April 1988 © *Financial Times*.

Extract 3.2 THE TIMES 29 FEBRUARY 1988.

FORECASTERS NOW DIFFER TO AGREE ABOUT GROWTH

Rodney Lord, Economics Editor

WHEN the Chancellor presents his new forecast for the economy a fortnight tomorrow, it is likely to look rather more attractive than the sober assessment which accompanied the autumn statement.

Forecasters ranging from the Thatcher sceptics at the National Institute of Economic and Social Research to the Thatcher enthusiasts at the Liverpool group, and including the pragmatic London Business School, are all agreed that the economy will grow by 3 per cent this year.

Although this is well below last year's 4.8 per cent, it is higher than the Treasury's autumn forecast of only 2.5 per cent. It also happens to be the same as last year's Budget forecast for 1987.

Since the forecasts were completed, the Central Statistical Office has announced its preliminary estimate of gross domestic product in the final quarter of last year, which showed a bigger increase than expected. And in recent years this preliminary estimate has subsequently been revised up by an average of 0.2 per cent. By fixing a higher starting point, this can only tend to increase the likely growth between last year and this year as a whole.

However, the increase in the growth rate—taking one year against another—is a little misleading about the immediate prospect. Because growth has been so rapid in the latter part of last year, even if there were to be no further advance at all from the present level, average GDP this year would be more than 2 per cent above the average for last year.

The LBS, for instance, whose latest forecast — like Liverpool's — is published today, has actually reduced the expected growth between the fourth quarter of last year and the fourth quarter of this year from 2.8 per cent last autumn to 2.2 per cent.

The main uncertainty facing the forecasters is how much of their income people will save. Rising pay increases and the prospect of tax cuts in the Budget suggest that disposable income will grow faster this year than last.

But savings are likely to be as low as they were in 1987. In the third quarter, the saving ratio dropped as low as 5 per cent and, for the first time since 1959, the personal sector was in overall deficit.

Although other countries such as the US and Sweden save less, this is very low for Britain by historical standards and suggests some recovery this year. Both the fall in the stock market and the possibility of higher inflation may encourage people to save more in order to rebuild some of their wealth. LBS therefore expects the savings ratio to rise from 6.5 per cent last year to 8.1 per cent this year, and the National Institute also forecasts a rise, though a slightly smaller one.

Of the other components of demand, investment should grow faster than last year. Industry is operating near to capacity, suggesting a need for further capital spending, while high profits offer the means to finance it.

But the contribution from net exports will fall further. The position facing Britain's exporters is the exact reverse of what it was a year ago. Demand in the world economy was then picking up as the fall in the oil price eventually began to work through, while British industry enjoyed the benefit of a big fall in the exchange rate.

Subsequently, demand has stagnated worldwide, especially in Europe, while the pound has risen 25 per cent against the dollar and nearly 10 per cent on average. With consumer demand still relatively buoyant, imports will go on growing rapidly, resulting in a widening balance of payments deficit.

The striking thing about the latest forecasts is how similar they are, bearing in mind the very different views of the economy which the three forecasting groups hold. Perhaps we are seeing a move in the middle ground of economic forecasting, as we have seen in politics.

The Liverpool group, as

Economic forecasts for UK 1988

	NIESR	LBS	Liverpool
GDP (%)	2.9	3.0	3.0
Inflation (%)	4.5	4.5	2.8
Unemployment (m)	2.3	2.6	2.3
Bal of pays (£bn)	−4.2	−4.1	−5.5

usual, is more optimistic about inflation, expecting a fall this year, while the National Institute and LBS both expect prices to accelerate slightly from 4.1 per cent to 4.5 per cent. But the Merseyside forecasters are the least sanguine about the balance of payments, expecting a deficit of £5.5 billion, compared with the £4.2 billion or so expected by both the other two.

On unemployment, Liverpool and the National Institute are in startling agreement that there will be a further large fall to 2.3 million, even if according to the Institute this has more to do with tighter benefits administration than higher demand for labour. LBS expects a more modest drop to 2.6 million.

It is only when we come to economic prescription that the gap begins to widen. While the Institute wants no tax cuts at all, Liverpool believes the Chancellor can "give away" £5 billion with prudence.

The Business School sits in the middle, concerned about "over-heating" in the economy but acknowledging the microeconomic benefits of tax reform. This is more like the spectrum of opinion we are used to.

Reprinted with permission from *The Times* 29 February 1988 © *The Times*.

---

gipsy fortune teller's notice 'Closed due to unforeseen circumstances'!). These different publication dates – note from Extract 3.1 that these range from December to April – and therefore slightly different information bases will inevitably result in at least marginal differences in the forecasts.

Macroeconomic forecasting may well have come some way from its original state, where it was seen more as an art than as a science; or perhaps the original forecasters were just a little more honest. Certainly, it is now a much more complex procedure, using considerably more sophisticated models, as befits the microchip age. Yet, if we were honest enough to concede in the previous chapter that our past records of GDP were less than fully accurate, then we would be foolish to expect a greater degree of accuracy to these forecasts; they provide invaluable information to government and business, but any forecasts can never be more than our best and most systematic guess (you can almost hear the forecasters wince at the use of such a word!). It is the destiny of every forecast to be proved wrong (but, hopefully, only marginally so) by events – hence the wry warning given by *The Economist* (20 December 1986): 'never forecast – especially the future'.

But the point remains. The basic model which we have developed in this chapter does allow us to predict, at least in qualitative terms, the possible course of future events. It also helps us to interpret the more sophisticated forecasts of the course of these events, as made by macroeconomic forecasting teams – and, if necessary, to check that these forecasts make sense. It is a useful and resilient model, which will be used repeatedly throughout the book.

CONCLUSIONS

1. The purpose of model building in economics is to simplify the complexity of the real-world economy, in order to permit the analysis and understanding of the main influences at work. This is intended to help both the explanation of past events and the prediction of future ones.

2. In the basic model, the total expenditure from all sectors is made up of household expenditure, or consumption, firms' expenditure on producer goods and inventories, or investment, expenditure on UK output by non-domestic households and firms (and even governments), or exports, and UK government expenditure; to calculate the total of expenditure received by UK firms, and therefore the demand for UK output, then both imports and expenditure taxation must be deducted from this total.

3. The macroeconomy, within the simplified context of the basic model, will adjust naturally towards equilibrium; this will occur when the output available is just sufficient to satisfy the total of planned expenditure from all sectors, or in terms of the symbols which have been used during the chapter:

$$Y = C + I + G + X - M$$

   all at their factor cost values.

4. The model can be used to analyse and predict the effect on equilibrium (and through this on the level of output, employment and income) of changes in the real world, by tracing how these might affect the different expenditure elements within the model.

5. For more formal prediction purposes, where the desire is for quantitative as opposed to qualitative guidance, it is necessary to develop the basic model into a more sophisticated computerized one, using systems of equations to describe the same relationships which are contained in the basic model. Despite their greater complexity, these forecasting models operate in the same way, in principle, as our own basic model.

6. The macroeconomic forecasts produced are used by government to monitor both the possible need for corrective policy, and the outcome of past policy actions as they influence the course of the economy. The same forecasts provide an invaluable source of data on the future economic environment for all businesses which will be operating within this. Thus macroeconomic forecasts are an essential data input to the strategic planning process for both government and the private sector.

66 *Understanding the Economy*

7. As a final, more technical point, care must be taken to distinguish between:

    (a) a movement along the various functions, which will occur during the adjustment of the economy towards its equilibrium level of income and;
    (b) a movement in the position of one or more of the functions which will reflect a change in the behaviour of the function in question, and will constitute a disturbance which will require a new equilibrium level of income.

    This distinction will be explored in greater depth in Chapter 4.

SELF-ASSESSMENT QUESTIONS

TRUE/FALSE QUESTIONS

3.1. Imports will tend to rise with the level of income, since they are related to consumption and investment expenditure.

3.2. Exports are a withdrawal, since they involve the loss of output from domestic markets; imports are an injection, since they add output to domestic markets.

MULTIPLE CHOICE QUESTIONS

3.1. In the basic model, with only the two sectors of households and firms, at the equilibrium level of income:

    (a) Stocks of inventories are equal to zero
    (b) The total of consumption plus savings equals income
    (c) The total of savings plus investment equals income
    (d) The consumption function has a 45° slope
    (e) The total of consumption plus investment equals income
    (f) The sum of the marginal propensity to save and the marginal propensity to consume equals unity.

3.2. In the completed aggregate expenditure model (that is, including trade and public sectors) an increase in the proportion of new income saved (or the marginal propensity to save) will:

    (a) Reduce the level of investment in the injection function and therefore reduce the income level;

(b) Reduce the slope of the consumption function (net of imports) and therefore the income level;
(c) Reduce the volume of import spending and therefore raise the net of imports consumption function, and therefore the income level;
(d) Raise the level of investment in the injections function and therefore the income level.

3.3. If the marginal propensity to consume is less than unity, an increase in income of 10 would cause consumption:

(a) To rise by less than 10;
(b) To remain at the same level as before, since only the marginal propensity is affected;
(c) To rise by more than 10;
(d) To rise by 10 exactly.

3.4. Given the same value for the marginal propensity to consume, if income fell by 10, would consumption:

(a) Fall by less than 10
(b) Remain unaffected
(c) Fall by more than 10
(d) Fall by 10 exactly?

3.5. In the basic model if $C = a + cY$, when the marginal propensity to consume is 0.6 and the value of a is 30, what would the total amount of consumption spending be at an income level of 240?

(a) 126
(b) 222
(c) 174
(d) 144
(e) 210

3.6. Given the same data, what would be the total level of savings at the income level?

(a) 96
(b) 66
(c) 114
(d) 126
(e) 30

EXERCISE

In terms of the complete aggregate expenditure model, what would be the effect on the equilibrium level of income of:

(a)   An upsurge of business confidence

(b)   An increase in propensity to import

(c)   A decrease in government expenditure?

Note: Solutions can be found at the end of the text.

Chapter 4

Consumption

> Introduction
> The national accounts data on consumption spending
> Consumption and income
> Consumption and savings
> Factors affecting the position of the consumption function
> Consumption and which year's income . . .?
> The consumption function and the multiplier
> Conclusions
> Self-assessment questions

INTRODUCTION

Where does the previous chapter leave us then? We have set up a basic model of the macroeconomy, and have used this to analyse the movement of the economy towards equilibrium, in response to the promptings of the different elements of expenditure. The next logical step must be to look in greater depth at the factors which influence the behaviour of the individual building blocks of the model. What determines the level of expenditure – or causes changes in that level – of consumption, or investment, or exports, or imports, or government expenditure, or taxation? We know that, together, these six elements will determine the level of economic activity – but what, in turn, determines *their* behaviour?

This chapter provides us with a more systematic analysis of consumption, the first of the expenditure elements. As with the other chapters in the book, it will try to explore some of the main practical, as well as theoretical, aspects of the topic. This allows it to consider a variety of questions. What is the level of consumption expenditure in the UK, and what share of output or GDP does it absorb? Do we consume relatively more or less of our output and income than other countries? If we do, does this impose any penalty upon us, now or in the future? Why have we only identified the relationship between income and consumption in our model; are there other, possibly equally important influences on consumption expenditure? In any case, which year's income are we talking about: this year's, or last year's, or some future year's income, or a mixture of all three? What is the relationship between consumption and saving? What do we mean when we say that the savings ratio in the national accounts is at possibly its lowest ever level in the UK? Should we be worried about this?

You will find that the chapter covers a wide range of material, and identifies some trends and problems which will recur throughout the book. The trends which have emerged in UK consumption expenditure over recent years carry very important consequences for macroeconomic policy. After reading the chapter, you should be able to understand:

- The factors which influence the shape, and the position of the consumption function
- The meaning of and the distinction between the terms 'marginal propensity to consume' and 'average propensity to consume'
- The interrelationship between consumption and saving
- Why both the position and the slope of the consumption function might change, and the effect that this will have on the level of economic activity
- How consumption expenditure will respond to a change in one of the other elements of expenditure, such as investment, or government expenditure, and
- The role and nature of the 'multiplier process' as the economy adjusts to disturbances, and the effect which this has on the response of GDP to these changes.

At first sight, you might feel a little disappointed by this apparent retreat into technical detail, when the whole new and exciting area of macroeconomic policy beckons. Please be patient! We cannot turn you loose onto advanced issues until you have a sound understanding of the basics of the subject. This is a hard lesson which even politicians must learn. After all, it could be argued that the continuing boom in UK consumption expenditure, which has caused so many problems over 1988 and 1989, was triggered as an unwanted and unintended side effect of major policy actions on taxation structure and domestic interest rates. It is not only the Sorcerer's Apprentice who can turn loose forces which, subsequently, he finds that he can neither control or cancel. Nigel Lawson was not, and will not be, the only Chancellor of the Exchequer to wince as well as to laugh at childhood memories of the classic Disney cartoon sequence . . .

Be patient, and try to learn what the magic spells mean and what they do, before you are tempted to invoke them.

THE NATIONAL ACCOUNTS DATA ON CONSUMPTION SPENDING

In Chapter 2, we dealt fleetingly with the national accounts data on consumption expenditure. The same data provides us with a useful starting point, and will allow us to explore the relative importance of consumption within the expenditure flows of the macroeconomy. How large is consumption expenditure, relative to the other elements which make up aggregate demand (that is, investment, exports and government spending)? What sort of share of our resources is claimed by consumption? Do we consume proportionately more, or less, than our international competitors? If so, does it matter?

This leaves us to quantify two main measures from the national accounts data. Firstly, how much of total UK expenditure is accounted for by consumption expenditure? We can answer this by taking consumption as a percentage of total domestic expenditure in the national accounts data. (Remember from Chapter 2 that TDE is the sub-total of all domestic expenditure elements, before the adjustment for the international trade flows.) Secondly, how much of total available output is taken up by domestic consumption expenditure? What we have to remember here is that imported goods and services will supplement the output which is available from our own domestic production.

Looking more formally at this second measure can introduce us to an important relationship which exists within any macroeconomic system, which is the balance which exists between aggregate or total demand, and the aggregate or total supply which is available to meet this. In Chapter 3 we showed that the economy adjusts naturally towards equilibrium, where available output is just enough to satisfy planned expenditure, or, in terms of the standard symbols:

$$Y = C + I + X - M + G$$

By some minor algebraic manipulation, we can rearrange this to the form:

$$Y + M = C + I + X + G$$

Table 4.1 UK consumption and GDP (£bn).

	Current prices			Constant 1980 prices		
	1976	1981	1986	1976	1981	1986
Consumption	75.9	153.0	234.2	125.6	137.4	161.3
Total domestic expenditure	128.3	247.1	378.4	215.9	221.7	259.9
Imports	36.9	60.8	101.3	51.5	56.4	75.1
GDP (Y)	126.6	254.1	374.9	220.3	227.9	259.9
Consumption as % TDE	59.2	61.9	61.9	58.2	62.0	62.1
Consumption as % of ($Y + M$)	46.4	48.6	49.2	46.2	48.3	48.1
Rate of growth (1976–86)						
Consumption	–	–	–	–	–	28.4%
GDP	–	–	–	–	–	18.0%
Imports	–	–	–	–	–	45.8%

(Source: *UK National Accounts*, 1987 edition, Tables 1.2 and 1.6. Reprinted by permission of Controller, HMSO.)

which gathers the two sources of output, GDP and imports, to the lefthand side of the equation (giving us a total for aggregate supply), and leaves the remaining expenditure elements from domestic and international markets (giving us a total for aggregate demand) on the righthand side. If we estimate the value for C as a percentage of $Y + M$, or aggregate supply, then this would provide a useful indicator of the resource claims made by consumption on available output.

This is a particularly useful arrangement of the equilibrium equation. In particular, it shows why excessive demand pressure (in terms of domestic production potential) spills over into increasing import purchases, as aggregate supply struggles to meet the level of demand.

Table 4.1 provides us with some of the basic data which allow us to examine the two measures; it covers three separate years over the period 1976–86. The first three columns of the table are stated at current prices; this simply means that they have been recorded at the actual, historic values of the years in question. In these terms, consumption expenditure has risen from £75.9 billion in 1976 to £234.2 billion in 1986. Total domestic expenditure (or TDE) has increased from £128.3 billion to £378.4 billion, and GDP from £126.6 billion to £374.9 billion over the same period. Given these values, it can be seen that consumption has risen from 59.2% to 61.9% of TDE over the period, increasing its share of aggregate supply (or GDP plus imports) from 46.4% to 49.2%.

Clearly, consumption is the largest of the expenditure elements; in comparison, government expenditure averaged a share of 21.5% of TDE and investment (covering gross domestic fixed capital formation and stocks/work-in-progress), a share of 17.5% over the same three years.

Table 4.2 International data on consumption.

(a) Consumption as a percentage of total domestic expenditure at constant 1980 prices.

	1976	1981	1986
USA	63.3	62.2	63.5
Japan	58.3	57.8	57.6
West Germany	56.5	57.7	58.2
Netherlands	59.8	62.1	60.1

(b) Rates of growth over period (1976–86) at constant 1980 prices (%).

	Consumption	GDP
USA	57.7	54.4
Japan	40.6	51.4
West Germany	22.0	22.4
Netherlands	10.6	11.9

(c) Consumption as percentage of aggregate supply ($\frac{C}{Y+M}$) for 1986.

USA	57.3
Japan	48.3
West Germany	43.1
Netherlands	37.2

Note: 1986 is latest available data for the Netherlands.

(Reprinted by permission of the OECD Department of Economics and Statistics, the *National Accounts*, 1987 edition and the *Quarterly National Accounts*, No. 1, 1988.)

The final three columns of Table 4.1 acknowledge that it is dangerous to use only historic, or current price values, when examining expenditure over a period of time; the existence of inflation, or rising price levels, within the economic system can easily distort the changes recorded in monetary values. In constant price terms, consumption showed a rather less spectacular rise from £125.6 billion to £161.3 billion, or by 28.4% over the decade; in comparison, TDE rose from £215.9 billion to £259.9 billion (an increase of 20.4%), and GDP from £220.3 billion to £259.9 billion[1] (an increase of 18.0%). This revised basis for the calculation shows that consumption grew by a substantially greater margin than either TDE, or GDP, which had the effect of increasing its

---

1. No, the figure for £259.9 billion for both TDE and GDP is not a misprint; for 1986 (in terms of 1980 prices) imports (£75,070 million) and exports (£75,087 million) were effectively in balance and cancelling each other out, so that TDE and GDP were left at the same rounded figure.

share of resources, from 58.2% to 62.1% of TDE, and from 46.2% to 48.1% of aggregate supply.

How does this sort of pattern compare to consumption expenditure's share of resources in other countries? Are UK households in any way greedy in their claims upon scarce resources, which have alternative uses? After all, the resources which are absorbed by consumption are not available for use in investment – which is the main mechanism by which technological change is absorbed into the productive base of the economic system. In the longer term, too little investment could result in out-dated production methods and products, and a resultant loss in competitive efficiency . . . all of which has a disturbingly familiar flavour in the context of UK experience over the last two decades. Or again, in the shorter term, if consumption is growing faster than GDP then, as we showed above, it can only be satisfied by drawing in an ever greater volume of imports to supplement domestic output levels – which could carry later problems for our international balance of trade[2] (the value of exports less the value of imports) . . . which again has an uncomfortably familiar feel for the UK economy.

Table 4.2 provides some reassurance here. Section (a) of the table shows the equivalent share of TDE for consumption in the USA, Japan, West Germany and the Netherlands. It would seem that the share of about 62% shown for the UK is not wildly out of step with the pattern experienced in these four countries; we would seem to consume relatively less than the USA, but noticeably more than any of the other three.

Section (b) of the table gives some food for thought, however. You will remember that we pointed out above that consumption expenditure in constant price terms grew by 28.4% over the decade, which was substantially greater than the equivalent increase of 18.0% in UK GDP. Compare these figures to those recorded for the other four countries. Japan, West Germany and the Netherlands all show a stronger rate of growth in GDP than in consumption over the period; only the USA exhibits the same pattern as the UK – but here the gap is one of only a few percentage points, rather than the yawning chasm of more than 10 percentage points shown for the UK. In each of these four countries, production has grown broadly in line with consumption.

It is worthwhile pausing for a moment to compare these countries' rates of growth in GDP over the period with the 18.0% figure achieved by the UK. GDP in the USA increased by 54.4%, in Japan by 51.4% and

---

2. Terms such as the balance of payments, or the current account, or the balance of trade will all be covered in Chapter 11. For the moment, it is enough to recognize that the balance of payments is a summary statement of the results of our international transactions in goods, services and capital. Treat, for the moment, the current account balance as the difference between exports and imports: a 'surplus' here implies that exports exceed imports; a 'deficit' implies that imports exceed exports for the period in question.

in West Germany by 22.4% (and, yes, these are all in terms of constant 1980 prices – we have not slipped in some current price measures to confuse you!). Only the Netherlands shows a lower rate of growth in GDP for the period (although their growth rate is understated for the reasons given in the Note to Table 4.2). Is there a message here that, while the UK is not yet too far out of line, there are clear symptoms of an emergent problem? If domestic output is growing so sluggishly, in terms of international comparison, can we afford to allow consumption to increase so rapidly?

The data from the national accounts would seem to have created more questions than it answered, but this is by no means unusual. One of the standard comments of experienced accountants (admittedly in the context of financial records of businesses, rather than the economy as a whole) is that 'accounting data seldom answer all your questions – they are more likely to suggest other questions which you should be asking'. From Table 4.2 there would seem to be both reassurance and cause for concern to be derived from international comparison. The UK's strong growth in consumption does not simply confine itself to making an eager market for domestically produced output. There is always a danger that at least some of this growth will leak away into a rising level of imports. If we want to quantify this danger, a brief glance back to Table 4.1 will show that imports to the UK rose by 45.8% over the period in question (and, remember, we were also becoming more self-sufficient in oil over the same period – a luxury not available to countries such as West Germany and Japan; how much *worse* might our import leakage have been without the resource base of North Sea oil?).

If we seem to be dwelling unduly on the *dangers* of a rapid rate of growth in consumption expenditure, it is only because this phenomenon has been a focal point of concern for UK macroeconomic policy since the mid 1980s – indeed, it has probably been the root cause of the growing problems faced by the UK government over 1988 and 1989. Extract 4.1 makes useful reading at this point. It does not only update the UK experience of rapidly rising consumption levels and the effect of this on imports from the data contained in our earlier tables. It also explores the possible causes of the problem, including the valid point that imports can also cover producers' goods such as raw materials and machinery and so on, which can be more properly attributed to the firms' sector; any surge for growth will tend to be preceded by a rise in such imports, as production capacity 'tools up' to meet the increase in domestic demand. However, the extract's identification of consumption growth as the main culprit in this instance is unequivocal.

Who said that national accounting data was boring? We have not even begun to analyse the factors which determine the behaviour of consumption expenditure, yet we have already identified the crucial role which it has played in our current problems within the UK economy. Can

Extract 4.1 FINANCIAL TIMES 28 JULY 1988.

THE BOOM GOES ON

WITH HER unexpected reshuffle this week, Mrs Thatcher appears to be saying that it will be Mr Lawson's job, and his alone, to get her out of the mess she fears he may have got her into. Whether Mr Lawson recognises that there is a challenge to meet is unclear. What is more obvious is his likely response to the fidgeting next door. If Mrs Thatcher will not allow him the best way to manage the economy – full membership of the European Monetary System – she is in a poor position to complain about the risks associated with alternatives.

What is the story so far? Our hero, the UK economy, continues to show great vitality, despite the oft-repeated prediction that a slow-down is just around the corner, as yesterday's current account figures remind one. The preliminary estimate of the current account deficit for the first half of 1988 is £5.6bn, £1.4bn more than the Treasury forecast for the year as a whole at the time of the budget, four months ago.

DRIVING FORCE

The figures also support evidence from the performance of unit labour costs that demand, not competitiveness, is the main cause of the current account deficit. After some months in the doldrums exports and especially exports of manufactures have made a strong recovery, it is just that imports are up still more.

It has been argued that growing imports of capital goods indicate that investment, not consumption, is the driving force. Neither facts nor inference are correct. Taking the latest quarter over the previous one, one finds that imports of capital goods have not been the most dynamic component, rising 6 per cent in volume when imports of cars rose no less than 14 per cent. Over the previous year, imports of capital goods rose by 20 per cent in volume, not that much faster than imports of manufactures as a whole. Moreover, even if the increase in imports were accounted for by capital goods, one would learn little about the source of demand growth, since there is no necessary connection between the two.

That the economy is in the midst of a private-sector-led "dash for growth" has long been obvious. Yet with huge reserves of unemployment, large net foreign assets, a creditworthy public sector, high underlying growth of productivity and low inflation, the UK has been in the best possible position to see such a policy through.

If all goes well, the unsustainably fast growth of demand will come to a natural end as higher rates of interest bite on the demand for credit. If it does not, a major inflationary upsurge can still be avoided by holding the exchange rate steady. The risk is that there would have to be much higher interest rates than any now contemplated. That would, indeed, produce a painful "stop" to the present "go" phase of the Lawson boom.

The question is not whether much higher inflation can be avoided. It can. The issue is rather the price. Mrs Thatcher can hope for a happy ending and Mr Lawson can do his best to produce it. Appropriately, given the role their spending has played in driving the boom, the principal characters in the story now are the citizens of the UK, in whom this Government has always placed its trust.

Reprinted with permission from *Financial Times* 28 July 1988 © *Financial Times*.

---

there be a better reason for acquiring a more systematic understanding of the influences which will determine the pattern of its behaviour?

CONSUMPTION AND INCOME

We have already stated that one of the main contributions of economics is that it tries to answer the question 'Why?' From Table 4.1 we can see that the absolute level of consumption expenditure has fluctuated from year to year – in constant price as well as current price terms. Why should this be so? Does consumption simply pick up variations in income, as the level of economic activity rises and falls? Or does it reflect other influences, such as the cost and availability of credit, or changes in the taxation regime which is being implemented by the government, or changes in household expectations on future prices, or future taxes, or future interest rates – or even future job security?

In Chapter 3, we listed a wide range of possible factors which might influence the level of consumption spending, looking at these in the context of modelling for macroeconomic forecasting purposes. We have now reached the point where we ourselves must try to select the main influences from this list, then to bring some degree of system and understanding to them.

From the start, we face the problem that we are constrained by the two-dimensional nature of our model. This means that we can only study directly the relationship between two variables, that is, between consumption and one other variable. This, in turn, means that we must select a single variable from the wider range of influences on the consumption decision by households. Logically, we should try to select the variable which we believe has the greatest single influence upon consumption – but this does not imply that we then ignore the existence of the other influences; we will show you how to build these into the model at a later stage in the chapter.

Which should we choose? The consensus would appear to be that available income has the greatest single impact on consumption. After all, it does provide the basis for the expenditure which is made by households: if income rises, then it is reasonable to expect that consumption expenditure will also rise; and if income falls then, sooner or later, consumption expenditure will also be reduced in response to this.

This was the reason why we showed the consumption function as a relationship between consumption and income, in our building blocks for the basic model. You will also remember that we argued that:

- If all of income was spent, then the consumption function would take the form of a line drawn at 45° from the origin;
- But it would be more reasonable to expect that only a proportion of additional income would be allocated to consumption; thus the consumption function would have a slope of *less* than 45°.
- And, since some basic consumption expenditure would occur even at very low levels of income, the consumption function would probably show some positive value for consumption, even at zero current income.

Taken together, these arguments provide us with a consumption function of the form illustrated in Figure 4.1.

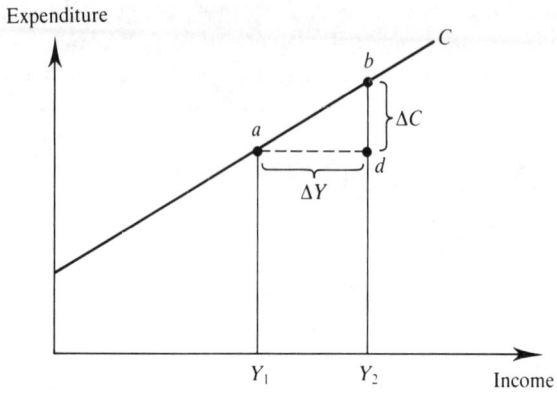

Figure 4.1 The consumption function.

What we must now do is fit this simplified concept of consumption into the more complex range of influences which we would expect in the real world. While this might seem to be a daunting task, the different influences can be divided into two broad categories, depending upon how they respond to the questions posed below:

(1) Do they affect the shape, or *slope* of the consumption function?
(2) Do they affect its *position*?

Given that we show the consumption function as a behavioural pattern against a range of possible levels of income in our two-dimensional model, it follows that the slope of the function will reflect the sensitivity of consumption expenditure to changes in the level of available income. If consumption is very sensitive to increases or decreases in income, then its slope will be relatively steep, showing that large changes in consumption will follow any given change in the level of available income. This type of consumption function would be similar to C_1 in Figure 4.2; as income rises from Y_1 to Y_2, the level of consumption spending will rise from aY_1 to bY_2. In contrast, if consumption is not particularly sensitive to changes in income, its slope will be relatively flat. C_2 would represent this type of function in Figure 4.2; in response to the same change in income, consumption will only rise from the initial level of aY_1 to dY_2.

This sensitivity of consumption to changes in the level of income is measured more formally by the **marginal propensity to consume**; this measures the ratio of the change in consumption to the change in income which has induced it. If the marginal propensity to consume is denoted by the symbols *MPC*, then:

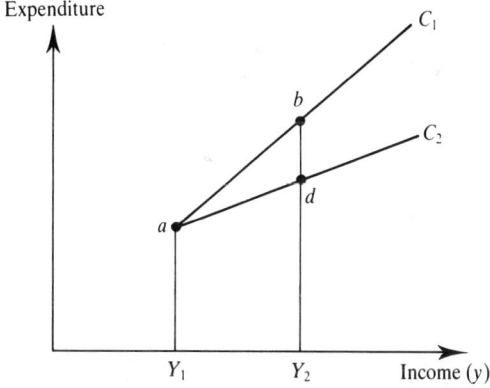

Figure 4.2 Consumption function: sensitivity to income.

$$MPC = \frac{\Delta C}{\Delta Y}$$

Table 4.3 provides a set of illustrative values which can be used to show how to calculate the *MPC* for any given change in income. For example, take the change of income from 700 to 800, in response to which the level of consumption rises from 680 to 760. What is the *MPC* over this part of the consumption function?

Table 4.3 Consumption, savings and income.

Disposable income (Y_d)	Consumption expenditure (C)	Savings (S)	Average propensity to consume $\left(\frac{C}{Y}\right)$	Average propensity to save $\left(\frac{S}{Y}\right)$	Marginal propensity to consume $\frac{\Delta C}{\Delta Y}$	Marginal propensity to save $\frac{\Delta S}{\Delta Y}$
400	440	−40	1.10	−0.10		
500	520	−20	1.04	−0.04	0.8	0.2
600	600	0	1.00	0.00	0.8	0.2
700	680	+20	0.97	+0.03	0.8	0.2
800	760	+40	0.95	+0.05	0.8	0.2
900	840	+60	0.93	+0.07	0.8	0.2
1000	920	+80	0.92	+0.08	0.8	0.2

$$MPC = \frac{\Delta C}{\Delta Y}$$

$$= \frac{760 - 680}{800 - 700}$$

$$= \frac{80}{100}$$

$$= 0.80$$

In other words, 80% of this increase in income is passed back into the macroeconomy via an increase in the level of consumption spending.

In terms of Figure 4.1, the *MPC* measures the gradient, or slope of the consumption function over the range of income in question. Think back to your basic geometry.[3] If:

$$MPC = \frac{\Delta C}{\Delta Y}$$

$$= \frac{bd}{ad}$$

This measures the gradient of the line *ab*, which is part of the consumption function.

If you take another look at Table 4.3 and Figure 4.1, you will see that they have something in common. In Table 4.3, no matter what change in income is taken, whether from 400 to 500, or 600 to 700, or 800 to 900, the value for the *MPC* remains the same at 0.80 (in each case, the change in consumption is equal to +80, divided by the change in income, which is equal to +100, giving a coefficient for the *MPC* of 0.80). The table shows a constant degree of sensitivity of consumption to changes in the level of income. Similarly, we are using a linear function in Figure 4.1, which means that any part of that function will have the same slope as the section *ab*, or the same value for *MPC*.

In short, where we have a linear consumption function, this implies that there will be a constant value for the *MPC* over the entire range of income covered by the model.

Up to this point, we have been analysing the relationship between *changes* in consumption in response to *changes* in the level of income. But it may well be that, for some questions, we are interested in a different aspect of the relationship between consumption and income; for example, we might want to know what *proportion* of any given level of income is taken up by consumption expenditure.

---

3. Or, better still, if you have a knowledge of calculus, then

$$MPC = \frac{dC}{dY}$$ which measures the rate of increase, and therefore the slope of the function.

This different aspect of the relationship is measured by the new concept of the **average propensity to consume**; this measures the value of the ratio between the absolute level of consumption expenditure, and the absolute level of income which supports this. For example, take the income level of 700 in Table 4.3, which supports a level of 680 in consumption expenditure; what is the average propensity to consume (or *APC*) at this level of income?

$$APC = \frac{C}{Y}$$

$$= \frac{680}{700}$$

$$= 0.97$$

In other words, at an income level of 700, 97% of that income will be taken up by consumption expenditure. Bringing the *MPC* into the analysis, if income rises beyond this point, then 80% of the additional income will pass through into additional consumption. The *APC* measures the pattern at a given point; the *MPC* measures what happens to that pattern, at the margin of change.

What does the *APC* measure in terms of Figure 4.1? Chip off a few more scales of rust from your memories of geometry. If:

$$APC = \frac{C}{Y}$$

and if Y_1 can be taken as the equivalent of the given income level of 700 in Table 4.3,

$$APC = \frac{aY_1}{OY_1}$$

This measures the gradient of the line *Oa*, which is the ray from the origin to the point on the consumption function above the income level in question. From Figure 4.1, you can see that this ray has a steeper slope than that of the consumption function, therefore the value for the *APC* will exceed the value for the *MPC* (as indeed it does, with 0.97 against 0.80).

We know that a linear consumption function results in a constant value for the *MPC*; does it also result in a constant value for the *APC*? A further examination of Figure 4.1 will show that this is *not* the case. Each point on the consumption function will have its own ray from the origin; each ray will have its own gradient, or slope; each point on the consumption function will therefore have its own value for the *APC*. Points towards the left end of the consumption function, that is, at the lower levels of income, will have rays with relatively steeper slopes – or higher values for the *APC*. A check back to Table 4.3 confirms that this is so; as you move from the income level of 700 towards lower levels of income, the *APC* rises steadily, and will exceed unity where consumption exceeds income. (This, in terms of the diagrammatic model, would cover all points to the left of the intersection of the consumption function and the 45° line; at the intersection, $C = Y$). Likewise, as you move along the consumption function to the right, each point will have a ray from the origin with a progressively flatter slope, or lower value for the *APC*. Table 4.3 again confirms that as you move to higher levels of income from 700, the value for the *APC* steadily declines.

You may feel that all of this is becoming just a little dry and technical (OK! Make that 'even more dry and even more technical' – after all, the customer is always right . . .) but, in fact, both concepts have a vital role to play in the more advanced theory of consumption. For this textbook, you will find that we focus almost entirely on the *MPC*; as such, treat the material on the *APC* as a safeguard against confusing in your own mind the two different relationships, that is, between the response of consumption to *changes* in the level of income, and the level of consumption as a *proportion* of level of income.

At the moment. our main interest lies in exploring what determines the *slope* of the consumption function; what we have established is that this reflects the value of the *MPC*, which measures the sensitivity of consumption behaviour to changes in the level of available income.

CONSUMPTION AND SAVINGS

Before moving on to the second category of influences on the consumption function, it is worth taking a little time to look at the relationship which exists between consumption, savings and income. Our preoccupation with the consumption function has tended to leave us with a blind spot in respect to savings.

However, this is easily rectified. If you check back to Figure 2.2, you will see that savings is a leakage from the income received by households, before consumption expenditure takes place. In other words, available income can be allocated either to consumption, or to savings (S), that is:

$$Y = C + S$$

and, by simple rearrangement, taking C over to the other side of the equation,

$$S = Y - C$$

Savings is therefore a residual from available income, after consumption plans have been implemented.

A glance at Table 4.3 will confirm this; at any level of income, say 900

$$S = Y - C$$
$$= 900 - 840$$
$$= 60$$

Note from the table that, while consumption will always have a positive value, savings can have a positive, or a negative – or even a zero value. When consumption exceeds income, for example, at the income levels of 400 and 500, it can only be sustained by dis-saving, that is, running down past savings balances, so that there is a negative flow of savings relative to that level of income.

The relationship between consumption and saving takes the form almost of a mirror image. If consumption grows faster than income (as we identified earlier in this chapter), then savings must decline relative to income; more formally, the 'savings ratio' will tend to fall, where there is an element of overheating, or excessive demand, in the domestic economy.

Take time to read Extract 4.2 at this point. It will provide you with some useful data on the value and trends of the UK savings ratio over recent years. In particular, it provides an excellent analysis of the possible causes of our recent savings behaviour – and a sound warning, yet again, of possible undervaluation of savings, as a result of the inaccuracies of national accounting.

More formally, the interrelationship between consumption and savings can be traced through into the more formal measures of *MPC* and *APC*. Once again, if:

$$Y = C + S$$

then, any change in income will be shared between consumption and saving, that is,

$$\Delta Y = \Delta C + \Delta S$$

If both sides of the equation are divided by ΔY, then

$$\frac{\Delta Y}{\Delta Y} = \frac{\Delta C}{\Delta Y} + \frac{\Delta S}{\Delta Y}$$

or, more simply,

$$1 = MPC + MPS$$

Extract 4.2 THE ECONOMIST 2 APRIL 1988.

SAVINGS
NEEDED: LOTS MORE MISERS

NOT for almost 30 years have the British saved as small a proportion of their disposable household income. In the fourth quarter of last year savings fell to only 4.3% of disposable income, compared with 14% in 1980. This was even lower than America's fourth-quarter savings ratio of 4.8%, and well below Japan's 1987 ratio of 18% and West Germany's 13%. When America's savings ratio fell, its balance of payments swung into massive deficit. If Americans had saved more, more of the government's budget deficit could have been financed by borrowing at home, rather than abroad.

British economists now wonder whether their economy might follow suit. Ominously, on the day after the savings figures for 1987 were published, February's trade figures showed that Britain's current-account deficit had widened dramatically in the first couple of months of this year.

Several reasons might explain the fall in the savings ratio in the 1980s:
- Lower inflation means that households do not need to put as much of their income aside to maintain the real value of their financial wealth.
- Easier access to credit has encouraged households to spend today and pay tomorrow, rather than saving up first.
- The rising value of houses and shares (until last October) made people richer. They have therefore felt less need to save.
- The population is aging, so

- The population is aging, so more people are running down their savings.

Some of the fears about the falling savings ratio may be misplaced. It does not necessarily mean that there will be less domestic cash available for investment, or that Britain will need to rely more on foreign capital. What matters is not just household savings, but the total savings of the private and the public sectors. Companies are currently flush with cash from which they can finance investment. And while the American federal budget moved deeply into deficit as household savings fell, Britain's budget has swung into surplus (or at least rough balance if the proceeds from the sale of public assets are excluded).

Nor is there much reason to fear that consumers have overburdened themselves with debt to finance their purchases of CD players or holidays to Val d'Isère. Because the value of the personal sector's financial assets has risen during the 1980s, its debt as a proportion of those assets has actually declined.

It is possible that the collapse of the savings ratio may be no more than a statistical illusion. Savings are one of the most unreliable parts of the national accounts. They are measured as a residual by subtracting consumer spending from personal disposable income, and so quite small errors in income or expenditure can produce a huge error in the level of savings. For example, if income had been under-estimated by just 1% in the fourth quarter of last year, and consumption over-estimated by 1%, then the true level of savings would be almost 50% higher than the official figure.

The national accounts are more likely to understate income than to overstate spending. Income figures are based on tax returns and so exclude money earned in the black economy. They may also seriously under-record the inflow of profits and dividends from abroad. If the measure of spending is accurate, but income too low, then savings will be higher than the figures in national accounts suggest.

Mr Steven Bell, the chief economist at Morgan Grenfell, has concocted an alternative measure of savings based on the personal sector's net acquisition of financial assets (ie, bank deposits and purchases of securities, less borrowing). This tells quite a different tale. The savings ratio becomes 14% last year instead of the official 6%. Although the ratio fell sharply at the start of the 1980s, it has—by Mr Bell's method of calculating savings—been broadly constant during the past five years.

It is true that figures on financial accounts are also rather unreliable, since unidentified transactions tend to be dumped into the personal sector. But Mr Bell believes that this alternative savings measure provides a more accurate guide than the official measure to both the level and the trend in the savings ratio.

WHEN GOOD NEWS IS BAD NEWS

If Mr Bell is right, and the savings ratio has not collapsed after all, should the Treasury rejoice? Ironically, it should probably start to run more scared. Most economic forecasters, including the Treasury, have reckoned that the low official savings figures show that consumers are becoming overstretched. They therefore expect savings to bounce back up in 1988, and consumer spending to slow down. This would help to slow the growth of domestic demand to a more sustainable rate and so dampen fears of overheating.

But if the true savings ratio is really much higher than the official figures suggest, then there is no reason for households to rein back consumption to rebuild their assets. The spending binge could continue. Morgan Grenfell's economists predict that the growth of consumer spending could quicken to 6% this year, up from 5% last year, compared with the Treasury's forecast of a slowdown to 4%. Continued rapid growth in consumer spending will suck in more imports. Morgan Grenfell have pencilled in a current-account deficit of £8 billion for 1988—roughly the same, at an annual rate, as during the three months to February, but double the Treasury's forecast of £4 billion. A deficit of £8 billion would be equivalent to 2% of Britain's GDP, which is not far short of America's expected current-account deficit this year of an estimated 2¾% of its GDP. *If they are correct, then last month's budget was dangerously generous. The British economy is already on full throttle. Soon, smoke could be pouring out of the engine.* [Author's italics]

Reprinted with permission from *The Economist* 2 April 1988 © *The Economist*.

This means that, over any given range of income, the sum of the *MPC* and *MPS* values must be unity. Again, you can check this in Table 4.3; here there is a constant *MPC* value of 0.8, which is matched by a constant *MPS* value of 0.2 (that is, every extra 100 of income results in an extra 20 of savings).

A little thought will show you that the same must be true of the two sets of values for *APC* and *APS*. If, as at the income level of 800, 95% of income is consumed, then the balance of 5% must have been saved; with an *APC* of 0.95 and a *APS* of 0.05, these two values must sum to unity. Note also that the 'savings ratio' discussed in Extract 4.2 is also the measure for the *APS*.

Stepping back from the technicalities of the relationship, simply bear in mind that when the text is focusing on consumption behaviour, the behaviour of savings will provide a mirror image to whatever fluctuations are under examination.

FACTORS AFFECTING THE POSITION OF THE CONSUMPTION FUNCTION

The second group of influences on the consumption decision were those which would alter the *position* of the consumption function. In effect, their influence would be to change the background conditions against which consumption would be planned relative to a given range of incomes. Households, in response to changes in these external factors, would tend to consume more, or less for any given income level than would have been the case before. As we pointed out before, in a two-dimensional model, we can only show directly the relationship between consumption and one other variable. Even if we wanted to illustrate the effects of one additional variable, for example the cost of credit, then we would need a three-dimensional model to show how both income and the cost of credit had a simultaneous influence upon consumption; and three-dimensional models can be difficult to construct and to interpret. If, however, we wish to cover several factors other than available income, then it becomes impossible to show the simultaneous effect of these graphically. Hence we are reduced to the clumsy device of relegating all factors other than income to 'background conditions', which are recognized, which are allowed to change, and which will have an effect on both the level of economic activity and upon the level of consumption expenditure.

Let's look at some of the main external, or exogenous (that is, existing outside the model) influences upon the consumption decision.

Direct taxation

Up till this point, we have talked loosely about 'available' income as the main single influence upon the level of consumption expenditure. Looking at this more formally, available income is really the net of tax income received by households (in effect, the inflow of income received by households at the top of the income loop in Figure 2.2) and available for either consumption, or savings decisions. The more correct term for this is **disposable income**.

If we start with any given consumption function, such as C_1 in Figure 4.3, then this simply indicates how consumers will react to different levels of GDP, or income, within the constraints of the given regime of direct taxation (that is, income tax).

What would happen if the government decided to change this taxation regime?[4] For example, what would happen if the government cut direct taxation, either by reducing the rates of taxation, or by raising the taxation thresholds for progressive taxation, or by increasing the allowances which could be set against taxation liability? This would affect income earned and received from all sources (for example, wages/salaries, self-employment, dividends, rent, interest). Disposable income would rise; more would be available for consumption expenditure, so that this

---

4. In both Europe and the UK there has been a substantial change in taxation philosophy and policy over the last decade, as governments have attempted to reduce the burden of personal taxation, to increase the incentive for households (and firms) to try to increase their earnings by greater productivity. See Chapter 10 for a more detailed discussion of **supply-side economics**.

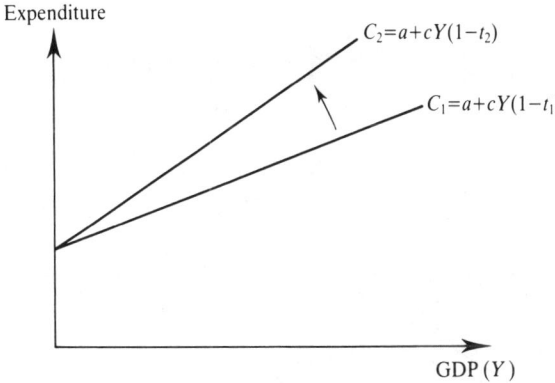

Figure 4.3 Consumption function and change in direct taxation.

too would tend to rise relative to the earlier consumption planned for any given range of GDP. At the same time, the benefits derived from the direct taxation cuts would tend to be greater at higher levels of income, so that consumption would tend to rise proportionately more for these higher levels. The effect would be to pivot the consumption function upwards, from C_1 to C_2, as shown in Figure 4.3.

In more formal terms, we are now saying that consumption[5] is a function of disposable income (Y_d), that is, we have revised the consumption function to:

$$C = a + cY_d$$

If disposable income is defined as income received, less direct taxation (T_d), then:

$$Y_d = Y - T_d$$

Next, if we take direct taxation as a simplified single rate of tax which is charged as a proportion (t) against income (for example, t could be a rate of 25% of income, that is, $t = 0.25$) this could be shown as:

$$T_d = tY$$

---

5. Note also that, within the formulation for the consumption function, that is, $C = a + cY_d$, the term c is the value of the *MPC*. It will measure the response of consumption to any change in income; if $c = 0.8$, then 80% of any additional income will flow back into the economy in the form of increased expenditure (or, conversely, consumption will fall by 80% of any decrease in income).

88 Understanding the Economy

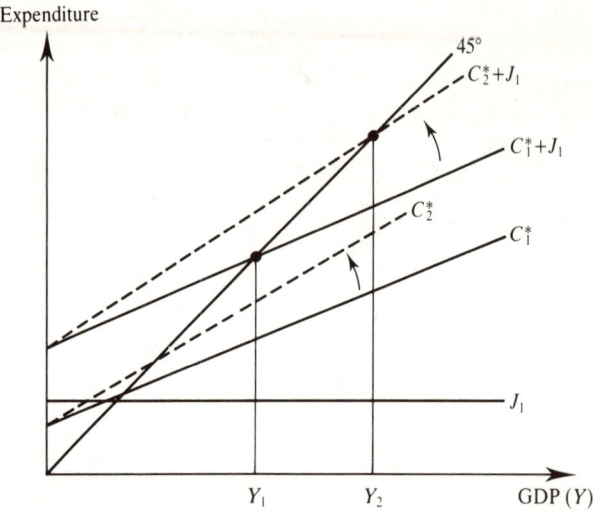

Figure 4.4 Effect of decrease in direct taxation on equilibrium income.

so that

$$Y_d = Y - tY$$
$$= Y(1 - t)$$

and

$$C = a + cY_d$$
$$= a + cY(1 - t)$$

This allows us to see more clearly why the consumption function pivots, following a change in the rate of direct taxation. This would change the value of t and, therefore, the value of the induced element $cY(1 - t)$; it would *not* affect the value of the intercept a, which would therefore anchor the consumption function to that intercept on the vertical axes, whatever adjustments were made to the rest of the consumption function.

It is interesting to follow the effects of these changes in taxation through to the full basic model, as developed in Chapter 3. We have illustrated this in Figure 4.4. If the consumption function has pivoted upwards, this will also cause the C^* function to pivot in a similar manner in the full model (remember, the C^* function is simply the consumption function, less imports), from C^*_1 to C^*_2. This in turn will be picked up by the aggregate expenditure function, raising this from $C^*_1 + J_1$ to $C^*_2 + J_1$. Note that there have been no changes in the injection function,

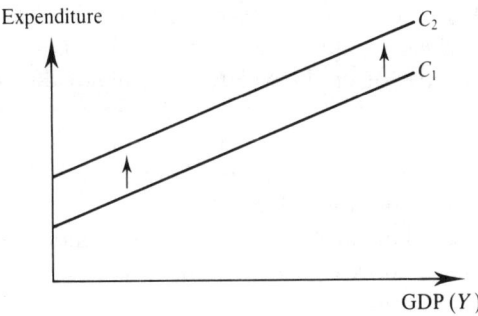

Figure 4.5 Consumption and changes in the cost of credit.

which therefore remains at its original value. Next, this movement in the aggregate expenditure function will change the equilibrium level of income. At the old equilibrium of Y_1, planned expenditure will now exceed available output, so that the economy will expand, that is, move to the right, towards the new equilibrium level of Y_2.

Therefore, one possible consequence of cutting the rate of direct taxation could be that the level of economic activity would rise; this is a point which is discussed in greater depth, in the context of supply-side economics, in Chapter 10.

The cost and availability of credit

The phenomenon of borrowing has an important influence on consumption expenditure. In effect, it allows people to anticipate future income in their current consumption expenditure. In any single time period, therefore, consumption decisions will reflect the current credit conditions which are available to households.

If there is a significant change on the availability, or the cost of credit, it will normally cause a revision in consumption decisions. For instance, should borrowing costs be reduced, or repayment terms permitted over a longer time period, then it is probable that there will be an upsurge in consumption expenditure, relative to the earlier decisions reflected in the original consumption function. This can be illustrated in terms of Figure 4.5. This shows that the consumption will rise from C_1 to C_2. Once again, the consequences of this revision in consumption behaviour can be followed through into the full basic model. Rather than reproduce this, try to visualize its effect in terms of Figure 4.4. The upwards movement of the simple consumption function would also raise the C^* function (but in parallel, as shown in the movement of the consumption function in Figure 4.5, rather than as a pivot, as illustrated in Figure 4.4). This would raise the aggregate expenditure function (or $C^* + J$ function), which would increase the level of equilibrium income. A reduction in the cost of credit will tend to make the macroeconomy expand. Conversely, if credit terms are made more severe (for example higher interest charges, heavier down payments, shorter repayment period), then consumption decisions are likely to be revised downwards, reducing the level of equilibrium income.

You will notice that, in the extracts to this chapter, higher interest rates have been identified as a possible policy weapon to curb the growth of consumption expenditure.

Expectations

This represents another important influence because it can affect the time pattern of consumption expenditure plans; therefore, it can dramatically change current consumption expenditure relative to current income levels. For instance, if rising levels of unemployment create a general feeling of job insecurity, consumption plans might be revised downwards from the pattern shown in the consumption function: some items of consumption expenditure, for example, higher priced consumer durable goods, which might have involved entering into a credit agreement, might be postponed temporarily; a conscious decision might be taken to build up savings balances purely as a precautionary, or contingency reserve. The effect of this change in expectations would be to move the level of the consumption function downwards; in terms of Figure 4.5, it would fall from a position corresponding to C_2 to a new position corresponding to C_1. If we were to follow the consequences of this for the full basic model, the C^* function would move downwards, bringing the aggregate expenditure or $C^* + J$ function down in sympathy, which would *reduce* the level of equilibrium income. This could well involve an increase in the level of unemployment – a sad illustration of how expectations can very easily become self-fulfilling.

To reinforce your grasp of the material, why not take a little time to set up the full model, and to trace for yourself how the economy would adjust to such a change in expectations; the text above should guide you through the various stages.

Alternatively, the expectations might be concerned with future price levels. If, for instance, households anticipate a substantial increase in the general price level in the following year, consumption plans for the present year might well be increased to take advantage of the lower current level of prices. This would cause the consumption for the current year to move upwards, as in Figure 4.5, with similar repercussions (and, quite possibly, forcing prices upwards to fulfil the expectations on price increases).

Household wealth

In Extract 4.2, a valid point is made that changes in the savings ratio can be caused by changes in household wealth. The very substantial increases over recent years in house prices and share values (probably two of the more important assets owned by households) have left people with more wealth than before, so that they may no longer desire to build up the same contingency reserve of savings. If savings are reduced relative to income, then this implies that consumption will then be increased, that is, the level of the consumption function will rise.

Therefore, changes in household wealth will also tend to change the position of the consumption function; consumption levels will tend to rise as household wealth increases, or fall if wealth decreases.

However, we need to treat this relationship with a little care. It is unlikely that wealth will change significantly under normal conditions in the short run; change will be a more gradual and long-term phenomenon. Its influence will tend to be greater in a consumption function which is more preoccupied with long-term patterns of consumer behaviour, as opposed to the short run consumption function with which we are dealing in this chapter. But, nevertheless, if short-term factors are dramatic enough to affect personal wealth levels substantially, then this change in wealth is likely to influence the position of the short run consumption function too.

Other factors might also influence the consumption decision, but direct taxation, the cost and availability of credit and expectations are probably the most important exogenous influences in the short run, in terms of our two-dimensional model of the consumption function. If you stop here to read Extract 4.3, you will find that this looks at the current behaviour of consumption, and its mirror image of savings, in the UK economy. You will find that we have already identified most of the influences which have been at work – but it is always reassuring to have our judgement confirmed and developed. The extract is useful, not only as a readable discussion of current trends and the problems which they appear to set for policy makers. It also underlines the role which perceived wealth plays in the consumption and saving decision, and suggests that the cost of credit possibly has a much lesser effect on non-durable consumption purchases (which account for about 90% of consumption spending) than most of us would have assumed.

Returning to the text, a very important point to grasp is that a change in the level of GDP will simply result in a movement along the *existing* consumption function, which shows the different levels of consumption expenditure which will result from different levels of GDP. In contrast, a change in one of the exogenous variables will change the background conditions against which consumption plans are made, which will be reflected in a revision of the *position* of the consumption function.

Extract 4.3 THE ECONOMIST 19 AUGUST 1989.

THE ECONOMY

ACACIA AVENUE AND THE TRADE DEFICIT

HOMO Britannicus, 1980s model, is a spendthrift. Last year people saved only 4½% of their disposable income, compared with 14% in 1980. This enthusiasm for consumption overheated the economy and pushed up inflation and the trade deficit. Mr Nigel Lawson, the chancellor of the exchequer, reckons that high interest rates will squeeze the public out of its profligacy. Consumer spending is now slowing, but it may take Britons an uncomfortably long time to learn about thrift.

The usual argument is that high interest rates squeeze consumption, by making borrowing more costly and by redistributing income from borrowers (who spend most of each extra pound) to savers (who spend less). But some recent research carried out by Mr John Muellbauer and Mr Anthony Murphy of Nuffield College, Oxford and the economics team of Credit Suisse First Boston, an investment bank, found no evidence that interest rates directly affected the 90% of spending that goes on non-durable goods as opposed to washing machines, televisions and the like. What they did find was one strong, indirect link between rates and spending—namely, house prices.

This finding supports the "life-cycle" theory of consumption. The theory says that people's spending this year depends not just on their income this year, but also on past and future income, and on their wealth. If they suddenly feel wealthier, they see less need to save to cover future spending, and will therefore rush out to the shops.

Which is what seems to have happened. As the prices of houses (about 60% of total wealth) and equities have boomed, Britons' illiquid wealth (excluding cash and bank deposits, that is) has risen from 3.6 times their disposable income in 1981 to a record high of 5.7 times last year. The researchers conclude that this is one of the main causes of the slump in savings.

The freeing-up of the financial markets has also encouraged newly wealthy Britons to spend. Deregulation has made it easier to borrow and hence "unlock" illiquid wealth. A couple moving house might get a larger mortgage than necessary and blow some of their capital on a boat or a car.

This argument says uncomfortable things to the government. Unless house prices fall relative to incomes, the savings ratio will continue to fall and demand will rise too fast. Although house prices are falling in the south, the Halifax Building Society's national figures still show a rise of 18% in the year to July. The ratio of house prices to earnings therefore remains at a record level. And the authors think that there is a lag between increases in wealth and increases in spending: they reckon that there is another 8% rise in spending to feed through.

What does this mean for the next couple of years? Suppose that non-housing wealth increases in line with income and average house-price inflation falls to zero by the end of next year. Then, according to the researchers' model, people's savings ratio will continue to fall this year, and spending on non-durable goods will accelerate later in the year. In 1990, although the savings ratio will rise, it will remain below its first-quarter 1989 level. So, Mr Lawson, demand may not slow enough to make a real dent in inflation and the trade deficit.

To boost savings, therefore, the government can either take the gentle road and allow wage inflation to reduce people's real wealth while house prices stagnate for several years, or it must inflict real pain on the housing market and push interest rates higher still so that prices fall sharply. That would be politically awkward ahead of an election: some voters would suddenly find their homes worth less than their mortgages. Yet double-digit inflation might be even more awkward.

Before you rush off to sell your house, though, a few crumbs of comfort. The CSFB study may be too gloomy. It probably has not taken full account of the impact of the slump in housing turnover, as opposed to prices, on spending. Lower turnover can do the same job as lower prices. The boom in housing activity led to a marked increase in equity withdrawal from the housing market to finance other spending. Likewise, the current slump in turnover (down a quarter on last year) will reduce consumption.

According to Goldman Sachs, another investment bank, equity withdrawal from the housing market—the difference between what people borrowed for house purchases and what was spent on houses—increased from £2 billion a year in the late 1970s to £18 billion last year. With fewer people moving house this year, they reckon that cash withdrawals could shrink by £5 billion and trim consumer spending by 2%.

Finally, Mr Lawson can also take comfort from the fact that interest rates do at least have a big direct effect on the 10% of spending that goes on consumer durables. Since Britain imports a high proportion of its durables, Mr Lawson's present medicine may at least help shrink the trade deficit.

Reprinted with permission from *The Economist* 19 August 1989 © *The Economist*.

In this case, the change has repercussions for aggregate expenditure, the level of economic activity, and income, as well as for the level of consumption expenditure.

CONSUMPTION AND WHICH YEAR'S INCOME . . .?

Even if we accept the simplification imposed upon us by the constraints of a two-dimensional model and agree that consumption is functionally related to the level of income, this may not provide us with full understanding of the relationship. After all, if consumption reflects household income, which particular year of income are we talking about? The current year's income? Or a mixture of current and past income? Or current and anticipated future income? Or even some more complex weighting of past, present and future income?

Up till now, all our model building has been within the context of the data for a single year, as measured by the national accounts; in terms of our model, this has led us to argue that current consumption (C_t) has been functionally related to current income (Y_t), or

$$C_t = c\ (Y_t)$$

But how realistic is this? More advanced theory suggests that there should be a more sophisticated pattern of influence. For example, Duesenberry has argued that there will probably be some form of 'ratchet effect' in consumption behaviour. As a community becomes more affluent, and its income rises towards a peak, then it will tend to raise its standard of living. This would happen, for example, as the economy moves into the boom phase of the trade cycle (the name given to the regular pattern of expansions and contractions which afflict all macroeconomies). But booms do not last forever; sooner or later the economy will pass into a recession phase, with falling levels of economic activity, and income.

When this happens, it is probable that the community will struggle to maintain its level of consumption (as in fact happened in the UK over 1979–81, when all other expenditure elements collapsed in our most savage and prolonged post-war depression). Households have, in effect, raised their expectations of what constitutes a 'normal' standard of living and, in the short term at least, they will change both their *MPC* and *APC*, as they fight to protect this standard. This type of behaviour will normally be 'bailed out', as the economy passes through the depression phase and moves back into recovery, when economic activity surges forward again, and incomes rise to rescue consumers from their temporary high spending position. If we accept this theory, then we must recognize that current consumption will reflect the influence of this previous income peak as well as its current level of income. In effect:

$$C_t = c(Y_{t-n}, Y_t)$$

where Y_{t-n} is the symbol for the income of the most recent peak year.

Broadening the range of influence still further, Modigliani, Brumberg and Ando have suggested that households reach their consumption decisons by viewing not a single year's income, but a whole series of past and anticipated future income flows, possibly even over the lifespan of the individual households which make up this sector. This 'Life Cycle Hypothesis' recognizes that, for the average household, income will fluctuate over the main earner's lifespan. During the early years, income will be relatively low (but anticipated to rise) and will probably be exceeded by consumption spending during these years, that is, by borrowing against future income. During the mid years – indeed the main period of the lifespan – income will rise to its peak, or to a relatively high plateau; it will typically exceed current consumption, the excess being used to repay past borrowing, or to build up savings for the final years of the lifespan. In these final years, with reduced income, the household must draw heavily on past savings, since even a reduced level of consumption will tend to exceed the income available for that period. It would follow then that the current consumption decision is taken against a lifespan profile of income, and is used to smooth out some of the fluctuations of the latter. It is an over-simplification to argue that only current income will influence current consumption.

Friedman's work on the 'Permanent Income Hypothesis' shares a lot of common ground with this view. He suggests that the rational consumer will plan current consumption against the context of some long-term average of income - even some estimated average of all future years' income. If there is a stable relationship (whether *APC* or *MPC*) between consumption and income, it is between current consumption and this estimated value for long-term, or 'permanent' income (Y^p), that is,

$$C_t = c(Y^p)$$

If permanent income rises by, say, 10% then consumption will be adjusted in proportion to this. But if current income for any single year diverges from this estimate of permanent income, the divergence will be treated as being transitory – a 'one-off' phenomenon – and may have *no* influence at all on current consumption.

For example, suppose that the average, or anticipated weekly earnings of the household is £150; this is the equivalent of weekly 'permanent' income. If, in a particular week, the earnings figure rises to £175 due to a one-off bonus, or extra overtime, then the extra £25 above the average is treated as transient income and does not affect consumption plans. Equally if in another week the earnings figure falls to £100 due to illness, this will be seen as permanent income of £150 less a transient income shortfall of £50 for that week. Once again, current consumption will not be affected, since this will be based on the permanent component, with households assuming that transient fluctuations, as deviations from the average, will sum to zero, that is, cancel out, over time.

Despite these more sophisticated arguments, we will continue to take the simpler view that current consumption is a function of purely current income. This simplified relationship is sound enough for our analytical purposes in this book. But do remember that it *is* simplified. In the heat of the macroeconomic policy debate, remember that consumption will not always move in a mechanical and automatic response to changes in GDP. This does not necessarily mean that it has a mind of its own! It simply reflects a more complex relationship than is convenient to use in our modelling.

THE CONSUMPTION FUNCTION AND THE MULTIPLIER

So far this chapter has discussed the factors which would change the entire position of the consumption function, and the factors which determine its gradient or slope. All that remains is to examine how the consumption function would respond to a change in one of the other elements of expenditure. To simplify the analysis, let us assume that there is neither an international trade sector (that is, no X or M), nor a public sector (that is, no G or T) in our model; this leaves us with only the basic two-sector model, covering households and firms.

We illustrate this response in Figure 4.6. We start from the point where the economy is already in equilibrium at the income level Y_1, with available output just enough to satisfy planned expenditure. Assume that there is a disturbance to the model, for example, in the form of a permanent increase in the level of investment, moving the injection

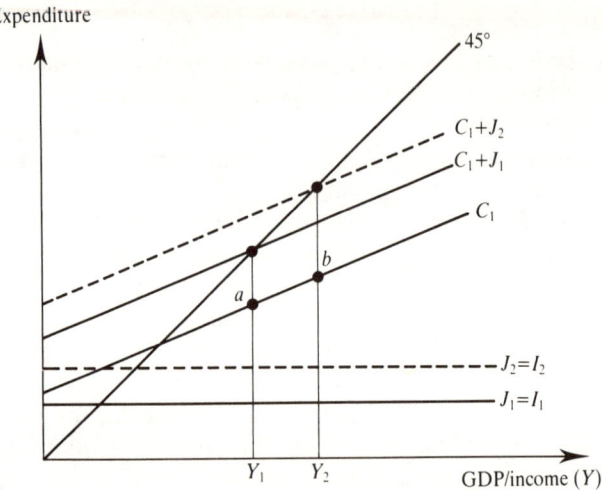

Figure 4.6 Consumption, income and an increase in the level of investment.

function up to J_2. This will raise the aggregate expenditure function to $C_1 + J_2$, in the model.[6] At the old equilibrium level of income, expenditure now exceeds available output, running down inventory levels. Output and employment are therefore increased, raising the income level. The process will continue until the economy reaches its new equilibrium level of income Y_2.

Note how the increase in investment has increased the level of income; since consumption is functionally related to the income level, the increase in income has raised the absolute level of consumption expenditure from a to b along the existing consumption function. Consumption does respond to a change in another expenditure element – but only because the latter affects the level of income and, through this, the level of consumption expenditure. Does this mean that consumption is totally passive, that it plays little part in the adjustment of the economy to change? Indeed, the reverse is true; consumption plays a key role in determining the extent of the adjustment process which is triggered by the disturbance.

Let's think more slowly through the course of events which would follow the type of disturbance illustrated in Figure 4.6. Assume that the permanent increase in investment amounted to 20; assume also that the

---

6. Be very aware that the change affects only the injection function; there has been no reported change in the background conditions for consumption, so that there is no need to revise the position of the consumption function. Households will move up or down the existing consumption function in response to changes in the level of income.

Table 4.4 Consumption and the multiplier process.

Round	Changes in income received	Changes in savings	Changes in consumption	Changes in expenditure
1	–	–	–	+20.0
2	+20.0	+4.0	+16.0	+16.0
3	16.0	3.2	12.8	12.8
4	12.8	2.6	10.2	10.2
5	10.2	2.0	8.2	8.2
6	8.2	1.6	6.6	6.6
7	6.6	1.3	5.3	5.3
8	5.3	1.1	4.2	4.2
9	4.2	0.8	3.4	3.4
10	3.4	0.7	2.7	2.7
11	2.7	0.5	2.2	2.2
12	2.2	0.4	1.8	1.8
13	1.8	0.4	1.4	1.4
14	1.4	0.3	1.1	1.1
15	1.1	0.2	0.9	0.9
16	0.9	0.2	0.7	0.7
17	0.7	0.1	0.6	0.6
18	0.6	0.1	0.5	0.5
19	0.5	0.1	0.4	0.4
20	0.4	and so on	–	–
and so on	–			
Overall change	+100.0	+20.0	+80.0	+100.0

MPC continued to hold the same value of 0.8, as has been used throughout this chapter.

Table 4.4 traced the response of the economy to such an increase in investment expenditure. It showed that the adjustment process would take the form of a whole new series of 'rounds' of expenditure, triggered by the increase in income generated by the higher level of investment spending.

The increase in investment of 20 is shown as the sole entry in round 1 of the table. In terms of the circular flow model of Figure 2.2, this represents additional income for the firms' sector, which will be used for payments to households for the input services used to produce these investment goods. Round 2 therefore starts with the receipt of this income, which can either be allocated to savings, or to consumption. From our assumed value for households' *MPC*, we know that 20%, or 4, of this additional income will be saved (that is, 0.2(20) = 4); the balance of 80%, or 16, will pass back into the economy in the form of additional consumption spending (that is, 0.8(20) = 16). But this second round of expenditure of 16 will *not* be on investment goods; it will follow the normal pattern of consumption spending and will flow to firms selling food, clothing, washing machines, holidays and so on.

Thus the expansion effect of the increase in investment is transmitted through consumption expenditure into a wider range of industries producing consumer goods. Moving into the third round of Table 4.4, this increase in the sale of output creates an additional income of 16 for households employed in these new industries; as before, part of this additional income will be saved (that is, 0.2(16) = 3.2) and the balance of 12.8 (that is, 0.8(16) = 12.8) will flow back into the economy as a new round of expenditure, transmitting the expansion to still more industries, as their goods and services are purchased.

By now you should be able to follow the process illustrated in the table, as it moves into the fourth, fifth, sixth and all subsequent rounds. The common feature in each is that the marginal flow of expenditure from one round becomes a marginal flow of income for other households in the next. Each time this happens, 20% of the flow leaks into household savings, so that the expenditure rounds become progressively smaller, and gradually reduce to an insignificant level – by which time, the economy is approaching its new equilibrium.

Note how, in our two-sector economy, savings is the only leakage from the system. In a more complex model, the various forms of taxation, or imports, would provide further leakages from the circular flow of income, which would accelerate the shrinkage in the flow of expenditure, and so reduce the extent of the adjustment process.

Note also how, if the various columns of the table are summed at the end of the adjustment process, this would show that both income and expenditure have increased by 100, in response to the original increase of 20 in investment.[7] The disturbance has therefore been magnified five times. This reaction of the economy to the disturbance is measured by a new concept, the **multiplier**; this measures the ratio of the final change in income (or ΔY) to the disturbance which triggered the adjustment, here the increase in investment (or ΔI). Where the multiplier is given the symbol k:

---

7. Two other points are worth noting: firstly, note how the increase in expenditure of 100 is made up of an increase in consumption of 80, plus the initial increase in investment of 20 – and see by how much more consumption has increased than investment; secondly, note how the total for the savings leakage is also 20 – at its simplest, savings has prevented all the expenditure going into consumer goods, and has reserved resources for investment, or producers' goods.

$$k = \frac{\Delta Y}{\Delta I}$$

$$= \frac{100}{20}$$

$$= 5$$

in our example above.

From the table, we know that consumption, in particular the *MPC* has had a major role to play in this magnification process. How can we show this, and evolve a formula which allows us to measure the strength of the multiplier?

By using some simple algebraic manipulation, we can both explore the nature of the multiplier and produce a more detailed final formula for calculation purposes. We know that, within our simplified economic system, there will be equilibrium when available output is just enough to satisfy planned expenditure, that is:

$$Y = C + I$$

We also know that

$$C = a + cY$$

so that we can restate the first equation as:

$$Y = a + cY + I$$

If we gather all the *Y* terms to the lefthand side of the equation, then:

$$Y - cY = a + I$$

which can be simplified to

$$Y(1 - c) = a + I$$

If we divide both sides by $(1 - c)$ then this becomes:

$$Y = \frac{1}{1 - c} \cdot [a + I]$$

Where does this leave us in our quest for the multiplier? A little thought should show you that we have now produced the formula for the multiplier. If $c = 0.8$, then

$$\frac{1}{1-c}$$

$$= \frac{1}{1-0.8}$$

$$= \frac{1}{0.2}$$

$$= 5$$

which was the multiplier's value. In short,

$$k = \frac{1}{1-c}$$

Thus any change within the square brackets will be magnified, or multiplied by this term, thus the value of which must exceed unity so long as c > 0, which will always be the case.

Returning to Figure 4.6 and Table 4.4, we can now see that the extent of the change in income will depend upon the size of the multiplier, which will reflect the value for the marginal propensity to consume which, in turn, will be reflected in the slope of the consumption function. If, for instance, the value of the *MPC* had been 0.9 (that is, 90% of the additional incomes passed on as consumption in each round), then the value of the multiplier would have been 10, and the final change in income from an increase in investment of 20 would have been 200. Alternatively, if the *MPC* had only been 0.6 (that is, 60% of income passed on as consumption each round), then the value of the multiplier would only have been 2.5 and the resultant change in income only 50. The higher the value of the *MPC*, the greater is the proportion of the additional income which flows back into the economy in the form of additional consumption spending, and the greater is the value of the multiplier. Or, in geometric form, the higher the *MPC*, the steeper is the slope of the consumption function, and therefore the aggregate expenditure function, and the greater is the distance between equilibrium levels for any given change in the level of the injection function.

Whatever the approach taken, it should be clear that the consumption function has an important role to play in the adjustment process which is triggered by any revision in the level of one of the exogenous elements of expenditure, be this investment, exports, or government expenditure.

CONCLUSIONS

1. Consumption is the largest of the expenditure elements within the UK national accounts; it makes up about 60% of total domestic expenditure, and takes up about 50% of aggregate supply (defined as $Y + M$).
2. This does not differ too much from the experience of our main international competitors – but there are worrying symptoms that, in the UK, growth in consumption is exceeding growth in domestic output, so that the aggregate supply can only match aggregate demand for the economy, if additional imports are sucked in. This does, in fact, appear to have been the case in the UK since the mid 1980s.
3. In terms of our simple theoretical model of the economy, the shape or slope of the consumption function is determined by the sensitivity of consumption to income or, more technically, the marginal propensity to consume. The greater the value of the marginal propensity to consume, the greater is the slope of the consumption function, and the greater the increase in consumption expenditure for a given change in the level of income.
4. At the same time, consumption expenditure is influenced by a number of factors: taxation, credit terms, expectations and household wealth all combine to provide a background context against which the consumption decision is made. A change in any one of these is likely to cause a revision in consumption behaviour, and the creation of a new consumption function in the model.
5. In more complex theory, the current consumption decision will be influenced not simply by current income, but by some view taken on past and anticipated future income. These more complex relationships are omitted from our more simple modelling procedures.
6. A change in the level of the injection function (which, in the full model, will include government expenditure and exports as well as investment) will also cause a change in the absolute level of consumption expenditure, because it will generally involve an adjustment towards a new equilibrium level of income. Consumption will change in response to the new income level, but this will involve a movement along the existing consumption function, rather than the creation of a new pattern of consumption behaviour .
7. The disturbance from the injection function, the change in income and the resultant change in consumption expenditure are all interrelated via the multiplier. This relates the overall change in income or economic activity to the change in injections, which creates the disturbance to the model. The extent of the adjustment process

depends upon the value of the marginal propensity to consume which determines the strength of the multiplier.

SELF-ASSESSMENT QUESTIONS

TRUE/FALSE QUESTIONS

4.1. Disposable income is that proportion of income received which households decide to allocate to consumption expenditure.

4.2. Expectations will have no effect on current consumption, since they relate to events in a future period.

4.3. The multiplier will apply equally to a negative adjustment, for example, to a fall in investment caused by greater business pessimism.

4.4. The multiplier can only operate where there is a simple two-sector economy (that is, households and firms).

MULTIPLE CHOICE QUESTIONS

4.1. An increase in the severity of credit terms (for example, shorter repayment periods, or higher interest charges) will:

(a) have no effect on the level of consumption, which will reflect current income levels;
(b) improve the economic health of the community, because less money will be borrowed;
(c) reduce consumption expenditure and the equilibrium level of income;
(d) reduce consumption but leave current income unaffected, since borrowing anticipates future income;
(e) reduce investment as well as consumption, lowering the level of income.

4.2. If there is an increase in the marginal propensity to consume:

(a) the consumption function will rise parallel to its previous position and raise the level of equilibrium income;
(b) the consumption function will rise parallel to its previous position, but nothing else will be affected; equilibrium income will be unchanged;
(c) the consumption function will have a flatter slope; it will pivot downwards, moving the intersection point of the 45° line and the aggregate expenditure function to the right, so raising equilibrium income;

(d) the consumption function will become steeper, moving the intersection point between the 45° line and the aggregate expenditure function to the left, thus lowering equilibrium income;
(e) the consumption function will become steeper, raising the slope of the aggregate expenditure function and the equilibrium level of income.

4.3. In the basic household/firms model (that is, excluding trade and the public sector), the value of the multiplier will depend on:

(a) the slope of the consumption function;
(b) the size of the initial disturbance, for example the change in investment;
(c) the extent of the final change in income which results from the disturbance;
(d) the value of the marginal propensity to save;
(e) the value for the average propensity to consume.

4.4. If the marginal propensity to save is 0.15 and there is a permanent increase in investment of 100, then the resultant increase in income will be:

(a) 118
(b) 15
(c) 667
(d) 115

Note: Solutions can be found at the end of the text.

Chapter 5

Investment Expenditure

> Introduction
> Investment in the national accounts
> A theory for investment behaviour
> Investment appraisal
> Other influences on investment behaviour
> A final reminder
> Conclusions
> Appendix 5A: The discounting technique
> Appendix 5B: The acceleration principle
> Self-assessment questions
> Exercise

INTRODUCTION

Investment is the second of the expenditure elements which must now be analysed in greater depth. You will remember that the term has a strict, technical meaning in its usage within economics. It represents the purchase of *physical* assets; it covers expenditure on producers' goods, such as premises, plant and machinery, tools and equipment, with a minor component for unsold output which is held as stock, or inventories. But, for the main part, investment is concerned with maintaining, or increasing the stock of physical productive capital in the economy.

From earlier chapters, you should be aware that investment has a key role to play within the macroeconomy. It is one of the expenditure elements which determines the equilibrium level of GDP and, through this, income and employment. At the same time, any change in the level of investment will, through the operation of the multiplier, produce a proportionately greater change in the level of economic activity. But these are essentially short-term effects and many would argue that investment has an even more important role to play in the longer term. Since it maintains or increases the stock of productive capital and, therefore, the output which can be produced by that stock of capital, it is a key component in the process of economic growth; too little investment can result in a weak and sluggish rate of growth for the economy. Or, at a more sophisticated level, since investment involves the purchase and installation of new capital goods, which will normally reflect the current level of technology, then investment becomes the transmission mechanism by which technological advance is built into the production base of the economy. Too little investment and the economy begins to lose its competitive edge, as outdated capital equipment results in higher costs, and outdated technology results in unwanted products. Would you want to buy an early 1970s desk calculator, when you could have a solar powered pocket calculator with a wider range of functions and at a fraction of the cost?

Up till this point, we have treated investment as being constant and autonomous with respect to income; in other words, we have argued that it is influenced by forces outside our model. The main purpose of this chapter must be to identify and explore these external forces, so that we can have a clearer understanding of why fluctuations might occur in the level of investment expenditure.

A brief word of warning: it will not be possible to produce a single, tidy theory which allows us to predict all aspects of the behaviour of investment expenditure. In part, this reflects the fact that several sectors are involved in the investment decision, and motivation differs between the sectors. Remember from the national accounts that the investment term of gross domestic fixed capital formation covers fixed investment by government and household sectors, as well as investment by firms. While firms' investment might plausibly be related to the profit motive, clearly this would be inappropriate for either of the other two sectors. Government fixed investment decisions will normally reflect social and political considerations, whereas households' investment in dwellings will normally reflect a combination of income, mortgage cost, and demographic influences although, realistically, the potential for capital gains on the market value of the house has had a growing influence on this decision, particularly in such locations as the South East of England (as you will remember from Extracts 4.2 and 4.3). Thus, if investment is defined purely in national accounts terms, it is unlikely that any single theory will be equally applicable to all sectors.

Even if, for the purposes of model building, investment is defined more narrowly as firms' expenditure alone, it must be remembered that this will still cover unsold stock and inventories, as well as fixed capital (that is, premises, equipment and so on). Once again, it is difficult to provide a single theory which copes convincingly with these short- and long-term uses of investment funds.

Apart from these definitional problems, any theory of investment faces difficulties in explaining the observed volatility of investment behaviour over time. From the early days of political economy it has been felt that firms' investment decisions have a 'rogue' or irrational element within them, reflecting sudden swings of optimism and pessimism within the business community. To some extent, it is possible to relate general feelings of optimism or pessimism to measurable factors (for example, changes in the level of GDP, or consumption expenditure); some swings, however, are less easily explained, and these reflect the 'animal spirits' element remarked upon by Keynes and others.

Our objectives for this chapter are to introduce you to some of the main influences on investment, and to try to build these into a simplified theory system, which will extend the understanding of the economy which is provided by the basic model. In more detail, we will look at:

- The share of resources which is typically allocated to investment in the UK;
- How this compares with the resource allocation practised in other countries – and what possible consequences might result from too marked a difference from their practice;
- How real firms try to reach a correct decision in their investment plans, or 'investment appraisal';
- What is meant by terms such as 'forecast profit stream', or 'user cost of capital';
- How to estimate the 'net present value' and the 'internal rate of return' for possible investment projects;
- The role played by the interest rate in investment decisions, or equally by influences such as business optimism or pessimism, or major waves of technological advance.

What follows may not result in a comprehensive theory of investment behaviour, but it should provide you with a solid awareness of the issues involved and an ability to apply this knowledge to assess the cause and possible consequences of past and future investment behaviour within the economy.

Table 5.1 Investment expenditure in the UK (1976–86) (£ billion).

	Current prices		Constant 1980 prices	
	1976	1986	1976	1986
Gross investment	24.5	64.2	42.2	46.5
private	14.4	51.4	25.0	36.2
government	5.4	7.3	9.1	6.1
public corporation	4.7	5.6	8.0	4.3
(private net of residences and vehicles)	9.4	34.6	16.0	25.6
As % of TDE				
gross	19.1	17.0	–	–
private	11.2	13.6	–	–
As % of GDP				
private	11.4	13.7	–	–
net private	7.4	9.2	–	–
Rates of growth				
gross investment	–	–	–	+10.2
private investment	–	–	–	+44.8%
GDP	–	–	–	+18.0%

(Source: *UK National Accounts*, 1987, Tables 1.2, 1.6, 12.1 and 12.2. Reprinted by permission of the Controller, HMSO.)

INVESTMENT IN THE NATIONAL ACCOUNTS

You may remember from Chapter 4 that investment in the UK amounted typically to about one-third of the level of consumption expenditure. In itself, there is nothing odd in this difference in magnitude; after all, investment involves the purchase of physical capital assets such as machinery and equipment, which can be used over many years to produce an output of consumption goods and services. It would be most abnormal in any economy if investment's claim on resources in any single year approached the same sort of share as that claimed routinely by consumption spending.

But what would constitute a 'normal' share of resources? How does the UK share compare with that of other countries? If there is a difference, does it matter?

Table 5.1 provides us with some of the data which are needed to answer these questions. It deals with the period 1976–86 and, if we reduce the cumbersome term of 'gross domestic fixed capital formation' to the more manageable term of **gross investment**, we can see that, in the UK, this rose from £24.5 billion in 1976 to £64.2 billion in 1986. Despite this increase, gross investment's share of Total Domestic Expenditure (TDE) fell from 19.1% to 17.0% over this period; part of the reason for this, you will remember, was that the share of consumption was rising. In constant price terms, the table shows that the increase in gross investment was predictably less dramatic; it rose from £42.2 billion to £46.5 billion, or by 10.2%, over the period.

However, this relatively sluggish performance conceals some very interesting trends. These have caused a very major change in the shares of the different investment components which make up the total for gross investment. In current and in constant price terms there has been a very substantial increase in the level of private investment (which covers both firms' investment *and* investment by households) which has raised its share from 58.8% to 80.0% of the total; even in constant price terms expenditure by this sector has increased by 44.8% and is now, by far, the dominant component of gross investment. But note how this increase in its relative share has been helped by the influence of government policy over the period. In constant price terms, government investment has been cut by about a third, while the privatization programme (and strict budgetary controls) have caused the investment expenditure of public enterprises to fall by almost one-half; as a result, their shares have fallen from 22.0% to 11.4% of the total in the case of government investment, and from 19.2% to 8.7% for public corporations.

Table 5.2 allows us to compare the UK pattern with data from some of our international competitors.[1] If we look first at the broad share of resources claimed by gross investment, we can see that the UK lies marginally below the USA in 1986 (17.0% of TDE, as against 18.1%), markedly below West Germany and the Netherlands (with shares of 20.3% and 19.6% respectively), and substantially below Japan (which allocated a massive 28.7% of TDE to investment). The same pattern applies if we focus more narrowly on private investment, within the total for gross investment. For the UK this represented 13.6% of TDE in 1986, against the 16.5% of the USA, the 16.0% of the Netherlands and the 21.6% for Japan; no equivalent breakdown is available for West Germany in the OECD national accounts.

Even if we sift out household expenditure on houses and vehicles

---

1. There is a data availability problem here. Only the full OECD national accounts publication breaks down the total for gross investment into its component parts; at the time of writing, the latest of these annual publications which was available was for May 1987 – which leaves 1985 as the most recent year for data. To allow comparison with UK figures for a full decade, the period 1975–85 has been used for the USA, Japan, West Germany and the Netherlands. This might pick up some minor differences in timing with the business cycle, but these should not be strong enough to falsify the comments made in the text of the chapter.

to leave us with a figure for net private investment by firms, this relative pattern is unchanged. This amounted to 9.2% of GDP in the UK in 1986, which compares to 11.1% for the USA, 11.4% for the Netherlands, and 16.3% for Japan.

We have argued in the Introduction to this chapter that persistent under-investment is a dangerous policy. Over the long term, it could result in the efficiency of productive capacity, or capital stock for the country, falling below that of its international competitors – partly because it has grown progressively older, and partly because it has become progressively more outdated in terms of current levels of technology. A casual observation of UK car showrooms, TV and audio systems, washing machines, dishwashers, refrigerators, other electrical appliances, shoes, clothing, floor coverings, or whatever, should underline this lesson. How many of these were once major items of UK manufacturing output – indeed, even to the extent that the UK held a major share in world markets? It might well be argued that changes in the international trade flows reflect the realities of the changing pattern of comparative advantage[2] in production between competing nations; but these changes, in turn, probably reflect the different rates of application of appropriate technological advances, at least as much as the more emotive claims of 'cheap' labour, or concealed government subsidy. The long-term development of the quality and the efficiency of any nation's stock of productive capital will depend upon the volume and the quality of its investment expenditure.

The data for the recent past, as shown in Tables 5.1 and 5.2 are not atypical; the UK has consistently 'under-invested' relative to other developed countries, from the post-war years to the present. In a very real sense, these shortfalls in investment were the seeds of the harvest which we have reaped since the mid 1970s. It is not enough to blame changes in world market conditions for our out-dated industrial structure and production attitudes. We alone are to blame. While government policy in recent years has certainly raised private investment in the UK towards a share of gross investment which is more comparable to that shown by these other countries, this is only the start of a long way back.[3]

---

2. See Chapter 11 on international trade and the balance of payments for a detailed discussion; for the moment, translate the term **comparative advantage** simply as the ability to produce at a lower cost level.

3. In passing, it is worthwhile looking at the share of government investment within gross investment for the Netherlands and Japan; while the UK policy has been to cut this share, to 'free' the economy for stronger private sector growth, Japan in particular seems quite happy with a much higher proportion for government investment (17.4%) of a much higher figure for gross investment. Government investment is not always a second best, or even 'bad' form of investment; it can make its own important contribution to the process of economic growth. If you are interested in following up the theme of the role for public sector investment, see *The Times*, 15 November 1983, p. 23, 'A cautious dose of investment could cure our ailing economy'. This

Table 5.2 International comparison of investment expenditure (1975–85).

	USA		Japan		West Germany		Netherlands	
	1975	1985	1975	1985	1975	1985	1975	1985
As % of gross investment								
private	82.7	88.4	72.1	75.3	N.A.	N.A.	81.4	85.9
government	12.3	8.6	16.2	17.4			18.6	14.1
public enterprises	5.0	3.0	11.6	7.3			N.A.	N.A.
As % of TDE								
gross	17.4	18.1	32.4	28.7	21.0	20.3	21.8	19.6
private	14.4	16.0	23.4	21.6	N.A.	N.A.	17.7	16.8
As % of GDP								
private	14.2	16.5	23.4	20.9	N.A.	N.A.	17.1	16.0
net private	9.9	11.1	16.4	16.3	N.A.	N.A.	11.8	11.4
Rates of growth (1975–85)								
gross investment	–	+54.1%	–	+40.2%	–	+15.7%	–	+1.7%
private investment	–	+64.7%	–	+49.8%	–	N.A.	–	+8.7%
GDP investment	–	+36.1%	–	+54.0%	–	+25.5%	–	+17.6%

Note: sectional breakdown of gross investment is not available for West Germany: OECD data only provided for gross figures: for Netherlands, public enterprise data not provided separately (included in private sector).

(Reprinted by permission of the *National Accounts*, OECD Department of Economics and Statistics, 1987, Tables 1 and 4 for each country.)

Extract 5.1 provides an interesting discussion on some of the problems of and frustrations in the current UK capital market. It explores the interesting criticism that the predominantly short-term gain horizon which afflicts players in the market, can have serious repercussions on the availability of long-term finance. If you are not too sure of what is meant by 'the short-term gain horizon' it is, at its simplest, the recognition that long-term investment projects will not yield their full stream of profits until some future date, but could impose short-term costs and weak short-term profits on the overall performance of the firm, which would reduce the firm's immediate profit earnings and, probably, its level of dividend payout to shareholders. Should the shareholders, in their turn, want to earn the maximum short-term return from the use of *their* funds, then they might prefer to switch those funds to uses which offer higher immediate profits. If this is so – and the topic of 'short termism' has been the subject of several heated, if unresolved, debates – then a supply-side constraint has been imposed on the highly developed capital markets of

---

3. (*cont.*) article was written to set out the main issues for debate, for a major symposium on the topic and is a useful outline of the main issues involved.

Extract 5.1 THE ECONOMIST 27 JUNE 1987.

INVESTING IN BRITAIN
LONG VIEWS ON SHORT-TERMISM

Do City firms let British industry down in their greed for short-term profits? Surely not, say the free marketeers—Britain's capital markets are among the world's most efficient. But, retort some economists, efficient markets may themselves discourage long-term investment. Who is right? According to a recent study by Deloitte Haskins & Sells, an accounting firm, more than 90% of British companies think that City firms take a view that is too short-term in making their investment decisions. They can cite plenty of circumstantial evidence.

Britain has invested less than other industrial countries—averaging under 20% of GDP between 1970 and 1986, compared with over 30% for Japan and 22% for West Germany. Electronics companies moan that the stockmarket depresses their share price if they announce long-term projects and that this is a brake on R&D. The high turnover of fund managers' portfolios—about 25% a year—and the way some pension-fund trustees are obsessed about topping monthly league tables are also given as evidence of short-termism.

Why might City institutions have a bias toward short-term rewards? There are at least two theories. First, though efficient in most senses, Britain's financial markets still have a few wrinkles that need smoothing. The biggest wrinkle is that investors and bankers lack information. This is the Bank of England's view. One senior London broker fears that analysts fail to understand complex industries like electronics, the business that complains loudest about short-termism. Solution: encourage shareholders and bankers to take a more active interest in their investments. Trustees, too, should be educated to lengthen their horizons, says Mr David Walker, an executive director of the Bank of England.

Improving the quality of information supplied in company accounts would be another help. Britain's Accounting Standards Committee plans to introduce new rules requiring firms to disclose their R&D spending, and to stop them hiding assets off their balance sheet.

The second theory is far more contentious. Instead of blaming short-termism on minor market imperfections, it blames the institutional structure of Britain's financial markets. Mr Colin Mayer, professor of corporate finance at City University Business School, argues that in highly competitive (hence supposedly efficient) financial markets shareholders keep at arm's length from their investments and banks have short-term profit motives. And the more competitive the markets, the more short term they will become.

The reason, says Professor Mayer, is lack of commitment between investors and firms. The perfect market breaks down because contracts cannot be written to cover future events. Banks have no incentive to bail out an ailing firm when the firm can shop around for better terms from a rival bank when it recovers. And a bank or shareholder can stop backing a firm's long-term strategy if a more immediately profitable opportunity comes along. So firms do not risk taking a long view.

Contrast Britain with Japan, he says. There, the banks have long-term relations with the firms they lend to (so much so that the debt they provide is like equity, he argues). Japanese banks will support struggling companies to protect a stream of future business. The stockmarket is peripheral to investment decisions, mainly because takeovers are rare. To western eyes, this smacks of an inefficient market. Look how well Japanese industry has performed, Professor Mayer says, and how economies with the "efficient" capital markets—America and Britain—worry most about their investment performance.

If too much competition in the financial world is indeed bad for industry, the case for far-reaching changes looks strong. The Trades Union Congress would be gleeful—it has long called for a national investment bank to plug shortfalls in long-term finance. Others want to expand the role of organisations like Investors in Industry, a successful semi-private institution that by-passes the arms-length capital markets. Owned jointly by the clearing banks and the Bank of England, it works closely with small companies to provide long-term finance.

To those on the other side of the debate, such recommendations are based on a false premise. They argue that the free-market case has the weight of over 50 years of theory and evidence on its side. First, the theory, rooted in the economics of perfect markets. On this view, banks compete to make profitable loans; only bad projects or firms will fail to get money. Shareholders stay at arm's length from their investments, but they nonetheless value firms on long-term earning potential. The more competition there is between financial firms, the better the capital markets do their job.

Then, the evidence. Three official studies have been made of the British financial markets: the Macmillan Committee report in 1931; the Radcliffe Committee Report of 1959; and the Wilson Committee report of 1978–80. Though the Macmillan Committee uncovered the famed "Macmillan gap" in funding for medium-sized firms, and the Wilson Committee thought small firms got a raw deal, both reports essentially gave the City a clean bill of health, even though the latter, commissioned by a Labour government, would have been expected to ferret out any City shortcomings.

Copious statistical analysis by economists shows the same thing from a different angle— that stockmarkets are rational and far-sighted. Hope flickered for critics of the City when a paper, published in February this year by two econometricians, Mr Stephen Nickell and Mr Sushil Wahdwani seemed to show that fund managers attach more weight to current than future dividends; and over five times more importance to current dividends than they would if the market were perfectly efficient.

It is easy to be sceptical about the sporadic resurrection of the short-termism debate. Professor Alan Budd of the London Business School explains it as a natural response to periods of bafflingly slow growth. And lots of takeovers may be evidence of inefficient managers, not of an inefficient market. An economist at the National Economic Development Office argues that firms grumble about the City because Britain has lost its comparative advantage in traditional industries: so finance is being diverted into services. Old-industry firms denied money for long-term investment

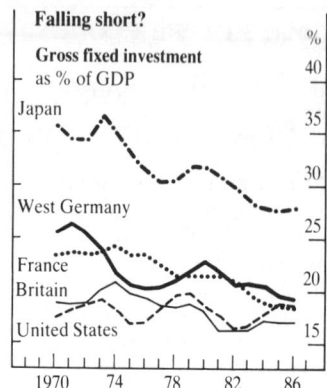

Falling short?
Gross fixed investment as % of GDP

are unfortunate victims of markets better at allocating capital than they are—the cruel but efficient face of capitalism. So "the market knows best" school of thought is still on top.

However, a glaring omission from research so far is a thorough comparative study of financial systems in different countries. The invisible hand may do a passable job at parcelling out cash, but other countries' financial systems, though more rudimentary or regimented, may do better. Professor Mayer and two fellow economists, Dr Jeremy Edwards and Dr Margaret Bray of Cambridge University, have begun a three-year study of capital markets in Britain, France, Japan, West Germany and America to find out.

Reprinted with permission from *The Economist* 27 June 1987 © *The Economist*.

---

the UK and the USA *in addition to* possible weaknesses in the demand for funds for investment purposes.

In case you feel that we are labouring the point a little, compare the UK rate of growth in GDP of 18.0% for the decade, with the 25.5% recorded for West Germany, or the 36.1% for the USA, or the 54.0% achieved by Japan. Is it purely a coincidence that all these countries have historically allocated a greater share of resources to investment than the UK? Is it simply an accident that the country which has habitually allocated the greatest share of GDP to investment has also achieved the greatest rate of growth in GDP? While economic growth will reflect many

Table 5.3 Investment behaviour over time (£ billion).

	Constant 1980 prices			Volume indices (1980=100)	
	Gross investment	Stocks	GDP	GDFCF	GDP
1966	34.0	1.4	171.5	81.9	74.4
1967	37.0	1.1	176.3	89.1	76.5
1968	39.3	1.7	183.6	94.6	79.6
1969	39.1	1.9	186.0	94.1	80.7
1970	40.1	1.4	190.3	96.4	82.5
1971	40.8	0.4	195.5	98.2	84.8
1972	40.7	−0.1	200.1	97.9	86.8
1973	43.4	5.0	215.5	104.3	93.4
1974	42.3	2.3	213.4	101.7	92.5
1975	41.5	−2.6	212.2	99.9	92.0
1976	42.2	1.2	220.3	101.6	95.5
1977	41.4	2.6	222.6	99.7	96.5
1978	42.7	2.2	230.6	102.8	100.0
1979	43.9	2.5	235.5	105.7	102.1
1980	41.0	−2.6	230.6	100.0	100.0
1981	37.6	−2.4	227.9	90.4	98.8
1982	39.5	−1.0	230.5	95.1	99.9
1983	41.6	0.7	238.6	100.1	103.5
1984	45.0	0.3	243.5	108.3	105.6
1985	46.4	0.6	252.6	111.6	109.5
1986	46.5	0.7	259.9	112.0	112.7

(Source: *UK National Accounts*, 1987, Tables 1.6 and 1.7. Reprinted by permission of the Controller, HMSO.)

factors other than the volume of investment expenditure, the latter does have a vital role to play within the growth process.

On rather less provocative ground, it is interesting to look at the behaviour of investment over time, to seek evidence of the nature of its volatility and 'animal spirits'; Table 5.3 provides UK data for the last 20 years, and Figure 5.1 reproduces the volume indices for investment and GDP in graph form.

What exactly is implied by the term 'volatility'? It would seem to suggest an erratic path, with dramatic and exaggerated fluctuations – possibly even with movements which run against the trend of economic activity. An examination of Table 5.3 would seem to confirm that UK investment has shown at least some, if not all, of these characteristics. There are strong surges in investment expenditure, against much more

Figure 5.1 The volatility of investment.

gentle rises in the level of economic activity, as measured by GDP: over 1966–67 the volume index for investment rose by over 7 points against a 2 point increase in GDP; or, more recently, trace the recovery surge of investment over 1981–84, as it rose from an index value of 90.4 to 95.1, then to 100.1, then to 108.3 by the last year of that period, against the more conservative increases in GDP from 98.8 to 99.9, then to 103.5, and finally to 105.6.

Equally, there have been hesitant stumbles in the level of investment, even against a relatively steady growth trend in GDP; note how the investment index fell over 1968–69, and 1971–72, and again over 1976–77 against rising GDP. And there have been years when investment has shown no clear trend, or even conviction; for example, trace its uncertain path over 1973–77 in response to the series of OPEC price increases (but note how these appear to have resulted in hesitancy, rather than major cuts in investment).

Finally, for a clear illustration of collapse look at the behaviour of investment in the downturn into recession from 1979. From a peak in its index value of 105.7 in 1979, investment plummeted by over 15 points to 90.4 in 1981, against an overall fall in the GDP index from 102.1 to 98.8 over the same period. Despite the relatively limited decline in GDP, the impact of the severity of the depression on business confidence can be traced in the fact that it took five years before the volume of investment recovered to pass the level set in 1979.

Figure 5.1 illustrates the relative paths of the two sets of indices in graphical form; it shows very clearly the marked differences in behaviour over 1979–84. But it is interesting for other reasons too. Note how the influences of changes in the level of investment can be traced in the movements of GDP (which is what we would expect from our multiplier analysis in Chapter 4), but their impact has been blurred and flattened by the behaviour of the other expenditure elements within GDP. This is particularly true of the 1979–84 period, where stubborn resistance of consumption to the negative effects of the depression, followed by its quick recovery into continued growth, cushioned the negative multiplier impact of the cuts in investment.

However, for evidence of real volatility, simply take a look at the behaviour of stocks or inventories over the 20-year period! While these movements may well reflect changes in the planned level of investment in inventories, the volatility also reflects the fact that stocks provide a 'buffer' between production and consumption. If there is a shortfall in demand, there will be an unplanned increase in investment in inventories, as unsold output is added to the target level of stocks. Conversely, if the level of demand is greater than was expected, it will be met at least in part by running inventory levels down below their target, or planned level. The result of these planned and unplanned variations is so haphazard that no attempt is made to produce a volume index for inventories.

One interesting trend emerges from the constant price data on inventories; the movement of the economy into major depression from the third quarter of 1979 has caused a major revision in stock-holding practice in the UK. Initially, over 1980–83, there were a series of savage cuts in the level of inventories held (remember, these are progressive cuts over the three-year period); this has been followed by four years during which only tentative (relative to the earlier years of the series) increases were allowed for inventories, despite the strong recovery of fixed investment expenditure. As a result, investment in inventories has fallen as a percentage of total investment (taken here as gross investment plus inventories) from a fairly 'normal' figure of 5.4% in 1979, to only 1.5% of the total by 1986.

For investment as a whole, therefore, there seems to be clear evidence of erratic – even unpredictable – behaviour. Where does this leave us in our task of providing a systematic explanation for these variations in the level of expenditure?

A THEORY FOR INVESTMENT BEHAVIOUR[4]

It is always interesting to observe and to speculate about movements in real-world data – but rather more difficult to explain *why* these

---

4. For another commonly used introductory model on investment behaviour, see Appendix 5B; this outlines the acceleration principle which links the level of investment to changes in the level of GDP. We have chosen to leave this alternative approach out of the main text to keep the latter as short and as simple as possible.

movements have occurred. Yet it is the latter which we must try to do, as economists. We have established that investment is relatively volatile; our task must therefore be to set up a simplified system of theory which allows us to analyse and at least partially explain this volatility.

As was the case with consumption spending, it is obvious that investment will reflect the simultaneous influences of a whole range of factors. For example, decisions on whether or not to increase the productive capacity, or capital stock, of the firms' sector will depend upon an assessment by individual firms of factors such as the pressure of utilization of existing capacity; the perception of future changes in this degree of utilization; on the potential profitability of the new ventures which are available; on the cost of, or return which must be made on any funds committed to these ventures; on changes in the business climate of optimism and pessimism; or on the response of production to new waves of technology (such as those spilling over from developments in North Sea oil exploration and extraction, or aerospace exploration – even possibly from Star Wars research).

Once again we are faced with the difficulty of representing these influences in two-dimensional form; this limits us to illustrating the behaviour of investment relative to one other variable which, ideally, should represent the strongest single influence on investment plans. Which, out of all the factors listed above, should we select?

While it is never a simple task to find a consensus among economists (although it is little more than a scurrilous suggestion that, if you laid all economists end to end in a line around the world, then they would still never reach a conclusion . . .), there is probably a strong degree of agreement that the rate of interest exercises a major influence on investment decisions. This follows because it sets a '**user cost**' on funds used for investment purposes.

At first sight, this might seem to apply only to funds *borrowed* by the firms' sector, or by its individual businesses; for the use of these funds, borrowers will normally have to pay the market price as represented by the market rate of interest.[5] But what happens if part of the funds used for investment are provided by the firm out of its retained profits, or business savings? Does the use of funds which the firm already owns also carry a user cost?

Indeed it should! After all, these funds could have been left in a riskless interest earning deposit account with a bank or building society, or used to purchase government securities, or relatively safe 'blue chip'

---

5. Realistically, there will not be a single rate of interest but a whole series of different rates, reflecting different durations of loan, different levels of security offered to and control by the lender, and different perceived rates of risk in the use of the funds; there may even be a distinction between actual (or 'nominal') and effective (or 'real') rates of interest to build in an adjustment for the effect of inflation. We ignore all this to keep the chapter as simple as possible.

private sector securities in the Stock Exchange. Retained profits will always have alternative uses; their true cost lies in the earnings opportunities which are forgone if they are not placed in these alternatives. This logic introduces you to one of the most important concepts within economics, the concept of **opportunity cost**; *the opportunity cost of any resource package is measured by what it could have earned in its next most valuable use.* When the author's daughter stands outside a football ground each Saturday and tries to decide whether to buy a match programme, or to spend her pocket money on sweets instead, then she is balancing the opportunity costs of her decision. The true cost of the match programme is the sacrifice of all the satisfaction she could have had from chewing sweets and disrupting her father's concentration – or, more normally, prayerful meditation. Alternatively, if she buys the sweets, then their opportunity cost will be the loss of all the pleasure she would have gained from reading the programme, and its official, authorized explanation of why the team were so unlucky as to lose their last ten games in a row.

Returning (with some difficulty!) to our central theme, even retained profits have a user cost; at this simple level of analysis, we will take their opportunity cost as the interest which could have been earned by lending these funds for others to use. Therefore, for internal and external funds,[6] the market rate of interest measures the user cost of capital; nothing is 'costless'.

So far so good. We can now start to build a new theory model which shows how the level of investment will be influenced by the rate of interest; at least we have identified the axes for the model shown in Figure 5.2. But what form does the functional relationship take?

Once again we must return to our commonsense knowledge of business. No rational firm will borrow funds unless it has reasonable expectations that it will be able to repay them, with interest, and still have the prospect of making a profit. In more formal terms, if the firm seeks to maximize its profits, it will embark on activities so long as the marginal benefit from them (that is, the revenue earned by them) exceeds the marginal cost involved (where this covers all the costs associated with the project, including user cost of the financial resources used).

---

6. If your heart remains unwrung by the misfortunes of the author's football team, your brain may be pondering about the user cost of funds raised by a new share issue for investment purposes. Again at its simplest, the yield expected on these shares (which will be one of the main influences on their market price) will be looking for some premium return over the relatively riskless alternative use of lending the funds at the market rate of interest. Even ordinary shares will reflect movements in the rate of interest; for example, if interest rates are expected to rise, ordinary share prices will tend to fall (so that the stream of dividends expected, provide a higher yield, and maintain the premium return over the more riskless use of funds). We have not distinguished between borrowed and subscribed funds in the text, again to keep things as simple as possible.

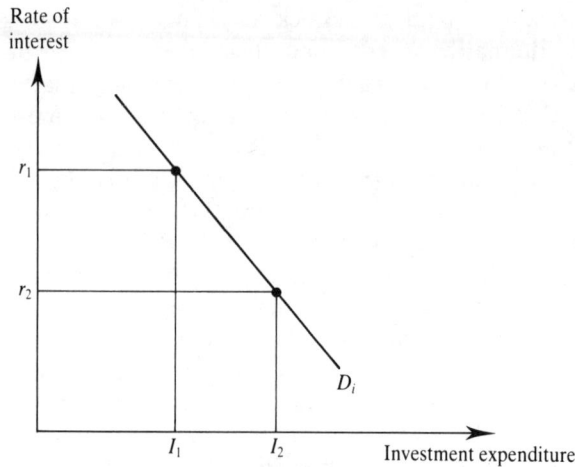

Figure 5.2 Investment and the rate of interest.

Thinking this through a little further, not all projects will have the same potential for profit. A few will offer the prospect of a really high return; rather more will offer the prospect of a relatively lower return. If, therefore, we were to set up a demand curve for investment funds (D_i) in Figure 5.2, it would tend to slope downwards from left to right. The higher the user cost of the funds, the fewer the projects which would be able to justify this in terms of profitability, and the lower would be the demand for funds; for example, at an interest rate of r_1, the demand for investment funds would be I_1, in terms of the model in Figure 5.2. Conversely, the lower the user cost of capital, the greater would be the number of projects which could cover the cost of borrowing, and the greater would be the demand for investment funds; in Figure 5.2, an interest rate of r_2 would result in a higher level of investment expenditure at I_2.

We have now produced a simple theory model which argues that the level of investment is functionally related to the user cost of capital, as measured by the market rate of interest, that is:

$$I = i(R)$$

Given the investment function derived from this relationship, as illustrated in Figure 5.2, we can identify the level of investment corresponding to any given rate of interest – or predict how the level of investment will respond to any changes in the rate of interest.

Even at this simple level, we can now look in greater depth at macroeconomic policy issues. For example, over 1979–81 the government was intent on reducing the rate of growth in the money supply; a consequence of this was that demand pressure pushed up the price of money, or the rate of interest. The period therefore experienced a series of marked increases in interest rates. Go back to Figure 5.1 and check what happened to the level of investment over this period. There were other influences, as we will discuss later, but the 'volatile' reduction in investment expenditure becomes rather less random and haphazard when we analyse the consequences of rising interest rates in terms of the model in Figure 5.2. Equally, might not the recovery of investment over 1981–84 have reflected, at least in part, the much lower levels of interest rate during this period?

For the first time, we are in a position to see one of the fundamental problems of macroeconomic policy. Frequently, a policy action taken to achieve one objective (here the control of inflation) can trigger an adverse side effect, which creates unwanted damage in other areas of the economy (here the level of investment, output and employment). Few policy actions are free from the risk of generating unwanted side effects. In more recent years, the government's decision to cut personal tax rates in the spring budget of 1988 (partly to simplify the structure of progressive tax rates, but mainly to improve the incentive to earn) has apparently, and predictably, triggered a major boom in consumer spending. To control the inflationary (and balance of payment current account) dangers of this, we have witnessed a series of major increases in interest rates over 1988 and 1989 (showing that the problems identified in Chapter 4 are still continuing). Can we anticipate that this increase in the user cost of investment funds will have an adverse effect on investment plans, as is being claimed by the CBI?

This must not, however, be taken as an argument for abandoning policy action altogether! We merely point out that it is important to be *aware* of the likely side effects, then to base the decision for action on a careful balancing of the predicted benefits of the policy against its possible costs.

INVESTMENT APPRAISAL

What we have at this point is a plausible relationship, which argues that the level of investment expenditure will reflect an interaction between the demand for investment funds and the user cost of capital, as represented by the market rate of interest. All theory models are, to some extent, simplified versions of real-world conditions; the crucial test which they must pass is that they can provide a reasonably accurate insight into real-world events and decisions. Our next task must therefore be to explore how well our new model reproduces the main characteristics of investment planning in the firms' sector. Is there a demand function for investment funds and, if so, what influences its shape and position?

Table 5.4 Estimation of the profit stream from a given project.

	\multicolumn{6}{c}{Year}					
	0	1	2	3	...	n
Revenue (R)	–	R_1	R_2	R_3	...	R_n
Cost (C)	C_0	C_1	C_2	C_3	...	C_n
Profit (Π)	–	Π_1	Π_2	Π_3	...	Π_n

Note: (when year 0 is the immediate present and profit is the difference between revenues and costs).

While macroeconomics is more properly concerned with the behaviour of firms in aggregate, for the moment it is easier to explore the practice of investment appraisal as it is carried out by the individual firm.

The purpose of investment appraisal is to establish whether or not resources should be allocated to a potential investment project. The basic criterion is that the project must justify the use of the funds allocated to it; it must yield at least a market rate of return on these funds.

When a single project is concerned, investment appraisal assesses the viability of this project, given the current user cost of the funding required. Where mutually exclusive projects are involved (that is, competing projects for a single purpose, so that selection of one eliminates the others), the purpose of investment appraisal is to rank the possibilities in terms of their relative profitability and, assuming that the basic criterion is met, select the best single project to ensure the most profitable use of funds by the firm. Where the projects are independent (that is, selection of one does not preclude the others) the purpose of investment appraisal is to rank the possibilities in order of their profitability, so that the firm's limited resources can be directed to the best uses, or the most profitable projects.

Each project will be assessed on the basis of its estimated flow of net income, or profit, over its lifespan; this involves estimating all revenues and costs which will be earned or incurred by the project. Table 5.4 sets out this process in conceptual form. The estimated revenues from the project are shown as R_1, R_2, and R_3 (or the revenues from the first, second and third years' sales) and revenues for all other years up to R_n, where n is the last year of the project's life. Against these revenues must be matched the costs incurred in achieving them; this is represented by C_1, C_2 and C_3 (or the costs incurred over the first three years of the project, shown as annual totals), up to C_n (the costs incurred in the last or nth year of the project). Deducting costs from revenue, yields an estimate of the profits, or net income of the project over its lifespan; Π_1 represents the profits from the first year, Π_2 the profits from the second

Table 5.5 Forecast profit streams.

	Project A	Project B
Capital outlay	1000	1000
Profit from year 1	200	0
year 2	200	0
year 3	300	300
year 4	300	400
year 5	400	500
year 6	300	500
	1700	1700

year, up to Π_n, the profits from the nth year of the project's life.[7] The remaining term C_0 represents the immediate cost of the capital outlay or investment in the project. Whereas the other subscripts represent values at the *end* of the year in question, the zero subscript in C_0 indicates that this cost must be met before the project can be launched.

To illustrate the process, assume that there are two mutually exclusive projects, A and B; both have the same capital outlay of 1000 involved; both have five-year lifespans; both face the same user cost of capital of 10%. The profit streams relating to the projects are shown in Table 5.5. Is either project viable? Which is the better project – or are both the same, since total profits add up to 1700 in each case?

Even an elementary knowledge of discounting will warn us that we cannot reach an accurate decision on project viability if we simply compare the raw data on future profits to the present figure for initial capital outlay; no common unit of measurement exists between, for example, the figure for Π_5 (the profit for year 5) and C_0 (the initial capital outlay for the project). Similarly, it would be quite wrong to add up the

---

7. Accountants would prefer the explanations to be given in terms of cash flows (which would also include all subsidies received and tax payments made). The revenue stream would become the inflow of cash from all sources, mainly sales; the cost stream would become the outflow of cash payments for all items, mainly raw material and running costs. The equivalent of the profit stream would be the net cash flow from the project. This would indeed provide a more accurate measurement of the timing of the benefits and responsibilities associated with the project (for example, normal terms of trade credit could delay cash payments by three to six months behind the recorded book figures for input purchases and output sales). The revenue, cost and profit version of the model has been used, despite its technical limitations, partly because its provides a simple conceptual illustration of the rather more complex real-world technique, and partly because it fits more easily into the microeconomic models of the individual firm's behaviour – which you may well be studying alongside this macro text.

various profit figures from Π_1 to Π_n; the resultant total would be meaningless. Where figures relate to a whole series of different time periods, from the present to the distant future, then the only common unit of measurement available is the present value equivalents of all the sums concerned.

If you have not encountered the concept of discounting future sums to their present value equivalents, then you must go straight to Appendix 5A of this chapter, where the technique is explained. Do not attempt to read further, until the discounting technique is thoroughly understood.

The next step in our investment appraisal process must therefore be to convert the raw data of our revenue, cost and profit forecasts into its present value equivalents. The rate of discount chosen should reflect the user cost of capital to the firm; it is represented here by the market rate of interest. Given this rate of discount (r), the present value of the stream of profits, or the net income from the project (Π_{pv}) calculated as follows:

$$\Pi_{pv} = \frac{\Pi_1}{1+r} + \frac{\Pi_2}{(1+r)^2} + \ldots + \frac{\Pi_n}{(1+r)^n}$$

or, more simply,

$$\Pi_{pv} = \sum_{i=1}^{n} \frac{\Pi_1}{(1+r)^1}$$

Whether or not investment funds should be committed to the project will depend upon the relationship between the present value of the profit stream, and the capital outlay or purchase price involved in embarking upon the project. The project should be accepted, so long as the present value of the profits, or the net income from it at least covers the investment outlay, that is:

$$\sum_{i=1}^{n} \frac{\Pi_1}{(1+r)^1} > C_0$$

This ensures that the earnings from the project cover running costs (C_1 to C_n), the initial capital costs (C_0), and the user cost of the funds allocated to the project (represented by the discount rate r). Any excess over the initial capital costs will imply that the project's profitability will more than cover the market rate of return on the funds used. Any deficit will imply that the profits will be insufficient to earn a market rate of return, so that the project must be rejected. If the two sides of the equation are equal,

Table 5.6 Discounted profit streams.

Year	Actual profits A	B	Discount factors	Discounted profits A	B
1	200	0	0.9091	182	0
2	200	0	0.8264	165	0
3	300	300	0.7513	225	225
4	300	400	0.6830	205	273
5	400	500	0.6209	248	310
6	300	500	0.5645	170	282
		Present value of profits		1195	1090
		Capital outlay		1000	1000
		Net present value		195	90

this implies that the project 'breaks even', in the sense that it just covers costs and provides the market rate of return on the funds allocated to it.

To return to the projects described in Table 5.5, we must calculate the present values for each of the profit streams, then compare these to the figure for capital outlay in each case. The calculations are shown in Table 5.6.

Note how, at the discount rate of 10% – or indeed for any given rate of interest – the more distant the sum the more heavily it is penalized by discounting, that is, the lower is its present value. In fact, the discount factor column can be interpreted as the present value of a future £1; given a 10% discount rate, this will have a present value of 90.9p if it is one year distant, 82.6p if it is two years distant, 75.1p if it is three years distant, down to 56.5p if it is six years distant. Thus, when you look at the timing of the profit flows of the two projects, the later inflow from project B is penalized; profits earned in more distant years are worth less, so that the present value of B's profits at 1090 lies below the present value of A's profit stream of 1195 – despite the fact that, in the crude profit data, they were identical. This should underline just how inaccurate are calculations which have been based on the crude, non-discounted figures.

Having calculated the present value of the forecast profit streams, the resultant figures must be set against the initial capital outlay involved; as we have already argued, the basic criterion for acceptance is that the project must show a present value figure for profits which at least covers the investment outlay. The difference between the two figures is known as the **net present value** (or NPV) of the project. Our acceptance criterion can now be restated in the rule that a project will only be viable when it shows a NPV value of zero or better, that is, when discounted future profits are shown to be sufficient to cover all the costs involved – including the user cost of the funds required by the project. In terms of this rule, both projects A and B are viable at the discount rate of 10%; Table 5.6 shows that project A has a NPV of 195 and project B a NPV of 90. And, since each has the same capital outlay of 1000, then project A, with its higher NPV value, is superior to project B.

Project selection is clearcut enough in this case, but when the projects have different values for capital outlay, selection cannot be based on a simple comparison of their NPV figures. For example, assume project X has a capital outlay of 800 and NPV of 400 (so that present value of profits would be 800 + 400 = 1200); project Y has a capital outlay of 500 and a NPV of 350 (present value of profits would be 850). While X earns a greater absolute net profit (400 against 350), it is, nevertheless, the relatively *less* profitable project. Relative profitability can be calculated by the **profitability index**, which is *the ratio of the present value of profit to the figure for the capital outlay*. The index values would be 1.5 (1200/800 = 1.5) for project X, and 1.7 (850/500 = 1.7) for Y. In other words Y is more profitable per £1 of capital outlay, or investment expenditure.

A glance at any set of discount tables (see Appendix 5A, Table 5.8 for an example of these) will show that the present value of the profit stream reflects the rate of discount used. If the rate of discount is increased, this reduces the present value of all future sums. Conversely, if the rate of discount is reduced, the present value of the profit stream rises.

Given the profit stream and the capital outlay figures for any project, it is therefore possible to estimate the rate of discount which will leave

$$\sum_{i=1}^{n} \frac{\Pi_1}{(1+r)^1} = C_0$$

so that the project 'breaks even', that is, shows a NPV value of zero. The discount rate which achieves this result represents the maximum user cost of funds which can be carried by the project. Since the figures for both the profit stream and the capital outlay will differ from project to project, then each individual project will have its own unique[8] solution rate of discount, by which the present value of the profit stream can be brought to the same value as the initial capital outlay, so that the NPV of the project is also brought to zero.

---

8. It is technically possible that the shape of the profit (or net cash flow) stream over time could result in a break-even equation which can be solved by more than one rate of discount; for simplicity, this possibility is ignored in the text.

Table 5.7 Estimation of internal rate of return for project A.

Year	Net cash flows	Discount factors at $r = 15\%$	PV (£)	Discount factors at $R = 16\%$	PV (£)
1	200	0.8696	174	0.8621	172
2	200	0.7561	151	0.7432	149
3	300	0.6575	197	0.6407	192
4	300	0.5718	171	0.5523	166
5	400	0.4972	199	0.4761	190
6	300	0.4323	130	0.4104	123
		PV	1022	PV	992
		C_0	1000	C_0	1000
		NPV	22	NPV	−8

Note: IRR is approximately

$$15\% + \frac{22}{30} = 15.7\%$$

(The denominator of 30 is the sum of the change in NPV in the project, as the result of a percentage point change in the rate of discount, that is: 30 = 22 + 8).

Let's return to our two illustrative projects to see how to find this solution rate of discount. From our earlier calculations, we know that project A shows a NPV of 195 at a discount rate of 10%, and project B a NPV of 90. If we concentrate on project A, what discount rate would bring its NPV to zero?

If you lack the mathematics (or a pocket calculator with the necessary programme) to solve the above equation for the project, all is not lost. We can provide the same solution by doing a series of trial and error calculations, during which we process A's profit stream through a series of alternative discount rates. What we have to do is to reduce its NPV from 195 to as near zero as we can manage; if we want to pull the NPV figure down, *then we must use a higher rate of discount*. (Check from the discount table in Appendix 5A that higher rates of discount pull down the present value of any future £1. For example, at 10% the present value of a £1 due in five years' time is just over 62p; if we were using a 12% discount rate, the present value of the same £1 would be about 57p; at 15%, it would be 50p.)

Table 5.7 shows the calculations for two rates of discount. At a 15% rate, project A's profit stream is reduced to a total present value of

1022, which leaves the NPV figure at 22; this tells us that we need a still higher rate of discount. But at the discount rate of 16%, the present value of the same profit stream has been reduced to 992, which leaves a negative NPV of −8; this rate is too high. Clearly, the solution rate of discount lies somewhere between 15% and 16%; we estimate it at 15.7%, using the simple proportionality calculation shown at the foot of the table.

The discount rate which brings the present value of the profit stream into equality with the initial capital outlay, or purchase price of the project is known as the **internal rate of return** on the project. In effect, it converts the forecast profits for the project into an estimated rate of return. This internal rate of return (IRR) represents the highest possible user cost of capital which can be carried by the project, while still allowing it to break even.

Where does all this leave us? From our earlier calculations we know that, at a market rate of interest of 10%, project A is viable; it will earn sufficient profits to cover all costs, including the cost of the investment funds committed to the project. The new IRR approach gives us the same answer: so long as the user cost of capital is less than 15.7%, project A will earn sufficient profits to justify this use of funds – so, at a 10% user cost of capital, A is clearly viable.

To make sure that you understand the technique, take some time to calculate the IRR for project B, using the same approach as was illustrated in Table 5.7; we estimate its IRR as 12.5%. As we already know from our earlier calculations, at a market rate of interest of 10%, this project also earns sufficient profits to justify the use of the investment funds required.

As a general principle then, we now have the rule that, for any single project, the firm will channel funds towards it, provided that the internal rate of return exceeds the user cost of these funds. But how do we choose between projects? We already know that A is more profitable than B (because it has a larger NPV value). This is confirmed by our IRR calculations; project A has a higher IRR value of 15.7, compared to the IRR value of 12.5 for project B. It is worth mentioning, in passing, that it is no longer necessary to calculate a profitability index when the capital outlay differs between projects; a simple comparison of the IRR values of the projects will indicate their relative profitability.

In short, each firm can now estimate the IRR values for all the potential new ventures or projects which lie before it, then rank these ventures in terms of their profitability in descending order of IRR value.

The result is now very similar to the model shown in Figure 5.2. Firms will invest in all projects for which the IRR exceeds the user cost of the funds involved. In other words, the demand function for investment funds simply reflects the relative profitability of the new projects open to the firms' sector. At a market rate of interest of r_1, funds will be allocated to all projects with IRR values equal to or greater than this user cost of capital; in total, I_1 funds will be demanded for investment purposes. At lower rates of interest, for example, at r_2, there will be more projects which will show IRR values which equal or exceed this new user cost of capital; therefore there will be a greater demand for investment funds, at I_2.

Firms, as individual entities, or as an aggregate sector, will make their investment plans on the basis of the user cost of capital, as represented by the rate of interest, and the range of projects which are open to them and which earn sufficient profits to justify this use of funds. Our conceptual model, as represented by Figure 5.2, corresponds very closely to the real-world practice of investment appraisal. As such, it is a useful addition to our understanding of the macroeconomy.

OTHER INFLUENCES ON INVESTMENT BEHAVIOUR

So far so good; our conceptual model appears to provide a useful insight into firms' investment planning practice. But now we must try to broaden the model to reflect the influences of factors other than the rate of interest. Earlier in the chapter we drew up a list of these. In this section we shall explore the influence on investment plans of two of the more important items on that list, namely:

- fluctuations in the state of business expectations, and
- changes in technology

How might these be built into our new investment model?

By its very nature, investment expenditure involves a long-term commitment to future production, taken in an uncertain world, using information which is far from perfect. No matter how scientifically we forecast, we are still guessing about future events and our performance against these events; with better information, we would quite possibly change both our guesses and our strategies. Investment, on the bottom line, is an act of faith. As such, it is highly sensitive to changes in expectations. Hence expectations have an important role to play within investment plans – indeed, some early theories of the trade, or business cycle attributed all of its fluctuations to changes in the level of investment, following swings in business optimism and pessimism.

Perhaps you doubt that hard-headed businessmen could be so fickle? If so, it is worth taking a little time to glance over Extract 5.2. The data here is from two regular surveys of investment intentions in the firms' sector, taken by the Confederation of British Industries (CBI) and the Department of Trade and Industry (DTI). If you look at the CBI data,

Extract 5.2 ECONOMIC TRENDS MAY 1988.

INVESTMENT IN PLANT AND MACHINERY
CBI INTENTIONS INQUIRY

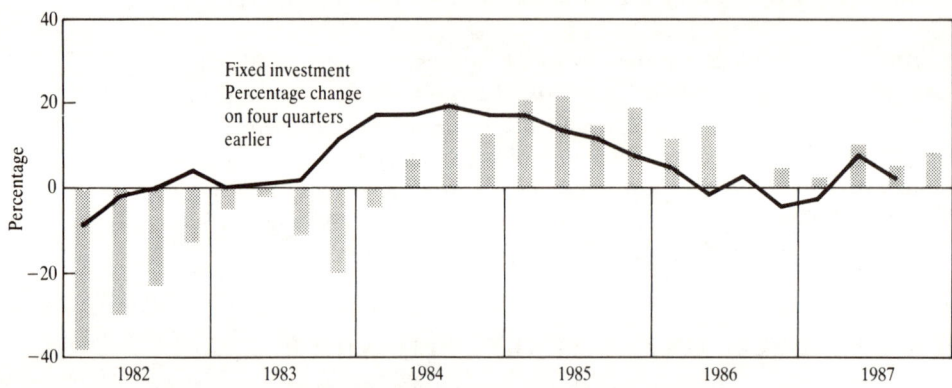

DEPARTMENT OF TRADE AND INDUSTRY
INQUIRY INTO INVESTMENT INTENTIONS:
MANUFACTURING INDUSTRY

Percentage change over previous year, in volume terms
Gross fixed investment (excluding leased assets)

	First December Forecast	First June Forecast	Second December Forecast	Second June Forecast	Actual
1976	Further reduction	Little change	−5 to −8	About −6	−5
1977	Large increase	Of order of +15	+10 to +15	+6 to +10	+5
1978	Strong increase	+20 or more	+10 to +13	+10 to +13	+7
1979	Rise, less than +8	Rise less than +8	+4 to +8	+2 to +5	+4
1980	Slight fall	Slight fall	−6 to −10	−8 to −12	−14
1981	Further fall	Fall of up to 8 to 12	−15 to −20	−15 to −18	−25
1982	Some recovery	Some recovery	−1 to −3	−3 to −5	−3
1983	Appreciable increase	Rise, around 5	Fall, up to 5	Fall, around 4	+2
1984	No recovery	Slow growth	Rise, around 10	About +12	+20
1985	Little change	Rise, around 6	About +7	Around +9	+12
1986	Slight fall	Slight fall	Rise, around 4	About +6	−1
1987	Little change	Small increase	Rise, around 3	About +6	
1988	Further rise	Further increase	Rise, around 12		
1989	Smaller increase				

Note: The figures in this table relate to manufacturing industry defined as Orders iii to xix. Standard Industrial Classification (1968) for 1983 and earlier years, and as Divisions 2 to 4, Standard Industrial Classification (1980) for 1984 onwards.

Source: *Economic Trends* May 1988. Reprinted with permission from the Controller, HMSO.

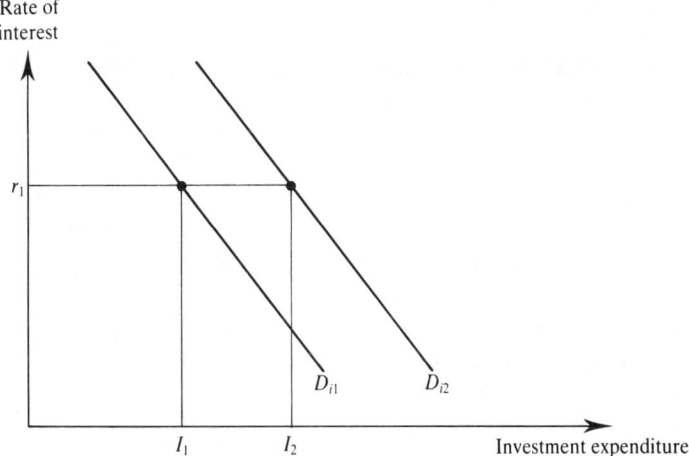

Figure 5.3 Effect of an increase in business optimism.

the quarterly bars show the intended percentage changes (with intentions moved forward one year to permit direct comparison with the actual change which occurred); the pattern which they sketch shows noticeably greater volatility of behaviour than the graph of the actual change. If, on the other hand, you look across the rows of the DTI inquiry, you can see how intentions were frequently subject to substantial revision over the period, and might not always be reflected in the actual changes which followed.

In terms of the model as set out in Figure 5.2, what would happen to the level of investment, given a constant rate of interest (and therefore user cost of capital), if there was a major upsurge in business optimism? For example, assume that major cuts in personal income tax rates were perceived by the business community to herald a prolonged boom in consumption spending, with its resultant pressure on existing productive capacity.

The simple answer is that the level of investment would rise, against the constant cost of capital. Why? Think through the consequences of the surge in optimism. At the very least, project sales forecasts ($R_0 \ldots R_n$) would be revised upwards, raising the expected stream of future profits from projects, which in turn would raise the IRR values for these projects, which would result in *more* projects justifying the allocation of funds at the same rate of interest. In terms of Figure 5.3, the demand function for investment funds would move outwards to the right, from D_{i1} to D_{i2}; as a result, given the same user cost of capital, r_1, the level of investment would rise from I_1 to I_2.

Conversely, a collapse in business confidence would have the opposite effect; investment plans would be revised downwards and the level of investment would fall. Think back to the cutbacks in investment over the years following 1979, and the hesitant, uncertain recovery in its level from 1981 up till 1983. How might this be explained by our model? This time, business perceptions of an impending crash would have adjusted project sales forecasts downwards, reducing anticipated revenue and profit streams, reducing forecast IRR values, so that fewer projects would appear to justify the then current cost of capital; the model as illustrated in Figure 5.3 would have run in reverse, with the demand for investment funds function moving to the left, resulting in a fall in investment for that year. With uncertainties and pessimism becoming almost cumulative (not least because the cuts in investment would trigger negative multiplier adjustment and *create* or at least exacerbate the very downturn which had been feared), the process of downward revisions in investment would spread over a number of years – and would need an awful lot of evidence that the recovery was indeed real and substantial, before a genuine upsurge in business confidence would allow investment to return to its previous higher level. In passing, it is only too probable that the 'batten down the hatches' mentality of a business community anticipating, then witnessing a major recession, would also result in savage cutbacks in the planned level of inventory investment – as can be observed in Table 5.3. It is therefore possible to build revisions in expectations into our new model of investment, by assessing the effect of these revisions on forecast profit streams and, through this, on the position of the demand function for investment funds.

This leaves us with the task of showing how the model would react to major changes in technology. These changes will tend to have two main influences on investment plans: firstly, they will create profitable opportunities for new or revised products; secondly, they will tend to change the relationship between inputs and output, with the effect of reducing production and other operating costs.

The first category of effect will move the demand function for investment funds out to the right, by generating a whole range of new ventures for the firms' sector. The second set of circumstances would also move the demand function to the right, but for a different reason; this time, by reducing the forecast values for $C_1 \ldots C_n$, technological change will tend to raise the expected stream of future profits, and the forecast IRR values from these, with the normal result that more projects will justify the use of funds at any given level of user cost of capital. In both cases, therefore, the technology changes would tend to move the D_i function to the right, as in Figure 5.3, which should raise the level of investment, at least until the economy has adjusted to the new opportunities which have been made available.

As you can see, the simple model illustrated in Figures 5.2 and 5.3 is marvellously resilient – yet we have by no means exhausted its explanatory powers. Take, for example, the impact of government taxation policy on the business sector. In practice, the investment appraisal process will normally work on net of tax and subsidy figures for the projects. Therefore, if the government increases the level of grants available for investment expenditure, the effect of this policy measure will be to reduce the net of grant purchase price, or capital outlay for the project; with this lower figure to set against the total present value figure of the profit stream, a higher rate of discount will be needed to bring the NPV value to zero, that is, the IRR value of the project will be *raised*. Similarly, if the government cuts the business taxation rate (or raises the threshold level of tax exemption for profits), then this will increase the net of tax profit stream and therefore the forecast IRR value for the project. Since all projects will be affected in a like manner, the effect of either taxation measure will be to move the demand function for investment funds to the right.

A FINAL REMINDER . . .

It may not be necessary, but we feel that a final reminder might not go amiss before we finish the chapter. We set out to identify what were the forces outside the basic model which determined the level of investment, and which caused fluctuations in this. Within the constraints of two-dimensional analysis, we have identified the rate of interest as the main influence on investment. A change in the interest rate would cause a movement up or down the demand function for investment funds; a change in any other influential factor, such as business expectations, technology or business taxation, would move the position of this demand function. In short, as was the case with the consumption function which we discussed in Chapter 4, some influences would cause a movement along the function, while others would cause a change in the position of the function.

However, when we return to our full basic model (which relates all the elements of aggregate expenditure to the level of income, or GDP), then you must remember that anything which causes a change in the level of investment expenditure on the horizontal axis of Figures 5.2 and 5.3 (which includes both changes in the rate of interest *and* anything which changes the position of the demand function for investment funds) will automatically result in a *new position* for the investment function in our basic macroeconomic model. The reason for this is that the basic model relates investment expenditure to the level of GDP alone; whether the new level of investment comes from a change in interest rates, or a revision in business optimism, or whatever, these are all influences which exist outside the model. Within the constraints of two-dimensional modelling, we can only show them as changing the horizontal level of the injection function and, as a result, the $C^* + J$ function. Figure 5.4 shows

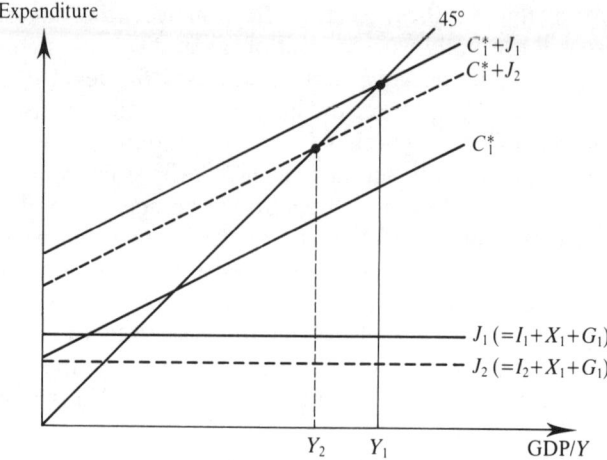

Figure 5.4 Effect on equilibrium income of a fall in investment due to a higher rate of interest.

how an increase in the rate of interest would affect the level of economic activity in the basic model. It would reduce the level of investment from I_1 to I_2, which would lower the injection function from J_1 to J_2. When this is picked up in the aggregate expenditure function, the latter would fall to $C_1 + J_1$ and the equilibrium level of GDP would fall from Y_1 to Y_2.

If you think through this a little longer, it will help you to understand a little more of the Chancellor's current dilemma in the UK. Increases in the interest rate were used to try to curb the level of consumption expenditure over 1988; by August 1989, the balance of trade position has moved into such a severe and persistent deficit that there is every possibility that the UK interest rate might have to be raised still higher. But high interest rates do not only affect consumption spending; they also have the unwanted side effect of raising the user cost of capital and, possibly, triggering a cut in the level of investment. The surveys of business investment intentions carried out by the CBI show an increasing degree of unease among respondents from the firms' sector. Therefore it could be that, in terms of our basic model, not only the C^* function but also the J function falls, causing a greater cut in the level of the $C^* + J$ function than was intended, creating the danger of a greater reduction in the level of GDP (a 'hard landing') than was desired . . . or is politic in the years before the next general election.

Once again your abstract theory has helped you to appreciate why there is a thin film of sweat forming on the brows of both the Chancellor of the Exchequer and the Prime Minister. Still think that economics has nothing to say about the real world?

CONCLUSIONS

1. In the UK national accounts, gross investment amounts to between 17% and 19% of total domestic expenditure. Once government and households' investment is deducted from this sum, the resultant figure for net private investment (which is the closest approximation we have to the term investment, as used in our model building) accounts for just over 9% of TDE.

2. While recent government policy has resulted in a marked switch towards private investment in the UK (reflecting constant price cuts in both government and public corporation investment), and while there has been a strong rate of growth in private investment over the last decade, there are still signs that the UK devotes a smaller share of resources to investment expenditure than some of our main international competitors. In the longer term, this could affect adversely the quality and efficiency of our stock of productive capital.

3. Investment behaves in a volatile manner over time, with marked and dramatic increases and decreases in the level of fixed capital formation as well as the residual element of unsold output, or inventories. It can even move in the opposite direction to trends in GDP.

4. One interpretation of this pattern of behaviour is that investment is more strongly influenced by factors other than the level of GDP – which is why it is treated as constant and autonomous in terms of the basic model.

5. Probably the main single influence on investment is the user cost of funds deployed for investment purposes; this will reflect the level of interest rates in the economy. There will normally be an inverse relationship between the level of investment and the rate of interest.

6. However, other factors will impose substantial pressure on investment plans. Among these will be changes in business expectations, major changes in technology, and government policy in business taxation. All of these will influence the demand for investment funds and changes in them will normally result in a change in the position of that demand function, as illustrated in Figure 5.3.

7. Whatever the change, whether in the rate of interest, expectations, or other factor, it will also cause a revision in the position of the investment function within the full model of income determination, where investment is depicted as constant and autonomous in terms of the income level.

8. The apparent volatility of the investment function in the basic model will not necessarily reflect a random or unpredictable element; most changes can be explained in whole or in part by our new model of

investment behaviour, as developed in this chapter. Thus, a fair proportion of the 'animal spirits' observed in investment are capable of systematic explanation and analysis.

Appendix 5A: The discounting technique

What would your reaction be if you were offered a choice between a gift of £100 from the royalties of this book, to be taken now, or the same sum to be taken in five years' time in the future? (OK! OK! Let's assume that the royalties from the sales of the book will be enough to cover the offer! Would you be indifferent between the two? Or would you prefer the bird in the hand (£100 taken now) to the bird in the bush (£100 in five years' time), even if the offer was made in writing and in your lawyer's presence?

If you have hesitated at all, you should be ashamed of yourself. Think about it a little. If the rate of interest is 10% per annum and is likely to stay at this level, then you could take the £100 from us now, deposit it in a bank or building society, earn 10% interest compounded annually, that is, paid into and accumulating in your account each year, so that your original £100 would be worth £161.05 in 5 years' time.

We could understand you being indifferent between £100 now and £161.05 in five years' time. But the original choice we offered you was no choice at all; you should have grabbed the money and run!

Let's look at it a little more formally. To accept a £1 in the future rather than the present involves postponing present consumption for future consumption. Since most people prefer the former, then they must be compensated for delaying consumption. This compensation is achieved by the market paying a rate of interest, compounded annually, for the use of the funds. If the market rate of interest (r) is 10%, as is the case in the problem set above, then the future value (V_f) at the end of the one year of a present sum (V_p) will be given by:

$$V_f = V_p + rV_p$$

(where rV_p is the annual rate of interest applied to the present sum)

$$= V_p (1 + r)$$

For example, £100 placed at 10% interest per annum will be worth

£100 (1 + 0.1)

= £110

at the end of the year. In effect, it takes £110 at the distance of one year into the future to 'be equal to' £100 in the present, in the sense that people will be indifferent between the two sums; *this means that future sums are worth less than present sums.*

If

$$V_f = V_p(1 + r)$$

as argued above, then, by rearrangement (dividing both sides by $(1 + r)$)

$$V_p = \frac{V_f}{(1 + r)}$$

This allows us to calculate the present value equivalent of a future sum at one year's distance, so that £100 in one year's time has a present value of:

$$V_p = \frac{100}{1 + 0.1}$$

$$= £90.9$$

This can be checked quite easily; it tells us that £90.9 placed at 10% interest for a year, will yield £100 at the end of the year – which, in fact, it does.

Likewise, over a two-year period, a present sum will accumulate compound interest so that its value at the end of that period (V_2) will be:

$$V_2 = (V_p + rV_p) + r(V_p + rV_p)$$
$$= V_p(1 + r) + r[V_p(1 + r)]$$
$$= V_p(1 + r)(1 + r)$$

therefore

$$V_2 = V_p(1 + r)^2$$

In other words, £100 at 10% per annum compounded will be worth

$$V_2 = £100(1 + 0.1)^2$$
$$= £100(1.21)$$
$$= £121.0$$

after two years.

As before, the present value equivalent of £100 in two years' time can be estimated by rearrangement. If

$$V_2 = V_p(1 + r)^2$$

$$V_p = \frac{V_2}{(1 + r)^2}$$

$$= \frac{£100}{(1 + 0.1)^2}$$

$$= £82.60$$

Table 5.8 Present value of £1 receivable at the end of each period.

Year	Percentage																			
	1	2	3	4	5	6	7	8	9	10	11	12	13	14	15	16	17	18	19	20
1	0.990	0.980	0.971	0.962	0.952	0.943	0.935	0.926	0.917	0.909	0.901	0.893	0.885	0.877	0.870	0.862	0.855	0.847	0.840	0.833
2	0.980	0.961	0.943	0.925	0.907	0.890	0.873	0.857	0.842	0.826	0.812	0.797	0.783	0.769	0.756	0.743	0.731	0.718	0.706	0.694
3	0.971	0.942	0.915	0.889	0.864	0.840	0.816	0.794	0.772	0.751	0.731	0.712	0.693	0.675	0.658	0.641	0.624	0.609	0.593	0.579
4	0.961	0.924	0.888	0.855	0.823	0.792	0.763	0.735	0.708	0.683	0.659	0.636	0.613	0.592	0.572	0.552	0.534	0.516	0.499	0.482
5	0.951	0.908	0.863	0.822	0.784	0.747	0.713	0.681	0.650	0.621	0.593	0.567	0.543	0.519	0.497	0.476	0.456	0.437	0.419	0.402
6	0.942	0.888	0.837	0.790	0.746	0.705	0.666	0.630	0.596	0.564	0.535	0.507	0.480	0.456	0.432	0.410	0.390	0.370	0.352	0.335
7	0.933	0.871	0.813	0.760	0.711	0.665	0.623	0.583	0.547	0.513	0.482	0.452	0.425	0.400	0.376	0.354	0.333	0.314	0.296	0.279
8	0.923	0.853	0.789	0.731	0.677	0.627	0.582	0.540	0.502	0.467	0.434	0.404	0.376	0.351	0.327	0.305	0.285	0.266	0.249	0.233
9	0.914	0.837	0.766	0.703	0.645	0.592	0.544	0.500	0.460	0.424	0.391	0.361	0.333	0.308	0.284	0.263	0.243	0.225	0.209	0.194
10	0.905	0.820	0.744	0.676	0.614	0.558	0.508	0.463	0.422	0.386	0.352	0.322	0.295	0.270	0.247	0.227	0.208	0.191	0.176	0.152
11	0.896	0.804	0.722	0.650	0.585	0.527	0.476	0.429	0.388	0.350	0.317	0.287	0.261	0.237	0.215	0.195	0.178	0.162	0.148	0.135
12	0.887	0.788	0.701	0.625	0.557	0.497	0.444	0.397	0.356	0.319	0.286	0.257	0.231	0.208	0.187	0.168	0.152	0.137	0.124	0.112
13	0.879	0.773	0.681	0.601	0.530	0.469	0.415	0.368	0.326	0.290	0.258	0.229	0.204	0.182	0.163	0.145	0.130	0.116	0.104	0.093
14	0.870	0.758	0.661	0.577	0.505	0.442	0.388	0.340	0.299	0.263	0.232	0.205	0.181	0.160	0.141	0.125	0.111	0.099	0.088	0.078
15	0.861	0.743	0.642	0.555	0.481	0.417	0.362	0.315	0.275	0.239	0.209	0.183	0.160	0.140	0.123	0.108	0.095	0.084	0.074	0.065
16	0.853	0.728	0.623	0.534	0.458	0.394	0.339	0.292	0.252	0.218	0.188	0.163	0.141	0.123	0.107	0.093	0.081	0.071	0.062	0.054
17	0.844	0.714	0.605	0.513	0.436	0.371	0.317	0.270	0.231	0.198	0.170	0.146	0.125	0.108	0.093	0.080	0.069	0.060	0.052	—
18	0.836	0.700	0.587	0.494	0.416	0.350	0.296	0.250	0.212	0.180	0.153	0.130	0.111	0.095	0.081	0.069	0.059	0.051	—	—
19	0.828	0.686	0.570	0.475	0.396	0.331	0.277	0.232	0.194	0.154	0.138	0.116	0.098	0.083	0.070	0.060	0.051	—	—	—
20	0.820	0.673	0.554	0.456	0.377	0.312	0.258	0.215	0.178	0.149	0.124	0.104	0.087	0.073	0.061	0.051	—	—	—	—

Table 5.8 (*cont.*) Present value of £1 receivable at the end of each period.

Year	1	2	3	4	5	6	7	8	9	Percentage 10	11	12	13	14	15	16	17	18	19	20
21	0.811	0.660	0.538	0.439	0.359	0.294	0.242	0.199	0.164	0.135	0.112	0.093	0.077	0.064	0.053	—	—	—	—	—
22	0.803	0.647	0.522	0.422	0.342	0.278	0.226	0.184	0.150	0.123	0.101	0.083	0.068	0.056	—	—	—	—	—	—
23	0.795	0.634	0.507	0.406	0.326	0.262	0.211	0.170	0.138	0.112	0.091	0.074	0.060	—	—	—	—	—	—	—
24	0.788	0.622	0.492	0.390	0.310	0.247	0.197	0.158	0.126	0.102	0.082	0.066	0.053	—	—	—	—	—	—	—
25	0.780	0.610	0.478	0.375	0.295	0.233	0.184	0.146	0.116	0.092	0.074	0.059	—	—	—	—	—	—	—	—
30	0.742	0.552	0.412	0.308	0.231	0.174	0.131	0.099	0.075	0.057										
35	0.706	0.500	0.355	0.253	0.181	0.130	0.094	0.068	0.049	0.035										
40	0.672	0.453	0.307	0.208	0.142	0.097	0.067	0.046	0.032	0.022										

In other words, £100 in two years' time is worth £82.60 in the present. (Check that £82.6 placed at 10% for two years will yield £100 at the end of the period – and remember that you are using compound interest.)

Generalizing, the present value of any future sum can now be estimated; for example, the present value of a sum in year n is:

$$V_p = \frac{V_n}{(1 + r)^n}$$

If, for instance, V_n represented project B's profit for year 4 as shown in Table 5.4, then its present value equivalent would be

$$V_p = \frac{400}{(1 + 0.1)^4}$$

$$= \frac{400}{1.464}$$

$$= £273.2$$

The calculation can be completed as illustrated above. Alternatively, it can be made by the use of discount factors tables (see Table 5.8 for an example of such a table). These tables have simply worked out the annual values for the discounting process, for example, the discount factor for year 4 at 10% per annum interest (DF_4) is:

$$DF_4 = \frac{1}{(1 + r)^4}$$

$$= \frac{1}{(1 + 0.1)^4}$$

$$= \frac{1}{1.4641}$$

$$= 0.683$$

Check from the table that this is the discount factor shown for year 4 at 10% interest.

Using either your formula or the discount tables you can now estimate the present value of any future sum, for any rate of interest.

You can now return to the text of the chapter and its worked examples.

Appendix 5B: The acceleration principle

In essence, this theory suggests that investment expenditure is a response to the changing pressure of the demand for output on the productive capacity of the country. If there is a rising demand for output against a given capital stock, then investment will be undertaken to increase the size of that capital stock. If the need to produce ouput levels off, or declines, then the need for investment, possibly even to maintain capital stock, is also reduced. More formally, the level of investment expenditure will reflect the changes which have taken place in the level of output which is required.

The theory argues that, in any single industry, there will be an optimum stock of capital for a given level of output from that industry. Equally, at the level of the national economy, for any given level of GDP or output, there will also be an optimum stock of capital, made up of the sum of all the optimum capital stocks from the different industries, reflecting their share of the overall output.

If K_t represents this optimum or desired capital stock for the nation and Y_t the GDP. or output level in question in period t, then the relationship between them can be shown as follows

$$K_t = wY_t$$

where w measures the 'capital:output ratio'. For instance, if Y_2 is 300, and K_t is 600 (since a given capital stock can produce output over a series of years, it could have a higher value than the output of a single year), then the value of w would be 2.

Output will vary over time. Realistically, so too will the value of the capital:output ratio, partly reflecting changes in technology, partly reflecting changes in the relative share of different industries in the output for a given period (if the weighting pattern changes, and each industry has its own capital:output ratio, then the overall, or average value of the capital:output ratio for the economy will also change). For simplicity, however, assume that the value of the capital:output ratio is constant over the time period in question. If so, as the level of output varies over time, so too will the optimum stock over capital; for example, if the output level in the second period is Y_{t+1}, then, given w:

$$K_{t+1} = wY_{t+1}$$

Thus, if Y_{t+1} is 330, and w is still 2, as in the earlier illustration, then K_{t+1} will be 660, that is, the optimum stock of capital will have to be increased. More formally,

$$\begin{aligned} K_{t+1} - K_t &= wY_{t+1} - wY_t \\ &= w(Y_{t+1} - Y_t) \\ &= 2(330 - 300) \\ &= 60 \end{aligned}$$

But this increase in capital stock as firms move towards the new optimum level represents net investment for the period, (I_{t+1}) therefore

$$\begin{aligned} I_{t+1} &= K_{t+1} - K_t \\ &= w(Y_{t+1} - Y_t) \end{aligned}$$

or,

$$I = w\Delta Y$$

where ΔY represents the change in the output level between the two years. This provides a new theory for investment behaviour, relating it not to the absolute level of income, but to the changes in the level of income or output. It shows that, if the level of output required rises between two periods, it is likely to trigger investment to increase the capital stock.

But why is this model described as the **acceleration principle**? This follows from the magnification effect, or boost it provides to the adjustment process within the macroeconomy. Think through the chain of events: if output rises (or falls):

(1) the resultant change in investment will normally be proportionately greater than the change in output which triggers it – because the capital output ratio will normally have a value greater than unity ($w > 1$);

(2) in turn, this increase (or decrease) in investment will set off a multiplier expansion (or contraction) within the macroeconomy, which will result in a proportionately greater increase (or decrease) in income and output – since the value of the multiplier will also normally be greater than unity;

(3) which will result in an even greater increase (or decrease) in investment, through the capital:output ratio . . .

(4) and an even greater multiplier expansion (or contraction) in GDP . . . and so on.

In other words, the effect of this model of investment behaviour is to add an additional magnification, or acceleration, to the adjustment process; hence its description as the **acceleration principle**, or simply the **accelerator**.

The model can be used to explain some aspects of investment behaviour. It is not wholly convincing as an explanatory insight into investment in fixed assets, where its behavioural pattern is just too mechanistic (can you believe that businessmen would respond so mindlessly to changes in past output, when the whole purpose of investment is to provide *future* output?), but it has been used in some macroeconomic forecasting models to provide at least a partial explanation/prediction contribution with respect to inventory plans.

SELF-ASSESSMENT QUESTIONS

TRUE/FALSE QUESTIONS

5.1. The purpose of discounting is to eliminate the effect of inflation on the value of money over time.

5.2. To obtain the present value of any project, the estimated profits or net income from the project must be added together for its lifespan.

5.3. The market rate of return must also be earned by the firm's retained profits, whether or not they are put to use as investment expenditure.

5.4. A change in the rate of interest will have no effect on the investment function portrayed in the basic model, since investment is related to the level of income in the latter.

'FILL IN THE BLANKS' QUESTIONS

5.1. Assuming that it has sufficient funds, the firm will accept all projects for which the internal rate of return (IRR) equals or exceeds (   ).

5.2. If a given discount rate leaves the present value of the project's profits below the capital outlay involved, this indicates that the IRR will be (   ) that rate of discount.

5.3. A decrease in business optimism will tend to move the demand function for investment funds to the (   ) and so (   ) the level of investment in the economy.

EXERCISE

This is designed to be used in conjunction with Appendix 5A on discounting. Students who already understand this technique might also find it useful to revise – if only to check the quality of their expertise!

A firm faces two projects, X and Y; the forecast profit streams for their six-year lifespans are shown below.

(a) If the firm's cost of capital is 10%, which if either of the projects will be viable?
(b) Which is the better of the two projects?
(c) What are the IRR values for the projects?

Use the discount table included in Appendix 5A. Postpone looking at the solution until there is no alternative strategy left . . .

	X	Y
Capital outlay	860	830
Profits: year 1	400	200
2	300	200
3	200	200
4	100	200
5	100	200
6	50	200

Note: Solutions can be found at the end of the text.

Chapter 6

Long-term Growth and Short-term Cycles

> Introduction
>
> The measurement of economic growth
>
> The UK business cycle
>
> The business cycle from 1970 to date
>
> Causes of the business cycle
>
> Comparison of economic growth rates
>
> A theory of economic growth
>
> Conclusions
>
> Self-assessment questions

INTRODUCTION

Two important relationships emerge from our consideration of investment expenditure in the previous chapter. The first is that the time pattern of resource allocation to investment expenditure will influence a country's performance in terms of economic growth; a habitually low level of investment will normally be reflected in a disappointing growth performance. The second relationship is also based on the time pattern of investment; with investment having a magnified effect on the level of economic activity through the multiplier, any volatility could well contribute towards the cyclical pattern of economic activity described as the business cycle. Given the importance of both relationships, it would seem to be an appropriate point to break off from our programme of detailed analysis of the individual elements of expenditure in order to consider these more general topics.

Economic growth is an important policy objective for any government. Apart from its main attraction, which is that it offers a way in which to raise the level of economic prosperity of the country concerned, it has the potential to contribute towards the solution of some of the other macroeconomic problems. For example, we have already discussed the problems of rising prices and imports which can be caused by an 'overheated' level of demand in the economy. One way to tackle these unwanted problems would be to curb demand, for example, by raising interest rates and the cost of credit. This has been the policy response in the UK over the summer and early autumn of 1988. But what if, in the longer term, we could deal with the excessive level of demand by raising our own capacity to produce goods and services, that is, by raising aggregate supply (or GDP)? The more we could produce, the smaller would be the residual of unsatisfied demand to spill over into import purchases – and place pressure on domestic price levels. In other words, economic growth might allow us to approach the problem through aggregate supply, just as short-term interest rates would allow us to tackle it through aggregate demand.

Or again, take the interrelated problems of high unemployment and the technological revolution. Technology tends to promote capital intensity (that is, the substitution of capital for labour in the production process). Partly as a result of this, the recovery of output from the lower turning point of the business cycle in 1981 was not strong enough to re-employ all the people who were in work before the depression struck – since the same level of output could be produced with a *smaller* labour force than before. How might economic growth help here? Its role on this occasion would be to provide a substantial and sustained increase in output which, even given the influence of new technology, would ensure that the demand for labour would recover, so that a real reduction could be made in the size of that grim mountain of the unemployed in the UK.

However, the path to economic growth is not necessarily a steady one; all economies are afflicted by a regular series of fluctuations in the level of economic activity. Described originally as the trade cycle, but referred to in more recent times as the **business cycle**, these fluctuations continue to frustrate and irritate the intentions of policy makers. Over a four- to five-year period, all countries can expect to endure periods of overheating (with all that this implies for rising rates of price inflation and possible balance of trade deficits). During the same time span, these bursts of high economic activity will normally alternate with periods of recession and even depression (when government preoccupation will tend to switch to the problems of idle productive capacity and rising unemployment levels). Such policy frustrations can pose a problem.

Should the cyclical fluctuations be suffered passively, or should some remedial action be taken to minimize and control the degree of fluctuation – possibly creating more stable conditions, which would reduce uncertainty and should encourage investment and a less disrupted run at economic growth? Or is short-term 'control' an illusion, which imposes costs and constraints in the long run on the very economic growth which we seek to pursue? Moving into an even more provocative area, is there any truth in the allegation that the causes of the cycle are *political* rather than economic, in the sense that governments of all parties have the primary objective of holding onto power, so that the economy is manipulated to be running into a boom period prior to elections, with the brakes slammed on subsequently to restore some control over economic events – and to build in a cynical capacity reserve for the next pre-election boom?

These issues have resulted in some of the most interesting literature in economic theory and research. Models abound which promise to offer insight and understanding; but much of this work is rather advanced for an introductory text. We feel, however, that the topics are too important to be ignored. Even a considerably simplified treatment will generate an appreciation of the issues involved in some of the most pressing problem areas of macroeconomic policy.

You may have realized that a common feature of economic growth and business cycles is that they deal with variations in the level of economic activity *over time*. This makes them rather different from the models with which we have dealt up till now, and which have been framed in terms of **comparative statics**. In other words, our models have had no real-time dimension: they have focused upon an opening level of equilibrium, whether for consumption, or investment, or even for the economy as a whole, then have tried to analyse the effect upon this of changes in one or more components of the model. They are timeless, in the sense that their prime interest is in the comparison of the initial and final equilibrium positions. If a particular set of events occurs, they argue, then this will be the final result, once all the forces have worked through the model, however long it takes.

But the real world economy moves through time; it takes time for the economy to *reach* its initial equilibrium position – and then to respond to any disturbances which create the need to search for a new equilibrium. It might take several years for such a disturbance to work through the macroeconomic adjustment process; indeed, the economy might never reach its new equilibrium, if further major changes render this irrelevant and trigger a fresh series of adjustments. Think back to the events over early summer to mid-autumn in the UK in 1988. We started with the bitter disagreement between Nigel Lawson and Margaret Thatcher about whether or not to use interest rate reductions to try to nudge down the international exchange value of the pound sterling.

Almost before the Chancellor could celebrate his victory and, more important, UK manufacturers could benefit from lower export prices, our over-heating domestic economy (which, in turn, resulted at least in part from the tax cuts of the spring budget working through into disposable income and consumption plans) had forced a whole series of *increases* in the interest rate, in an attempt to cool down demand pressures. But this increase in UK interest rates attracted international capital; and, as the owners of these international funds bought sterling to enter the UK money and capital markets, this drove up the exchange rate for sterling . . . so that neither the domestic interest rate nor the international exchange rate was given the chance to move to the levels which the Chancellor had wanted.

The study of the path of the economy over time and between its equilibrium points is known as **dynamic path** analysis. A great deal can be learned from its record of the adjustment process.

Think of it in purely human terms. Suppose that the author weighs himself and gazes in consternation at his current equilibrium state. Gathering his courage, he resolves to diet. Three months later, he looks approvingly at the New Improved Author, as reflected both in the mirror and on the scales. Comparative statics analysis would take the form of single frame snapshots of the bulging 'before' and the more streamlined 'after', and would permit comparison of the old and the new equilibria; clearly, there had been a major improvement. But think of what we could learn from a study of the dynamic path. What would a video of selected moments within the three months tell us? It would show the initial determination; the brave refusal of favourite foods; the resistance and heroic resolve in the face of pressure from overweight, hedonistic and thirsty friends; the initial success as the scales spiralled downwards. But to eat is human and to forget divine. What about the sneaked chocolate biscuits from the kitchen; that 'absentminded' second helping of apple crumble; the crafty pints quaffed for 'purely social' reasons at Old Whatsit's retiral presentation; the mistake of eating the dog's laxative chocolate (a non-recommended way of losing weight quickly . . .)? Without knowledge of the dynamic path, who would have believed that the splendid, athletic creature from the second equilibrium snapshot was one and the same as the shifty degenerate who fell so often (and with so much pleasure) by the wayside *during* those three months. Might not an awareness of these lapses during the dynamic path undermine any confidence that the New Improved Shape would continue to be a lasting equilibrium – whereas the snapshots would not even pose the question?

Knowledge of the pattern of events over time is an important component of economic analysis. Some knowledge of the characteristics and problems of economic growth and cyclical fluctuations will help a great deal in building an understanding of the role of the public sector (or G and T in terms of the basic model). Equally, it will help to identify why so much interest is taken in the net balance from our international trade flows (or X and M in terms of the basic model). While within the constraints of an introductory text, you cannot possibly be given any real depth of expertise in these complex areas of theory, it is nevertheless important for you to have at least an appreciation of the issues involved.

After reading this chapter, you should be able to:

- Recognize the problems involved in the measurement of economic growth;
- Be aware of the nature of the business cycle and be able to identify the factors which produce this pattern of economic fluctuations;
- Assess the UK's growth performance against that of our main international competitors;
- Analyse in simple terms some of the key influences on the rate of economic growth in any country;
- Identify some of the main causes for the relatively poor rate of economic growth in the UK.

THE MEASUREMENT OF ECONOMIC GROWTH

The most logical place to start is with a formal definition of the term **economic growth**. We all have some broad idea of what is implied by the term: an economy which is growing is one where more goods and services are produced each year. But, while this is broadly correct, it does not help us to sort out the problem of measurement. Can we measure growth simply by looking at the year to year movements in GDP, stated in terms of constant prices to remove the possible distortion of inflation? After all, this is what our opening definition would suggest. Or should we recognize that, to produce more goods and services, an economy must increase its productive capacity, and therefore its potential to produce output? Should we derive some measure of *potential* output, or GDP?

Neither measure is completely satisfactory. If we decide to measure growth through the changes in real (that is, constant price) GDP over time, then this has the important advantage that we are measuring what has actually been achieved; and the data is readily available in our national accounts. But there is still a major disadvantage; the data can be adjusted to avoid the distortion effect of price inflation, but it will still reflect the additional distortions imposed by the short-term fluctuations of the business cycle. Figure 6.1 shows how the second set of distortions can occur.

All economies experience a similar type of cycle to the stylized version shown in Figure 6.1; the essential feature is that GDP oscillates around a rising trend line, as the cycle swings between booms and slumps,

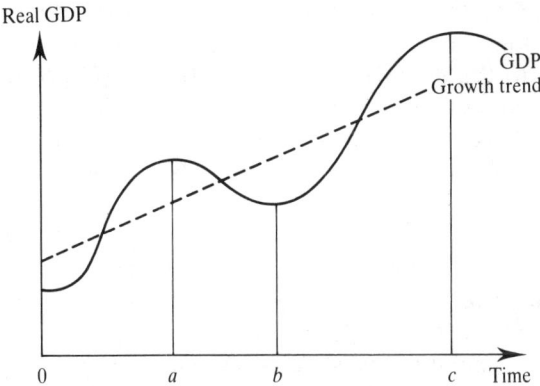

Figure 6.1 A stylized model of the cycle.

completing the sequence every four to five years. Over the time period 0a in the model, the economy moves through its recovery phase (broadly the upswing section below the trend line) into its boom phase (broadly from the trend line to the upper turning point of the cycle, above a). Over the next time period ab, the economy turns into recession (broadly the downswing of the cycle down to the trend line) and, ultimately, depression (the section of the downswing below the trend line to the lower turning point above b). Over the final time period bc, the economy moves again through a new recovery phase into a new boom.

Consider what would happen if we simply measured growth over the time period bc. We would pick up what would seem to be a strong surge of growth – but would be confusing long-term economic growth with the short-term recovery and boom phases in the business cycle; no doubt this period would include some real economic growth (as measured in terms of an increase in our potential to produce output) but this would be swamped with the clutter of noise and distortions imposed on our data by the short-term cycle. At best, we would *overstate* the economic growth for the period in question. Conversely, if we measured growth over the time period ab, we would pick up the distortions imposed by the downswing; we would record negative growth, that is, a reduction in output – despite the fact that investment in some industries over the period would be raising our productive potential and our capacity for economic growth. At best we would *understate* this economic growth.

Indeed, if we work purely from real GDP data, we are in danger of confusing long-term economic growth, as measured by increased production potential, with short-term variations in the degree of capacity utilization of that production potential. In effect, we should be interested more in the trend line than in the cycle of real GDP.

If, despite the danger, we decide to pursue this course, then we must do either of two things. Firstly, we must measure growth only between like points in the cycle, for example, from the upper turning point above *a* to the upper turning point above *c*. Or, alternatively, we must measure output movements over a much longer period of time, during which a whole series of business cycles will tend to cancel each other out, or at least impose a relatively minor influence on our measurements.

Given these difficulties, most economic theorists argue strongly that economic growth should be measured in terms of potential output which, in turn, would reflect the growth over time of our production potential. In its favour, this approach eliminates the problem of misidentification caused by the short-term influences of the cycle. But it is still not without major problems. In practice, how should we define and measure our 'potential output', given that this will be the end product from an amalgam of labour and capital inputs (and their assumed quality or efficiency) and technological change? Obviously, it will be the output which we are capable of producing at some high level of economic activity – but how high . . . and could we realistically expect to achieve this assumed level of efficiency? Most countries have some series of estimates of potential output, or full employment output – but you have to hunt very hard to find the series, then take a lot of time to read the footnotes! How realistic a measure is potential output? For example, British Leyland had enough productive capacity in the mid/late 1970s to produce *all* the new car units sold in the UK in any single year. The problem was that not enough people wanted to buy British Leyland cars, so that a very large part of that productive capacity lay idle – draining resources from the company and contributing substantially to its vicious circle into decline. It's not enough to be *able* to produce output; this capability is meaningless, unless you are also able to *sell* it.

There is a final problem, which results from the partial view provided by our system of measurement, and for which there is no easy answer. As economists, we define and measure growth as long-term changes in output; if we explicitly recognize inputs at all, our measure deals with increases in capital, or productive capacity. This narrow focus does not consider the effect of growth – or the business cycle – on the other main input of *labour*, or employment. This ommission has the potential to lead us into all sorts of problems with both our measure and our terminology, since movements in the level of the labour input do not always mirror events in the level of output. Can we talk about 'recovery' when unemployment figures are spiralling up, as they did over the early 1980s? Can we talk about 'boom' and 'growth', when many many thousands of people find it impossible to connect with a meaningful job, especially in areas such as the North of England, or Scotland, or Northern Ireland? Certainly unemployment levels have begun to respond to the recovery in output over recent years – but how much of this is real, and how much simply a reflection of a variety of major changes in the registration and measurement of unemployment? Separating the economics from the bitter political debate, we would simply pose the question: 'Is it not a little dangerous to focus measurement exclusively on output movements, when these provide only a partial insight into the state of the economy?'

For the purposes of this introductory text, we will define economic growth – and business cycle movements – as changes in real GDP over time. We are well aware of the potential for confusion (and for partial vision). With the former in mind, it would seem that the next logical step is to look in a little more detail at the nature of the business cycle in the UK over recent years.

THE UK BUSINESS CYCLE

As we have stated earlier, the business cycle is the term used to describe the regular fluctuations in the level of economic activity which occur over time, with periods of boom and prosperity alternating with periods of slump and depression. Normally, as shown in the stylized form of Figure 6.1, the cyclical fluctuations take place against a clear growth trend in real output.

It is useful to start by analysing the cyclical fluctuations which have been experienced by the UK economy over the last 35–40 years. This series of cycles are covered by two figures: the path of GDP movements over the period 1950–70 is shown in Figure 6.2; the data for the more recent period of 1971–87 are shown in Figure 6.3.

For any analysis of the cyclical path of GDP, it is normal to make a series of adjustments to the current price data, to minimize the dangers of distortion, and to present the cycle in its clearest form. Firstly, the effect of price inflation must be eliminated, so that the behaviour of real output trends over time can be studied; the data series should therefore be stated in terms of the prices of a single base year (taken as 1963 for the data series of Figure 6.2, and 1980 for Figure 6.3).[1] Secondly, to eliminate possible distortion from changes in subsidy and indirect taxation policy over time, the series should also be stated in terms of factor cost values, rather than at market prices. Finally, the use of annual figures for GDP tends to damp down the fluctuations which have occurred – quarterly series allow the fluctuations to be traced more clearly; but if quarterly

---

1. It has not been possible in either period to obtain a constant price data series, as at a single year; the government tends to change the base year every five or six years. We have therefore had to convert each series to a single base year (1963 in Figure 6.2, and 1980 for Figure 6.3). The simple conversion formula used may have resulted in minor inaccuracies in the *level* of GDP, but it should not have affected in any substantial way the cyclical pattern of either data series.

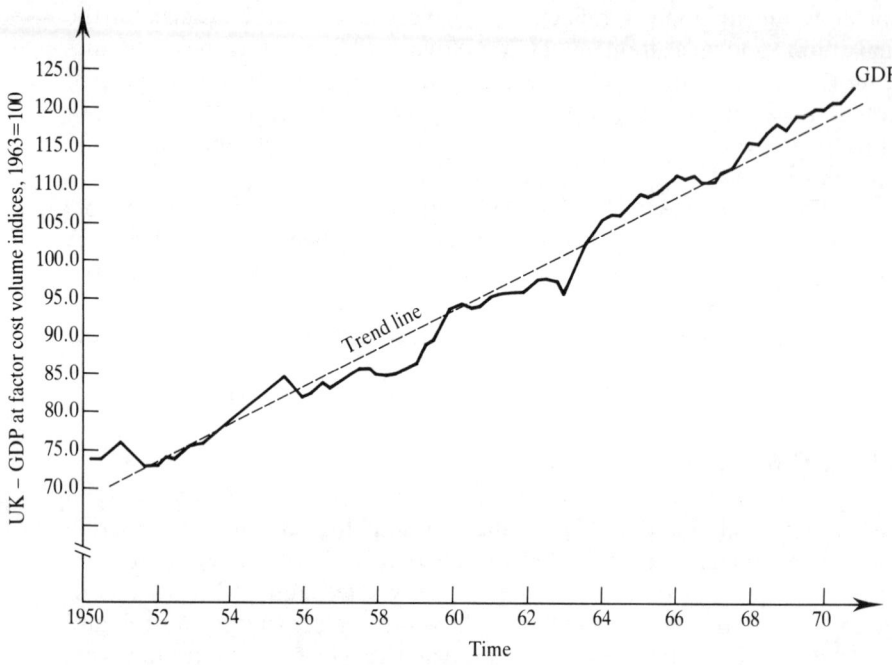

Figure 6.2 The business cycle 1950–70. (Source: various issues of the *National Institute Economic Review*. Reprinted by permission of the National Institute of Economic and Social Research.)

data is used (as is the case in both data series) then this should have been adjusted for seasonal variations over the period.

If we look at the data for 1950–70, as shown in Figure 6.2, it is possible to identify some clear characteristics for this series. One of the first points to note is that much of the cyclical fluctuation is caused not by expansion alternating with decline, but simply by variations in the rates of growth from period to period. Consider this for a moment; if, in a series of successive periods, an economy grows by 2%, then 4%, then 6%, then 5%, then 3%, then 1% . . . then back to a rising sequence from 2% again, we have created a cyclical pattern *in which there is no decline*, simply a slowing down in successive rates of growth. While the above series is contrived for effect, it does in fact explain a fair number of the fluctuations in real GDP which occurred over the first period of 21 years. In fact, there have only been four clear periods of decline in output, namely for 1951/52, 1955/56, 1962/63 and 1966/67. None of these recessions/depressions was particulary severe and, indeed, the greatest divergence between output and the growth trend, over 1956–60, was caused more by a plateau in growth rather than an absolute depression.

The second point follows from the existence of steady economic

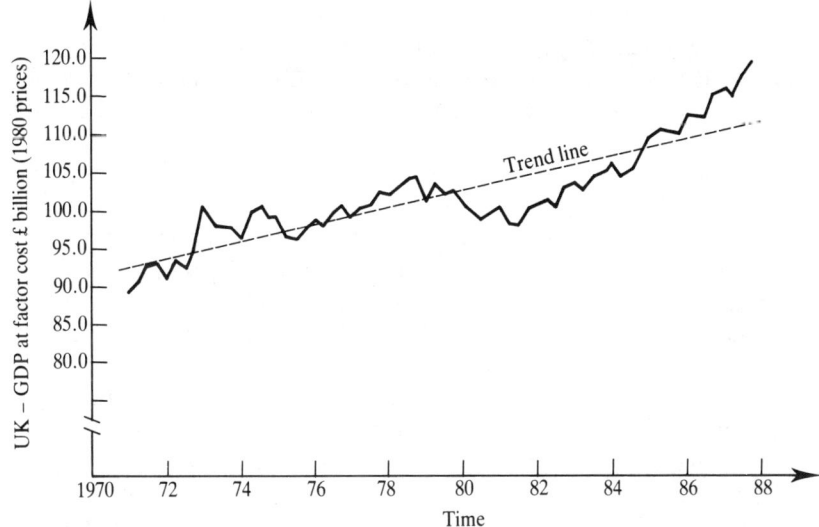

Figure 6.3 The business cycle 1971–87. (Source: *Economic Trends*. Reprinted by permission of the Controller, HMSO.)

growth over the period; this has allowed successive booms to result in ever higher output peaks over time. As a reflection of the same growth influence, even the lower turning points in the cycle represent successively higher output levels. Indeed, one of the remarkable features of the cycle is that, typically, each trough represents a higher level of output than all but the most recent boom; the output consistent with depression towards the end of the period (for example, for 1966–67) far exceeds the best years of peak activity from only two to three years earlier in the past.

The third point is concerned with the regular duration of the cycle. To measure duration, we must make sure that we are covering an entire cyclical series; we can do this if we take the time between either successive upper turning points or, alternatively, between lower turning points. For the earlier period illustrated in Figure 6.2, the duration of the cycle appears to have been about four to five years, and can be traced more clearly from the succession of lower turning points. For those interested in the historical aspect of the cycle, this represents a marked change from the more traditional duration of 9–12 years of the cycle over the nineteenth and early twentieth century in the UK. A similar change in pattern towards a shorter duration of business cycle has been observed in most countries.

We have already stated that the cycle will normally occur against a trend of long-term economic growth; Figure 6.2 shows that this is indeed the case – the regression equation for the trend line indicates an average rate of growth of 2.5% per annum for the period.[2] However, the trend line shown in Figure 6.2 is measured from real GDP (taken over a series of four cycles to minimize the danger of distortion). What sort of growth would have been recorded if we had measured the path of potential output for the period? If we take full employment output as an acceptable equivalent for potential output, then this would take the form of a gentle curve, or 'ceiling', which would lie just above the output peaks of quarter 1 of 1952, quarter 2 of 1955, the first quarters of 1965 and 1966, and the third quarter of 1968.[3] If you can visualize such a ceiling, you will see that one of the remarkable characteristics of the cycle over the 1960s in particular, was the success of a series of governments (from both main parties) in the UK in keeping the economy running so close to its target level of full employment. In retrospect, these were probably the high years of Keynesian macroeconomic policy – internationally, as well as in the UK. In the current climate of hostility towards interventionist policy in Thatcher Britain, it is worth remembering that the discredited Keynesian policy makers in earlier governments did record some real and sustained successes over the 1960s, whatever problems they encountered in the mid 1970s.

To summarize our main findings on the business cycle for the years between 1950 and 1970, we could say that this period was characterized by a steady growth trend behind the cycle, a duration of around four to five years for the cycle, and a relatively gentle pattern of oscillation.

THE BUSINESS CYCLE FROM 1970 TO DATE

Figure 6.3, covering the later period of 1971–87, provides some interesting contrasts to the earlier pattern. To deal with these in a systematic fashion, it is useful to divide the data into three time periods, these being from 1971–79, then from 1979–84, and finally from 1984 to the end of the data series in 1987.

Over the first of these periods, it is possible to trace the disruptive impact on the economy of the quadrupling of oil prices by OPEC. It is no longer the case that the cyclical oscillations are largely caused by variations in the periodic rates of growth. The adverse effects of the

---

2. The regression equation for the trend line in Figure 6.2 was $Y_e = 94.97 + 2.50x$, where Y_e gives the estimated trend line values for GDP and x represents the year (as expressed as a time interval from the central point of the time series). For those few who are interested, note the lower growth rate implied by the regression equation for the trend line in Figure 6.3, which was $Y_e = 101.98 + 1.12x$ (that is, 1.1% per annum, as opposed to the 2.5% in the earlier equation).

3. See, for example, D.C. Rowan: *Output, Inflation and Growth*, Ch 20, p. 429

substantial increases in energy and raw materials costs which followed the OPEC oil price revisions can be traced in the three sharp declines in real output, for 1973–74, then for 1975–76, and finally for 1978–79. A simplistic analysis might blame these price shocks for the uncertain path of real GDP and the relatively low growth performance over the period, but this would be quite unfair. The graph shows that, on each occasion, GDP recovered relatively quickly from the disturbance – and it must also be remembered that, with our reserves of North Sea oil coming into production during the latter half of the 1970s, the UK benefited to some extent from high oil prices.[4] But, equally, there were adverse influences from factors other than the pricing decisions of the OPEC cartel. During the mid to late 1970s, the UK suffered from relatively severe price and cost inflation, which tended to reduce our competitive efficiency in world markets (damaging export sales), and simultaneously left our domestic markets over-priced and vulnerable to increased import penetration. The resultant fall in demand for UK output would also have had the effect of slowing down the rate of growth in GDP, and contributing to the uncertain path of the latter over 1973–79.

If we move on to examine the second period of 1979–84 in Figure 6.3, we will see that this shows several unique characteristics in terms of the UK's post-war experience of the cycle. The most noticeable of these was that the decline in real GDP from £103.9 billion in the third quarter of 1979 to £98.2 billion in the third quarter of 1981 (both figures in constant 1980 prices) represented the most prolonged and severe recession/depression sequence in the recent history of the cycle. We would have to go back about 50 years to trace a similar experience. While the pattern from Figure 6.2 is that the trough level of GDP normally exceeds all but the most recent output peak, in Figure 6.3 we would have to go back to the third and final quarters of 1975, before we found a similar level of output to that of the lower turning point in 1981. It represented a very severe fall in real output – and was reflected in an equally severe fall in the level of employment, as the demand for labour fell in response to the cuts in output; unemployment rose from 1.36 million in December 1979 to 3 million by end September 1981. Secondly, note the length of time it took for real GDP to cross the trend line again. Not only did it take from the third quarter of 1979 to the second quarter of 1981 before the cycle moved into its recovery phase; it took until the third quarter of 1984 before the cycle moved from recovery into boom (remembering that recovery was defined as the upswing section below the trend, and boom as the upswing section above the trend). In short, the

---

4. If only because the high grade North Sea oil had a ready international market (which generated export sales) and, simultaneously, provided us with at least some possibility of import substitution (which would have reduced imports).

combined phases of recession, depression and recovery amounted to an unprecedented 20 quarters, or five years' duration.

Why should the economic collapse have been quite so severe and prolonged? This is a question to which we shall return at several points throughout the book. For the moment, we can suggest three possible and partial explanations. Firstly, the speed and severity of the recession resulted in a collapse in business confidence, which had a catastrophic effect on investment, as we know from the previous chapter. This caused a series of downward revisions in the level of investment – which would have exacerbated the rate and the depth of the decline. Secondly, the UK's international trade flows were adversely affected by two separate influences during this period: the relatively high rate of inflation in the UK resulted in a serious loss of our competitive efficiency, as we have already argued. At the same time, the combination of high domestic interest rates (triggered by attempts to control the rate of growth in the money supply) and the existence of vast and valuable oil reserves in the North Sea, resulted in a historically high value for the UK exchange rate. These influences combined to price our exports out of world markets, and to lay open our domestic economy to relatively cheap import goods and services.

Taken together, these factors would cause the injection function to fall substantially, with both investment expenditure and export sales dropping; at the same time, consumption net of imports (that is, the C^* function) would also have fallen as the import component rose. Overall, aggregate expenditure, or the $C^* + J$ function in the basic model, would have fallen markedly, pushing the economy into contraction as it tried to move to its new and lower level of equilibrium GDP.

The third possible explanation stems from another unique feature of the period. Until this point in time, governments had run broadly Keynesian macroeconomic policies. In previous years, the automatic response of any government to a perceived threat of depression had been to 'lean' against the cycle, and try to stimulate aggregate expenditure; the following chapter will discuss this policy response in detail. However, the new government in power at the start of the recession was firmly committed to the ideals of monetarism; again these will be discussed in later chapters. For the moment it is enough to say that no major short-term action was taken to try to influence the level of aggregate expenditure. It is central to the monetarist philosphy that the government's prime responsibility is to achieve a stable monetary environment, then leave the economy to adjust itself towards equilibrium against this background of stability. For the first time in many years, the downturn was left to run unchecked. Many economists have argued that this non-interventionist stance was responsible, to a greater or lesser extent, for contributing to the severity of the trough, and the prolonged uncertainties of the recovery phase. It is impossible to assess the effect with any accuracy. We pass no comment on the issue, beyond identifying that there was a unique and tidal change in macroeconomic policy from 1979.

On less contentious ground, there is also much of interest, and grounds for speculation, contained in the data for 1984–87. At first sight the data appears to behave in a manner which is similar to that identified in Figure 6.2; real GDP rose more strongly, and the pattern of oscillations was again more in the form of variations in rates of growth between periods (negative movements were relatively minor). On the basis of this data, there have been strong political claims that the UK has become one of the fastest growing economies of recent years – which would be welcome news indeed.

Such an interpretation of the data should set some warning bells ringing in your mind, when you remember our earlier discussion of the problems of measurment of economic growth. If your data is a series of real GDP figures, then there is always the danger that you will *not* be measuring the long-term phenomenon of economic growth, but will simply be picking up the short-term distorions of the business cycle. Given the unprecedented severity of the previous trough, to what extent does recent UK data simply reflect a recovery in the degree of utilization of existing capacity, and to what extent does it show *real* economic growth, in the sense that productive capacity and potential output have been increased? We have no data series for potential output over the period, against which we can judge and answer these questions. We are left to speculate. Even the possible proxy measurement of full employment output offers little real guidance; apart from the fact that the UK has been running well below this ceiling, with even current unemployment figures lying in the range 2.0 to 3.0 million,[5] we have no accurate

---

5. It is, frankly, difficult to deal with unemployment statistics over the last 10 years, without being accused of either statistical inaccuracy or political bias. At the root of the problem is the fact that there have been a large number of changes in the method of registration for unemployment benefit and, therefore, recording of unemployment statistics. The picture is further complicated by the variety of retraining and self-employment training courses, which have removed many people from the unemployment statistics, at least for a temporary period. Finally, determined government measures to investigate and prosecute benefit abusers have resulted in a substantial number of people withdrawing claims of eligibility – sometimes on the basis of unfounded fear and ignorance. Whatever the reasons, it is the end result which gives us cause for statistical concern; it is difficult to compare unemployment data for the period before 1979 to recent and current data, since each is the product of a different philosophy and a different system of measurement. It is the equivalent of comparing counts of apples to apparently equivalent counts of oranges, when all they have in common is that they are both edible fruits. Depending upon your political viewpoint, either the pre-1979 figures overstate true unemployment, or the current data understates the true number of people seeking employment. We do not wish to step into the violent political debate on the issue; we merely acknowledge the uncertainty about the figures. If unemployment was measured in the same fashion as for the pre-1979 data, then the 1988 figure would be substantially in excess of its 'official' level; various guesstimates would add anything from 250,000 to 1,000,000 (or even more . . .) to this recorded level.

knowledge of the growth path of the ceiling. As we struggle to disentangle short-term cyclical from genuine long-term growth influences, our measurement problem only serves to underline why theorists would prefer all measures of growth to be made in terms of potential output.

In conclusion, Figures 6.2 and 6.3 have shown us that there is no such thing as a 'normal' business cycle. Each cyclical series, while conforming to the broad stylized form of Figure 6.1, has its own characteristics, affecting the degree of oscillation, or the duration of a particular sequence of stages, or the apparent background context of economic growth. Why this should be so is the next question which we should try to address.

CAUSES OF THE BUSINESS CYCLE

The phenomenon of the trade or business cycle has intrigued generations of economists and we have been left with a rich inheritance of both rudimentary and sophisticated models, which seek to explain the causes of the cyclical fluctuations in real GDP over time. To some early theorists, the over-correcting swings of business optimism and pessimism, with the resultant volatility in the level of investment and, through this, in the level of economic activity, explained many of the observed fluctuations. More recently, others like Paul Samuelson drew attention to the effect of possible interaction between the independent theory models of the multiplier and the accelerator, both of which have been discussed in earlier chapters. It is possible, by varying the values of the multiplier and the accelerator and the lag systems built into each, to create a whole series of different cyclical patterns of response to a disturbance by the macroeconomy. Some assumed value combinations result in a **damped cycle**; here the disturbance creates major initial fluctuations, which gradually diminish as the economy 'homes in' to its new equilibrium value, as shown in Figure 6.4. Other value combinations create the possibility of an **explosive cycle**; here the pattern of cyclical fluctuations of GDP becomes ever more violent, diverging further and further from both the old and the new equilibrium levels of GDP, as shown in Figure 6.5. Some of the most interesting and lasting contributions to the theory of the cycle, such as that put forward by J.R. Hicks, take up the concept of an explosive cycle and show how this could be constrained by the growth over time of some form of **ceiling** and **floor** for the macroeconomy; in terms of this type of model, the observed cycle simply traces the dynamic path of the economy as it ricochets between these two sets of constraints.

Interesting though these models are, there is a danger that the price of their elegant simplicity is too high; their simplifying assumptions and strict formal modelling relationships can result in a stylized and rigid interpretation of the cycle, when its main observable characteristic has

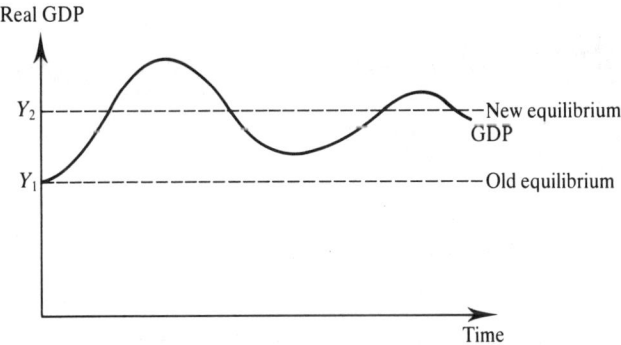

Figure 6.4 'Damped' business cycle.

been its complexity and variability of nature over time. We would argue that it is possible to provide an adequate depth of understanding on the basis of the simple theoretical models which we have already set up – and, simultaneously, leave scope for variation over time in the relative importance and timing of the influences which are identified below.

In what follows, we will simply try to identify groups of possible influences which, at different points in the business cycle, will tend to push, or pull, or turn the dynamic path of real GDP into cyclical fluctuations. We make no attempt to build all of these suggestions into a systematic model.

Depression phase

Let's take the final stages of the **depression** phase in the cycle as our starting point. From observation, we know that this point in time will be characterized by substantial excess capacity in capital stock and in the labour market. This will result in a low level of investment, with very little new productive capacity being set up and replacement investment (for capital equipment which has become obsolescent, or inefficient from extensive usage) may possibly be held at an even lower value than is needed to maintain existing capacity at its present level. Wage demands will, generally, be non-aggressive and job security will tend to be the dominant objective; even substantial changes in working practices or manning levels may be accepted, as necessary for survival. Prices of goods and services will tend to be held constant, or will be rising sluggishly, reflecting the low level of demand and unsold output.

Ignoring the possibility of deliberate government reflationary measures,[6] recovery may be generated from one or a combination of

---

6. See Chapter 7 on fiscal policy and Chapter 8 on monetary policy for a detailed discussion of what is involved for both reflationary and deflationary policy measures.

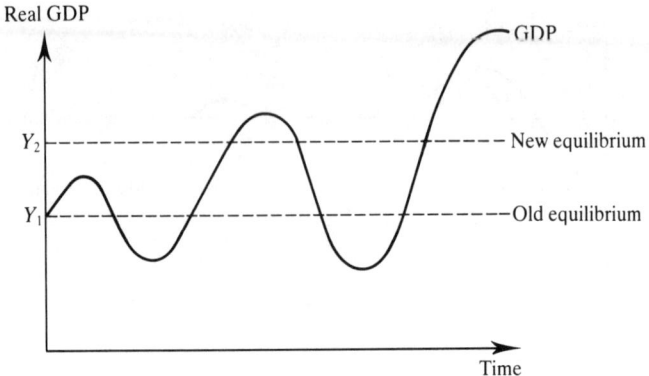

Figure 6.5 'Explosive' business cycle.

several impulses:

(1) Unreplaced capital usage may finally bring actual capital stock down to a level more appropriate for current demand; if so, then a higher level of replacement investment will be needed to maintain capital at that level, that is, there will be an increase in investment.

(2) If the rate of interest falls, as a result of the low demand for credit from households and firms, reflecting in turn the low level of economic activity, then this will tend to move firms down their demand function for investment funds. Even in the depressed conditions of this stage in the cycle, more projects will offer an IRR value which would justify the risk of the new and lower user cost of capital – which should also increase the level of investment (this time it would be net investment, that is, it would involve *adding to* existing productive capacity).

(3) Since most developed countries experience some degree of inflation if, at steady exchange rates, UK prices are held constant or rise more slowly than those of our main competitors, then our goods and services should gradually become more price competitive, in world and in our own domestic markets; exports could rise and imports could fall, as our output becomes relatively cheaper.

Any one or more of these events would cause the injection function to rise (reflecting higher investment and export levels); at the same time, the C^* function (the consumption function net of imports) could also rise, if there is a switch from imports to UK produced goods. The combined effect of these upward movements would be to raise the aggregate expenditure function, which should cause the economy to expand towards a new and higher level of equilibrium GDP. If the economy does respond in this manner, then we have passed beyond the lower turning point of the cycle, and have moved from the depression into the early stages of the recovery phase.

Recovery phase

From observation, we know that the upswing will normally begin to gain in momentum as the economy moves through the **recovery** phase towards boom. What we must now try to identify are the influences which might generate this increase in momentum. Once again, we can isolate a number of possibilities from our existing body of knowledge on the macroeconomy. Firstly, as excess capacity disappears, and as income and employment levels rise through the multiplier adjustment response to the set of disturbances which created the upturn, it is not unreasonable to expect an upward revision in business expectations. From our knowledge of investment behaviour, an increase in business optimism would cause a revision in investment appraisal estimates, which will tend to move the demand function for investment funds to the right, creating even higher levels of investment *at the existing user cost of capital*, or rate of interest. Secondly, if the accelerator principle is considered, as soon as output begins to expand (which it must do as soon as we pass the lower turning point of the cycle), through the capital:output ratio this will signal the need for a larger optimum stock of capital. This will not only increase the net investment element (that is, investment made to increase productive capacity) within gross investment. Any increase in investment will automatically trigger its own multiplier adjustment process, which will cause a further expansion in both expenditure and income, which could be picked up again by the accelerator and translated into still further increases in investment.

In short, we could expect the recovery process to take the form of a series of upward revisions, both in the level of investment and in the multiplier expansionary response to these. We are not talking simply of a single wave of investment decisions. It will take time to purchase and install the new capital goods, during which the continuing multiplier expansion process will be placing ever greater demand pressure against existing capacity. Business people would have to be rather less than human to resist such pressure. It is very likely that there would be a series of waves of investment, as different industries within the firms' sector respond to the ever expanding ripples of the recovery phase, when it affects their particular markets.

Given that both the multiplier and the capital:output ratio are likely to have values greater than unity, it should be clear that the recovery, once started, is likely to develop its own momentum, as increases in investment have a magnified effect on income and, in turn, the increases in output required have a magnified effect on investment.

Boom phase

The influences identified above should combine to provide a reasonable explanation for both the lower turning point, and the upswing through recovery into the **boom** phase of the cycle. From observation, we know that this latter phase will be characterized by an increasingly full use of all resources, with rapidly rising prosperity and expenditure levels, with buoyant business optimism as past successes fuel the appetite for further ventures. Unemployment will have fallen steadily, almost to the point where it has reached a hard core level, a residual of the people who, for various reasons, find it difficult to enter and remain in employment. But if the achievement of reasonably full employment is still a genuine policy objective, why should the boom ever end?

Experience has shown that sooner or later the momentum of the upswing will be checked, again reflecting a number of influences:

(1) Once excess capacity has disappeared and the economy reaches full employment, output can only be increased via greater capital intensity, that is, net investment and revised manning levels will be needed. But, at some stage, the capital goods industry will itself face a maximum output constraint, and be forced to 'queue' new investment orders; thus the physical capacity of the capital goods industry at least will set a constraint on the rate of increase in output.

(2) As output rises more slowly, there is a danger that demand pressures will spill over into price inflation. This could have a number of adverse effects on domestic output levels:

(a) Firms will compete to attract inputs which will allow them to raise their level of output; this will tend to bid up the prices of labour and capital;

(b) Rising production costs and interest rates will both tend to discourage investment (the first will reduce the IRR value of possible projects and move the demand function for investment funds to the left; the second will move firms up the relevant demand function for investment funds);

(c) Rising production costs and prices will affect UK price competitiveness in world and domestic markets, with falling exports and increasing imports a possible consequence of this.

(3) If we bring the accelerator into the analysis, this will translate the slowdown in the rate of increase in output into a *fall* in the level of investment. Why? Remember that the accelerator is a mechanical relationship which links the level of investment to the rate of change in output. (In case you have forgotten, the relationship would take the form of $I = w\Delta Y$, with w being the value of the capital:output ratio; don't say that we don't look after you!) Therefore, if GDP rises from 200 to 220 and then again to 230 over three successive periods, and if we keep the assumed value of w at 2, investment in period 2 would be 40 (or 2[220 − 200]), but would fall to 20 in period 3 (or 2[230 − 220]). Investment has therefore fallen while output is still increasing (purely because the rate of increase in output has slowed down); and, if investment has fallen, this will trigger a *negative* multiplier adjustment, which will ultimately cause income to fall.

These factors will combine to ensure that the momentum of the upswing will gradually die. At first, this might reflect only the physical constraint on expansion of bottlenecks as discussed above; it will be an enforced slowdown. But, ultimately, the other effects described will lower the level of the injection function and the net of imports consumption function. In terms of the basic model, the equilibrium level of income will fall, creating the upper turning point, and the economy will slide down into the recession phase of the downswing.

At this point, it is interesting to look at Extract 6.1, from *The Economist*, of 23 July 1988. You will be able to trace in this not only some of the symptoms of the final stages of a boom phase, but also the changes in expectations – in this case from euphoric to worried (indeed, by the end of August 1988, *The Economist* had become quite scathing in its level of criticism) – which also take place during the cycle. And (or do our eyes deceive us) is there also a tacit admission in the closing paragraph that political and economic cycles are at least a little intertwined?

Recession phase

The stylized models of the cycle, such as those shown in Figures 6.1, 6.4 and 6.5, all suggest that once the **recession** phase has been entered, the

Extract 6.1 THE ECONOMIST 23 JULY 1988.

LAWSON COOLS IT

BY ATTACKING the way in which Mr Nigel Lawson has been managing the economy, Sir Alan Walters, the prime minister's former economic adviser, may possibly have persuaded the chancellor of the exchequer to stay in his job. Faced with the news that Sir Alan may be back in Number 10 Downing Street late next year, Mr Lawson is quite cussed enough to decide not to open the way for any weak-kneed replacement for himself at Number 11 who might be bossed about by Mrs Margaret Thatcher, with Sir Alan at her elbow.

Sir Alan left Downing Street for a job at the World Bank in Washington five years ago. He has returned every two or three months to talk to the prime minister. A monetary purist, he complained that Mr Lawson was wrong, earlier this year, to cut interest rates to 7½% in order to hold down the pound against the D-mark. In a newspaper article last week, arguing the case against British membership of the European Monetary System, he said interest rates might have to go to "some 11% or 12% in the coming months". An embarrassed Downing Street has now told him to shut up.

No doubt Sir Alan misjudged the impact of his remarks on a City already feeling that Mr Lawson had lost control of inflation. Interest rates have risen six times since June 2nd, most recently (thanks to Sir Alan) on Monday. Now the City, seeing June's roaring money supply and record lending by banks and building societies, expects a seventh rise.

Sir Alan's anxieties are shared by Mr Lawson's cabinet colleagues, some of whom have begun to worry that the chancellor is not frightened enough by signs that the economy is overheating. The chancellor may not do much to discourage them. It would suit him well if nervous ministers were clamouring for a tougher fiscal stance as they negotiated their bids for the coming public-spending round. In fact, the evidence of overheating is still unclear. Take two indicators, inflation and the balance of payments.

Certainly, inflation is picking up. Retail prices rose by 4.6% in the year to June, up from 3.3% in February, and the rise looks likely to hit 6% later this year. Higher mortgage rates will see to that. This may be only a temporary blip, but it comes at a bad time for bosses negotiating a pay round.

The current-account deficit, expected to reach £10 billion this year, is another sign of overheating. Although it is true that the deficit may be much reduced by statistical revisions, the trend is clearly deteriorating.

The deficit may, of course, simply be the counterpart of a capital inflow, caused by the desire of foreigners to invest in Britain's prosperity. If this inflow goes into investment, that will generate the exports to finance foreign borrowing. So argues James Capel, a firm of London stockbrokers. In the first five months of this year imports of consumer goods rose, in volume, by only 10%; imports of capital goods rose 18%. James Capel argues that the investment boom will help to increase productive capacity, so industry can meet higher demand.

Not so, says another broker, Goldman Sachs. Its economics team points to a recent survey by the Confederation of British Industry, which found that the proportion of firms operating below capacity had fallen to its lowest level recorded since the survey began in 1958. And, according to Goldman Sachs's estimates, even if manufacturing investment grows by the expected 16% this year, this will raise the capital stock by only 5%. That in turn will allow non-inflationary growth of barely 4%—not enough when domestic demand is surging by 7% a year.

Goldman Sachs's team also doubts that the trade deficit mainly reflects imports of capital goods. Although imports of consumer goods have been relatively weak, so have exports, falling by 4% in volume in the first five months of 1988. Indeed total exports look weak in relation to world trade, while imports have grown, on average, as fast as they usually do, compared with domestic demand. Manufacturers, constrained by capacity, may have switched their production from exports to take advantage of surging demand and healthy profit margins at home.

The Treasury denies that the economy is overheating. But it

is clearly worried about the growth of domestic demand. If so, then why has Mr Lawson timidly nudged up interest rates half a point at a time, rather than stamping on expectations with one bumper increase? Because, says the Treasury, it does not want to push up sterling. Small increases are less likely to shift the exchange rate than a large jump. Besides, the game has changed. When the government was a large seller of gilts (government securities), it had to raise interest rates in large jumps. Push rates up by dribs and drabs, and the market stops buying gilts, because it expects a further rise. Since the government is no longer a net seller of debt, it can afford a softly-softly approach.

Mr Lawson may now have done enough to contain the boom. Some economists believe that interest rates are a blunt weapon to use to cut consumer borrowing, and that they tend to hurt investment more. However, work by one merchant bank, Morgan Grenfell, suggests that consumers are more sensitive to interest rates than they used to be, and that rates are now high enough to check the boom, if only they are given time to work. Morgan Grenfell's economists point out that the personal sector has recently switched from being a net lender of assets with floating interest rates (like mortgages) to being a net borrower. So whereas in the past the personal sector as a whole was better off after a rise in interest rates, now its disposable income will fall.

The increase in the mortgage rate on August 1st, probably by an average of two percentage points, will be the biggest rise for four years. It could have considerable impact on demand. For not only will it discourage home buyers from taking out larger mortgages (which account for two-thirds of total personal borrowing), but the higher monthly repayments will leave all mortgagors with much less to spend.

Even so, Mr Lawson may reckon that it would be wise, before Sir Alan might arrive in Downing Street, to make quite sure he has slain the inflationary dragon. If he decides to stay at the Treasury, Mr Lawson might also consider that a tough stance now would leave more room for a convenient pre-election expansion in the early 1990s. Tory backbenchers, to judge by their rapturous support for him this week, are becoming quite fond of their capable, arrogant chancellor. Who knows what might happen if he won them a fourth election? Why, they might even wonder whether he would make a prime minister one day.

Reprinted with permission from *The Economist* 23 July 1988 © *The Economist*.

---

downswing will normally tend to gather momentum. Why should this be so? Once again there are several possible explanations. Firstly, it takes time for the multiplier adjustment to work its way through its response to a disturbance; if the injection function has moved downwards, then the contraction process triggered by the multiplier's response to this will tend to be lagged – if only because planned consumption is normally resistant to pressures for cuts. But this is only a delay in the inevitable and, sooner or later, the negative multiplier adjustment will become fully operative, and will magnify these cuts. At the same time, investment expenditure is likely to suffer from several, cumulative downward revisions as excess capacity begins to build up and business prospects deteriorate. Expectations are likely to be revised downwards, moving the demand function for investment funds to the left, and reducing the level of investment at the existing user cost of capital, or rate of interest. Once again, if we bring the accelerator into our analysis, this will add its own pressure for further cuts. As output moves from positive growth into negative decline, the accelerator will signal the need for a reduction in the required stock of capital, which will halt not only net or expansion investment, but could also result in cuts in the normal level of replacement investment. As the recession deepens, it is very likely that the level of investment will fall to the point where it is no longer sufficient to provide replacement investment for existing capacity, so that the stock of productive capital is allowed to decline towards the lower level required. Just as the upswing of the cycle tended to gather momentum, so too the downswing will tend to send the economy lurching into full depression.

As the economy approaches its lower turning point, however, the momentum of the downswing will tend to level out, as the factors which will ultimately generate recovery begin to grow in influence. Unreplaced capital usage will gradually bring actual capital stock down to its desired level. The slackening demand for credit will gradually reduce interest rates. Falling rates of wage increase and crisis-inspired searches for efficiency will gradually reflect in more competitive production costs and prices. With improving price competitiveness, some benefits should be reaped in terms of export sales and import substitution. As firms begin to suspect that the lower turning point is at hand, some longer term investment plans will be reactivated, in preparation for the recovery. In short, the business cycle will gradually reach the point of recovery, as analysed earlier in this section.

There it is then; we have taken you through the full business cycle and used your existing knowledge of macroeconomic theory to produce an explanation for the cyclical path of real GDP. We would stress that we have not provided you with a systematic model of the cycle; far from it – indeed our explanation is more of a patchwork quilt than a model! But it is useful. Look over it again, and think how different cycles could be prompted by different influences: perhaps fluctuations in the level of investment provide the key to some cyclical series; perhaps our own competitive efficiency and its consequences for international trade flows lies more at the roots of other cycles. There is no truly 'normal' cycle, each differs in magnitude and shape. Some may have no real depression phase; recession may take the form of a brief plateau before recovery and boom are reactivated. Others, like the most recent downturn, may have a crushing and prolonged trough in activity. Some may have no sustained boom, before the combination of internal pressures and the impact of unexpected external events precipitates the recession; others, such as the current upswing, may show a prolonged boom in the face of all economic predictions.

Of course our explanation is messy, unstructured and complex; but at least it allows room for manoeuvre, with scope for different weightings of pressure and different shapes of cycle. It provides an insight into the complex workings of the latter – and this was what we set out to do.

COMPARISON OF ECONOMIC GROWTH RATES

It is now time to return to our theme of economic growth, which is the long-term phenomenon against which the short-term fluctuations of the business cycle occur. We have still to answer several of the questions which were raised in the introduction to this chapter. To do so, firstly, we must examine the data for longer term GDP movements, so that we can estimate the rate of economic growth which has been achieved by the UK. Next, we must compare this to the growth rates which have been recorded in other countries – using these as a standard against which to compare our own performance. Finally, once we have established the nature of any difference, we must then explore why such a difference in rates of growth could emerge.

At first sight, the long-term growth performance of the UK economy would seem to be satisfactory. A series of estimates have placed our rate of growth over the last 120 years or so at a little in excess of 2% per annum. This has been a remarkably steady rate of growth,[7] and has provided the potential for substantial gains in prosperity for all sectors of the macroeconomy over the period.

The main grounds for criticism of the UK's performance come from a comparison of our achievements against those of other countries. If there was any danger of complacency, this should evaporate rapidly after a glance at the contents of Tables 6.1 and 6.2; the message from these tables, particularly from Table 6.1, is that the UK has had one of the lowest rates of economic growth of any developed country – and this as a long-term pattern, rather than as a freak result over one particular period.

Table 6.1 deals with the rates of economic growth achieved by a selection of countries over the period 1955–82. These countries are all members of the Organization for Economic Cooperation and Development (OECD); we have shown all of the 'major' economies, that is, the group of seven nations which together account for about 85% of the total OECD output, but have selected only four nations from the other 17 'minor' economies, which together make up the balance of 15% of OECD output.

If we look at the first period of 1955–65, we can see that the average annual rate of growth of 2.8% for the UK is substantially lower

---

7. Surprisingly, while you would expect the strong domestic and international trade of the Victorian economy to have achieved a strong rate of growth, this has not been the case when average growth has been estimated for that period (reflecting possibly their more severe trade cyclical fluctuations?). Growth has been estimated as 2.3% per annum for the period 1870–1913, then at 1.6% per annum average for 1913–57 and, as you can see from Tables 6.1 and 6.2 at 2.8% per annum for 1957–67, and 2.2% per annum for 1969–79. Over the entire period, there has been a remarkably steady growth rate of a little over 2% per annum.

Table 6.1 Growth of real GNP/GDP[1] in OECD areas.

	Average per annum (percentage)		Annual rates (percentage)		
	1955/65[2]	1969/79	1980	1981	1982
USA	4.0	3.0	−0.2	1.8	−0.5
Japan	10.2	5.4	4.2	3.8	3.8
West Germany	5.1	3.2	1.8	−1.0	1.3
France	5.7	4.1	1.2	0.5	2.5
UK	2.8	2.2	−1.8	−2.0	0.3
Italy	5.5	3.3	4.0	0.0	1.0
Canada	4.5	4.3	0.0	3.0	1.0
Total above	N/A	3.5	1.0	1.3	1.0
Belgium	3.4	3.6	2.5	−1.3	1.0
Denmark	3.6	2.5	−0.2	−0.5	3.3
Netherlands	4.9	3.5	0.5	−2.0	0.5
Norway	3.8	4.5	3.8	1.3	0.0
Total all OECD countries	N/A	3.3	1.4	−0.3	1.5

Notes: 1. All above countries show GNP data apart from France, UK and Italy where growth measured is real GDP.
    2. 1955/65 data taken from Maddison, A. (1967) *Economic Growth in the West*.
(Reprinted by permission of *OECD Economic Outlook*, December 1981.)

than that achieved by all other nations named in the table. It lies well below the USA's 4.0% and Canada's 4.5%: West Germany with 5.1%, Italy with 5.5% and France with 5.7% have all achieved about double the UK rate of growth; Japan, with a remarkable annual figure of 10.2%, has grown at nearly four times the UK's rate. All four 'minor' nations have all exceeded comfortably the UK rate of growth – indeed the Netherlands' very strong growth rate of 4.9% for this period stands comparison with the growth performance of any of the 'major' European economies.

For the second period of 1969–79, it is noticeable that all the growth rates have been reduced . . . and equally noticeable that the UK's relative performance is still pretty much the same as before. Our average growth rate of 2.2% per annum still lies well below the performance level of the other 'majors' (for which the group average was 3.5% for the period) and, while the gap has closed a little, France (4.1%), Canada (4.3%) and Japan (5.4%) have all grown at about double the UK rate.

Table 6.2 Growth of real GNP/GDP[1] in OECD areas.

	1983	1984	1985	1986[2]	1987[2]	Average 1980–87
USA	3.6	6.4	2.7	2.8	3.0	2.5
Japan	3.2	5.1	4.5	2.3	2.8	3.7
West Germany	1.8	3.0	2.5	2.8	3.0	1.5
France	0.7	1.5	1.4	2.0	2.3	1.5
UK	3.4	3.0	3.5	2.3	2.8	1.4
Italy	−0.2	2.8	2.3	2.3	3.0	1.5
Canada	3.1	5.5	4.0	3.0	2.8	2.8
Total above	2.9	5.0	3.0	2.5	2.8	2.4
Belgium	−0.1	1.3	1.1	2.0	2.0	1.1
Denmark	2.0	3.4	3.8	2.8	0.5	1.9
Netherlands	1.4	2.3	1.8	1.5	1.5	0.9
Norway	4.5	5.6	4.2	4.3	2.0	3.2
Total OECD	1.6	2.6	2.5	2.5	2.5	1.8

Notes: 1. As before, France, UK and Italy use real GDP, all other real GNP.
      2. These are forecast rates of growth.
(Reprinted by permission of *OECD Economic Outlook*, December 1987.)

Looking down to the 'minor' group's rates of growth, the UK's performance is again relatively weak – indeed, from the full list of the 17 minors, only Switzerland with an average rate of 1.4% per annum, had a lower rate of economic growth for the period. Out of the total OECD membership of 24 countries, the UK was the second lowest in terms of growth performance.

It is interesting to speculate why rates of growth were lower for this second period, especially since trade levels were booming over the late 1960s and the early 1970s. Obviously, different countries would be affected by different sets of circumstances, but there were two sets of influences which were common to all. The first, and probably the main influence was the impact over the mid and late 1970s as OPEC imposed a series of substantial increases on the price of crude oil – taken cumulatively, these had the effect of more than quadrupling its price over five or six years. In the short term, there is little that a country can do to change its pattern of energy and raw material usage (crude oil is an important raw material as well as a source of energy); as a result, most oil-importing countries lurched into heavy current account deficits in their balance of payments (that is, payments due for imports exceeded the receipts earned by exports). A common response to this deficit position was that nations tried to reduce the deficit by bringing in **deflationary** macroeconomic policies,[6] attempting to cut their aggregate expenditure and, through this, their purchases of other, non-oil imports. But if all nations seek to cut their import purchases, then they are simultaneously cutting each other's export sales (since one country's imports are another country's exports). In terms of our basic model, both the C^* function (reflecting the impact of the deflationary measures on C) and the J function (reflecting the loss of exports – and further possible cuts in I) would fall, causing the economies concerned to contract towards a new and lower equilibrium level of GDP. At best, there would be a marked slowdown in economic growth (as measured in terms of real GDP) towards the end of the period, which would have the effect of reducing the annual average rate of growth for the period as a whole.

But it is interesting to speculate further. A second possible influence might have been the resurgence of monetarism and the consequent decline of Keynesian policy during the 1970s. Apart from the growing academic momentum of monetarism, at practical policy level there was a developing apprehension about the cumulative effects of **fiscal deficits** (that is, where the total of government expenditures exceeded the total of its receipts from taxation) from Keynesian **reflationary** policies.[6] Taken with the major increases in costs following the OPEC price increases, there was a growing awareness and experience of severe inflationary pressure. Even diehard Keynesian economies such as the UK had to concede substantially tighter monetary targets as the price for borrowing rights from the International Monetary Fund (IMF) towards the later years of the 1970s. To the extent that Keynesian policies weakened, and governments embraced the stricter disciplines of monetarism, then the short-term effect would be that economic recession (as discussed in the previous paragraph) would be allowed to proceed without a serious attempt at its correction – which once again would have an adverse effect on average rates of growth in GDP for the period as a whole.

Returning to Table 6.1, the final series of annual growth rates are interesting, not because they provide an accurate measure of economic growth, but because they show how the different countries weathered the trough of the business cycle over 1979–82. The impact of the downturn can be traced in the real GDP patterns of all the countries – even Japan, where annual growth fell to about 4%! But what is clear, once again, is that no single country was affected more adversely than the UK, for which output fell by 1.8% over 1980, and by a further 2.0% over 1981, followed by an uncertain recovery of 0.3% for 1982; in comparison, the average figures for the 'majors' group were growth rates of 1.0%, 1.3% and 1.0% for those three years. Only the Netherlands, over 1981 and

1982, appeared to suffer to the same extent; all other economies appear to have declined less, then to have recovered more strongly than the UK.

In short, Table 6.1 contains two grim messages for the UK. Firstly, we had the poorest economic growth performance out of all the 'major' countries and, indeed a relatively poorer performance than almost all the 'minor' OECD members. Secondly, we appeared to suffer more severely than any other country from the last major downturn in the business cycle.

In contrast, Table 6.2 shows some remarkable differences in pattern from this earlier period. If we judge solely from the annual rates of growth (which is always a dangerous procedure), then it would seem that the UK had been transformed into one of the fastest growing OECD economies over 1983 to 1987. For example, against the average for the entire OECD group of 1.6% for 1983, 2.6% for 1984 and 2.5% for 1985, the UK's annual rates of growth were 3.4%, 3.0% and 3.5%; only Canada, the USA and Japan out of the seven 'majors' performed better over these three years. Even the OECD forecast rates for 1986 and 1987 (yes, forecasts; remember the problems of data lags which were discussed in Chapter 2) would seem to suggest a relatively stronger performance level from the UK than we would have expected from Table 6.1.

Had someone waved a magic wand over the UK to galvanize its growth performance, after years of sloth and self-indulgence? Have the new monetarist and supply-side policies achieved more than traditional Keynesian policies could ever offer? Some politicians and even economists would argue so most vehemently.

Once again there should be a gentle and by now familiar sound of warning bells ringing in your mind. The events from 1982 to 1987 must be interpreted with care; in effect, the data neither proves nor disproves the claims which have been made upon it. Firstly, 1983–85 is too short a period over which to measure growth by movements in real GDP rather than in potential output. It is quite impossible to separate the influence of the short-term recovery phase of the cycle from any genuine economic growth which might have occurred. After all, we suffered more severely in recession than anyone else, and were recovering from a much more depressed lower turning point – why should our recovery not have been relatively stronger than most? Secondly, if we follow our established practice of measuring growth over decades, or at least longer periods, then the average figures for 1980–87 should bring us up short in our tracks. Once again, our average annual rate of growth figure of 1.4% for the period is *below* the average of the seven 'majors', which was 2.4% – and was even below the average for all 24 OECD members of 1.8%. We can certainly take comfort from the fact that we have closed the gap between ourselves and countries such as Italy, France and West Germany; this is a real and important achievement. But the USA, Canada, Japan – and 'minors' such as Denmark and Norway – are still well ahead of us, which should at least provide a target for the future.

Of course the abnormally severe depression experienced by the UK has had the effect of damping down our average performance for the period – but, equally, it has also exaggerated our apparent 'growth' over 1983–85. We can't have it both ways! Always remember that 'there are lies, there are damned lies, and there are statistics'. What the table really shows us is that there is room for real optimism about the possibility that we have improved our relative growth performance – but it is still too early to be certain, whatever the politicians might claim . . . Such caution (could it even be honesty?) is one of the reasons why economics has the reputation of being 'that dismal science'!

A THEORY OF ECONOMIC GROWTH

As always, the economist must seek to probe beneath the level of a simple description of events, and try to produce a systematic analysis of *why* these events have taken place. We have already seen that different countries manage to achieve different rates of economic growth and, in particular, we have seen that the UK's historical performance (at least up to 1982) has been very weak indeed. Why should such differences occur – and why should we have lagged so persistently behind others? Clearly each country will have unique influences from its own set of institutions, its own cultural attitude, and its own pattern of comparative advantage, as reflected in its pattern of industrial production, and all of these will have some influence on its growth path. But it is still possible to identify a *process* of growth which is common to all economies; it is by looking at how each country deals with the key aspects of this growth process that we might be able to offer a more convincing explanation for the different rates of growth which we can observe in practice.

Obviously, an important topic such as economic growth has generated its own specialist field of literature over the years. Some of the resultant models are very sophisticated indeed and lie well beyond the realms of an introductory text such as this. But it is still possible to use a relatively simple model[8] which:

- is based on techniques which have already been developed in the text;
- identifies some of the main influences on and problem areas in the growth process;

---

8. The model which is used in the text has been derived from the independent work of R.F. Harrod over the late 1930s and E.D. Domar over the late 1940s. It is one of the variety of introductory models which are used in what has become a somewhat complex and advanced area of theory.

- recognizes explicitly that growth of productive capacity alone is not sufficient; the resultant output must also be sold.

Despite its limitations, you will find that this model will provide you with a useful understanding of this very complex topic.

The first building block of the new model is the **capital:output ratio**, which we have already used in the theory of the acceleration principle.[9] This ratio is derived from the argument that, for any given level of output (Y), there will exist an optimum stock of capital (K) which can produce this; the capital:output ratio (w) measures the numerical relationship between the two, that is:

$$\frac{K}{Y} = w$$

For example, if the level of output is 200 and the optimum stock of capital to produce this is 400 (remember that the same stock of capital can be used many times to produce this level of output, so that it is quite possible that $K > Y$), then the value of the capital:output ratio will be 2.

If the reciprocal of our equation is taken (those of you with rusty maths can relax; you can do anything to an equality – even turn it upside down – so long as you do the same to *both* sides), then:

$$\frac{Y}{K} = \frac{1}{w} = \sigma$$

What the revised version of our equation now shows us is that we can measure the potential output (Y) which can be produced by any given stock of capital (K), to establish the **productivity per unit of that capital** (σ). Using the same illustrative values for K and Y,

$$\sigma = \frac{Y}{K} = \frac{200}{400} = 0.5$$

Bringing in another building block, let us keep the analysis as simple as possible by assuming that both technology and work practices are held constant over the period of the analysis, so that each new (or marginal) unit of capital will have the same productivity as any existing unit. In other words, we can restate our equation to show that:

---

9. The capital:output ratio was introduced in Appendix 5B to Chapter 5, as the basis for the acceleration principle in investment. It is *not* essential that you have read this Appendix as a precondition for understanding the growth model, since the latter is not concerned with the accelerator.

$$\frac{Y}{K} = \frac{\Delta Y}{\Delta K} = \sigma$$

The new building block is of course investment; as a matter of definition, we know that investment is any expenditure in the firms' sector which increases the stock of capital (for example, from purchases of premises, or equipment, or machinery and so on). Therefore, if:

$$I = \Delta K$$

then

$$\frac{\Delta Y}{I} = \sigma$$

or (by multiplying both sides of the equation by I),

$$\Delta Y = I\sigma$$

To be more explicit, since we are dealing with potential output (or the output which could be produced by the full utilization of the stock of capital), let us add a subscript (p) to this change in output, to leave it in the form:

$$\Delta Y_p = I\sigma$$

After all the algebra, where are we? Earlier in the chapter, we pointed out that one of the methods of measuring economic growth was to measure the increase in potential output (ΔY_p) over time. We have therefore evolved a growth equation which shows that the rate of economic growth in any country depends upon two separate factors, these being:

- The level of net investment (I), which is defined as additions to the productive capacity of the economy, and
- The productivity of that investment (σ).

From Chapter 5, we already know that countries devote different percentages of their GDP to investment expenditure. We can now see why a country such as Japan, which has sustained a very high level of investment, has also achieved such a high rate of growth; equally, we can understand why it is no accident that the UK, with its relatively low level of investment, has also shown a very poor growth record historically. The model has therefore given substance to our argument that it is a dangerous policy for any country to run with a low level of investment expenditure. In a sense, we were already aware of the role of investment in the growth process (although, in fairness, our earlier argument was based more on the theme of technology transmission through investment – a dimension which is excluded from the present simple model).

But the model has drawn our attention to a new aspect of economic growth. Just how productive has been our investment in the UK, relative to that of our main international competitors? More specifically, what sort of value do we show for σ relative to them?

From the equations above, we know that:

$$\sigma = \frac{\Delta Y}{I}$$

It is possible to derive a crude estimate of the value of σ from the national accounts data for our group of countries – but bear in mind that what follows is a very tentative and rough estimate from generally available data, rather than a careful exercise in empirical research. For a start, we can measure ΔY from changes in constant price GDP at factor cost. Similarly, we can use gross domestic fixed capital formation (GDFCF) as a proxy for I, although it is not a truly accurate measure of changes in the economy's capital stock – if only because it includes both government and household expenditure, as well as the type of firms' investment which we really want to measure.

Table 6.3 shows the results of our calculations: I has been estimated from the flow of GDFCF over the period; ΔY has been measured as the increase in GDP over the period – and both elements have been measured in terms of constant 1980 prices. If we look first at the earlier period of 1973–79, we can see that our tentative estimates have drawn attention to a new weakness in the UK economy; our investment expenditure was substantially less productive than the 'norm' for other countries. Our σ value or, to give it its proper title, our **incremental output:capital ratio** (IOCR) of 0.05 was roughly half of the IOCRs of Japan, West Germany, the Netherlands and the USA for the period. UK growth has been relatively weak not only because we have invested less, *but also* because we appear not to have made a particularly productive use of that limited investment. Indeed, our estimated IOCR value diverges even further from the norm than does our pattern of relative investment.

Why should this be so? Out of a rich vein of specialist literature on the topic, some economists have argued that too high a proportion of UK investment has gone to the public sector and to public enterprises, where it has been put to uses for social rather than economic objectives, so yeilding a relatively low productivity in terms of output. Others have suggested that the firms' sector has been blameworthy in channelling its

Table 6.3 Comparison of incremental output : capital ratios (constant 1980 prices).

	1973–79		1980–86	
UK (£billion)				
I	297,469		298,238	
ΔY	16,307		24,826	
σ		0.05		0.08
USA ($million)				
I	3,396,596		3,232,396	
ΔY	362,215		423,463	
σ		0.11		0.13
Japan (billion yen)				
I	472,856		481,435	
ΔY	43,902		50,168	
σ		0.09		0.10
West Germany (million D-mark)				
I	2,077,960		1,899,610	
ΔY	187,390		95,910	
σ		0.09		0.05
Netherlands (million guilders)				
I	486,790		389,070	
ΔY	48,940		11,360	
σ		0.10		0.03

Notes: 1. I was taken as total of GDFCF from national accounts data; ΔY is change in real GDP at factor cost over period.

2. Apart from the UK the other countries had 1980–85 as second period, from OECD national accounts.

investment towards industries such as food, drink and tobacco, or textiles, or petrochemicals, which have shown a less dynamic growth at international level than many other sectors of industry; in other words, we may have been investing in the wrong type of industries. Some economists have argued that we have diverted too high a proportion of investment into idle stocks or inventories. Some feel that the root cause of the problem has been that either weak management, or intransigent labour has opted for a lower and less productive level of technology than was possible, that is, the quality of our technology transmission has been poor. Still others have shown from empirical research that, once the investment has been made, it has been substantially under-utilized – or has been badly used, due to the slow development of the necessary skills by workforce and management.

Whatever the cause, our simple exercise shows us one of the main benefits of modelling. It identifies problem areas, and focuses the search for causes – and, hopefully, possible solutions.

Once again, the estimates for 1980–86 offer some comfort, and provide some support for the argument that there has been a genuine improvement in the UK's growth performance over recent years. Tentative though our estimates might be, they suggest that there has been a marked improvement in our IOCR value, from 0.05 to 0.08. Not only does this raise us closer to the levels of productivity of investment which were enjoyed by our competitors in the earlier period, it has also (given the apparent deterioration in the IOCR values of West Germany and the Netherlands in this second period) raised us up the 'league table' and left us in a relatively stronger growth position.

How real is this apparent improvement – for is it ever a bad thing to retreat back to commonsense to provide a crude check for results? It could very well be picking up genuine developments which we have already acknowledged. From earlier chapters, we know that public sector and public enterprise investment have been cut drastically, with a much stronger emphasis laid on economic as opposed to social objectives: in addition, we know that there has been a substantial cut in the level of inventories within investment expenditure; and there have been major efforts to 'streamline' manning levels and working practices throughout the period. While such changes have also imposed social costs as part of their price, a more narrow view of their benefits would be that each would help to improve the IOCR value for the UK. It is beyond the scope of this text to say whether or not the benefits would outweigh the costs, but we would argue strongly that policy makers must be aware that there are two sides to any coin, and proceed only when there is a strong likelihood of a clear net benefit.

Extract 6.2 makes interesting reading at this stage. It is a review of the OECD's short-term projections for the UK. It has two quite separate themes which are of interest: firstly, it provides a relatively objective and external view of the short-term economic pressures associated with the extended boom phase in the UK cycle; and, secondly, it also explores some of the underlying improvements in the growth potential of the UK economy.

Already, our simple growth model has provided us with a great deal of thought-provoking material. But it has still a contribution to make, and one which goes straight to the Achilles heel of any approach which measures growth solely in terms of *potential* output. Yes, we are back to the awkward problem that the output must also be sold, if the benefits of growth are to be reaped.

Extract 6.2 THE ECONOMIST 20 AUGUST 1988.

THE ECONOMY
PRAISE FROM PARIS

WHAT better holiday reading for a chancellor of the exchequer than the latest report on the British economy from the Organisation for Economic Co-operation and Development? The OECD's praise is lavish, compared with its recent lukewarm assessments of the Japanese and West German economies.

The OECD is less worried about accelerating inflation and the deteriorating trade figures than are those City analysts still at their desks. This may be partly because its economic forecasts are somewhat out of date: as usual, they were first published in its "Economic Outlook", and prepared in early May, before the latest interest-rate rises, and before it was clear how fast the economy was growing. For example, the OECD predicts that Britain's current-account deficit will reach £5¾ billion this year, rising to £7½ billion next. In the first six months of 1988 alone, the deficit totalled £5.6 billion.

Like practically everybody else, the OECD thinks that the current rapid pace of growth in domestic demand is unsustainable. The vital question is whether it will slow down of its own accord. The OECD's economists still stick by their central forecast: the economy will slow gradually, inflation will remain under control.

Were the personal savings ratio to continue to fall and domestic demand to remain buoyant, inflationary pressures and the current-account deficit would both increase. If the inflow of foreign capital, now financing the deficit, were to stop, sterling would sink and interest rates and inflation rise. If domestic demand does not slow, says the OECD, Britain will need a tougher budget next March.

The OECD devotes less attention to short-term prospects than to the longer-term improvement in the economy's supply-side performance. This is now the eighth year of continuous expansion; British industry's profitability has swung from being the lowest in the OECD to one of the highest; and, whereas productivity growth has continued to slow or remained constant in most countries in the 1980s, in Britain it has improved significantly. Only in Japan has labour productivity grown faster this decade.

Moreover, Britain is the only country apart from Japan which has had a relative improvement in capital productivity compared with the 1970s. So industry's efficiency gains are even more impressive when measured in terms of total factor productivity (ie, the weighted average of the growth in labour and capital productivity). That still leaves plenty of room for improvement. Output per worker in Britain is, on the OECD's reckoning, still a third lower than in America and a quarter lower than in West Germany or France.

Can the recovery be sustained? If, as the OECD argues, Britain's improved performance is mainly the result of supply-side measures such as labour-market reforms, financial liberalisation, deregulation and tax reform, then Britain may be able to look forward to many more years of the same. However, this is only half the story. Some of Britain's boom has been the result of looser macroeconomic policies than the government intended. The Treasury's projections for nominal GDP growth have repeatedly been revised upwards. The government's microeconomic reforms have indeed allowed supply to respond faster to demand. But they have not yet been so revolutionary that expansion can continue at the pace of the first half of this year.

Reprinted with permission from *The Economist* 20 August 1988 © *The Economist*.

In terms of theory, we know that any economy will tend to adjust towards an equilibrium level of GDP, where available output is just sufficient to satisfy the planned levels of expenditure. To keep our analysis as simple as possible, let us exclude both the public sector and the international trade sector from the model, so that our equilibrium condition can be stated as:

$$Y = C + I$$

Our final building block has been described as the **paradox of investment**. What does this mean? Up till now we have been dealing with equilibrium in the context of a single period; as such, we have treated it solely as an element within aggregate demand, as in the equation above. For a dynamic path analysis, we must recognize that investment does not only affect the righthand side of the equation; by increasing productive capacity, it also affects aggregate supply (Y), or the lefthand side of the equation, for the following period. The central issue of the paradox of investment is that, if Y rises between periods, while aggregate demand remains unchanged, then we are no longer in equilibrium – planned expenditure will now fall short of available output.

In short, we have now focused on the point to which we have referred at several stages in this chapter: it is not enough to have the potential to produce output; unless aggregate demand rises alongside potential output (Y_p), excess capacity will emerge in the economy.

But how can aggregate demand be raised? In our simple model, the main problem is that the level of consumption expenditure is *passive*, in the sense that it is functionally related to the actual, or realized level of GDP; it will not rise of its own accord, but only if the level of GDP rises first, when it will respond to this. Thus it is investment itself which must provide the impetus to cause aggregate demand to rise. The full meaning of the paradox of investment is that, having increased aggregate supply, investment must itself increase in the following period to ensure that aggregate demand rises alongside potential output, and equilibrium is maintained (in other words, to ensure that planned expenditure rises to absorb the increase in available output).

This allows us to return to our final building block in the model. We know that, if there is a change in investment, this will raise the level of income and consumption through the multiplier. To distinguish actual, or realized GDP from potential output, let us give it the symbol Y_r. If, therefore, there is an increase in investment (ΔI), then the resultant increase in actual GDP (or realized sales) will be:

$$\Delta Y_r = \frac{1}{1-c} \times \Delta I$$

Since $1 - c$ also gives us the marginal propensity to save (if 80% of additional income is consumed, the balance of 20% must be saved), then we can rewrite the equation as:

$$\Delta Y_r = \frac{1}{s} \times \Delta I$$

or,

$$\Delta Y_r = \frac{\Delta I}{s}$$

Adding this building block (which is only a slight reformulation of the familiar multiplier) to the growth model, allows us to examine a new aspect of the growth process over time. Just as there can be an equilibrium in any single time period, so too there can be an equilibrium, or steady and sustained rate of economic growth. If, starting from an equilibrium position, both potential output and realized sales of output grow at the same rate, then we will remain in equilibrium over time. In other words, for an equilibrium rate of growth to be held, then ΔY_p must grow at the same rate as ΔY_r over time. If:

$$\Delta Y_p = \Delta Y_r$$

and, as we know already,

$$\Delta Y_p = I\sigma$$

and, as we have shown in the final building block,

$$\Delta Y_r = \frac{\Delta I}{s}$$

we can substitute both of these terms into our equilibrium equation to show that, for an equilibrium rate of growth to be achieved:

$$I\sigma = \frac{\Delta I}{s}$$

This, in turn can be rearranged (multiply both sides by s) to show that:

$$\Delta I = sI\sigma$$

which can be further rearranged (divide both sides by I) to

$$\frac{\Delta I}{I} = s\sigma$$

The lefthand side of this final equation shows us the rate of growth in investment over time, which will keep us at a steady, equilibrium rate of growth. For example, if we use the normal illustrative values of $c = 0.8$ (so that $s = 0.2$), and the capital:output ratio $w = 2$ (so that its reciprocal $\sigma = 0.5$), then the necessary annual growth rate of investment is

$$\frac{\Delta I}{I} = 0.2(0.5)$$

$$= 0.1$$

or 10% per annum. If we could maintain a growth rate of 10% per annum in investment expenditure, then we would hold a steady equilibrium rate of economic growth.

If, for any reason, the rate of growth in investment diverges from this annual rate, then we fall off what has been described as the **razor edge of growth**, that is, the tightrope which gives us an equilibrium rate of growth. For example, if investment growth falls below 10%, then aggregate demand will not grow sufficiently alongside aggregate supply, or potential output. Excess capacity will emerge, which is likely to cause a downwards revision in the next period's investment plans – which will exacerbate the problem, and create even more excess capacity. There is no margin of forgiveness; if we slip off the razor edge, then we slide progressively away from steady growth – at least in terms of our modelling.

But where does all of this algebraic manipulation leave us in terms of the real world? Does this final theory of an equilibrium growth rate in investment carry any real-world message for us?

Indeed it does. Firstly, it stresses the point that aggregate demand must also grow to support our growth in potential output. In our simple model, the entire burden of providing that impetus falls on investment. But this is only a two-sector model. In the real world, the burden can be shared with any other of the injection function elements; in particular, if exports can be increased steadily, this will help to support our growth rate. Countries such as Japan, West Germany, Italy and France have leaned heavily on the success of their international trade flows to augment their performance in economic growth; it doesn't matter where you sell your increased output – so long as you sell it and prevent excess capacity from developing. It is not so clearcut whether rising sales to the government sector would have the same effect; in the short run, perhaps, but in the long run we begin to drift into the position where the public sector claims an ever increasing share of resources, with both fiscal and monetary side effects.

Secondly, our abstract theorizing has drawn attention to another important aspect of economic growth. We finished up by showing that

$$\frac{\Delta I}{I} = s\sigma$$

that is, the equilibrium growth rate for investment would be set by the values of the marginal propensity to save, and the incremental output:capital ratio. We have already discussed the apparent improvement in the value for σ in the UK; we can now see that this could improve the rate of growth in investment and, through this, our performance in economic growth. But what about the UK value for s, in the equation? What are the implications of the fall in the savings ratio which has been experienced recently in the UK, as a consequence of the developing momentum of the consumption boom?

In terms of simple theory, and our two-sector model, it will also pull down the rate of growth in investment; savings, or non-consumption, provides the resources for investment. Does this mean that the recent recovery in UK investment is under threat? Not necessarily in the short run, because the real world offers the additional source of finance from the international sector, via international capital flows. Indeed, it would seem that much of the recent increase in UK investment has been funded by international capital – to leave the Brits free to go out and enjoy their consumer boom party! It is a nice trick, if you can pull it off in perpetuity. The danger for the UK lies in whatever set of circumstances might cause this international flow of capital to dry up. Who will then fund our investment plans if it is still party time – and if the government is still determined to cut its investment expenditure to a minimum? It is no accident that, during September 1988, the government had been arguing that UK savings must also be encouraged; not only would this help to damp down the rate of growth in consumption spending, it would also address a potential source of weakness in our growth process.

Who said economic theory had nothing to do with the real world? Our primitive (relative to the specialist literature on economic growth) little model has:

- Helped us to identify why the UK performance in economic growth has been historically weak, and
- Drawn our attention to a potential source of weakness, which could undermine what appears to have been a genuine improvement in our growth performance over recent years.

CONCLUSIONS

1. All countries experience cyclical fluctuations in income and output levels over time, although the severity of these fluctuations will vary both between countries and, within any single country, over different business cycles. Both boom and depression will be temporary phases rather than permanent features.

2. In the UK, as in most other countries, there is clear evidence that the business cycle in the post-war era has taken place against a background of a rising trend in output, or economic growth. Against this trend, cycles have normally been minor fluctuations, from which recovery has been relatively quick. Only the most recent recession and depression of 1979–82 have diverged from this pattern, both in terms of the severity of these phases in the cycle, and in terms of the duration of the trough – it took until 1984 before the previous peak level of output of 1979 was exceeded.

3. From international comparison, it would appear that the UK's average rate of economic growth (at least in the post-war period up to 1982) has been substantially lower than that of any other developed country. Further, the recession and depression phases of the most recent cycle appear to have affected the UK more severely than any of our main international competitors.

4. While the cyclical fluctuations in output reflect through into the level of employment, there are additional influences at work in the form of technological changes and input substitution. The 1970s and early 1980s have exhibited substantially higher levels of unemployment than the 1960s. In particular, the decline in output from 1979 to mid 1981 resulted in a considerably greater decline in the demand for labour. When the initial recovery in output did materialize, it merely slowed down the rate of increase in unemployment. It has taken the later cyclical phase of the boom to make a real inroad into the grim mountain of unemployment in the UK. The recovery in employment has been complicated by the tendency of technological change to reduce the requirement for labour per unit of output, so that real output must show substantial and sustained growth before any benefits are felt in the labour market. It will take a very considerable and prolonged run at economic growth if unemployment is to be reduced to anything like the levels felt to be 'normal' up until 1975.

5. Economic growth must therefore be a prime economic objective for any government. As such, it is important that we should be able to understand why the UK rate of growth was so relatively low in the past – if only so that we can try to ease constraints and try to improve our future performance.

6. Our analysis has suggested that there are two main reasons for the past weaknesses in our growth performance. Firstly, we have invested less than have our main competitors. Secondly, the productivity of our investment has been much lower than others have achieved. Over the 1980s there have been signs that we have improved our performance in each of these areas of weakness, and recent figures for real GDP do suggest that it is possible that our rate of economic growth has improved in response; it is still too early – since economic growth is a long-term phenomenon – to be sure.

7. However, we are also able to identify two possible sources of weakness, which might have an adverse effect on future performance. Firstly, the recent decline in our savings ratio has only been compensated by international capital flows; there is a danger that a longer term effect could be to constrain the rate of growth in our investment expenditure. Secondly, if this occurs, we must seek to support the increase in our potential output by a demand element other than investment. Since exports provide an alternative source of growth, we must ensure that our macroeconomic policies do not undermine this potential. To remain price-effective in world markets, we must guard against rising cost pressures from inflation in the UK, and we must be careful not to let the UK exchange rate rise to a level where it damages potential sales. As at autumn 1989, there is a real danger that the rising momentum of the consumption boom could be creating unwanted inflationary pressures. Simultaneously, the policy measures which are being used to contain this boom, that is, the wave of increases in the rate of interest, could well cause an unwanted increase in the exchange rate . . .

8. There is evidence that real improvements have been achieved in terms of our growth performance over the 1980s. With somewhere between 2.0 and 3.0 million still unemployed, it would be sad indeed if we were to allow these improvements to drift away from us.

SELF-ASSESSMENT QUESTIONS

TRUE/FALSE QUESTIONS

6.1. The business cycle is concerned with short-term variations in income and output and has little influence on levels of employment.

6.2. Simply to hold unemployment at a steady level over the next few years, real output must rise steadily in the UK.

6.3. Over the period 1982–87, the UK had one of the fastest rates of growth in the world.

6.4. A country's rate of economic growth depends upon its level of investment expenditure over time.

MULTIPLE CHOICE QUESTIONS

6.1. Trade cycle data is stated in terms of constant prices and at factor cost adjusted values.

(a) To eliminate growth trends and permit a study of the cycle;
(b) To eliminate the influence of exchange rate variations;
(c) To identify movements in real output of goods and services;
(d) To exclude the effect of changes in production costs;
(e) To exclude the effect on expenditure values over time of price and expenditure tax changes.

6.2. The rate of increase in the upswing will gradually be checked, reflecting that:

(a) Full employment of labour creates an absolute constraint on output;
(b) Full employment of labour necessitates a switch to more capital intensive production methods;
(c) Once households have satisfied their consumption plans for the period, they will tend to revert to routine expenditure;
(d) Increasing use of credit has forced up the rate of interest, causing revisions to consumption and investment plans;
(e) The multiplier adjustment process has been completed and income has reached its new equilibrium level.

6.3. The economy will move into recession due to influences such as:

(a) Loss of business confidence that the boom will continue;
(b) Falling levels of investment caused by the slower rate of growth in output as the boom levels off;
(c) A decline in the capital:output ratio as capital wears out, reducing the influence of the accelerator;
(d) Rising production costs reflecting the competition for scarce labour in full employment conditions;
(e) Falling levels of imports as price levels rise.

FOOD FOR THOUGHT

The text appears to argue that economic growth is automatically a desirable target for any government. Does this mean that there are no potential disbenefits associated with growth? If there are problems, or areas of criticism, what would you expect these to be?

Note: Solutions can be found at the end of the text.

Chapter 7

Fiscal Policy

> Introduction
> The national accounts data on expenditure and taxation
> Fiscal policy: the Keynesian context
> The basic fiscal model
> The fiscal multipliers
> Fiscal policy: the lessons of experience
> Conclusions
> Self-assessment questions

INTRODUCTION

Now that we have explored the nature and causes of the short-term business cycle and the longer term phenomenon of economic growth, both of which combine to make up the background environment for macroeconomic policy decisions, we are ready to return to a more detailed examination of the factors which influence the government's expenditure (G) and taxation (T) plans. These can no longer be treated as 'constant and autonomous' within our basic model of the economy. If they are set by forces outside the model, we must now try to analyse these forces.

Fiscal policy is the term used to cover the government's strategic intentions as it plans its expenditure and estimates the taxation (and possibly borrowing) which will be needed to cover this. The topic is a controversial one and brings you face to face with one of the main conflict areas between the Keynesian and the monetarist viewpoints. Should taxation be set simply to cover and balance government expenditure – and, conversely, should this expenditure be set with its taxation implications in mind? Or is it possible for a government to use a deliberate imbalance between its expenditure and taxation plans to try to influence the course of the economy? Indeed, is it possible to *control* the macroeconomy by the use of fiscal policy? Or, is this apparent influence and control quite illusory, is its effect little more than a short-term disruption to the course of events? Is it even possible that its undesired side-effects set up a series of long-term constraints on the flexibility and efficiency of the macroeconomy, penalizing productivity and growth – so that we should try to use it only minimally as a policy instrument?

Whatever your initial stance on the issue of government intervention in the working of the economy (and we would urge that you 'shelve' any purely *political* prejudices for the moment since these can only act as a block against fresh learning and understanding), we would defy you not to become interested in this debate. It deals with issues which are vitally important to every single person within the economy, whether involved as a participant, or as an observer from the sad ranks of the unemployed. It is important to be aware of its strengths and its weaknesses, its potential and its limitations. It is not our intention to argue either that fiscal policy is 'right' or 'wrong'. If we are to argue any particular theme it would be that there is an equal danger in both a mindless belief in its potential for control and influence, and in an equally mindless rejection of fiscal policy as an ineffective, if not damaging, policy instrument. Over-simplified, black and white arguments are dangerous, when there is no clearcut case for acceptance, or rejection. Our intention is to try to set out both sides as simply as possible, then to leave you to make up your own minds.

In this chapter, we will try to:

- Establish the broad magnitudes of government expenditure and taxation receipts in the context of the UK economy;
- Compare the UK position with the pattern which emerges from the national accounts of some of our main international competitors;
- Explain the role perceived by Keynesian economists for fiscal policy in the influence and control of the macroeconomy;
- Analyse how the basic model will respond to deliberate changes in government expenditure, benefit payments, and taxation;
- Examine and compare the multiplier adjustment process triggered by each of these policy changes;
- Discuss some of the main problems associated with fiscal policy as a practical policy instrument;
- Identify some of the undesired side-effects of this policy.

Table 7.1 UK government expenditure versus GDP (£billion).

	Current prices			Constant 1980 prices		
	1976	1981	1986	1976	1981	1986
Government final consumption expenditure	27.0	55.5	79.4	47.0	49.1	51.4
Government share of GDFCF	5.4	4.6	7.3	9.1	4.0	6.1
Total government expenditure (G)	32.4	60.1	86.7	56.1	53.1	57.5
GDP	126.6	254.1	374.9	220.3	227.9	259.9
Rate of growth in total G				–	–	+2.5
Rate of growth in GDP				–	–	+18.0
Total G as share of GDP				25.5	23.3	22.1
Local authority as percentage of government final consumption				40.2	38.9	38.6

(Source: *UK National Accounts*, 1987, Tables 1.2, 1.6, 9.1 and 12.1. Reprinted by permission of the Controller, HMSO.)

THE NATIONAL ACCOUNTS DATA ON EXPENDITURE AND TAXATION

From earlier chapters, you will remember that government expenditure (G) is one of the elements of aggregate expenditure or demand in the basic model, and that it appears also as one of the expenditure elements in the national accounts. You should remember also that, in the national accounts, there is a government expenditure element for public sector investment in the measurement of Gross Domestic Fixed Capital Formation (GDFCF). In Table 7.1, both of these elements of expenditure are added together to show that total government expenditure (that is, the total of final consumption and GDFCF expenditure) amounted to £32.4 billion in 1976, rising to £60.1 billion in 1981, and again to £86.7 billion in 1986.

In constant price terms (to eliminate any distortion caused by price inflation), total government expenditure rose from £56.1 billion in 1976 to £57.5 billion in 1986, showing a growth rate of 2.5% over the period against the growth of GDP (also in constant prices) of 18.0% over the same period. This very sluggish rate of growth in expenditure is interesting; it reflects a strong government conviction that public sector involvement in the economy had been allowed to grow too rapidly in the past, resulting in too large a claim upon economic resources, to the detriment of the private sector. As a result, the relatively firm control on expenditure over the 1980s (which you will notice has hit government investment more severely than it did final consumption – with govern-

Table 7.2 International comparison of government expenditure and GDP.

	Constant prices (1980)	
	1976	1986
USA ($billion)		
Total government expenditure	491.7	632.4
GDP	2,403.3	3,180.1
Rate of growth in government expenditure	–	+28.6%
Rate of growth in GDP	–	+32.3%
Government expenditure as percentage of GDP	20.5	19.9
Japan (billion yen)		
Total government expenditure	30.8	44.7
GDP	197.4	297.7
Rate of growth in government expenditure	–	+45.1%
Rate of growth in GDP	–	+50.8%
Government expenditure as percentage of GDP	15.6	15.0
West Germany (billion D-marks)		
Total government expenditure	266.8	322.4
GDP	1,322.7	1,608.5
Rate of growth in government expenditure	–	+20.8%
Rate of growth in GDP	–	+21.6%
Government expenditure as percentage of GDP	20.2	20.0
Netherlands (billion guilders)		
Total government expenditure	67.3	72.6
GDP	311.1	361.2
Rate of growth in government expenditure	–	+7.9%
Rate of growth in GDP	–	+16.1%
Government expenditure as percentage of GDP	21.6	20.1

(Reprinted by permission of the *OECD National Accounts*, Table 1.4 for each country.)

ment GDFCF falling from £9.1 billion to £6.1 billion in constant price terms) has resulted in total government expenditure falling from 25.5% to 22.1% of GDP over the period.

Table 7.2 allows us to compare this UK pattern of resource allocation to the public sector with that of the four regular databases for the USA, Japan, West Germany and the Netherlands. Two interesting points emerge from the comparison. Firstly, the reduced UK figure of 22.1% of GDP is *still* significantly higher than for any one of these countries; government expenditure amounts to about 20% of GDP in the

USA, West Germany and the Netherlands – and only about 15% of GDP in Japan (reflecting the greater weighting given to resources allocated to private sector investment in that country). Secondly, the severity of the UK controls can be judged by comparing our 2.5% growth rate for government expenditure over the period with the much more rapid rates of growth in these other countries. For example, government expenditure in real terms grew by 20.8% over the same period in West Germany, 28.6% in the USA and 45.1% in Japan. Only the Netherlands, with its lower growth of 7.9% was anywhere near the UK. However, despite these rapid rates of growth, note how, in each country, growth in government expenditure was held *lower* than the growth in GDP for the period, so that its share of GDP *fell* over the decade.

Table 7.3 allows us to look in a little more detail at government expenditure and taxation receipts in the UK. You will notice that there is a distinction drawn between 'current' and 'capital' items. These are standard national accounts terms which apply equally to households, firms and government sectors, and distinguish between income and expenditure generated out of current production activities, that is, ongoing, routine economic activities during the year, and transactions associated with adding to wealth, or the stock of capital assets.

If we continue to focus on government expenditure, your first glance at this new table is likely to confuse you. (What do you mean 'even more than usual'?) The figures which we have been quoting in earlier tables as total government expenditure lie well below the total figures shown here. For example, our earlier total of £86.7 billion for 1986 is only about half of the new figure of £166.2 billion (the total for current and capital expenditure) in Table 7.3. That should be enough to wake up even the most somnolent reader!

The explanation is that, so far, we have been dealing only with government final consumption and the government's share of gross domestic fixed capital formation. These, however, are only two of the items which make up the wider list of all forms of expenditure, as shown in Table 7.3. The government also makes payments in respect of subsidies, and debt interest on the outstanding balance for sums which have been borrowed by government.[1] But the greatest single source of difference between the two tables is caused by the inclusion of **transfer payments**, or the 'grants' and 'transfers' items in Table 7.3.

From Chapter 2 you will remember that GDP measures the money

---

1. Subsidies, you should remember, were part of the factor cost adjustment made to GDP at market prices (to calculate GDP at factor cost, you added subsidies and deducted expenditure taxes from GDP at market prices). Go back and revise! The term **national debt** is given to the total of all outstanding sums which have been borrowed by successive governments over the years, and the debt interest payments shown here represent the sum needed to 'service' that debt.

Table 7.3 UK government receipts and expenditure.

	1976	%[1]	1986	%[1]
Current receipts				
Taxes on income	19.0	38.0	52.4	33.5
Taxes on expenditure	16.3	32.6	62.3	39.9
Social security contributions	8.4	16.8	26.1	16.7
Rent	1.9	3.8	4.0	2.6
Interest and dividends	2.4	4.8	5.9	3.8
Others	1.2	2.4	2.9	1.9
Total	49.2		153.6	
Current expenditure				
Government current consumption	26.1	46.6	76.9	46.3
Subsidies	3.4	6.1	6.5	3.9
Grants to personal sector	12.7	22.7	50.5	30.4
Debt interest	5.3	9.5	17.0	10.2
Others	1.7	3.0	4.8	2.9
Total	49.2		155.7	
Current balance	0.0		−2.1	
Capital receipts				
Taxes on capital	0.8	1.6	2.7	1.7
Capital expenditure				
GDFCF	5.4	9.6	7.4	4.5
Grants and transfers	1.4	2.5	3.1	1.9
Total	6.8		10.5	
Capital balance	−6.0		−7.8	
Overall balance	−6.0		−9.9	

Note: 1. Percentages relate to total of current and capital receipts and to total of current and capital expenditure.

(Source: *UK National Accounts*, 1987, Table 9.1. Reprinted by permission of the Controller, HMSO.)

value of the flow of transactions for final goods in the economy; it meters the value of the trade in goods and services, where payment is made in exchange for the product or the service received. In stark contrast, transfer payments do not result from any transaction within this flow; they are payments received without the need to exchange any product, for example, state pensions, unemployment benefit, invalidity benefit and so on. They are simply transfers of income, taken as taxation from some sectors of society, and allocated as benefit payments to other sectors of society. They transfer purchasing power between groups in society – at its simplest, they perform the Robin Hood function of taking from the rich to give to the poor. Whether you are on Robin's side – or support the Sheriff of Nottingham – will depend largely upon which group enjoys your membership!

By convention, transfer payments (because there is no balancing transaction of production) are excluded from the measurement of GDP; hence they did not appear in our earlier tables. But, at £50.5 billion for 1986, or 30.4% of our new total for all aspects of government expenditure (plus a further £3.1 billion of capital expenditure), they are very much a major element in the government's planning of its expenditure, and therefore of its fiscal policy; hence the inclusion of this broader table in the text.

This method of treatment can and does create confusion. For example, a frequent accusation against 'profligate' public sector expenditure by its political opponents is that it amounts to 40% of GDP, which is indeed a dramatic and intuitively excessive figure. But, wait a minute, we said earlier that UK government expenditure had already been cut to 22% of GDP, which was only slightly above the 20% figure for three of our international comparisons. Which is the correct figure, 40% or 22%? Certainly, the total for government expenditure in Table 7.3 of £166.1 billion in 1986 does amount to 41.5% of GDP for that year – but how should this figure be interpreted? After all, the bulk of the difference lies in the existence of transfer payments, which are switches of income between groups in society, and do not really constitute a claim for public sector use of these sums. Is it fair to accuse even the most profligate of governments of spending pensions, or sickness, or unemployment benefits? Of the two figures, the 22% share of GDP is probably the more accurate reflection of the genuine public sector claim on resources. The rather more shocking figure of 40% is yet another example of how statistics can be presented to achieve almost any desired effect – and should help to instil in you a healthy scepticism about any form of quotation from 'official' statistics . . .

Returning to our analysis of Table 7.3, you may feel that the 22% share is still excessive; this may be so, but the data suggests that any excess is only marginal, relative to our main competitors – unless, of course, all governments are equally skilled in securing more than their fair share of shoulder space at the feeding trough!

Whatever the case, all government expenditure must be covered by income received by the government, or by borrowing to 'balance the books' for the year. Table 7.3 showed how taxation and National Insurance contributions are by far the main sources of income for the government, accounting for 87% of total receipts in 1976 and 90% in 1986. A further glance at the table will show that, despite the income contribution from other minor items such as rent, or interest and dividend receipts, when total receipts were compared to total expenditure for the year, the government was left to fund a deficit of £6.0 billion in 1976, and £9.8 billion in 1986. We hasten to add that this is not always the case; 1977 stands in magnificent isolation as the only year over the decade from 1976–86, when there was a current surplus in the UK national accounts – admittedly a surplus of only £861 million – but at least it proves that such an occurrence is possible! And, from provisional figures for 1987 and 1988, it would appear that the UK has moved into a clear surplus position for these years, to confirm that a current deficit is not necessarily a way of life for governments.

If we turn now to a closer consideration of the data on taxation receipts, the effect of government policy can be traced in the changing pattern of the taxation figures. Fiscal strategy over the decade from 1976–86 has reversed the relative importance of direct taxation and expenditure taxes, as income earners for the government. Direct taxation has fallen from 38.0% of total income in 1976 to 33.5% in 1986, with expenditure taxes rising from 32.6% to 39.9% to more than compensate. This reflects a firm Thatcherite belief that excessive direct taxation reduces incentive and blunts initiative – and therefore the potential for improvements in competitive efficiency and the rate of economic growth. When we discuss **supply-side economics** later in the book, we will explore the foundation for this belief. For the moment, we will simply state that there has been a substantial change in the pattern of taxation in an attempt to achieve the benefits identified above.

To remain even-handed in our treatment, we must also acknowledge that there have been strong counter-arguments to these changes in taxation policy. Direct taxation tends to be **progressive** in its impact, both in the sense that higher income earners will pay a greater absolute amount of taxation than lower income earners, *and* in the sense that most direct taxation systems place successive levels of earned income into a series of 'bands', with the marginal tax rate (that is, the rate of taxation levied on each band of income) rising through the bands. As a result, taxes are levied relatively more heavily on the richer sections of society, on the argument that these sections can more easily afford to carry the tax burden. In contrast, expenditure taxes are **regressive** in nature; they involve the same payment per unit purchased (as part of the market price of goods and services) by rich and poor alike, but will tend to weigh relatively more heavily on the lower income groups of society. Think about it; who is going to find the greater difficulty in paying the VAT element in the cost of a pair of shoes, Richard Branson or the widowed pensioner lady who lives down the street? Our intention is not to force you into a moral judgement, but simply to underline the fact that the same sum of money can have a vastly different importance to two consumers, where one is relatively rich, and the other relatively poor. Therefore, it has been argued that the switch in taxation policy towards a greater emphasis on regressive expenditure taxation has imposed social costs, as well as creating the potential for social benefits in the form of incentives for growth. Once again, it is important that the final policy decision is made in terms of the balance of *net* benefit, rather than on the inaccurate and tub-thumping rhetoric of gross benefit alone.

Table 7.4 allows us to compare the UK pattern of government current income receipts and expenditure with that of our four regular international competitors. Because of the differences in both fiscal philosphy and data presentation, it is not easy to make a straightforward comparison. Certainly it would appear that the UK places substantially more reliance on expenditure taxation than any of these other countries. Our figure of 39.9% of total government receipts lies well above the figures of 21.2% for the Netherlands, 25.9% for Japan, 26.6% for the USA, and 27.3% for West Germany (which could reflect the influence of relatively high taxation in the UK on items such as car tax, or customs and excise duties on alcoholic drinks and tobacco). At the same time, West Germany and the Netherlands appear to gather their funds for social security transfer payments more directly from their social security contributions, than is the case in the UK. Their contribution figures of 36.1% and 37.0% are well in excess of the UK figure of 16.7% – indeed our figure is still substantially lower than the USA's 22.9% of total receipts from this source. This, in turn, will tend to make the direct taxation burden relatively lower (since the UK relies more on this form of taxation to raise funds for social security payments), which is clearly the case for West Germany and the Netherlands. Possibly, a more accurate assessment of the contribution from direct taxation would be gained by adding together the figures for this and for social security contributions (on the grounds that both are normally deducted from earned income to leave **disposable income**). On this revised basis, the UK's figure of 50.2% of total income from this source compares with that of 62.4% for the Netherlands, 63.5% for West Germany, 64.6% for the USA and 68.6% for Japan – indicating that we diverge quite substantially from the fairly similar pattern in these other countries.

Some differences can also be traced in the pattern of expenditure between countries. This is most noticeable in the relative importance of social security benefits and grants; these amount to 46.2% of expenditure in the Netherlands, 41.5% in Japan, 32.9% in West Germany and 28.5% in the USA – compared to the UK figure of 30.4%. It is noticeable that in

Table 7.4 International comparison of current government income and outlay (1986).

	USA $ (billion)	%	Japan yen (billion)	%	West Germany D-M (billion)	%	Netherlands guilder (billion)	%
Receipts								
Direct taxes	546.3	41.7	31.3[1]	68.6	237.1	27.4	57.6	25.4
Indirect taxes	347.7	26.6	11.8	25.9	236.4	27.3	48.0	21.2
Social security contributions	300.4	22.9	—[1]	—	313.0	36.1	83.9	37.0
Others	115.0	8.8	2.5	5.5	79.8	9.2	37.3	16.4
Total	1,309.4	100.0	45.6	100.0	866.3	100.0	226.8	100.0
Expenditure								
Current consumption	778.6	52.3	32.6	36.1	381.7	46.0	68.2	29.4
Subsidies	26.3	1.8	3.7	4.1	40.7	4.9	7.7	3.3
Social security benefits and grants	425.0	28.5	37.5	41.5	273.5	32.9	107.2	46.2
Others	259.8	17.4	16.5	18.3	134.7	16.2	48.9	21.1
Total	1,489.7	100.0	90.3	100.0	830.6	100.0	232.0	100.0
Balance	−180.3		+13.2		+35.7		−5.2	

Note 1. Included in direct taxes figures; breakdown not given.

(Reprinted by permission of *OECD National Accounts*, 1988, Table 6 for each country.)

all countries (possibly rather more marked in the case of the UK) there has been a sharp increase in the relative importance of this item over the decade, reflecting the increase in numbers unemployed and, to a lesser extent, in the number of surviving pensioners. Government final consumption expenditure again varies in relative importance, with the UK figure of 46.3% of expenditure for 1986 lying somewhere in the middle of the range, as set by 29.4% for the Netherlands, and 52.3% by the USA.

For those cynics who doubt the ability of governments to live within their means, Table 7.4 shows that both West Germany and Japan achieved a healthy current surplus balance for 1986, while the Netherlands and the USA were in deficit. The Netherlands figure of £5.2 billion, or 1.4% of GDP, is relatively minor, but the very substantial deficit balance of $180.3 billion (or 5.7% of GDP) for the USA is part of a continuing trend in that country, and is the cause of some concern both to domestic USA observers, and to world financial markets in general.

Table 7.5 has been provided to give a little more depth of detail for those interested in the breakdown of some of the main items of revenue and expenditure for the government. From this you will see that, excluding transfer payments, education (£19.5 billion in 1986), the health service (£19.4 billion) and defence (£18.6 billion) are the three largest single categories of government expenditure, and make up collectively some 35.5% of total expenditure. This overall share is almost identical to that shown in the 1976 figures, but there has been some shuffling between the expenditure heads, with education being the main sufferer, falling from 13.5% of total expenditure in 1976 to 12.0% in 1986. Outside these main items of expenditure, the other expenditure headings have relatively minor and unchanging shares over the period. The main change in relative importance affected the housing and community amenity item, which fell from just under 9% of total expenditure in 1976 to 5.5% by 1986, reflecting the government's policy commitment to cut public sector investment in and associated subsidies given to housing (GDFCF fell from 40% to 20% of this category of expenditure over the period). The somewhat large figure of £18.8 billion for 'other' items of expenditure in the table is dominated by the £17.0 billion payment of debt interest due by the government (or 10.5% of government expenditure for the year).

It is noticeable that the largest single item of expenditure is the bill from the range of social security benefits, or transfer payments; this accounted for 30.9% of total expenditure in 1986, against its 24.2% share in 1976, reflecting a substantial increase over the period both in the numbers unemployed and in the numbers of people surviving to claim pensions from the state. It is a sobering thought, that if grants to universities and colleges had grown at the same rate as social security benefit payments (an increase of 3.5 times) or, to a lesser extent, defence over the period (2.7 times), then this textbook could have had three

Table 7.5 Analysis of government expenditure and taxation in UK (1986).

	£ (billion)	%
Expenditure		
General public services	6.8	4.2
Defence	18.6	11.5
Public order and safety	6.7	4.1
Education	19.5	12.0
Health	19.4	12.0
Social security	50.2	30.9
Housing and community amenities	8.0	4.9
Recreational and cultural affairs	2.2	1.4
Agriculture, forestry and fisheries	2.4	1.5
Mining, mineral resources and manufacturing	1.9	1.2
Transport and communication	3.7	2.3
Other economic affairs and services	3.8	2.3
Others	18.8	11.6
Total	162.2	100.0
Taxation on income		
Income tax		
Wages and salaries	34.1	23.8
Dividends, interest, rent	6.4	4.6
Social security benefits	1.3	0.9
Life assurance and mortgage relief	−4.2	−2.9
Petroleum revenue	2.7	1.9
Corporation tax	12.0	8.4
Social security contributions		
Employers	13.3	9.3
Employees	12.0	8.4
Self-employed and non-employed	0.8	0.6
Total	78.5	(54.7)
Taxes on expenditure		
Personal sector		
Durable goods	3.6	2.5
Other goods	22.1	15.4
Services (including rates)	14.1	9.8
Total	39.8	27.7

Table 7.5 (*cont.*)

	£ (billion)		%
Personal sector capital formation		1.8	1.2
Other sectors expenditure taxes			
Government			
Current	3.8		2.6
Capital formation	0.0	3.8	–
Companies and public corporations			
Current	14.5		10.1
Capital	1.6	16.1	1.1
Overseas			
Taxes on UK exports		0.8	0.6
Total expenditure taxes		62.3	(43.4)
Taxes on capital			
Death duties		0.9	0.6
Taxes on capital gains		1.6	1.1
Others		0.2	0.1
Total		2.7	(1.9)
Development land tax			
Capital transfers			
Total tax revenue		143.5	(100.0)
Income from			
Rent, interest, dividends and			
all other sources		12.8	
Total government income		156.3	

Note: totals may not conform to sum of individual values, due to rounding.
(Source: *UK National Accounts*, Tables 9.4 and 9.5. Reprinted by permission of the Controller, HMSO.)

authors, and could have been three times as long for you to read. We leave you to work out the net benefit in this case!

Switching our attention to the main items within taxation receipts, the table shows that income tax on wages and salaries at £34.1 billion in 1986, was the largest single revenue raiser for the government on the range of income taxes shown, with the other main direct taxation elements being social security contributions (that is, National Insurance) from employers and employees, totalling £25.3 billion, and corporation tax on firms of £12.0 billion. Other points of interest in this first category of direct taxation are the tax relief claimed on life assurance and mortgages (amounting to about one-eighth of the total of tax collected from private sector wages and salaries), and the contribution received from petroleum revenue taxation – although tax, price and activity level changes have reduced this source of income from its peak of £7.4 billion in 1985 to the much more modest total of £2.7 billion in 1986.

In terms of receipts from expenditure taxes, the table shows that these are drawn mainly from the private sector's expenditure on goods and services, and from the firms sector's current expenditure. Those of you with a grudge against the Chancellor's customs and excise duties on beer, wines, spirits and tobacco will find the £8.7 billion total raised by this contained within the £22.1 billion figure for 'other goods'. Those with a similar grudge towards local authority rates payments (soon to be replaced with the Poll Tax) will find the £6.5 billion raised from the private sector contained in the 'services' figure of £14.1 billion; you might even be interested to know that this private sector contribution amounted to 43% of total rates receipts of £15.1 billion for 1986. Indeed, this provides a timely reminder that all the tables deal with the combined data from central and local government, a fact which affects some items (for example, education which is mainly a local authority responsibility, and is one of the main expenditure claims on the grants which they receive from central government) rather more than others. To gain some idea of the size of the local government 'bite' overall, local authority expenditure amounted to 39% of government final consumption in 1986.

The relatively minor role played by taxes on capital is clearly shown in Table 7.5; in total, these raised £2.7 billion in 1986, mainly from taxes on capital gains and death duties.

It is easy to become lost amid such a wealth of statistical data. Perhaps it might be useful to summarize the main points which have emerged. Government expenditure (excluding transfer payments) currently amounts to about 22% of GDP in the UK. It is covered mainly by government receipts from taxation and other minor sources, such as rents, or interest and dividends received. The problems of controlling expenditure, of raising taxation revenue to pay for it (and, if necessary, of borrowing to cover the balance) are not just local difficulties which are experienced only in our incompetent UK economy. All countries face the same problems, must try to decide on priorities, and must make agonized choices between expenditure and taxation plans. In any country, the price of an electorally popular move to reduce the much resented taxation burden must always be paid in terms of the other elements in the equation; stark choices will have to be made in cutting expenditure plans for education, or health – or borrowing will have to be increased. Likewise, however well intentioned the desire to increase the funding for health, or education, or defence, or benefit payments such as pensions, invalidity allowance, or student grants, then the bill must be presented in the form of taxation increases – or increased borrowing. Given the bitterness of the pill, is it surprising that the borrowing option has been exercised to at least sweeten the taste, by governments of all political shades and in all countries?

With this sober point in mind, it is interesting to read Extract 7.1, which explores the fiscal dilemma which currently confronts the centrally planned Russian economy. It shows that, whatever the basis of the economic system, the harsh truth remains that wants and needs will always exceed available resources – a truth which provides economics with its foundation stone of the human dilemma. Given relative scarcity, choice is unavoidable. But what should we choose, and on what criteria should choice be based? And can we live with the consequences of that choice? The extract merely underlines the fiscal problems which face all governments, of whatever political colour. If there is a state, then there will be a flow of expenditures and a counterflow of taxation and other receipts; all policy decisions will have an effect on these flows, or on the financing of the difference between them.

Extract 7.1   THE ECONOMIST 8 OCTOBER 1988.

BUDGET PERESTROIKA

Russia now seems to have a much bigger budget deficit than America has. But is a communist deficit the same as a capitalist one?

FOR Russia to admit to serious budget worries is new. Put it all down to Mr Mikhail Gorbachev's reforms. *Glasnost* is producing greater openness about Soviet finances. And *perestroika*, or economic "restructuring", is making those finances even messier than they were before.

By some measurements Russia's budget deficit is now right up at Latin American levels, far above North American ones. Even under *glasnost*, Soviet officials release few figures, saying only that the situation is "alarming". But according to estimates by Plan-Econ, a research outfit in Washington, Russia's budget deficit rose from an annual average of 20 billion roubles ($32 billion at the official, distorted exchange rate) in 1980–85 to 55 billion roubles in 1986, 95 billion roubles in 1987, and perhaps 120 billion this year. As a share of Soviet GDP, PlanEcon reckons, the budget deficit has risen from under 3% in 1980–85 to about 14% this year. America's deficit is 3% of GDP.

Why has the Soviet deficit increased so dramatically? For the usual reasons. State spending in the Soviet Union rose by 9% a year (in nominal terms) in 1986–87, after annual rises of 4% in 1983–85; government receipts have hardly risen at all. Mr Gorbachev has been throwing money at his economic problems, investing heavily in an effort to modernise industry, and paying workers more to win their support.

Still, the differences between President Gorbachev's budget difficulties and President Reagan's (or President Bushaki's) matter more than the similarities:

Spending. Almost the entire Soviet economy is state-owned, so compared with America the state has many more bills to pay. It supports a massive bureaucracy, finances most investment and pays out billions of roubles in subsidies for food and for loss-making enterprises. This difference in the scale of the public sector helps to explain why defence looms so large in America's budget (28% of outlays in 1987) and yet, according to official figures, is fairly small in Russia's. Another reason is that Soviet statistics have been doctored to hide the true size of military spending, much of which is concealed under other headings, and with understated prices for military equipment.

Revenues. In America nearly half of all federal receipts in 1987 came from income taxes. In the Soviet Union less than one-tenth did. Far more important to Russia are the so-called "turnover taxes" on consumer goods. Turnover taxes are especially high on alcohol—which is why Mr Gorbachev's anti-vodka campaign has left a big hole in the public finances. Taxes on booze brought in some 12% of state revenues in 1984, the year before Mr Gorbachev came to power, but only about 9% last year.

Bridging the gap. Unlike the dollar, the rouble is not a convertible currency. So Mr Gorbachev cannot rely on an inflow of foreign capital to make his books balance (although high-priced sales of consumer imports from the West could help boost revenues quite a bit). The central bank simply has to print more roubles. The result is inflation, either suppressed (longer queues) or open (higher prices). As the budget deficit widens, both problems are growing worse.

What is to be done?

The Soviet press is beginning to come clean about inflation, which until recently, officially, barely existed in Russia. Now it is recognised that inflation is already far more serious than previously admitted.

Mr Gorbachev and his advisers have some brave ideas for cutting spending and boosting revenues. The problem is timing. Can new policies bite quickly enough to avoid a big burst of inflation?

On the expenditure side, the aim is to slash spending on bureaucrats and on loss-making factories. Millions of bureaucrats are to be redeployed to work that produces wealth instead of stifling it. Factories will have to cover their own costs, or eventually be closed down. In the new, cost-conscious climate, wage rises should be linked closely to rises in productivity. Cuts in defence spending should be possible if a

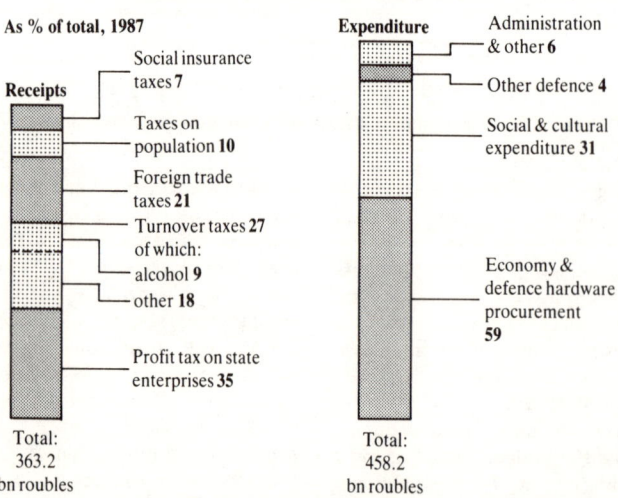

deal reducing conventional forces in Europe can be worked out. But both a new deal on arms and a new efficiency in the economy are likely to take years, if they can be achieved at all.

On the revenue side, the anti-alcohol campaign is being relaxed slightly. Mr Gorbachev is hoping to increase output of (and hence tax revenue from) other types of consumer goods much faster than he has managed so far: more cars, and more privately produced (ie, non-subsidised) food. The good idea of selling off state housing is gaining support, as is the more dubious one of selling imports of consumer goods at a fat mark-up.

Optimists hope that this mix of policies will do the job: the budget will be brought under control; Mr Gorbachev will introduce his price reform in 1990-91 as planned; and as promised he will do so without making anybody poorer. The more likely outcome is that painful price rises will be unavoidable. If so, Mr Gorbachev will have to decide whether to try to suppress them with artificial controls, or to bring about much freer markets and what would amount to an open devaluation of the rouble. He will be wiser to choose the latter.

Reprinted with permission from *The Economist* 8 October 1988 © *The Economist*.

FISCAL POLICY: THE KEYNESIAN CONTEXT

Fiscal policy, for any government, will therefore involve a careful weighing of priorities, an ability to choose between desired alternative policy options, and a clear awareness of the short and longer term consequences of any given policy action. From the previous section it would appear that any government must make its expenditure – or its taxation – plans within the general constraint that the two sides of the equation are kept broadly in balance. This conforms to the traditional view (and, to a lesser extent, to the current UK government philosphy) that the state is no different from the average household; both must learn to live within their means and to try to avoid overspending, which can only be covered by borrowing and debt.

But this, in turn, could create problems for the government in the pursuit of its normal macroeconomic policy objectives. For example, most governments would at least pay lip service (and some would genuinely subscribe) to a set of objectives which would include the achievement of:

- Relative price stability and the avoidance of the problems of price inflation;
- A satisfactory rate of economic growth, with the safeguards and improvements this implies for general prosperity;
- A position of broad 'external' balance in trading relationships with other nations, to minimize the risk of disruption to the domestic economy from exchange rate and interest rate problems;
- Reasonably full employment.

A little thought would show that these policy objectives will not always and automatically be achieved; the tide of economic events is likely to frustrate one or more of the objectives. In times of prosperity, employment may well be high, but, as the boom phase develops, excess demand pressures are likely to drive prices upwards and, by drawing imports into the country, create a deficit in external trade (imports exceeding exports). Conversely, as demand pressures decline during recession and depression, it may be possible to achieve a greater degree of price stability and a better external balance – but, at the same time, unemployment is also likely to rise to uncomfortable levels.

At the root of the problem lies the fact that, even if we simplify matters by excluding the longer term objective of economic growth, there is a substantial degree of inherent conflict between policy objectives. It is almost a rule of thumb that improvement in some objectives can only be achieved at the cost of unacceptable deterioration in others – particularly if one single objective is pursued excessively. For example, it has been argued that attempts to achieve and maintain unrealistically high levels of employment over the 1960s were the root cause of much of the inflationary pressure and our subsequent loss of international price competitiveness in the 1970s. Equally, in the early 1980s, the policies which were designed to squeeze price inflation from the UK economic system have been blamed for prolonging and possibly exacerbating the severity of that depression in the UK, with its post-war record levels of unemployment.

Returning to the fiscal debate, if a government were simply to try to hold a broad balance between expenditure and taxation, this would leave it in a purely passive position – both with respect to its response to the changing tides of economic events (the ebb and flow of which can be traced in the course of the various extracts used in the book) and with respect to its ability to achieve its stated policy objectives. Indeed, if it tries mindlessly to balance its budget, this could have a positively damaging effect on the economy. As the level of economic activity rises when the economy is moving into boom, so too will the government's receipts from taxation on incomes, expenditure and business profits. If the government were to take this opportunity to raise its own level of expenditure (possibly by implementing plans which were postponed from earlier periods) alongside the rising flow of taxation receipts, then this would *add* to the already strong demand pressures, and could well contribute to the conflict of objectives and the resultant policy problems which would be generated by that boom. Conversely, as the economy moves into recession, easing the pressures on the policy objectives for inflation and external balance, the employment position will normally deteriorate; and, if the government sought to reduce its expenditure plans to reflect the falling taxation revenues from the lower level of economic activity, this withdrawal of demand would further weaken the capacity utilization position within the economy, and *exacerbate* the problems associated with depression.

During the major depression of the late 1920s and early 1930s there developed a belief that fiscal passivity was unnecessary, even undesirable.

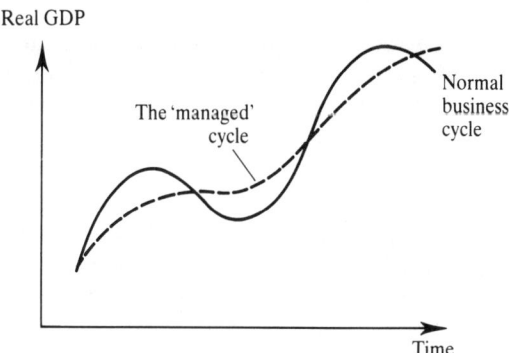

Figure 7.1 The 'managed' business cycle.

It was argued that the government could use the powers provided by instruments such as fiscal policy to influence the tide of economic events. If, during the drift into recession and depression in the business cycle, the root cause of the problem lies in an inadequate level of aggregate demand, then the government should attempt to raise this, and stimulate a recovery towards a higher level of economic activity. This might well create a temporary fiscal imbalance, if policy measures resulted in expenditure exceeding tax revenue. But the borrowing involved could be repaid at a later date, from future budget surplus periods. Given the cycle, if excessive aggregate demand was the predominant characteristic of the later stages of the boom phase, then the government could counter and correct this by manipulating its own expenditure and revenue plans, in a deliberate attempt to damp down the growth in demand, and so ease the pressures on the economy; for example, it could reduce its own level of expenditure, or demand, creating a situation of fiscal surplus.

In essence, the argument here (described as 'Keynesian' economics, but also reflecting contemporary theoretical developments in Scandinavia[2]) was that fiscal policy, far from being passive, should be contra-cyclical. Rather than going along with the cycle, the government should 'lean against' it. The conceptual results of such a use of fiscal policy are shown in Figure 7.1. This shows the familiar pattern of economic activity which is associated with the business cycle, where a series of booms alternate with a series of slumps or depressions. Keynesian economists argued (and here it must be stressed that this view, while based on the seminal contribution of the *General Theory of Employment, Interest and Money* written by John Maynard Keynes and published in 1936, was more accurately attributable to the consensus which emerged from the work of several generations of economists and practitioners over the 1950s and 1960s) that it was possible to control and 'flatten' this path of fluctuations

---

2. In fact, Sweden in 1935 was the first country to run a deliberate fiscal deficit, as a result of its own academic debate on this issue. The UK, admittedly delayed by the disruption of the war, followed a decade later.

for the economy. If fiscal policy was used to reduce excessive demand pressure during periods of boom, and to stimulate and revitalize demand during recessions, then a **managed cycle** would result. This, in turn, would minimize the social costs of inflation during the boom phases of the cycle, and of unemployment during the slumps. Further, it was argued, if the cycle could be controlled and made less volatile in this manner, there would result a much higher average level of capacity utilization in the economy, which could reduce the perceived degree of uncertainty and risk associated with investment, encouraging the latter and permitting a faster rate of economic growth.

It is difficult now, in the more cynical and self-seeking 1980s, to understand the degree of excitement and conviction felt by protagonists of these **demand management** policies. In place of the previous helplessness in the face of economic fluctuations, there was a new belief that the level of economic activity could be influenced – even controlled – by careful and consistent use of the fiscal policy instrument, to the benefit of all. To understand the basis of this belief, it is important that we return to our model of the macroeconomy and use this to trace how the process of influence and adjustment was perceived to operate.

THE BASIC FISCAL MODEL

What did demand management policy involve and, within this, what was the role for fiscal policy? It is possible, with the benefit of hindsight, to produce a simplified and conceptual framework, which provides a fairly accurate description of the system of control and influence, as it was envisaged to operate by Keynesian policy makers of the time.

- Firstly, the government had to take responsibility for defining a coherent and feasible set of macroeconomic policy objectives and for deriving a clear set of policy targets for the economy from these;
- Next, it would use the results from available macroeconomic forecasts to identify the current position of the economy and its likely future movement from this;
- By comparing these forecasts to the policy targets, then it would be possible to estimate the probable gap between events and the desired position for the economy;
- Given this gap, the forecasting models could be used to simulate the probable effects of different fiscal policy corrections, and therefore to select the best fiscal strategy;
- Finally, this fiscal strategy could be implemented, to adjust the level of aggregate demand and to correct or to influence the path of the economy towards its desired policy targets.

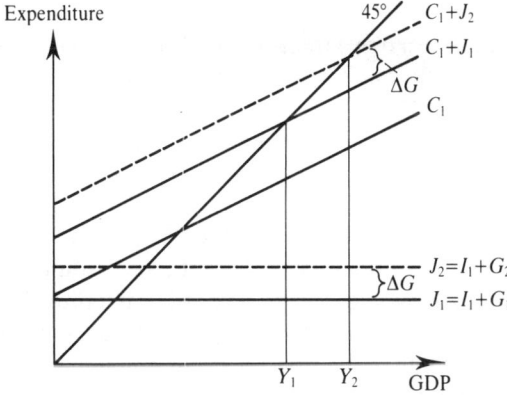

Figure 7.2 Fiscal reflation: increase in government expenditure.

Clearly, all of this implied a readiness to intervene in the workings of the economy, taken with a belief that aggregate demand could be influenced *and* that the manipulation of aggregate demand would trigger a controlled response from the economy. It is possible to use our basic model to trace the foundations upon which these beliefs were based.

For the sake of simplifying the analysis which follows, exclude the foreign trade sector from our conceptual macroeconomic system; this leaves us to deal with the domestic households, firms and government sectors. As always, equilibrium will occur where the output available is just sufficient to satisfy the expenditure plans of these sectors, so that the model will adjust towards the GDP level where:

$$Y = C + I + G$$

The righthand side of the question represents aggregate demand, or the total of all demands in the simplified economy. The government can influence this in either or both of two ways.

Firstly, it can influence aggregate demand *directly*. Since government expenditure is a component of aggregate demand, any deliberate changes in the level of government expenditure will raise or lower the level of the injections function and, through this, the level of the $C + J$ or aggregate demand function. For example, let us assume that the government's policy need is to *reflate* the economy, that is, to raise the level of economic activity. Figure 7.2 illustrates how this might be achieved; to raise the level of economic activity, if the government raises its own expenditure from G_1 to G_2, then this will cause the injections function to rise from J_1 to J_2, with the vertical movement representing the increase in government expenditure (ΔG). As a result, the aggregate demand function will rise from $C_1 + J_1$ to its new higher position of

$C_1 + J_2$ (with the vertical distance between the two functions again reflecting the increase in government expenditure, ΔG). This increase in aggregate demand will cause the economy to move from its old equilibrium position of Y_1 to the new higher equilibrium level of GDP represented by Y_2. The government has directly influenced the level of aggregate demand and has caused the economy to reflate by raising its own level of expenditure.

Conversely, if the government's policy need was to cause the level of economic activity to contract, or *deflate*, then it would simply reverse the above procedure. It would cut its level of expenditure, which would cause the injections function to move downwards by the amount of the ΔG adjustment; this would cause the aggregate demand function to fall, which would move the ecomony to a new and lower level of GDP. Simply run the model, as illustrated in Figure 7.2, in reverse – so that the economy would move from Y_2 to Y_1.

A second possibility is that the government could influence the level of demand *indirectly* by influencing the expenditure plans of either (or both) the households' or the firms' sector. Let's assume again that the government wishes to *reflate* the economy, that is, to cause the level of economic activity to rise; this might well be its perceived policy need, in response to an economic forecast that the economy was heading into recession.

For example, assume that the government wishes to reflate by indirectly influencing the level of *investment* expenditure (or *I* in the basic model). A number of options exist. One possibility would be to use taxation policy; if business taxation rates were reduced, or if taxation allowances were increased to reduce the burden of business taxation, then after-tax business profits would be greater. This would not only provide more internal funds from which investment expenditure could be drawn; it would also raise the net of tax profit stream in investment appraisal calculations for new ventures, which would raise the internal rate of return values for these, which would cause the demand function for investment funds to move to the right. Even at an unchanged user cost of capital there would be an increase in the level of investment. A similar effect would be gained if larger grants were awarded to defray the effective cost of the capital outlay of an investment project, or other allowances made (for example increasing the permissible rate of charging depreciation of the asset against taxable profits) to defray the burden of taxation on new ventures. Again, these would raise the internal rate of return (net of tax) on new ventures, moving the demand function for investment funds to the right, and increasing the level of investment expenditure against any given rate of interest.

Whichever method was used, the effect, in terms of the basic model, would be identical to that illustrated in Figure 7.2 – with the difference being that it would be an increase in investment (ΔI) which would cause the injection function to rise from J_1 to J_2 (in other words, J_2 would now comprise $I_2 + G_1$). As before, the upwards revision in the level of the injection function would cause the level of aggregate demand to rise, and would push the economy from the original equilibrium position of Y_1 to the higher level of GDP represented by Y_2. Once again, fiscal policy has been used to influence the level of aggregate demand – but this time it has operated indirectly, by seeking to encourage investment and to increase expenditure plans in this sector.

While the process of indirect influence of investment expenditure plans could be reversed to deflate or reduce the level of economic activity, it must be remembered that a lower level of investment would have adverse long-term repercussions on economic growth and, possibly, international competitiveness. It is therefore unlikely that the government would deliberately select investment expenditure as a target for deflationary fiscal policy, when the intent is to force the level of economic activity to contract.[3]

A second possibility for indirect influence would be to use fiscal policy to manipulate households' *consumption* expenditure plans, as the remaining element of aggregate demand; this could be achieved through the government's influence over the amount of income available for consumption expenditure. Up till now we have treated consumption as being functionally related to GDP, that is, we have used a consumption function of the form:

$$C = a + cY$$

This was permissible only so long as there was no government sector. When we add the public sector to our model, we must recognize that this introduces household taxation into our simplified economic system. As a result, not all of the income earned from factor payments (which, you will remember, was one of the flows from which we could measure GDP) will be available for allocation to consumption and to saving. In short, we must now recognize that consumption expenditure is functionally related to **disposable income**, which we can define as:

> the income which remains for households after all adjustments for taxation and transfer payments have been made.

It might help if we set this down a little more formally; we have now revised the consumption function to the form:

---

3. In passing, it is worth noting that just such an adverse result could follow from a side-effect of *monetary* policy; if short-term interest rates are raised to discourage consumption expenditure – as has been the case over 1988 and 1989 – this could affect longer term interest rates and, through these, cause a downward revision on investment plans. CBI surveys of investment intentions have shown a steady downward trend in response to the government's clearly stated intention to hold interest rates high until inflation is brought under control again.

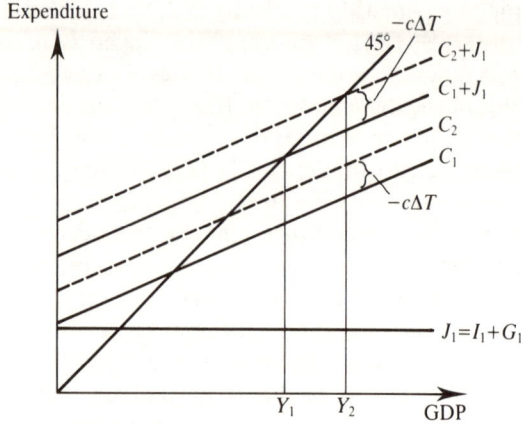

Figure 7.3 Fiscal reflation: reduction in lump sum taxation.

$$C = a + cY_d$$

where Y_d is the symbol for disposable income. Disposable income, in turn, is simply:

$$Y_d = Y - T + B$$

where Y represents the normal factor incomes from all sources as derived from GDP, T represents all forms of taxation payment charged on households (including local government taxes, such as the old system of rates payments, and the new 'Poll Tax', or Community Charge, as well as normal central government taxes), and B represents all the income paid to households in the form of transfer payments, such as pensions, student grants, unemployment benefit, invalidity benefit and so on.

We can now trace the possible methods of indirect influence of consumption expenditure through fiscal policy. Once again, if our illustrative government wants to reflate the economy, it can do so in either of two ways. Firstly, it can reduce the tax payments due to be made by households, for example, by reducing National Insurance contributions, or increasing tax allowances. Secondly, it can raise the sums due to be received in the form of benefit or transfer payments, for example, by increasing pension rates, or raising the range of rates applied in the calculation of all other benefits. In either case, with T falling, or B rising, disposable income is increased. Figure 7.3 traces the response of the economy to such changes. The increase in disposable income results in an increase in consumption spending over the same range of GDP; the consumption function rises from C_1 to C_2. This, in turn, raises the aggregate demand function from $C_1 + J_1$ to $C_2 + J_1$. The effect of the taxation or benefit payment adjustment is therefore to make the economy expand from its initial equilibrium position of Y_1 to a higher level of economic activity, as represented by Y_2. Once again, fiscal policy has been used to reflate the economy, using the influence which the government has on disposable income to trigger a revision of consumption expenditure plans.[4]

Should the intention be to deflate the economy, for example in response to a set of economic forecasts which predict an excessive level of demand, then the government would attempt to *reduce* the level of disposable income available to households, either by raising the burden of taxation, or by reducing the flow of income from benefit payments. The response of the economy can be followed by running the model of Figure 7.3 in reverse; the consumption function would fall, causing a downwards revision in the aggregate demand function, and a contraction in the level of economic activity.

THE FISCAL MULTIPLIERS

The above section shows how the government can influence the level of aggregate demand, either directly through G, or indirectly by seeking to influence expenditure plans for C and I. The basic model allows us to predict the direction of the response but, as yet, can say little about the *quantitative* results of the policy action. If, for example, the government wishes to raise the level of GDP by £100 million, must it raise its own level of expenditure by this amount? Or raise benefit payments by that amount? Or reduce taxation by that amount? Indeed, does it matter which of the three options it chooses?

To explore these questions, we must return to the concept of the multiplier. Fiscal policy action, whether it takes the form of an increase in G (or B) or a reduction in T represents a disturbance to the macroeconomy; this will trigger an adjustment process, during which the effect of the initial disturbance will be magnified. In other words, the impact of the fiscal adjustment will be augmented by the existence of the multiplier. Look again at either Figure 7.2 or 7.3. Compare the size of the disturbance (the vertical movement in the function concerned) with the size of the resultant change in GDP (the movement along the horizontal axis); in each case, the final change in GDP is greater, because of the operation of the multiplier.

It is a relatively simple matter to show this in algebraic form. If we continue to use the simplified economic system where, in equilibrium:

---

4. An alternative (but rather more complex) source of reflation would be that the government increases disposable income by cutting the rate of income tax. This too would have the effect of moving the consumption function upwards – however, this would take the form of a pivot, with the consumption function remaining anchored at its existing intercept on the vertical axis (after all, at zero income there will be no benefit from a change in tax rates). For illustrative purposes, the more simple 'lump sum' tax or benefit change has been used in Figure 7.3.

210 Understanding the Economy

$$Y = C + I + G$$

and keep consumption functionally related to disposable income, or

$$C = a + cY_d$$

with disposable income still taking the form

$$Y_d = Y - T + B$$

then, by substitution

$$C = a + cY - cT + cB$$

and, substituting this into our opening equation,

$$Y = a + cY - cT + cB + I + G$$

This can be rearranged, by collecting all the Y terms on the lefthand side, to the form

$$Y - cY = a - cT + cB + I + G$$

This, in turn, can be simplified to

$$Y(1 - c) = a - cT + cB + I + G$$

Dividing both sides by $(1 - c)$ leaves us with a familiar multiplier type of formulation,

$$Y = \frac{1}{1 - c} \times (a - cT + cB + I + G)$$

If any of the terms within the brackets change, then this will cause the income level to change; the relationship between the initial disturbance and the final overall change in income will be influenced by the size of the multiplier.

For instance, if G rises from say 50 to 60 then, given a marginal propensity to consume of 0.8:

$$\Delta Y = \frac{1}{1 - c} \times \Delta G$$

$$= \frac{1}{1 - 0.8} \times (+10)$$

$$= \frac{1}{0.2} \times (+10)$$

$$= 5 (+10)$$

$$= +50$$

In other words, an increase in government expenditure of 10 will cause the income level to rise by 50, since the value of the multiplier is 5 in this illustration. More formally, the **government expenditure multiplier** is:

$$k_g = \frac{1}{1-c}$$
$$= 5$$

given the above value of 0.8 for the marginal propensity to consume.

Where does this leave us in answering our opening question: by how much should government expenditure be increased, to raise GDP by £100 million? We can now find the answer to this question by a simple rearrangement of our basic formula: given that

$$\Delta Y = k_g \times \Delta G$$

we are left with

$$\Delta G = \frac{\Delta Y}{k_g}$$

Given that the desired increase in GDP is £100 million, and that the illustrative value of our government expenditure multiplier is 5, then

$$\Delta G = \frac{100}{5}$$
$$= 20$$

In other words, an increase of £20 million in government expenditure will activate the normal multiplier adjustment, which exists in any economic system, and (in terms of our simple illustrative model[5]) raise GDP by £100 million to its target level. Our simple model shows that we can not only predict the direction of the response of the economy; we can also control the extent of that response through the size of the fiscal adjustment.

Returning to our opening series of questions, would a reduction in

---

5. The simple multiplier value is exaggerated, because it only takes account of the leakage in savings from each round of expenditure and income generation. In reality, the formulation for the multiplier is rather more complex and builds in a whole series of additional leakages to each round of expenditure and income generation, reflecting direct taxation charged on earned income, expenditure taxation charged on consumption, import content of expenditure, and the loss (or gain, if deflation is involved) of income from benefit payments, as the level of unemployment falls (or rises, in the case of deflation). These additional leakages have the effect of weakening the value of the multiplier, here illustrated at 5, to somewhere between 1.25 and 1.50. Clearly, with a smaller multiplier value, the ΔG needed for a given ΔY will be *greater* than is implied by the text of the chapter – without in any way altering the basic principles discussed in the latter.

taxation of £20 million secure the same effect? To answer this, we must return to our original formulation and examine it in more depth. If:

$$Y = \frac{1}{1-c} \times (a - cT + cB + I + G)$$

then we can identify two important points which follow from the term $(-cT)$ within the brackets above. Firstly, income will move in the opposite direction to that of the taxation adjustment; hence the minus sign. Secondly, and probably less obvious at first sight, only a proportion of the increase in disposable income caused by the decrease in taxation, will pass though into extra consumption expenditure; this follows from the presence of the marginal propensity to consume in the term. If you are struggling a little with this formal analysis, retreat back to your commonsense. What would your own response to a tax rebate? You would probably add it to your normal earned income, and treat it in the same fashion as this; for most people (excepting the author's wife!) this would involve saving a proportion of the tax rebate, then spending the residual proportion on consumption.

Thus, if taxation is reduced by £20 million, for example, by cuts in National Insurance contributions, or local government taxation payments:[6]

$$\Delta Y = \frac{1}{1-c} \times (-c\Delta T)$$

$$= \frac{1}{1-c}(-0.8 \times -20)$$

$$= \frac{1}{1-c}(+16)$$

This is an extremely important result; due to the savings leakage, only £16 million of the £20 million tax cut would pass through into additional expenditure, creating the disturbance which activates the multiplier adjustment. If we run through our model to its conclusion then, with the value of the multiplier still at 5, the tax cuts of £20 million would only

---

6. Changes in the rate of income tax trigger a rather more complex multiplier process and response from the economy, and are ignored for this introductory treatment. But the *direction* of the response will be as before. For example, assume that the taxation rate is reduced: as described in footnote 4 on p. 207, this will cause the consumption function to pivot upwards (taxation will only affect the cY_d term, not the intercept a), which will cause the aggregate demand function also to pivot upwards, which will cause the economy to move to a new and higher equilibrium level of GDP. Get out a pencil and a piece of paper and draw the model to show this (or, conversely, to show the effect of an increase in taxation).

cause the level of GDP to rise by £80 million, which is short of the intended increase of £100 million.

In technical jargon, economists say that the £1 of taxation cuts is less **high powered** than the £1 of government expenditure. This is *not* a political point! We are simply drawing attention to the fact that, while the entire amount of government expenditure passes through into the multiplier adjustment process, only a *proportion* of taxation cuts will do so, due to the fact that the latter operate on disposable income, and are therefore subject to the leakage represented by the marginal propensity to save.

It is possible to show the same effect in a different manner; if we return to the equation

$$\Delta Y = \frac{1}{1 - c} \times -c\Delta T$$

then this can be rearranged into the form

$$\Delta Y = \frac{-c}{1 - c} \times \Delta T$$

For the normal value of the marginal propensity to consume of 0.8, we can now recalculate the value of the **taxation multiplier** (k_t)

$$k_t = \frac{-c}{1 - c}$$
$$= \frac{-0.8}{1 - 0.8}$$
$$= \frac{-0.8}{0.2}$$
$$= -4$$

Thus, we can predict the effect of reducing taxation by £20 million:

$$\Delta Y = k_t \times \Delta T$$
$$= -4 \, (-20)$$
$$= £80 \text{ million}$$

More important, we can now calculate the necessary cuts in taxation which would raise the level of GDP by £100 million. If:

$$\Delta Y = k_t \times \Delta T$$

then

$$\Delta T = \frac{\Delta Y}{k_t}$$

$$= \frac{100}{-4}$$

$$= -25$$

In other words, to cause the level of GDP to rise by £100 million, taxation cuts of £25 million would have to be made; these would trigger the multiplier adjustment which would raise the level of GDP by the desired amount.

These different multiplier values can be used to illustrate an interesting proposition, known as the **balanced budget theorem**. This explores what would happen if government expenditure and taxation receipts were changed by the same amount, for example, if expenditure and taxation were both raised by, say, 10. Clearly, the government expenditure change would raise the level of income; at the same time, the increase in taxation would reduce the level of income. Would the effects cancel out? In fact they would not. Income would rise by 50 from the charge in government expenditure (or 5 times 10); to offset this, income would fall by 40 from the increase in taxation (or minus 4 times 10). The net effect would be that income would rise overall by the amount of the change in government expenditure, reflecting the stronger fiscal multiplier for the latter. More formally,

$$\Delta Y = k_g \times \Delta G + k_t \times \Delta T$$

$$= \frac{1}{1-c} \times \Delta G + \frac{-c}{1-c} \times \Delta T$$

Since $\Delta G = \Delta T$, that is, both change by the same amount and in the same direction, then

$$\Delta Y = \frac{1}{1-c} \times \Delta G + \frac{-c}{1-c} \times \Delta G$$

$$= \Delta G \left(\frac{1}{1-c} - \frac{c}{1-c} \right)$$

$$= \Delta G \left(\frac{1-c}{1-c} \right)$$

$$= \Delta G$$

That is, GDP will rise by the amount of the increase in government expenditure.

In terms of the simple fiscal model used in this section, one of the implications for the balanced budget theorem is that a neutral budget, where balanced changes are made in G and T, would *not* have a neutral effect on income. The income level would move in the same direction and to the same value as the change in government expenditure, because of its relatively stronger fiscal multiplier.

In rather less depth, fiscal changes which involve benefit payments will face a similar leakage to the taxation cuts case; once again the reason for this is that the change in benefit payment affects disposable income, and is therefore subject to savings as well as expenditure plans. In terms of a basic formula, if

$$Y = \frac{1}{1-c} \times (a - cT + cB + I + G)$$

then

$$\Delta Y = \frac{1}{1-c} \times c\Delta B$$

or,

$$= \frac{c}{1-c} \times \Delta B$$

But note that there is no minus sign this time; GDP will respond in the same direction as the change made to benefit payments. As before, the equation can be rearranged into a formula for a separate benefit multiplier k_b, where:

$$k_b = \frac{c}{1-c}$$

However, there are grounds for suspecting that the marginal propensity to consume for those in receipt of the increase in benefit payments would be higher than the marginal propensity to consume of the community as a whole; benefit recipients are likelier to be living closer to the poverty line and are therefore unlikely to be able to save as much from the extra disposable income as would be the normal case. Indeed, it is possible that their marginal propensity to consume could be close to unity (that is, their marginal propensity to save could approach zero), in which case the value of k_b could be very similar to that of the standard multiplier value of k_g. Depending upon the value allocated, it is possible to rearrange the fiscal formula for benefit change to allow an estimation of the amount of benefit increase which would be needed to raise GDP by the desired amount.

Simply to illustrate the process, assume that benefit recipients have a marginal propensity to consume of $c' = 0.9$; our fiscal formula would become

$$\Delta Y = \frac{c'}{1-c} \times \Delta B$$

with

$$k_b = \frac{0.9}{1 - 0.8}$$
$$= 4.5$$

Given this information,

$$\Delta Y = k_b \times \Delta B$$

and

$$\Delta B = \frac{100}{4.5}$$
$$= 22.2 \text{ million}$$

In other words, an increase in benefit payments of £22,222,222 (plus 22 pence for those of you who believe in real accuracy!) would activate a multiplier expansion which would raise the level of GDP by the desired £100 million.

FISCAL POLICY: THE LESSONS OF EXPERIENCE

Where does all of this technical analysis leave us? Conceptually at least, it suggests that fiscal policy could be a powerful policy instrument through which to influence and control the dynamic path of the economy. Given a coherent and feasible set of policy targets, forecasts could be used to define the gap between the actual and the desired state of economy. Any necessary correction could be achieved by fiscal policy, using this either to manipulate the level of aggregate demand directly (via changes in government expenditure), or indirectly (via the effect of taxation changes on consumption and investment expenditure). Normally, several options would be available, each with its own process of multiplier adjustment. The government could then select the course of action which seemed most suitable, or efficient, in the circumstances.

At this stage, you should be able to appreciate some of the

enthusiasm and commitment felt by Keynesian economists over the 1950s and 1960s. What an incredible weapon of economic planning appeared to be in their hands! If it could be made to work as well in practice as was suggested by theory models, a whole new era of controlled economic progress would open up. During the initial period of enthusiasm for demand management policies, there can be little doubt that many economists felt that fiscal policy represented a major and exciting new breakthrough. With this new policy instrument, anything was possible. A contemporary leading economist (A.R. Prest in 1968) was driven to remark on this degree of confidence which existed; the predominant view, he suggested, was one of '101% certainty of the rightness of Keynesian principles, and 99% certainty of their practicality'.

It is always cheap and easy, from the advantaged position of hindsight, to dismiss such a viewpoint as 'naive', and even dangerous. But these people were at the very beginning of a major new learning curve, when both enthusiasm and confidence would most naturally be at its maximum. It takes years of trial and error to accumulate from practical experience a more balanced and, generally, less dogmatic view of the new policy measures. What works in theory does not always translate into practice in the more complex world of reality.

By now you should be accustomed to retreating into a commonsense check on new material. Let's check back through the three main stages of practical demand management, as outlined above. Firstly, how realistic is it to expect that any government's policy objectives will always be clear, coherent and feasible – and capable of being interpreted into a series of achievable and quantified targets? Extract 7.2 makes sobering reading. Even allowing for the distortion effect of politicians seeking to stimulate interest and win support, and their willingness to promise anything, to postpone and tidy away all the difficult decisions until it's too late for the electorate to change their mind, the confusion and unreality of objectives which emerge from this atmosphere are all too depressingly familiar in most countries. Is the government always likely to have a clear view of what we should be trying to do – or even of what we are probably capable of doing? Short-term political horizons pose very real problems for framing and implementing long-term strategies. It is all too easy to let objectives degenerate into bland and meaningless genuflections – or to be hyped up by a frenzied PR exercise, into targets which have little real possibility of independent, let alone joint achievement.

Secondly, even if we have a clear and consistent set of targets, how realistic is it to expect that economic forecast results will always provide simple and uncomplicated guidance to policy makers? Different forecasting groups run different simulation models, use different assumptions, make different educated guesses – and may even have differing access to provisional data. In Chapter 3, we have already illustrated how the ongoing stream of forecast publications from the different teams will

Extract 7.2 FINANCIAL TIMES 2 NOVEMBER 1988.

Economic issues in the US election

THERE THEY GO AGAIN

Benjamin Friedman

Remember Ronald Reagan's promise to balance the budget by 1983? And to do so despite cutting taxes, beefing up America's defences and, above all, keeping Social Security benefits sacrosanct?

Here we go again. The Republican platform assures us that "with the help of the Gramm-Rudman Law and a flexible spending freeze, a balanced budget can be expected by 1993." But it gives no clue to what part of spending would be flexible and what would be frozen except that, once again, Social Security is sacrosanct, and that it is the Democrats who are soft on defence spending.

The Democratic platform says: "Reducing the deficit requires that the wealthy and corporations pay their fair share and that we restrain Pentagon spending." But it gives not a hint about what that fair share is, and the further discussion of defence contains no proposals that can be translated into budget savings.

To make matters worse, as the election campaign has unfolded, both Vice President George Bush and Governor Michael Dukakis have presented their respective lists of new government initiatives for the 1990s. Each will only make the Government's fiscal imbalance even wider.

Both Mr Bush's lack of specifics and Mr Dukakis's emphasis on "competence" suggest that, whoever wins, the next administration's approach to narrowing the budget deficit will primarily consist of another well-intended attack on the traditional three-headed monster Wastefraudandabuse. Surely no informed American voter expects this battle to enable the new President to balance the budget by 1993 any more than David Stockman's "magic asterisk" – billions of dollars of "future savings to be identified" – enabled Mr Reagan to do so by 1983.

Meanwhile, the election campaign is nearly over and no one has forced the candidates to address the real economic issue the US now faces. Since 1980 the federal government's borrowing has absorbed nearly three fourths of the net saving done by all American families and all American businesses combined.

This chronic fiscal imbalance, not pointless disagreements over how many jobs have been or are likely to be created, ought to have been the real issue in this year's campaign. Under current US tax and spending policies, the deficit will only widen further – except to the extent that the Social Security system's growing surplus offsets part of it. And to use the Social Security surplus to finance an ever larger deficit in the Government's other operations, rather than to build up a sizeable trust fund as it was intended to, will only solve one problem by creating another. Without the growing trust fund balance, the only way to cope with the baby boom generation's retirement, beginning in about 25 years, will be to slash retirees' benefits or raise payroll taxes to extraordinary levels. Either one generation will not get what it has paid for, or another will pay as none before ever has.

Fixing the deficit problem ought to have been the chief economic issue in the campaign because the prosperity Americans are enjoying today is a false prosperity, an illusion based on borrowed time and borrowed money. With so little of US private saving left after the Government finances its deficit, the US is not investing in the plant and equipment it will need to deliver advances in the average citizen's standard of living. President Reagan's rhetorical dedication to saving and investment notwithstanding, in the 1980s the US has devoted a smaller share of national income to net business investment than at any time since the Second World War. Investment in infrastructure has shrunk as well. So has investment in educating and training the work force. It is no surprise that the much touted business expansion experienced in the 1980s is the first in 50 years not to have brought any increase in the earnings of the average working man or woman, after taking account of inflation.

The threat posed by the continuing fiscal imbalance is all the greater because so much of America's borrowing in the 1980s has been from foreign lenders. As a result, the stagnating incomes Americans will receive in the future will be all the more painful in that a growing share will go merely to service foreign debts. When Mr Reagan took office, the balance of what foreigners owed Americans over what Americans owed foreigners amounted to some $2,500 for every US family of four. When either Mr Bush or Mr Dukakis takes over, the balance will be about $8,000 per family in the other direction. America has exchanged its role as the world's biggest lender, with all the international influence that that position usually conveys, for a new role as the world's biggest debtor.

It is plain to everyone that Americans cannot continue indefinitely along their current path, watching their economic prospects erode and their debts mount, and pretending all the while that closing a few tax loopholes, or achieving some management efficiencies, will stem the source of this corrosion. Yet that is just what both parties have done in the campaign. Neither will say what parts of current spending are to be cut, and both oppose a tax increase. The conventional wisdom is that to do otherwise would be political suicide because the voters will turn on whoever is responsible enough to tell the truth.

The truth is that 73 per cent of last year's spending went for defence, Social Security, Medicare and Medicaid, and interest on the national debt. Where will Mr Bush or Mr Dukakis cut?

The truth is also that, political rhetoric aside, there has been no major disagreement between President Reagan and the Congress over the total amount (in contrast to the composition) of federal spending. The Republican platform points to "the relentless spending of Congressional Democrats," while the Democratic Platform assails "seven years of 'voodoo economics' (and) fiscal irresponsibility." But in fact the savings voted by Congress on the defence spending Mr Reagan proposed came sufficiently close to offsetting the excess it voted beyond his proposals for non-defence programmes that, on average during 1982–87 (the 1981 budget was Jimmy Carter's), government outlays for all purposes other than interest on the national debt came to just $15bn per year more than Mr Reagan requested. The average deficit during these years was £184bn.

Finally, the truth is that solving the problem will require steps far more serious than either Mr Bush or Mr Dukakis will admit – including cuts not just in government programmes that no one will miss, but in highly visible areas that millions of Americans care about deeply; or an increase not just in nuisance taxes, but in the income tax or something like it; or, more likely, both major spending cuts and a sizeable tax increase. Such actions would be hard enough to take even under the best of circumstances. They will be impossible without the kind of national consensus that, in a democracy, can come only from open discussion of the problem and debate about the alternatives.

A presidential election ought to provide the opportunity to reach for just such a consensus. That, however, would require leadership. This year's candidates are not running, but running away. So far, no one is calling them back.

Reprinted from *Financial Times* 2 November 1988 © Benjamin M. Friedman.

---

typically produce a range of results. With luck, the major forecasts will all point in the same direction; given Murphy's Law (which can be loosely translated from its original Dublin vernacular into 'If anything can go wrong, it probably will . . .'), it is equally possible that they will point in different directions, and suggest quite different policy responses. For example, over the first two years of the 1980s, the Treasury forecast was feverishly reassuring us that the lower turning point in the business cycle had been turned, that recovery was imminent, and that the boom phase was only a few short months away (only to be contradicted by the next –

and still declining – set of provisional data). The more Keynesian orientated National Institute forecast and, to a lesser extent, the OECD forecast both argued that we were still on the cycle's downslope and looking for a turning point. Simultaneously, the Cambridge Economic Policy Group (CEPG) warned that a yawning chasm of decline lay before us, and that crisis level changes were needed to both our international trade practices and our fiscal stance, if we were to survive.

Where then was the clear and unequivocal guidance for the policy maker from this sophisticated network of economic forecasts? What sort of policy response could cover all three viewpoints? Which should be trusted? Was the Treasury too much under the influence of a (then) beleaguered government, which was desperate to find some sign of success for its policies? Were the other groups too Keynesian in their loyalties, and too ready to discredit the new policy direction of monetarism? Whichever viewpoint we accept, it would imply a quite different policy response. If we were in the recovery phase then, given the delay which policies would experience in working through to their real-world economic response, reflation could result in an embarrassingly high level of demand and an overshoot of the boom phase into inflation and external balance problems; the response suggested by the Treasury forecast was clearly a cautious one – even to the point of passivity. On the other hand, if we were to accept the National Institute and OECD view, then possibly some minor reflation would be needed, to ease the economy from depression into recovery. And, if we were to believe the CEPG forecast, then (apart from instant emigration!) really major reflationary policy action, coupled with strict importation controls would have been the possible response.

We have already conceded that we do not always have a clear idea of where we want to go, in terms of genuine and achievable policy objectives. We have just been driven to admit that it is quite possible that we might not have any truly accurate set of forecast data, from which we could judge our divergence from these targets. What happens if the third stage of fiscal corrective strategy is undermined by a doubt that fiscal policy might not be capable of achieving the degree of control which is needed to influence the economy with confidence and accuracy?

What appear to have been the main problems which have emerged from practical experience of *using* fiscal measures as an instrument of demand management control and influence?

Firstly, we have learned that it is not always easy to exert quick and **flexible control** over the three main fiscal variables.

For government expenditure, experience has suggested that there are a number of severe problems which hinder adjustment, particularly to deflationary measures. The administrative framework of government is vast and complex, and covers local authorities as well as central government. The need for change must be communicated through the various departments and authorities. Acceptance of the need for change, and of the modifications to policies which will be necessary to allow this change to be implemented, is far from automatic. Apart from the frictions which will exist within any large organization such as central government, the determination of local authorities to pursue their own independent policies in response to their own internal objectives, has proved to be a major conflict area with successive governments – not least in the current UK context, where a radically reforming right-wing central government has fought a bitter and prolonged battle of trench warfare with a group of equally radical and resistant left-wing local authorities.

Even where the need to cut is accepted, this simply throws into sharp relief the opportunity costs of the alternative uses of the funds in achieving prized objectives. Should the cuts be made against education, or defence, or housing, or social services? Should they be spread equally across the board, or fall disproportionately on selected areas? Such decisions are difficult, and organizational resistance to threat is automatic. Experience has shown repeatedly that the cuts tend to be minimized, and the bargaining process prolonged – with both of these responses creating major problems for fiscal control.

Equally, there can be genuine reasons for delay. For instance, the existence of indivisibilities complicates the ability to make cuts (or indeed to increase expenditure marginally). It might be feasible to leave some government projects in a partially finished state, for example, a completed section of motorway, or part of a housing, or industrial estate. Others are likely to be quite invalid until they are fully completed, for example, hospitals, schools, water and sewerage facilities. The ability to cut could therefore depend upon the phasing of project starts and completions, every bit as much as on the political and organizational will to cut.

While the resistance to change is likely to be stronger for cuts, there are also features which will slow down the response to plans for increasing expenditure. Revised bids for funds will have to be made between competing uses for the extra funds. External factors, such as the lags involved in obtaining planning permission, tendering for contracts and so on, will also add to the delay.

In short, the evidence is that government expenditure is rather less flexible and sensitive to the need for change, than is implied in theory.

Benefit payments at first sight appear to offer a more promising tool. If the extra funds can be directed quickly to the recipients, the increase in expenditure will follow equally quickly – and with a marginal propensity to consume which must be close to unity, the benefit pound must be almost as 'high powered' as the government expenditure pound.

But, in reality, the speed at which additional funds can be channelled to benefit recipients is constrained by the ability of the administrative structure to absorb the changes involved. A decision to increase pensions may take several months before it can be implemented; where eligibility for benefit is being widened, some time will be needed to draft and put into effect the new procedures involved.

However, the problems of using benefits as the fiscal target become significantly worse when deflation is the intention – simply because it is people who are affected. Who should suffer the proposed cuts? Pensioners? The sick? Widows? The unemployed? Should the cuts be achieved by 'targeting' resources on the more needy sub-groups within each category and reducing, even abolishing payments to the rest? Will there be organized opposition? How much – and how electorally damaging – support will be drawn from the public? The truth is that benefit payments will tend to operate on a 'ratchet' principle; they can be raised, but are very resistant to reductions – even when these are achieved in real, as opposed to money terms (that is, where benefit rates rise at less than the rate of inflation, so reducing the purchasing power of the transfer payment).

Inflexibilities in the other fiscal variables would appear to throw much of the burden of adjustment onto the taxation system. As with benefits payments, changes in taxation would appear to affect households and firms relatively quickly. But practical experience has drawn attention to a number of possible problems in this area as well. Once again, the administrative structure for tax collection in the UK finds it difficult to respond quickly to changes in taxation policy; the awareness of such difficulties will constrain the government's freedom to vary tax rates. Secondly, if the intention is to deflate, there is evidence that a series of increases in tax rates could ultimately have an adverse effect on incentive, reducing the willingness to provide effort, or to take risks; it might even tend to promote tax evasion at all levels, which will reduce the potential taxation 'take' of the government – and increase the potential burden of government expenditure on those still paying taxes in a more honest fashion. Thirdly, if the intention is to reflate, recent experience has shown that reductions in direct taxation rates have the power to trigger severe intersectional hostility within the economy, as the apparent gap widens between the relatively rich and the relatively poor; to what extent is the potential for efficiency gains undermined by the very real social friction generated by shifting the tax burden, or reducing government expenditure plans to accommodate these tax cuts? Finally, there is also some evidence that repeated changes in taxation rates and allowances could create an element of uncertainty, which can have an adverse effect on investment plans (particularly for small firms) and, indirectly, economic growth.

Leaving, for the moment, the world of practical difficulties we can also draw on some of the earlier theoretical material on consumption behaviour to identify another, and possibly major, problem for fiscal policy. The response by households to tax induced changes in their disposable income could be less sensitive where these are felt to be transitory in nature. If it is accepted that consumption decisions are based on a wider time horizon than simply current income, then fluctuations in current disposable income might have less influence on consumption than is indicated in the simple theory models – remember the influence of the permanent income, or the life cycle hypothesis, as discussed in Chapter 4.

The above are all known as **discretionary** or deliberate changes in fiscal policy; they are made with the intent of influencing the level of economic activity, and are weakened by the relative inflexibility of the main fiscal variables. Before moving on, it is important to draw your attention to a built-in element of fiscal flexibility which exists in any fiscal package; we are, of course, referring to the operation of the **built-in stabilizers** of the fiscal system. Stabilizers in a ship are intended to damp down and minimize the amount of movement of that ship in rough seas; built-in stabilizers perform a similar function for the macroeconomy.

The essence of the stabilizer is that it does not take the form of a deliberate policy response to a recognized problem; it happens automatically and simultaneously. For instance, as the economy moves into the boom phase of the economy, two simultaneous fiscal adjustments will follow: firstly, as the levels of income and expenditure rise, then so too will the taxation payments received by the government, from income tax, corporation tax and VAT; secondly, as the rising demand for labour cuts down the number of persons unemployed, then fewer people will be receiving unemployment and other supplementary benefit payments from the government. In short, taxation receipts will rise and government expenditure on transfer payments will fall as the economy moves into boom, creating a fiscal surplus and providing a check to the rate of growth in aggregate demand. Extract 7.3 analyses just how this built-in stabilizer effect contributed to the Chancellor's ability to find room for further taxation cuts, or increases in expenditure (and also complements the insights given by the two earlier extracts into the interrelationship between the government's expenditure plans and the constraints imposed by current taxation receipts, this time in a UK context). Conversely, if the economy were to move into recession and depression, the built-in stabilizers would again tend to work in the opposite direction, and so counterbalance the decline to some extent: taxation receipts would be reduced, to reflect falling levels of income, profits and expenditure; benefit payments would increase, as the numbers unemployed rose.

However, it is essential that you realize that these are *minor* adjustments to the government's fiscal stance. Just as a ship's stabilizers won't eliminate all movement, and passengers can still have good reason to become seasick, so too the fiscal stabilizers will only reduce the pace of the movement into expansion or contraction. Their function is *not* to correct and cure; this is more the intended purpose of, or role for discretionary fiscal policy. Rather, the role for the fiscal stabilizers is more akin to taking aspirin tablets to ease the symptoms or pain, *without*

Extract 7.3 THE ECONOMIST 5 NOVEMBER 1988.

SEE HOW THE MONEY ROLLS IN

AFTER months in which his reputation was dented by rising interest rates and a growing balance-of-payments deficit, Mr Nigel Lawson has pulled off another political coup. His autumn statement ingeniously managed to seem generous to backbenchers without frightening the City. The doubts may grow later.

The booming economy is pouring tax revenue into the chancellor's lap. He now expects a budget surplus of £10 billion in 1988–89, compared with the £3 billion surplus he expected last March. Even if, as the Treasury forecast assumes, he runs another budget surplus of £10 billion in 1989–90, he could in theory have room for annual tax cuts of £3 billion–5 billion next March.

He has been suggesting that he will not take advantage of that. At present it seems he will be wiser not to. For the boom which has boosted tax revenues has also aggravated inflation and the external payments deficit. So, having stumbled into domestic debt repayment by accident, Mr Lawson may be tempted to turn it into policy.

By the end of the 1990s, the proportion of old people relative to taxpayers will be rising fast. Perhaps, ministers muse, they should aim to pay off a good chunk of the £170 billion national debt. As they do, the cost of debt interest will shrink. Public spending on programmes will be able to grow faster than the economy, while the total, which includes debt interest, magically holds constant its share in GDP.

In spite of the vast budget surplus, the boom is uncomfortably strong. If, as Mr Lawson has repeatedly said, inflation is the judge and jury of his economic policy, he is now on probation. He now thinks retail prices will rise by 6¼% by the end of 1988, against the forecast of 4% he made just seven months ago. They are almost certain to have risen even faster by early 1989.

The forecasts in the Treasury's autumn economic statement say, in effect: "See, no harm done." If they prove correct, Mr Lawson is about to achieve a strange and difficult feat. The statement predicts that the inflation rate will fall from an (undisclosed) peak of 7% or so in the first half of next year, to 5% by the fourth quarter, and "assumes" that by 1991 it will be back down to 3%. All the while domestic demand will be strong enough to keep the economy growing robustly, with unemployment flat or falling. Such painless disinflation is rare, especially in Britain.

One implication of the numbers is that the Treasury now regards Britain's sustainable growth rate as over 3%. That is why it believes real growth at that rate in 1989 should be consistent with an easing of inflationary pressure. The Treasury might be right—after all, the economy grew by 4% last year and will grow by 4½% this year. But a chancellor who really cared about getting inflation down would not count on it. Periods of inflation often begin with an optimistic reassessment of how much demand the economy can stand.

The City's immediate reaction to the forecasts was to say that inflation might fall as the chancellor claims, but only if demand is squeezed a bit more tightly than he is predicting; or else that the economy might grow at 3% next year as Mr Lawson says, but at the cost of a bit less progress on inflation. The first of these possibilities explains why another rise in interest rates may come during the next few months.

What is true for inflation is truer still for the chancellor's forecast for the external current-account deficit. In his budget in the spring, he predicted that the deficit would be £4 billion in 1988; the new forecast is for £13 billion. Only a small improvement, to £11 billion, is expected in 1989. But merely to keep the deficit in check seems to call for some fancy footwork.

Specifically, the Treasury is counting on export volumes rising by 5½% next year (after a rise of only 1½% in 1988) while growth in import volumes shrinks to 4½% (from 12%). The decline in expected imports assumes that savings recover. Even so, it is hard to square with the 3% of expected increase in domestic demand—especially since the chancellor's aim is to keep sterling steady. That, together with relatively high inflation, implies a steady decline in international competitiveness.

Reprinted with permission from *The Economist* 5 November 1988 © *The Economist*.

treating the underlying cause of that pain. Their role is therefore important, but limited.

The *second* set of problems which have emerged from practical experience are all concerned with the lags or delays which exist within the system of fiscal analysis, policy formulation, policy implementation, and economic response. Fiscal policy cannot be considered solely in terms of comparative statics, as we have been guilty of doing in our simple fiscal models; the framing and implementation of fiscal strategy will take place against the dynamic path of the business cycle. Taken against this dynamic context, there is a very real risk that fiscal actions could have inappropriate – even embarrassingly wrong – results. Why should this be so?

Practice has shown that there is a real likelihood of delays at various stages in the fiscal process, and that these delays could create problems for the correct **timing of the impact** of fiscal action. The first set of lags are all concerned with problem recognition and the acceptance of the responsibility to respond. For example, the delay in data availability for analysis and forecasts will provide a first, unavoidable lag; this lag could lengthen before the trends shown by the data draw attention to the emergence of a problem; it could lengthen still further, before policy makers are driven to the decision that they must take action to counter the problem. The second set of lags are all concerned with policy implementation: firstly, the appropriate policy response will take time to formulate; then it must be negotiated through the labyrinth of government machinery; even when acceptance of the need for and correctness of the policy response has been won, there will probably still be implementation lags (as discussed in the section above). Nor are we finished yet, for there will be a final set of lags which are concerned with the response of the economy to the fiscal policy 'nudge'. The fiscal disturbance will trigger the multiplier, which operates through a series of rounds of expenditure (or progressive expenditure cuts, where the fiscal action has been deflationary), *all of which take time*; it could easily take between 12 and 18 months before 80% of the adjustment process is complete.

Where does this leave you then in terms of your ability to control the economy? Would you like to drive a car down the motorway when you could only see out of the rear view mirror, and when steering, brakes, gear changes and acceleration are all subject to a delayed response? In fiscal terms, when the lags are either unanticipated, or are longer than has been anticipated – since there is no reason why they should conform to a standard pattern – then this creates two major dangers to the overall objective of stabilizing the economy.

Firstly, by the time the fiscal measures start to impact on the economy, they could provide a 'correction' which is wrong, either in degree or in direction. Reflationary measures taken before the lower turning point could begin to affect the economy *after* that turning point, and result in a (possible dangerous) boost to and exaggeration of progress through the recovery phase. Or, as Nigel Lawson discovered over 1988, effective taxation cuts taken in the middle stages of a boom phase, could contribute to an exaggerated consumption boom, with the initial applause turning into swingeing criticism as both inflation and external trade deficits lurch far beyond the levels forecast. Extract 7.3 underlines the strength of this embarrassment. Alternatively – as the OECD argued in the early 1980s, when analysing the very severe decline of the UK economy relative to that of other member nations – measures taken to control the excesses of a boom may well impact on the dynamic path during the following slide into recession, accelerating and exacerbating the collapse into depression.

Secondly, fiscal policy is run by politicians, who are only too human! We have already said that there will be lags; impatient policy makers, monitoring the apparently limited responses of the economy to their policy changes, could well be tempted to judge that this limited response reflected 'too gentle' an initial policy nudge, and then add an additional policy correction to an adjustment process which had still to achieve its full momentum or impact. For example, only two or three of the multiplier's expenditure round responses might have taken place, with several more relatively strong expenditure rounds to follow (even allowing for the fact that progressive leakages weaken the strength of each successive round of expenditure). This additional fiscal correction could very easily result in an ultimate over-correction. Imagine what would happen if you were braking your car to a halt, in heavy traffic, as you approached some traffic lights – only to have a nervous passenger slam on your handbrake . . .

In both cases, there is a distinct possibility of fiscal policy having a destabilizing effect on the dynamic path of the economy through its business cycle phases. Sadly, this is not merely a conceptual possibility; there has been some evidence of real-world destabilization in several countries during the high years of traditional Keynesian policy intervention.

The *third* set of problems which have emerged from our experience of practical fiscal policy usage are all concerned with the unanticipated and undesired **side-effects** which could be triggered by policy action. It seems impossible to divorce any form of policy from its unwanted side-effects, some of which could counteract the operation of the policy and the achievement of its initial objectives. Experience has shown that there are two major side-effects which could affect the operation of fiscal policy, as outlined above.

Firstly, there is the **crowding out** effect. Assume that the intent of fiscal policy is to raise the level of economic activity, and that it takes the form of an increase in government expenditure. As the level of economic activity rises, it will tend to drive up the rate of interest (as we will show in the next chapter). This, in turn, will increase the cost of credit and of capital. To the extent that consumption and investment expenditure are interest sensitive, they will be reduced, creating an offsetting effect to the increase in government expenditure in the aggregate expenditure function. At worst, in the view of some monetarists, the offset will be complete, so that fiscal policy has no net effect on the level of income and output, but merely 'crowds out' private sector expenditure; the government will simply be making the purchases which would have been made anyway by households and firms. Realistically, there will tend to be some 'crowding out' effect if interest rates rise – but it is likely to be less than total, in the light of recent evidence on the interest sensitivity of private sector expenditure plans. Nevertheless, the possibility of its existence (and its implications for the share of resources claimed by the public sector) has been one of the reasons why Thatcherite policies have made a central objective out of reducing the scale of government involvement and intervention in the economy. It is also one of the reasons why tentative (and frequently disguised, because it conflicted with a declared monetarist stance) reflation in the UK over recent years has taken the form of *taxation* reductions, rather than increases in either government expenditure or benefit payments. In fairness, however, this type of adjustment is also central to supply-side policy, which has probably provided a more accurate description than monetarism of the UK government's stance from the mid 1980s; this will also be dealt with in a later chapter.

Secondly, there are a number of potentially embarrassing **monetary repercussions** which can be triggered by fiscal policy. If anything, the Keynesian policy maker's view tended to be rather tunnel visioned, and dismissive towards possible monetary influences – to the point of exaggerating and distorting J.M. Keynes's own view. Again assume that the intention is to raise the level of economic activity by increasing government expenditure, or reducing taxation, or both. Such a policy could leave expenditure greater than taxation receipts, that is, create a fiscal deficit. The way in which this deficit is funded is likely to be crucial, in terms of the final effect of the fiscal measures. If the funds, for example, are raised from the public by a sale of government stock to them, this could lower bond prices and raise interest rates, which would trigger the 'crowding out' effect discussed above. Alternatively, if the deficit is funded by creating new money this could add a further – and monetarists would argue a stronger – reflationary effect to that intended in the fiscal package (although one which they would see as purely temporary in nature, and damaging to price inflation and international competitiveness in the longer term).

The repercussions of monetary changes on the course of the economy are analysed at greater depth in subsequent chapters. At this stage, we would merely point out that fiscal policy cannot fully be divorced from its monetary implications, and that these could exaggerate and distort the economic response which is intended by the fiscal measures. Such a view is not simply a monetarist 'knock down' of the potential for the use of fiscal policy as a control device within the macroeconomy; it is a view which would probably be accepted by many neo-Keynesian economists (a cumbersome term which would simply embrace all economists who would still accept the need for some intervention and guiding influence in the running of the macroeconomy).

At the end of this brief outline, what can we say about the potential usefulness of fiscal policy? Does it have a role – or does it conjure up so many demons that it is better left firmly locked up in Pandora's box? At the very least, fiscal policy makers have gradually become aware that the economy is a much more complex organism than it appeared to be originally. Neither the policy need nor the policy response is ever likely to be as clearcut and uncomplicated as tends to be implied by the simplified and purely conceptual models which were used earlier in the chapter. Whatever the rightness, or wrongness, of the underlying Keynesian principles involved, experience has shown that the practicality of simple fiscal corrections is less certain than was originally felt to be the case. Therefore, in many countries, there has been a retreat from the Keynesian principle of control and influence, into monetarism and its advocacy of return to the greater reliance on free market forces, and/or a switch of emphasis towards supply-side, as opposed to demand management policy influence.

However, this does not imply that you should ignore the basic fiscal models which we have dealt with earlier in this chapter. However discredited the Keynesian ideal, the models have an embarrassing power to predict some of the adverse side-effects of the other policies. For example, if you make substantial cuts in government expenditure, what will happen to the level of economic activity? Or again (and don't send the proof to the Chancellor!), what would happen to the level of activity and consumption demand if you make a substantial cut in households' taxation? If a policy action involves a clear fiscal adjustment – whatever its philosophy and intention – this *will* have an impact, via the appropriate multiplier, on the economy; and this impact can still be analysed and predicted by the simple fiscal models such as we have used. Their underlying Keynesian philosophy may well have been discredited, at least for the moment, but the models still work and have relevance.

CONCLUSIONS

1. If government expenditure is defined as government final consumption and government gross domestic fixed capital formation, then it accounts for about 22% of GDP currently in the UK, having been reduced from just under 26% during the last decade. This figure still

lies a little above the comparative figure of 20% for the USA, West Germany and the Netherlands – and well above the figure of 15% for Japan.

2. The figure of 40% of GDP which is frequently quoted in evidence of the 'excessive' claim of the public sector on economic resources, includes additional payments made by the government on subsidies, national debt interest and, particularly, transfer or benefit payments (which account for 30% of that all-inclusive total of government expenditure). Since transfer payments are not spent by the government, but by their recipients, such as the elderly, the ill, the unemployed, it is a little unfair to accuse the government of using such funds! Indeed, the UK appears to pay rather less in social security benefits than West Germany and the Netherlands.

3. Government expenditure must be broadly matched against government income from taxation and other sources; the main sources of revenue in the UK are from taxation on income (including business profits) and on expenditure, and from National Insurance contributions. There is evidence that there has been a clear switch in emphasis from direct taxation towards expenditure taxation over the last decade, which implies that the UK system of taxation has become more regressive in nature than has traditionally been the case.

4. Until the late 1970s in the UK, consistent use was made of fiscal policy to counterbalance the economic fluctuations of the business cycle, and to attempt to stimulate investment and to raise the rate of economic growth. There was a strong Keynesian tradition, which sought to influence the level of aggregate demand either directly, through variations in the government's own expenditure or indirectly through changes in taxation (which might affect either net of tax business profits, or households' disposable income).

5. The effects of these changes were magnified by the multiplier adjustment process which was triggered by them. While this multiplier process was common to all fiscal changes, only the government's own expenditure changes would pass in their entirety into the multiplier; taxation and benefit changes would operate on consumption expenditure plans by influencing disposable income – and would therefore be subject to an additional leakage from savings.

6. However, over the 1970s in particular, there developed a greater awareness of practical difficulties inherent in the operation of fiscal policy. For example, an essential requirement for fiscal correction is that the contents of the fiscal package should be capable of quick and certain control. In reality, while government expenditure, benefit payments and taxation policy can influence aggregate demand, the process of control is less precise, less immediate and less certain than it would need to be for confident and accurate management of the level of aggregate demand.

7. To some extent, some flexibility can be given to fiscal policy from the automatic operation of the built-in stabilizers in the fiscal system. Undoubtedly, the operation of the stabilizers contributes towards damping down cyclical fluctuations. But it does not eliminate the need for discretionary policy changes, where the objective is to alter the direction of the economy, rather than simply to minimize the degree of the fluctuation.

8. The existence of lags in the decision, formulation, implementation and response stages of fiscal policy poses problems for policy makers, and creates the danger that their actions might move out of synchronization with the cycle, turning fiscal policy into a destabilizing instrument. Impatience with the speed at which the policy is working its way through the economic system should also be guarded against, or it could result in unnecessary policy supplementation and ultimate over-correction.

9. Finally, it must be recognized that fiscal policy, in common with most other policies, can generate some conflicting and undesirable side-effects. Care must be taken, particularly over periods of successive fiscal deficits, to avoid 'crowding out' and inflationary repercussions. This lesson in particular has been a difficult one for traditional UK Keynesian economists to accept.

10. Because of the range of problems associated with fiscal policy, its use – indeed the whole Keynesian principle of interventionism – has been widely discredited in recent years. Over the last decade, there has been a clear swing internationally towards the principles of monetarism and supply-side economics, both of which emphasize the return to a greater degree of dependence on the operation of free market forces, to create a more efficient and prosperous economy. But the insight into the workings of the macroeconomy given by the basic model, and its fiscal extension, are still important. Fiscal actions, whether deliberate or simply reflecting the unintentional side-effects of other policies, will still affect the economy as shown by the theory model. Simply because they have become unfashionable does not mean to say that the fiscal relationships no longer operate within the economy. Perhaps we should try to build on experience, rather than to reject it totally?

SELF-ASSESSMENT QUESTIONS

TRUE/FALSE QUESTIONS

7.1. It is not possible to achieve simultaneously the government's macroeconomic objectives of full employment and a stable price level.

7.2. When fiscal policy is used in a contra-cyclical manner, the imbalances recorded in each period will tend to build up into a cumulative total of borrowing.

7.3. An increase in government expenditure will raise the level of income and consumption expenditure, moving the position of the latter function upwards, in terms of the $C + J$ model. Conversely, a reduction will reduce income and lower the consumption function.

7.4. Whether fiscal policy chooses to reflate by raising G or reducing T it will have the same effect of raising aggregate expenditure and therefore income by the same amount.

MULTIPLE CHOICE QUESTIONS

7.1. If the government wishes to reduce the level of economic activity by
using fiscal policy it should:

(a) Reduce direct taxation,
(b) Raise expenditure taxation,
(c) Reduce business taxation,
(d) Reduce benefit payments,
(e) Reduce Government expenditure.

7.2. One pound of government expenditure is more high powered than a pound of tax cuts in reflation because:

(a) It is more likely to be spent on capital goods rather than consumption goods;
(b) It affects disposable income more quickly and directly than taxation changes and possible rebates;
(c) It carries the full weight of the government's authority;
(d) It gives in to the multiplier expansion process without any initial loss or leakage in savings;
(e) It is exempt from savings leakages during all the expenditure rounds of the multiplier process.

7.3. The 'Balanced Budget' theorem shows that, if G and T are both reduced by an indentical amount, the level of economic activity will:

(a) Remain the same, since the two multiplier processes, one expanding and one contracting income, will cancel each other out;
(b) Rise, since the reduction in taxation will increase incentive;
(c) Fall by the amount of the government expenditure reduction;
(d) Fall by the total amount of government expenditure and taxation cuts;
(e) Rise, since the government expenditure multiplier is more powerful than the taxation multiplier.

7.4. The inclusion of income related taxation and benefit payments in the multiplier formulation, has the effect of:

(a) Raising the value of all the multipliers (for government expenditure, taxation and benefit changes) since more terms are included in the multiplier formulae;
(b) Making the government expenditure multiplier more 'powerful' than ever, since taxation and benefit multipliers will be reduced;
(c) Raising the value of the benefit multiplier against that of the taxation multiplier;
(d) Reducing the value of all the multipliers, particularly those for taxation and benefit changes;
(e) Reducing the value of all the multipliers since all will be affected equally by the additional tax leakage and benefit adjustment.

Note: Solutions can be found at the end of the text.

Chapter 8

Money and Monetary Policy

Introduction

The nature of money

The demand for money

The supply of money

The banking sector and money creation

Monetary policy

Problem areas in monetary policy

The rate of interest

Conclusions

Self-assessment questions

INTRODUCTION

Earlier chapters have largely ignored the role played by money in the economic system. Its existence has been accepted implicitly: the constant flow of transactions within and between sectors has always assumed some interchange of payment and receipt. The closest we have come to dealing explicitly with money was when we acknowledged that some fiscal actions could have unwanted side-effects, as a result of their monetary consequences.

Such a low key treatment would appear to suggest that money is not particularly important in the working of the economic system, that its role is the relatively neutral one of facilitating payment to record and settle the more important flows of transactions within that system. Nothing could be further from the truth.

Money represents a major new dimension which exists alongside the circular flow models of Chapter 2, and the basic model of the economic system which was derived from these. Certainly, money provides the payment system which underpins the transaction flows recorded in our models, but its role and influence extend far beyond this basic contribution. Consider the simple act of saving which, from our circular flow models, we know is a leakage out of current income earned by both households and firms. What form do these savings take? What happens to them when they disappear from the model? Equally, we are well aware that some households and firms will want to make purchases which exceed their current incomes, and which can only be funded by borrowing against future incomes. But where do the borrowed funds come from? To whom and under what terms must the repayments be made? To complicate matters still further, the acts of savings and borrowing are not confined to households and firms. The government (central and local) will also be involved as a borrower, for example, to finance benefit and other payments while waiting for taxation and other receipts, and as a saver, for example, if the flow of government income exceeds its planned level of expenditure, as was discussed in Extract 7.3. Finally, there will be a constant flow of money and capital within the international trade sector; much of the recent UK investment expenditure has been funded by international monetary flows.

The truth is that there is a **money market** functioning alongside the final goods market (and the labour market) with which our simple models have been concerned. Its role is to channel funds from savers to borrowers (and back, in the form of repayments) both within and between the various sectors of the economy. This interflow of funds is managed by a complex network of the central bank for the economy (the Bank of England in the UK) and the wide range of **financial intermediaries** which are active in the money market. Conceptually, the role of the financial intermediaries is simple enough; they simply match the needs of savers and borrowers, bringing system and supervision to the constant flow of funds between the two groups. The reality is rather more complex. The specific needs of individual savers and borrowers differ widely. Some savers will want easy, even instant access to their funds; others will be prepared, if suitably compensated by premium rates of interest, to give up instant access – but will still have different views on what constitutes an acceptable degree of risk in the use of their funds. Some borrowers might want to use funds for only a short period of time, for example, to fund the purchase of a car, TV, automatic washing machine, holiday, or to hold inventories. Others will want to use the funds (and to repay this use) over a much longer period, for example, to purchase a house, or a factory, or machinery, tools and other equipment.

To operate successfully – not least in the enhanced state of competition since the **big bang** largely broke down the boundary fences between types of financial institution in the UK in 1987 – financial intermediaries have had to develop highly specialist knowedge of particular types of transaction and well structured links both with the appropriate groups of clients and with the network of the money market as a whole. Additionally, they have had to learn to work through a portfolio of activities, to balance risks and to average out the different time flows and needs involved in the turnover of funds between clients. How else could such widely divergent demands (for example, the savings of pensioners be matched to the investment borrowing of firms) be defined and satisfied? Without such skills, who else could provide systematic knowledge of the best sources of appropriate funds for particular uses – or the most profitable (or safest) uses of funds for particular types of savers?

Some financial intermediaries operate within the **banking sector**: for example there are discount houses, which are highly specialist operators who borrow very short term – even less than 24 hours – funds to hold and realize financial assets such as treasury and commercial bills, or certificates of deposit (CDs); there are the commercial or 'clearing' banks, who specialize in servicing the needs of individuals and small to medium sized firms; merchant banks, who have developed particular expertise in acting as bankers and advisers to large depositors and borrowers; Trustee Savings Banks, with a traditional (but currently rapidly diversifying) focus on small savers; and there is the Girobank and National Savings scheme, run by the government, and targeted on servicing (not to mention raising money from!) small savers. **Non-bank** and **other financial intermediaries** cover a further range of financial institutions: there are building societies, gradually moving from their traditional role of providing mortgages on housing and other properties, into a wider and more generalized (and profit orientated, in contrast to their traditional trustee, non-profit-making stance) range of banking services; finance houses, which deal mainly with hire purchase loans for consumption (and firms') expenditure; unit and investment trusts, which take small savers' funds and use them to hold a professionally managed portfolio of financial assets; and there are life assurance, and pension funds, which organize contractual savings from current income, through professionally managed portfolios, into future lump sum payments (for example, on death or retirement of the client) and pension systems.

The money market consists of an extremely complex network of specialist institutions and clients, and deals with all transactions involving short-term funds. However, it should not be seen as a *single* market. Rather, it consists of a series of specialist sub-markets, such as the discount market, the CD market, the interbank market, local authority market, finance house market, even Eurocurrency markets.

Money, therefore, does not merely validate the operation of the final goods and labour markets with which our earlier chapters have been preoccupied. Its influence on these other markets is complex and powerful. As such, we can no longer ignore its existence; the time has come to explore its nature, its role and its main patterns of influence on the economy. However, a word of caution is needed at the start. The subject money and monetary policy is an extensive and complex field of study in its own right within economics; it would be quite impossible to cover all the relevant topics, or even to deal adequately with the main topics within this field, given the constraints of a single chapter, and an introductory book. The aim here is, therefore, to provide you with a generalized understanding, rather than a specialist knowledge of the subject. Even this brief and superficial treatment should provide you with an invaluable additional insight into the workings of the economic system, and the problems involved in its control.

In more detail, the objectives of this chapter are to provide you with a sound, if limited, base of knowledge on the following topics:

- The nature and role of money;
- The different types of demand for money and the factors influencing them;
- The nature of the money supply and the problems associated with its measurement;
- The role of the commercial banks in providing money and, indeed, 'creating' money;
- The relationship between the government, and the money market;
- The influence of and the control exercised by the Bank of England over the process of money creation and the money supply;
- The nature of open market operations as carried out by the Bank of England, and their possible consequences on the economy;
- The nature of the other instruments which might be used as part of monetary policy in an economy;
- Some of the main strengths and weaknesses of monetary policy and its use by the government;
- The way in which the demand for and the supply of money interact to establish the rate of interest.

THE NATURE OF MONEY

If our intention is to analyse the workings of the money market, then our first logical step must be to define what the term **money** means. At first sight this might seem quite unnecessary. After all, we all know what money is: we can all jingle coins in our pockets or purses; those more fortunate among us can even rustle £5 notes (we academics can just about remember the feeling!); practising, or intending Yuppies can flex their plastic cards and look superior. But what about that grey-haired old lady, trying to buy her novelty calendar with her TSB chequebook? Is she offering money? Or what about that strange, sunburned academic, trying to convince the university bursar that he has raised overseas research funds, and flourishing a plastic bag full of cowrie shells? Is he offering money, or is he just slightly more demented than the normal academic?

It may surprise you to be told that one of the most difficult tasks in macroeconomics is to provide a clear and consistent definition of money; we shall explain why when we return to the topic later in the chapter.

For the moment, we will use a simple and powerful – if rather general – definition: *money is anything which, in the economic system concerned, is generally acceptable in payment of a debt*. In any modern society, money would automatically include items such as notes, coins, plus cheques and credit cards – since all of these will normally be accepted in settlement of a transaction. This acceptability, in turn, will normally reflect on how well the monetary unit performs against the traditional functions which it is expected to fulfil.

Firstly, the monetary unit must be a recognized **medium of exchange** through which the flow of transactions in the economic system can take place. Households and firms all produce goods or services; they sell their output, or factor services for money, then use the latter to buy the goods or inputs which they need. Without the common link of money, the economic system would be reduced to barter. Rather than goods and services being sold, they would have to be exchanged directly for other goods and services. The pig farmer wanting a washing machine would have to find a washing machine producer, or owner, who was looking for a pig; exchange would take place within the constraint of having to establish a *coincidence of wants*. Money therefore acts as a lubricant for trade.

Secondly, money must be capable of being used as a **unit of measurement**. This means that it must not only be capable of acting as a common good in terms of which all other goods are valued, but that it must also be 'divisible' – in the sense that it can be broken down into any set value, whether £5000, or £5, or even 5p. This will permit relative values to be established objectively over a range of goods and services. Otherwise, the relative values of any two goods would be set on an *ad hoc*, subjective basis for each transaction, and would vary depending on factors such as bargaining skills and intensity of want of the participants. How many pigs would have an equivalent value to one washing machine? Would the relative values established in that transaction be acceptable in all similar transactions? How would a third good, say an economics textbook be valued . . . in terms of pigs, or washing machines – or should these be revalued in terms of textbooks?

Thirdly, money must be capable of acting both as a **standard of deferred payment** and as a **store of value**. Not all transactions involve immediate settlement. The provision of 'trade credit' is a common practice within the firms' sector, whereby inventories can be purchased without payment for one, two, or even three months – by which time they should have been converted into sales, providing the funds for settlement. The short-term debt must be able to be expressed and ultimately settled in terms of the monetary unit of that economic system, be it pigs or pounds sterling. Equally, the monetary proceeds of any transaction must be capable of being carried forward into later time periods. The washing machine can be sold now, and the proceeds held in money form, as a store of value, or a reserve of purchasing power, until some future date.

There is nothing academic or abstract about these functions of money; if anything they are even more important to a complex economy than a primitive one. Without an acceptable money unit, it would be impossible to trade complex goods and services on any sort of systematic basis, so that output, employment and income would all suffer. In a sense, the nature of the monetary unit is less important than its acceptability; many items such as shells, sharks' teeth, tobacco, gold, silver, warehouse receipts have all provided acceptable monetary units and therefore a basis for trade. Indeed, in the immediate post-war period in Germany, following the collapse of confidence in the monetary unit, cigarettes, fountain pens and bars of chocolate all acted as acceptable monetary units for transactions. What constitutes 'acceptability' will vary from society to society, and also over time. How would any of these societies have reacted if you had offered a small rectangular piece of plastic in payment for your new outrigger canoe, or bale of tobacco leaves, or Zeiss 10 by 50 binoculars, or whatever?

The essence of money is that it is generally acceptable in settlement of a debt. In our modern society, our old lady could happily pay for her calendar by using her TSB chequebook, or even a cheque drawn on her building society deposit account. So long as our demented academic, and the bursar, and the clients all believe in the monetary powers of the cowrie shells in the plastic bag, the research study could take place; after all, if we accept 'plastic money', why not the more aesthetically pleasing shells? In any case, as Extract 8.1 shows, the whole concept of money is on the brink of a new revolutionary form; it could become little more than an electronic pulse passing through a computer. But, even here, isn't it interesting that the idea is being tested in Edinburgh, Leeds and

Extract 8.1 THE SCOTSMAN 17 NOVEMBER 1988.

LAST OF THE BIG SPENDERS

Kiss your money goodbye ... soon you will be able to dispense with cash. Andrew Garfield reports on the dawning of the plastic revolution

THE cashless society is well nigh upon us. It arrives in Edinburgh sometime next year, but only on trial. The Scottish capital, along with Leeds and Southampton, has been chosen as a showcase for a system which could eventually provide the infrastructure for the brave new world of tomorrow, where money will be obsolete and everything from petrol to pet food will be paid for by plastic.

Like spaceships, electronic mail and star wars, cashless shopping has always featured as an essential part of the Boy's Own view of future lifestyles.

The reality, sadly, is more humdrum than the gleaming electric walkway and plexiglass-domed future so beloved of the science fiction writers of yesteryear.

Shopping electronically won't change much of the way we live now. But it will be more convenient. For one thing, it does away with the bother with cheque books, biros which don't write, and those fiddly credit card devices which get your fingers covered in ink, whilst the lady behind you who just wanted a pair of tights fumes in a fast-lengthening queue.

Most customers already seem to prefer to get their money from cash dispensers rather than have to talk to bank clerks face to face: Scots more so than the English, according to surveys. This bodes well for EFTPOS (electronic funds transfer at point of sale) terminals which work pretty much the same way, except they do away with the cash; instead, the customer gets the goods (or services) whilst the bill is automatically charged to the credit card or current account of their choice.

The detail — which shops, which cards — will vary, but the principles stay the same. For the average shopper EFTPOS will be just another stage in an evolution which has taken humankind from conch shells through bank notes to plastic. Already, but for the relatively small proportion of coins and notes actually in circulation, money is little more than computer data.

The real revolution comes only after EFTPOS has made the leap from the laboratory into the high street and is beginning to establish itself as the main way to pay.

Not until then will the real reason why the banks have spent millions on its development become plain for all to see. It is the biggest revolution in banking since gold coins went out and one which none of the banks can afford to miss out on.

EFTPOS has been a glint in bankers' eyes for decades. Ever since the Chinese invented bank notes, paper has been the bane of the lives of moneylenders and merchants; when the Italians invented double-entry book-keeping the march of paper became unstoppable.

Electronic funds transfer will sweep away the paper, and more importantly, the vast army needed to process it.

In Belgium, which has the most advanced EFTPOS network in Europe, getting and paying for petrol at 2am in the morning is probably easier than at 2pm in the afternoon. But the pumps will be unmanned.

The next technological generation, the smart card, in operation in France and already being tested in Britain, has the potential to do away with the street newspaper seller, too.

But that is nothing compared with the savage competition which electronic banking could really unleash. The choice between cash, cheque or plastic in our pre-EFTPOS age is pretty much one of convenience. EFTPOS will make it equally convenient to use Visa, Access or any one of a number of direct-debit cards which the banks and retailers will thrust into your hands.

The race is on to decide which of the big institutions will control the main payment systems of the future. EFTPOS will strengthen the banks' monopoly over our money.

The British clearing banks set up a committee on EFTPOS as long ago as 1975. It took until 1985 before they were able to agree on what to do about it. Three years on, EFTPOS UK, the company they set up to provide a single UK-wide EFT system, has an electronic banking system which works in the laboratory but which it has yet to test on real people.

With all this at stake, the banks' patience has been running out. Last year, Barclay's became the first major bank to break ranks. Increasingly conscious that other countries had systems already operating and that it was only a matter of time before a competitor jumped the gun, Barclays launched its Connect card in England last year.

SWITCH, involving the Royal Bank of Scotland, Midland and National Westminster, followed last month. The Clydesdale Bank set up its Counterplus system in Aberdeen seven years ago, but having stalled because of its commitment to EFTPOS UK, has now decided it cannot wait either and is busily signing up retailers to its system.

The nightmare that everyone wanted to avoid — a repeat of the babel of competing systems that has grown up around the various cash dispenser networks — looks close to repeating itself, and it will be repeated again once banks start fighting it out over a future European EFTPOS network.

The trouble is that none of the banks can afford to be left behind when we come to "roll-out", that time two or three years hence when EFTPOS UK finally gives the go-ahead for its national system to be set up, and the system is rolled out like a carpet to cover the whole of the UK.

The when and how of "roll-out" hinges on how the people of Edinburgh, Leeds and Southampton take to the first tentative steps of the cashless society. They had better like it.

YOUR GUIDE TO THE CASHLESS SOCIETY

EFTPOS

(Electronic Funds Transfer at Point of Sale): The technology enables customers to pay for anything electronically. By inserting a plastic card into a terminal at the supermarket check-out, cash desk, or petrol pump and tapping in a personal identification number purchases can be paid for immediately without coins, notes or cheques. The money will be debited directly from your account or added to your credit card bill. EFTPOS is a boring word for a revolutionary concept, unfortunately it is too late to exchange it for something more graphic.

Electronic cheque

Direct debit — just like a cheque you fill in the amount and it is deducted from your bank account, your signature being your PIN number.

Magnetic stripe

(or magstripe): The brown strip on the plastic card which stores all the data needed for the machine to process your transaction. Magstripe cards are the basis for most automatic teller machines and EFTPOS systems available. They're far cheaper to manufacture than the alternative smart card, but not as secure or as versatile which is why they will eventually be superseded.

Electronic wallet

A rechargeable card that can operate independently of a terminal. It can be filled with smallish amounts, typically £20, and spent on low-value goods, like newspapers.

Smart card

A card with a built-in microprocessor. France has opted for the next generation technology, which is reprogrammable and therefore more versatile. It is also more secure. Its potential applications are mind-blowing and more are still being discovered. It costs nearly eight times as much as conventional cards, though the price is falling by the month.

Some 2,500 students at Loughborough University are using smart cards in a test being carried out jointly by GEC and Midland Bank. The Merit card can be used for EFTPOS, as an electronic purse in the student shops, bars, cafeterias, and to buy travellers' cheques. It also tracks all spending, which can be read off at information points on the campus.

Starting next Monday at a squash club in Northampton, members will be provided with Barclays smart cards which will do everything from booking a court to devising a fitness programme. It will even tell doctors what drugs not to give a holder if he or she collapses from a heart attack on the court.

On-line

The terminal will check with HQ before authorising any transaction. Easier to stop fraud, but costly and time-consuming.

Off-line	Multifunction card	Security
Terminal will let the payment through provided it is below a certain limit, and then sort out the details, usually at the end of the day, though by then it may be too late.	Why carry 20 pieces of plastic when one will do? Increasingly cards will double up with their cheque guarantee, debit, credit, you-name-it function all on the same piece of plastic. Cure for bulging wallets.	No system is foolproof, but how secure it is will depend on how much you can spend. Encryption is the key, coding the data so it can't be spent. But if hackers can get into the Pentagon they can get into a bank computer. But there again if you're mugged with a wallet full of fivers, how secure is that?

Reprinted with permission from *The Scotsman* 17 November 1988 © *The Scotsman*.

Southampton, to explore its *acceptability* to the public, every bit as much as to identify the infrastructure which will be needed to service the new money form?

THE DEMAND FOR MONEY

If there is a money market then, conceptually at least, it can be treated in a similar fashion to the market for any other good, or service. There will be a demand for money, and a supply of money, both of which will interact to set a price (or rate of interest) for money. Our first main task must therefore be to look systematically at the reasons for holding money balances, that is, to ask why there is a **demand for money**.

The simple Keynesian analysis of the demand for money provides a useful introductory statement of the factors which influence that demand. It suggests that there are three main reasons why firms and households will want to hold money balances (as opposed to converting income payments instantly into goods and services).

Firstly, there will be a **transactions demand for money**, to meet the everyday payment needs of households and firms. Payments for the routine flow of transactions in both intermediate and final goods will normally be made either out of cash balances or, more normally, by a series of entries in the banking accounts of the parties concerned. Participants in all sectors will normally maintain some balances of money to finance their transactions. A contributory factor to the need to hold such balances is the fact that there is frequently a lack of synchronization between the intermittent receipt of income and the need to make expenditure from this. For example, a household may receive a monthly income, but there will be a daily stream of expenditures; therefore the income, or at least part of the income, will have to be held as a money balance to fund these routine expenditure needs (although credit card usage and monthly settlement of the total outstanding has eased this particular problem for many).

Secondly, there will be a **precautionary demand for money**. Whereas the transactions demand for money is concerned with planned expenditure, this second component of demand is related more to holding money balances to cover possible items of *unplanned* expenditure. It reflects the desire of households and firms to maintain contingency balances, either to cover unexpected emergencies, or to take advantage of unexpected opportunities. Essentially, this reflects the element of uncertainty in transaction flows; at its simplest, it represents the holding of a money reserve which might seldom, if ever, be used.

What are likely to be the main influences on these two demands for money, that is, what factors will influence the total level of balances held for each purpose? Transaction balances have the prime objective of convenience and access, and reflect the basic role of money as a medium of exchange. It is therefore likely that the level of economic activity, or GDP (as a proxy for the flow of transactions[1]), is likely to be the strongest single influence on the size of transaction balances (D_t) held by the households' and firms' sectors. The greater the level of economic activity, the greater will be the flow of transactions, and the greater will be the level of money balances held to fund these transactions. The precautionary demand for money (D_p) is less easy to analyse: to some extent it will also reflect the level of economic activity, or income earned by households and firms (if only because the latter provides the ability to build and maintain reserve balances); but precautionary balances also contain aspects of the store of value function, since they are held over time as reserve purchasing power. It is therefore possible that precautionary balances will also be sensitive to the rate of interest (which could affect either the level of such balances held or, more likely, the financial form in which the balances are held). But it is customary to simplify this relationship for introductory analysis by arguing that both demands will be influenced only by the level of GDP, or in terms of a more formal specification:

$$D_{t,p} = f(Y)$$

Thirdly, Keynes drew attention to the possibility of a **speculative demand for money**, whereby money is held as a financial asset in its own right (that is, its short-term certainty of value becomes attractive to wealth holders, relative to the possibility of capital losses in the market value of other forms of financial assets). Wealth can be held in a variety of forms, such as money, financial assets (for example, government and other fixed interest securities, or shares), and real assets (for example, houses, cars, jewellery and so on). Taking these broad groups in turn, money has the attraction of providing immediate liquidity (that is, convertibility into instant purchasing power) and, in the short run, relative certainty of

---

1. Since the total number of transactions will include intermediate ones as well as final goods, remember that their total value is not the same as that of GDP.

value; as against this, it offers little or no return for funds held in this form.[2] Financial securities (which are conventionally simplified to fixed interest securities and described as 'bonds', in the subsequent analysis), offer a return and the possibility of capital gains, in the sense that if their market value rises they may be sold for a higher value than their initial purchase price; equally, there is the danger that their market value could fall below the initial purchase price in certain circumstances. Real assets provide the owner with the benefits from a stream of services from their use and may, or may not, offer the possibility of capital gain (or loss) on resale.

Why should people want to hold part of their wealth in money balances (in addition to normal transaction and precautionary balances) when the return offered is lower than that provided by other financial assets? One explanation is that, if wealth holders anticipate that the market value of their bonds is likely to fall in the near future then, depending upon the transaction costs involved, it could well be in their interest to sell the bonds before the expected capital loss is incurred. In other words, to avoid the possibility of capital losses, they will transfer at least a proportion of their bond holdings into the certain short-term value and liquidity of money balances, with the intention of moving back into bonds at a more opportune moment. Thus money balances are held as a speculation against possible capital losses; this is the speculative demand for money.

These capital gains, or losses, will reflect movements in the market prices of the bonds. In turn, one of the main influences on bond prices lies in the expected and actual behaviour of interest rates. Should the rate of interest rise, this implies that the yield (or the earnings) from existing fixed return securities will become relatively less attractive. For example, if a bond is bought for £100 when the rate of interest was set at 10%, it will yield a fixed sum of £10 per annum as the 10% return on that purchase price. Should interest rates rise to, say 15%, then this £10 per annum return will seem less attractive, compared to newly issued bonds which are yielding £15 per £100 bond. Some bond holders will opt to sell their existing bond holdings and transfer their funds into the new bonds with their higher rate of return. As a result of this selling, the price of the older bonds will tend to fall; the process will continue until the price of these original bonds has fallen to about £67, when the fixed £10 per annum will represent a yield of about 15%, which is once again consistent with current market conditions. In short, if the rate of interest rises, bond

---

2. Much depends on how money is defined: if only cash and current accounts are included, the return will be zero (although some of the English and Scottish clearing banks have begun to offer interest on current accounts, to match the competitive pressure from the larger building societies); if the definition is widened to include demand saving deposits, then some interest return is possible.

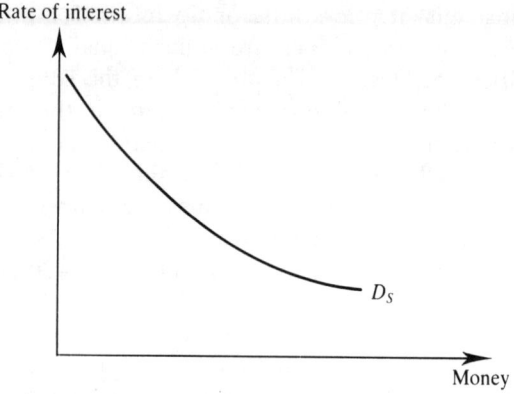

Figure 8.1 The speculative demand for money.

prices will tend to fall, as market forces bring the rate of return on existing bonds into line with the current level of interest rates.[3]

Conversely, if interest rates fall from 10% to, say, 5% then the £10 per annum return on the older bonds would be superior to the current market rate. As wealth holders bid for these bonds their price would be driven upwards; once again, the process would continue until the price rose to £200, when the £10 per annum would represent the same 5% yield as elsewhere in the market.[3]

Bond prices tend therefore to vary inversely with the rate of interest: if the interest rate rises (or is expected to rise), bond prices will fall; if the rate of interest falls (or is expected to fall), bond prices will rise.[4] Since bond prices reflect actual and expected changes in the rate of interest, it can be argued that the speculative demand for money (D_s), which is the alternative asset form, is also associated with these expectations, that is,

$$D_s = f(R)$$

The broad nature of this relationship is illustrated in Figure 8.1. It implies that wealth holders will compare the current rate of interest to their own perceptions of what represents the normal range of interest rates. As the

---

3. In both cases, it is also assumed that the bond is not close to its maturity date, when the market value will tend towards the principal due for repayment.

4. At the same time, equity prices will also tend to reflect yield movements in bonds; if the return on bonds rises in reponse to changes in the rate of interest, equity prices will also tend to fall under selling pressure (as people switch to the more attractive bonds), raising the yields of these alternative financial assets. Thus share prices too will tend to vary inversely with the rate of interest.

actual rate of interest rises, more and more wealth holders begin to feel that actual rates have become relatively high, compared to their own subjective view of the norm. They therefore anticipate that, in the future, interest rates could fall; in turn, if this happens, bond prices will tend to rise, offering the possibility of capital gains. They will thus tend to adjust their wealth holdings so that they can take advantage of this possibility; to do so implies that they will move from money balances into financial assets, so that the speculative demand for money is low. Conversely, as the actual rate of interest falls, more and more wealth holders will begin to feel that it is relatively low, compared to their subjective view of the norm. They will thus anticipate that, in the future, interest rates could rise again; this would tend to reduce bond prices, creating the danger of capital losses. To avoid the latter, providing that the transaction costs involved do not offset the potential gains from the switch, they will tend to convert at least part of their bond holdings into short-term, speculative money balances. The lower is the interest rate, the greater will be this speculative demand for money.

If you feel that the above is too complicated in its reasoning, then you might prefer a simpler analysis of the relationship between money and the rate of interest. Once again, start from the assumption that there is a simple choice between money and bonds as alternative financial assets. Money offers convenience, but zero or little return (and here there is a problem in how 'money' is defined, as you will discover in the following section when we deal with the problems of measuring the money stock; depending upon the definition used, some forms of money can carry substantial interest earnings). In contrast to this, bond holders enjoy interest payments from the bonds. In this simpler analysis, the higher is the rate of interest, then the higher is the return from bonds, and the less attractive are non-earning money balances in comparison; the demand for money will be relatively low at high rates of interest. Conversely, at low rates of interest the more convenient money balances sacrifice less in terms of interest forgone (that is, the opportunity cost of holding money balances is less); therefore there will be a greater tendency to hold money as a financial asset. If you prefer this simpler approach then, once again, you are arguing that within the overall demand for money there will be a functional relationship with the rate of interest, as well as with the level of economic activity, which leaves you with the same type of demand for money function as is discussed below.

Returning to our Keynesian framework, what happens when we draw the three components of the demand for money together? The text above has argued that the demand for transactions and precautionary balances will tend to vary directly with the level of money income; equally, the demand for speculative money balances will tend to vary inversely with the rate of interest. Thus the overall demand for money will reflect both influences simultaneously.

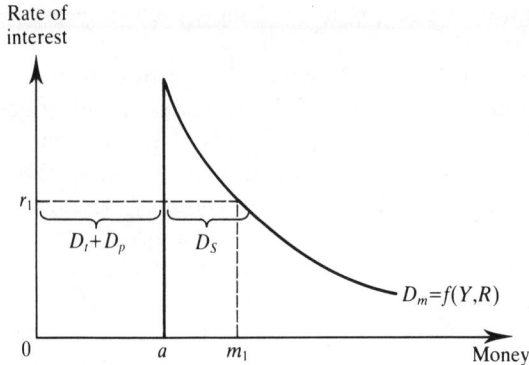

Figure 8.2 The total demand for money.

Figure 8.2 illustrates the results of this simultaneous influence; it shows that the demand for transactions (D_t) and precautionary (D_p) balances is determined by factors other than the rate of interest; they are indicated to be constant and autonomous relative to the latter. The speculative demand for money is grafted on to these to complete the total demand for money function. For any given rate of interest, for example, at r_1, the demand for money can be identified, here as Om_1, with Oa representing the demand for transactions and precautionary balances, and am_1 the demand for speculative balances at this rate of interest. Obviously, different rates of interest would result in a different overall demand for money – not because of any change in the demand for transaction and precautionary balances, but simply reflecting the adjustment in the demand for speculative balances consistent with that rate of interest.

While our main purpose at the moment is to focus on the relationship between the demand for money and the rate of interest, it is worthwhile digressing to consider the effect on the demand for money of an increase in the level of economic activity. As the flow of transactions increased, this would move the demand for transactions and precautionary balances out to the right, causing the whole demand function to move in the same direction. (See Figure 8.3 to trace this movement, but do not try to follow that particular analysis any further at this point; we shall return to it later in the chapter.)

THE SUPPLY OF MONEY

Now that we have built up some understanding of the factors which influence the demand for money, our next logical step must be to return

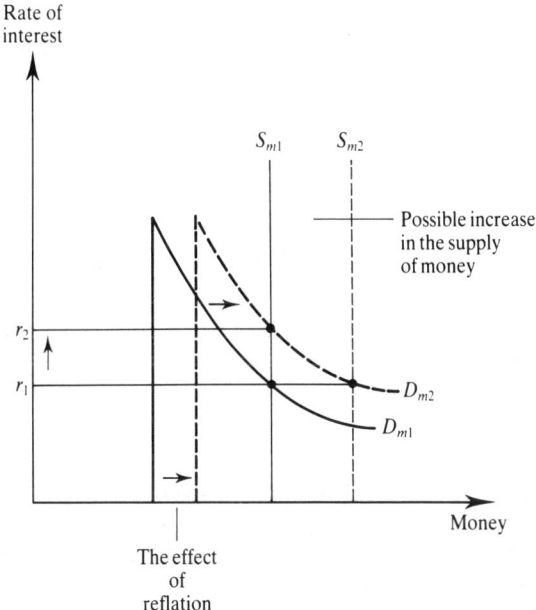

Figure 8.3 Demand for money, supply of money and the equilibrium rate of interest.

to the vexed question of the definition and the measurement of the **supply of money**.

At first sight, this should be a relatively simple matter; but it has proved to be extremely difficult to select a single definition and measure which provides a clear and unequivocal insight into the behaviour of money and the money market. Where do the problems lie? Even if we discard the more exotic forms of money, such as sharks' teeth and cowrie shells (after all, our academic could *never* have convinced the bursar, who once did nightschool classes in accountancy!), we still face all sorts of difficulties in providing a list of items which would be accepted as money in a modern, developed economy.

Until now, we have used a very broad definition of money; we have defined it as anything which is generally acceptable in payment of a debt. The problem is now to try to explore what could conceivably be included in the term 'anything'. If we retreat to our commonsense, then two of the more obvious items would be cash and cheques drawn on firms' and households' banking accounts. If we start from this position, then we are using what used to be described as the 'narrow' view of money in the UK. The M1 measure of money includes notes and coin in circulation, plus sterling 'sight' deposits held by households and firms in the commercial banks. Sight deposits are simply those deposits from which payment can be made on demand, for example, transferred by cheque. They may, or may not, be interest bearing.

Perhaps we might feel that this is too restrictive a view of money; after all, what is to stop firms and households from transferring sums of money from their precautionary or other interest bearing balances *into* their sight deposits, then using these for transaction purposes? If we take this *broader* definition of monetary items, we are using the official M3 (formerly sterling M3) measure of money. This adds to the M1 figure the total of all private sector 'time' deposits in the banks, together with public sector sight and time deposits. Time deposits are simply those funds which have been deposited on the basis that notice must be given before withdrawal. In recent years, there has been a considerable growth in the use of fixed term deposits (for example one month, or three months, or even one year or longer); the longer the term of notice – and therefore the longer the period for which the financial intermediary is given use of the funds – the greater is the premium of interest paid.

Does this exhaust the range of possibilities? Not really. Building societies (particularly the larger ones) have been moving increasingly into offering general banking services – indeed the whole distinction between commercial banks and building societies is likely to become progressively more blurred with the new freedoms given to the latter under the Building Societies Act of 1986. Is there any difference in acceptability between a cheque drawn on a commercial bank account and one drawn on a building society account? Both will be honoured if there is a sufficient balance available (or an agreed loan has been arranged). Equally, what is to stop firms and households from transferring sums from other types of building society deposits (with, or without notice, depending upon the terms of the deposit) into an account from which payment can be made by cheque? If we broaden our definition to cover this new range of money balances, then we are conforming to the UK government's new M4 measure of the money stock.

By now you must feel as if you have strayed by accident into a set of motorway travel directions – but you have still a fair number of miles to go. If we have now conceded that our definition of money should include financial assets, or near-money forms which can be switched into purchasing power, what about National Savings deposits, or certificates of deposit, or a whole range of financial instruments in routine use within the trading flows of the money market? The M5 measure of money in the UK (formerly PSL2, that is, measuring public sector liquidity) adds just such a range of items to the M4 measure to give us the broadest definition of money in general use in the UK.

Your retaliation is likely to be immediate (provided that you have not fallen asleep): 'What about M0 and M2?' you could ask, with heavy irony, 'after all, these are the only numbers you have missed out . . . .'.

Money and Monetary Policy

```
                Notes and coins in
                circulation with
                the public
                       │
 plus   Private sector
        non-interest-
        bearing sterling
        sight bank                    plus   Banks' operational
        deposits                             balances with the
                                             Bank of England
                       │                            │
 equals Non-interest-bearing          equals  M0
        component of M1 etc.
                       │                            │
 plus   Private sector interest-bearing  plus  Private sector interest-bearing retail sterling
        sterling sight bank deposits           bank deposits
                       │                            │
 equals M1                            plus   Private sector holdings of retail building
                       │                     society shares and deposits and national
                       │                     savings bank ordinary accounts
                       │                            │
 plus   Private sector sterling time bank deposits  equals  M2
                       │
 plus   Private sector holdings of sterling bank
        certificates of deposit
                       │
 equals M3 (previously £M3)
                       │
 plus   Private sector holdings of building society   plus   Private sector holdings of foreign currency
        shares and deposits and sterling                     bank deposits
        certificates of deposit
                       │                                       │
 less   Building society holdings of bank deposits    equals  M3c
        and bank certificates of deposit, and notes
        and coin
                       │
 equals M4
                       │
 plus   Holdings by the private sector (excluding
        building societies) of money-market
        instruments (bank bills, Treasury bills,
        local authority deposits), certificates of tax
        deposit and national savings instruments
        (excluding certificates, SAYE and other
        long-term deposits)
                       │
 equals M5 (previously PSL2)
```

Figure 8.4 Relationships among monetary aggregates and their components.

Brace yourself! There *are* M0 and M2 measures of money in official use in the UK, providing relatively narrow and technical measures of the money stock; but, out of deference to your state of confusion and mental exhaustion, we shall not define these in detail in the text. The chart given in Figure 8.4 sets out the family tree of measures in use in the UK, and shows how these are interrelated to each other.

To give you some idea of the relative magnitudes involved, Table 8.1 shows the change in values for the different money measures over the year from September 1987 to September 1988. For example, the money supply as defined by M0 rose from £15.5 billion to £16.8 billion over the 12-month period, an increase of 8.8% (which was rather above its target range of 1–5%). M1 increased by 17.4% to £104.1 billion, and M3 by 22.5% to £215.8 billion; neither was given an official target, but both rates of growth were embarrassingly high, and provide yet another indicator of 'overheated' demand within the economy over the period concerned. The new M4 measure showed a money supply figure of £346.4 billion, and M5 a figure of £362.0 billion, with increases of 17.9% and 17.1% respectively for the 12 months – again reflecting very strong rates of growth.

Which is the 'best' measure and therefore definition of the money supply? It is fair to say that government preference (covering both main parties) has been fickle, and that no single measure has proved to be consistently satisfactory in its performance, for reasons which we will discuss later. For example, at relatively high rates of interest, firms and households tend to switch some of their sight deposit balances into time deposits, to benefit from the higher return on funds there; this has created some discontinuities and distortions in the behaviour of M1 over time. Another current measurement difficulty might follow if a sufficient number of commercial bank customers choose to transfer their business to building society cheque accounts, to benefit from interest paid on these transaction balances. This would cause the M3 measure to reflect a decline (or a slower rate of growth) in consequence (but, simultaneously, accelerate the growth rate of M4). No single measure seems to be free from the problems of a changing composition in the way in which financial assets are held. As a result governments tend to select a set of measures which, in combination, they feel should provide a more accurate insight into developments in the supply of money. Historically, UK governments have tended to use some combination of M1 and M3, or M3 and M5 (or PSL2, as it was known in the past). Probably the current favourites would be a combination of M0, M3 and M5; but, given the potential for embarrassment from the rapid rates of increase in the latter two, the public emphasis has been firmly placed on M0.

Extract 8.2 explores the possible value of using the new M0 measure. You might feel that *The Economist* is being a little bit cynical about the government's record on money measurement, or at least about

Table 8.1 UK measures of the money supply (£billion).

	Sept 1987	Sept 1988
M0[1]		
Notes and coins	15.3	16.6
Deposits at the Bank of England	0.2	0.2
Total	15.5	16.8
Other measures of money supply		
Notes and coins	12.6	14.3
Sight deposits	76.1	89.8
M1	88.7	104.1
UK private sector time deposits	87.4	111.7
M3	176.1	215.8
Private sector holdings of building society shares, deposits and CDs	128.0	147.8
Less Building society holdings of M3	(12.1)	(17.2)
M4	292.0	346.4
Private sector (excluding building society) holdings of money market instruments	4.7	4.2
National Savings deposits and certain securities	10.3	11.4
M5	307.0	362.0
M2[2]		
Notes and coins	12.6	14.3
Non-interest-bearing sight deposits	31.3	35.1
Private sector retail interest bearing deposits with banks	47.0	57.3
Private sector retail shares and deposits with building societies	88.9	104.3
National Savings Bank ordinary accounts	1.7	1.7
	181.6	212.7

Notes: 1. average for month
      2. end of month figure
(Reprinted by permission of *The Bank of England Quarterly Bulletin*, November 1988.)

Extract 8.2 THE ECONOMIST 18 JUNE 1988.

Britain's monetary policy

HANG ON A M0

MR NIGEL LAWSON, Britain's chancellor of the exchequer, retains much of his personal credibility as an inflation-fighter even though the details of his monetary policy have lately been good for a laugh and not much else. Broad money, variously measured, has been growing horribly quickly. Sterling, which had therefore been deemed chief monetary anchor, was deemed otherwise in March by the prime minister; exchange-rate policy has since been patched up, though none too convincingly. Throughout, the figleaf to conceal all this embarrassment has been M0.

This skimpiest measure of money—cash, in a word—has been all but ignored by the City. It is the only measure still honoured with a formal target by the Treasury (though officials pay due regard, of course, to all the other Ms, and to everything else you may care to mention). By not-so-pure chance, it is also the only one that has not been sounding an inflation alarm.

Guess what? Now that M0 looks set to grow disturbingly above its new target range, a City economist has produced a study which could well persuade everybody to start taking it seriously, as yet another sign of mounting inflationary pressure. Mr Stephen Hannah, formerly a Treasury official, now of County NatWest, argues in his bank's current financial bulletin that M0 is not the "Mickey Mouse aggregate" it has so far been taken for. It has, he says, a role as a warning signal for inflation—though a subtly different one from that envisaged by yesteryear's orthodox monetarists.

Early monetarism thought of "money" as a store of liquidity and hence as a source of future spending power. By squeezing this source, for instance with high interest rates, the government could reduce future demand in the economy and thus put downward pressure on inflation. This view of money as liquidity has several implications. First, the appropriate measure is a broad one—such as M3, the Treasury's previous target aggregate—because readily cashable bank deposits are as much a source of future spending power as cash. Second, changes in "money" might precede changes in demand by a year or more. Third, since money-as-liquidity is spending power, squeezing it should squeeze spending too.

None of this applies to M0. It is too narrow to pose as money-as-liquidity; therefore there is no reason to expect changes in it to change spending later; which also means that squeezing it is unlikely to have any direct effect on future inflation. So while the government has played down the broad measures, saying that changes in financial markets have broken the link between money-as-liquidity and spending, the City has been ignoring M0, saying it has nothing to do with monetarism.

Mr Hannah points out, however, that M0 is a reliable indicator of present, as opposed to future, demand. He shows that M0 growth has tracked quarter-by-quarter growth in demand, measured by money-GDP, fairly reliably since the early 1970s. This makes sense: M0 is not so much money waiting to be spent as money in the act of being spent. Very narrow money, in other words, is a plausible coincident indicator of demand. Untidily, Mr Hannah finds a slightly stronger statistical link between M0 and demand in the following quarter than between M0 and demand in the current quarter. Let that pass. Note too that M0 grows more slowly than money-GDP, because of gradually increasing efficiency in the use of cash. But what matters is that this gap is stable, at an annual average of four and a half percentage points.

A coincident indicator of demand—one that gives no advance warning—might seem of little use. Why not look at money-GDP directly? The answer is that money-GDP figures take months to emerge and do so only in quarterly form. M0 figures are quickly available on a weekly basis. If Mr Hannah is right, they give a useful—and worrying—snapshot. The measure is growing at nearly 6% a year. Allowing for the 4½% gap between its growth and that of money-GDP, this suggests that money-GDP is still growing at least as rapidly as last year's rate of 10%. This compares with the Treasury's budget forecast of 7½% for the year to next April.

If the long-term growth of supply in the economy is 3% a year, all this implies a risk that inflation is set to rise to 7% or so. It is time the Treasury dropped its M0 target: it is going wrong, and it might mean something.

Reprinted with permission from *The Economist* 18 June 1988 © *The Economist*.

the way in which it has tended to abandon (in setting official growth targets) those measures which have grown more rapidly than was intended. In its defence, *The Economist* has argued consistently for real monetary control, against a background where governments of all parties (and probably all nations), have tended to react to real-world statistical feedback which appears to contradict cherished political dogma, by either changing the statistics, or looking for a less embarrassing measure . . .! Our modern conversion to the religion of public relations has proved to be even more far reaching than the one experienced by Paul on the road to Tarsus.

Table 8.2 provides some interesting international comparisons, both on the money supply measures which are in preferred use in the various countries, and on the rates of growth associated with these over the previous 12 months (to February/March, 1988). Once again, it is noticeable that the UK rates of growth in M0, M3 and M5 are relatively high against the context of money growth in other countries – reflecting the 'overheating' of the UK economy.

It is easy to bog down amid such a welter of definitions and measures. It is therefore useful to stand back and consider some of the main points which can be drawn from the above discussion.

There are two vitally important aspects of money measurement which we would draw to your attention. Firstly, it is not an easy task to set down a hard and fast definition of the range of items which make up the supply of money, due in part to the ability of wealth holders to switch balances between different types of money and near-money financial assets. This carries important implications for any government which seeks to set itself a range of **monetary targets** for its macroeconomic strategy; it is likely to find that these targets will be difficult to achieve in their stated form.

Secondly, if you look again at the detail of the money measures in Table 8.1, you will be surprised at just how *little* of the supply of money is under the direct control of the government. Even if we take the 'narrow' measure of M1, notes and coins (the only items which are firmly and directly under the control of the government) account for only about 14% of the total in each of the years shown; for the 'broad' measure of M3, notes and coins amount to only about 7% of this new figure for the money supply. This is a point of major importance; the balance – between 85% and 93% of the supply of money (as measured by M1 or M3) is in the hands of the clearing banks, which are independent, profit making organizations. Thus, if the government wishes to control the rate of growth of the money supply, it must first control the routine operations of the commercial banking system. Since the latter are responsible to their shareholders and customers, as well as the government, it is at least possible that there might be a conflict of objectives between the government and these financial institutions – a view which might be

Table 8.2 Money aggregates: recent trends and targets. Percentage changes, seasonally adjusted at annual rates.

		Last observation	Last 12 months	Last 6 months	Last 3 months	Average last three monthly changes	1987 targeting Actual outcome	1987 targeting Official range	Official target 1988
United States	M1	Feb. 1988	3.7	3.4	2.3	3.7			
	M2	Feb. 1988	3.7	4.7	4.8	7.2	4.0	5.5–8.5	4–8
	M3	Mar. 1988	5.4	6.2	6.7	8.5	5.4	5.5–8.5	4–8
Japan	M1	Feb. 1988	8.3	5.0	3.1	15.2			
	M2+CD	Feb. 1988	12.0	12.1	10.7	11.5	11.8	11	12
West Germany	M1	Feb. 1988	9.0	7.0	7.3	16.2			
	M3	Feb. 1988	6.0	6.2	7.4	8.3			3–6
	CBM	Feb. 1988	8.1	8.4	8.9	8.7	8.1	3–6	
France	M2	Feb. 1988	3.7	4.1	3.1	−0.3	4.1	4–6	4–6
	M3	Feb. 1988	8.6	7.3	5.7	2.4	9.2	3–5	
	L	Feb. 1988	11.5	11.0	8.4	5.6			
United Kingdom	M0	Mar. 1988	5.3	4.8	2.4	1.8	4.3	2–6	1–5
	M3	Mar. 1988	21.0	17.7	12.0	18.2			
	PSL2	Mar. 1988	15.8	14.1	11.5	15.7			
Italy	TDC	Feb. 1988	12.8	11.2	11.8	11.6	13.1	11	11
	M2	Feb. 1988	7.8	3.2	−0.3	−1.0	8.5	6–9	6–9
Canada	M2	Mar. 1988	6.1	4.0	6.9	12.7			

(Reprinted by permission of the *OECD Economic Outlook*, No. 43, June 1988.)

strenuously denied in formal circles, but is nevertheless a possible, if not probable context for monetary control.

Why might such conflict exist? To answer this apparently simple question, we must look in a little more depth at both the lending activities of the banking sector and at the government's periodic attempts to control these through monetary policy.

THE BANKING SECTOR AND MONEY CREATION

Banks are financial institutions which make and receive payments on behalf of their customers, provide cash on demand, and administer a whole range of additional customer facilities ranging from financial advice to security and legal services. In terms of the analysis which follows, they have two key characteristics:

(1) They are independent, private sector organizations, which will seek to maximize profits like any other member of the firms' sector.
(2) They must also maintain an adequate level of liquidity, in the sense that they must always be able to meet any cash or settlement demands made upon them, by their customers or other banks.

At first sight, liquidity and profitability are conflicting objectives, in the sense that maintaining a liquidity reserve will divert funds away from more profitable (and simultaneously less liquid) uses. At one extreme, the bank would maximize its liquidity if all its deposits were held simply in cash form – but the return or profit would be zero from such a use of funds. Conversely, it would be at its most profitable if all its funds were put into high return uses, such as providing overdrafts to customers – but here liquidity would be poor, despite the fact that some of these loans are, technically, repayable on demand.

To simplify the analysis of business behaviour at introductory level, it is normally assumed that firms have a single objective, which is to maximize profit in the short and the long run; resources will always be deployed to secure the maximum gain from any situation. But banks do not fit comfortably into this simplifying assumption, since their need to maintain adequate liquidity represents a second major objective. Conceptually this can be dealt with in either of two ways. Firstly, it could be argued that to earn profits, banks must have deposits and, to attract these deposits, they must be able to demonstrate liquidity and security. Thus the maintenance of liquidity is an integral part of the behavioural pattern for profit maximization. As a second option – and this is the approach adopted here – the apparent short run conflict of liquidity and profitability can be conceded. Then the behavioural assumption for the

Table 8.3 UK banks' balance sheet (30 September 1988).

	£billion	£billion	%		
Liabilities (sterling £billion)					
Deposits					
Sight	115.0				
Time	215.0				
Certificates of deposit	36.7	366.7	87.0		
Items in transmission etc.		12.0	2.8		
Capital and other funds		42.7	10.1		
Total liabilities		421.4	100.0	(for comparison, assets October 1981)	
Assets (sterling £billion)				(£billion)	%
Notes and coin		2.4	0.6	1.5	1.2
Balance with the Bank of England		1.3	0.3	0.5	0.4
Treasury bills		0.7	0.1	0.7	0.6
Other bills		7.7	1.8	2.1	1.7
Market loans		122.2	29.0	37.9	31.1
Total		134.3	31.8	42.7	35.0
Investments (including government stock, one year or more)		20.6	4.9	6.7	5.5
Advances					
UK public sector	1.9				
UK private sector	224.5				
Overseas	13.2	239.6	56.9	62.5	51.3
Other		26.9	6.4	10.0	8.2
Total assets		421.4	100.0	121.9	100.0

(Reprinted by permission of the *Bank of England Bulletin*, November 1988, Table 3.1.)

banks becomes that they will try to maximize profits, subject to the constraint that they must always maintain an adequate reserve of liquidity.

This is *not* an arid academic point. Banks do have to walk a tightrope between profitability and liquidity, and it is possible to trace how they solve the problem, from an analysis of their balance sheets.

The balance sheet of any firm can be represented by the formula:

$E + L = A$

where E is the equity, or the owners' contribution to the business; L represents the liabilities, or the sums owed to third parties; and A represents the assets owned by the business. At its simplest, the lefthand side of the equation shows the *sources* of the funds which are held by the business; in contrast, the righthand side of the equation shows the *uses* to which these funds are put, as the firm seeks to achieve its objectives, or – in terms of simple theory – to maximize profits.

Table 8.3 provides a collective balance sheet for the UK banking sector which is suitable for our purpose. From this you will see that the total equity figure amounts to £42.7 billion as at September, 1988; liabilities are predominantly the customers' deposits held by the banks, which amounted to £366.7 billion, with items in transmission making up the balance of the total of £421.4 billion, for the lefthand side of our equation.

But our main interest lies in the deployment of assets by the banks; this shows us how banks have used the funds available, to allow themselves to maximize profits, subject to maintaining an adequate reserve of liquidity. Note how the balance sheet lists the assets in a pattern of declining liquidity and, simultaneously, increasing profitability.

The first two items in the table, notes and coin and balances at the Bank of England, represent completely liquid uses of funds – but have the disadvantage of providing a zero to very low return. These uses account for about 1% of total assets.

The next batch of items, treasury bills, other bills, and market loans, all represent funds held in financial assets which are short term in nature, and are quickly convertible into more liquid forms, with little danger of capital losses. For example, the discount market handles a constant flow of purchases and sales of discounted treasury and other bills (broadly the equivalent of post-dated cheques, which will be honoured on their due date, which is normally 90 days or less). While these represent slightly less liquid uses of funds, they do offer a slightly higher rate of return in compensation. Taken together, these first five items amount to 31.8% of total assets, as at September 1988, and represent the banks' use of funds to provide a reserve of liquidity.

The two remaining items, namely investments (including longer dated government stocks) and advances – represent the most profitable uses of the banks' funds but, simultaneously, are the least liquid forms of assets, and carry a real danger of capital losses. Together, they make up 60.8% of total assets.

Comparative figures are shown for asset deployment in October 1981; the broad pattern is the same, but there are some interesting variations in the weighting for particular items. The essential differences reflect the comparison of asset deployment between the mid point of a severe depression phase and a probable peak of a major boom phase in the business cycle. Note how the liquidity reserve for the depression year is substantially higher, at 35% of total assets; this could reflect the banks' collective prudent assessment of the higher risks in the economic environment at that time. At the same time, advances were markedly lower at 51.3%, reflecting households' and firms' pessimism at the lower turning point in the cycle, with a resultant lack of demand for credit (which could also explain why the banks were rather more liquid than normal).

It is possible to trace the same broad pattern of asset deployment by the banking sector over the latter part of the nineteenth and the entire twentieth century in the UK. This reflects a formula derived from their years of experience in the prudent management of funds; the banks have found that they will be able to meet any foreseeable claim for funds, if they hold 30–33% of their total assets in relatively liquid forms. While this represents a crude simplification of the commercial banks' policy intentions, it does show an accepted trade-off pattern in asset deployment which permits them to balance the conflicting objectives of liquidity and profitability.

This formula also provides us with a clear insight into banking practice; if only a proportion of sums deposited need to be held in a liquidity reserve, then the balance of the funds are available for use in earning profits. In particular, they are available for use as loans and advances, which are the form of asset use which yields the greatest return, and therefore profit to the bank. This practice is known as **fractional banking**, in that only a proportion of deposits will be held as a reserve against demands for payment by customers.

But this, in turn, takes us to a new and important aspect of the money supply. If customers' deposits provide funds for making loans and advances to other customers, and if cheques drawn against these agreed loan limits will be honoured, then bank credit (and credit from any similar financial intermediary) provides a means of payment which will also be accepted in payment of a debt. If the banks can create credit, then they are also **creating money**, in terms of our definition. Thus, loans and advances are an integral part of the supply of money and are the main reason why there has been such a rapid rate of growth in the M3 and M5 measures of money stock.

Indeed, broadening our argument, any access to credit which will permit purchases, is providing money in terms of our definition that 'money is anything which is acceptable in payment of a debt'. Even **plastic money**, or credit cards, by financing payments act as money – and the instant credit offered by them is also money. However, in this latter case, borrowing on credit cards – despite the fact that it catches the headlines – is only a tiny part of the whole of consumer borrowing. From Bank of England figures as at the autumn of 1988, over 80% of all recent households' borrowing has been on mortgages. Only 15% of personal sector debt is currently on consumer credit – and it is this latter figure which includes credit cards; the Bank estimates that credit cards account for less than 5% of the total, with 40% or more of credit card holders repaying their instant credit within the interest-free period. In short, despite their ubiquitous presence, 'plastic money' credit cards are simply used as a convenient method of payment, virtually as an alternative to the chequebook, and are settled from the same account which would have honoured the alternative instrument of cheques.

But let us not be diverted from our main theme. If banks can offer credit then they can create money, and the behaviour of the money supply figures will simply provide a measure of the banking sector's activities in its pursuit of profit. Is this ability to create money an open-ended power? How much credit can be offered on the basis of a new wave of deposits into the banking system?

Money creation by the banks reflects their ability to offer credit to households and firms. This activity is constrained by the need to maintain an adequate reserve of liquidity. It is possible to set up a simplified model which shows how the money creation process operates and responds to its constraint. To set up the model, assume that:

(1) The banks have only two possible uses of funds, these being as a reserve of liquid assets (unspecified, but corresponding to the first five items in Table 8.3), and as profit earning assets (simplified to cover only advances).

(2) The banks attempt to hold a liquidity reserve amounting to 30% of total assets (this figure is illustrative, but is based on past and current UK practice).

(3) The banks operate uniformly and simultaneously in their response to an increase in their liquid reserves, by creating additional advances.

(4) Bank customers spend to the full extent of their agreed borrowing power.

(5) Recipients of this expenditure pay it back into their own banks, without holding part as a cash balance (which would represent a leakage from the system depicted in the model).

Given these assumptions, the process by which money is 'created' is shown in Table 8.4. Here the catalyst is provided by an injection into the banking system by some external agency; for example, if the government buys back £90 million of its securities from the public, the latter will pay their receipts from this transaction into their accounts at the various banks. The banks can either hold these funds in idle liquidity, or use them to earn profits. In terms of the assumptions made, the banking

Table 8.4 Illustration of the money creation process.

		(£m)		(£m)
1.	The initial round			
	Banks receive	90	Hold	27
			Lend	63
2.	The second round			
	Deposits rise by	63	Hold	18.9
			Lend	44.1
3.	The third round			
	Deposits rise by	44.1	Hold	13.2
			Lend	30.9
4.	The fourth round			
	Deposits rise by	30.9	Hold	9.3
			Lend	21.6
5.	The fifth round			
	Deposits rise by	21.6	Hold	6.5
			Lend	15.1
6.	The sixth round			
	Deposits rise by	15.1	Hold	4.5
			Lend	10.6
7.	The seventh round			
	Deposits rise by	10.6	Hold	3.2
			Lend	7.4
8.	The eighth round			
	Deposits rise by	7.4	Hold	2.2
			Lend	5.2
9.	And so on			

system will hold 30% of the inflow (that is, £27 million) as a liquidity reserve and advance the balance of £63 million to households and firms. The latter, again given the assumptions, will spend to the limit of these agreed advances, and the recipients of this expenditure will pay the £63 million into their banking accounts. This creates the possibility of a second round of credit creation; the banks can hold the new wave of deposits in idle reserve, or attempt to use it to earn profits. If they again hold 30% (or £18.9 million) of the new deposits of £63 million as a liquidity reserve, which will meet all normal demands for payment, this leaves the balance of £44.1 million for making new advances, in this simplified model.

The process of adjustment to the initial disturbance will continue as shown in the various 'rounds' depicted in the table. In the third round, recipients of the expenditure from the second round will again pay this into their accounts; the banking system will again hold 30% of this new and third wave of deposits (that is, £13.2 million) as a liquidity reserve, and lend out the balance of £30.9 million. As the process continues over the fourth and subsequent rounds, the adjustments involve progressively smaller figures, since the need to maintain liquidity reserves at each stage of the process acts as a leakage from the process of expansion. The process will continue until the sums involved become zero.

The total deposits created, against which cheques can be drawn and honoured in payment, can be calculated by adding up the column of bank receipts, that is, £90 million in round 1, £63 million in round 2, £44.1 million in round 3 and so on. If the table had been completed for the full adjustment process, the total change in deposits would have amounted to £300 million; as it is, by the end of round 8, £282.7 million have been accounted for. The amount of this attributable to an increase in the level of advances (the true 'money creation' in the process) can be calculated by adding the 'lend' items in the table, that is, £63 million from round 1, £44.1 million from round 2, £30.9 million from round 3 and so on. Again, if the table had been completed, these items would sum to £210 million; by the end of round 8, £197.9 million have been accounted for. But what has happened to the first wave of £90 million of new deposits into the banking system, the initial disturbance which triggered off the whole adjustment process? If the 'hold' items are added together, that is, £27 million from round 1, £18.9 million from round 2, £13.2 million from round 3 and so on, then these would add to £90 million, had the table been completed; by the end of round 8, they sum to £84.8 million.

Thus, overall, the initial injection of £90 million has been held by the commercial banks as a liquidity base, on the basis of which they have made advances of £210 million, so that deposits in total have increased by £300 million. Once again, there is clearly a form of multiplier process at work, in the sense that the end result is substantially greater than the initial disturbance which triggered the adjustment. This new multiplier is known as the **money multiplier**, or the **credit multiplier**; if we give this the symbol k_m, then a formula can be derived[5] which shows that:

---

5. The formula for the money multiplier can be derived as follows. We know that a liquidity reserve (R) must be held as a proportion (ρ) of total deposits (D), or, in algebraic form,

$$R = \rho D$$

From the text, we know that if the reserve base changes, so too will total deposits, that is,

$$\Delta R = \rho \Delta D$$

By rearrangement (divide both sides by ΔD) we can show that:

$$\Delta D = \frac{1}{\rho} \times \Delta R$$

therefore

$$k_m = \frac{1}{\rho}$$

$$k_m = \frac{1}{\rho}$$

where ρ represents the liquidity reserve ratio which is in operation. Taking this a little further, and using the values from Table 8.4, if ΔR represents the initial increase in the reserve base (from the settlement of customers' cheques by the Bank of England in the table), and ΔD the resultant change in total deposits, then:

$$\Delta D = k_m \times \Delta R$$
$$= \frac{1}{0.3} \times +90$$
$$= +300$$

that is, with our new money multiplier, we can now estimate the final increase (or decrease) in total deposits which will follow from any increase (or decrease) in the liquidity reserve base of the banking sector.

Given this increase in total deposits, it is a simple matter to calculate the amount of credit, or money which has been created by the banking sector. This will simply be the additional loans and advances (ΔA) which have been made during the money creation process, as illustrated in Table 8.4; and these are simply the different between the change in total deposits and the initial change in the reserve base of the banks, that is,

$$\Delta A = \Delta D - \Delta R$$
$$= 300 - 90$$
$$= 210$$

To summarize the above, we now know that the practice of fractional banking allows the banking sector to increase the amount of credit offered to customers (and therefore to create money) when there is an increase in the level of assets held as part of their liquidity reserve. Changes in the money supply, as measured in its broader forms such as M3 or M5, will largely reflect changes in the level of credit offered by financial intermediaries, such as the banks and the building societies. The consumption boom which initially boosted, but latterly has troubled the UK economy over 1988 and much of 1989, has been largely fuelled by credit – which is one of the reasons why the interest rate has been subject to repeated increases over this period.

But, before we deal with the interest rate, there is one vital question which we must now consider. The supply of money will normally be a key target for the government in the implementation of its macroeconomic policy. But we have shown that the supply of money is largely in the hands of financial intermediaries such as banks and building societies. Can the government *permit* these independent, profit making organizations to decide on the level of money stock which is needed to allow the economic system to function, or must it take steps to *control* the money supply ... which involves imposing its will upon these independent members of the firms' sector?

MONETARY POLICY

How might the government seek to influence the actions of the financial intermediaries and, in particular, their apparent power to create money? In any economy, the **central bank** provides the vital link or channel through which the government can influence, or even transmit instructions to, the independent organizations which make up the money market. In the UK, the central bank is the Bank of England; as central bank, it must act both as:

(1) the government's bank and
(2) the bankers' bank

As the government's bank, it has several key responsibilities. Firstly, while the government holds minor working balances elsewhere in the banking system, its main financial transactions are carried out by the Bank of England, which deals with the major group of official accounts such as the National Loans Fund, the Paymaster General Account and the National Debt. Secondly, on behalf of the government it is responsible for the issue of legal tender, which is the term given to the notes and coin which, within the UK, must be accepted in settlement of a debt. Thirdly, it is responsible for managing the ebb and flow of the government's debt. If government borrowing requires a new issue of stock, this will be placed on the market at a set price; it is the Bank's responsibility to take up whatever is unsold at the date of issue and release this 'on tap' as it feels there is a demand for the stock in the market. This avoids new issues depressing bond prices, thus raising yields and placing upwards pressure on the rate of interest. Conversely, if an issue of government stock is approaching its maturity, the Bank will seek to purchase this as it is available, over a period before the redemption date – again to smooth the flow of transactions and prevent major unwanted disturbances to bond prices and the rate of interest. Finally, in its management of the government's debt, the Bank will seek to minimize the outstanding balance, by employing any surplus funds to reduce the amount of debt, and avoid unnecessary interest payments by the government.

While the Bank of England continues to deal with a few old established private accounts, it does not normally deal directly with the public. Its other major customers, apart from the government, are made up of the financial institutions in the UK. For example, the banks all maintain an account and balance with the Bank of England. This serves a dual purpose: firstly, it acts as one of their key liquidity reserve items, to be drawn on if they are short of cash in response to customers' demands; secondly, it is used routinely to settle inter-bank indebtedness, for example, from the daily clearing of cheques deposited and drawn in payment.

Within its duties as the bankers' bank, one of the Bank of England's main responsibilities is to act as a *lender of the last resort*. If a dire shortage of cash develops within the banking system, the Bank will lend against appropriate assets. While, if it was an absolute emergency, the Bank could lend directly to a commercial bank (provided that the problem was one of a genuine and temporary shortage of cash, and did not reflect more serious and deep rooted problems in the latter's investment policy, or general management of finances), the normal UK practice is to deal with such cash shortages in a more indirect fashion through the discount houses. The latter specialize in holding portfolios of treasury bills, gilt edged (that is, government) stock, commercial bills and so on, funded by short-term borrowing from the commercial banks and other institutions. If the commercial banks, in response to their own urgent cash needs, withdraw their funds from the discount market, or attempt to raise cash by selling treasury and other bills to the market, then the discount houses can borrow from the Bank of England to balance their position, against the security of the financial assets which they hold. In return for this right of access to the Bank, the discount houses must be prepared to take up the treasury bills issued each week by the central bank. The discount houses thus act as intermediaries between the Bank of England (or central bank) and the commercial banks.

From the above, you will realize that the Bank of England has an important role to play in the day-to-day transactions carried out by both the government and the financial intermediaries; it is this overlapping role within the money market which allows it to act as a transmission channel for the government's intentions towards that market, through **monetary policy**.

Given the stated objectives for the chapter, we will provide only a general description, rather than a detailed study, of the operations within the money market which are described as monetary policy. In particular, we will focus on two important aspects: firstly, its use to influence the cost and availability of credit; and, secondly, its influence on the level of demand (and therefore the level of economic activity) as portrayed in our basic model.

While the practice of monetary policy varies between countries and, over time, within any single country, there are a number of common policy instruments which can be used either by the central bank or, more directly, by the government itself. As with Chapter 7 on fiscal policy, the emphasis and comment on the material which follows are both on the UK system. The main policy instruments are explained below.

The manipulation of short-term interest rates

Until August 1981, the Bank of England published a Minimum Lending Rate (MLR) (previously known as the Bank Rate) which acted as an indicator for the whole structure of short- and medium-term interest rates in the UK. Technically, the MLR was the rate at which the Bank would discount first class bills to the discount houses. Since this represented the short-term rate of interest at which it was prepared to give funds to the discount houses, then the latter had no choice but to adjust their own rates in accordance with this, so transmitting the Bank's signal through to their routine business with the commercial banks and, therefore, through to the pattern of interest rates offered and charged by the latter. In general, the commercial banks would adjust their rates automatically in response to changes in the MLR, partly in acceptance of the government's intention, as represented by the signal, and partly reflecting their own awareness that the Bank could, if it had to, drain cash from the market and drive them to the discount houses, and the new rates of interest which had been imposed there.

Since 1981 the MLR has, technically, been abandoned; the Bank no longer takes the official responsibility for setting or administering the market's short-term rates. This, in a sense, was an inevitable consequence of the new monetarist thinking of the time. A central belief of monetarism is that free markets should be allowed to generate their own solutions, so that the traditional system of Bank control over interest rates was seen as an embarrassing anachronism; as opposed to a system of 'adminstered' rate changes, it was felt that market forces should be allowed a greater role in determining the structure of interest rates. Apart from this point of principle, the decision also reflected the government's intention at that time to concentrate more on the control of the money supply; if growth in this was to be constrained, then surges and variations in the demand for money would result in more volatile movements in short-term rates, and it was felt that market forces, as opposed to an administered price system, would achieve a greater degree of flexibility in response.

By now you must be resigned to the fact that nothing in economics is ever quite as simple and straightforward as it seems! While the above is still pretty much the 'official version' of events in the market, what seems to have emerged in practice is that the freedom to fluctuate is more apparent than real. The Bank has acted to hold very short-term rates (the seven-day rate has become the key rate in this respect) within a narrow band. It now publishes on a daily basis the rates at which it has conducted its dealings – which gives the same sort of guide to the Bank's view of appropriate rate levels as did the MLR, without having the formality of the latter. As before, there is the same ultimate power to drain cash from the market and drive the commercial banks back to the discount houses, and their greater direct dependence on the Bank for funding. In short, we seem to have adopted the very British solution of carrying on as before, while claiming that a totally new and superior set of procedures is in operation . . .

While the Bank's influence on medium-term interest rates (such as the key three-month rate) is less direct, these would still not appear to be left totally to market forces. In practice, much of the dealing reflects expectations on the future movements of the short-term rates (which are still heavily influenced by the Bank); and, on occasions where the Bank has disagreed with the assessment of market forces, it appears to have moved to communicate its own views on dealing rates in this part of the market. Overall, therefore, it would seem that the theory of a greater freedom of movement for interest rates operates in practice only so long as the level and trend are broadly consistent with the Bank's own views – which leaves the system still semi-administered, rather than completely free to market forces.

Extract 8.3, which is a compilation of comments on the Bank's influence over interest rates, drawn from the Mais Lecture given by the Governor of the Bank in May 1987, is interesting – not only for the insights which it provides into the mechanics of the system, but also for its studied diplomacy in disavowing that there is any intention to control!

In terms of monetary policy, what would happen if the Bank were to exert its influence on the market to *raise* the structure of interest rates? How might this affect the level of economic activity in the economy?

Interest rates in the money market determine the cost of credit to firms and households, through the borrowing rates which are charged by the banks and the other financial intermediaries. If interest rates were to be increased – as they were on five separate occasions in the UK over 1988–89 – then this would also increase the cost of credit. Here the chain of influence can become a little uncertain. If we assume that there is a reasonable degree of sensitivity to cost, the increased rates should discourage borrowers, and so constrain the growth in demand for credit (and therefore the supply of money). It might even cause the level of borrowing to fall, which would tend to reduce aggregate demand (with either C or J falling, in terms of the basic model) and the level of economic activity.

However, the evidence on the degree of interest rate sensitivity is rather mixed; marked increases in the cost of credit on several occasions

Extract 8.3 BANK OF ENGLAND QUARTERLY BULLETIN AUGUST 1987.

THE INSTRUMENTS OF MONETARY POLICY

Extracted from the 7th Mais lecture, when the Governor of the Bank of England discussed some of the problems of using policy instruments: the extracts all deal with interest rates

Introduction

Outside commentators on monetary developments sometimes create the impression that those responsible for operating monetary policy sit in front of a battery of switches and levers, each one of which will produce a precise and certain response in some area of the financial markets or directly in some more distant part of the economy. I can assure you that there is only one switch in my room, and that is the light switch.

In practice we have only a very limited range of instruments, though they can often be used tactically in different ways, and their effects can vary depending upon the particular circumstances prevailing at the time.

The operation of interest rate policy

There is a popular perception that the monetary authorities dictate the general level of interest rates, and it is of course true that we are able to exert a very considerable influence on it. But the extent of our influence should not be exaggerated. The financial markets are themselves an immensely powerful influence which we can never afford to ignore. At times, if market sentiment is uncertain and if the authorities are relatively confident in their view of the appropriate policy stance, the Bank's lead may be readily followed. But at other times, if we sought to impose a level of rates against strong market opposition, we are liable to be forced to change our stance. This could result from pressures at other points on the money-market yield curve beyond the point at which we were ourselves operating, or in the foreign exchange or gilt-edged or equity markets, any or all of which could have effects on the wider economy that were inconsistent with our policy aims at the time. We need always therefore to try to work with the grain of the markets to achieve the required effects.

This is true whatever the particular technical arrangements for exerting official influence on interest rates that are in place. Some people have read into the changes in those arrangements that have occurred over the years—from Bank rate to minimum lending rate to our present somewhat more flexible method of operation through the rate at which we purchase eligible commercial bills from the discount houses—much greater significance than is justified. While it is the case that the particular technical arrangements can provide for a greater or lesser *degree* of market or official influence, and that the relative influence exerted by the market and the Bank can change with circumstances, both influences are always present.

Operating within this constraint, the Bank can vary its tactics flexibly in order to try to achieve different effects on sentiment. Often our aim will be to slow the momentum of an interest rate movement sought by the markets rather than obstruct it altogether. In that case we need to think ahead to the possibility of further moves, and there are major tactical decisions to be made as to whether a move made sooner rather than later, or a larger rather than a smaller move, will produce the best eventual outcome from a policy perspective. In some circumstances, as for example last autumn, delaying a move can result in a smaller eventual move than the markets were suggesting; in others, such as the ½% reduction made ahead of the Budget this year, the judgement was that, had we delayed further, until the facts of the Budget were known to the markets—which would normally have been desirable—the pressure would have intensified for an overall larger reduction than the eventual 1% that seemed prudent to us at the time on policy grounds.

In seeking to influence the size and timing of interest rate changes we can operate with a higher profile—through publicised 2.30pm lending to the market, for example, which is the equivalent of the earlier MLR announcement: or we can operate more discreetly through varying the scale of assistance in relation to the market's needs or the terms on which we lend privately to the discount houses. When there is an interest rate change we can either follow a move in base rates initiated by the clearing banks or we can choose to anticipate a move that they might make on the basis of the rates prevailing in the interbank market.

Depending on market perceptions of the stance of policy, and the strength of prevailing pressures, these different tactics can have different effects on sentiment in the financial markets, and that in turn, as interpreted by the media, can have different effects on the perceptions and behaviour of the wider economy.

Conclusion

Chancellor, I have deliberately set out in this lecture to explain some of the limitations that apply to the operation of monetary policy, because I believe that this central part of the Bank of England's function will be better understood if there is a clearer perception of what we can and what we cannot hope to achieve. I am frequently asked why we do not take some particular action, for example, to raise or lower interest rates, to have this or that impact on some other particular aspect of the economy, such as the exchange rate or the growth of consumer borrowing, which my questioner sees as self-evidently desirable. I hope to have explained to you that the process of monetary management is rarely as simple as that: our ability to achieve selective effects is circumscribed and we need to be conscious of the *overall* effects of what we do.

The reality is the following:
- The instruments of monetary policy are limited, indeed in essence we are dependent upon a single instrument—the short-term interest rate.
- Our understanding of the precise effects of interest rates on the economy is limited, though I have no doubt of the direction of those effects in the round, and no doubt that they are powerful.
- Our ability to determine interest rates is limited, though, here too, I have no doubt that it is a powerful influence.

But we have a clear understanding of the aim of monetary policy. This aim, too, is limited —though, I would argue, crucially important. Monetary policy cannot, of itself, deliver a strong economy or full employment or greater industrial efficiency. It can lay an essential foundation for the achievement of those aims by resolutely pursuing the stabilisation of the value of money. That, I can assure you, remains our central banking purpose.

Reprinted with permission from *Bank of England Quarterly Bulletin* August 1987 © Bank of England Quarterly Bulletin.

---

in the past appear to have made little impact on the demand for borrowed funds. This might have reflected both the expectation and the effect of prolonged inflation (which would reduce the real burden of interest payments); equally, over 1980–81, it might have reflected the desperate straits of firms' borrowing, where instant liquidity – at whatever cost – might have been seen as the price of short-term survival in the harsh economic climate imposed by the trough of the cycle. More recently, with a large proportion of credit flowing into house purchases, it is very likely that the potential for capital gains from soaring house prices has far outweighed the costs of the credit needed to make these purchases, in the minds of borrowers. Whatever the cause, the essential feature to grasp is that where there is no real sensitivity to the cost of credit, then the weapon of interest rates will tend to have a limited short-term impact on the level of aggregate demand. It is very likely that this is the reason why the level of demand has been so resistant initially to the Chancellor's attempts to control it; in the longer term, as higher interest rates begin to bite through increased mortgage repayments, and effectively reduce the income available for other uses, then their constraining effect is more likely to be felt.

Open market operations

These represent the second main instrument of monetary policy, and have the potential to operate more directly upon the supply of money (or at least the borrowing component of this) as defined earlier in the text. **Open market operations** are the description given to:

> the transactions carried out by the Bank of England in the open market, whereby it buys or sells existing government securities by dealing directly with the public, with the intention of influencing the liquidity reserves of the commercial banks, and so triggering a multiple adjustment of their deposits and advances.

Note how it makes use of the principle of fractional banking, which we discussed in the previous section.

For example, assume that the Bank *purchases* existing government securities from the public on the open market; it will pay for these purchases by cheques drawn on itself. These cheques will be paid in by the members of the public to their sight or time deposits in the banking sector; in turn, when the commercial banks present the cheques for payment to the Bank of England, the amounts involved will be credited to their balances at the Bank, thus raising their liquidity reserve. If you look back to Table 8.4, you will be able to trace the consequences of this type of open market activity on the level of credit offered by the banks; an increase in their liquidity base allows the banks to use these funds to support a multiple expansion of loans and advances. You will remember that we calculated that an increase of £90 million in banks' reserves from this source would result in an increase in total deposits of £300 million, including an increase in the level of advances of £210 million. The size of the money multiplier, which would determine the extent of the overall increase, would be set by the reserve ratio which was in operation, that is,

$$k_m = \frac{1}{\rho}$$

In terms of the illustration in Table 8.4, with a reserve ratio of 30% the value of the money multiplier would be 3.33, so that the impact of the open market purchases on total deposits would be magnified by this amount.

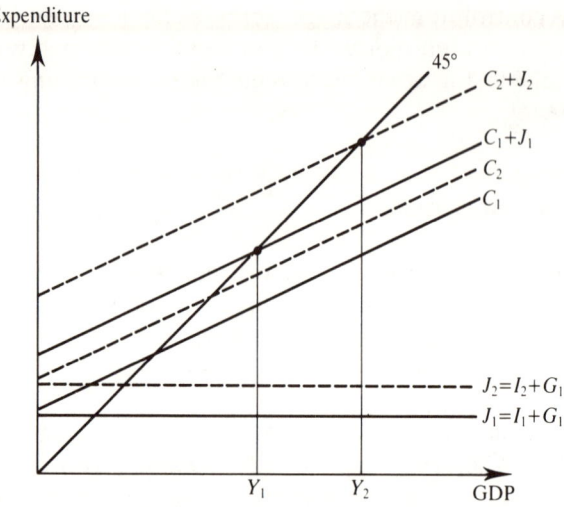

Figure 8.5 Effect of a reduction in interest rates.

If we think beyond this expansion of the money supply into its possible effect on the level of economic activity, then we can use our basic model to trace the consequences of the open market purchases on the market for final goods and services. If, as a result of the increase in their liquidity reserves, the commercial banks are placed in a position where they can support a greater volume of credit to households and firms, this should result in additional borrowing by both. In terms of Figure 8.5, this would raise both C and I to provide a new and higher level of aggregate expenditure of $C_2 + J_2$; this, in turn, will cause the economy to expand from Y_1 to the new and higher equilibrium level of GDP at Y_2.

Indeed, there is a second possible reason why open market purchases could cause a reflation of demand in this way. It is quite possible that the Bank's activities in purchasing bonds could drive up their market price; this would reduce bond yields, which might place downward pressure on interest rates – making credit cheaper as well as more easily available. If this occurred, it would provide an additional reason for a rise in the level of borrowing (and therefore C and I expenditure) by households and firms.

Conversely, if the Bank *sold* government securities to the public, the latter would pay by cheques drawn against their deposits or agreed advances in the commercial banks. The Bank would take payment for these cheques by deducting the amounts concerned from the commercial banks' balances at the Bank of England (then passing the cheques back to the banks, where they would be deducted from from the customers' balances). This would reduce the commercial banks' liquidity reserve, and could force a multiple contraction in their advances.

For example, if the open market sales amounted to £100 million, and the banks' reserves fell by this amount, then the commercial banks would have to rearrange their asset deployment by reducing the level of outstanding loans and advances, until the new lower reserve figure once more represented 30% of total assets. We can use the money multiplier to calculate the scale of adjustment which would be necessary; total deposits would have to fall (ΔD) by:

$$\Delta D = \frac{1}{\rho} \times \Delta R$$

$$= 3.33(-100)$$

$$= -£333 \text{ million}$$

(and by a further £333,333.33p for those of you who demand total accuracy!) This would imply that advances would have to be cut (ΔA) by:

$$\Delta A = \Delta D - \Delta R$$

$$= -333 - (-100)$$

$$= -£233 \text{ million}$$

The open market operations, this time by reducing the commercial banks' liquidity reserves, would trigger a multiple contraction of advances via the money multiplier. The commercial banks' response to open market sales would be to call in advances due for repayment, and to refuse or reduce the number of permissions for new advances requested by households and firms, until total assets were brought back into line with available reserves. Not only would this be reflected in the broader measures of the supply of money (either as a cut, or as a reduction in the rate of growth – depending upon what was happening to other sources of borrowing). In terms of our basic model, the effect would be the opposite of that illustrated in Figure 8.5; C and I would both fall, reducing the level of aggregate demand, and forcing the economy to contract towards a lower equilibrium level of income. Open market sales are therefore deflationary in their effect.

As before, the sales of these bonds on the open market could trigger a complementary side-effect. If the Bank has to raise the rate on government bonds to make them more attractive to buyers, this could exert upward pressure on interest rates; indeed, as credit becomes more difficult to obtain, market forces could drive interest rates upwards, at least initially. Thus open market sales could be accompanied by an increase in the cost of credit, which would tend to nudge C and I in the same downwards direction as that caused by the reduction in the availability of credit discussed above, reinforcing the revisions in consumption and investment expenditure plans.

A distinction should be drawn between the Bank's activities in open market operations, and those transactions which are concerned with the shorter dated bills in the market. The former involves a transaction between the Bank and the public, whereas purchases of eligible bills involves transactions between the Bank and the other financial institutions. Secondly, the effect of open market operations is to influence the commercial banks' liquidity reserves and, through this, their levels of advances. In comparison, if the Bank buys eligible bills, the adjustment takes place *within* the commercial banks' liquidity reserves, that is, short-term bills are reduced and balances at the Bank increased; there is thus no net change in the commercial banks' liquidity reserves, and so there is no knock-on effect to advances and the supply of money.

However, any dealings, for whatever purpose, between the Bank and the public will have the type of consequences illustrated above. For example, if the Bank releases new stock on behalf of the government by selling it to the public, then these sales will reduce the commercial banks' balances at the Bank. Conversely, if it buys stock to smooth a redemption (that is, spreads the flow of its purchases of a stock which is approaching its maturity date), its payments will ultimately raise commercial banks' balances at the Bank. Should the Bank feel that these events could have a disruptive effect on the supply of money, it might decide to run *offsetting* open market operations to minimize, or even neutralize the adjustment. In general, open market operations represent a device which can be used by the central bank either to influence the level of loans and advances offered by the commercial banks (and so the supply of money) or, alternatively, to change the liquidity position of the commercial banks and drive them to the discount market, where the Bank can impose its own views on short-term interest rate levels and, ultimately, on the cost of credit.

Manipulation of the reserve ratio

While the commercial banks can create money by increasing the volume of bank credit, they cannot create reserves. The amount of reserves available, taken with the reserve ratio in force, sets the limit to credit creation.

In some countries the government, via the central bank, has legal powers to vary the required reserve ratio to be observed by the commercial banks. By doing so, they can influence the level of bank credit which can be supported by a given level of reserves, without having to use open market operations to change the level of funds held in this reserve. To illustrate, take a simple case where the banking sector held an initial liquidity reserve of 300, had advances and loans of 700, and therefore total assets of 1000; if the liquidity reserve ratio was 30%, then these total assets would be fully covered. But suppose that the government, through legislation, raised the required reserve ratio to 40%. Clearly, total assets must be adjusted until the reserve figure of 300 represented 40% of total assets; equally, in our simplified balance sheet, the only way such an adjustment could be made would be by reducing the level of advances. To reduce total assets to 750 (so that the reserves balance of 300 satisfied the new legally imposed reserve ratio of 40% for this figure), advances would have to be cut to 450. Thus, raising the required reserve ratio will force the commercial banks to reduce advances and, therefore, the supply of money (and, conversely, reducing the legal reserve ratio would permit the banks to increase the level of advances). As before, these changes in the supply of money would have repercussions on consumption and investment plans (by affecting the availability of credit), so that this instrument of monetary policy would also have reflationary or deflationary consequences on the market for final goods and services.

This type of legislation has never applied in the UK, but there have been some interesting variations in the government's attitude towards the financial assets which should be included in this reserve ratio. Until 1971, the commercial banks were allowed to operate to the pattern which had been proved to be prudent from practical experience, that is, that liquid and near liquid assets (as identified in Table 8.3) should be held at about 27%–28% of total assets. Over the period 1971 to 1981 the government, through the Bank of England attempted to impose a tighter technical control over the system, by requiring the commercial banks to maintain their **reserve assets** at a ratio of at least 12.5% of their **eligible liabilities**. 'Eligible liabilities' consisted mainly of sterling deposits; reserve assets consisted of selected items from (and, in some case, specified maximum proportions of) balances at the Bank of England, money at call, treasury and local authority bills, plus short-dated (less than one year to maturity) government and nationalized industry bonds (but excluding certificates of deposit with a maturity of more than two years). The intention was that the traditional 30% ratio should *not* be disturbed, but that the composition of items which would normally be included within this should be subject to greater control.

The position since 1981 is that the Bank of England has reverted to the system underpinned by the traditional liquidity ratio; the reserve ratio requirement was ended. There has been an inconclusive discussion about the possibility of using a more narrowly defined liquidity reserve measure (**monetary base control**), corresponding to the very liquid assets included in the M0 measure of money, or **high powered money** (so called because of the very high value such a ratio would give to the money multiplier, if it were to be used). But the only specific current requirements are, firstly, that the commercial banks should maintain a cash ratio of at least 0.5% of their 'eligible liabilities' at the Bank; the commercial banks themselves can decide whether or not to exceed this in providing a working balance for their settlement and other needs. Secondly, the commercial banks must hold a minimum proportion of 4% of their 'eligible liabilities' in secured deposits with the discount market (to permit the discount houses to function in the bill market). But both of these measures should be seen as requirements which are intended to ensure the smooth and efficient operation of the money market, rather than to act as constraints, or a control mechanism.

Other measures

There are three other possible tools of monetary policy, as it has been operated in the UK. These tend to be relatively minor, in the sense that the main thrust of monetary policy will normally be exercised through the manipulation of short-term interest rates and open market operations described above. However, the following have made a contribution at some stage in the past, and are still technically available for future use:

Special deposits

The success of open market operations depends upon the commercial banks being on the margin of their liquidity reserve; in particular, open market sales will only influence the level of borrowing if these reserves are driven below their minimum safe level. But in practice, the banks have tended to hold a reserve which is substantially in excess of this minimum ratio; frequently, available reserves could support a greater level of credit than appears in the banks' balance sheet. This 'surplus liquidity' may be a prudent practice, from the viewpoint of the commercial banks but it does represent a possible cushion against the open market operations carried out by the Bank of England, and so might frustrate the full deflationary intentions of the latter. For example, if the liquidity reserve amounts to 35% of total assets, then open market sales must reduce these reserves to 30% of total assets before the commercial banks need to consider *any* response in their lending policy. Nor is this simply a conceptual point; banks are very sensitive about their independence, and have been slow on occasion to respond to the Bank's signals for control – after all, offering credit is the most profitable use of banks' funds.

Accordingly, the Bank has the power to call for the commercial banks to lodge sums at the Bank, when they feel that there is surplus liquidity in the banking system. These special deposits earn a relatively low rate of interest for the commercial banks, but their essential feature is that they cannot be included in the computation of the reserve ratio, that is, they are effectively withdrawn from the liquidity reserve. In this way actual liquidity reserves can be brought more into line with the margin of liquidity, so that open market operations can have a more direct and immediate effect. Equally, when the need for control of the money supply has eased, the special deposits can be released in whole or in part by the Bank, thus boosting the liquidity position of the commercial banks. No special deposits have been called since summer 1980, but the government has stated that the power to do so has been retained.

Supplementary special deposits
The history of attempted monetary control is a fascinating topic in its own right. There has seldom, if ever, been an open and obvious conflict between the commercial banks and the Bank of England; but, on occasion, eyebrows have been seen to be raised and – in moments of extreme stress – copies of the *Financial Times* have been opened, or closed, in first class rail compartments with rather more noise and flourish than has been strictly necessary. Money market emotions run deep. While both sides would probably deny the allegation vehemently, there are grounds for suspecting that the banks have tended to be a little evasive towards central control at times. This has been reflected in the emergence of a series of experimental policy instruments, which have been used intermittently, with patchy if any success, then ultimately abandoned. For example, supplementary special deposits (nicknamed 'The Corset' – almost certainly by an irreverent tabloid) were introduced in 1973 to try to impose some control over the rapid growth in the supply of money. Under this scheme, growth in excess of a specified rate was penalized by requesting the bank concerned to make a non-interest-bearing deposit with the Bank, proportional to the amount of excess growth. This instrument was used from 1973–75, again in 1977, and again over 1980–82 but, like most forms of direct control, it has been dropped (partly on grounds of principle and partly because it was felt to blunt the competitive response of the financial intermediaries to changing conditions in the money market).

Hire purchase credit
This provides another device by which the government can influence the availability of credit. For example, if the minimum proportion of the total debt required for the initial deposit is increased and the repayment period reduced, this makes borrowing via HP contracts less attractive, and should have significant effect on consumer expenditure. Conversely, if reflation is desired, the credit terms can be eased with lower initial deposits required, and greater repayment periods permitted. With more attractive credit opportunities, consumption expenditure should be increased – as in fact has happened as a result of the relaxation of credit

terms in the car industry from autumn 1982. Whether credit is being eased or tightened, there is no direct control over the cost of HP credit. Nevertheless, there is a strong indirect influence, in the sense that the interest charged by the finance houses will reflect market rates, which are still at least partially under the control of the government.

While HP controls do offer a relatively strong link to consumption expenditure, there has been a reluctance over recent years to chop and change the terms of credit in response to policy needs. It is felt that this form of control is too 'industry specific', in the sense that its effect tends to be concentrated on those consumer goods industries which are heavily dependent on this form of credit (for example, cars, furniture, stereo systems, refrigerators, washing machines and so on). The preferred form of 'control' has been to operate through the structure of interest rates and therefore on the ultimate cost of credit – with an eye to the fact that banks and building societies have been competing increasingly for short- and medium-term credit customers, and placing extra pressure on the specialist market niche of the finance houses. In a sense, competition in interest rates has been encouraged, and allowed to determine both the overall volume of credit taken up and the pattern of distribution of this business between the different forms of financial institution.

PROBLEM AREAS IN MONETARY POLICY

The instruments which have been described above are used individually or collectively to implement the government's monetary policy. In essence, they represent different methods which can be used by the government, through the Bank of England, to supervise and influence the activities of the various financial institutions which make up the money market. In particular, they provide an additional constraint on the ability of the banking sector to 'create money', and therefore provide the means through which the government can maintain some degree of control over the supply of money.

Before we turn to a more critical assessment of the effectiveness of this package of measures, it is useful to distinguish between monetary policy and the **monetary management** activities of the Bank of England. Much of the Bank's routine involvement in the money market is intended more to ensure the efficient operation of this market and to smooth out unwanted disturbances, than to effect changes in the supply of money; this is very much its 'management' role within the market, as it supervises cash flows, government borrowing, bond prices and interest rates. The term of **monetary policy** is therefore confined to deliberate initiatives and actions which are intended to influence the supply of money and through this, possibly, to influence the level of economic activity.

As with fiscal policy, there is always the danger that a simplified and outline presentation of a policy instrument can leave the reader with a false impression of its actual – as opposed to its theoretical – power. On the face of it, monetary policy has a great deal to offer. Unlike fiscal policy, it does not face a limited number of decision and action points (such as those associated with the main and autumn mini-budgets). The government's central bank is involved in the day-to-day operation of the money market, so that there is an apparent scope for monitoring and adjusting policy in pursuit of monetary targets. But care must be taken here not to translate the simple point of greater *access* into a case for more accurate and flexible *control*. Monetarist economists have argued consistently that the influence of monetary control on the economic system is through a series of time lags, which can be prolonged and which can vary for reasons which are still not fully understood. They insist that, given the possibility of unpredictable delays in response, monetary policy should not be used for short-term manipulations, but should be held as an instrument controlling the longer term expansion of money and the creation of a more stable environment for business and consumption decisions.

Again in its favour, many economists would argue that monetary policy is more acceptable in its side-effects than fiscal policy. Compare how each policy would operate, if the government's intention was to reflate the economy. Under fiscal policy, the expansion in income triggered by the increase in government expenditure could drive up interest rates (as we will discuss in the following section) and so 'crowd out' interest sensitive private sector expenditures, creating an offsetting effect on the intended expansion. In contrast, should reflation be carried out by monetary policy, then this could take the form of an increase in the supply of money (for example, by open market purchases, followed by a multiple expansion of credit). As argued above, this would spill through directly into expenditure on real assets and, indirectly, through a reduction in the rate of interest and the consequent stimulation of interest sensitive expenditure. In other words, reflation by monetary policy would reduce the rate of interest and stimulate private sector expenditure, in contrast to the increase in the rate of interest and crowding out of private expenditure which would result from fiscal policy.

However, all is not sweetness and light. Practical experience has shown that some serious problems can be anticipated in the use of monetary policy. Firstly, there is an informational problem. While financial data is more quickly and more comprehensively available, which helps monitoring and problem identification, there are still major problems of *interpretation* of the trends and events which are contained in this data. Which money stock measure(s) should be used? Indeed. which can be fully trusted? **Goodhart's Law** (propounded in probable exasperation by a senior adviser to the Bank) is the broad financial equivalent to Murphy's Law; it states that whenever a target measure of money is chosen, then this will immediately begin to behave in a quite abnormal and unpredictable fashion. In effect, the monetary target is distorted by the attempts of financial institutions to find ways and methods of easing – if not defeating – the control system which the target represents. It is this behavioural problem which has resulted in the constant chopping and changing of money supply measures – and the increasing unwillingness of the UK government to set official targets. This is why only the very narrow M0 is still given an official target – and even this takes the form of a wide range, rather than a single growth rate. Advisers to the Bank, as they mull over the information contained in their chosen set of measures (such as M0, M3 and M5 currently) have a disturbingly similar appearance to ancient priests brooding over the omens contained in chicken or animal entrails; the worrying fact is that the modern priests might not have the same degree of accuracy in their interpretations and prophesies . . .

Secondly, many economists would argue that the system of control is less certain than it might appear to be. Much of the supply of money, however defined, is an integral part of the profit earning activities of the independent commercial banks; and even they might have limited control over events. In the case of reflation, even if credit expansion is made possible by open market operations, it will not take place if households and firms are unwilling to borrow – which may well be the case in conditions of depression and uncertainty (remember the relatively high liquidity reserve figure for 1981 in Table 8.3). The commercial banks cannot be *made* to increase the supply of money. Conversely, to reduce the supply of money for deflationary purposes, the level of advances from the commercial banks must be cut. But the whole history of monetary control in the UK is one of lukewarm and partial responses to signals for deflation. Even when the combined weight of open market operations, special deposits, supplementary special deposits and 'management meetings' with the Governor of the Bank has brought the commercial banks under some sort of effective constraint, households and firms have still been able to obtain funds from 'fringe banking' financial institutions – in some of which (for example, finance houses) the commercial banks have had an ownership interest, and to which they have frequently redirected customers which they were not able to serve 'over their own counters'. Even where severe credit charges have been imposed as a rationing system (for example, when short-term rates have been raised repeatedly, as over 1988–89), neither households nor firms have shown the expected sensitivity to this in their borrowing requests, at least in the short term. Response is therefore nowhere near as clearcut as our illustrations in the text might seem to suggest; it is more likely to be imperfect and delayed. However, it must be stressed that our criticism is not that monetary policy *cannot* change the supply of money; it is simply that it might take longer to do so than you would expect, due to the indirect system of control via the independent commercial banks, and their relationship with equally independent households and firms.

Thirdly, even if the Bank were able to measure, interpret and control the supply of money, then there would be a real possibility that the interest rates which would emerge in the money market would become embarrassingly volatile, and embarrassingly high on occasion. The truth is that the past and current imperfections in the system of control have tended to absorb some of the surge and ebb pressures of demand, by permitting leakages and overspills from the system of control. If these forgiving leakages were to be stopped, then the normal fluctuations of demand would crash like waves against the cliff of a fixed stock of money, with unwanted if spectacular results. Do we want greater variations in interest rates? Do firms with investment projects and households with extensive bank loans or mortgage borrowing want substantial, if temporary, increases in credit costs? One of the reasons why the monetary base proposals did not really go beyond the discussion stage was that the authorities suspected that the answer would be a loud 'No' to both questions. There is a strongly held, and very British belief that the money market (and through the rate of interest which emerges from this, the real economy) *benefits* from its known imperfections in control . . . The more efficient is the control over the stock of money, the more savage are the implications for the price of money, that is, the rate of interest.

Finally, there is a further source of problems, in the possible side-effects of monetary policy on international trade flows. If, for instance, the government seeks to impose strict controls on monetary growth, as a result of which domestic interest rates are driven upwards, then this could well attract international funds to the UK economy (to benefit from the higher return there), which could raise the exchange valuation of the pound sterling (as we will discuss in Chapter 11). This, in turn, would tend to drive upwards the price of UK exports in world markets and, simultaneously, reduce the price of imported goods and services in our own domestic markets. As a result, export sales could fall, and import penetration of domestic markets could rise, both weakening the demand for UK output (reducing both the J and the C^* functions, in terms of the basic model), so causing the level of economic activity and employment to contract. There is some evidence that this unwanted side-effect of the government's macroeconomic policy over 1979–81 (which was trying to halt inflation and to damp down inflationary expectations) was a contributory cause of the severity and the duration of the depression phase of that cycle.

THE RATE OF INTEREST

But where does all of this leave us? We set out originally to explore the relationship between the money market and the real economy. The basic structure for our investigation has been that if there is a market, then there is also a demand for money which interacts with the supply of money, to set the price of money – or the rate of interest. Our first task was to build up an understanding of the factors which would influence the demand for money. Figure 8.2 summarizes the behavioural pattern for this demand. Our second main task was to explore the nature of the supply of money. This involved not only an exploration of the problems of providing a clearcut definition of the financial assets which operate as money, but also the realization that any broad definition of 'money' will cover assets and activities which are, for the most part, outside the direct control of government. This, in turn, has taken us through the government's attempts, via monetary policy, to exercise some control over the supply of money – and we have seen that this is far from a certain and accurate process.

How can we reduce all of this into a simple model? Figure 8.3 gathered all the main items of information together, to show how demand and supply interact to establish the rate of interest in the money market.

Earlier in the chapter we argued that the demand for money would be a function of both the level of income and the rate of interest. In terms of the model, the demand for transactions and precautionary balances sets the position of the demand for money function, while the demand for speculative balances determines its slope, or sensitivity to the rate of interest.

For a simple model, it is possible to treat the supply of money as being determined administratively by the government, as an absolute amount for any given time period; this allows the function to be depicted as vertical and therefore unaffected by the rate of interest. In turn, this implies that the government has full control over commercial banks' deposit levels and credit creation policy, as well as over the issue of notes and coin. This we know is very much an over-simplification; equally, it implies that the commercial banks are insensitive to the rate of interest in their credit creation policy, which is very much a further simplification. Nevertheless, whatever the slope of the supply function (that is, vertical or steeply positive), our simplifications do not interfere with the functioning of the model.

Given the functions as they are shown in Figure 8.3, the equilibrium price, or rate of interest will be set where the quantity demanded equals the quantity supplied of money, opposite the point of intersection of the two functions: above this point, supply will exceed demand, so that interest rates will tend to drift downwards; below this point the reverse is true, and interest rates will tend to be bid upwards as firms and households search for funds. Given the initial functions of D_{m1} and S_{m1}, the rate of interest would emerge as r_1.[6]

As with any other equilibrium, should the position of the functions be revised, this will normally result in the emergence of a new equilibrium. When discussing the side-effects of fiscal policy, reference was made to the possible problem of increased government expenditure 'crowding out' investment. This possibility can now be explored in terms of our new model; Figure 8.3 also showed that, as the economy reflates in response to the increase in government expenditure, as magnified by the multiplier adjustment process, then the demand for transaction and precautionary balances is also likely to increase. This will cause the position of the demand for money function to move outwards from D_{m1} to D_{m2}. Against an unchanged supply of money, S_{m1}, this will force up the rate of interest to r_2. To the extent to which consumption and investment are sensitive to the rate of interest, these planned expenditures will be revised downwards, creating an offsetting effect within the aggregate expenditure function of the basic model (that is, while G will increase within the J function, I will also fall, and the C function might also be revised downwards. The 'cancelling out' effect could be partial or even total, depending upon the extent to which the interest rate rises, and the degree of sensitivity shown towards this increase by investment and consumption expenditure plans). But the end results are that the overall expansion of the economy in response to the increase in government expenditure is rather less than was anticipated, and resource allocation to private sector expenditure is reduced, 'crowding out' the latter.

It is interesting to pursue this point a little further. Should the government wish to avoid 'crowding out', it could do so by allowing the supply of money to increase (in terms of Figure 8.3, the money supply function would move to the right), so that the new S_{m2} cut the higher demand function D_{m2} opposite the original interest rate of r_1. With no change in the rate of interest, there would be no short-term revisions in either consumption or investment expenditure plans . . . so there would be no 'crowding out' experienced. It might be yet another over-simplified judgement, but traditional Keynesian policy makers have been accused of allowing 'permissive' increases in the supply of money, in their determination to hold interest rates at a level which would encourage investment expenditure and, therefore longer term economic growth. Chapter 9 will show how these increases in the supply of money could well, in the longer term, have triggered the inflationary pressures which so undermined both the actual and the anticipated return on investment,

---

6. Again this is a simplification; rather than a single rate of interest, there will be a whole range or structure of interest rates, with each rate reflecting factors such as duration of loan, security (or collateral) available, perceived degree of risk and so on.

that substantial damage was caused to the latter and to the UK's rate of economic growth from the mid to the late 1970s.

At this stage, we have no wish to explore the point. It is sufficient to use it as a possible example of how it is dangerous to ignore the role of money in the macroeconomy. Perfectly praiseworthy actions taken in the present can, if they have monetary implications, come back to haunt the policy makers at some future date. Long and difficult though this chapter may have seemed at times, it should have been invaluable in releasing you from a tunnel-visioned view of the macroeconomy. Behind the comfortable clarity of the basic model of the economy, there lies the very complex and additional dimension of the money market. It is dangerous – if not downright foolish – to examine either market in isolation from the other; actions taken in one will generally carry consequences for the other, and the feedback from these consequences is very likely to influence, or even distort, the anticipated results of that original action.

CONCLUSIONS

1. Money is anything which, in the economic system concerned, is generally accepted in payment of a debt. It must act as a medium of exchange; it must also provide units of measurement in terms of which the relative values of other goods can be set; it must also be capable of being used as a standard of deferred payment, and as a store of value.

2. The transactions demand for money is essentially linked with its function as a medium of exchange. The precautionary demand for money, while it also reflects an end use in this role, also contains some aspects of the store of value function, in that precautionary balances will tend to be held over time as a reserve of purchasing power.

3. The demand for speculative balances is linked more firmly with the store of value function of money. While money balances will generally yield a low or zero return, their short-term certainty of value is attractive to wealth holders as a form in which their wealth can be placed, when capital losses are feared in other forms of financial asset.

4. While a conceptual definition of money is relatively easy to provide and understand, it is extremely difficult to provide a definition which yields a convincing and clearcut measure of the supply of money in practice. The problem lies in where the boundary line is drawn between money which is used for transaction purposes, and other money balance and near-money financial assets which can quickly be converted into cash. In most countries, therefore, the behaviour of

money is measured through a combination of different money supply definitions. In the UK, the combination which is currently used covers the M0, M3 and M5 measures of money – all of which have been growing rather more rapidly than is comfortable over 1987–88.

5. A related problem is that the supply of money consists of any financial item which is acceptable in payment of a debt; as such, it embraces notes, currency, and deposit and overdraft accounts from which payment can be made on demand by the commercial banks (and, increasingly, by the major building societies). But these financial intermediaries are independent organizations, with their own profit earning objectives. The practice of fractional banking (where only a proportion of new deposits are held as a liquidity reserve) permits these financial intermediaries to create credit. This, in turn, leaves a very large proportion of the money supply outside the direct control of the government and its central bank, the Bank of England.

6. Since the supply of money is normally a key policy target for any government, some degree of control or influence must be exerted by the central bank of the 'money creation' powers of the financial intermediaries. The various methods of control are described collectively as the instruments of monetary policy: in the UK the first main instrument of control over the level of credit which is offered is through the Bank's ability to influence the cost of credit via interest rates in the money market; the second main instrument of control is provided by the ability of the Bank to influence the banking sector's liquidity reserves through open market operations, with these changes in reserves triggering either a multiple expansion or contraction of credit.

7. Provided that the commercial banks respond as stated, and households and firms are sensitive to the cost of credit, then monetary policy offers a potentially powerful weapon of economic policy. Changes in the supply of money should influence aggregate expenditure in both of two ways: firstly, the changes should lead directly to adjustments in the level of planned expenditure on wealth held as real assets; and secondly, changes in the money supply should be reflected in changes in the rate of interest and, through this, in the level of borrowing and expenditure by households and firms.

8. If the independence of the commercial banks hinders their response to government policy (particularly if there is surplus liquidity in the banking system) then institutional factors might hinder and delay the supply of money response to monetary policy promptings. This is equally true where households and firms seek a source of credit

with determination and some degree of tolerance to interest charges. Conversely, if reflation is sought in conditions of uncertainty and low expectations, then the availability of credit or of surplus cash balances might not necessarily pass automatically into higher levels of expenditure. The ability in practice to control and deliver changes in the supply of money might be rather less convincing in the short term than would be suggested by the theory models – a problem which is shared with fiscal policy.

9. The rate of interest is set by the interaction of the demand for and the supply of money. If the demand for money increases, for example if there is a substantial rise in the level of economic activity and therefore in the demand for transactions and precautionary balances, then against a fixed supply of money this will drive up the rate of interest. Conversely, if the supply of money rises against an unchanged demand for money, this will tend to drive interest rates lower.

10. Given the possibility of interest rate sensitivity in both consumption and investment expenditure plans, it must always be accepted that changes in the rate of interest in the money market could have real consequences for the level of aggregate demand in the market for final goods and services. The same is true for changes in the supply of money in the money market, where these involve changes in the availability of credit to households and firms. The two markets are therefore interrelated, and it is dangerous to view one in isolation from the other. If the government seeks to reflate the economy, it will probably drive up interest rates, which could have an adverse feedback on consumption and investment plans. If the government seeks to cut the supply of money (for example in an attempt to curb inflationary pressures), the subsequent increase in interest rate levels is likely to have a strong deflationary effect on the level of demand and economic activity. Neither is simply a theoretical point; governments have repeatedly ignored – and then been surprised by – the strength of the adverse feedback between the markets.

11. Control of the economy is therefore rather more complex than might be suggested by the introductory macroeconomic models. Policy makers must constantly be aware of events in both markets and, in framing policy for either market, must bear in mind the possible repercussions of that policy in the other market. Simplistic solutions will seldom, if ever, apply. This is a major conclusion which will be taken up again and explored in depth in the following chapter on inflation.

SELF-ASSESSMENT QUESTIONS

TRUE/FALSE QUESTIONS

8.1. Whether the M1, the M3, the M4, or the M5 definitions of money is used, only a minor proportion of the items involved are under the direct control of the government.

8.2. The commercial banks' power to 'create' money simply refers to the ability to make further loans and advances in response to any increase in their liquidity reserves.

8.3. When the Bank of England purchases eligible bills from the commercial banks this will raise the liquidity reserves of the latter and permit a multiple expansion of credit.

8.4. When monetary policy seeks to expand the supply of money and reduces domestic interest rates, this could also cause the international value of the pound sterling to fall and, through this, affect the UK's international trade flows.

MULTIPLE CHOICE QUESTIONS

8.1. The power of the UK commercial banks to 'create' money is limited in practice by:
   (a) The extent to which they can issue their own notes;
   (b) The extent to which the government, through the Bank of England, is prepared to provide notes and coin;
   (c) The need to maintain a reserve to meet demands for cash;
   (d) The willingness of households and firms to take up advances, when these are available from commercial banks;
   (e) The trust of the public in the banking system.

8.2. The rate of interest is set by the interaction of the demand for and supply of money; it will, therefore:
   (a) Rise if there is a contraction in the supply of money;
   (b) Be unaffected if there is a fall in the level of economic activity;
   (c) Rise if there is an increase in income levels;
   (d) Fall, if there is a fall in income levels and an increase in the money supply;
   (e) Rise if there is an increase in income levels and also in the supply of money.

8.3. Given similar assumptions to those behind Table 8.4, if commercial banks hold 25% of their total assets as liquidity reserves, by what amount could they increase their advances if £40 million of liquid assets are injected into the banking system?

(a) £120 million
(b) £160 million
(c) £133.3 million
(d) £93.3 million

8.4. Again given these assumptions, what would be the effect on the level of advances if the Bank of England sold £21 million of government securities to the public, and the banks liquidity rates was held at 33% of total assets?

(a) Increase by £63.6 million
(b) Decrease by £63.6 million
(c) Increase by £42.6 million
(d) Decrease by £42.6 million

What would happen to the commercial banks' reserves in the correct answer?

8.5. In response to open market purchases by the Bank of England, the commercial banks would have to:

(a) Call in customers' advances and conform to the lower liquidity reserve;
(b) Sell treasury bills to the discount houses to restore the liquidity reserve to an adequate level;
(c) Increase their level of advances to customers in response to their greater liquidity reserves;
(d) Absorb any surplus liquidity by transferring assets from their balances at the Bank to items with a higher rate of return (but lower degree of liquidity);
(e) Sell longer term investments in government securities or private sector stock, in order to reinforce their liquidity reserves.

8.6. An increase in the supply of money through appropriate monetary policy would cause:

(a) An upwards revision in expenditure or real assets, which would boost output and investment;
(b) An increase in expenditure and income, with the latter being picked up in the transactions and precautionary demands for money, raising interest rates and reducing investment expenditure;
(c) A reduction in interest rates, stimulating investment and, through the multiplier consumption expenditure;
(d) Funds to be available to purchase financial assets, driving up market prices and the rate of interest and reducing real investment expenditure;
(e) An increase in speculative balances which would depress the market value of securities and discourage investment expenditure.

Note: Solutions can be found at the end of the text.

Chapter 9

Inflation

> Introduction
> The measurement of inflation
> The need for policy correction
> The Keynesian view of inflation
> The role of expectations
> The Keynesian view of the role of money in inflation
> The monetarist view of inflation
> The monetarists' cure for inflation
> Conclusions
> Appendix 9A: Monetarism and the quantity theory
> Self-assessment questions

INTRODUCTION

Up till now we have taken care to deal with macroeconomic analysis within the simplified context of constant prices. In our modelling, we have always assumed that output and capacity could be smoothly increased to cope with any rise in the level of demand, so that there would be no problem in the form of unsatisfied demand spilling over into price increases. In reality, neither the UK nor any other economy is likely to experience such convenient conditions. It is only too probable that production constraints will occur, so that domestic production finds it difficult to match any surge in the level of demand expenditures. It is even likely that these bottlenecks and constraints will come into effect long before the economy is working at its full production capacity. Prices are, therefore, unlikely to remain constant and it is now time to build a recognition of this new phenomenon into our analysis.

One result of this more complex modelling is that we find that there is a less clearcut link than we have hitherto assumed between changes in the level of expenditure and the response of real output and employment. This, in turn, robs both macroeconomic policy and the whole issue of intervention of much of their simple clarity. Up till now it has seemed obvious that, if the government wanted to increase the level of economic activity, it could simply raise the level of aggregate demand through either fiscal or monetary policy measures; such an increase in aggregate demand (represented by an upward movement of the $C + J$ function in the model) would move the economy to a higher equilibrium level of GDP, with the level of employment rising to reflect the higher level of output implied by this adjustment. But, if we abandon the protection of our assumption about constant prices, then we must recognize that the increase in aggregate expenditure could affect prices every bit as much as real output and employment.

Where does this leave us in terms of the predictions which we can draw from our models? To what extent might attempted reflation be dissipated in price increases (even if the effects of international trade are still ignored) rather than focused on its intended targets of real output and employment? If capacity constraints exist in the real world – or if there is any substantial degree of friction in the response of input markets (whether capital or labour) to planned changes in output – can output and employment policy targets be achieved at all? Worse still, if price increases build up a momentum under excess demand pressure, will they stabilize again when this excess pressure is removed? Indeed, do prices rise only in response to demand pressure, or might the root cause lie in supply-side influences such as rising costs, or profit margins, reflecting the possibility of production inefficiency, or union militancy, or monopolistic greed? Is it even possible that prices increase simply because the participants in the macroeconomy *expect* them to increase?

If you have been impatient to get away from simplistic modelling and its equally simplistic conclusions, your wish is about to be fulfilled! If you have wondered why both economic advisers and policy makers have dithered in the face of clearcut media advice (although it must be stressed that economists never dither; we only recheck our conclusions . . .), soon you will gain some understanding and sympathy for them. Away from the simplified world of introductory models, there may be no simple answer – or, if there is, it may not be the answer we would want to hear.

Whereas the 1950s and 1960s were associated with a policy commitment to prevent the recurrence of a depression of the magnitude and the duration of the early 1930s, the main policy preoccupation from the mid 1970s has been to prevent, or to bring under control, the punitive spiral of price inflation – whatever the social costs imposed on the community, simply because to do nothing could result in even greater social costs. Nor has this bitter experience been confined to the UK; it has affected all countries to a greater or lesser degree over this period.

This chapter will try to guide you through some of the main issues in the complex debate about the phenomenon of inflation. While there is a greater degree of consensus on causes and possible cures than was the case in the early 1980s, there is still a fair amount of controversy. This chapter makes no attempt to resolve this; it simply suggests that you try to suspend any initial prejudices (which are very probably derived from your political beliefs), try to keep an open mind, then make your own decision. To help you to do so, the main themes of the debate will be presented in as balanced and objective a fashion as possible.

The objectives of the chapter are to cover the following topics:

- What is meant by the term **inflation**?
- How is the rate of inflation measured, and how does the UK experience compare to that of our main international competitors?
- Why do governments attempt to control inflation?
- What do we mean by the terms **demand-pull** and **cost-push** inflation?
- How did Keynesians originally view the causes, and the cure for inflation?
- Where did the short run **Phillips Curve** fit into their macro-economic policy thinking?
- Why did this prove to be unstable, and what is the role of **expectations** in the process of accelerating inflation?
- Why do monetarists argue that the **quantity theory of money** lies at the root cause of all inflations?
- What is the monetarists' **transmission mechanism**, and what are its implications for policy?
- In broad outline, what is the monetarist view on corrective policies for inflation?

THE MEASUREMENT OF INFLATION

Everyone knows that inflation is concerned with rising prices. But, at any moment in the multitude of markets which make up the macroeconomy, some prices will be rising, some will be constant, and some could even be falling. Furthermore, behind the market for final goods such as TV sets, or cars, or holidays, or even hairdressing services (for those who, unlike the author, still need them), there are the various input markets in which prices will also be changing. What is happening to the price of labour in terms of wages and salaries? What is happening to the price of capital in terms of the market rate(s) of interest? What is happening to the price of land, both directly and in terms of its influence on land-using commodities such as houses and office space? With which particular set of prices is inflation concerned?

In macroeconomics, we deal in broad aggregates, rather than in specific prices. As a simple starting point, therefore, we can use the definition that:

> *inflation occurs when there is a significant and persistent increase in the price level in general.*

We are not concerned with the fact that some prices will rise at a faster rate than the overall average, or that some will rise at a lower rate, or even fall. Inflation measures the overall impact of rising prices.

While a variety of statistical measures[1] exist, the most frequently used official measure of the rate of inflation in the UK is provided by the **retail price index** (the RPI). This looks at the consequences of price changes through the eyes of consumers. In effect, it measures the cost of purchasing a representative bundle, or 'basket' of goods and services by the average household. Its monthly publication provides one of the key indicators of the state of the economy to both the media and to politicians. The index is based on two components: firstly, there is the physical collection and quantities of items of regular expenditure; secondly, there is the price or cost of the individual items.

To define the representative bundle of goods and the relative importance (or 'weight') of each item, the RPI draws on the Central Statistical Office's survey of the expenditure patterns of a sample of households (the **family expenditure survey**, or FES). The items are broken down into the main categories of expenditure, such as food, alcoholic drink, tobacco, housing, fuel and light, clothing and footwear, durable household goods, transport and vehicles, miscellaneous goods and services (even meals bought and consumed in restaurants, for those of you who can still afford such a luxury). The 'weighting' given to each category, and to the items within each category, broadly reflects the proportion of total expenditure as shown in the FES. The behaviour over time of this wide range of prices is established by sampling visits of teams of inspectors who, quite literally, shop around to record prices and price

---

1. For example, we have detailed statistical series on producer and wholesale prices; or again, we have the tax price index, which is another key measure which was set up by the Thatcher government to show how changes in taxation, as well as prices, can affect the purchasing power of consumers' disposable incomes over time.

Table 9.1 Consumer prices: UK index of inflation.

	Index of retail prices[1] (15 Jan 1974=100)	Internal purchasing power of the pound (1976=100)
1974	108.5	145
1975	134.8	117
1976	157.1	100
1977	182.0	86
1978	197.1	80
1979	223.5	70
1980	263.7	60
1981	295.0	53
1982	320.4	49
1983	335.1	47
1984	351.8	45
1985	373.2	42
1986	385.9	41
1987	–	–

Note: 1. This data is for annual averages, rather than for the monthly series.
(Source: *CSO Abstract of Statistics*, 1988 edition: Tables 18.5 and 18.7. Reprinted by permission of the Controller, HMSO.)

changes over different regions. Drawing on this raw data, indices are established for individual items, then for expenditure categories, then for the 'basket' as a whole.

Table 9.1 shows the behaviour of the RPI (15 January 1974 = 100) over the period 1974–86 in the UK. You can use it either to assess the position over the period as a whole, showing that the index has risen by about 286% over the 12 years; or, it can be used to trace the surges of particular phases of inflationary pressure, such as the impact of some of the OPEC oil price increases in the mid 1970s, or the consequences of the new government's increases in VAT and non-oil energy prices in the early 1980s. The second column of the table shows a related index calculated by the CSO from the RPI; this traces the falling real purchasing power of the pound and gives, perhaps, a clearer view of one of the main consequences of inflation in an economy. It shows that by 1986, the pound could buy only 41% of the basket of goods which it could command in 1976; in effect, after 10 years we now hand three one-pound coins over the counter, instead of the single one-pound note which was enough before . . .

Such a revelation can be embarrassing to any government, and the monthly publication of the RPI will frequently be awaited with some trepidation by senior politicians. Currently, the UK government has found that its claims to have brought inflation under control are suffering from the consequences of the very policy instrument which has been chosen to *provide* that control. From the extracts shown in earlier chapters, you will remember that the Chancellor of the Exchequer chose to increase interest rates quite substantially, to damp down the inflationary (and balance of trade) effects of a major consumption-led boom. A side-effect of this policy has been that the resultant increases in the mortgage rate of interest on housing has risen significantly, and has added anything up to two percentage points to the rate of inflation as recorded by the RPI (entering the index through the housing category of expenditure). This embarrassment is so acute that the government has seriously considered the possibility of *excluding* the mortgage rate from the index, so that the effects of the corrective policy do not appear as an additional symptom of the problem to which it is addressed.

Extract 9.1 is interesting, not only because it discusses the problems of producing weights which accurately reflect the pattern of expenditure for the average household, but also because it provides an excellent range of opinions on the government's proposal; its conclusion would appear to be that there is a better case for *increasing* the weighting given to housing-related expenditure, rather than banishing at least part of the item to spare the government from its short-term blushes. There is always unease when a government appears to react to unfavourable statistics by changing the basis upon which those statistics are calculated; after all, the purpose of these objective data is to draw attention to emergent problems from whatever source, policy or economic events. Faced with the unhappy precedent of the constant modifications to the recording of unemployment, there would appear to be a consensus that the RPI should be left to record housing costs as at present – or at least that the weighting given to elements such as mortgage interest, or even the new community charge,[2] should be adjusted upwards to give a more accurate reflection of the share of total household expenditure which is normally allocated to these items.

Table 9.2 provides some broad guidance on the relative rates of inflation experienced in consumer prices by our normal set of five countries, over the period 1961–87. Looking first at the average annual rates of inflation recorded for all member countries in the OECD, it is

---

2. Since the debate of Extract 9.1, there has been a further suggestion that the new Poll Tax (or community charge) should also be excluded from the RPI measure of inflation – where it would influence the latter through the weighting for housing costs. The view taken by an all-party committee was that the Poll Tax should continue to be *included* in the measurement of inflation, since 'any alteration would be viewed with great suspicion by the public'.

Extract 9.1 THE SCOTSMAN 6 FEBRUARY 1989.

WEIGHTY DECISIONS ON FAIR INFLATION FIGURES

Angus McCrone

AN EXTRAORDINARY statement from the Employment Secretary, Norman Fowler, accompanied last month's announcement that the rate of inflation had risen to 6.8 per cent in December.

Mr Fowler observed: "Over the last few months mortgage interest rates have been an important factor in the recent increases in inflation." So important in fact, said the Employment Secretary, that the rise in prices other than mortgage interest payments had remained practically unchanged since July, at 5 per cent.

So far so good. But then, the next paragraph began: "Higher interest rates have been necessary in the fight against inflation."

The two sentences together suggest something very strange — that the Government's chosen weapon against inflation, high interest rates, is also the major cause of inflation. The cause and the cure are therefore the same.

"The Government does face a paradox," says Joe Roseman, economic analyst at Phillips & Drew, the City stockbroker. "But I do have sympathy with what they're saying — the high mortgage rate will feed into increases in the retail price index in the short term."

The Government's critics are not at all sympathetic, and ministers are involved in some frantic head-scratching over how to prevent their counter-inflation policy scoring even more own goals by pushing up the inflation figures further in 1989.

To the anger of the Opposition, Mr Fowler, whose department compiles the retail price index, and the Chancellor, Nigel Lawson are concentrating not on changing the policy, but on how to change the statistics.

The retail price index is a measure of the change from month to month in the cost of a representative "basket" of goods and services of the sort bought by a typical household.

A crucial aspect of this basket is how much weight is given to each item in the basket — for instance is food a bigger area of spending for this typical household than housing costs or clothing?

In the RPI calculations for 1988, food was given a weight of 163 out of the total basket of 1,000, housing costs were given 160, including just 42 for mortgage interest payments, clothing was given 72 and alcohol 78.

Chancellor Lawson has already started distancing himself from the official RPI figures by talking of "underlying inflation", which is the same as the RPI with mortgage interest payments stripped out. He says that this measure shows inflation at only 5 per cent, instead of the 6.8 per cent and rising of the official RPI.

Even observers sympathetic to the Government's economic policy are strongly against Mr Lawson and Mr Fowler removing mortgage interest payments from the RPI.

Mr Roseman at Phillips & Drew said: "This is simply not on. To strip out the fact that debt has increased and house prices have gone up is out of order. Every industrial country has some representation for housing costs in their inflation figures."

And Dr Andrew Sentance, head of the economic trends department at the CBI, commented: "People who are arguing to exclude housing costs altogether are going a bit too far. We have to find a satisfactory way of having housing costs in the index."

In fact there is a strong argument that the RPI has been greatly understating the impact the last five years' huge increases in housing costs have had on the pockets of consumers.

With both house prices and the mortgage rate at very high levels, people are having to spend a much larger proportion of their money on mortgage interest payments than the 42 out of 1,000 suggested by the 1988 RPI weightings.

The 1988 weightings give local authority rates 43 points, one more than mortgage interest payments — a relation totally out of step with the situation in South-east England and elsewhere. In the South-east, for example, the average mortgage for a young couple is probably at least £40,000, equivalent to about £400 a month in repayments.

If both are relatively well off, this might be 25 to 30 per cent of their combined salaries, not the 4.2 per cent suggested by the RPI weights. So should mortgage interest payments be given a heavier weight in the basket?

In March, the Government is due to publish the new basket weights to be used for calculating the RPI from February 1989. One possibility is that ministers will swallow their unhappiness about mortgage interest payments being in the RPI, and that the new RPI will give interest payments much more weight than the present 42 out of 1,000.

If this happens, then the official inflation rate is likely to go even higher in the short term than it would have done with the 1988 weights. This could mean the headline inflation rate breaking through the 8 per cent barrier some time in the first half of 1989.

Alternatively, mortgage interest payments might be washed out of the RPI weights altogether — producing overnight a nice-looking inflation rate of about 5 per cent, but certain to provoke fury from the Government's critics and accusations of massaging the figures.

It would have another disadvantage too. At the moment, increases in the mortgage rate tend to cause big rises in the headline inflation rate, but when the mortgage rate comes down, there tends to be an equally big fall in official inflation.

As Phillips & Drew says: "It is a pity that Mr Lawson was not as trenchant in his criticisms when mortgage interest payments flattered the published inflation figure."

With mortgage rates probably near their peak, and house prices unlikely to rise much this year, some much more flattering falls in inflation might come Mr Lawson's way late this year or in 1990.

There is a third possibility — a compromise in which the RPI would continue to include the effects of rising house prices, but would not include the volatile mortgage interest rate. Such a proposal is being put forward by Mr Roseman and his colleague Bill Martin at Phillips & Drew.

The P&D team says: "Alternative methods of calculating shelter costs produce a rather less volatile inflation measure. The reduced volatility is an advantage, making it easier to gauge the underlying trend in retail price inflation."

This would, claim Mr Roseman and Mr Martin, also reduce the risks of increased mortgage rates sparking off higher wage claims.

This is a point on which employers, and their representatives, the CBI, are also concerned.

Dr Sentance commented: "The RPI is, whether we like it or not, used by employees as a point of reference for pay bargaining. It's in employees' interests to have a realistic indicator."

But to people other than Government ministers and employers, all this might seem a little beside the point. After all, when mortgage rates do go up, they hit the pockets of ordinary people — if you have to pay more for housing, then that leaves less to spend on the other items in the basket, like food and alcohol.

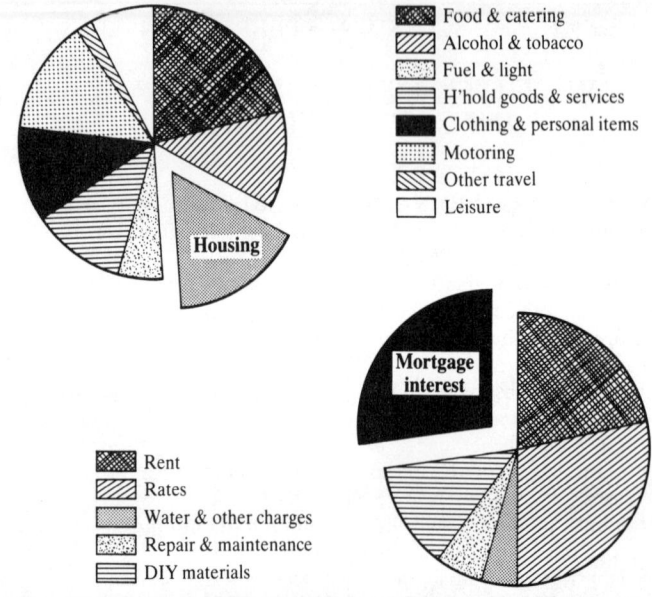

How the items in the RPI are divided up (above) and how the housing proportion is sub-divided

Reprinted with permission from *The Scotsman* 6 February 1989 © *The Scotsman*.

Table 9.2 Consumer prices: average annual rate of increase.

	1961–70	1971–77	1978	1979	1980	1981	1982	1983	1984	1985	1986	1987
UK	4.1	13.9	8.3	13.4	18.0	11.9	8.6	4.6	5.2	6.1	3.4	4.2
USA	2.8	6.6	7.7	11.3	13.5	10.4	6.1	3.2	4.7	3.5	1.9	3.7
Japan	5.8	10.7	3.8	3.6	8.0	4.9	2.7	1.9	2.5	2.1	0.4	−0.2
West Germany	2.7	5.6	2.7	4.1	5.5	5.9	5.3	3.0	3.2	2.2	−0.2	0.2
Netherlands	4.0	8.3	4.1	4.2	6.5	6.7	6.0	2.8	3.9	2.3	0.2	−0.5
Total OECD	3.3	8.5	7.9	9.8	12.9	10.5	7.8	5.3	5.8	4.5	2.6	3.2

(Reprinted by permission of *OECD Economic Outlook*, issues 29 (Table 21), 35 (Table 23) and 43 (June 1988, Table 22).)

clear that there is a pattern of rising rates of inflation up to a peak figure of 12.9% in 1980, followed by a steady decline in the rate of increase in prices as member countries fought to bring inflation under control over the period 1981–87. Within this overall pattern, it is possible to trace the impact on member countries' inflation rates caused by the major increases and subsequent adjustments in the price of oil (which is both a source of energy and a major raw material in its own right) by the OPEC cartel over the mid 1970s.

Using the OECD average as a standard for comparison, it can be seen that the UK rate of inflation was substantially in excess of this 'norm' over the period up to and including 1982; indeed the UK inflation rate of 18.0% in 1980 was almost 50% higher than the OECD average of 12.9% for this year. While the marked improvement in the UK rate of inflation gradually narrowed this gap and even allowed us to fall below the OECD average for 1983 and 1984, our annual rate of inflation has gradually drifted above the norm again for the last three years of the period – a worrying trend which has continued over 1988 and 1989.

Comparison with the USA, Japan, West Germany and the Netherlands makes even grimmer reading. At no stage throughout the entire period did the UK manage to hold its inflation rate at the same level as these major competitors; even our very real achievements in inflation control over the period from 1982 seem very ordinary when compared to the remarkably low figures recorded by Japan, West Germany and the Netherlands in particular. The message is clear enough: there is no case for resting on past achievements; there is a need for an even greater improvement in our control of inflation, if we are to remain competitive. The sensitivity of UK financial markets to this need is so great that, when the then Chancellor, Nigel Lawson, accidentally omitted the routine reassurance on inflation control from a public lecture in the autumn of 1988, the resultant fall in share prices had to be countered with an official statement, issued on the following day, that this still remained a key priority within government policy.

THE NEED FOR POLICY CORRECTION

Before we begin to analyse the possible causes of and cures for inflation, it is important that we pause and think through the reasons why most governments accept that they have a clear duty to control and minimize the rate of inflation. This was not always the case. Until the early 1970s, many governments saw inflation as a transient problem which was associated with the boom phase of the business cycle. If, during this phase, aggregate demand for goods and services exceeded the available supply, then this would normally result in an increase in the general price level (and in input markets, as the firms' sector competed for resources to service this demand). But boom phases would be followed in the cycle by recession, depression and recovery, during which prices would tend to stabilize again. Inflation was viewed as an inevitable but periodic problem. Even where inflation persisted throughout most of the cycle, some observers argued that a minor or **creeping inflation** could confer benefits to the economy concerned; with rising money profits and money wages, firms and households would enjoy a feeling of affluence and optimism, which could only have a positive effect on investment and the economic growth which would result from this.

From the mid 1970s a consensus gradually developed that the 'party time' euphoria generated by inflation could not be sustained. As inflation rates rose steadily, it became obvious that inflation imposed its own variety of hangovers . . . and that these hangovers were increasing in their frequency and severity. What are these problems, and what are the 'social costs' which are associated with them?

The first and most obvious problem is that inflation erodes the purchasing power of the monetary unit. We have already seen in Table 9.1 that the steady inflation over the decade from 1976–86 reduced the purchasing power of the pound by about 60%. This erosion of purchasing power, and its threat to real standards of living, is particularly serious for those sections of society which live either on relatively fixed money incomes (such as pensioners, recipients of other state benefits, or students), or whose bargaining power is so weak – or its exercise unacceptable to members – that their money incomes grow more slowly than the ongoing rate of inflation (for example nurses, or academics). Not only does this loss of purchasing power create hostility and frustration among the sections of society who are 'losers'; even the 'winners' who have real bargaining power and are prepared to use this, find that their apparent gains are lost in the face of continuing inflation, and tend to become more aggressive still. At one level, the response of the labour market to the erosion of the purchasing power of their money incomes triggers a redistribution of income between different bargaining groups within the market (in favour of the 'winners' and at the expense of the 'losers'). At the same time, and this takes us into our following point, this random process sends confusing signals into the labour market. Relative wages between industries and professions should reflect the state of demand and supply in each case (that is, the greatest increases should be won where there is a relative shortage, so that further trained resources are attracted to this sector of the market); if they reflect instead a random pattern of militancy and opportunism, then this will only coincidently provide accurate guidance for resource movement.

The second main problem is that continuing inflation distorts the signals for resource allocation in the market for final goods and services. In any economic system which is dependent wholly, or largely on market forces, resources will be switched between uses in response to relative profitability which, in turn, should reflect demand and supply conditions for the various items within final output. It is changes in this pattern of profitability which move resources from declining to expanding industries and so keep the pattern of production in tune with the constantly changing pattern of market opportunities. But profit is the margin between price and costs, and will therefore be affected by changes in production costs which are caused by the random bargaining pressures which we discussed in the previous point. The problem is compounded by the fact that prices do not rise on a broad front, each at the same rate of inflation. Where inflation is substantial and persistent, the routine of price changes can also take on a random pattern, which further distorts the profit margin's reflection of the changing pressures of demand. The less accurate are adjustments to prices and costs, then the less accurate is the resultant pattern of profits and losses, so that the signals for resource movements become random and blurred.

Just another boring textbook point of theory? Not really. The more distorted the reflection of demand and supply conditions within the economy, the less efficient and smooth is the movement of resources between uses, and the slower is the response of the economy to the changing pattern of opportunities offered by the market. Who wants to buy mid-1970s flared trousers, or 1960s hula-hoops? Who wants to take the gamble of investment in new technology when future prices, costs and profits are so uncertain? Is it purely an accident that the UK, with one of the worst inflation records in Europe, was beginning to develop so many of the signs of a 'stranded' economy during the 1970s, with its pattern of industrial production geared more to the past, than to the present or the future? Was it totally surprising that abysmally low levels of investment in the domestic economy existed in the early 1980s, while investment capital poured out of the country into economies with substantially lower rates of inflation, and higher (or more certain) return on investment?

The third problem is that continuing and substantial inflation can introduce a serious distortion into a country's pattern of international trade. GDP measures the money value of the domestically produced output of goods and services which is sold both at home and in world markets. Where a country such as the UK experiences a prolonged period of more rapid inflation than that which is recorded by its main competitors – and Table 9.2 provides little reassurance on this point – then it is probable that (given reasonably steady exchange rates) it will find that its goods are relatively expensive (and relatively outdated, if investment levels have also suffered) in both sets of markets. Obviously, this creates major problems. Where there are close substitutes, as there will be if output from the world's producers competes within the same market, then consumers will tend to choose the cheaper substitutes. If these substitute goods have also a more up-to-date technological content, then the higher priced goods are even more disadvantaged. If domestic producers struggle to hold prices at a more competitive level, while their own production cost levels are rising rapidly, then the profitability of the goods will suffer (which will discourage investment and tend to lock the country into a vicious circle of outdated technology and design). Such a country could expect to suffer the double blow of declining export sales and increasing expenditure on imports. This, in turn, could well have two adverse effects on the economy: firstly, reflecting the switch of demand to externally produced goods, domestic productions levels – and therefore employment – will suffer. Secondly, at least initially, the fall in export receipts and the increase in import payments is likely to create a trade deficit in the balance of payments. Once again these symptoms should be very familiar in a UK context, not only historically, but even in more recent events, as described in the extracts to earlier chapters.

The fourth problem is that inflation, if left unchecked, tends to build up its own momentum. While there was no clear evidence on this point up till the mid 1960s, international experience since then has been that inflation rates tend to accelerate over time. Few economists would now argue that it is possible to maintain indefinitely a 'comfortable' rate of inflation. The upwards drift of the inflation rate in the later years of Table 9.2, continuing over 1988 into at least the early months of 1989 (when the RPI for February showed an increase in the rate of inflation to 7.5%, the highest since the early 1980s) would seem to confirm this observation.

What causes the inflationary process to develop its own momentum? At this stage in our analysis of the phenomenon, it is possible to provide two interrelated explanations. Firstly, we know that the main consequence of inflation is that the purchasing power of the monetary unit is eroded. Therefore, if an inflationary process is triggered by excessive aggregate demand (for example, during the boom phase of the business cycle), it will erode the purchasing power of money incomes; this will tend to trigger more aggressive bargaining for wage settlements in the following period, as groups of workers try to compensate for lost purchasing power, and the higher cost of living. At the same time, given the existence of unsatisfied demand, firms find it relatively easy to pass on this increase in production costs by raising final output prices still further; therefore, there is a form of 'knock-on' effect, which will tend to prolong the duration of the inflation.

Secondly, as firms and households gain experience of *continuing* inflation, they will learn to build in an allowance for expected inflation into their future plans. Firms will forecast the likely rates of increase in raw material and labour costs; given a greater awareness of the effects of inflation on the real value of business profits than was the case in the past, they will tend to set future prices to cover costs and protect real profits. Simultaneously, in wage bargaining in the labour market, claims will begin to reflect not only a correction element for unanticipated past inflation; they will also contain a new element for anticipated future inflation. The effect of this learning process can be to not only sustain inflation, but to gradually increase the rate of inflation experienced. It is yet another case where expectations can become self-fulfilling. Therefore, the international experience from the early 1970s onwards has been that, without firm control, creeping inflation will gradually develop into a jog-trot and, ultimately into a gallop. Inflation appears to develop a life of its own, with price increases becoming more frequent, and the extent of the price adjustments ever greater.

This grim threat takes us into the final problem associated with unchecked inflation; there is always the fear that inflation can degenerate into **hyper-inflation**. As we have indicated above, practical experience suggests that the rate of inflation tends to accelerate over time, so that the erosion of the purchasing power of the monetary unit will also accelerate. There is a danger that, at some point, this will result in so rapid a loss in the real value of money that public confidence in the monetary unit collapses. Once again, this is by no means a theoretical point; there have been occasions where the inflationary process has been so severe that it has created a crisis of confidence, which has resulted in the breakdown of the currency system in question. If money loses its real purchasing power on a weekly, daily, or even hourly basis, as happened in early post-war Germany, how can it remain acceptable as a standard, or a store of value, or as a medium of exchange? The problem is compounded by the fact that no one can quantify the threshold point beyond which hyper-inflation develops, or the further threshold rate which results in a collapse of the monetary unit, and the reduction of the economy to a barter system, until a new and more acceptable monetary unit is found. Do they occur when inflation reaches 50% per annum, or 100%, or 200%, or 500%, or even higher . . .? Countries such as Israel, or Argentina have survived staggering annual equivalent rates of inflation without monetary collapse. There is no evidence that hyper-inflation will *always* result in a breakdown of the currency, but the fear that this might happen is so great that there is a strong conviction that the process of inflation must be controlled long before this is a possibility.

For all of these reasons, therefore, most governments accept that they have a major responsibility to set up their policies in such a way that their domestic rate of inflation is kept within reasonable bounds. In a sense, it is the one form of intervention in a market-based economy which has not come under serious challenge – although Keynesian and monetarist economists might differ as to the causes of the problem, and the curative measures which are necessary.

THE KEYNESIAN VIEW OF INFLATION

Given that governments generally accept their responsibility for the control of inflation, our next task must be to analyse how they might do so. The most sensible starting point would seem to be from the simple and familiar basic model of the economy.

Inflation was originally viewed as a symptom which was associated with a particular phase in the trade cycle. As the economy passed from the recovery into the boom phase of the cycle, all the expenditure elements would be rising rapidly and would, sooner or later, overshoot the output available to meet them. Given normal constraints on resource availability, this would generate two sets of pressure symptoms:

(1) Prices for goods and services would rise, reflecting the relative scarcities caused by the excess demand;

(2) The balance of trade would move into deficit at least in the short term, as imports were sucked in and as intended export items were diverted to the domestic market, to satisfy these excess demand pressures.

To keep the analysis as simple as possible for the moment, we will continue to exclude the international trade sector from the basic model; we shall be dealing with this in Chapter 11. This leaves us free to focus on the effect on the price level of excess demand pressure.

But what exactly do we mean when we talk about **excess demand** pressure? In our basic model, when planned expenditure exceeds available output (taking the economy out of equilibrium), the economy has always been able to expand its level of output to restore inventories to their planned level, and to meet the higher level of demand. In other words, excess demand has been a temporary phenomenon which has been satisfied and eliminated by an automatic adjustment to supply, or output. But this has only happened because we have built in the modelling assumption that there will always be spare capacity within the economy; where there is no constraint on production, the economy can then respond freely to any expansionary impulse. If we are to make our model more realistic, then we shall have to drop this simplifying assumption; capacity constraints can and do exist. We must modify our

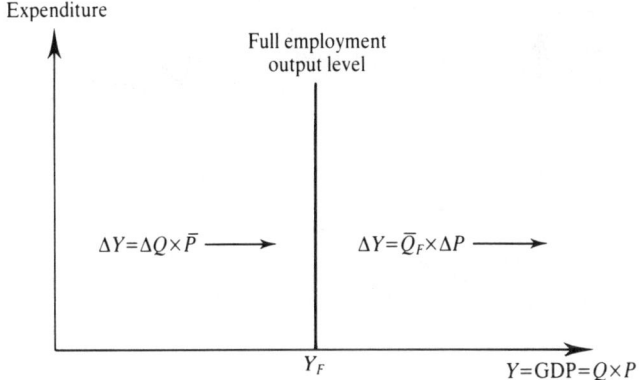

Figure 9.1 The composition of GDP during expansion.

model to recognize that this is so. In Figure 9.1 we show the model with a capacity constraint identified at the GDP level of Y_F; this constraint can be described as **the full employment level of output**, that is, it corresponds to the real output level which is consistent with full employment[3] and the given stock of capital in the economy.

Next we must recognize that GDP has two component parts: firstly, there is the component of the physical (or real) output of goods and services, whether these be cars, or kettles, or catering services; secondly, there is the list of the prices at which the different final goods and services are sold. For the moment, let us assume that up to the point of the constraint of maximum output, any increase in expenditure can be met by an increase in output at constant prices, that is, that the consequent rise in GDP (ΔY) will reflect:

$$\Delta Y = \Delta Q \times \bar{P}$$

where ΔQ represents the change in real output, and $\bar{P}$ indicates that prices are unchanged.

However, if demand pressures try to push the economy beyond the capacity constraint of Y_F, we must recognize that real output cannot be increased beyond this point (it is, after all, the maximum output which can be produced from available resources), so that GDP can only rise by selling the same output $\bar{Q}_F$ at higher prices than before (ΔP). In other words, if the economy tries to expand beyond (that is, to the right of) the full employment output constraint, it will only result in rising prices, so that changes over this range of GDP will take the form of:

$$\Delta Y = \bar{Q}_F \times \Delta P$$

as shown in Figure 9.1.

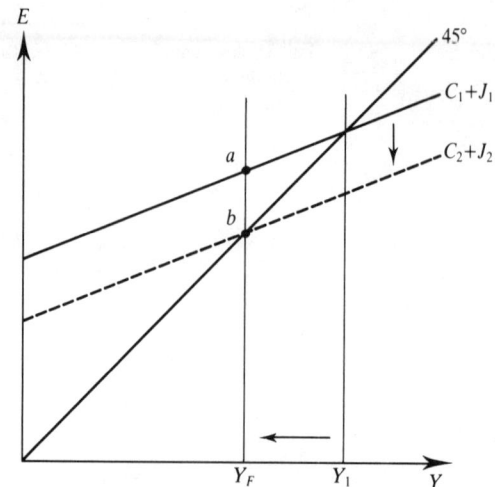

Figure 9.2 The correction for an 'inflationary gap'.

How does equilibrium GDP emerge in this new and modified version of our basic model? In fact there is no change to our normal solution to the model; equilibrium will still occur when available output is just enough to satisfy the expenditure plans of households, firms and the government, that is, where the aggregate demand (or $C + J$) function intersects the 45° line.

Therefore, in terms of our modified model, inflation can only occur if the equilibrium level of GDP lies to the *right* of Y_F which, in turn, implies that the aggregate expenditure function must intersect the 45° line to the right of the constraint, as in Figure 9.2. Given the position of $C_1 + J_1$ in this model, there is an **inflationary gap** of ab at the full employment level of output; at this point, the planned expenditure of aY_F would exceed available real output of bY_F, driving up prices as firms, households and government all tried to realize their expenditure plans. The economy would move into equilibrium at Y_1 level of GDP but this (in the absence of international trade) would simply reflect the fact that the maximum output of Q_F had been sold at increased prices (that is, $Y_1 > Y_F$, only because the prices are higher in the former case).

Why might the aggregate expenditure function be in such a position? It might have risen to this level because the soaring business optimism during the boom phase had caused repeated upwards revisions to the investment and aggregate expenditure functions. It might have followed from an error in government demand management policy, for example where fiscal reflation had proved to be excessive and had resulted in over-correction. Alternatively, it could have been caused if the delayed timing of the full impact of past fiscal measures had brought an intended reflation (targeted on the recovery phase of the cycle) into phase with the boom. It could have been the result of an over-ambitious, or careless monetary policy, for example if the commercial banks' liquidity reserves had been raised to permit an excessive expansion of credit, or if interest rates had been nudged too low, stimulating too great a volume of borrowing by households and firms.

Whatever the reason, the *cause* of inflation would take the form of excess demand within the economy. The *cure*, in terms of the model illustrated in Figure 9.2, would be to eliminate the excess demand pressure by fiscal, or monetary policy. For example, government expenditure could be cut and/or taxation rates increased; alternatively, special deposits could be called and open market sales could be carried out by the Bank of England to reduce the liquidity base of the commercial banks until a contraction of credit was forced upon them. Whether fiscal or monetary policy was used (or even a mix of the two policies) then, assuming that both C and J components were affected, the aggregate expenditure function could be reduced to $C_2 + J_2$, as shown in Figure 9.2, which would move the equilibrium level of income from Y_1 to Y_F, and eliminate price inflation by bringing expenditure plans into line with available real output.

This is a useful starting point, but it must be seen as a simple analysis, based on a simple model, and with a simple solution. The problem is that it is an analysis which does not correspond fully to the observable facts of inflation. There are probably three main complications which conflict with the simple results of our analysis so far:

(1) There will be a lag between policy action and the resultant control of the aggregate expenditure function;

(2) Prices will tend to rise before, as well as after the constraint of Y_F has been reached;

(3) Prices could continue to rise, even after excess demand pressures have been eliminated from the economy.

Let's look at each point in turn, to see how our analysis must be developed. The first point reflects one of the weaknesses of the simple model, in that it lacks any time dimension; it fails to indicate how long it will take for the aggregate demand function to move to $C_2 + J_2$, and bring the economy back to equilibrium at the full employment level of output, Y_F. Until it does so, there will be excess demand, and inflation will be experienced. From earlier chapters, we know that it can take many months before the full impact of fiscal or monetary policy measures 'works through' into the economy. Over the summer and autumn of 1988 – and the following spring and summer of 1989 – there was a classic example of this type of lagged response, as the Chancellor's increases in the interest rate appeared for a long period to be having little or no effect on consumption and investment plans. Therefore, we must accept that, even after the policy correction has been made, it will normally take some time (almost a full year in terms of our example) before the aggregate expenditure function responds fully to the promptings of policy. This is one reason why price inflation cannot be turned off, as by flicking a switch.

The second problem takes us into an interesting area of the debate. Unlike our simplified conditions in Figures 9.1 and 9.2, most countries experience rising prices long before the full employment level of output is reached.[3] This simply reflects the fact that relative scarcities and bottlenecks exist in many sectors of the macroeconomy, driving up costs and prices well in advance of the ultimate constraint of full capacity. One area where this is particularly noticeable is in the labour market. When demand levels for final output are high, this creates an environment within which firms are likely to offer higher wages to attract labour as they try to increase their individual levels of production; simultaneously, organized labour can also demand higher payments to reflect its increasing scarcity value. Demand pressures can therefore trigger increases in wage costs, at a relatively early stage in the expansion process towards Y_F. These, in turn, will tend to be passed on to consumers in the form of higher prices for final output – which creates the possibility of inflation *before* the constraint is reached.

The inflationary process is therefore likely to contain **cost-push** as well as **demand-pull** pressures, with final output prices rising in response to both influences. As we have described it above, the root cause of inflation remains the excess demand pressure for final output, and cost-push inflation, or rising input prices, is induced or triggered by the pressures placed on input markets by the demand for final output.

It is possible to explore the behaviour of labour input costs in a little more depth by looking at the short-term **Phillips Curve**. This was the product of research work carried out by Professor A.W. Phillips in the late 1950s on the relationship between the rate of increase in wages ($\dot{W}$) in different periods, and the corresponding rates of unemployment (U) in the UK labour market. Figure 9.3 illustrates the function which 'fitted' the data for the two variables over the period 1861–1957.

As would be expected, this shows a clear pattern of trade-off between the two variables. Using the rate of unemployment as an indicator of the level of economic activity, the Phillips Curve shows that

---

3. Technically, full employment does not imply total or 100% employment of the labour force. At any given time there will be a proportion of the labour force involved in transfer between jobs, for example, moving from declining to expanding industries, training for better jobs or, for various reasons, unable to work. The term 'full' employment indicates that all labour, other than this normal core or level of unemployment, is employed. For example, if this core of unemployment normally makes up, say, 5% of the labour force, then 'full' employment indicates that the other 95% are in employment.

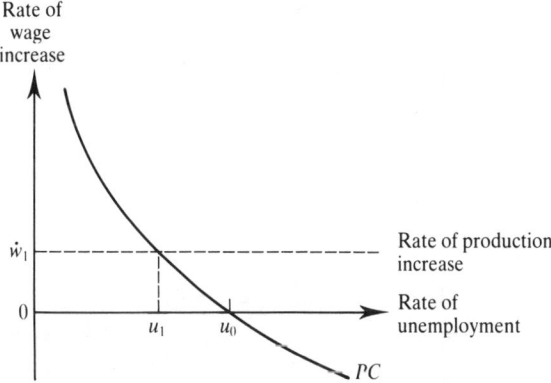

Figure 9.3 The Phillips Curve.

(over the period for which recorded data was available) the lower the rate of unemployment and the greater the demand pressure on the labour market, the higher was the resultant rate of wage increase. Conversely, the higher the rate of unemployment and the weaker the demand for labour, the lower was the resultant rate of wage increase. Indeed, historically, at sufficiently high levels of unemployment (for example at or beyond u_0 in Figure 9.3), wages have either been constant, or have even fallen.

In passing, it is worth noting that not all wage increases are inflationary; for example, up to the rate of increase corresponding to $\dot{w}_1$, rising wage costs could be absorbed by normal increases in productivity for the period, without prices having to be raised. But, if wages increase beyond this level, then production costs will rise and contribute to the inflationary process.

So far we have developed some understanding of the two separate components of inflation: demand-pull inflation reflects the pressure of excess demand on prices, as illustrated in Figure 9.2; cost-push inflation is the result of these demand pressures for final output being transmitted into input markets, such as the labour market, and is illustrated in Figure 9.3. It is possible to bring together the two threads of demand-pull and cost-push inflation into a slightly more sophisticated model, and use this to develop our understanding of the process of inflation. This time, our interest lies in exploring how the separate elements of real output and the price level, which together make up GDP, behave in response to increases in demand – before as well as after we reach the constraint of full employment output.

The new model is set out in Figure 9.4. Its vertical axis measures the general level of prices (P), and its horizontal axis the level of real

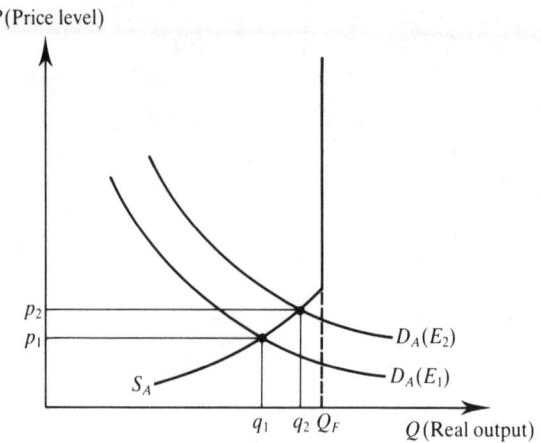

Figure 9.4 The model for inflation.

output (Q) in the economy. From our new knowledge of cost-push inflation, we would expect the **aggregate supply function** (S_A) to have the shape indicated: even before maximum capacity output is reached, increasing costs will tend to drive up prices, as output expands; at the same time, the function will become vertical above full employment output, Q_F, reflecting the fact that this represents an absolute constraint on the level of output which can be produced from the economy's existing resource base.

This builds the phenomenon of cost-push inflation into our model, but how can we transfer our demand level information, as contained in the aggregate expenditure function of Figure 9.2? Figure 9.5 shows us the familiar equilibrium condition in our normal model; at Y_1, available output is just enough to satisfy the expenditure plans of the various sectors of the economy ($C_1 + J_1$). Looking at this equilibrium situation from a slightly different viewpoint, E_1 measures the total expenditure from all sectors at this equilibrium level of GDP. How much real output (Q) could we buy with this absolute amount of expenditure? Surely, it would depend upon the price level – the higher the price level, the less would be our command over real output; the lower the price level, the greater would be the amount of real output which we could purchase. Think about it in more personal terms; if you have £100 to spend on records, obviously you can buy more of them if their average price is £5 (when you can buy 20 records), than if their average price is £6.67 (when you can only buy 15 records) or, worse still if their average price is £10 (when you will be limited to 10 records). The higher the average price level the fewer records you can buy; alternatively, the higher the average price level, the less real output you can buy with a given total for

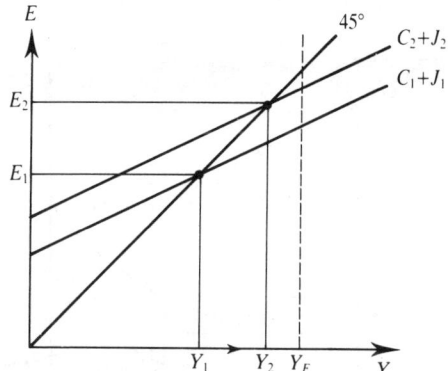

Figure 9.5 Reflation in the basic model.

expenditure. We can transfer this information more formally into Figure 9.4, by constructing the **aggregate demand function** which is a rectangular hyperbola[4] for the expenditure level E_1; this shows the different amounts of real output which can be purchased by E_1 over different possible price levels.

As always, the macroeconomy will adjust towards equilibrium, which will occur when available output (S_A) is just enough to satisfy the total of planned expenditures, as represented by $D_A(E_1)$. In other words, the economy will tend to settle at the q_1 level of economic activity, with a corresponding price level of p_1. Our new model shows the same type of equilibrium as before, but in a form which allows us to look at the separate elements of real output and the price level, rather than at their combined value of GDP.

How does this help us to analyse the process of inflation? Looking at Figure 9.5, we can see that the equilibrium level of GDP (Y_1) lies below the level of GDP consistent with full employment (Y_F). If the government were to attempt to move the economy closer to Y_F, it could use either or both of fiscal and monetary policy to raise the aggregate expenditure function to $C_2 + J_2$ (assuming that both elements of aggregate expenditure were affected by the policy correction); in our model, this would raise the equilibrium level of GDP to Y_2; but this would cause the level of expenditure to rise from E_1 to E_2 at this higher level of economic activity. Taking this information back to our new model in

---

4. For those of you who have forgotten your geometry, the key property of this exotic curve is that all the rectangles drawn from any point on the curve to the two axes are equal in area. This is a mathematical property, and cannot be blamed on economics; we are simply using this characteristic! Since the D_A function links price and real output coordinates, then this implies that the sum of PQ will give the same total expenditure, regardless of the point chosen on the function.

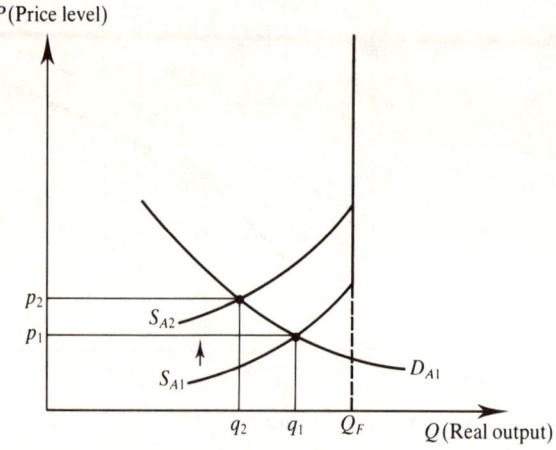

Figure 9.6 'Cost-push' inflation.

Figure 9.4, we can show that the effect of the government's reflation would be to raise the level of aggregate demand to $D_A(E_2)$. The economy would adjust towards its new equilibrium position, where the aggregate supply function intersects the new aggregate demand function. From Figure 9.5 we know that the level of GDP will rise; from Figure 9.4, we can draw the additional information that this increase in GDP will be caused by an increase in the price level (to p_2) *as well as* an increase in the real output component (from q_1 to q_2). In other words, part of the reflationary policy impulse would be dissipated in an increase in prices; this could result in a smaller expansion in real output (and through this a smaller reduction in the rate of unemployment) than was intended by policy makers, at the cost of introducing inflation into the general price level of the economy – despite the fact that there is still spare capacity in the economy.

Up till now we have argued that cost-push pressure, as suggested by the short-term Phillips Curve of Figure 9.3, is really **demand induced**, in the sense that wage (and other input) costs rise under the pressure of rising demand. However, there is a further reason why countries might experience rising prices, even where there is spare capacity within the economy. It is possible that prices might rise to cover increases in costs, which have nothing to do with demand pressures in the input markets. The classic illustration of this type of 'pure' cost-push inflation was provided by the series of OPEC price increases over the mid 1970s, affecting both energy and raw material costs. Figure 9.6 shows how the effect of such increases in input costs would be to raise the aggregate supply function from S_{A1} to S_{A2} – with the new upward sloping section indicating that this change in production costs was due to conditions quite outside the normal Phillips type of relationship. (Just as the slope of the consumption function reflects the relationship between consumption plans and income, but a change in the position of the consumption function reflects a change in *other* influences, such as the cost, or the availability of credit, or consumption expectations). Given the aggregate demand function D_{A1}, the economy was originally in equilibrium at q_1 real output and p_1 price level. The effect of the OPEC oil price increases, by raising the position of the aggregate supply function, was to move the economy to a new equilibrium, which involved the price level rising from p_1 to p_2 – and the level of real output contracting from q_1 to q_2 (with the implication that the level of employment also contracted, raising the level of unemployment).

There would be a similar effect for any increase in the costs of imported materials or foodstuffs. So long as this increase in costs takes place at constant exchange rates (for example, reflects a world shortage in the items, as a result of which their prices rise in world markets), then we are still looking at 'pure' cost-push inflation, and measuring its consequences on the economy. But, if the increase in import prices reflects a fall in the UK exchange rate, then we must be careful with our analysis; it is quite possible that the exchange rate has fallen because of a severe balance of trade deficit – which might itself have been caused by domestic inflationary pressures, with excess demand 'sucking in' imports to supplement domestically available output. In this case, while the aggregate supply function would behave as indicated in Figure 9.6, we would no longer be dealing with 'pure' cost-push, but would have returned to the more familiar world of induced cost-push inflation.

So far we have managed to explain why there are time lags in bringing aggregate demand under control, and why countries can experience rising prices well before reaching the constraint of full employment output. This takes us to our third point, which was that many countries have experienced a continuation of price inflation, even *after* any excess demand pressure has been removed from the economy. For example, in the UK, by February or March 1989, it was beginning to look as if the Chancellor's interest rate increases had finally brought the rate of growth in consumer credit under some sort of control – yet the RPI was indicating that the annual rate of inflation had crept up to 7.5% (its highest since the early 1980s) and, worse still, there was evidence that wage increases in the labour market were beginning to drift to progressively higher and higher levels of settlement. Why should input costs continue to rise even after the original demand-pull pressures have worked themselves out in the economy?

Before we consider the possible reason for this pattern of behaviour, let's look at its consequences; we can use our new model in Figure 9.7 to explore the possibility, and to extend our understanding of the cost-push phenomenon.

Assume that the economy is in equilibrium at q_1 level of real

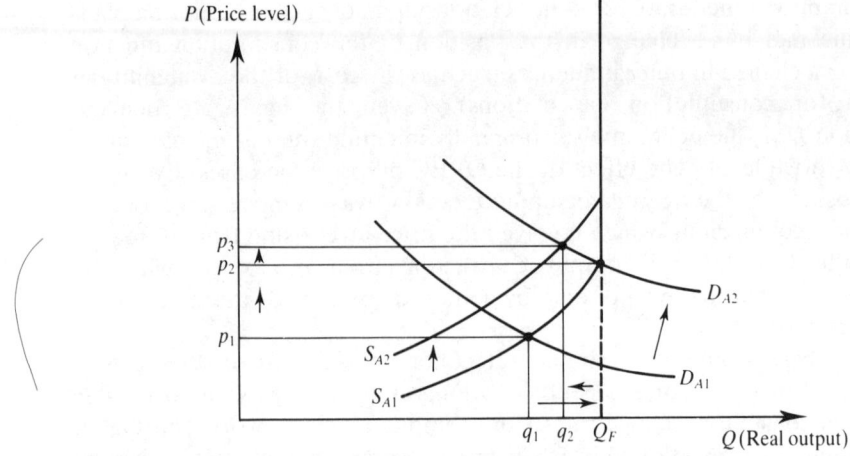

Figure 9.7 'Induced' cost-push inflation.

output and p_1 level of prices; this would imply a level of economic activity which lies below the full employment level of output. Assume secondly that the government decides to raise the level of aggregate demand from D_{A1} to D_{A2}, in an attempt to cut the aggregate supply function S_{A1} above the real output level q_F, and so to achieve full employment. The model shows that, as a result of demand induced cost-push pressures, the improvement in real output would be achieved, but at the cost of prices rising from p_1 to p_2. In other words, the improvement in employment would be accompanied by a substantial increase in prices, as inflation is introduced into the economy (note how we are *not* dealing with the type of excess demand identified in Figure 9.2; there is no question of trying to push the economy beyond Q_F).

So far our model reflects fairly accurately the 'normal' inflationary experience of most countries over the late 1950s and 1960s. But, over the 1970s (even if we ignore the genuine cost-push adjustments which followed the OPEC price increases) it became clear that input costs, particularly labour wages, were rising far beyond what could have been expected from any past correlation of demand pressure and changes in wage rates. If we were to build this into our model, what would be its effect? In Figure 9.7, we can see that the rising labour costs would move the aggregate supply function upwards to S_{A2} (because we need a new function to illustrate the new labour cost conditions). But, if we change the position of the aggregate supply function, this will make the economy move from Q_F to a *third* equilibrium position, where D_{A2} cuts the new and higher aggregate supply function S_{A2}. In short, our model has shown us that there is a danger that expansionary policy could result not only in an induced movement up the original aggregate supply function; if it triggers a free-for-all in the labour market, it could result in a new and higher aggregate supply function, reflecting a new wave of cost-push inflation, which would raise the price level still further from p_2 to p_3. Nor is this the only adverse effect; the model shows that the level of real output would *fall* from q_F to q_2, defeating the government's policy intention of trying to achieve full employment.

Don't make the mistake of assuming that Figure 9.7 merely illustrates an interesting theoretical possibility. It provides an analytical description of events which not only afflicted real-world economies over the 1970s, but which also shook the very foundations of international government macroeconomic policy. The frightening experience of governments internationally was that policies, which had apparently worked in the past, had suddenly ceased to cope with economic conditions – indeed all the signs were that these policies were worsening the problems which they sought to cure, as inflation spiralled ever upwards. What had changed?

THE ROLE OF EXPECTATIONS

To understand what was happening, we must go back to the simple Phillips Curve as illustrated in Figure 9.3. This was originally interpreted by policy makers as showing a stable relationship – after all, it did represent a behavioural pattern established over almost 100 years. Policy makers had long recognized that there was a conflict between the two major macroeconomic objectives of maintaining full employment, and holding prices stable; it was accepted that it was impossible to achieve both objectives simultaneously. The Phillips relationship merely underlined this problem; the more successful the attack on unemployment, the greater would be the inflationary pressures which would be generated in the labour market.

The only way to resolve such a conflict was to seek a **trade-off**, or compromise between the two objectives, taking the form of a simultaneous and partial achievement of each. In short, policy makers must be prepared to settle for less than full employment, and less than zero inflation – but try to ensure that the blend which emerged was acceptable.

Figure 9.8 shows conceptually how such a trade-off might be established. Note how the vertical axis has been changed to show the rate of *price* increase directly, rather than the rate of annual wage increases which would cause this inflation; but the curve retains its shape, and operates under the same general principles as before. Conceptually at least, policy makers should be able to define the maximum rate of unemployment which would be socially acceptable (in the context of the pursuit of their other objective of keeping inflation under control); this is

312 *Understanding the Economy*

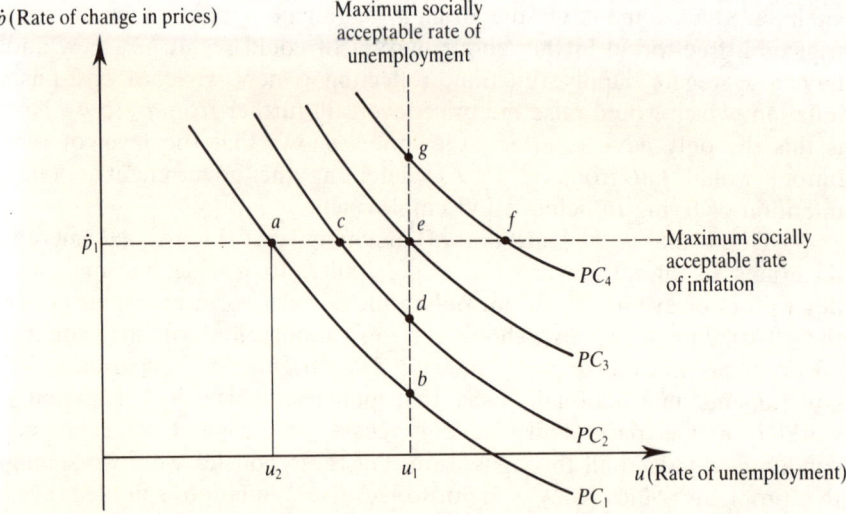

Figure 9.8 The breakdown of the short run Phillips Curve.

represented by the unemployment rate of u_1 in in model. At the same time, policy makers should have some view of the maximum rate of inflation which would be socially acceptable (in the context of their pursuit of the other main objective of holding unemployment as low as possible); let this be represented in the model by $\dot{p}_1$, with u_2 the corresponding point on the other axis. When the Phillips Curve is superimposed on this information, we can identify the **trade-off zone** of ab on the curve; at any point within the range ab, there is a partial but acceptable achievement of both objectives. Therefore, if policy makers were to set their macroeconomic policies to keep the economy running at a level where the unemployment rate lay between u_1 and u_2, then they would have achieved an acceptable compromise in terms of their policy objectives for unemployment and inflation.

Conceptual though the above argument is, it does reflect the policy makers' attitude towards the advice offered by the Phillips relationship in the context of the continuing conflict between objectives; policy was operated in broadly this fashion over much of the 1960s. With hindsight, this was an inappropriate – even dangerous – use of the information provided by the Phillips Curve. The essence of the relationship which had been identified was based on a long-term series of cyclical movements up and down the scale of economic activity; periods of slack had averaged out with periods of pressure. So long as inflation (whether demand-pull or cost-push) was minor and transient, people would not be too aware of its erosive effect on the purchasing power of their money incomes; in more technical terms, they would suffer from **money illusion**, and be happy to register only the money value (or nominal value) of their earned incomes. Only in these conditions would wage increases simply reflect changing levels of demand pressure in the labour market.

However, where the economy is held deliberately within a narrow range of activity, which eliminates periods of substantial slack in capacity, and which results in a continuing experience of inflation, then we are introducing new conditions into the economy, and into the labour market in particular. Further, if policy makers in their enthusiasm (or in a mistaken belief of the completeness of their control over the economy) hold the level of economic activity too close to point a in the trade-off range over a prolonged period of time, then inflation is no longer a minor and transient irritation. A **learning curve** effect is likely to develop, as people become increasingly aware of the consequences of inflation on their planned standard of living, and new behavioural patterns will tend to develop.

Money illusion is unlikely to persist when increases in money wages are frustrated, or 'caught out', by the effects of **unanticipated inflation**. Then it is but a small step from this recognition of events to the decision that future wage bargaining will reflect, in addition to its normal response to labour market conditions of relative scarcity:

- A new element, representing a retrospective compensation for any lost purchasing power in the previous bargain, as a result of higher inflation than was anticipated and, possibly,
- A new element representing workers' forecasts or expectations of the rate of inflation for the period ahead, during which the wage bargain would run.

The effect, in terms of the model in Figure 9.8, is little short of disastrous. Given rates of unemployment become associated with successively *higher* rates of wage increase, and therefore inflation, than would be expected from the historical pattern. In effect, the position of the Phillips Curve drifts upwards, indicating that changes are taking place in the background conditions for the relationship. This, in turn, carries implications for the trade-off zone; note how, if the Phillips Curve rises from PC_1 to PC_2, the zone is narrowed to cd on the new curve. If the Phillips Curve drifts still further upwards to PC_3, then there is no trade-off zone left at all; there is one point, e, in the model where both unemployment and inflation objectives can be satisfied simultaneously – and then only at maximum socially acceptable rates in both cases. If the Phillips Curve rises above this level, for example, to PC_4, then *no* compromise is possible; policy makers must either hold unemployment at its maximum socially acceptable level and suffer the non-acceptable rate of inflation corresponding to g or, conversely, hold inflation at its maximum socially acceptable level and suffer a non-acceptable level of unemployment, at a rate corresponding to f in the model. Only one policy objective can be achieved, at the expense of the other.

Over the 1970s in most countries, the Phillips Curve relationship between unemployment and inflation deteriorated in just the manner which we have described. By the mid to late 1970s, it was generally accepted that the Phillips Curve relationship had broken down completely; countries were confronted with the new and frightening phenomena of high and rising unemployment existing simultaneously alongside high and rising inflation rates. Not even attempts to suppress the symptoms, such as the wide variety of prices and incomes policies which were used internationally to try to contain the rates of increase in labour costs and prices, seemed able to do much to halt the accelerating crisis.

At least we have now some sort of explanation for the upward movement of the aggregate supply function in Figure 9.7. Before, we were only interested in looking at the effects of abnormal increases in input costs, such as wages; now we can relate these increases to the breakdown of the Phillips relationship.

But the model in Figure 9.7 contains a further message which we have still to draw to your attention; inflation, *if left to itself* should be finite. While the model is timeless, in the sense that it does not specify how long it will take for prices to move from the initial equilibium level p_1 to the final level p_3, it nevertheless implies that once prices have reached this higher equilibrium level then they will stop rising, provided that there is no further change to the information contained in the model. The inflationary process will only continue beyond this point if either aggregate demand, or aggregate supply, or both, are revised upwards again.

How might this happen? Economists now believe that a government could, inadvertently, prolong the process of inflation. For example, if policy makers are so focused on their objective of achieving full employment, then they might be tempted to counter *any* contraction of real output (such as the movement from Q_F to q_2 in Figure 9.7) with an almost automatic reflationary response; this would raise aggregate demand beyond D_{A2}, and set off a whole new series of inflationary adjustments (with the economy moving to a new equilibrium where D_{A3} intersected S_{A2}). This type of response was not uncommon internationally in the 1970s. But this is not the only danger; it is also possible that there is a more sophisticated problem connected with the government's setting of its macroeconomic policy targets. What if a government defines the concept of full employment too ambitiously? What if the policy target of q_F is either impossible to achieve, or to sustain without damage to the economy? What exactly does the nebulous concept of 'full employment output' imply?

By now we are moving into rather deeper waters. With the benefit of hindsight, many economists would now concede that it was both wrong and dangerous for governments to select some arbitrary and low level of unemployment to represent the condition of full employment output, whether this was taken as 3%, or 2%, or even lower. The capacity constraint should not be set solely in terms of what society, or policy makers, feel is desirable; its definition should be based on economic characteristics. In each country there will be a particular rate of unemployment, a **natural rate of unemployment**, at which inflation will be stable. Should the government seek to reduce unemployment below this level, to achieve an arbitrarily set policy target figure, then the result will be that inflation is triggered. This will not be the once-and-for-all inflation which we drew by implication from Figure 9.7; rather it will be the continuously accelerating inflation which we witnessed in the progressive breakdown of the Phillips relationship in Figure 9.8. This, in turn, would result in a further series of upward revisions in the aggregate supply function depicted in Figure 9.7, giving the latter almost a life of its own and creating the prospect of continuing – possibly even worsening – inflation.

Over recent years, the concept of the natural rate of unemployment has tended to blend into the cumbersome, but more descriptive term of the **non-accelerating inflation rate of unemployment** (or the NAIRU for short). But where does the NAIRU, or its predecessor the natural rate of unemployment lie ... at 2% unemployment ... or 5% ... or 10%? It would seem that there is no single, magic number. The NAIRU reflects a series of institutional and cultural influences in each country (most of which result in imperfections in the adjustment of the labour market); as such, it will vary from country to country – and from time to time within a single country. In effect, the NAIRU measures the level of unemployment within the labour market which results from immobilities and rigidities. If the proportion of the labour force which lies in the older (and less easily absorbed) age groups increases over time, then this demographic change will tend to cause the NAIRU to rise. Similarly, if the unemployment is concentrated geographically, for example, as a result of closures of older industries in particular regions, and the unemployed are unable (because of cost) or unwilling (because of age or social ties) to move to other regions where expanding industry is concentrated, this too will cause an upward movement in the NAIRU. Another possibility, proponents of the theory argue, is that persons who are unemployed take longer to search for and accept alternative work: for example, it may be that the only job prospects which are available offer poorer conditions, or lower paid work than they have come to expect from their previous career experience; or, if the level of benefit payments is reasonably high, there may be a reduced incentive to take very low paid employment. Either reason would tend to cause an upward drift in the NAIRU. Finally, there is the tragic problem of the long-term unemployed, who appear to drift beyond desperation and active search

Table 9.3 Estimates of NAIRU values – OECD and UK.

(a) OECD estimates.

	Coe and Gagliardi	Actual rate of unemployment
1967–70	2.1	2.2
1971–75	4.2	3.0
1976–80	7.6	5.4
1981–83	9.4	10.0

(b) UK estimates (males).

	Layard and Nickel	Actual rate of unemployment
1955–66	2.0	2.0
1967–74	4.1	3.8
1975–79	7.8	6.8
1980–83	10.7	13.8

(Reprinted by permission of Coe D.T. and Gagliardi F. *Nominal wage determination in ten OECD economies* (working paper, March 1985). Layard R. and Nickel S. *The cause of British unemployment*, (National Institute Economic Review, No. 111, Feb. 1985).)

into depression, apathy, and loss of self-confidence. Research shows that they are less likely to continue to look for work, or to make a positive impression on job interview, or to be capable (at initial re-entry) to take the job pressures and responsibilities which, previously, they would probably never even have noticed. As the proportion of long-term unemployed rises, this too will tend to pull up the NAIRU.

Accepting that the threshold rate will vary between countries and over time, is it possible to give even a broad idea of where the NAIRU threshold will lie? Table 9.3 provides a summary of results from some of the research work on the topic. This work would seem to confirm our earlier comments; apart from the fact that there has been a clear upward drift in the NAIRU values estimated for both the OECD member countries as a whole and, even more so, for male unemployment in the UK, note how the *actual* rates of unemployment lie below the NAIRU estimates from the mid 1960s right up to the end of the 1970s, with the implication that this could cause inflation to accelerate.

Extract 9.2 provides a useful series of points for consideration. It

Extract 9.2   THE ECONOMIST 14 MAY 1988.

AMERICA AT FULL EMPLOYMENT

The sharp drop in America's unemployment rate in recent years should, on past experience, have pushed wages up. It hasn't

THE number of jobless Americans fell last month to 5.4% of the labour force—a 14-year low, and down from a peak of 10.7% in December 1982. Europe's average unemployment rate still stands at 11%. Economists have been predicting for at least a year that America's tightening labour market will soon lead to higher pay, and hence higher inflation. The unexpectedly large drop in unemployment in April greatly added to the financial markets' fears of higher inflation.

Those fears may be wrong, because wage claims remain modest. Hourly wage rates rose by only 2.9% in the 12 months to April—slightly higher than last year's average rise of 2.5%, which was the smallest increase for 40 years. The 2.9% rise is equivalent to a real pay cut of 1%.

At first sight this seems to contradict the theory of the NAIRU—the non-accelerating-inflation rate of unemployment (sometimes called the natural rate of unemployment or the full-employment rate). This once controversial concept is now accepted in some form by most mainstream economists. NAIRU's true believers say that every economy has a certain rate of unemployment that is consistent with stable inflation. If the actual rate of unemployment is above the NAIRU, the greater risk of redundancy encourages workers to moderate their pay claims. If the jobless rate falls below the NAIRU, workers will be able to flex their industrial muscles and wages will accelerate. The gap between the actual jobless rate and the NAIRU is therefore an indicator of the slack in the labour market.

So why aren't wages rising more quickly in America now that unemployment has fallen below most economists' estimates of the NAIRU? The reason is presumably that a country's NAIRU is not fixed in stone. It can vary over time depending upon factors such as the level of skills, demographic change, wage bargaining procedures, social-security laws and various other labour-market rigidities.

Most econometric studies suggest that in Europe the NAIRU rose sharply between the early 1970s and the early 1980s, to around 8-9% in Britain, France and West Germany (see table). Government meddling in labour markets was partly to blame. More recent experience suggests that the NAIRU has since risen further in these countries. In America, on the other hand, estimates of the NAIRU suggest that it has hardly budged from around 6% over the earlier period, and there is evidence that it has fallen in the 1980s. Thus it is possible that America's unemployment rate is still slightly above its new "full employment" rate, thus explaining the continued wage moderation.

Why is the NAIRU so much lower in America than in Europe, and why has it fallen during the 1980s?

• The power of American unions has dwindled, partly reflecting the tough line the Reagan administration took with the air-traffic controllers, and also the impact of the strong dollar in the first half of the 1980s. In recent years unions have been prepared to forgo wage rises in exchange for job security. Union membership has fallen from over 25% of the workforce in 1980 to around 18% today, compared with 40-50% membership in most of Europe. Deregulation has sharpened competition; employers are less willing to concede inflationary pay claims.

• Unemployment benefits, already meagre in comparison with many European countries, have become less generous and harder to get. This has increased the incentive to go out and look for a job. In 1980 44% of the unemployed were claiming unemployment benefits; today the proportion is 30%.

• Many European labour markets are still riddled with rigidities such as strict hiring and firing rules. Wage differentials also tend to be smaller in Europe than in America, preventing wages from responding quickly to changes in the demand and supply of different skills. Minimum wages have squeezed differentials in several countries, but America's minimum wage has been frozen since 1981. Its real value has fallen by almost a quarter.

Today 95% of all hourly paid workers receive more than the minimum rate.

In many European countries, particularly Britain, even when unemployment rose above the estimated NAIRU it failed to moderate pay claims. This is the converse of America where low unemployment is now failing to reignite wage inflation. One popular explanation is that the NAIRU may itself depend on the actual level of unemployment—ie, as the jobless rate rises it drags the NAIRU up with it, so higher unemployment does little to reduce wage pressure.

This phenomenon—known as hysteresis—may reflect changes in long-term unemployment. The longer somebody is out of work, the more discouraged he becomes. He searches less keenly for work and therefore has less impact on wage negotiations. So as the proportion of long-term unemployed rises, downward pressure on wages falls at any given level of total unemployment. Hence, the NAIRU rises. Conversely, as long-term unemployment shrinks, the NAIRU could fall. In several European countries two-fifths of the jobless have been out of work for more than a year. In America the proportion has fallen to 8%.

This suggests that America may have been enjoying a virtuous circle falling unemployment reduces the NAIRU, allowing unemployment to fall further without triggering higher inflation. Europe's circle is, in contrast, vicious.

Unemployment rate required to keep inflation stable (NAIRU) %		
	1971–1975	1981–1983
America	6	6½
Japan	1	2
West Germany	1½	8
France	3½	8
Britain	4	9
Italy	7	6½
Canada	7	7½
Holland	4	10½

Reprinted with permission from *The Economist* 14 May 1988 © *The Economist*.

---

provides some additional information on the different NAIRU estimates for a more detailed range of countries than was shown in Table 9.3. Also there is an interesting discussion of what causes the NAIRU threshold value to differ between countries, and to change over time in any country. Finally, it offers the prospect of a downwards movement in the NAIRU, to set against the depressing trend of upwards drift which was experienced over the 1970s and 1980s.

It is probable that we have identified yet another example of why economics has been labelled (wrongly!) as 'that dismal science'. In terms of the cause and control of inflation, economic theory may have told us something which we would have preferred not to hear. If we accept the theoretical arguments which lie behind the concept of the natural rate of unemployment, or the NAIRU, then government attempts in many countries to push the rate of unemployment below this threshold to unsustainable and ultimately destabilizing levels, have caused much of the cost-push pressure and the inflationary spiral of the 1970s. The pathway to inflation, as well as to that other and warmer place, is paved with good intentions . . .

Milton Friedman has been a leading exponent of this school of thought. In his view, the simplistic short-term Phillips Curve – as it has been intepreted and used by policy makers – is a dangerous and unstable concept, because it ignores the role played by expectations. Figure 9.9 sets out a simplified version of his argument. If we start from point *a*, we

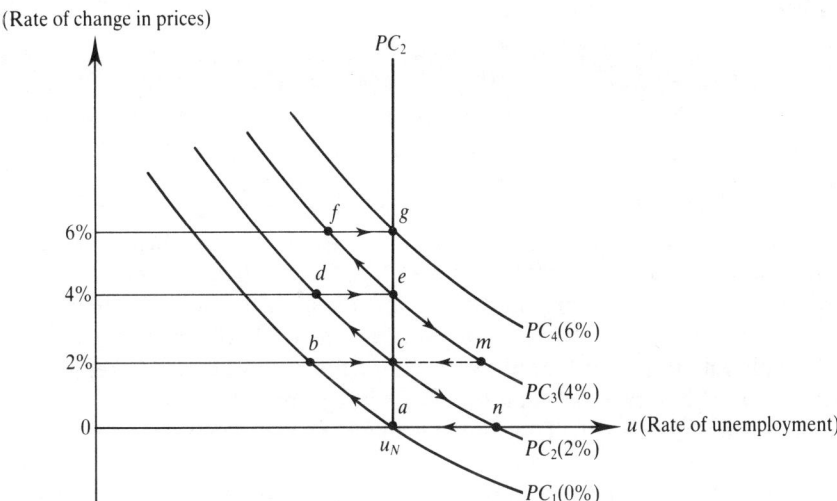

Figure 9.9 The long run Phillips Curve.

have a situation where inflation is stable at zero per cent per annum: neither workers nor firms expect inflation, since there is no experience of inflation. This stable relationship can only exist where the labour market is itself in equilibrium, that is, where the demand for labour is just enough to take up the available supply of labour (allowing for the natural rate of unemployment, u_N).

Should the government try by reflation to reduce unemployment below this level, Friedman argued, then *in the short term* there would be a movement up the short run Phillips Curve PC_1, which was based on zero inflation expectations; the economy might move up to point b, where inflation of 2% per annum would be experienced. If policy makers, recognizing the dangers of ever-accelerating inflation take action to hold the inflation rate at this level of 2% then, as demand is restrained, the cost-push pressures will gradually move the economy back to a higher level of unemployment, that is, back along the path between b and c. If inflation is held at 2% per annum indefinitely, then a new equilibrium position of c will emerge. At this point, workers will expect this rate of inflation and allow for it in their bargaining; simultaneously, firms will pass on cost increases in their 2% per annum revision in prices, so that neither party is worse off. Real incomes, that is, the purchasing power of the higher nominal or monetary incomes, is now the same as before at point a.

This exercise can be repeated as often as government policy tries to achieve a lower level of unemployment than u_N. For example, a second reflation could move the economy up PC_2 to point d, with the rate of inflation rising from 2% to 4% in the process; if corrected, the economy would drift back towards a third equilibrium at point e, where workers and firms, once again, correctly anticipate the annual rate of inflation as being 4%. Likewise, the economy could move up the new PC_3 to point f and a 6% per annum inflation, before drifting back to equilibrium at point g and PC_4.

The essence of Friedman's argument is that there can only be a stable equilibrium at u_N, where both workers and firms correctly anticipate the rate of inflation, and so hold their real incomes constant – whether nominal incomes and prices are rising at 0%, or 2%, or 4%, or 6%, or whatever. In the long run there is *no* trade-off possible between unemployment and inflation; even where the government is prepared to accept a higher rate of inflation, it cannot permanently stay at a lower rate of unemployment. The 'improvement' in the unemployment rate is part of a condition of disequilibrium (that is, participants have not anticipated correctly the rate of inflation) and the movement back towards equilibrium will simply restore unemployment to its natural rate. The **long run Phillips Curve** is therefore a vertical line above u_N, joining together all the points such as a, c, e and f where the rate of inflation has been correctly anticipated by the public and by firms.

Does this mean that the original point a is a sort of Garden of Eden, to which it is impossible to return, having committed the original sin which took us from a to b (with Keynesian policy cast in the role of the serpent, in terms of Friedmanite thinking . . .)? Unlike the biblical tale, return is possible – but at the cost of a higher level of unemployment than that associated with u_N. If we start from point e on PC_3, where inflationary expectations are of 4% per annum, policy makers could deliberately *deflate* the economy, so that it moves to a level of unemployment and inflation consistent with point m on that short run Phillips Curve (note how you can move in either direction along the Phillips Curve). If position m is held, and the public and firms begin to anticipate the lower rate of inflation of 2% per annum associated with this, then the economy will begin to adjust back along the path mc towards the stable point c and the lower Phillips Curve of PC_2. Further deflationary policy could push the economy down PC_2 to point n, where zero inflation is experienced again. If this rate of inflation is then held by policy makers, the participants of the macroeconomy will adjust their inflationary expectations back to zero, and we will have returned to long run equilibrium at point a. In short, Friedmanites would argue, to defeat inflation policies must be pursued which deflate the economy and break the rising spiral of expectations about future inflation.

Extract 9.3 is interesting to read, in the context of the short run and the long run Phillips Curves. It underlines the fact that wage push is a phenomenon which is by no means confined to the UK. It shows how real wages (that is, the real purchasing power of money or nominal wages) are

Extract 9.3 THE ECONOMIST 1 AUGUST 1987.

THE WAGES OF INFLATION

In the 1970s big wage increases helped stoke inflation; today wage moderation has helped to douse inflation. For how long?

AVERAGE wages in the big seven OECD countries increased by only 3% last year, compared with an average annual rise of 11% during the 1970s. The typical American worker has had a pay rise of little more than 2% during the past 12 months—the smallest increase since the second world war. In real terms, his pay packet is now worth 8% less than in 1978. Despite rising inflation this year and falling unemployment, there are few signs that American wages are about to take off.

The rate of increase in both nominal and real earnings throughout the OECD has fallen sharply. The slowdown is particularly marked in Italy and France. Italy's annual rate of wage increases declined from 23% in 1981 to 5% last year. Only in Britain and West Germany have wages bucked the trend. The average British worker has had a real pay rise of 20% in the past five years. In West Germany, despite negative inflation last year, workers have stuck out for wage increases of 3% at least. This has brought them a big gain in real terms.

In Japan, where consumer prices have also fallen, the growth of nominal earnings has fallen too. This is partly because profit-related bonuses are a big chunk of Japanese workers' total take-home pay. The appreciation of the yen has cut profits, and this in turn has squeezed wages.

The wage moderation of the 1980s is partly explained by tighter monetary and fiscal policies. Tight monetary policies have reduced inflationary expectations and meant that the money to pay much higher wages is simply not there. But the slowdown in pay rises also reflects a fundamental shift in the pattern of wage setting: the effect of microeconomic measures to make labour markets more efficient.

In a new study*, the OECD has examined the progress which governments have recently made in loosening labour-market regulations and other institutional drags. It reports:
• Social security benefits have become less generous. During the 1960s and 1970s, replacement ratios (unemployment benefits as a percentage of average wages) rose steadily. Since the beginning of the 1980s, they have fallen in nine of the 16 countries considered by the OECD.
• Minimum wages have been frozen in nominal terms in some countries, implying a cut in real terms. America's minimum wage has fallen by about a fifth in real terms since 1980. But France's has risen by roughly the same amount over the same period.
• Trade unions are on the defensive in most countries. Fewer days have been lost by strikes in the 1980s than in the 1970s. West Germany and France have given businesses more leeway in changing their hiring and firing laws.
• Almost all governments have tried to squeeze public-sector pay. Governments have been prepared to sit out prolonged strikes rather than give way to union demands—eg, in the disputes involving air traffic controllers in America in 1981 and British coal miners in 1984–85.
• Indexation of wages to prices has been scrapped or weakened in several countries, including Italy, France and Holland. In America and Canada fewer workers are now covered by cost of living agreements.
• Incomes policies have become less popular, as governments have instead attempted to deregulate labour markets and to encourage a closer link between pay and the profits of individual companies or industries. Yet France, Spain and Australia all still have incomes policies.
• Wage-setting practices have become more flexible. In America, in particular, workers have accepted pay freezes or even pay cuts. Some industries have introduced two-tier wage levels—eg, airlines—with new workers doing the same jobs being paid less than existing employees.

How have these microeconomic changes affected wage developments? Most analysts agree that in the short run at least there is a trade-off between unemployment and wage inflation (known as the Phillips curve): the higher the rate of unemployment, the lower the pay rises workers are likely to accept.

Weaker trade unions and less

generous unemployment benefits might make wages more responsive to unemployment—ie, the short-run Phillips curve would become steeper, resulting in a bigger decline in wage growth for a given rise in unemployment. Alternatively, the policies might lower inflationary expectations, or influence other variables which determine wage rises; this would shift the short-term Phillips curve rather than change its slope.

The OECD concludes that some microeconomic measures have helped to moderate wage growth—for instance, by lowering inflationary expectations, but it finds little evidence that they have altered the way wages respond to unemployment and inflation. If the OECD is right, the short-term trade-off between unemployment and wage inflation is no better today than in the 1970s: a fall in unemployment would probably be followed by faster wage rises. But because most countries' current unemployment rates are well above estimates of the level of unemployment which is consistent with stable inflation, the risk of a big pick-up in wage inflation is limited. The wage-price spiral of the 1970s is dormant, but it probably is not dead.

* Microeconomic changes and macroeconomic wage disinflation in the 1980s. OECD Economic Studies, spring 1987.

Reprinted with permission from *The Economist* 1 August 1987 © *The Economist*.

---

frequently adversely affected by the inflationary process at or immediately following the point where money wages have risen most dramatically. Finally, it details some of the measures which, internationally, have helped economies to move back down to lower short run Phillips Curves in the later years of the 1980s (where the curve has 'shifted', rather than simply changed its shape, in terms of the extract's discussion).

Where does all of this leave us? Are you thinking back with nostalgia to the simple world of the basic model with which you started the chapter? We hope not, for you have just been taken through one of the most hotly debated areas in macroeconomic policy. Simply because the real world is more complex than you – or the original Keynesian policy makers – believed is no reason for panic or rejection. Perhaps it is time to draw back from the detail of the argument, in order to assess its overall pattern. What we have seen is that the experience of the escalating problems of the 1970s proved to be a depressing one to Keynesian policy makers. Through their eyes, the economy had simply ceased to respond to the promptings of tried and trusted policies. Unemployment and inflation rates were rising simultaneously, to historically high levels, not simply in the UK but in all countries which operated within the principles of Keynesian macroeconomics. As awareness of the complexity of the problem developed, policy instruments too became increasingly complex, when governments sought to grapple with rising prices and money incomes (whether interpreted as symptoms, or causes). Despite this, control continued to slip, with achievements amounting to little more than transient 'pauses' in the inflationary process.

To many economists, it seemed that the heyday of traditional

Keynesian policy was drawing to its close. Just as Keynesian beliefs had once overtaken the ruling body of thought described as 'classical economics' in the 1930s, when the latter seemed to be overwhelmed by the tide of real-world events, it now appeared that Keynesian economics, in turn, was failing to deal convincingly with current economic conditions. Was the time again ripe for change in macroeconomic thinking?

THE KEYNESIAN VIEW OF THE ROLE OF MONEY IN INFLATION

Obviously, we are coming to the point where the alternative views of the monetarist school must be introduced and considered. Before we do so, however, it is interesting to look briefly at the role of money in the process of inflation, as perceived by Keynesian economists. All but the most extreme of the Keynesian school would have accepted that money had a key influence, possibly as a cause (where monetary policy had created the excess demand) and certainly on the *duration* of the inflationary process. Indeed, most would have agreed that if the supply of money was held constant, then the wave of inflation would ultimately 'burn itself out', leaving prices to stabilize, as implied by Figure 9.7.

Why should this be the case? One explanation is that, as price levels rise, additional transactions and precautionary money balances will be needed to fund and cover the same real *volume* of trade. Therefore, one consequence of inflation will always be to increase the demand for money balances. In terms of Figure 9.10, the demand for money function would rise from D_{m1} to D_{m2}, having been pushed to the right by the increased demand for transaction and precautionary balances. If the supply of money is held constant at S_{m1}, this increase in the demand for money would drive up the rate of interest from r_1 to r_2.

This adjustment in the money market would then feed back into the market for final output. Following the increases in the interest rate, interest sensitive expenditures would be revised downwards (although, as we have witnessed over the summer and autumn of 1988 – and even into the spring of 1989 – in the UK, there could well be a lag in this response to the higher cost of credit). This would reduce consumption and investment expenditure, causing aggregate expenditure either to fall or, at least, to stabilize. This takes us back, once again, to the conclusion suggested by Figure 9.7 which is that, provided there is no further upward adjustment to either the aggregate demand or the aggregate supply functions, then the inflationary process should wind down and prices stabilize again at their new, higher equilibrium values.

A similar effect could be argued, if we were to include briefly in our model the world trade flows of an open economy. If domestic costs and prices are rising faster than those of world competition (given

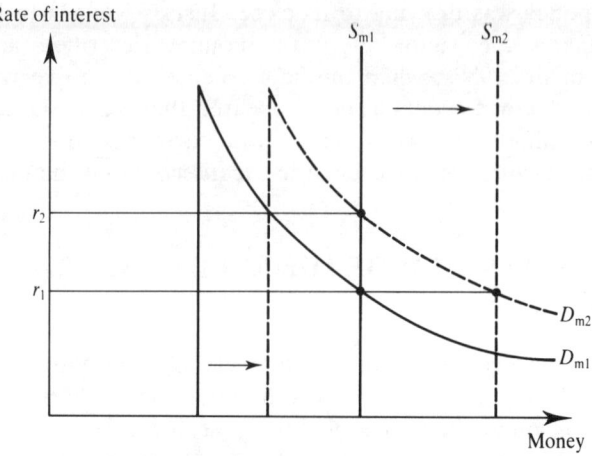

Figure 9.10 Effect of inflation on the rate of interest.

constant exchange rates, to keep the model as simple as possible) then the resultant price disadvantage in world and domestic markets is likely to cause export sales to fall and import purchases to rise. For example, it was by no means a coincidence that the UK government was embarrassed in the spring of 1989 to report that not only had inflation risen to 7.5% (and was expected to go at least a little higher), but also that the UK had recorded its third-worst ever deficit in the balance of trade. Returning to our basic model of Figure 9.2, if we were to adjust this to include international trade flows then the effect of an increase in imports would be to reduce the consumption of UK goods, while the fall in exports would also reduce the level of the injection function; these would combine to reduce aggregate demand, as shown in the model, to $C_2 + J_2$, which would cause the equilibrium level of GDP to contract. Taking this information through to our (by now well worn and tattered from excessive use!) model in Figure 9.7, the resultant fall in expenditure would lower the level of aggregate demand, and so provide a second corrective force which should bring to a halt the process of inflation.

Thus the inclusion of the money market, or of international trade, should provide influences which would combine to bring the process of inflation to a halt; in a sense, any inflation will contain the seeds of its own cure. For inflation to continue indefinitely, it must be *validated* by the government, for example if the latter responds to the rising level of unemployment, or falling levels of investment expenditure, with a naive or mechanistic reflationary policy. If reflation is attempted by expansionist monetary policy, then this would move the supply of money function from S_{m1} to S_{m2} in Figure 9.10, which would cancel out the corrective influence provided by the constant money supply. If reflation is attempted through the medium of fiscal policy, this would not only raise the level of aggregate demand in Figure 9.7 and perpetuate the inflationary spiral; it is at least possible that the need to fund a fiscal deficit could result in an increase in the supply of money[5] which, once again, removes this corrective influence. (Indeed, some of the more extreme monetarists would argue that the only short-term effects which might follow from a fiscal reflation would be caused by the increase in the supply of money which this might imply!)

Therefore, if you believed that only monetarists were prepared to acknowledge a role for money in the analysis of inflation, you can now see that this was very much an over-simplification. Keynesians as well as monetarists would accept that, if the money supply is held constant, the duration of any wave of inflation will be limited. For inflation to be sustained, whatever its initial cause, the process of inflation must be validated by an increase, or a series of increases in the money supply.

THE MONETARIST VIEW OF INFLATION

However, monetarists would go much further in defining the role of money in inflation. They would argue that excessive increases in the money supply are the prime and only cause of any inflation. Rising prices, or cost-push influences such as rising wages, falling exchange rates and rising import costs are merely symptoms of a process started by an excessive growth of the supply of money. Milton Friedman argues: 'inflation is always and everywhere a monetary phenomenon'.

Most economic models are based on a combination of theoretical analysis and empirical testing of that theory. In the case of monetarism, the initial research which led to a resurgence of interest in the role of money was the massive study *A Monetary History of the United States, 1867–1960*, by Milton Friedman and Anna Schwartz. This examined the interrelationship in the USA between the rate of growth in the money supply, and its effect on prices and the level of economic activity over the period. In broad summary, its conclusions were that:

(1) Substantial changes in the money supply were generally followed, after a lag, by changes in the price level and the level of economic activity;

---

5. When there is a deficit (that is, $G > T$) this must be funded by some form of borrowing. The government could print more notes. It could borrow from the Bank of England. If it issues bonds, these could be used as collateral by the public to raise loans (for example, see Black, J., *The Economics of Modern Britain*, p. 103). All involve an increase in the supply of money.

(2) Substantial increases in the money supply normally resulted in periods of severe inflation in prices;

(3) Substantial reductions in the money supply were normally followed by periods of severe recession;

(4) Periods of stable prices and output levels were generally preceded by a stable money supply, or by a money supply in which there had been only a minor rate of growth.

These empirical observations were consistent with the analytical predictions of the **quantity theory of money**, which had been formulated by Irving Fisher in 1911. Using a minor variation of the original formulation,[6] this could be stated as:

$$MV \equiv PQ$$

where M represents the supply of money for the period (take care not to confuse it with the symbol for imports), V represents the income velocity of circulation (that is, the number of times during the national income accounting year that a unit of money is employed in income transactions), P represents an index value of the general price level, and Q the real (or physical volume of) output produced during the period.

In simple terms, the lefthand side of the identity, covering the money supply and the number of times it is used, will give us a figure for total expenditure or aggregate demand; the righthand side, covering the output produced and the list of prices at which this was sold, provides us with a figure for GDP or aggregate supply for the year. The model is a tautology, in the sense that at the end of any year (in a closed economy, where there is no international trade), actual spending will always equal output sold and held in inventories.

If this relationship holds in any single year over a period of time, it will also hold during that series of years; as such, it can be differentiated with respect to time. As a result of this exercise (see Appendix 9A, if you are brave enough to confront the simple differential calculus involved; otherwise, just trust the result!) the quantity theory can be restated as

$$\dot{M} + \dot{V} = \dot{P} + \dot{Q}$$

where $\dot{M}$ represents the annual percentage rate of change in the money supply, $\dot{V}$ represents the annual percentage rate of change in income velocity of circulation, $\dot{P}$ represents the annual percentage rate of change

---

6. Fisher used the form $MV \equiv PT$, where T represented the volume of transactions which were carried out in the period; we have converted this term to a measure for real (or the physical volume of) output, Q.

in the price level (that is, the rate of inflation), and $\dot{Q}$ represents the annual percentage rate of change in real output.

It is interesting to compare the views of pre-Keynesian or 'classical' economists with those of modern monetarist or 'neo-classical' economists on this version of the model. The classical economists argued that the value of V (the income velocity of circulation) would reflect institutional and technical factors, such as the frequency of income payments to households, or the pattern of use of the banking system. These arrangements would change only slowly over time; in terms of our variant of the model, $\dot{V} = 0$. This would leave only the rate of growth in the money supply, on the lefthand side of the equation, to affect both the rate of growth in prices and real output on the righthand side of the equation. However, their belief was that real output would be determined by real factors, such as the size of the labour force, the amount of capital stock, and the general level of technology, rather than by the supply of money. Since these real factors would also change only slowly over time, the original quantity theory view was that changes in the money supply would affect only the residual term of the price level (or $\dot{P}$, in our version of the model). Thus, changes in the money supply would normally result in broadly proportionate changes in the general price level.

The same broad conclusion emerges from modern quantity theorists. Monetarists argue that V is a stable function of known variables and, normally, will exhibit only modest fluctuations over time. Given a reasonably stable value for V so that $\dot{V} = 0$, the quantity theory relationship once again resolves to the interaction between the rate of growth in the money supply ($\dot{M}$), and the rate of growth in the nominal or money value of GDP (that is, $\dot{P} + \dot{Q}$) over time. Friedman argues that 'there is a consistent though not precise relationship between the rate of growth in the quantity of money and the rate of growth in nominal income. If the quantity of money grows rapidly, so will nominal income . . .'[7]

It is not, however, an instantaneous relationship, in the sense that both elements in the righthand side of the equation will respond immediately and in equal proportion to any variations in $\dot{M}$, on the lefthand side of the equation. Friedman argues from his empirical studies that, typically, there will be a delay of between six and nine months on average in the response of GDP to a change in the money supply. Further, he argues, that in the initial response of GDP, output (or $\dot{Q}$ in our version of the model) will typically be affected much more strongly than the price level (or $\dot{P}$); indeed, the initial value for $\dot{P}$ could be very small in the short run, following variations in $\dot{M}$. From his studies, on average it could be 15–24 months before the initial change in monetary

---

7. See Milton Friedman, *Money and Economic Development*, New York: Praegar, 1973.

growth ($\dot{M}$) begins to have a significant effect on inflation ($\dot{P}$). This applies equally to expansions and contractions in the rate of monetary growth. But he stresses that these figures are based on *worldwide* averages and should not be taken as a precise relationship for any single country.

To summarize, the view which emerges is that in the short run – which could extend over several years – monetary changes will tend to affect primarily output, so that increases in the money supply would appear to benefit real output and employment levels. However, this effect is only a transitional one. Ultimately demand pressures on final output and inputs will drive up prices and wages, eroding the gains achieved in output and employment. In the long run, therefore, changes in the money supply will affect only prices. 'What happens to output over longer periods depends on real factors: the enterprise, ingenuity and industry of the people; the extent of thrift; the structure of industry and government; the nature of competition in industry; the relations among nations . . .'[7]

Reverting to our formulation of the quantity theory model, another aspect of Friedman's arguments can be illustrated. If:

$$\dot{V} = 0$$

(that is, if velocity is relatively stable over time), then if the government can hold

$$\dot{M} = \dot{Q}$$

(that is, if it can hold the rate of growth in the money supply equal to the rate of growth in real output over time), then

$$\dot{P} = 0$$

(that is, there will be no price inflation).

This is a tremendously powerful result, in the context of the analysis of inflation; as we have presented it above, it has sometimes been described as 'Friedman's 4% rule'. To explain this somewhat cryptic description, the average annual rate of growth in real output for the USA has been about 4%. Friedman argued that if the annual rate of growth in the money supply was held to 4% per annum, price inflation would be squeezed from the system; the general price level would become more stable, and price movements would tend to reflect only relative scarcities and surpluses of individual items.

Sadly, governments are all too human and, in most countries, it is far from easy for the government (through the central bank) to control exactly the credit creation activities of its financial institutions; as a result, the discipline implied by the Friedman rule has proved to be too demanding and austere for most countries to observe. Our version of the model shows only too clearly the consequences of slippage; if:

$$\dot{M} > \dot{Q}$$

then it follows that

$$\dot{P} > 0$$

In other words, if the rate of growth in the money supply is permitted to exceed the rate of growth in real output, then price inflation will occur. Completing the original Friedman comment 'inflation is always and everywhere a monetary phenomenon . . . *in the sense that it can be produced only by a more rapid increase in the quantity of money than in output*'.

Now you can see why we got so heated up about the problems of defining, measuring and controlling the money supply in the previous chapter! Taken in the context of the UK economy, the rate of growth in the money supply has regularly exceeded the long run average rate of growth in real output which, until the later 1970s at least, was a little above 2% per annum. It makes little difference which of the multitude of M measures we select; they have all embarrassed successive governments. Given the predictions of the quantity theory, whether the excessive rate of increase in the money supply was deliberate (as where the money supply was allowed to increase permissively to hold down interest rates and encourage investment), or accidental (as where the fiscal deficits incurred in reflation were funded by creating new money), or institutional (as where the development of fringe banking activities and the evolution of 'plastic money' created greater sources of and access to credit), the end result could only be a series of waves of price inflation.

A quick glance back to the money supply statistics of the previous chapter will show that not even the 'monetarist' policies of the early Thatcherite government were beyond blame. Despite their success in bringing the UK rate of inflation down over the early to mid 1980s, the purist would still argue that there was 'excessive' growth in the UK's money supply. The purest purist of all, Milton Friedman, was asked in a current affairs programme on television how he would rate the UK government's policies in their attempt to follow the recommendations of his theories. He blinked once behind his spectacles and smiled: 'If they were my students, I'd give them an "A" for intentions – and a "D", or maybe even an "E" for performance,' he quipped. The 'A' grade speaks for itself; in the American University system, the 'D' grade is a marginal, and the 'E' grade a clear fail . . . If that was his view in the early 1980s, when the UK's faith in monetarism was at its zenith, what would he have made of the recent rates of increase in all our measures of the money supply – even the hotly disputed M0? If the quantity theory could help us to analyse the errors of earlier and well intentioned Keynesian policy makers, might it not still hold . . . even for professed monetarist policy makers? Here is the root cause of the repeated and swingeing criticism made by *The Economist* in the various extracts; if you permit an excessive rate of increase in the money supply then, after a lag, you will discover that you have triggered both an upwards spiral of inflation *and*, in an open economy, a series of major balance of trade deficits (since imports will be sucked in to augment the rate of increase in domestic output, or $\dot{Q}$).

Perhaps you might feel that the quantity theory approach is a little too stark in its simplicity, and too mechanistic in its assessment of cause and effect for a real-world economy. If so, it is possible to add a little flesh to its bare bones by sketching out the monetarists' view of the **transmission mechanism**, or the process by which excessive increases in the money supply generate the various symptoms of inflation within the economy.

Money balances, they would argue, are just one single asset among a portfolio of other assets, each of which represents a way in which money can be held. Households and firms will choose a pattern of allocation between the different asset forms which maximizes their utility (or satisfaction). An unexpected increase in the supply of money will leave them with greater money balances than they need for normal transaction purposes. These excess money balances will normally be reallocated into other forms of asset; there is no reason why some of this reallocation should not be into real assets (such as stereo systems, furniture, dishwashers, cars and so on). Compare this monetarist perception of the very direct link between the money supply and aggregate demand to the rather more involved and indirect Keynesian link, where changes in the supply of money affect first of all the rate of interest and, only then, through the response of interest-sensitive expenditures, aggregate demand.

Returning to the monetarist analysis, this surge in purchases will create a scarcity for final output which will tend to drive up the prices of the affected items and, simultaneously, encourage firms to compete for additional inputs as they seek to increase their own individual levels of output and profit. This will transmit demand pressure into cost-push pressure in all input markets; rising input prices, whether for labour, for raw material, or even for capital are merely *symptoms*, rather than a *cause* of inflation.

Taking the analysis a little further, in any economy which is open to international trade, rising domestic prices will tend to cause exports to fall (either because domestic goods have become relatively more expensive in world markets, or because goods destined for output are switched into easier domestic sales), and imports to rise (as additional goods are sucked in to satisfy domestic demand). This is a familiar experience in the UK. If the resultant balance of trade deficits cause the exchange rate to fall, raising the cost of imports of necessary foodstuffs and raw materials, then this new set of cost-push pressures must also be recognized to be a symptom of demand-pull inflation, rather than a cause of the problem.

The longer the inflation continues, the more households and firms will be made aware that rising prices are eroding the real value of their money incomes. As we have discussed earlier, their attempts to correct for past unanticipated inflation, and to forecast and allow for future rates of inflation, will feed through into more aggressive attitudes in wage bargaining and price setting. These inflationary expectations are likely to become self-fulfilling and sustain, or even increase, the inflationary pressure.

If the inflation accelerates beyond some critical rate, the falling real value of the currency unit may encourage households and firms to convert their money income more quickly into real assets, either to consume, or hold as a 'hedge' against inflation (for example, the late 1970s witnessed a major surge of purchases of houses, stamp collections, antique silverware, furniture and porcelain, in a deliberate attempt to hold wealth in a form where capital gains from the purchases would protect the wealth holder against the erosive influence of inflation). This implies a probable increase in the income velocity of circulation (so that $\dot{V} > 0$), which would add to the pressures generated by the lefthand side of the quantity theory equation.

In short, the monetarists would argue that:

(1) Excessive increases in the money supply are likely to create inflationary pressure on prices, whatever apparent short-term benefits are achieved in terms of output and employment;

(2) Wage-push and 'imported' inflation are symptoms of an ongoing inflation; the only true cause is given in (1) above;

(3) Inflation, once started, will tend to build up its own destructive momentum;

(4) There will be lags in the transmission mechanism, which could vary between countries, or even between different waves of inflation in any one country;

(5) These lags would not only operate during the expansion process of an inflation; they would also operate during deflationary policy changes, creating difficulties and delays in achieving control over the process of inflation.

Friedman himself comments that 'it is a long road to hoe to stop an inflation that has been allowed to start. It cannot be stopped overnight. That really is the main reason why you shouldn't let one get started.'[7]

THE MONETARISTS' CURE FOR INFLATION

By now you should be well aware that Keynesians and monetarists put forward different interpretations of the cause, and possibly even the course of an inflation. These differences are also reflected in the policy solutions which are offered by the two schools of thought.

To Keynesian policy makers, grappling to contain the escalating problems of the 1970s, there developed a perception that inflation had become an increasingly complex phenomenon, which required an increasingly complex set of curative policies, embracing a mix of fiscal and monetary policies, prices and incomes policies, consensus planning policies, manpower forecasting and retraining policies, and policies designed to influence the overall volume and the geographical pattern of investment spending.

In stark contrast, monetarists argued that there was not merely a simple cause of inflation (an excessive rate of increase in the money supply); there was also a simple cure for inflation (that is, to stop the excessive rate of growth in the money supply). Policies aimed at symptoms such as unemployment, or wage bargaining, or declining levels of domestic investment expenditure, would have no lasting effect and little short run benefit. The only real solution would be to tackle the root cause of the problem and, with sustained determination, to bring the rate of growth of the money supply under control.

The very simplicity of the monetarists' argument was probably as strong an attraction to harried governments as was its content, which offered the potential for halting the frightening spiral of inflation. The remarkable fact is that while few governments had not at least a broad commitment to Keynesian principles in the early 1970s, even fewer were not committed to monetarist principles by the end of that decade. This represents a truly remarkable wave of conversions – some, admittedly, more whole-hearted than others.

In this brave new world of monetarism, what were the more detailed instructions for policy makers seeking to bring the rate of growth of the money supply under control, so to eliminate inflation? At its very simplest, since borrowing is one of the major components of the money supply:

(1) Public sector borrowing must be cut, ideally by reducing government expenditure, rather than by raising taxation (see Chapter 10 on supply-side economics) and, simultaneously,

(2) Private sector borrowing must be constrained or reduced by influencing, through monetary policy, the cost and availability of credit for households and firms.

In terms of the monetarists' transmission mechanism, if the rate of growth in the money supply is cut, then households and firms will soon find that their actual money balances are less than is needed for planned expenditure. To some extent, they might raise money balances by selling other forms of financial assets (which would depress the prices of the latter, and, as a result, raise yields and interest rates). But a major part of their response will be to revise downwards their planned expenditure. This will ultimately cause real output and employment levels to fall. As a result firms, facing unsold output and rising inventories, will hesitate to raise prices and will be more resistant to wage demands. At the same time, organized labour, facing rising unemployment, will tend to reduce its degree of militancy in wage negotiations. Gradually, once the public becomes aware that the government's stance is firm on the issue (and that it has no intention of 'bailing out' workers or firms from the consequencies of their inflationary settlements), then inflationary expectations will be revised downwards. Ultimately, inflation should be squeezed from the economic system. With improving price competitiveness (given that exchange rate movements do not distort the position, for example rising in response to increasing UK interest rates) domestic output should benefit from rising export sales and from falling import purchases in domestic markets. This should help domestic output levels to recover – which, in turn, should stimulate investment – so that the economy should begin to move into recovery. The existence of spare capacity in the recovery phase should ensure that there is no immediate resurgence of inflation, so that the recovery should be sustained into a more extended run at economic growth.

In reality, while the economy might well follow the path described by theory, it is extremely unlikely that the correction and control of inflation will be either quick, or painless. Friedman himself has always argued that, just as the initial effects of an increase in the money supply will boost real output and employment rather than prices in the short term, in a similar fashion cuts in the rate of growth of the money supply will hit real output and employment levels for some time, before the rate of inflation begins to decline.

In a very real sense, the acceptance of the need to break free from the vicious circle of inflation must be *forced* upon the players, as a result of the pain which is experienced from a continuation of their present behavioural pattern. Most pains have a threshold level which must be exceeded before a response is triggered; so too with inflation. Output must fall and unemployment must rise for some time before the control policies begin to bite on their target of price increases. This problem is compounded by the role which is played by expectations within the economic system. Expectations are based upon current observation and past experience; if the past experience has been that the government will always validate inflation when unemployment becomes a matter of social concern, then this is a very major expectation to balance against any government's current declarations that 'there is no alternative' to the present policies of control. The bigger the party, the worse is the hangover, as most students would confirm. The more rampant and prolonged the inflation, the greater are the immediate social costs of bringing expectations, and then inflation, under control.

With reference to the UK experience over 1979–82, there is still a very substantial area of dispute. To monetarists, the severity of the cyclical downturn and its social costs of savagely high levels of unemployment, were both necessary and inevitable. They would argue that the policies of the government were justified by their success in reducing the UK's annual rate of inflation, and bringing this more into line with the OECD average. Few Keynesians would dispute the need for firm control, but most would probably concur with both the National Institute of Economic Research and the OECD view that the correction was too sharp and too severe, so that a substantial part of the misery of the UK's decline into a prolonged depression was self-imposed and unnecessary.

It is not the purpose of this chapter to argue the case for one or other of the two viewpoints; we have tried to discuss both viewpoints as objectively as possible, with the intention of letting you work through the arguments and then make up your own mind.

We might volunteer some observations, without any intent to affront either school of thought but with the probability of bringing outraged cries from both (economists are great believers in objectivity – until it is their own views which are under attack!). It is probably true that Keynesian policy was accompanied with a relatively permissive regime in the control of the money supply. It is also probable that the role of expectations was underestimated in Keynesian thinking. We have seen how both these elements are crucial in the generation and duration of inflation. But the faults do not lie exclusively in one school of thought. The simple monetarist models discussed above tend to ignore both the time element and the institutional difficulties involved in bringing the growth of money under real control. These institutional factors embrace not only the resilience of expectations, but also the very real independence of financial intermediaries which are in the midst of a technological revolution, as well as the uncertainties of decontrolled competition; as we have pointed out before, there is no direct control over the supply of money. It probably took a lot longer to control inflation than was anticipated, and the social costs of disinvestment and unemployment were considerably higher than anyone would have predicted. An obsessive concentration on a single macroeconomic objective is unlikely *not* to achieve some improvement in that objective – but at a severe cost in terms of the conflicting objective which is being ignored. In the 1960s and early 1970s, an obsessive drive towards full employment did much to send world inflation rates lurching upwards. In

Extract 9.4 THE ECONOMIST 3 DECEMBER 1988.

BETTER THAN IT LOOKS

MARGARET THATCHER'S proudest claim is that she has transformed the British economy. Until just a few months ago it was hard to disagree: productivity growth was convincingly up, unemployment sharply down, inflation safely in check, foreign assets piled high. In the spring her chancellor, Mr Nigel Lawson, crowned these achievements by cutting tax rates deeply at the same time as he raised public spending and put the budget into surplus—a stunning feat of public finance, made possible by stronger economic growth than in any of the other big industrial economies bar Japan. But that was the last of the good news.

All of a sudden the economy looks horribly old-fashioned. In the six months to October the external deficit on current account was £9 billion, or 4% of GDP (at an annual rate); in other words, proportionately one-third bigger than America's. To stop the pound from plunging, the Bank of England has pushed interest rates from 7½% in May to 13%. A triumphant budget followed by a vicious monetary tightening: this is too much like the economics of the 1960s and 1970s that Mrs Thatcher and her ministers said they had abandoned for ever. After nine years of Thatcherism, can the British economy really be back in its earlier dismal rhythm—a burst of unsustainable growth ending in a burst of high inflation and a balance-of-payments crisis?

The government's embarrassment is intense because, for the moment, it lacks a convincing answer to that question. Mr Lawson tells Parliament that Britain is suffering from "a bit too much of a good thing", while Mrs Thatcher drums her fingers ominously. The Labour party again has cards to play; its economics spokesman can tell Mr Lawson that Britain has the biggest trade deficit, the highest interest rates and the second-highest inflation rate in Europe. In certain parts of the prosperous, property-owning, mortgage-servicing democracy that the Tories set out to create, Mr Lawson's bullish appraisals and "vigorous" use of interest rates now qualify him to be strung up with barbed wire. Something has gone wrong, sure enough. But what?

Spend, spend, crunch

Britain is suffering from too much demand. In the spring the Treasury forecast that real domestic demand would rise by 4% this year. That would have been consistent with a gentle slowing of economic growth

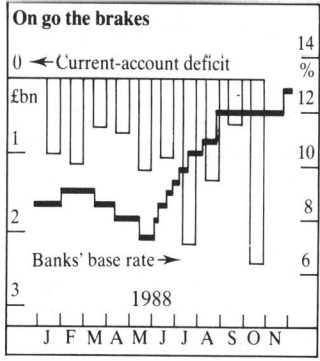

from 1987's 4%, alongside stable inflation and a tolerably small current-account deficit. In fact domestic demand is set to grow by 6% or more this year—half as much again as the Treasury said. Much of the excess is due to faster-than-expected consumer spending, financed to an unhealthy degree by a continuing boom in credit. This burst of spending has fuelled both the deterioration in the balance of payments and an upward creep in inflation.

To cool the pace of demand, the Treasury is relying exclusively on higher interest rates. That is why the price of money has nearly doubled in seven months, and why it may rise further. Next year demand will ease, says Mr Lawson, and the economy's growth will slow to a rate—3%, say, against this year's 5%—that can be maintained without higher inflation. There will be discomfort, especially for those who have taken on lots of floating-rate mortgage debt. But there will be no recession, and soon all will be well. The Treasury's only mistake was in failing to spot the strength of demand earlier—an understandable error, because the first few months of 1988 were overshadowed by fears that demand would collapse after the stockmarket crash.

Such is the case for the defence, and it is mostly sound. Mr Lawson has a good chance of steering the economy down to a soft landing next year. This is partly because the Tories' economic achievement is real, not imagined. The supply side of the British economy really has been transformed by nine years of Thatcherism. The reward for deregulating the economy, for curbing the restrictive powers of trade unions and for promoting competition is not just a higher achievable rate of growth, but greater resilience in the face of short-term strains like the present squeeze.

The proper charge against Mr Lawson is that his approach to managing demand is adding pointlessly to these strains. This is nothing new. The microeconomic (supply-freeing) part of Thatcherism has always worked much better than the macroeconomic (demand-managing) part. In 1979–81 Britain suffered a recession that was deeper than it needed to be because the Treasury followed a doctrine of monetary control that, in the end, proved unworkable. Since then its macro-policy has changed once or twice a year. Monetary targets of every kind have come and gone. Fiscal policy was at first a servant of those targets, then a tool for managing demand in its own right. Now it has no role at all.

All of which makes Mr Lawson's impatience at having to explain, yet again, his one true macroeconomic policy rather comical. Worse, though, he is now repeating an earlier mistake. Dearer money feeds into Britain's published inflation rate through its effect on mortgage payments. So Mr Lawson is trying to get inflation down by first putting it up. His predecessor, Sir Geoffrey Howe, did the same when he virtually doubled value-added tax in 1979: that fed the wage-price spiral and made the task of disinflation all the harder. This year's acceleration in the retail-price index may indeed be just temporary, as Mr Lawson says; but if it spurs wage demands it could drag the underlying rate of inflation up to meet it.

A tighter fiscal policy would cool demand without this drawback—but it has an even bigger point in its favour. The chancellor wants both to peg sterling and to control the pace of demand in the economy. To do that he must expect, sooner or later, to need two instruments of policy: only by coincidence will a given level of interest rates stabilise the pound and keep demand on track. In this, Mr Lawson has been lucky for most of the past seven months. But the latest rise in interest rates sent sterling up; the Bank of England had to swap pounds for foreign currency to hold it steady. The government is tightening monetary policy with one hand (higher interest rates) and loosening it with the other (intervention against the pound).

The long-running confusion over the aims and instruments of macro-policy has sapped the Treasury's credibility. In one unnoticed sense Mr Lawson has actually come to rely on the loss of confidence. To check demand he needs to keep interest rates higher than those abroad. But if moneymen believed his resolve to keep sterling steady, he would be unable to do it. He can drive a wedge between British and foreign interest rates only to the extent that investors expect sterling to fall. For lack of fiscal policy, the chancellor has fashioned a tool of policy from the markets' refusal to take him seriously.

By the time of Mr Lawson's next budget, the growth in demand is sure to have slowed —maybe by too much. Lower inflation and a shrinking trade deficit will help to restore his battered reputation. That being so, Mr Lawson had better in the meantime rediscover either the case for fiscal policy or the case for letting sterling float where it will.

Reprinted with permission from *The Economist* 3 December 1988 © *The Economist*.

---

the UK at least, a similar obsession with the control of inflation has caused very severe social costs in terms of unemployment. Having suffered so much, this is why it is so sad to see the rate of inflation begin its familiar upwards drift again.

Where does present UK government policy lie, and how serious is the emergent problem? Extract 9.4 is broadly optimistic, resting this view on the real achievements which have been made; but it does underline the fact that the government has been drifting between the more clearly defined macroeconomic policy stances, whatever its strident claims for continuity. In a sense, this drift reflects the practical realities of the debate; monetarist policies have been given their chance, and there is a greater awareness now of their limitations, of their short-term social costs, of the harsh austerity of their programme. Control can be achieved, but not by the single and painless wave of a magic wand. Once again we can see that, in economics, there is seldom a quick and simple solution.

CONCLUSIONS

1. Inflation occurs when prices in general are rising substantially over time; these price increases will affect not only the price of final output, but also the price of the inputs needed to produce that final output.
2. Inflation, if left unchecked, imposes major costs upon society as a whole: it causes a major erosion in the purchasing power of money incomes; it creates an opportunistic and random pattern of relative wage increases within the labour market; it obscures relative profitability, so creating problems for resource movement and the adjustment of the industrial structure to the changing pattern of market opportunities; it can build up its momentum, as households and firms learn to anticipate inflation, and to build this into their wage settlement and pricing plans; it could degenerate into hyper-inflation, which might cause a collapse of confidence in the monetary unit of the economy.
3. The rate of inflation experienced by the UK has typically been higher than the inflation rates achieved by its main competitors, which has had an adverse effect on the demand for UK output. While major improvements have been made from the rates of in excess of 20% experienced over 1979–80, and inflation has been brought down towards the OECD average over 1983–84, there is clear evidence that a new surge of inflationary pressure has been creeping back into the UK economy over recent years; this, in turn, has contributed to a deteriorating net balance in our international trade flows.
4. In simple Keynesian terms, inflation is caused by the pressure of excess demand in the market for final goods and services; as such, in the simple model, the cure lies in deflationary demand management policies. In more sophisticated modelling, it can be shown that the demand pressures on final output will induce cost-push pressures in the markets for inputs, which will provide a secondary impulse to the process of inflation; in Keynesian policy terms, various forms of prices and incomes policy, and consensus planning were used to try to contain these cost-push pressures.

5. Over the 1960s and early 1970s, it seemed possible to achieve an acceptable trade-off between the conflicting policy objectives of full employment and the control of inflation. From the mid-1970s, this possibility of trade-off appeared to deteriorate, partly as a result of genuine cost-push pressures (such as the increase in energy and material costs associated with OPEC), but mainly as a result of rising expectations about future inflation, which finally caused a breakdown of the relationship depicted in the short run Phillips Curve. By the late 1970s, most countries were experiencing substantial unemployment and price inflation simultaneously.

6. Keynesian theorists were not unaware that money had a substantial role to play in the process of inflation. For inflation to be sustained, it was generally accepted that it must be validated by permissive increases in the money supply. If the latter were held constant, it was accepted that inflation would normally burn itself out.

7. Monetarists argue that money had an even stronger role to play; the only possible cause of inflation is where there has previously been an excessive rate of growth in the money supply. In simple terms, if the rate of growth of the money supply is allowed to exceed the rate of increase in real output then, if the income velocity of circulation is stable, the end result will be price inflation.

8. In the short run, they argue, an increase in the rate of growth of the money supply will affect real output and employment levels more than prices. But, as wages and production costs rise, the initial beneficial effect on output and employment is eroded. In the long run, the only lasting effect of the increase in the money supply will be on the price level. Real output and employment will, in the long run, be influenced by real and not monetary factors.

9. Given that the cause of inflation lies in an excessive rate of growth in the money supply, to their minds the only possible cure for inflation is to bring the growth in the money supply under control. This will result initially in a severe deflation of real output and employment levels but, sooner or later, inflationary expectations will be defused and prices will become more stable. This starkly simple solution contrasts with the complex network of control instruments developed by Keynesian policy makers in the mid-1970s, just as its implicit acceptance of the need for (transient) high levels of unemployment as part of the costs of control, clashes with the Keynesian preoccupation with maintaining as full a level of employment as is possible. A further point of initial conflict lay in the definition of full employment; monetarists argued that this should be defined to allow for the natural rate of unemployment (or the NAIRU) for the economy – which implied a rather higher equilibrium level of unemployment than was initially acceptable to Keynesians.

10. To some extent, the bitterness of the debate between Keynesian and monetarist protagonists has eased; mainstream economists would concede that each school has valid points to make. All but the most rabid of Keynesians would concede that a greater degree of control must be maintained over the growth rate of the money supply, than was the case in earlier policy making. All but the most rabid of monetarists would concede that there are severe problems and costs associated with a dedicated control over the supply of money. Probably the most important difference in viewpoint lies in the respective schools' attitudes towards government intervention. On balance, Keynesians would still be prepared to intervene by either monetary or fiscal means should they feel that the market economy was taking too long to reach an acceptable solution to events. In sharp contrast, monetarists are convinced that intervention should be minimized and the government's role confined to setting monetary growth at a reasonable rate over long periods of time, to ensure a stable general price level, within which market forces can operate with greater certainty. Apart from this difference in principle, both would agree that inflation, if left unchecked, can develop a dangerous momentum, which would impose its own severe long-term social costs on the community. How best it should be tackled, will depend upon the theoretical base held by policy makers – and even here, in the UK at least, there has been a drift of interest from the potential of demand-side control towards the opportunities of supply-side reforms, as we will explore in the following chapter.

Appendix 9A: Monetarism and the quantity theory

As stated in the text, the quantity theory formulation can be adapted to the form:

$$MV = PQ$$

where M = stock/supply of money, V = the income velocity of circulation, P = index of price level, and Q = the level of real output.

Where this equality results for each year over a series of years, it is possible to differentiate the equation with respect to time. This would give us the result:

$$V \times \frac{dM}{dt} + M \times \frac{dV}{dt} = Q \times \frac{dP}{dt} + P \times \frac{dQ}{dt}$$

340 Understanding the Economy

This in turn can be rearranged to show that:

$$\frac{M}{M} \times V \times \frac{dM}{dt} + \frac{V}{V} \times M \times \frac{dV}{dt} = \frac{P}{P} \times Q \times \frac{dP}{dt} + \frac{Q}{Q} \times P \times \frac{dQ}{dt}$$

(since M/M, V/V, P/P and Q/Q all equal one, adding them to the differentiated equation does not disturb the equality). This, in turn, can be simplified to show that:

$$MV \left(\frac{1}{M} \times \frac{dM}{dt} \right) + MV \left(\frac{1}{V} \times \frac{dV}{dt} \right) = PQ \left(\frac{1}{P} \times \frac{dP}{dt} \right) + PQ \left(\frac{1}{Q} \times \frac{dQ}{dt} \right)$$

This can be further simplified if we divide the lefthand side by MV and the righthand side by PQ (once again, since $MV = PQ$, we are still not disturbing the equality); this would leave us with:

$$\left(\frac{1}{M} \times \frac{dM}{dt} \right) + \left(\frac{1}{V} \times \frac{dV}{dt} \right) = \left(\frac{1}{P} \cdot \frac{dP}{dt} \right) + \left(\frac{1}{Q} \times \frac{dQ}{dt} \right)$$

The final step is to shorten this cumbersome statement into the form:

$$\dot{M} + \dot{V} = \dot{P} + \dot{Q}$$

where $\dot{M}$ represents the percentage rate of change in the money supply over time (which is what $[1/M \times dM/dt]$ measures, $\dot{V}$ represents the percentage change in velocity over time, $\dot{P}$ is the percentage change in prices over time (or the rate of inflation) and $\dot{Q}$ is the percentage change in real output over time.

SELF-ASSESSMENT QUESTIONS

TRUE/FALSE QUESTIONS

9.1. If inflation were to be eliminated, all prices would be stable and constant over time.

9.2. The Phillips Curve relates the level of unemployment in the labour market for any given period to the level of money wages which will result in that period.

9.3. All cost-push pressure from the input markets is merely a symptom reflecting excess demand pressure for final output. As such, it will ease when demand pressures are satisfied.

9.4. Monetarists believe that reflationary policies will always have a greater initial impact on output and employment than on prices.

MULTIPLE CHOICE QUESTIONS

9.1. The concession of higher money wages will not necessarily damage output and employment levels since:

   (a) These will depend on demand levels which will benefit from the higher wages;
   (b) Productivity gains from improvements in technology and manning practices could absorb the higher price of labour without raising the price of final output;
   (c) The government will always reflate when the level of unemployment rises, so validating the higher money wages;
   (d) The higher price of labour will force firms to use it efficiently by adopting a better technology;
   (e) The labour force has a right to be paid an adequate level of money wages.

9.2. If the money supply is held constant during a period of inflation, then the latter will burn itself out because:

   (a) People will gradually lose confidence in the monetary unit and expenditure will fall;
   (b) The decline in the real value of the monetary unit will reduce the real value of taxation receipts, and force the government to cut its expenditure;
   (c) Once the commercial banks have reached their credit ceilings, there will be no money to fund further transactions;
   (d) The shortage of cash and credit will ultimately increase the rate of interest and result in reductions of consumption and investment expenditure;
   (e) The fall in the real value of wealth holdings will result in an increase in savings to restore the latter, as a result of which consumption will fall.

9.3. In terms of the quantity theory, an increase in the rate of growth of the money supply will:

   (a) Cause an increase in the income velocity of circulation;
   (b) Cause output and employment to rise in the short run;
   (c) Cause output and employment to rise in the long run;
   (d) Cause prices only to rise in the short run;
   (e) Cause prices only to rise in the long run.

9.4. In terms of monetarist transmission mechanism, the price of final output will rise because:

   (a) Unexpected increases in money balances resulting from the increase in the supply of money will spill over into additional purchases of real assets, driving up the prices of the latter;
   (b) The increase in the money supply will reduce interest rates, stimulate investment and possibly consumption expenditure, creating a scarcity of final

output and raising the general price level;
(c) Unreasonable wage demands from monopsonistic labour market institutions will push up production costs and therefore prices, to protect profit levels and investment;
(d) The pressure of government expenditure will create a scarcity of resources for the private sector, raising production costs and prices;
(e) The falling real value of the monetary unit will tend to force prices upwards to protect profits and investment.

9.5. Keynesians would tend to argue that inflation:

(a) Is a simple problem caused by aggregate expenditure setting $Y_e > Y_F$; as such the cure lies in deflationary fiscal policy, which would move the aggregate expenditure function downwards to a more appropriate position;
(b) Is less important a social problem than unemployment; policy should therefore be set to minimize the latter, as the lesser of the two evils;
(c) Is caused largely by cost-push disruptions from organized labour; the power of the latter should therefore be weakened, so that wage bargains reflect realistic market forces;
(d) Reflects weaknesses in the operation of market forces; part of its cure must be to substitute a greater degree of central planning;
(e) Has a number of contributory causes, which can only be tackled by a set of policies designed to influence both the aggregate demand and aggregate supply functions.

9.6. Monetarists would tend to argue that inflation can be cured if:

(a) An incomes policy is used to constrain wage demands and help to reduce cost-push pressures within the economy;
(b) Institutional bargaining forces in the labour market have their monopsonistic power reduced, so that wage settlements can reflect more accurately the market conditions for final output;
(c) The government refuses to react to rising unemployment levels, so that workers and firms are faced with the market consequences of their actions;
(d) Target rates of monetary growth are set for the period ahead, and a determined attempt is made to hold the actual rate of growth of the money supply to these targets;
(e) All forms of government subsidy and intervention are reduced, to ensure that final output is produced as efficiently as possible for world and domestic markets.

Note: Solutions can be found at the end of the text.

Chapter 10

Supply-side Economics

> Introduction
> The root of the problem
> The enhancement of competition
> The role for tax cuts
> Supply-side theory: a broad assessment
> Conclusions
> Self-assessment questions

INTRODUCTION

At several points in the text, reference has been made to the term **supply-side economics**. To many economists, this has the potential to be the greatest single breakthrough in economic thinking since the Keynesian revolution. Therefore, this chapter must introduce you to some of the radical arguments associated with this new body of theory, otherwise our treatment of macroeconomic policy would be incomplete. At the same time, it is important for you to realize that the topic is not 'just another piece of abstract theory'; supply-side economics has had a revolutionary impact on practical government policy in both the USA and Europe.

What exactly does supply-side theory involve? Before we get down to looking at its main content it is vital that you should recognize its main difference in *principle* from the macroeconomic policy which we have discussed in earlier chapters. Keynesian policy emerged as a response to a perceived situation of **market failure**; market forces alone seemed to be incapable of breaking free from the periodic dislocations of the business cycle in general, and from the very high unemployment and severe depression conditions of the early 1930s in particular. The essential principle of Keynesian economics was that some degree of intervention was needed, to 'nudge' – or even to correct – market forces towards a more acceptable equilibrium.

As we have already seen, Keynesian policy itself appeared to be running into difficulties in many countries over the mid and late 1970s, as it sought to deal with the gradually worsening problems of inflation, low economic growth, and rising unemployment. Many economists felt that these difficulties were rather more than a temporary embarrassment; in their opinion the struggles of Keynesian policy reflected the more serious symptoms of **intervention failure**. In other words, government intervention was failing to achieve a satisfactory solution or equilibrium for the macroeconomy (and, in the view of some, might even be causing the economy to under-perform). This conclusion resulted in a major revival of interest in and development of pre-Keynesian economic models; in a very real sense, the wheel had turned completely back to its original theoretical point of departure. As a result, the common feature of much of this new theoretical preoccupation was a renewed belief in the efficiency of market forces, as the other side of the coin of mistrust and lost confidence in government intervention and activity.

We are familiar with one of these theoretical rehabilitations; monetarism, as we have already noted, was based on the revival and extension of the classical quantity theory of money. But this was only one of several emergent strands of theory and research. Another major development came in the form of a rekindling of interest in the classical theory of public finance, as a result of which economists began to explore the impact of taxes on individual incentive and corporate behaviour. A series of central themes began to build up from the work of economists such as Martin Feldstein, Michael Boskin, Robert Mundell and Arthur Laffer; these themes were first described collectively as **supply-side economics** by Herbert Stein in 1976. In a remarkably short space of time, this new view was embraced as a worthwhile cause by the *Wall Street Journal* (through Jude Wanniski, the associate editor of the editorial page of this influential newspaper), then adopted as a theoretical basis for policy reform by the Republican party, before emerging to provide the foundation stones for many of the policies implemented by the Reagan and Thatcher administrations in particular. Few new waves of theory have ever swept so quickly through public as well as professional awareness, into high fashion 'buzz-words' and radical new policies.

It is often the case that a highly descriptive buzz-word is difficult to translate into a formal and informative definition; this is very much the position with supply-side economics. As the name implies, this new body of theory is concerned with the behaviour of the aggregate supply function.

Keynesian demand management policy had emphasized the role of aggregate demand in setting the level of economic activity. Policy makers were well aware of the importance of aggregate supply but, if there was a considered opinion, it would have been that aggregate supply was too slow and imperfect in its response to government prompting, and that aggregate demand offered a greater potential for influence and control.

In sharp contrast, supply-siders argued that the greater potential for influence lay in the aggregate supply function. They believed that the position of this function and its freedom to move over time were both constrained by a number of factors; *if these constraints could be eased or removed, then aggregate supply could bound forward to offer major increases in terms of output, employment and economic growth.* To release these constraints would involve radical changes in two main fields of policy: firstly, the government must act to deregulate markets and to promote competition within markets; secondly, the government must reform its tax structure, to reduce the 'wedge' of taxes which had been driven between households' and firms' earned income, and the net of tax disposable income which they derived from this. The purpose of the first set of changes would be to reduce inefficient government intervention in the detailed working of the economy, and so to improve overall efficiency. The purpose of the second set of policy reforms would be to restore incentive to the players in the economic system, and so to improve work effort and productivity. The combined result of the two sets of policy measures would be to move the aggregate supply function to the right.

Consider Figure 10.1. Using the model developed in the previous chapter, this shows us the familar inflationary effect of an increase in aggregate demand, from D_{A1} to D_{A2}; once again we can see that, as real output rises from its original level of q_1 towards the full employment constraint of real output level Q_{F1}, inflation begins its upward spiral, with prices rising from p_1 to p_2, and real output rising to q_2. But, what if we could find a means of moving the aggregate supply function from S_{A1} to S_{A2}? This would take us from the opening intersection of aggregate demand and aggregate supply at point a to the new intersection at point b. Note how this would imply a major increase in real output from q_1 to q_3, at the original price level of p_1. At best, we could increase the level of economic activity, and possibly reduce the level of unemployment, all at constant prices; our supply-side policies could help us to eliminate inflation *and* to increase the rate of economic growth (since any increase in potential output, which would follow from the movement to the right of the aggregate supply function, would represent economic growth). At worst, even if the increase in aggregate supply is not enough to allow us to achieve q_3, it should still raise economic growth and allow us to hold the rate of inflation lower than would otherwise have been the case.

It is small wonder that the arguments of supply-side economists fell

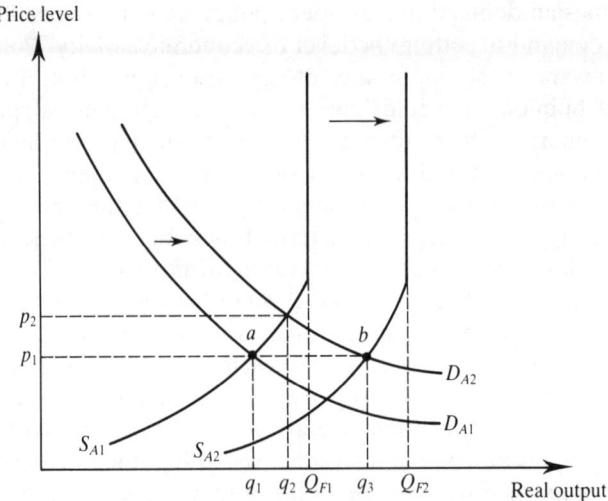

Figure 10.1 Effect of an increase in aggregate supply on prices and output.

on such ready ears. At a stroke the new policies seemed to offer a way forward to dealing with the dominant economic problems of the 1970s; in most countries, policy makers were only too conscious of their inability to influence the rising tides of inflation and unemployment, and only too aware of their worsening rates of economic growth. And where in the world is there a public which does not believe that there is too much government 'red tape' and that tax bills are far too high?

But how could such policies work? Why should they succeed where Keynesian policies had failed? If intervention and investment subsidies could not raise economic growth, why should less intervention do so? Would a return to a greater reliance on free market forces not simply turn back the clock to the very conditions which Keynesian policy had sought – and ultimately failed – to cure? Would tax cuts be enough to restore incentive, so raising effort and output, or would they simply raise aggregate demand and degenerate into renewed inflationary pressure? Could a complex modern economy respond to theories and beliefs which had originated in the eighteenth and nineteenth centuries?

The objectives of this introductory chapter to the topic of supply-side economics are:

- To provide a simple supply-side analysis of the nature of the problems which were acting as constraints on economic growth;
- To discuss the role of enhanced competition in producing increased efficiency in supply-side policies;

- To analyse the role of tax cuts in increasing the incentive to work, save and invest;
- To assess some of the possible problems which might be experienced in the implementation of supply-side theory.

THE ROOT OF THE PROBLEM

The central themes which have emerged from the supply-side literature can be traced back to the very roots of economic theory. Adam Smith in 1776 in his book *An Inquiry into the Nature and Causes of the Wealth of Nations* argued strongly that production and wealth would be maximized if the markets for goods and services were liberated from the tyranny of government control. A nation's wealth was not maximized because the government, or producers set out with this intention. Far from it, each producer would seek to satisfy his [*sic*] own self interest and, 'by pursuing his own interest he frequently promotes that of society more effectively than when he really intends to promote it'. With producers behaving in this manner in the myriad of fragmented markets which make up any economy, it is almost as if 'an invisible hand' gathers together their atomistic efforts into an overall solution which provides the greatest good for all.

At first sight, you might feel that there is a strong element of mysticism in any belief which argues that the total sum of independent, self-seeking and unrelated effort provides an optimal solution for all. Yet, in terms of more advanced modern neo-classical theory, this is exactly the solution which emerges. While, in an introductory macroeconomic textbook it is not appropriate to discuss the detailed analytical framework which supports Smith's view that resources are allocated most efficiently within a system of free and competitive markets, there is no reason at all why we should not explore some aspects of the argument, where these can be considered in broad, commonsense terms.

If all producers are motivated by self-interest, then the natural result is that they will compete against each other in the various markets within the economy. The main result of this competition is that it will promote efficiency: if a producer becomes careless and inefficient, then his (or her) costs will rise, so that less profit will be made when matching competitors' prices; or again, if consumer tastes and preferences change, then the producer must respond quickly and accurately to these changes, or risk losing customers (and their revenue) to competitors. Competition between producers, each seeking to maximize personal or corporate gain, provides a harsh and continuing discipline. Simply to survive, the producer must become and remain efficient. If he (or she) fails to do so, then potential new entrants are queued up to move into the space which the unsuccessful producer will leave behind in the market.

This simple theme is capable of further and important development. Competition implies a continuing battle for survival, within which individual producers seek to establish a 'competitive edge' which will yield at least a transient advantage in terms of profits. The possibility of personal gain provides an incentive for the individual to search through the noise and clutter of the market place for new and more profitable ways of servicing customers. In terms of modern neo-classical theory, it is the role of the entrepreneurial producer to operate at the margin of change, in order to identify emergent market opportunities, then to assemble and organize the resource package which is needed to exploit these opportunities, and to convert them into successful businesses. The entrepreneur is a vital catalyst in the process of adjustment, which matches resource deployment to the changing pattern of market opportunities.

To the supply-side economist, the two essential elements of the equation are that markets are fully competitive and that the individual players within markets have the incentive to operate to maximize their personal, or corporate gain. It is when these two conditions are not met, that an efficiency problem emerges – with all the familiar attendant symptoms of low productivity, poor economic growth, unemployment and inflation.

Looking at the first element in the equation, supply-siders would argue that, during the 30–35 years of active Keynesian policy, there was a gradual erosion of freedom and a diminution of competition within markets. To some extent this reflected natural weaknesses in market structure, such as the development of imperfect monopolistic and oligopolistic markets,[1] where producers set up entry barriers against new competition to protect their existing market shares and profits. However, supply-siders also believe that competition has suffered from the steady encroachment of government into the market structure. This might have taken the form of the government acting as a producer in its own right, as in the old 'nationalized industries' or state monopolies for steel, coal, electricity, gas, telecommunications, water and so on. Or it might have been that the government has acted as a large and even dominant customer (in more technical terms, as a **monopsonist**), imposing design,

---

1. The terms **monopoly** and **oligopoly** refer to markets where there is restricted competition, because of the limited number of producers in the market, and both frequently result in restrictive practices or collusion between firms, where the intention is to protect or increase prices and profits, for the benefit of the producers and at the expense of consumers. In a monopoly, as the name suggests, there is a single producer (or a coordinated group of producers acting as a single firm). In an oligopolistic market, there is a small number of independent and competing producers; but the pressures of competition can be so disliked that the oligopolists will frequently collude or come together to agree prices and market shares, in an attempt to protect or even to increase profits.

quality standards and cost conditions on producers, for example in civil engineering and defence contracts, or in local authority housing contracts. Most frequently, government involvement has been through the imposition of regulations and controls on producers, to ensure safety standards for customers, or working conditions for employees, or permissible contents for the product, or planning and developmental constraints on proposed industrial expansion, or standards and penalties for the control and treatment of pollution, or whatever.

Some supply-siders believe that there has developed almost an adversary type of relationship between producers and the government. Like the relative giant of Gulliver in the tiny kingdom of Lilliput, producers have woken up to find themselves tied down by a network of fine threads. Each individual thread, or rope, might be so light and fine in itself that it imposes no recognizable burden or check; but their collective and combined effect might be to hold the giant as a helpless victim. However well intentioned the individual bureaucratic controls on producers, their overall effect has been to hedge producers in with so many constraints that neither they, nor the markets in which they operate, can function in an efficient fashion. As a result, the economy as a whole has been gradually overwhelmed and dragged into stagnation.

The second main problem, in the eyes of supply-siders, is that self-interest has become almost a condemnatory term; added to this, progressive taxation systems have reduced the individual's incentive to take the risks, and to make that additional effort which is needed to keep the economy operating successfully at the margin of change. At the best of times, taxation drives a wedge (the **tax wedge** effect) between effort and the reward received for that effort. The greater the tax burden, the bigger is the wedge, and the less is the incentive to make any additional effort.

The **Laffer Curve** is one of the best known models from supply-side theory; according to Jude Wanniski of the *Wall Street Journal*, this was reputedly drawn for the first time, with a ballpoint pen on a Washington restaurant napkin, by Arthur Laffer to illustrate to Donald Rumsfield, the White House Chief of Staff, how tax rates could affect incentive. The resultant curve is shown in Figure 10.2; it shows the total tax revenue received by the government from different levels of tax rates. At zero taxes, the government revenue from taxation is zero. As tax rates rise initially, so too does government revenue – but at a decreasing rate, as the public become more resistant to the increasing level of taxation. At some point, shown here as tax rate t^*, government revenue from taxation will reach its maximum of R^*. If tax rates rise beyond this, people will tend to switch to lower taxed alternatives (such as leisure activities), or divert their activities into finding tax loopholes – or even into operating in the informal, or 'black', economy to avoid taxation. From Figure 10.2, you can see that if the tax rate is raised from t^* to t_1, then government

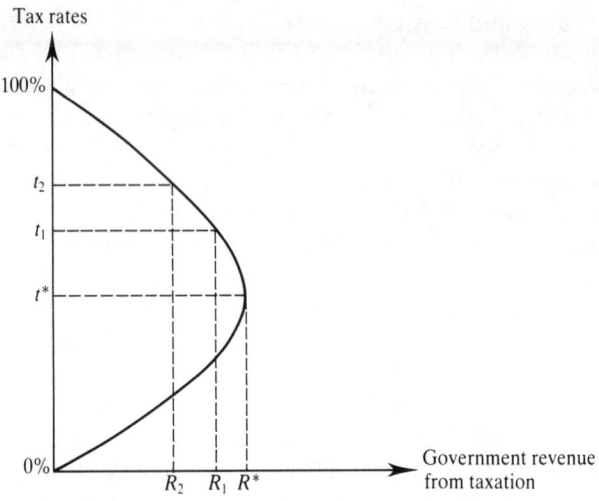

Figure 10.2 The 'Laffer Curve' and effect of tax rate changes on government revenue from taxation.

revenue could actually fall (from R^* to R_1 in the model). Taken to the extreme, if the tax rates are raised to 100% then no one will work (or at least no one will declare income for taxation) since the entire reward is taken by the government; the result is that, once again, government revenue from taxes falls to zero.

The problem is that the model is purely speculative, in the sense that the shape and position of the Laffer Curve have not been determined from empirical research results. It illustrates a very plausible behavioural pattern, and there is some empirical support for its main message that excessive taxation can be counter-productive. But, if it does exist, where does the critical tax rate of t^* lie? It could be at 50% of taxable income, or 40%, or 30%, or whatever. In the late 1940s, long before anyone had heard of supply-side economics, Colin Clark had argued that any tax burden in excess of 25% of GNP would discourage both effort and output ... and had been largely ignored. Nearly 40 years later, Laffer was arguing that – wherever t^* lay – there was a distinct probability that USA marginal tax rates in the mid 1970s were *above* this level, creating a strong disincentive effect. In this view he found ready and powerful support from Ronald Reagan. Another folk tale (to lay alongside the restaurant napkin) is that one of the reasons why Reagan was such a quick convert to supply-side economics was that, in his own experience as a film actor (OK ... if you are a perfectionist you can find your own term!) he had found that it was only worth his while making three movies a year, because of the size of the tax wedge for any fourth film.

Retreating as quickly as possible from the world of B movies, if the economy was operating on the backward sloping section of the Laffer Curve, then it would follow that *if tax rates were reduced*, a greater incentive would be provided to stimulate the self-interest and effort levels of both households and firms. Nor would the government lose out. The lower marginal rates of taxation would operate on a greater volume of taxable income, so that the government revenue from taxation would rise; in Figure 10.2, if the tax rates are reduced from t_2 to t_1, then the government revenue rises from R_2 to R_1.

Supply-siders were quick to point out that any continuing process of inflation would exaggerate the disincentive effect of taxation. There are two reasons for this. Firstly, taxation is levied on money incomes. Let's go back to the equilibrium condition of the long run Phillips Curve which we considered in the previous chapter, and assume that households and firms are correctly predicting the rate of inflation, so that money incomes and prices are rising at the same rate, as a result of which *real* incomes are constant. But if money incomes rise, so too will taxation deductions (for example, 30% of £1000 is a greater sum than 30% of £900); net of tax real income will therefore fall. The second reason why inflation exaggerates the disincentive effect is that most economies operate with a system of progressive taxation on incomes, that is, taxable incomes are allocated into bands (or tax brackets), with higher incomes being subject to higher marginal rates of taxation. For example, in the UK in 1979 the standard rate of tax (that is, the marginal tax rate for the first band of taxable income) was 33% . . . and the marginal tax rate for the top band of taxable incomes was 83%. (Academics can remember the first, but have only read about the second marginal rate in textbooks!) To return to our argument, if money incomes are rising alongside inflation, then there will be a tendency for people to find that part of their incomes spill over into higher tax rate bands; this phenomenon is known as **bracket creep**. Once again, the result of inflation is to increase the tax which is deducted from money incomes, so reducing net of tax real income. The effect of inflation is therefore to increase the size of the tax wedge, and so to reduce the incentive for extra effort.

Where does all of this argument leave us? To supply-siders, we have weakened the two essential conditions for growth which were identified earlier in this section: markets have become less free and competitive, and therefore less efficient; at the same time, the pursuit of self-interest has been blunted by cultural mistrust and, more important, by the disincentive effect of excessive taxation. As a result, we are left with the problems of stagnating productivity and economic growth rates, working through the macroeconomy into the twin evils of high unemployment and increasing inflation.

Just as the monetarists came up with a disarmingly simple solution to an apparently complex problem, so too did the new supply-side missionaries. If part of the problem was that the force of competition within markets had been constrained and weakened, then the solution would be to remove these constraints and restore effective competition. If the other part of the problem was that personal (and corporate) incentive had been blunted by excessive levels of taxation, then the relevant solution here would be to *reduce* tax rates. The result, they argued, would be that there would be a major increase in efficiency, productivity and growth. In terms of Figure 10.1, we would be able to move the aggregate supply function to the right, increasing output, employment and prosperity – and reducing the effect of inflationary pressures on the economy.

There is always a danger that, when a complex and fiercely debated series of theoretical arguments are simplified to provide an introduction to the topic, the result comes out in such black and white terms that you wonder why anyone (even an economist) could ever dispute the logic of the analysis and the proposed solution. Why are we not all supply-side economists? The obvious answer is that there are normally two sides to any argument. However, before we examine some of the problem areas, let's look in a little more detail at the way in which competition might be increased, and at the interrelationship between efficiency, incentive and economic growth. For the moment, all we ask is that you remain aware that there is still a great deal of controversy surrounding the claims of supply-side economics; when we have finished our outline of supply-side theory, then we will return to look at some of the worries and the counter-arguments which have been advanced. Then, once again, we will leave you to make up your own mind!

THE ENHANCEMENT OF COMPETITION

It is one thing to argue that constraints on competition should be removed, so that markets can operate with greater freedom and efficiency. It is quite another thing to identify which constraints should be removed, and how best to increase competition and promote the operation of market forces within the economy. In following through the translation of the conceptual advice into practical policies, it is interesting to see how a real world government has tackled this particular strand of supply-side theory.

UK government policies, since 1979, have been very strongly influenced by supply-side arguments. Indeed, while the link between theory and policy is more normally illustrated in the context of the Reagan administration, many observers would suggest that the radical and continuing policy reforms of the Thatcher government provide a still more comprehensive case study. It is possible to identify three distinct supply-side themes in recent UK policy; these cover the topics of deregulation of markets, privatization of state-owned economic activities, and the promotion of small business start-ups.

Deregulation is intended to remove constraints on competition which have developed either from official licensing procedures, or from the natural specialization and restrictive practices which have evolved within markets. For example, until recently, would-be operators on long distance and local coach travel had to obtain licences from the relevant transport authorities; this system of licences had been introduced to impose stricter safety standards and to define the conditions of service provision for customers but had, in effect, become a **barrier to entry** behind which monopolistic operators could control the provision and the price of services to the public. The Transport Act of 1980 removed much of the licensing restriction on new entrants, while still seeking to protect safety standards for the public. This triggered a massive expansion in the number of businesses competing for long distance coach travel, causing substantial reductions in fares, and a considerable switch in the pattern of travel towards this relatively cheap mode of transport. More recently, licence restrictions have been eased on urban and other local services, with a similar pattern of expansion in the increase in the number of operators competing for the main routes within these areas.

Another high profile act of deregulation resulted in the 'Big Bang' changes of institutional practice within the capital and money markets in 1986. These ended a number of long established restrictive practices within these highly specialized markets, broke down compartmental walls between different activities and institutions, and permitted the entry of foreign firms. This has triggered a continuing process of entry and merger, which has imposed a substantial degree of change on the numbers, identities, resource base and the range of services offered by the various financial institutions – and not without some very dramatic and well known casualties.

Similar but less publicized deregulation of professional private sector restrictive practices has been experienced by other markets such as opticians, and solicitors involved in house conveyancing. However, arguably the greatest single act of deregulation in a European as well as a UK context has been the decision of the European Commissioners to break down member state boundaries and to create a single and unified European market by 1992, within which any producer can operate in any member state to serve any internal market within the Community.

All of these illustrations reflect policy changes which have increased both the number of participants, and the areas in which they can compete – with the clear intention of stimulating competition and efficiency within the markets concerned.

Privatization provides the second – and fiercely contested – theme of UK government policy, where motivation has been drawn from supply-side objectives. It has been a fundamental belief of Thatcher governments that the state's claim on resources and its involvement in the economic system as a player in its own right, should both be reduced. In part, this reflects a perception that state involvement is, almost by definition, inefficient and cumbersome; the other side of this particular coin is an equally strong conviction in the efficiency of private ownership and control of resources within the discipline of competitive markets. In part, the supply-side arguments for the transfer of ownership have provided a welcome additional weapon to the government, when it was seeking to reduce the public sector borrowing requirement in its pursuit of control over the money supply. To an unknown extent, supply-side theory has provided a respectable platform for a long held and bitterly nursed opposition to the actions which brought about the public ownership of the industries concerned in the first place. History contains many examples of theory providing a public justification for actions which would have been taken in any case! Whatever the motivation, the UK government's privatization programme has involved the sale to the general public via share issue on the capital market of a variety of government owned concerns, or nationalized industries.

It is not appropriate for this chapter to become involved in this most bitter of controversies; rather, we would prefer to try to look at some of the main points as objectively as possible (and, once again, probably offend everyone . . .). How might privatization increase both competition and efficiency in the markets which are affected by this exercise? Certainly, if the privatization has involved the breaking up of a state monopoly into a series of units, each of which is passed into private sector hands to compete against each other and possibly even against additional new entrants to the market, then there is a clear link to the objective of increasing competition. The break up of the National Bus Company, and the exposure of local authority transport services to private operators would provide at least a conceptual fit to this argument. Another possibility is that, if the transfer to private ownership results in corporate objectives being formally restated in terms of commercial rather than social targets, this could perhaps result in the achievement of greater efficiency against this more narrow set of measures. The tremendous gains in productivity and profitablity recorded by British Steel, as it has prepared for privatization, would seem to support this type of argument – although it must be noted that this particular element of policy does not increase the number of businesses competing, but simply tries to make the same single business more competitive. Finally, it has been argued that the discipline of producing a satisfactory return to shareholders within the capital market will ensure that real efforts are made to improve the quality of both product and performance (as has been claimed for British Gas, and the British Airports Authority).

For every argument in favour of privatization, opponents have raised at least one counter-argument. For example, if we take the final point in the previous paragraph, there is a specialist area of theory in managerial economics which has explored the actions and efficiency of large organizations, where ownership rests with external shareholders and control with salaried professional managers. Many of these models show that the discipline of reporting to external ownership is less in fact than it might appear to be in theory, and that the tendency is for managers to continue to pursue their own private set of objectives, subject to the constraint that enough profit is earned and distributed in dividends to keep the shareholders 'off the back' of the management team. In effect, within any large organization there is always a danger that a compromise will be sought between the owners' and the managers' interests, which will involve a lower effort level than is truly consistent with maximizing shareholders' wealth. Undoubtedly, the transfer of ownership from the the state to private shareholders will have some effect on the operational efficiency of the organization – but it is possible that these gains might turn out to be rather more elusive to reap in full than is expected.

At the root of much of the unease is the fact that much of the UK programme of privatization has simply transferred a continuing monopoly from public to private ownership. There is no reason why a private monopolist should be better behaved or more efficient than a public or state monopolist; if anything, there is every reason to fear the opposite. The potential for monopolistic abuse is so great that the international practice has always been to view *any* monopoly with suspicion.[2] It is not surprising, therefore, that this form of privatization has been heavily criticized externally, as well as within the UK, with several leading international economists expressing doubt about the real potential for efficiency gains.

The **promotion of small business start-ups** represents the third theme which is at least partially rooted in supply-side economics. If the objective is to increase competition within markets, then the most obvious way to do so is to increase the number of participants within these markets. At the same time and on a more sophisticated level, there is strong evidence that the UK has a relatively weak entrepreneurial culture, with education, career and social experience all conditioning people to follow the role model of the career employee, with risk taking

---

2. When you deal with this model in microeconomic theory, you will find that there is a potential for monopolists to create an artificial scarcity of output and, as a result, to cause both prices and their own profits to rise to levels which could not be sustained in more competitive markets. Indeed, this potential to increase profit has frequently resulted in otherwise independent producers coming together to act in collusion as a **cartel**, so that total profits for the industry as a whole are increased, then allocated among the participants. Such actions reduce the level of consumer benefit and, in protection against this, most countries have set up policing agencies which have the power to investigate and take action against current or potential monopolies.

in the form of self-employment, or in launching innovative ventures, typically left to others – rather than perceived as a personal career opportunity. The UK government has launched an unprecedented[3] campaign of support for small businesses, in an attempt to deal with both problems. Firstly, while one single new entrant small business is unlikely to pose much threat or pressure to established firms within a comfortable market, a significant number of energetic and aggressive new entrants, each pursuing its own self-interest is, like a party of unruly schoolchildren, more likely to waken and activate sleeping giants. Secondly, the promotion of self-employment is a quite deliberate attempt to stimulate a new and more entrepreneurial culture (as well as its other objective, which is to contribute towards a reduction in the level of unemployment); it is hoped that the rehabilitation of the principles of self-help and self-advancement through setting up successful small businesses, will encourage individuals to act more along the lines of the entrepreneurial model described by Adam Smith and the classical economists. All successful big businesses have started from some relatively insignificant seeds in the past; who knows which of today's entrepreneurs, searching for business opportunities at the margin of change, will come up with the ideas which will provide the new 'sunrise industries' of the future?

While our intention is to present, rather than to dispute the case, it is important not to join mindlessly in the euphoria and enthusiasm which surrounds this major new policy initiative. From the limited statistical evidence which is available, it would not seem that the marginal flow of new starts is focused on the margin of change; to the contrary, it appears that the vast majority of new starts (and failures) are concentrated on the 'easy entry' service industries which are already well represented in our industrial structure. Equally, there is some evidence that the increased competition which has been generated has a disturbing and anarchic element, as ill-prepared, inexperienced *but subsidized* new entrants struggle frenetically for a survival foothold, frequently at the expense of more efficient and established businesses – which might even be *displaced* by successive waves of new entrants which, in turn, struggle and perish in

---

3. After the Bolton Committee of Inquiry into Small Businesses in 1971, the tempo of favourable legislative measures increased steadily (despite the Committee's own recommendation that the policy stance should remain neutral) over the 1970s. Under the Thatcher government it grew explosively, as small businesses were made the subject of a major policy initiative; the government claims to have passed 104 small business measures during its first five years of office. In addition to this central government interest, there has developed a complex network of public and private sector promotional and training agencies, as local authorities, private sector sponsored Enterprise Agencies, and a bewildering variety of joint venture arrangements have attempted to deal with deindustrialization and unemployment at a more local level. From decades of neglect, the pendulum has swung to the opposite extreme; the supporting infrastructure for small business has become a major growth industry in its own right.

large numbers once the subsidy element is removed. It is far from clear that such markets are achieving genuine improvements in efficiency, for all the noise and clamour of competition within them.

The above is very much a descriptive sketch of the UK government's competition policy, and of its attitude towards the difficult topic of state intervention. But it is enough to provide a flavour. At the same time, it is probably fair to say that many of the government's supply-side policy initiatives are not really intended to be presented as a carefully thought-through solution to the problem of imperfectly competitive and inefficient markets – whatever the politicians themselves might believe. Rather, the policies have been launched and given the opportunity to prove themselves . . . in a very similar manner to the launch of any new small business venture. Both offer prospects of success; each must face and overcome many major problems before that success can be established.

If we accept these measures on this basis, where does it leave us? The government's intention has been to remove constraints on competition, to free the operation of markets from what Adam Smith once described as the 'tyranny' of intervention and control. Undoubtedly, such actions have created opportunities for growth; but opportunities must be seized. Once again we have returned to the key role of incentive within a market economy. Our next step must be to consider the scope for taxation reform in influencing incentive and, through this, the response of individuals and businesses to the new opportunities which have been made available.

THE ROLE FOR TAX CUTS

One of the main benefits which appears to be offered by supply-side economics is the potential to 'free' aggregate supply and, as a result, to increase the rate of economic growth. The next stage in the supply-side argument is to consider how this growth can be achieved – not so much through government policy's traditional focus on offering subsidies for the improvement of the capital and labour resource base, as on a new use of taxation policy to influence the incentive to work, save and invest.

One of the fascinating aspects of this argument is that it defines a new role for fiscal policy. Whereas conventional fiscal policy sought to influence the level of economic activity through its focus on the level of aggregate demand, the new school of thought would focus it exclusively on factors which influence the behaviour of aggregate supply. The result of this switch in emphasis is intriguing: traditional fiscal policy was heavily criticized as having little other than a transient, or short-term influence on the economy; under supply-side usage, fiscal policy is seen to have a new and *long-term* influence on the economy. What provides the basis for these claims?

To understand this new role for fiscal policy, we must go back to our earlier analysis of economic growth. From Chapter 6 you will remember how we set up and developed a simple growth model which identified the critical elements in the growth process as:

$$\dot{Y}_p = \dot{I} = s\sigma$$

where $\dot{Y}_p$ measures the rate of change, or growth, in potential output (which is broadly the same as the rate of increase in full employment output which, in turn, is measuring the movement to the right of the aggregate supply function which we used in Figure 10.1), $\dot{I}$ measures the rate of growth in investment expenditure, s is the marginal propensity to save, and σ represents the incremental output:capital ratio (or, more loosely, the changing productivity of capital).[4]

Within the limitations of this simple model, the rate of economic growth will rise if we can use government policy to raise the value for $\dot{I}$ which, in turn, implies some improvement in the ratio values for s and σ. Let's try to trace how supply-side arguments for taxation reduction might be reflected in one or more of these growth elements.

If we start with the potential for improvement in the productivity of capital then we could argue that this will reflect influences such as the efficiency with which managements organize labour resources, and the work effort which both groups are prepared to make. We have already discussed the supply-side view that taxation is excessive; in more technical terms, supply-siders would argue that it is the *marginal* tax rates which are excessive, that is, the rates of taxation which operate on the income from any additional effort. If a person expects to lose 50%, or 60% – or even 83% for top income earners in the UK in 1979 – of the money income earned from additional effort, then this will reduce substantially his or her interest in making that effort. Why work overtime, or work harder for payment by results wage systems, if you only get the residual of 50%, or 40% – or even 17% – of the additional income earned?

Supply-siders believe that progressive tax systems should be simplified into fewer tax bands, and that the marginal rates of taxation for all tax bands above the standard or basic rate should be reduced; such fiscal changes, they claim, would increase the incentive power of additional earnings and, through this, create a surge of new effort which would be reflected in the growth rate of GDP. This argument has been largely accepted by the UK government. Over a fiercely criticized series

---

4. Another key influence, with which we will deal a little later, is the *quality* of the investment expenditure which is made. If this is in low technology, low productivity equipment, it will do little to enhance the productive potential of the capital stock of the economy; while if it is in high quality assets, then this will provide another source of improvements in productivity from the labour force which uses this capital equipment.

of taxation reforms, it has tried to reduce the income tax disincentive to work by simplifying the progressive tax structure and by reducing all marginal rates – particularly those paid by top income earners. By 1988 the basic rate of tax had been cut to 25% of taxable income, and the top rate pulled down to 40%. These taxation reforms were simply following the trail which had been blazed by the Reagan administration in the USA, where income tax rates were reduced by almost a quarter during the first three years of the 1980s by a very pro-supply-side government.

The interrelationship between taxation and incentive applies equally to the firms' sector; supply-siders argue that a reduction in business taxation rates could have a double beneficial effect. Firstly, the tax cuts would increase net of tax profits, which should result in increased retained profits, which could be used as an internal source of funds for investment. Secondly, if tax rates are reduced (or taxation allowances, such as the permitted rate of depreciation of new asset purchases against profits, increased), then the effect of this would be to raise the net of tax income stream from new ventures. The resultant higher NPV figures for these ventures would move the demand function for investment funds to the right, as argued in Chapter 5, which would tend to result in a higher level of investment for any given level of interest rates. In short, the tax cuts could trigger not only an increase in the demand for investment funds but also an increase in the level of internal funds available for investment purposes.

At a more sophisticated level, you will remember that we made a distinction in Chapter 6 between the quantity or amount of investment, and the *quality* of that investment and its usage. In case you have forgotten the details, we pointed out that not only did the UK allocate a relatively small share of resources to investment, but there was also evidence that much of our investment expenditure was allocated to low quality (that is, low technology content) capital goods. It is interesting to apply supply-side arguments to this particular source of weakness in the UK's performance. Firstly, it could be claimed, tax cuts would increase the forecast net of tax return on more expensive and better quality capital equipment; at its simplest, it would improve the NPV for such projects, once the discounted stream of future income was set against their higher initial capital outlay. Secondly, the reduced personal taxation wedge would provide a greater incentive to management and workers to accept the opportunities offered by more innovative investment, since they would have a greater self-interest in the potential increase in earnings which this could provide. Once again, a reduction in personal and business taxation could feed through into clear gains in both the quality of capital and the productivity derived from this by both management and labour resources.

To summarize the argument so far, it is the view of supply-siders that cuts in personal taxation would provide a greater incentive for additional work effort from management and labour resources, which would raise the value of σ for any given stock of capital. At the same time, cuts in business taxation could improve both the quantity and the quality of that capital stock through increased investment expenditure – providing a further boost to σ as well as $\dot{I}$, in terms of our growth equation.

This leaves us with only the element of s to consider from our growth model; how might savings respond to changes in taxation? Supply-side theory argues that tax cuts would provide a double boost to savings. Firstly, any reduction in the tax wedge will increase households' disposable income, from which savings are drawn; some economists would add that the marginal propensity to save will increase as income rises (reflecting a curvilinear, rather than a linear consumption function, with the absolute amount of consumption expenditure rising more slowly at higher levels of disposable income). A second effect of personal tax cuts would be that net of tax interest earned by savings would increase (the interest earned on savings is treated as additional income to households, and taxed at the appropriate marginal rate), which would also increase the incentive to save. Both responses to tax cuts should benefit the final term s in our simple growth model, and help to raise the rate of economic growth in that model.

So there we are: if we are prepared to accept supply-side arguments, as they have been presented here, then it would seem that fiscal policy could be used to raise the values for σ, s and $\dot{I}$ in terms of our economic growth model. This in turn would allow us to raise $\dot{Y}_p$, which would move the aggregate supply function of Figure 10.1 to the right or, more formally, increase our rate of economic growth.

SUPPLY-SIDE THEORY: A BROAD ASSESSMENT

From this outline presentation of the supply-side case, it is easy to see why many economists feel that its radical policy suggestions (to deregulate markets, to increase incentive by cutting tax rates) represent the most exciting potential breakthrough in economic thought since the heady days of the Keynesian revolution. Of course our relatively one-sided presentation of the many controversial issues in the theory has over-simplified the position. But, at the same time, all major theoretical developments start off with a '101% belief in the correctness and a 99% belief in the practicality of their policies'. The message is never so clear and obvious as when it is fresh, new and relatively untested. As a result, all major theory developments have had their share of arrogance and tunnel vision. Keynesians argued that, if there was unemployment and spare capacity in the economy, then this was because the level of demand was too low. Monetarists insisted that if there was inflation, it could only have been caused by an excessive increase in the supply of money. Neither school was initially prepared to countenance doubt, or admit the possibility of other views. Why should supply-siders be different in the strength of their belief and the stridency of their claims?

It is important to realize that each school, in turn, has had a major message to pass on to policy makers, however hotly that message has been challenged and debated, however tattered its banner has become by the close of hostilities. Each has provided its own vital insight into particular aspects of a very complex macroeconomy. Many years ago, Giovanni Guareschi wrote a marvellous series of short stories about Don Camillo, a village priest, and his arch enemy (and, when needed, his greatest friend) Peppone, the Communist village mayor; all the battles of religion and politics were fought out by these giant adversaries in their little village in Northern Italy. In an inspired moment, Guareschi likened the truth about religion to a large, beautiful and complex room with many windows: each window would give its own particular view of the room and its treasures; if a person climbed up to look through one of these windows, he or she would find no reason to doubt the accuracy of this partial vision – and would be prepared to defend it against any alternative vision with words or, if necessary (which it frequently was in the stories!), with fists. Certainly, each vision would contain its own elements of truth, but it would only be part of the whole truth. To understand the whole truth, to get a truly accurate description of the room and all its treasures, we must bring *together* all the combatants' views, from each and every one of the windows – by a process of reason, tolerance and cooperation, rather than by conflict and domination. So too with economics: each theory contributes its own insight; each contains its own constraints and the distortions imposed by its partial vision. We must learn to accept the importance of the first – and to beware of the dangers of the second.

The contribution of supply-side economics lies in its recognition that the macroeconomy has a considerable capacity to respond to performance improvements within aggregate supply. This is a message of major importance. We have already outlined how supply-side policy could improve the various elements in our equation for economic growth and, through this, benefit output, income and employment. It is equally possible to identify its potential contribution in the context of the quantity theory model, as developed in Chapter 9; you will remember that we showed there that:

$$\dot{M} + \dot{V} = \dot{P} + \dot{Q}$$

where $\dot{M}$ represented the rate of growth in the money supply, $\dot{V}$ the rate of change in income velocity of circulation of that money supply, $\dot{P}$ the rate of increase in prices (or the rate of inflation) and $\dot{Q}$ the rate of increase in real output (or economic growth). In terms of this model, the effect of supply-side policy would be to increase the value for $\dot{Q}$. If we look at the inflation implications of this improvement, it would mean that a higher $\dot{M}$ could be matched to the higher $\dot{Q}$, with $\dot{P}$ still held at zero (as was the case in our illustration of supply-side policy in Figure 10.1) or, if there was an excessive increase in the money supply, then the higher value for $\dot{Q}$ would absorb part of this and reduce the consequent pressure on prices.

Here again we can see that supply-side theory offers a potentially important contribution. However, all new theories generate friction, and supply-side theory is no exception to this general rule. It is scarcely an exaggeration to say that for every point which we have made in favour of the new body of theory, at least two counter-arguments have been made!

Rather than simply knock down what we have struggled to build up, we feel that it would be more sensible to consider some of the opposing viewpoints (or the views through alternative windows) within a relatively simple framework. All new theories appear to experience three common problem areas as they make their transition into practical policies. Their proponents find, as they struggle to implement the new policies, that:

- There are weaknesses in the basic assumptions upon which the theory has been built;
- Basic relationships prove to be rather more complex – or even ambiguous – than was originally believed;
- Side effects emerge to embarrass, or even operate against the intentions of the theory and the policies which are derived from it.

Let's start off by looking at some of the warnings and criticisms which might come under the category of inherent problems in the assumptions of supply-side theory. Firstly, supply-side theory is firmly founded on the concept of self-interest, and the potential of the individual to act for self-gain and self-improvement. In seeking to stimulate this self-interest, the reform of the progressive tax structure has resulted in a switch of taxation from direct to regressive taxation and, simultaneously, in a widening in the pattern of distribution of income and wealth between individuals. While this might well provide a greater degree of incentive, there is also the opposite argument, which is that it could also generate friction and hostility within society from the coexistence of extreme poverty and extreme wealth; such frictions could be exacerbated by the cutbacks in welfare and other government expenditure programmes which have been designed to permit the tax cuts, or to sharpen the differential between employment and 'idleness'. In short, the price of greater individual incentive could well be a greater degree of social tension, some economists have argued.

Secondly, supply-side theory argues for the removal of or a reduction in the amount of regulations and constraints which are imposed on markets, on the grounds that the unhindered operation of free market forces should create greater efficiency within the economy. But many of these regulations and constraints were imposed to prevent or contain abuses from some producers within the market system (the 'unacceptable face of capitalism', to quote Edward Heath, an ex-Prime Minister). Some economists are worried that deregulation could result in a return of these abuses (has human nature changed all that much?), or in a serious lack of action on issues such as environmental pollution. The pursuit of private interest within a competitive environment has all too often resulted in individuals and businesses imposing **external costs** on society, when the desire to minimize private costs has been reflected in a wilful neglect of the consequences of production, or its waste products, on others. If market forces are not compelled to recognize social costs, then they will tend to function on the basis of the lower and rather more selfishly defined private costs.[5] Any efficiency gains are likely to be measured against this correspondingly narrower definition (for example, as increased profits to the individual firm and its owners), rather than against the more accurate context of society as a whole (for example, excluding the problems of acid rain damage, industrial illness, sub-standard drinking water quality, possibly even the 'clusters' of child leukaemia, or various types of cancer around nuclear, or nuclear waste treatment establishments). Yet these social costs must still be paid, in cash or in kind, by society; as such, they should also be set against the reported gains in efficiency.

Thirdly, there is an implicit belief that 'market forces' will ensure

---

5. If social costs are not included in the firm's calculation of production and distribution costs, then the price will be based on these private costs and will, as a result, be artificially low. This will tend to stimulate demand and, as a result, the level of production and the pollution which is caused by both consumption and production will be higher than is necessary. Think of the problems of lead and other pollutants within car exhaust emissions; it has been estimated that it would increase production costs by £400 1000 if engines were to be modified to reduce this type of pollution to an acceptable level (which is by no means zero pollution). If car manufacturers were to **internalize** the social costs of pollution from car usage, prices would rise by at least the amount of these extra pollution treatment costs, which could have an effect on sales and, possibly profit. There is therefore a strong case in most producers' minds *not* to deal with pollution control until they are pressured into so doing by legislation, or public opinion. This reluctance to 'clean up' their own contribution to pollution applies to state as well as private producers; fossil fuel burning power stations are probably the major component in our exports of acid rain to Scandinavia. UK governments' track record of evasive and cynical denial of all evidence (which has earned us the unsavoury title of 'the dirty old man of Europe') simply underlines that the State is every bit as reluctant as private sector producers to recognize their responsibility for preventing or treating the social costs created by their own actions, or the actions of their consumers – due to the implications which this might have for their total costs and prices.

that the pattern of production changes in response to movements in *consumer* tastes and preferences. Classical economists used the term **consumers' sovereignty** to underline the fact that resource deployment must ultimately reflect the wishes of consumers within society ... the consumer was king. But economists such as J.K. Galbraith have pointed out that consumers can only choose from the range of goods and services which have already been provided by producers – and that their choice is heavily influenced by the advertising and publicity campaigns which are orchestrated by these producers. Galbraith and many other economists would argue that if any single group is sovereign, it is the producers rather than the consumers. A return to a dependence on free market forces could well increase the power and influence of this already powerful group.

The second group of criticisms and reservations are all concerned with the fact that basic relationships can turn out to be rather more complex and ambiguous, than is initially realized (for example, remember the problems of latter-day Keynesian policy, as discussed in Chapter 9). Here the main force of criticism appears to focus on the relationship between tax cuts and the incentives provided by these. We must bear in mind that the modelling relationships between tax, effort, savings, investment and growth are rather more complex than we have shown in this introductory text. However, given this caveat, it is still possible to draw attention to three areas where theoretical debate, or empirical evidence, appears to cast some doubt over the strength of the likely response to tax cuts.

If we start with the basic relationship between tax cuts and work effort, then cuts in the marginal rate of tax will alter choice at the margin between work and leisure, in favour of the former;[6] but, at the same time, the resultant increase in disposable income and affluence will make it possible to achieve a desired standard of living with *less* work than before.[7] The two elements within the overall response to tax cuts could therefore operate in different directions, which might well result in a smaller *net* increase in work effort in practice, than has been promised by supply-side theorists.

There is a second potential problem in the response of savings to tax cuts. Certainly, cuts in direct taxation will increase disposable income

---

6. In more technical terms, this is the **substitution effect** of the tax cut; work has become less heavily taxed, therefore the rational person might be prepared to switch some leisure time into additional work effort, in response to the incentive of higher net of tax income.

7. This is the **income effect** of the tax change, which has made individuals and businesses more affluent than before at the same level of earnings. The overall response to the tax change will result from the combination of the substitution and the income effects, as these are experienced for the macroeconomy as a whole.

and so permit an increase in savings, possibly even increasing the marginal as well as the average propensity to save. A further boost to this conclusion is provided by the fact that interest earned on savings is also subject to tax, so that a cut in income tax will increase the net of tax return from savings. However, if households have some *target* or planned level of savings in mind, then the effect of tax cuts could be to allow this target to be achieved more quickly than before; this leaves a greater share of disposable income for possible increases in consumption expenditure. This at least raises the possibility that cuts in the tax rate could result in a lesser increase in savings than has been argued by supply-side theorists. In terms of simple empirical evidence, few governments have been more enthusiastic about the supply-side message than the UK government; yet, as at March 1989, the UK savings ratio has fallen to its lowest level for 33 years, as discussed in Extract 10.1 . . . While this undoubtedly reflects a number of factors, there nevertheless remains some cause for concern.

If we turn our attention to business savings, or retained profits within the firms' sector, then there is also a fear that cuts in personal and business taxation designed to increase net of tax profit, will not necessarily result in an increase in *retained* profits, which will be held for future investment expenditure purposes. At least at small firm level (and, as we have already argued, this is a major dimension within government policy), empirical research suggests that the practice[8] has been for owners to draw on or to distribute the increased net of tax profits, or to neutralize the incentive effect of lower taxation by allowing costs to rise and efficiency to fall, as 'organizational slack' develops within the business. Retained profits, as a source of investment funds, have not responded significantly to the taxation changes. If this practice is general to all sizes of business, the effect could be to weaken substantially the response of investment to cuts in taxation. Economists have always been aware that tax is an important influence on incentive and the level of work effort; but it is only one of several possible influences. Supply-side theorists have tended to view the tax/incentive link almost as a *sine qua non*; but this is an over-simplification, and could result in apparently 'irrational' responses of effort level to tax changes.

The final category of potential weaknesses are all concerned with the emergence of unanticipated and unwanted side-effects which could at best embarrass and, at worst, act counter to the intentions of policy makers. At this early stage of supply-side policy, some economists have identified two possible areas of embarrassment. Firstly, despite the predictions of the Laffer Curve, the very substantial tax cuts which have been made in the USA have been accompanied by the development of a very major fiscal deficit (that is, excess of government expenditure over

---

8. See, for example, *The Performance of Small Firms* by Storey D.J., Keasey K., Watson R. and Wynerczyk P., Croom Helm, 1987, Chapters 4 and 5.

Extract 10.1 FINANCIAL TIMES 30 MARCH 1989.

SAVINGS RATIO FALLS TO ITS LOWEST LEVEL FOR 33 YEARS

Ralph Atkins, Economics Staff

THE PROPORTION of income saved by the UK personal sector fell last year to the lowest level for 33 years, according to official statistics released yesterday.

Growth in consumer spending outstripped increases in incomes to continue a decline in the savings ratio since the early 1980s, the Central Statistical Office (CSO) figures show. However, the ratio picked up slightly in the last three months of last year.

Other CSO figures showed that profits of non-North Sea oil companies grew by a fifth last year. This was accompanied by exceptionally strong dividend payments, which in turn fed through to boost personal incomes.

However, gross trading profits of North Sea oil companies fell by 19 per cent in the last three months of the year and were 36 per cent lower than in the corresponding period a year before.

Together, the figures underline the buoyancy of the UK economy last year with both incomes and profits rising rapidly. In spite of the steep rise in interest rates, growth is likely to continue into the early part of this year.

Mr Kevin Gardiner, UK economist at Warburg Securities, said: "There is a lot of momentum out there and it is extremely difficult to see it dropping overnight."

Personal savings as a proportion of after-tax incomes fell to 4.1 per cent, down from 5.6 per cent in 1987 and the lowest since 1955. In the fourth quarter it stood at 4.1 per cent, up from 3.1 per cent in the previous three months.

The CSO said past figures for the savings ratio have been revised sharply upwards, largely because of revisions to figures for wages and salaries. Previously the ratio had been shown as falling to 1.3 per cent in the third quarter.

The savings figures, calculated as the difference between personal disposable incomes and consumer spending, are treated with scepticism by most economists because of large inaccuracies in national financial accounts, although the general trend is rarely disputed. The CSO said recent figures could be substantially revised.

Real personal disposable incomes, after deducting taxes and social security contributions, increased by 5 per cent last year. That was the fastest growth rate since 1979, highlighting the rapid growth in living standards.

Gross trading profits of non-North Sea industrial and commercial companies fell by 6 per cent in the fourth quarter of 1988. However in 1988 as a whole, profits were 20 per cent higher than in 1987.

Reprinted with permission from *Financial Times* 30 March 1989 © *Financial Times*.

---

taxation receipts). The UK government has tended to be rather more circumspect in its tax cuts; it has balanced the potential revenue losses from lower rates of income tax, with increases in both expenditure taxes and National Insurance contributions over the 1980s. However, returning to the USA's experience, some economists have argued that there is a real danger that the attempts to finance this fiscal deficit could drive up the market rates of interest. This, in turn, could create a type of 'crowding out' effect, which could have an adverse effect on interest sensitive expenditure such as investment by increasing the cost of capital. Therefore, the tax cuts should have a *direct* effect on investment, by providing larger net of tax profits as encouragement, but they might also have a negative *indirect* effect on investment, should a fiscal deficit cause interest rates to rise.

It would seem possible that the second and unwanted side-effect is currently being experienced by the UK. The fact that supply-siders dislike the Keynesian model has not prevented that model from operating as described in earlier chapters. Tax cuts may well raise aggregate supply in the long run; but, in the short run, they will also raise disposable income and consumption and, therefore, aggregate demand. If aggregate demand rises more quickly, or more strongly than aggregate supply in the economy's initial response to the tax cuts then, ironically, this side-effect could trigger the very inflationary pressure which supply-side economics was supposed to cure. This type of difficulty was predicted in the USA in 1981 by the Council of Economic Advisers to President Carter: they estimated that a 10% cut in tax rates would tend to have a limited initial effect on aggregate supply, which would increase in response by a limited 0.5–0.9%; in contrast, the Council estimated that aggregate demand would rise by about 2%, creating inflationary pressure within the economy. Again in terms of general empirical observation, the extracts contained in earlier chapters have traced the steady upwards 'creep' in the rate of inflation in the UK, following the Chancellor's tax cuts in 1987 and 1988. Even allowing for the fact that other forces might well have contributed to this phenomenon, there is still the possibility that we are experiencing one of the side-effects of supply-side policy . . .

It is important not to become bogged down or confused by the clamour of claims and counterclaims in the debate on supply-side economics. The most important claim which can be made by any theory is that it can also appear to work in practice. There is at least a *prima facie* case to be made that supply-side policies have had a major impact on the economic performance of the UK. Extract 10.2 provides a useful and interesting discussion of some of the main achievements which have been claimed. You will find that we have already identified and discussed many of these over Chapters 6–9. All we would say at this late stage in the chapter is that you must beware the perils of any set of statistics: as the extract reveals, the UK shows up well in any table relating to rates of change in productivity and growth; but the problem is that our absolute levels of productivity, and unit labour costs are still very close to the relegation zone of any international league table and, with our spiralling earnings and inflation rates, we must be careful before we claim any lasting victory in the economic battle.

Another important test of any theory is the amount of *lasting* interest which is taken in its views by practical policy makers. Here too, supply-side theory scores well; apart from the USA and the UK, supply-side theory arguments have influenced policy in a number of other European countries. Surprisingly, the message has not only found a ready interest in right-wing countries such as West Germany; even socialist

Extract 10.2 THE ECONOMIST 3 DECEMBER 1988.

SCHOOLS BRIEF
Britain's supply-side miracle

IN the early 1960s Britain was the second richest (behind America) of the Group of Five big industrial economies (America, Japan, West Germany, France and Britain); today its GDP per person is at the bottom of the league. In the past 20 years Britain's GDP has grown by an average of 2.2% a year—well below the 2.9% average of the G5.

Since British employment was virtually the same last year as in 1967, labour **productivity** also increased by an average of 2.2% a year. Of the big five economies, only America did worse—and that was partly because America managed to expand the number of jobs by more than 50%.

However, that 20-year comparison conceals a big change. Britain's productivity growth did lag behind that of the other big economies in the 1960s and 1970s—but it has improved sharply, both in relative and in absolute terms, in the 1980s. Total output per head has gone up by an average of 2.5% a year since 1980. Only Japan has had faster productivity growth. The average for the G5 countries was a little under 2%. In manufacturing, Britain's productivity has topped the league. Has the British disease at last been cured?

In the slow lane

Ever since Britain became the first workshop of the world, other countries have shown a distressing ability to catch up and overtake. One excuse was that Britain was the first country to industrialise. By 1960, for example, farming accounted for less than 5% of GDP, compared with 30% in Japan, 23% in France, and 14% in West Germany. That meant less scope for labour to shift from (low-productivity) farming to (high productivity) industry. But this did not explain the poor performance of **manufacturing** itself.

As in all the big industrial economies, manufacturing's share of GDP has fallen, from 28% in 1967 to 22% in 1987, while services have jumped to 65% of GDP. But whereas elsewhere the absolute volume of manufacturing output continued to grow, Britain's manufacturing production was no higher at the end of the 1970s than it had been ten years earlier.

By the late 1970s it was clear that something was seriously wrong with the British economy. Economists laid the blame on:

• Steeply progressive personal **taxes**. Top marginal tax rates of 98% on investment income (pejoratively labelled "unearned" income) and 83% on income from employment severely blunted incentives to work and invest.

• Overly powerful and inflexible **trade unions**.

• Excessive **government** interference in the economy. Too much regulation hampered the efficient working of markets, it was argued, and too much public spending "crowded out" private business. Public spending grew from 38% of GDP in 1967 to a peak of 48% in 1984.

• Investment **subsidies**. These promoted the wrong sorts of capital spending. The real failing of British industry was the quality of its investment, not the quantity. The rate of return on capital of non-oil companies fell from 12% in the 1960s to 3% in 1980–81—the lowest in the G5, by a wide margin.

• The goal of **full employment**, pursued through policies of demand management, with too little regard for the effects on inflation and long-term efficiency.

The results were painfully clear by the 1970s. Britain was hit harder than most economies by the quadrupling of the oil price and the world-wide explosion of inflation. For most of that decade Britain had the highest inflation rate of the big five, the weakest external balance and the slowest economic growth.

In electing Margaret Thatcher in 1979, the British voted for a sharp change in economic policy. The chief goal was no longer to maintain jobs now at any cost. Instead it was to defeat inflation, in the belief that this would create more and better jobs in the longer term. So short-term demand management was abruptly dumped in favour of improving the economy's **supply side**.

This implied a reversal of the traditional roles of economic policy. In the previous quarter of a century macroeconomic instruments (i.e., monetary and fiscal policy) had been used to boost growth and employment, while microeconomic measures, such as prices and incomes policies, were used to check inflation.

Now, macroeconomic measures were to be directed at controlling inflation: the **medium-term financial strategy** (announced each year as part of the government's budget) began to set targets for monetary growth and government borrowing several years ahead. Microeconomic policies, meanwhile, sought to boost output and jobs by making markets work better—through deregulation; the abolition of controls on prices, wages and capital movements abroad; tax cuts (which have now cut the top marginal rate of income tax to 40%); trade-union reform; and the privatisation of nationalised industries.

The government has already **privatised** more than a third of what was owned by the state in 1979, including British Telecom, British Gas and British Airways. The state industries' share of total employment has fallen from 9% to less than 5%.

Miracle or myth?

Between 1979 and 1987 Britain's GDP grew on average by 1.9% a year, still well below the OECD average of 2.4%. This is partly because Britain suffered a much deeper recession in 1979–81 than other countries. In 1981 364 of the country's economists wrote a letter to *The Times* warning that there could be no recovery without a change of policy. In the space of a few months, without a change of policy, the recovery began. Since then growth has averaged almost 3% a year. This is slightly faster than America and well ahead of West Germany and France.

Better productivity has increased **profits**. The rate of return on capital rose from 3% in 1981 to 10% last year. This is, however, less than the rate of return in Britain in the 1960s and in the other G5 economies today.

The improvement in labour productivity is not just due to an increase in the amount of capital per worker (though there has been such an increase). Britain is the only big industrial economy apart from Japan which has seen a relative improvement in the productivity of capital (ie, output per unit of capital) since the 1970s. The change in the efficiency of British industry therefore looks even more impressive when measured in terms of **total factor productivity** (ie, the weighted average of labour and capital productivity). In the other four big economies total factor productivity remained stable or fell.

The government's critics argue that the increase in productivity happened mainly because the least productive factories and workers were shed during the recession of the early 1980s, and that this, as a matter of mere arithmetic, raised the average productivity of the rest. The charge is partly true. But there is also strong evidence that individual firms are much more productive thanks to more flexible working practices, more harmonious labour relations and better management.

For example, in the 1970s British Steel was one of the most inefficient steel producers in the world, producing 40% less steel per worker than rival firms in West Germany. Today, on the eve of privatisation, it is the most efficient and profitable steel firm in the world. In 1980 an average of 14.5 man-hours went into a tonne of steel; today less than six. The workforce has fallen by two-thirds.

That was the cost of Mrs Thatcher's economic miracle: fewer jobs. **Unemployment** rose by more than in other countries, to a peak of 12% of the labour force in 1986. However, the government's critics are now being silenced by its steady fall, to 8% this year—only a whisker above the OECD average.

The blame for the sharp rise in unemployment lay with the failure of the British labour market as much as with the government's austere policies. Despite high unemployment, British **real wages** have risen by 20% since 1982, compared with increases of just over 10% in Japan and West Germany, 3% in France and a fall of 1% in America.

Britain's labour market is riddled with *rigidities*: trade unions use their monopoly power to improve the wages of their members, the housing market impedes mobility between regions, and inadequate training restricts mobility between occupations. Firms in the south-east complain of shortages of skilled labour, while dole queues remain long in the north.

Legislation has helped to tame the unions. The number of days lost through strikes has fallen. Union membership has dropped from about 50% of total employment in 1980 to 38%. This partly reflects the decline of smoke-stack industries, the traditional recruiting ground for trade unions. Nevertheless, union membership remains high compared with

America's 18%. A recent worrying sign: as the threat of unemployment has receded, the unions have seemed ready to flex their muscles again.

Oiling the wheels

The introduction of the Thatcher government's economic experiment coincided with a big structural change in the economy—namely the transformation of Britain from an oil importer into an **oil exporter**. Moreover, this happened just at the moment when OPEC pushed up the price of oil. It is difficult to disentangle the effects of the two.

Today Britain is a biggish oil producer—the only country among the G5 to be self-sufficient in oil. North Sea production peaked in 1985 at 2½m barrels a day, but the country should remain self-sufficient until the end of the century. In 1985 oil accounted for 6% of GDP and 21% of exports. The slump in oil prices has since cut those proportions to 3% and 11% respectively.

North Sea oil brought two direct benefits to the British economy. It generated extra revenue for the Treasury, allowing it to reduce borrowing or cut taxes by more than it otherwise could. And it shielded the economy from OPEC's price rise in 1979. Consumers still paid world prices, but Britain's import bill was reduced relative to the costs faced by oil importers.

But perhaps the biggest benefit of North Sea oil was that it cushioned the economy against the harshest short-term effects of the Thatcher government's policies. Without oil revenues the balance of payments would have deteriorated sharply and incomes would have fallen more severely. In such a climate the policies might have proved politically unsustainable.

As Britain moved into surplus in its oil trade, it became a net **importer of manufactures**— for the first time since the industrial revolution. In the late 1960s exports of manufactures had been almost twice manufactured imports. Now they are 10% less. The decline in Britain's share of world exports of manufactures—down from 12% to 7% in the 20 years from 1960—has stopped in the past few years. But imports still account for an increasing share of domestic sales.

The government argues that the deterioration in manufacturing trade was inevitable. In becoming an oil exporter, Britain needed to export relatively fewer manufactured goods to pay for its imports. So, goes the argument, the pound was bound to appreciate, making manufacturing less competitive.

Well, up to a point. The rise in the real exchange rate was due as much to tight monetary policy (ie, high interest rates) as to oil. Arguably, if different policies had been pursued, the balance of payments might have adjusted to the fact of North Sea oil at a higher level of manufacturing output.

Tight monetary policy and the resulting over-valuation of the pound in the early years of the Thatcher government had a truly vicious short-term effect on industry. But, as a recent book* suggests, this (partly unintended) squeeze could well prove to be a good thing in the long run. It put much greater pressure on industry to become efficient than a more gradual approach would have done. The economy, in other words, needed a shock. Mrs Thatcher gave it one.

There is still plenty of room for improvement. Despite the recent acceleration in Britain's productivity growth, output per manufacturing worker is well below that in the other big economies. Comparing levels of productivity (as opposed to changes in productivity, as this brief has done) is notoriously difficult. However, one estimate says that Britain's output per manhour in manufacturing last year was 30% less than Japan's, 40% less than America's, and half West Germany's.

If levels of productivity in Britain and America continue to grow at the same relative pace as they have since 1980, it will be roughly 45 years before the average British manufacturing worker produces as much as his American counterpart. Britain's supply-side miracle is, as yet, no more than work in progress.

* *The Economy under Mrs Thatcher*. By Geoffrey Maynard. Published by Basil Blackwell.

Reprinted with permission from *The Economist* 3 December 1988 © *The Economist*.

politicians, such as France's President Mitterand have conceded ground in their policies – while over May and June 1989 in the UK, there has been a major change of policy attitude within the Labour Party, as the leadership has committed official Opposition strategy to a continuation – as opposed to scrapping – of many of the radical new policies.

However, we have tried to show that there are still counter-arguments and worries and, if we are dealing with the long-term phenomenon of economic growth, there is still a lot of evidence to be gathered and analysed. If there is a one sentence conclusion to the debate (and no economist would feel comfortable with such a proposition!) it would be that there are benefits to be reaped from a 'freeing up' of the economy, such as has been argued by supply-siders, but a great deal has still to be proved before it can be argued that supply-side theory is the *only* way forward.

CONCLUSIONS

1. As with monetarism, supply-side economics represents a withdrawal from the interventionism of Keynesian economics, and a rekindling of interest in the classical economics view that efficiency is more likely to be achieved if individuals are left to pursue their own self-interest within free and competitive markets.

2. The essential arguments of supply-side theorists are that the government should act to deregulate markets and to reduce their own presence in or influence over them, so as to stimulate competition, efficiency and productivity; simultaneously, the government should reform its tax structure by reducing at least the marginal rate of tax, so providing a greater individual incentive for entrepreneurial and other forms of work effort, which would contribute towards the gains in productivity and growth.

3. In sharp contrast to the Keynesian view that the level of economic activity could be more easily influenced and controlled by demand management policies which were focused on the level of aggregate demand, supply-siders argue that there is an even greater potential for positive influence and improvement in performance if aggregate supply, rather than aggregate demand is the prime target for policy.

4. The supply-side view of the problems of the 1970s was that these had been caused by the gradual erosion of freedom to operate within the market system, combined with an excessive level of government activity. This problem had been exacerbated by the gradual build up in the tax burden carried by households and firms, partly designed to produce a more egalitarian distribution of income, and partly a consequence of the need to fund the excessive

level of government involvement. The burdensome tax structure had stifled individual initiative, and the proliferation of constraints and regulations had hampered the ability of the market system to adjust to change and to grasp emergent opportunities within this. The result was that rates of productivity and economic growth had declined, with stagnating production levels failing to cope with the artificially high level of demand, creating unnecessary inflationary pressure within the economy.

5. These arguments have been largely accepted by both the USA and the UK governments over the 1980s. In the UK, the Thatcher administration has been very active in its attempts to deregulate certain key market areas, removing barriers to competition, and arguing that the increased pressure which this would bring to bear on participants would enforce a greater degree of efficiency in operation. At the same time, the UK government has pursued an active policy of privatization, which has involved the transfer of ownership by share issue of several major state undertakings from the public to the private sector. Finally, the government has provided very positive policy support for small business start-up, which is seen to satisfy the government's twin objectives of restoring a more entrepreneurial culture, and increasing the number of participants and therefore the degree of competition within markets.

6. Similarly, the UK government has introduced several major reforms of the tax structure within the economy, simplifying the progressive system of taxation, reducing its marginal rates of taxation and, to a considerable extent, transferring part of the tax burden to regressive taxation measures such as expenditure taxes and National Insurance contributions. These reforms have sought to implement supply-side theory's recommendations, in an attempt to provide a greater degree of incentive for work effort, savings and investment within the economy.

7. If supply-side arguments are accepted, then the combined result of these reforms would be to raise productivity levels, the propensity to save, and investment, all of which would permit an increase in the rate of economic growth and, simultaneously, provide substantial assistance in the control of inflation within the economy.

8. However, as is normally the case with new policy initiatives, there is still a considerable degree of controversy surrounding this radical return to the principles of classical economics. Its promotion of individual self-interest has been reflected in a radical retreat from accepted standards of social responsibility and welfare provision, and has created a substantial degree of friction with the growing disparities in income and wealth distribution. There are worries that increased market freedom could result in abuse, or in the evasion of

major social responsibilities such as those connected with our new and higher awareness of the dangers of environmental pollution. There has been an active and acrimonious debate on the relationships which are crucial to supply-side theory, with many senior economists openly doubting the strength (and in some cases even the direction) of the response of individuals and corporate decision makers to the new system of taxation. In common with other major theoretical initiatives, such as Keynesian and monetarist economics, some embarrassing side-effects appear to have been experienced when theories have been translated into policies, noticeably the possibility of a new type of 'crowding out' effect, and the fact that tax cuts appear to have a stronger short-term influence on aggregate demand than aggregate supply, creating the very inflationary pressure which supply-side theorists have claimed to reduce.

9. For the moment, therefore, most economists would view the arguments of supply-side theorists with a great deal of interest. It may well be that attempts to intervene in the working of the market system, with the intention of improving the solutions offered by this system, have imposed an unjustified burden of costs and constraints; or again, it might not – for some economists would reject totally this fundamental belief of supply-siders. Few economists would dispute the case in theory for the efficiency of resource allocation within a market system; after all, the analysis of the operation of such a system provides the core material for the subject of modern economics. Even in practice, centrally-planned economies, such as Yugoslavia, Poland, Russia and China have accepted this truth and have released an increasing share of resource deployment to free market forces within their economies.

10. But economists have been aware for many years of potential and actual problems which are associated with the operation of free market forces and the pursuit of individual self-interest. Equally, it is apparent that some of the empirical evidence on the effect of supply-side policies has been ambiguous, and that there are some emergent difficulties in the translation of theory into policy. Hence, not all economists have adopted the claims of supply-side theorists with confidence and conviction; to many, the short-term record of these radical policies has been promising, but final judgement has been deferred until a longer period of evidence is available for analysis. History shows that initial euphoria can dwindle, as unanticipated difficulties emerge, as governments either over-react or under-react to both the opportunities and the threats revealed by the new policies, as the economy displays its genius for behaving in ways which no one could have anticipated – however easy it is to

SELF-ASSESSMENT QUESTIONS

TRUE/FALSE QUESTIONS

10.1. Keynesian policy focused on aggregate demand because it was felt that the aggregate supply function was little more than an absolute constraint on the economy and, what is more, a constraint which could not be influenced by government policy.

10.2. Supply-side theory argues for a reduction in the degree of state intervention, on the grounds that this inhibits the efficient operation of free market forces, which can cause a decline in productivity and a reduced performance in economic growth.

10.3. The Laffer Curve argues that if tax rates are reduced, this will provide the incentive for an increased volume of effort and, simultaneously, reduce the search for methods of tax evasion, so that government revenue from taxes should actually rise.

10.4. The effect of inflation is to increase the 'tax wedge' effect which, in turn, will have an adverse effect on work effort.

10.5. Supply-siders argue that cuts in the marginal rate of taxation will not only increase the rate of economic growth, but will also reduce the danger of inflation.

MULTIPLE CHOICE QUESTIONS

10.1. One of the main purposes of the UK government's privatization programme has been to increase competition and efficiency, because:

(a) A private sector monopoly will always be more efficient than a state monopoly;
(b) Private shareholders will impose a far greater degree of control through ownership on the professional managers, than would have been the case under state control;
(c) The use of resources by the private sector is always more efficient than their use by the public sector;
(d) Where the state monopoly is broken down into independent and competing

private sector organizations this will result in efficiency gains;
(e) Because prices will fall when the organization is run within the private sector.

10.2. Cuts in personal and business taxation will result in increased investment and economic growth because:

(a) Households and firms will have a greater net of tax income from which investment expenditure could possibly be made;
(b) Business confidence will rise, moving the demand function for investment funds to the right, at the current rate of interest;
(c) Forecast net of tax profit from new ventures will rise, increasing both their NPV rating and moving the demand function for investment funds to the right;
(d) The government will have to cut its own expenditure, which will release resources for usage in the private sector;
(e) Ventures which might otherwise have 'gone underground' into the black or informal economy, will be formally declared and registered in investment statistics.

10.3. Tax cuts could trigger a version of the 'crowding out' effect on investment expenditure because:

(a) People will have more money to spend on consumption goods;
(b) Businesses will divert funds from investment usage to reap the higher net of tax return from risk-free interest gained within the financial markets;
(c) The government will be forced to borrow to finance its fiscal deficit, which will drive up interest rates and the cost of capital;
(d) The higher net of tax return will encourage people to save more, which will withdraw these funds from investment usage;
(e) The government will be forced to cut its welfare payments, which will reduce income and savings, so that less funds are available for investment purposes.

Note: Solutions can be found at the end of the text.

Chapter 11

International Trade and the Balance of Payments

> Introduction
>
> The rationale for trade
>
> The UK trade flows
>
> The balance of payments
>
> The exchange rate
>
> 'To be (a member of the EMS) or not to be . . .?'
>
> Conclusions
>
> Self-assessment question

INTRODUCTION

You will have realized that the international trade sector has been excluded from our models and our analysis over the chapters on fiscal policy, monetary policy, the debate on inflation, and supply-side economics. We have followed the normal convention for an introductory text of dealing with these topics within the simplified framework of a 'closed' economy, where only purely domestic flows of transactions are involved. No doubt you will be first to agree that some of the material

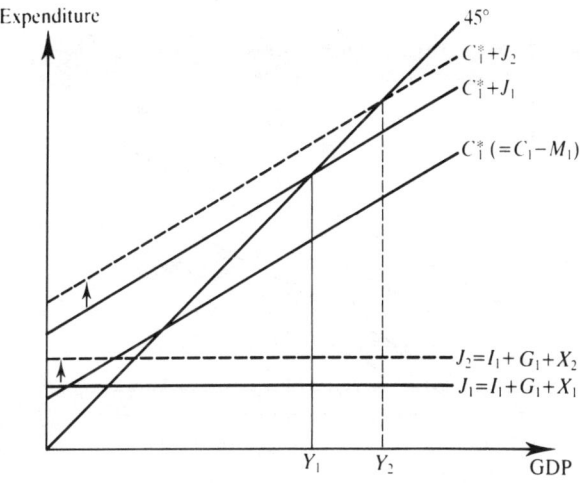

Figure 11.1 Effect of increased exports on GDP.

was quite difficult enough without building in the additional complication of trade and capital flows with the rest of the world economy ... However, any treatment of macroeconomic analysis would be very incomplete if it were to leave you without at least an awareness of some of the complex issues and problems which are introduced when we move back into a more realistic 'open' economy.

In case you have forgotten how the international trade flows of exports and imports influence the level of economic activity, Figure 11.1 reminds you of the basic model. From this you can see that exports and imports are both components of the aggregate expenditure function, and will therefore help to set the equilibrium level of GDP towards which any country will adjust. Additional export sales represent additional demand for UK output; in terms of the model, an increase in exports would raise the level of the injections function to J_2, which would raise aggregate demand to $C^*_1 + J_2$, so setting up a disturbance which would cause a multiple expansion of income and employment, and take the economy to the new higher level of equilibrium GDP of Y_2. This illustrates the important role which the export market has played in underpinning employment stability and economic growth in countries such as Japan, West Germany, and Italy. Conversely, lost export sales can set up a multiple contraction of domestic output, income and employment – an experience with which the UK has been only too familiar in the past.

Likewise, Figure 11.2 will remind you of the influence of imports on the domestic economy; it shows how imports represent a leakage from

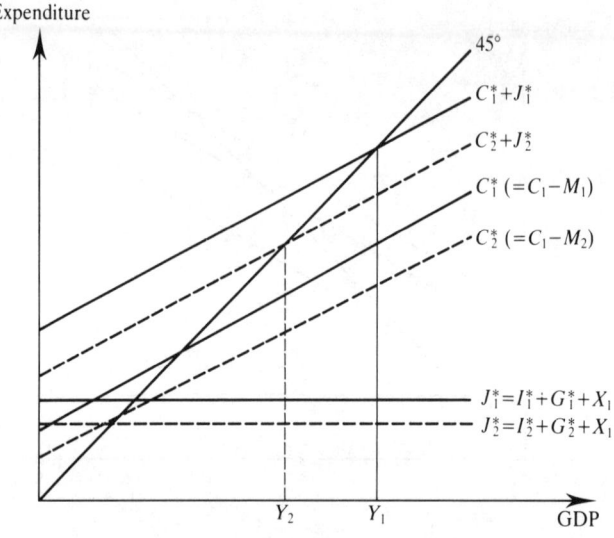

Figure 11.2 Effect of increased imports on GDP.

UK consumption and, realistically from investment and even government expenditure (to show this let C^*, I^* and G^* represent these expenditure elements *net* of import content in each case). An increase in the propensity to import – for whatever reason – will divert domestic expenditure from domestic output, reducing income and employment. In terms of the model, both the net injections and the net consumption functions will fall, reducing the aggregate expenditure function, and triggering a multiple contraction within the economy to the new and lower equilibrium level of GDP at Y_2. This is no abstract point of theory; in the UK, we have been only too familiar with the depressing phenomenon of rising import penetration into domestic markets. But, equally, if domestic output could be made more attractive by pricing, design, or marketing then major gains could be won back by import substitution, that is, by causing a switch of consumption expenditure from imports back to the equivalent domestic products.

However, the influence of the international trade goes far beyond these simple modelling illustrations. Its existence introduces a whole new and major series of complications for our domestic macroeconomic policy. Consider what would happen if government policy was to promote a surge in our rate of economic growth. One of the first consequences of this policy would be that imports of equipment and raw materials would be sucked in by the increase in UK producers' investment expenditure. Next, the surge of income from the resultant multiplied expansion could well spill over into consumer imports before domestic production capacity could be activated to cope with the higher levels of demand. If you think back on some of our earlier extracts, you will remember that Nigel Lawson's initial reaction to the deteriorating balance of trade position for the UK was to judge that this was merely a side-effect of our preparation for economic growth.

Or, to take a different example, one of the dangers if we seek to raise domestic interest rates to curb consumer demand pressures is that this could well attract a substantial inflow of international capital into the economy – which is likely to raise the UK exchange rate. This, in turn, will tend to make UK exports more expensive in world markets, which will make life rather more difficult for exporters than they, or the policy makers would prefer.

By now you should be familiar with the conflict which exists between the objectives of maintaining price stability, and holding a reasonably full level of employment within the domestic economy. What we are now seeing is a new source of conflict, this time between the objectives which are set for the domestic economy, as against those which relate to our external trading position. The current series of major deficits in the UK's external balance over late 1988 and early 1989 are simply yet another attack of a long established malaise.

Despite the difficulties and complexities which it introduces, it is essential that we should bring the additional dimension of international trade and capital flows into our analysis, if only because it allows us to deal with issues which are central to macroeconomic policy. Why do we trade at all in world markets? What seems to be the problem in our international trading performance? Should we try to protect ourselves, either as a single nation or as one of a cooperating group of nations (as in the EEC) from fair and unfair world competition? Why has the UK suffered so badly from import penetration into its domestic market? Will the proposed single European market of 1992 simply exacerbate the problem? What do we mean when we talk about 'invisibles' and what role do they play in our settlement of international indebtedness? What is an 'exchange rate' and why is it so important that the Chancellor and the Prime Minister could find themselves in such bitter disagreement over the appropriate policy? Where, if at all, does the European Monetary System fit into our trading relationships? What do we mean when we talk about a 'trade deficit', or indeed about a 'balance of payments problem'? How healthy is the UK balance of payments? Why have recent years seen an increased volume of international capital movements? What attracts – or repels – international capital? Does it matter if much of UK investment is funded from this source – or if it is international capital which appears to fund our growing trade deficit?

International trade and the balance of payments are each major fields of theory in their own right; in an introductory text it is impossible to provide anything other than a relatively superficial treatment of a few of the main topics within a very complex area. The objectives of this chapter are to:

(1) Discuss briefly the rationale for international trade between nations;
(2) Provide a general analysis of the nature and geographical pattern of the UK trade flows in exported and imported goods;
(3) Distinguish between the trade flows of goods and services in the UK balance of payments to identify the part played by 'invisibles';
(4) Explore the nature of the short- and long-term capital and banking flows in the balance of payments;
(5) Look at the funding implications of the balance of payments;
(6) Consider how exchange rates are set and explore the factors which influence the international valuation of domestic currencies;
(7) Discuss the problem of measuring international competitiveness;
(8) Analyse some of the main problems for macroeconomic policy which are created by operating within a fully open economy;
(9) Explore, in outline, the case for and against the UK's full membership of the European Monetary System.

THE RATIONALE FOR TRADE

Why trade at all? Events over recent years in both the UK and the USA, which have seen rising import penetration of domestic markets and export sales struggling in world markets, seem to have given new life to **protectionist** arguments. But such reservations are not new. Great economists such as David Hume, David Ricardo, Adam Smith, and John Stuart Mill were writing on the same broad issues of international trade and protectionism as long as 200 years ago.

The basic rationale for trade is that nations, like individuals, can benefit from specialization. The benefits are possibly more obvious in the case of individuals. It is conceptually possible that an academic economist could grow his (or her) own food, make his own clothes, build his own house, devise his own transport, and provide his own entertainment (not necessarily from watching videos of great debates in economics!). But, apart from their number of hands, economists suffer from a high incidence of thumbs; the standard of living of the self-sufficient economist would be low indeed. It was no accident that economists were the first to develop the argument for specialization . . . This states that, if the individual were to concentrate on his (or her) most efficient form of activity, he could maximize the output generated from his own particular skills, or resource endowment, and exchange any unwanted surplus for the output of other specialists. Since all output would be produced efficiently by specialist experts, the starving economist would be able to obtain goods from others at a far lower resource cost than he himself could match – just as they could benefit from his more efficient economic services in providing market forecasts, or carrying out investment appraisals, or even in just curing insomnia. Specialization of activity and exchange of surplus would benefit all individuals.

So too with nations – while each could probably produce most or all of the necessary range of goods and services, it is very probable that the production of some items would involve an inefficient use of resources. Bananas could probably be grown at Cape Wrath – but not as efficiently as mountain sheep could be reared there.

Each nation has a limited endowment of resources; each has its own pattern of particular aptitudes reflecting, for example, climatic conditions, soil quality, historical skills, or technological knowledge. If prosperity is to be maximized from the use of these limited resources, they must not be squandered on wasteful, or inefficient uses. Ideally, the limited resources should be applied only to selected items, where the nation enjoys a relative efficiency or **comparative advantage**. While such specialization will result in surplus production of the items selected, the surplus output could be exchanged through international trade for goods which have been produced more efficiently elsewhere. Not only would specialization and international trade ensure the most efficient production uses of limited resources in global terms; it would also ensure that consumers would be provided ultimately with a better range of goods, at more advantageous prices, than would be possible under a regime of self-sufficiency.

It is also important to realize that the balance of comparative advantage need not rest permanently with any single country. For example, over the 1960s and 1970s Japan appeared to enjoy a clear comparative advantage in industries such as electronics, steel and shipbuilding. But, during the 1980s, there have been signs that the balance of advantage has swung over to the emergent industrial power of South Korea, in steel and shipbuilding at least. The pattern of relative strengths and weaknesses is constantly changing and, unless this is successfully anticipated and new opportunities developed to provide the foundation for further growth, then past success can all too easily be transformed into current decline. In a very real sense, part of the economic problems of the UK have reflected our sluggish recognition of and adjustment to these facts of life.

Moreover, to draw full benefit from comparative advantage specialization, it is not a sufficient condition simply to be able to produce efficiently; it is also essential that the goods and services which are produced are *sold*, in domestic as well as world markets. At its simplest, the level of export sales and import purchases will reflect the strength of the demand for them in their respective markets. In turn, the demand for any item will tend to reflect factors such as relative prices (UK prices compared to world competitors' prices), trends in income and prosperity of consumers, and the attitude of consumers towards the quality, design and performance of the goods in question.

Looking first at the price of UK exports, three distinct components can be identified, these being:

(1) Production costs in the UK;
(2) Profit margins in the UK;
(3) The UK exchange rate, that is, the rate at which the pound sterling prices are converted into foreign currency prices in world markets.

These three elements will combine to set the world price of UK exports. If UK production costs, or profit margins, grow out of line with those of our main competitors then, at constant exchange rates, the price of UK goods in world markets will rise and export sales will probably decline. Equally, if production costs and profit margins grow broadly in line with those of our competitors, but the exchange valuation of the pound rises, then again UK exports will suffer a price disadvantage in world markets. Conversely, if UK production costs and profit margins rise more slowly than in competing countries, or if the UK exchange rate falls (with relatively stable UK production costs and profit margins), or if world production costs rise more rapidly than ours, then the UK's exports should become relatively cheaper in world markets, as a result of which the demand for them should rise[1] (and economic activity levels respond as in Figure 11.1).

Similar factors will operate to determine the level of demand for imports to the UK economy. Simply, if imports are relatively cheaper (whether from competitors' lower production costs, or profit margins, or from movements in the UK or the other countries' exchange rates), then they will be more attractive than domestic output, and demand for them should rise as demand switches to them from domestic output. This, in

---

1. The response of consumers to price changes in UK exports will depend upon the **price elasticity** of the goods concerned, that is, the degree of sensitivity of world customers towards these price changes. The text of the chapter assumes that there is a substantial degree of elasticity, that is, world consumers are relatively sensitive to price changes, so that an increase in the price of UK goods (for whatever reason) will trigger a marked contraction in the volume of exports sold, so that the receipts from export sales will fall. Conversely, if the price of UK goods falls, this will stimulate a marked increase in the volume of sales so that the receipts from exports will rise. This might well be a rather more clearcut reaction than empirical evidence would always support which, in turn, could simply reflect the fact that factors such as product quality, performance, or even simply promotional sales effort will also have an important influence in consumers' decisions.

turn, will tend to depress the level of domestic economic activity.

However, there is a danger that this focus on relative prices might understate the effect on UK trade flows of the other important influences on consumer demand. The demand for exports and imports will also reflect movements in consumers' income in the markets concerned. If consumers become more prosperous, for example as the domestic or even the world economy moves into the boom phase of the cycle, then demand and consumption expenditure levels will normally rise. In the course of doing so, it is probable that the amount of expenditure on imported goods and services will also rise – as Chancellors of the Exchequer have discovered to their embarrassment in recent times. Conversely, the severity of the recession and depression experienced in most countries from the late 1970s into the early mid 1980s slowed down the rate of increase in world income levels. This, in turn, was picked up in a more sluggish performance by UK exports in world markets.

A final vital influence on the demand for exports and imports is provided by consumers' perceptions – or tastes and preferences – of the goods in question. If customers believe (whether that belief is rooted in fact or not is of no consequence) that UK goods are of lower quality, or dated in design and function, or less reliable in terms of delivery and after sales performance, then this too will have an adverse effect on the demand for UK output. Lack of competitiveness need not be confined to relative prices; indeed, if UK goods are felt to be significantly inferior, then it could take a very substantial improvement in relative prices before these goods become genuinely attractive again to consumers, in domestic as well as world markets.

THE UK TRADE FLOWS

Now we have at least some tools with which we can begin to analyse and interpret the real-world trade flows between the UK and our main trading partners. How much do we earn from exports? How much do we spend on imports? What seem to be the main trends within these trade flows? Who are our main trading partners? Why have the extracts in earlier chapters of the book traced a course of increasing concern with the UK's trading performance over recent years? How does our performance measure up to that of our regular trading competitors of the USA, Japan, West Germany and the Netherlands?

Table 11.1 summarizes some of the main data on the UK trade flows.[2] It shows that, over the period, exports rose from £25.2 billion in

---

2. The data which follows relates to trade flows in *goods* produced and consumed in the UK. Services are normally produced for a purely domestic market, such as window cleaning, retail distribution, dentistry, legal advice, education. Where the services are produced for consumption

Table 11.1 (a) UK international trade flows (£billion). (b) Volume indices for UK trade flows (1985 = 100).

(a)

	1976	1981	1986	1987
Exports	25.19	50.67	72.68	79.42
Imports	29.12	47.32	81.39	89.58
Net balance	−3.93	3.35	−8.72	−10.16

(Reprinted by permission of the *Annual Abstract of Statistics*, 1983 (Table 13.1) and 1989 (Table 13.1).)

(b)

	1976	1981	1986	1987
Exports	65.1	83.3	103.6	109.0
Imports	63.6	75.8	106.9	114.4

(Source: *Economic Trends*, May 1989 (Table 15). Reprinted by permission of the Controller, HMSO.)

1976 to £72.7 billion in 1986 and £79.4 billion in 1987. Once again we have to guard against the distortion effect of price inflation; section (b) of the table shows that the *volume* of exports rose from an index value of 65.1 in 1976 (with 1985 = 100) to 109.0 in 1987, which represents a growth in real exports of 67.4% over the period – which is still a considerable achievement although, even if this has received less publicity than the bad news.

In contrast, expenditure on imports rose from £29.1 billion in 1976 to £81.4 billion in 1986 and £89.6 billion in 1987; this represents a real increase from a volume index of 63.6 in 1976 to 114.4 in 1987 – an increase of 79.9% over the period.

Given the multitude of individual transactions which take place between countries, it would take a remarkable coincidence to leave an exact balance between the two trade flows of exports and imports. Table 11.1 shows that there has been no such coincidence over the period. Imports exceeded exports by £3.9 billion in 1976, then by £8.7 billion in 1986 and £10.2 billion in 1987, leaving an **external trade deficit** for each of

---

2. (*cont.*) by non-resident households and firms, for example, tourism, or specialist financial and insurance services, they are shown as 'invisible' or non-tangible items of trade. The trade flows in invisibles will be dealt with in the following section on the balance of payments. This conventional treatment can be a little confusing at first, since up to now we have made no attempt to distinguish between goods and services in the domestic flow of transactions in the 'closed' economy, on the grounds that they are both forms of economic activity which generate income and employment.

International Trade and the Balance of Payments

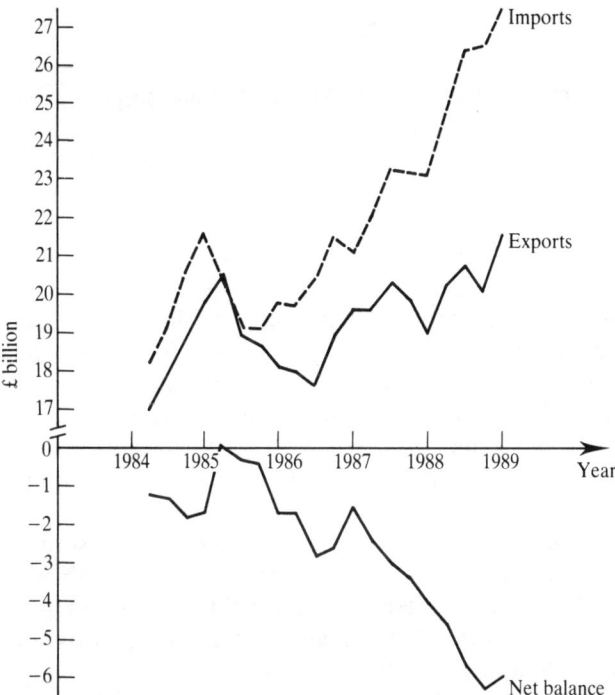

Figure 11.3 UK net balance of exports and imports. (Source: *Economic Trends*, May 1989. Reprinted by permission of the Controller, HMSO.)

these years; indeed only 1980, 1981 and 1982 out of the entire period showed a positive annual balance in external trade, with the 1981 figure of £3.4 billion representing by far the largest surplus.

Figure 11.3 updates the trade figures, on a quarterly basis over the last five years. It makes sobering, if not depressing reading. Out of the 20 quarters under analysis, there was only one (the second quarter of 1985) when there was a positive net balance, that is, when export earnings exceeded imported goods and services; in each of the remaining quarters, there was a negative net balance, or an external trade deficit. The normal pattern of UK trade flows, at least during these recent years has been for import purchases to exceed export earnings in our trade flows, leaving a series of deficits on external trade. The chart also illustrates the marked deterioration in the UK's external trade position from 1985; as a result of the very marked increase in expenditure on imports over this period, the quarterly net balance increased from about zero to a net deficit of over £6.3 billion by the end of 1988.

Why should this be so? It is possible to provide a very simple explanation in terms of our basic equation for macroeconomic equilibrium. We know that the economy will be in equilibrium when the available supply of output is just enough to satisfy the total of planned expenditures. In an open economy, this can be stated as:

$$Y = C + I + G + X - M$$

This equation can be rearranged, by transferring imports from the right to the lefthand side (and, remember, it will change its sign as it moves across – in response to mathematical rather than economic laws . . .), to show that:

$$Y + M = C + I + G + X$$

This is a useful statement; it groups together the different elements of aggregate demand on the righthand side, and gathers the two sources of available supply, namely domestic output and imported goods into the lefthand side. With very little imagination it can be seen that any excessive level of demand (relative to supply capacity) in the economy will spill over from domestic output and suck in additional imports from abroad.[3]

Earlier chapters traced how growing demand pressures have been developing in the UK economy; from our simple model above, we could therefore predict a growing deficit in external trade (always assuming that exports do not rise to match the higher volume of imports – and this is unlikely, for evidence suggests that excessive domestic demand in the UK has tended to absorb or 'poach' a share of the goods intended for export). But we can do still better than this. In the previous section, we argued that export and import trade flows would be influenced by relative prices between the UK and the world economy. From Chapter 9 you will remember that we identified an upwards drift in the UK's rate of inflation relative to the rest of the OECD member nations from about 1985–86 onwards. This would tend to make UK goods more expensive in both world and domestic markets. To make matters worse, the UK exchange rate has also tended to rise over 1987 and 1988 (from $1.43 or DM2.87 at the end of 1986 to $1.79 or DM3.18 by the end of 1988). The combined effect of these two trends would be to raise the price of UK exports and, simultaneously, reduce the price of imports to the UK. Small wonder, taking all three explanations into account, that there has been such a marked deterioration in our net balance of trade!

---

3. We must exercise a little care here; we are talking about the exports and imports of goods, whereas the terms X and M in our basic model may have implied that they were dealing with goods *and* services, as for all the other elements in the equation. Once again we are back to the problem of 'invisibles' in our measurement of the flow of international transactions. For the moment, translate X and M as applying only to goods, to remain in the accurate context of this section – although the broader interpretation of the symbols does not affect the principle of our analysis (for example, the rising affluence associated with growing domestic demand in the UK has resulted in an increase in the number of holidays taken abroad, whether taken in terms of the number of tourists, the duration or the frequency of holidays – which implies an increased consumption of import services, if we take the broader meaning of M).

Extract 11.1 provides some useful material at this point – although some of its comments will perhaps be better understood after you have read the next section on the balance of payments, and have dealt with the additional dimensions of international capital flows and the funding of the deficits. *The Economist* discusses the possible causes of the recent deterioration in the UK's trade position, and in the competitiveness of UK manufacturers. At the same time it shows how the growing strength of domestic demand over 1986–88 has tended to drive up input costs in at least the labour market. You should be familiar with much of its comments: we identified the UK's improved growth performance in Chapter 6; we cautioned about the emergence of a 'party time' mentality in Chapter 9; and, in Chapter 10 we showed how supply-side tax reforms had affected aggregate demand as well as their intended longer term target of aggregate supply – with pretty much the same effect as a late guest bringing in an additional carrier bag of alcoholic goodies to the party, just when the original supplies were drying up! Extract 11.1 and Figure 11.3 do little more than identify and trace the unhappy course of the resultant hangover . . .

Table 11.2 allows us to explore a different aspect of our international trade performance. We already know that there has been a substantial increase of 67% in the volume of exports over the period 1976–87. In the bottom half of the table, it is interesting to trace how UK manufacturers have raised the share of their output taken up by export sales from 24% to 30% over the period (indeed from 19% to 30% if we take the longer period of 1971–87); as we have already remarked, this is a very real achievement which has been overshadowed by the problems associated with the imports trade flow. Obviously, not all industries have contributed equally to this performance. Some, such as timber and wooden furniture, or paper and publishing do not appear to have been particularly active in exporting. Others such as textiles, electrical and electronic engineering, chemicals, and metal manufacturing have shown a very substantial increase in the proportion of their output directed into export sales. Still others, such as mechanical and instrument engineering, while showing a minor deterioration in their export position, still remain major exporters.

The import data from the table continues to spread an aura of gloom. Overall, the degree of import penetration rose from 23% to 35% of home demand for manufactured goods over the period 1976–87, which represents an increase of more than 50% over those 11 years. This deterioration can be traced in every industry with the exception of two, namely food, drink and tobacco, and paper and publishing. Some have been particularly badly affected by the changing pattern of the trade flows, such as metal manufacturing, the chemical industry, electrical and electronic equipment, footwear and clothing, textiles – and not least our beleaguered car industry and its component suppliers. Not only has this

Extract 11.1 THE ECONOMIST 15 APRIL 1989.

FASTEN YOUR SEATBELTS

THE economy could be in for a bumpy ride. "I have never made any promises of soft landings or semi-soft landings," Mr Nigel Lawson warned a House of Commons select committee on April 10th. Britain's chancellor of the exchequer made it plain that he was prepared to increase interest rates further—and hence accept slower growth—if necessary, to prop up sterling and squeeze down inflation.

Britain's retail-price index for March, due on April 14th, was expected to show a 12-month rise nudging 8%. Even after stripping out mortgage-interest payments, the inflation rate has jumped from 3.7% to around 5.7% over the past year. The headline figure is likely to fall in the second half of this year as the increases in the mortgage-interest rate drop out of the 12-month rate of change, but the Treasury's forecast of 5½% by the end of the year already looks too optimistic.

The tighter labour market is pushing up pay settlements. Unit labour costs—already up by 8.4% in the whole economy in the year to the fourth quarter of 1988—are likely to accelerate as output and productivity slow.

Pressure on wages will grow if sterling weakens, pushing up import prices. The pound looks increasingly vulnerable. Britain's large current-account deficit is being financed by short-term capital inflows which could suddenly go into reverse. With a $47 billion chest of foreign reserves, the Bank of England has plenty of ammunition with which to defend sterling but, if the pound comes under sustained attack, interest rates would have to rise.

Slamming on the brakes

It is still not clear whether base rates of 13% have been enough to slow the pace of domestic demand. The strongest impact has been on the housing market. The surge in mortgage lending fuelled the boom of the past couple of years, as higher house prices encouraged consumers to spend more, and households withdrew equity to finance other purchases. The slump in the housing market—in turnover as well as prices—in the south of England should help to reduce consumer spending. New mortgage lending is down a fifth on a year ago. The Treasury's current favourite measure of money, M0 (mainly notes and coins), has also slowed sharply. It rose by only 0.2% in the past six months compared with 6.0% in the previous six.

The signals from the real economy are more mixed. The

Manufacturers' competitiveness*

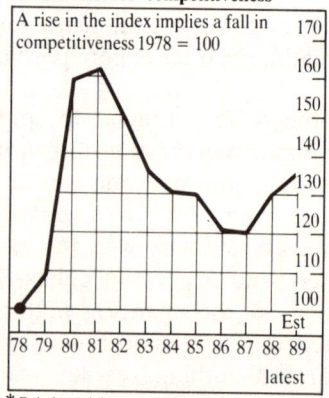

A rise in the index implies a fall in competitiveness 1978 = 100

* Relative unit labour costs in common currency

volume of retail sales jumped 3.1% in February, but is little higher than last summer. Imports have held up strongly. At the same time, output is holding up better than consumer demand: manufacturing production in the three months to January was 7% higher than a year earlier. The big question is whether manufacturers, who have been constrained by capacity, can sell more of their output abroad as domestic demand stalls.

Mr Peter Walker, the sole remaining wet in the cabinet, thinks not. Britain's non-oil current-account deficit has never been bigger, he told the Tory Reform Group on the same day that Mr Lawson was trying to reassure the Commons committee. Mr Lawson's reply would be that Britain's current-account deficit can easily be financed. Many smaller OECD economies—Denmark, Belgium and Australia, for instance—have run large deficits for long periods. For a bigger country like Britain, which has an internationally traded currency, this may be less easy. True, America has run a current-account deficit of around 3% of GDP for five years. But America is a unique case, since it can finance its deficit in its own currency. Of the other six big economies, none has run a deficit anywhere near to 3% of GDP for longer than one year. Britain's is now 3-4% of GDP.

However, the freeing of international capital flows may mean that it is now easier for a large country like Britain to finance a deficit. Indeed, this may be the reason why the current account has deteriorated so much. Because capital moves more freely, the trade deficit, rather than inflation, is now the main symptom of excess demand. The 7–8% increase in real domestic demand in Britain last year was the fastest since the war. In the past, such excess demand would have pushed up prices a lot; instead, higher interest rates attracted the foreign capital needed to pay for imports.

Mr Lawson also claims that the current-account deficit can be reduced to a manageable size without the pound falling. He gave several examples to the Commons committee of countries (Japan, West Germany, Holland and Austria) which, in the late 1970s and early 1980s, achieved swings from deficit to surplus of around 3% of GDP, without a sharp currency depreciation. What he failed to mention was that all of them except Japan also suffered at least one year of falling output and rising unemployment.

What is more, apart from Austria, these countries started off with much smaller deficits, of 1–1½% of GDP. Britain's larger deficit makes sterling more vulnerable and leaves the government with much less room for manoeuvre. Austria succeeded in transforming a current-account deficit of 4.5% of GDP in 1977 into a surplus by 1982. But Austria is much smaller than Britain; and some of its success may have been due to its corporatist system of agreements between unions, employers and the government, which this government is hardly likely to want to copy.

Mr Gavyn Davies, an economist at Goldman Sachs, an American investment bank, has examined previous cases where the big seven industrial economies have tried to run current-account deficits on Britain's scale. All have come to grief. Not one moved back to balance without a depreciation of its currency and consequent inflation. And, in all cases, domestic demand was forced to grow much less than the world average. As a rule, the smaller the fall in the currency, the more painful the slump in domestic demand.

If all the burden of adjustment in the current account has to fall on domestic spending, with no improvement in competitiveness, then a much sharper slowdown in domestic demand will be needed. But a soft landing and a cheaper pound might prove a worse combination, if it left inflation stuck at a higher level than abroad. There are other reasons why a depreciation may not make much sense: while manufacturers' competitiveness has deteriorated by more than 20% since the end of 1986, sterling's trade-weighted value is now close to most estimates of purchasing-power parity.

Indeed, a hard landing may be the best thing for Britain's longer-term economic health. A short, sharp slump in output and a small rise in unemployment would snap the wage-price spiral, halt inflation, and allow the economy to perk up just in time for the next election—although Mrs Thatcher might have to soldier on to the last minute, in 1992, to see a real revival.

Reprinted with permission from *The Economist* 15 April 1989 © *The Economist*.

---

industry's export performance dropped sharply, but imports make up virtually 50% of domestic sales — and this does not take full account of the very grey area of the true import content of 'UK' car producers such as Nissan Datsun, or Toyota, or General Motors' Vauxhall, or Ford Motors . . . or even 'British' Leyland and its Honda engines and designs . . .

Table 11.3 provides a geographical breakdown of the UK's trade flows, and should cast a little factual light on some rather vexed questions which have been asked over the years. Who are our main trading partners? Should we ever have turned our backs on our Commonwealth markets? Do our EEC partners drain far more benefits from us than we do from trading membership of the Community? Why is there such a

Table 11.2 Import penetration and export sales ratios for products of manufacturing industry.

	1971 %	1976 %	1987 %
Imports/home demand			
Metal manufacturing	19	24	42
Chemical industry	19	25	41
Mechanical engineering	19	29	38
Electrical/electronic engineering	18	32	49
Instrumental engineering	37	54	58
Motor vehicles and parts	15	29	48
Food, drink and tobacco	17	18	18
Textiles	17	26	47
Footwear and clothing	14	26	39
Timber and wooden furniture	26	28	31
Paper, printing and publishing	18	22	22
Total all manufacturing	17	23	35
Exports/manufacturers' sales			
Metal manufactures	18	18	41
Chemical industry	27	34	46
Mechanical engineering	37	45	43
Electrical/electronic engineering	24	37	43
Instrument engineering	46	56	52
Motor vehicles and parts	35	43	34
Food, drink and tobacco	4	6	12
Textiles	20	26	32
Footwear and clothing	10	15	21
Timber and wooden furniture	3	6	5
Paper, printing and publishing	8	10	11
Total all manufacturing	19	24	30

(Source: *Annual Abstract of Statistics*, 1983 (Table 12.2) and the *Monthly Digest of Statistics*, May 1989 (Table 15.10). Reprinted by permission of the Controller, HMSO.)

Table 11.3 Geographical breakdown of UK trade flows (£billion).

	Exports				Imports			
	1981	%	1987	%	1981	%	1987	%
EEC	20.5	43.5	39.4	49.7	21.7	42.5	49.6	52.9
Rest of Western Europe	6.8	14.3	7.6	9.6	7.8	15.3	12.9	13.8
USA	4.6	9.6	13.0	16.4	6.1	11.8	10.8	11.5
Japan	0.6	1.3	1.5	1.9	2.2	4.3	5.5	5.9
Australia/New Zealand	1.1	2.3	1.6	2.0	0.8	1.6	1.2	1.3
Other developed countries	1.8	3.7	0.9	1.1	2.2	4.3	0.7	0.7
Oil exporting countries	4.8	10.1	5.2	6.6	3.7	7.2	1.7	1.8
Other developing countries	5.8	12.4	8.5	10.7	5.6	11.0	9.3	9.9
Centrally planned economies	1.3	2.8	1.5	1.9	1.0	2.0	2.1	2.2
Total	47.2		79.2		51.1		93.8	

(Source: *Annual Abstract of Statistics*, 1983 (Tables 12.5 and 12.6) and the *Monthly Digest of Statistics*, May 1989 (Tables 15.5 and 15.6). Reprinted by permission of the Controller, HMSO.)

degree of apprehension over our trading links with countries such as Japan, or South Korea?

Even in 1971, two years before the UK entry into the EEC, it represented by far our most important trading partner; the affluent, fast growing member nations of the Community accounted for about 30% of all exports from and imports into the UK. It is fascinating to trace from Table 11.3 how these trade flows have developed. The European market took up £20.5 billion or 43.5% of our total export sales in 1981; by 1987 it had absorbed £39.4 billion of exports or just under 50% of our total sales in world markets. By 1987 the USA[4] had become our second largest export market with 16.4%, or £13.0 billion of sales. The major trading partners within the rest of Western Europe group were Sweden (with £2.3 billion of export sales in 1987), Switzerland (with £1.8 billion) and Norway (with £1.2 billion). Our main export markets within the very large group of other developing countries were India (with £1.1 billion of sales), Hong Kong (with £1.0 billion) and Singapore (with £0.6 billion). It is noticeable that there had been very little change in the relative importance of exports to the Japanese market, which accounted for between 1% and 2% of total sales.

Looking through the details of our trade flows in imports, it can be

---

4. Technically, the USA data is for the North America group in the tables relating to exports and imports by country; but the United States account for 85% to 90% of the total, with Canada accounting for all but a very small residual of the balance.

seen that the EEC bloc is also our main source of imports, with purchases rising from £21.7 billion in 1981 to £49.6 billion in 1987 – accounting for 52.9% of total import purchases in this year. Our main trading partners from the rest of Western Europe were again Switzerland (from whom we imported £3.3 billion of goods and services in 1987), Norway (from whom we also imported £3.3 billion) and Sweden (£3.0 billion). Imports from the USA rose from £6.1 billion to £10.8 billion over the period, but remained at between 11% and 12% of our total imports bill. Our main sources of imports from other developing countries were Hong Kong (£1.5 billion in 1987), Taiwan (£1.0 billion), South Korea (£0.9 billion) and Brazil (£0.6 billion).

One point which emerges from the table is that our trade flows with Commonwealth countries such as Australia, New Zealand and Canada have always been relatively minor; the lingering criticism of the UK's decision to align itself with Europe rather than the Commonwealth has always been based on a false and exaggerated conception of the strength of the trading links which existed between the countries – whatever the political and social ties. On a quite separate issue, it is clear that there has been a substantial shift in the pattern of trade with Japan. While exports rose from £0.6 billion to £1.5 billion over the period, this merely restored the Japanese share of UK exports to its previous and 'average' level of about 1.8% of this total trade flow. In contrast, over the period imports from Japan exploded from £2.2 billion to £5.5 billion, more than doubling their total value and sharply increasing their contribution to our total imports to 5.9% by the end of the period – and leaving an external trade deficit of some £4000 million for 1987. And remember, this does not pick up the full influence of Japanese production bases which have been set up in the UK, in car assembly, construction machinery and equipment and electronics. To a lesser extent, the UK faces the same problem of a strong net deficit in its trade with South Korea; against the imports of £936 million we could only set an export total of £427 million in 1987, leaving a trade deficit of some £509 million – although, obviously, it is very unlikely that the trade flows with any single nation will every truly balance. Finally, trade with the centrally planned economies (such as Russia, Poland, Czechoslovakia, Romania and so on) can be seen to hold its position as a stable but minor element within the UK trade flows.

THE BALANCE OF PAYMENTS

While the information contained in the previous section provides us with a valuable insight into the UK's involvement in international transactions, it is a very limited insight. Trade flows between nations have their counterflows of international payments. For every French or West German car imported into the UK, some subsequent payment from the

UK will have to be made. For every bottle of malt Scotch whisky sold to Japan, some future payment will be received by the UK in settlement of the transaction.

At the same time, the trade flows with which we have been dealing are by no means a complete record of all the transactions which take place between the countries concerned. Firstly, we have dealt only with physical goods such as cars, foodstuffs, clothing, shoes, oil, machinery and other capital equipment; these tangible products are described as **visible trade**. But, there is also a very active international trade in services, or intangible products. What about that 'Under 35' holiday you took last year, and your brave but unsuccessful attempt to empty the European wine lake? Or, on a more serious level, what about the Greek shipping company which always insures its vessels and their cargo with Lloyd's of London? Your own holiday activities (even the ones which you would rather forget) are all imports of services: Lloyd's business with the Greek shipping company is an export of services; both sets of services involve economic transactions between the countries, and are described as **invisible trade** items.

Or how do you handle the trade credit offered by a West German exporter to a British importer, or the subsequent payment in settlement? What happens if the British importer decides to buy 'future' DM, based on advice that sterling is likely to depreciate heavily against the DM during the period of credit? Or how do you deal with a long-term capital movement, as when an American firm either opens up a new factory in the UK, or expands an existing one? Where can you show the expenditure flow of UK firms and households, when they purchase foreign stocks and shares, in the belief that they will enjoy a greater return from these than would be possible in the UK capital market? Or the inflow of international capital, to take advantage of an increase in the UK domestic rate of interest? These are all described as banking and **capital** flows, and are every bit as much a flow of international transactions as the sale of exports, or the purchase of imported holiday services.

To develop a broader and more comprehensive understanding of the full range of international activity, we must turn to the more complete analysis which is provided by the UK's statement of its balance of payments. This gathers together all the items or transactions which involve a payment or receipt between the UK and all other international participants. Each item within the statement can be categorized either as a debit, or as a credit entry. A debit item involves the settlement of a debt with a foreign participant, and will take the form of an *outflow* or payment of pound sterling or foreign currency; in terms of Table 11.4, it appears as a minus item. In contrast, a credit entry involves the settlement of a debt to the UK by a foreign participant, and will take the form of an *inflow* or receipt of pound sterling or foreign currency; in

Table 11.4 The UK balance of payments (£billion).

	1981	1986	1987
1. Current account			
Visible trade			
Exports	+50.7	+72.7	+79.4
Imports	−47.3	−81.4	−89.6
Visible balance	+3.4	−8.7	−10.2
Invisible trade			
Exports	+57.3	+77.2	+80.0
Imports	−53.8	−68.7	−72.5
Invisible balance	+3.5	+8.5	+7.5
BALANCE OF TRADE	+6.9	−0.2	−2.7
2. Capital transactions			
Investment overseas by UK residents			
Direct	−6.0	−11.5	−15.4
Portfolio	−4.5	−25.2	+6.5
Investment in UK by overseas residents			
Direct	+2.9	+4.2	+6.0
Portfolio	+0.3	+8.4	+10.8
Net foreign currency transactions by UK banks	−0.2	+10.1	−1.4
Net sterling transactions by UK banks	−0.5	−0.4	+3.9
Private sector lending and borrowing with overseas banks	−1.2	+1.0	−2.2
Changes in external assets and liabilities	−0.7	+2.1	+2.8
TOTAL CAPITAL ACCOUNT	−9.8	−11.3	+11.0
3. Official financing			
Current account	+6.9	−0.2	−2.7
Capital account	−9.8	−11.3	+11.0
Balance for financing	−2.9	−11.5	+8.3
Changes in official reserves	2.4	−2.9	−12.0
Balancing item	0.5	14.4	3.7

(Source: *Annual Abstract of Statistics*, 1989 (Table 13.1). Reprinted by permission of the Controller, HMSO.)

Table 11.4 it appears as a plus item.

The balance of payments records all transactions which affect the international demand for and supply of the pound sterling in relation to other countries. In the case of a debit item, such as the import of a Japanese colour TV set, we cannot pay the Japanese manufacturer in sterling; the debt will have to be settled in terms of the yen valuation of the item. To settle the debt, sterling must be supplied to purchase the necessary amount of yen. Conversely, if a Japanese tourist comes on holiday to the UK (that is, we export the service of UK holidays), he/she will buy or demand sterling for expenditure in the UK, in exchange for Japanese yen. In effect, all debit items affect the international supply of sterling, and all credit items the international demand for sterling, as part of the process of making payment or settlement of the transaction. As we will see in the following section, it is the events which take place within the balance of payments which affect the behaviour of the exchange rate for sterling.

However, to return to the balance of payments, this will normally be split into three broad sections.

Firstly, there is the **current account**. This summarizes the results for the period of all the trade flows of goods and services which have taken place between the UK and its trading partners; the resulting net balance is described as the **balance of trade**.

In Table 11.4, you will see that the trade flows are split into the two sub-categories of **visibles** (or tangible goods like cameras, watches, foodstuff and machinery) and **invisibles** (or intangible services). The figures which make up the visible balance are the same as those in Table 11.1. You might be interested to know how these have benefited from the UK supplies of North Sea oil (which provides us with a flow of exports, and can also be used domestically to reduce the UK's imports in oil). The net surplus balance in our oil trade amounted to £4.1 billion in 1986 and £4,2 billion in 1987; in other words, without this cushion the visible trade balance would have been over £4 billion worse in each of these years. Those oil reserves are finite, and the exploitation of later fields is likely to be more difficult in the future; if, as some forecasts have predicated, there is a decline in the oil surplus to figures of below £2 billion then it is very probable that visible trade deficits could become increasingly dramatic in the near future . . .

The invisible trade figures cover a wide variety of services and other items. For example, they cover earnings from sea and air transport, tourism, and financial services. A second main sub-group of invisibles covers receipts by UK residents of interest, profits and dividends from abroad (which we have already met in the national accounts in Chapter 2 under the heading of 'net property income from abroad', and which represent earnings from the ownership of foreign productive, financial and other assets), with the counterflow of similar payments made from

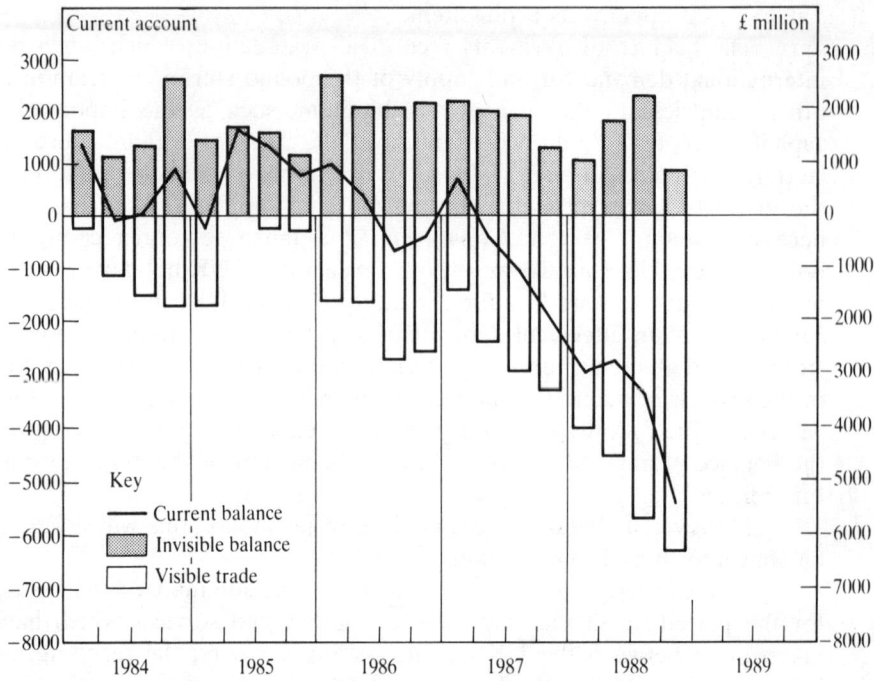

Figure 11.4 UK balance of payments. (Source: *Economic Trends*, May 1989. Reprinted by permission of the Controller, HMSO.)

UK activities to overseas residents. Finally, invisible transactions also include government and private transfers, such as UK grants, contributions and subscriptions to international organizations, or private gifts of money or assets to and from the UK.

From Table 11.4 you will see that invisible trade recorded a positive net balance for each of the three years, and this is very much a characteristic of the UK current account records; credit entries for invisibles have always exceeded debit entries, so that this element in our trade flows does much to offset the normal deficit from visible trade. Figure 11.4 provides a dramatic update and illustrates the roles played by both elements in the current account position. From it you can see just how heavily the UK has come to rely upon its invisible earnings; part of the severe deterioration in our current account balance has been due to the recent and relatively weak quarterly figures for invisible trade.

Normally when commentators become alarmed about a 'balance of payments crisis' in the UK, they are referring to the balance of trade deficit recorded in the current account, rather than to the overall position of the balance of payments as a whole. How serious is the problem at present, given the data in earlier tables and the concern expressed in Extract 11.1? In Table 11.5 we show the comparative position for our regular countries of comparison, and you will find that these are anything but reassuring. The extract was worried that the UK deficit in the current account was running at 3–4% and probably worsening. From the table you will see that the USA (which has also been heavily criticized by both American and international comment) is in a similar position; here the deficit has grown from 0.6% to 3.3% of GDP from 1980–86. In each other country there has been a strong movement into a current account surplus of between 4% and 5%, with the international trading strength of West Germany very evident in the table.

How concerned should we be about the UK's performance in international trade? We are a very open economy, and our international trade flows take up a substantial proportion of GDP and total domestic expenditure (TDE); for comparison purposes, UK exports absorbed 26.3% of GDP in 1986, and imports to the UK amounted to 26.9% of TDE. Perhaps major deficits are an unavoidable part of these circumstances? It is an argument which has been used, but which carries little real merit. The open economy condition is equally true of West Germany, and even more true for the Netherlands, neither of which shows such a worrying deficit balance. At its simplest, a persistent and severe deficit position in a country's balance of trade reflects the fact that its demand for world goods and services is rather stronger than the world's demand for its goods and services. In short, its domestically produced output must be relatively expensive and/or relatively unattractive in both domestic and world markets. This surely must be a cause for some concern – even if, technically, a current account deficit is not of itself a crisis, so long as it is willingly financed from elsewhere in the balance of payments.

The **capital account** is the next broad section of the balance of payments statement; this summarizes the results of all the capital and banking flows to and from the UK economy.

In Table 11.4 you will see that the first two items in the capital account are concerned with capital movements from investment activities. This can cover either *direct* investment, for example, setting up or expanding production capacity; or it can be *portfolio* investment, which deals with purchases and sales of stock in existing businesses. The table identifies the substantial investment outflows from UK residents which have been so much a part of the 1980s. These probably reflect a combination of the relaxation of exchange controls (which has been part of the liberalization of capital markets which has occurred over this period), and the perception by UK firms and households that a greater return could be earned outside the UK. Whatever the case, the net capital outflow for this heading has increased steadily from £2.4 billion in 1977 to a peak of £36.8 billion in 1986; the credit entry for portfolio

Table 11.5 Current account position: OECD members.

	USA ($billion)		Japan (billion yen)		West Germany (DM billion)		Netherlands (billion guilders)	
	1980	1986	1980	1986	1980	1986	1980	1986
Exports of goods and services	273.3	290.2	32.9	38.1	391.9	584.5	176.8	232.0
Imports of goods and services	288.1	429.3	35.0	24.8	401.1	485.0	178.6	214.7
Current account balance	−14.8	−139.1	−2.1	+13.3	−9.2	+99.5	−1.8	+17.3
Exports as percentage of GDP	10.2	6.9	13.7	11.5	26.5	30.2	52.5	54.0
Imports as percentage TDE	10.7	9.9	14.4	7.8	27.0	26.4	52.7	52.1
Current account balance as percentage of GDP	−0.6	−3.3	−0.9	+4.0	−0.6	+5.1	−0.5	+4.0

(Reprinted by permission of the *OECD National Accounts*, 1988 (Table 10 for each country).)

investment of £6.5 billion in 1987 is the first of its kind for a decade, and has helped to reduce the net capital outflow to £8.9 billion for that year. In contrast to this substantial outflow, investment in the UK by overseas residents, both in the form of direct and portfolio investment, has shown a steady positive net inflow; indeed the total has climbed steadily over 1985–87 from its previous range of £1 billion to £5 billion to reach a new and substantially higher peak of £16.8 billion, with the main growth taking place in portfolio investment. You will remember how we have drawn attention to the decline of the UK savings ratio in earlier chapters; here you can trace at least in part how much of our recent investment expenditure in the UK has been funded by international capital.

The next two rows of Table 11.4 are both concerned with short-term flows of money into and out of the banks in the UK and abroad. The use of net figures can be misleading; for example, the figure of −£1.4 billion for net foreign currency transactions by UK banks in 1987 conceals gross flows of £45.6 billion lending abroad, as against £44.3 billion borrowing. The sterling lending and borrowing activities have always been very much smaller; for example in 1987 the net credit entry of £3.9 billion reflects the difference of £4.6 billion lending abroad, as against £8.5 billion borrowing. These short-term money flows cover, among other elements,[5] the movement of funds seeking to avoid anticipated falls, or to take advantage of possible gains in exchange rates, or in response to the changing advantages offered by the international pattern of interest rates. From time to time in the past, very large movements of 'hot' (or short-term advantage) money have taken place and large net negative balances have developed, drawing a crisis level response from UK governments; this has led to a view that, while short-term money movements may help at times to balance deficits in the current or elsewhere in the capital account, they are not necessarily the most stable of support systems. A rumour, a sudden panic, or a marked change in the pattern of international advantage could lead to a very dramatic reversal of the flow, with pretty much the same effect as pulling out the rug from underneath the stately tread of the family butler and his tray of drinks . . .

The final items in the capital account are, in relative terms, minor. They cover both private sector lending to and borrowing from foreign banks and, under the title of 'changes in external assets and liabilities', the net balances from the flows of identified trade credit between firms in different countries, inter-government loans by the UK, and subscriptions to international lending bodies.

---

5. A large proportion of the banks' activities are concerned with their operation within the Euro-currency market. Probably triggered by the American capital outflows of the 1960s, Euro-markets developed as governments and firms borrowed the dollars against a variety of interest earning securities which were acceptable to the dollar holders; the Euro-bond emerged to be traded in the Euro-dollar market, and international capital market activities now cover a massive flow of trade in a variety of currencies.

Aggregating the entries in the capital account of the balance of payments shows that there was a net inflow of £11.0 billion in 1987, as against the outflows of £9.8 billion in 1981 and £11.3 billion in 1986.

There is no reason in the real world[6] why the net balance of capital movements should exactly equal the net balance of the current account; it is more normal that there will be an overall net dificit or a net surplus for the different periods which are under analysis. The final broad section within the balance of payments deals with the **official financing** of the final net balance struck from the trade and capital flows for the period; it is part of a residual adjustment, which ensures that the balance of payments will always and ultimately balance. If, for instance, the trade and capital flows resulted in a net credit or inflow for the year, then this will be reflected in an increase in the UK's reserves of gold and convertible foreign currencies (or be used to repay past borrowing). Conversely, if the aggregation of the trade and capital flows results in a net deficit or outflow, then this must be financed by drawing on reserves, or by raising fresh borrowing from the International Monetary Fund (IMF), as in 1976 when the new higher prices of oil imports to the UK placed our reserves under serious pressure.

From Table 11.4 it can be seen that the combination of the current account deficit and the capital account surplus in 1987 left a net surplus of £8.3 billion for that year. As a result, official reserves were *increased*[7] by £12.0 billion from that year's flow of international transactions. If you are still fully awake, you will realize that this still leaves a balance of £3.7 billion to be accounted for. This final figure is tidied into the **balancing item** for the balance of payments, a title which gives it a degree of mystique and possibly even of nebulous respectability. The real truth of the matter is that the balancing item is simply the residual which cannot be accounted for in our records of international transactions; it is no more than a shamefaced entry for 'errors and omissions'. It reflects the

---

6. In the more abstract world of pure theory, if the exchange rate is left completely free to find its own equilibrium level, it will fluctuate until it finds a value which equates the demand for sterling to the supply of sterling. If the demand for the currency (in the form of all the credits or inflows) is to be equal to the supply of the currency (in the form of the total of debits or outflows), then the balance of payments will be left with a zero balance – without any need for official financing. Thus, if there is a current account deficit, the exchange rate will operate until this is matched exactly by a capital account surplus; conversely, a current account surplus will be matched by a capital account deficit.

7. Yes, you may well blink given that the £12.0 billion is preceded by a minus sign; however, since the purpose of the exercise is to show a final zero balance for the overall balance of payments, the statement has adopted the convention of showing increases in official reserves as a use or outflow (−) of the surplus, or as a source of payment or inflow (+) to offset any final deficit. Out of deference to any confusion which you might already be experiencing as you work your way through the intricacies of the balance of payments statement, the author felt that it was kinder to introduce this new complexity in a footnote which you might never read.

impossibility of registering and recording every single transaction which has taken place between the UK and the rest of the world. The Bank of England has a very accurate knowledge of the movements which have occurred in our reserve balances; the balancing item fills the gap between these known changes and the recorded volume of transactions for the year. The residual can be positive or negative; over the last decade it has varied from one negative entry of £2.4 billion, to a range of positive entries between £0.5 billion in 1981 and a massive £14.4 billion in 1986 (with this figure being almost three times greater than previous highest residual error value). In comparison, the figures for 1987 show a very respectable degree of accuracy, and are only £3543 million out of balance . . .!

THE EXCHANGE RATE

In a closed economy the flow of transactions is carried out in a single domestic, currency. In an open economy, where there is international trade and capital movements, then economic activity will take place in a variety of currencies. For transactions to take place at all, it is essential that a relative valuation is set on the currencies of the trading partners, both at the point of sale and at the point of settlement (since payment can 'lag' the transaction by up to several months, during which time the currencies will normally fluctuate in value).

The **exchange rate** is *the rate at which one currency converts into the other*. For example, on 4 July 1989, £1 of sterling would have converted into either $1.58, or DM3.05, or 223.04 yen – or at a list of specified rates into any recognized currency.[8] These rates of conversion vary from day to day, and even during the course of a single day; you should be able to see a typical list on the financial pages of your daily paper.

The exchange rate for any currency represents its 'price' on the foreign exchange market. Given the spread of time zones for the main financial centres of New York, London, Zurich, Frankfurt, Hong Kong and Tokyo, and given the immediacy of modern information and telecommunication systems, this market offers the possibility of a 24-hour trading day for its operators.

For any single currency such as sterling, the exchange rate is set largely through the interaction of the demand for and the supply of that currency, at any given moment of time. The demand for sterling will reflect the total of the inflows, or credit items in the balance of payments. If foreign households and firms wish to make a payment in settlement for

---

8. Obviously the exchange rate can be viewed from the opposite direction too; given the exchange rate values quoted in the text, a USA dollar would buy 63p of sterling, a DM 33p and 2 yen would just about buy 1p.

UK exports, or if they want to purchase UK physical or financial assets, their first step must be to buy sterling (since the transaction will be carried out in terms of the domestic currency). Conversely, the supply of sterling will result from the total of all outflows or debit items in the balance of payments. This time it is the UK households and firms who must sell sterling to buy foreign currency, to pay for the imported goods and services, or to purchase the foreign assets in the domestic currencies of their trading partners.

In a completely free market, the exchange rate will fluctuate and interact with the flows of demand and supply, until it finds a level which brings the market into equilibrium, that is, where the demand for the currency is just enough to absorb the available supply. Where a currency is left in this manner to find its own level in response to market pressures, this is described as a **floating exchange rate**.

Such a system will involve frequent, and even substantial revisions in the level of the exchange rate, both as it searches for its equilibrium level, and as this equilibrium level is itself affected by changes in the volume of supply and demand over time. If, for any reason, there is a surge in demand which creates a relative scarcity of the currency in the market, then the exchange rate will tend to rise. Conversely, if there is a marked increase in the volume of outflows or debit items, then there will tend to be an excess supply of the currency relative to the demand for it, which will cause the exchange rate to fall. Speculative movements of capital into or out of the UK have placed severe short-term pressure on the sterling exchange rate on several occasions in recent years. Or, as an example of more permanent pressure, West Germany's persistent trade surplus has placed a continuing upwards pressure on the DM exchange rate, establishing it as a 'strong' currency. In contrast, a 'weak' currency would be one where there is a persistent deficit position, a predicament not unknown to the UK, French and Italian economies in the past.

These constant variations in the level of exchange rates can create problems for trade partners; if exports are sold or imports purchased under a fairly routine three-month trade credit period, what would happen if the sterling exchange rate were to fall sharply between the date of the transaction and the date when settlement was due? To illustrate, let's take the case of a UK firm which sells a crate of 25 bottles of malt whisky to a West German importer at a price of £12 per bottle. At a current exchange rate of DM3.05 to £1 sterling, this would imply that the West German importer would have to pay DM915 in settlement of the transaction. If the UK exchange rate falls over the intervening three months to, say, DM2.95 then our delighted German importer would need to sell only DM885 to buy the £300 sterling needed to pay the UK exporter.

What does it matter, you might ask? After all, the UK firm still gets its £300 and is no worse off. But what if you were involved in a similar transaction over the same time period, and had contracted to pay £500 for accommodation and transport charges to your local tourist agency, to cover a (purely cultural) visit to a selection of West German breweries? When you went to pick up your tickets, your apologetic tourist agency would have to ask you for a surcharge; whereas your £500 would originally have purchased the necessary DM1525 to cover all your holiday bills, at the lower exchange rate of DM2.95, you would need to pay £516.95 to let you pay the same bills. Just as well the brown paper bags come free on the flight . . .

Fixed exchange rate systems provide a sharp contrast to this constantly shifting network of floating exchange rates; as the name implies, exchange rate values are agreed and fixed between the currencies of the member nations, and the resultant pattern of 'parity' values is then held for as long as possible. The Bretton Woods agreement of 1944–71 provides an example of this type of system; originally set up to ensure some stability in the vulnerable years following the Second World War, it continued to function (with periodic amendments for individual currencies) for many years after its introduction. It operated as follows: the value of its 'central currency', the USA dollar, was fixed in terms of gold; the values of all the other major currencies were then fixed in terms of the USA dollar. Finally, the International Monetary Fund (IMF) was set up to monitor the operation of the system, to provide credit to countries which had moved into serious (but temporary) deficit problems, and to approve any necessary changes, or **realignments** in exchange rates where situations of permanent imbalance developed in particular countries.

Where currencies are traded in an open market, it is almost impossible to operate with a system of rigid or unchanging rates. However correct the agreed parity values might be initially, the constantly changing surges of demand and supply for the different currencies will inevitably create conditions where the agreed exchange rates do not clear the markets for particular currencies. Therefore a fixed exchange rate system will normally permit some degree of fluctuation around the agreed central value for currency (for example, in the Bretton Woods agreement, exchange rates were allowed to fluctuate within a narrow band of 1% around agreed parity values), but the central bank will be expected to intervene in the market through buying and selling their currency, 'leaning against' the market to hold rates within this band.

The European Monetary System (or EMS) is a current example of a fixed exchange rate agreement between member countries. This system covers nine currencies; the UK, Greece and Portugal are the only EEC states with currencies outside the EMS parity grid. As with the Bretton

Woods agreement, there is some degree of freedom within the grid: the Italian lira and the Spanish peseta are allowed to fluctuate by 6% on either side of their central rate; the seven remaining currencies have a much narrower 2.25% margin for fluctuation.

As you will know from earlier extracts, the UK is not a member of the EMS. The exchange rate value for sterling is determined largely by the operation of market forces – but the government reserves the right to intervene (that is, to buy or sell sterling with deliberate intention to influence the exchange rate) where it disagrees with the valuation which is emerging from the market. For example, should a strong upwards revaluation of world oil prices push up the sterling exchange rate (given the UK reserves of North Sea oil), the government might choose to sell sterling to reduce or counteract this influence. Conversely. if the combination of a UK trade deficit and capital outflows have resulted in an excess supply of sterling driving down the exchange rate, then the central bank would very probably step in to sell foreign currency reserves and to buy some of the unwanted sterling, again smoothing out the fluctuations in the rate of exchange. This 'mixed' system of market forces and periodic intervention is described as a **managed** or **dirty float**, indicating that it is not a 'pure' system of floating exchange rates.

Extract 11.2 provides an insight into the extent of the intervention which might be needed in such a system, and describes the international response of central banks to a series of current influences affecting the USA dollar and its effect on other currencies. It might help if you think through these events in terms of their implications for the demand and the supply of dollars; deal separately with the 'encouraging trade figures', then the subsequent 'profit taking', and finally the drop in USA interest rates.[9] Note how the central banks' intervention was designed to prevent these short-term fluctuations from interfering with necessary longer term adjustment in relative currency values.

A recurring theme associated with both the periodic realignment of currencies within a fixed exchange rate system and the intervention activities of central banks responsible for managing a dirty float, is that a currency can become **over-valued** or **under-valued** within the foreign exchange market. What does this imply?

---

9. If you are struggling with the interest rate effect, remember that international capital will be seeking its best return based on interest rates (and the possibility of capital gains from appreciation of the currency). If USA interest rates fall relative to other international rates then, provided the potential gain from the transaction outweighs its costs, some international capital will move out of the USA towards other higher interest rate countries; dollars will be sold to purchase the new entry currency, which will push down the American exchange rate. Also, if international capital owners speculate that the exchange rate is about to fall sharply, or to continue to fall then, rather than taking the risk of a capital loss from holding dollars, they will sell dollars and move out. Either way, the capital flight will add to the excess dollars left from profit taking, to create an excess supply condition in the market for dollars.

Extract 11.2 THE TIMES 17 JUNE 1989.

Intervention holds US currency below DM2 and lifts sterling

CENTRAL BANKS TAME DOLLAR SURGE

Colin Narbrough, Economics Correspondent

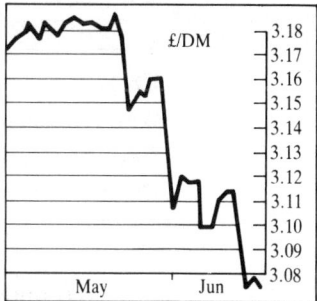

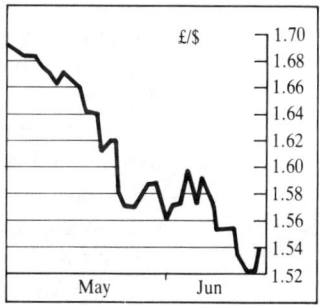

The world's leading central banks yesterday appeared to have tamed the rampaging dollar, at least for this week, after a co-ordinated burst of intervention which came to the timely rescue of the troubled pound.

On Thursday night, the banks, reinforcing profit-taking and a shift of sentiment for the dollar, stepped in on a massive scale to magnify the dollar's fall, pushing it down four cents against sterling in a jittery New York market.

This gave the pound a much-needed respite, allowing it to stage a dramatic comeback to close at $1.5455, after only managing $1.5180 in London.

The attack on the dollar followed its sharp rise on Thursday's encouraging US trade figures, which pushed the American currency to its highest levels against the yen for more than two years and its best against the mark since end-1986.

But the high-flying moment was brief, as profit-taking and a full-point drop in the US long bond rate sent the dollar heading down.

It was at this point that the central banks made their move, selling dollars to the market to bring the currency off still faster.

The central banks, including the Bank of England, have been intervening all week against the dollar, fearful that its continuing rise will delay the vital readjustment needed between the US — with its huge twin trade and budget deficits, and the big surplus economies — Japan and West Germany. The British Government, reluctant to raise base rates again to defend the pound, was also intervening in self defence.

Overnight, the Bank of Japan, keen to prevent the higher dollar from fuelling inflation in the Japanese economy, sold dollars repeatedly, helped by the US Federal Reserve Board.

Shortly after 8am yesterday, the Bank of England, the Bundesbank and other European central banks joined in after an early telephone conference between the bank leaders.

The timing of the assault on the dollar was left to the dealing departments at Threadneedle Street and in other centres.

Some technical charts show that the dollar can fall back to support between DM1.95 to DM1.97, but most analysts believe the dollar remains on an upward trend and will rise again from the intervention level after some consolidation.

The market was very thin yesterday, causing choppiness in the dollar movements.

Dollar sales started in Europe at about DM2.0045, pushing it to DM1.9925 at the Frankfurt fix.

The intervention by the Bundesbank was its first since late May, confirming that it had not abandoned intervention as a policy.

The dollar ended in Europe almost four pfennigs below Thursday's close after a stormy day of rises and falls. Its consolidation at the lower level after the previous day's six pfennig drop was expected to keep the US currency below DM2 until the market plucks up the courage to take on the central banks' defence line.

The dollar ended at DM1.9905 yesterday, close to its DM1.9920 opening. On Thursday it finished at DM2.0285.

Dealers said the Bundesbank sold dollars at DM1.9925 — the level apparently agreed with the other banks.

In London, sterling ended at $1.5330, an increase of one-and-a-half cents from Thursday's finish.

Reprinted with permission from *The Times* 17 June 1989 © The Times.

Table 11.6 Real and nominal exchange rates.

	Start of period	End of period
UK price index	100	125
West German price index	100	105
UK nominal exchange rate	3.20	3.05
UK real exchange rate	3.20	3.63

To understand such a judgement, we must go back to basics. The purpose of the exchange rate is to convert prices between currencies at the points of sale and settlement. As such, it has an important influence on the international competitiveness of a country's goods and services. If the sterling exchange rate is rising then, given constant domestic prices and profit margins, this will simultaneously raise the world price of UK exports and reduce the UK price of imported goods and services (in both cases because the pound sterling will command greater amounts of the foreign currencies). Conversely, as we have already illustrated with our UK/West German examples, if the sterling exchange rate falls then the world price of UK exports is reduced, and the UK price of imported goods and services rises. In each case, the change in the UK exchange rate makes UK output less or more competitive with world trade.

But does this mean that a fall in the sterling exchange rate will *always* make domestic production more competitive? It is tempting to agree, given our earlier illustrations, but it would be quite wrong to do so. The crux of the matter is that we have always viewed the exchange rate changes against a backgound of constant domestic prices; in these circumstances, exchange rate changes do have a direct influence on international competitiveness. But what happens if UK prices do *not* remain constant. For example what would happen if, while the sterling exchange rate fell from DM3.20 to DM3.05, UK prices rose by 25% against a West German inflation rate of 5% over the same period? Does the fall in the UK exchange rate still make UK goods and services more competitive? Table 11.6 sets out the illustrative values of the exchange rates and price indices.

To answer these questions, we must consider whether or not the fall in the exchange rate has *offset* the higher UK rate of inflation. This means that we must learn to distinguish between the **nominal exchange rate** (E_N) and the **real exchange rate** (E_R). The nominal exchange rate is the rate which is quoted in the market; in our example, the UK nominal exchange rate has fallen from DM3.20 to DM3.05 over the period. The real exchange rate is derived from the nominal exchange rate, by building in an adjustment for any underlying differences in price movements between the countries. In terms of a simple formula:

$$E_R = \frac{E_N \times P_{UK}}{P_G}$$

where all the values refer to the same time period, E_R is the real exchange rate, E_N is the nominal exchange rate, P_{UK} is the price index value for UK goods for that period and P_G is the price index value for West German goods.

Given the illustrative values in Table 11.6, we can see that there will be no difference between real and nominal exchange rates for the start of the period (since the price indices are both at their base year value of 100, leaving the ratio of the indices equal to unity). However, for the close of the period:

$$E_R = \frac{3.05 \times (125)}{105}$$

$$= 3.63$$

What does this tell us? It shows that, after the different rates of increase in output prices are taken into account, the real exchange rate (which is the true measure of the UK's competitive position) has risen from DM3.20 to DM3.63, which means that the position of UK exporters has *worsened*. The decline in the nominal exchange rate has not been enough to compensate fully for the UK's higher rate of inflation. In consequence, the world price of UK exports will have increased, and imported goods and services will be cheaper in the UK domestic market. This will normally have an adverse effect on the demand for UK produced output and, through this, on the level of employment in the UK.

Read Extract 11.3 at this point. This discusses how the growing German trade surplus with its fellow members within the EMS is placing pressure on the nominal central rates. Note how the extract points out that the reason for the widening trade gaps must lie in differing levels of international competitiveness '. . . and hence in real exchange rates'. Does the solution lie in judging that the DM is under-valued? Or does the pressure on the parity grid simply reflect that other currencies, such as the French franc and the Italian lira are over-valued? If the solution lies in a 'Sunday afternoon huddle of finance ministers' agreeing to a realignment of nominal exchange rates, which currencies should move in which direction – and by how much? Note particularly how the extract argues that the only sure way for countries to achieve a readjustment which works would be for the deficit countries to do better than average in terms of productivity gains and cost restraint . . . which takes us back to the ratio of the countries' price indices in our formula, and real exchange rate movements.

Extract 11.3 THE ECONOMIST 3 JUNE 1989.

STRAIGHTEN EUROPE'S SNAKE

Desirable though the prospect of monetary union is, it should not rule out one last realignment of European currencies

WHILE the rising dollar and the huge trade imbalances between America, Japan and West Germany grab headlines, another growing imbalance tends to get overlooked: West Germany's surplus with its fellow full members of the European Monetary System. This could threaten not just the present stability of the EMS, but Europe's plans for economic and—looking further ahead—monetary union.

West Germany's trade surplus with America fell from DM28 billion in 1986 to DM17 billion ($9 billion) last year. But its surplus with other EMS members jumped from DM30 billion to DM46 billion, almost eight times the 1983 figure. Worse still, when America's external deficit shrinks, the imbalances within Europe are likely to get worse. Mr William Cline of the Institute for International Economics forecasts that if America's deficit is reduced by $100 billion by 1992 through a slowdown in its domestic demand and a depreciation of the dollar evenly against other currencies, this would leave West Germany's overall trade surplus virtually unchanged. The deficits of France and Italy would almost double.

So what? Such EMS imbalances hardly matter if, as at present, they are being financed willingly. And, in theory, they will matter even less within a single European market. An obvious solution would be for West Germany to grow faster and hence import more from its neighbours. But Germany's real GNP grew by 3½% last year, and its fiscal policy has been more expansionary than that of any other EMS member in the past three years. In that case, the reason for Europe's widening trade gaps must be differences in competitiveness—and hence in real exchange rates.

The central rates of the EMS have remained fixed in nominal terms for almost 29 months—the longest period of stability in the system's ten-year life. Inflation differentials have narrowed, leading some people to conclude that nominal exchange rates do not need to change. Yet West Germany's growing surplus with other countries at the same time as its domestic demand is buoyant suggests that the D-mark is undervalued—partly, perhaps, because earlier realignments never compensated fully for inflation differentials. On one estimate the French franc, the lira and the currencies of other deficit countries need to be devalued by at least 15% in real terms against the D-mark.

The grinding path to competitiveness

The surest way to achieve a real devaluation is also the hardest—by the deficit countries doing better than average on productivity and cost restraint. The alternative—a Sunday afternoon huddle of EEC finance ministers, eventually agreeing on nominal realignments—cannot guarantee a lower real exchange rate for the franc, the lira and the rest: the benefits of devaluation can be eroded quickly by faster inflation. But there is now less risk of that happening, because EEC countries have sensibly abandoned or diluted wage indexation. As a result, the higher import prices that follow from a devaluation do not get embedded throughout the economy within months.

Even more important, European economies need to get ready for the not-too-distant day when they become a monetary union. That does not mean they should act as if the day has already dawned and nominal exchange rates can no longer be changed. Unless the pressures from growing imbalances are relieved before a union is set up, they could bust it in its vital early years. Even before then, the deficit countries might turn protectionist, threatening the 1992 programme.

Reprinted with permission from *The Economist* 3 June 1989 © *The Economist*.

Within this context, it is interesting to examine the additional concept of the **purchasing power parity exchange rate** (E_P). This estimates what the nominal exchange rate value must be if the differential inflation rates are to be fully offset, and the real exchange rate held constant at its opening value, so that the country's competitive position is unchanged. Returning to our illustrative example in Table 11.6, what nominal rate would leave UK output in an unchanged competitive position as at the end of the period? We can estimate this from the formula:

$$E_P = \frac{\bar{E}_R \times P_G}{P_{UK}}$$

where $\bar{E}_R$ represents the constant real exchange rate value, and P_G and P_{UK} represent the closing price index values for the two countries. Taking the values from Table 11.6,

$$E_P = \frac{3.20(1.05)}{1.25}$$

$$= 2.69$$

In other words, to retain purchasing power parity (that is, an unchanged position on world and domestic prices, and so an unchanged level of competitiveness) the sterling exchange rate would have to fall to a nominal value of DM2.69 by the end of the period. Returning to Extract 11.3, if the intention is to remove the competitive disadvantage which has developed, then our Sunday afternoon huddle of ministers should be resetting the nominal exchange rates at their purchasing power parity values – a major realignment which, in some cases might well be judged to be politically impossible, and in others to be too disruptive to other domestic macroeconomic objectives (for example, the fall in nominal rates will increase the price of imports and will raise the rate of domestic inflation).

Even outside the rigidities of a fixed exchange rate system, the managed adjustments of the nominal exchange rate under a dirty float system is unlikely to compensate completely for the loss of competitive advantage caused by an excessive (that is, relative to main international competitors) rate of domestic inflation. Therefore, a predictable consequence of rapid domestic inflation is that the country's international competitive position will be steadily eroded – with all the familiar problems of declining export sales, rising import penetration, trade deficit, and weakened peformance in domestic output and employment. Once again we can see why the recent drift in the UK rate of inflation carries such serious implications.

'TO BE (A MEMBER OF THE EMS) OR NOT TO BE . . .?'

The essence of any good soliloquy is that it should be long on words, strong in emotions and, ideally, generate as little action as possible despite its anguish. The debate on whether or not the UK should become a full member of the EMS clearly satisfies all of these conditions. The UK's dialogue of hesitation can be traced back to the creation of the 'snake' of European currencies in 1972 (when it was certainly not helped by the humiliation of having to withdraw from tentative trial membership after only a few weeks, as a result of speculative pressure on the sterling exchange rate in the foreign exchange market), through the European Monetary Co-operation Fund of 1973, and through the formation and subsequent operation of the EMS from its inception in 1979. To judge from Mrs Thatcher's reaction to the Delors Report[10] of June 1988, it is still far from certain that any real action will be taken by the UK . . . and it is beginning to become clear that the other EMS members have a diminishing interest in the UK's final decision. Few Shakespearian Hamlets would have had the courage to milk an audience's attention and sympathy to such a point of substantial indifference.

Extract 11.4 shows that there has been far from unanimity on the matter. Nigel Lawson firmly believed that, if the UK had entered in the mid 1980s when both our rate of inflation and our nominal exchange rate were at an ideal level for entry, then much of our current difficulties with inflation and trade deficits could have been avoided. In contrast, Margaret Thatcher is equally – if not more – convinced that these current problems originated in Mr Lawson's attempt to 'shadow' the DM over spring 1988. Why should two such senior Ministers take diametrically opposed views on UK entry into the EMS? No treatment of exchange rates would be complete without at least a brief consideration of some of the issues involved, and the extract provides a useful introduction to the topic.

It is important to begin by acknowledging that the UK is already a member of the EMS in every respect, apart from formal participation in the parity grid or the **exchange rate mechanism (ERM)**; the term 'full membership' therefore implies the taking of this final step. What advantages would full membership offer?

---

10. This report was prepared for discussion at the 26 June 1989 'summit' meeting of European leaders; it was the product of a committee of central bankers from member nations, chaired by Jacques Delors, the President of the EC. Its purpose was to set out the various stages by which the EMS would develop into full monetary union, whereby there would be a permanent fixing of EMS parities (with a logical development being a single common currency) and the establishment of a European central banking institution. It represented a three-stage development plan, with the completion of the EMS representing the first of these stages.

Extract 11.4 FINANCIAL TIMES 14 JUNE 1989.

AGREEMENT TO DIFFER LEAVES EMS TIME BOMB TICKING

Peter Norman and Simon Holberton on the strains between the Chancellor and the Prime Minister

MR NIGEL LAWSON, the Chancellor, this week set a time bomb ticking under his already volatile relationship with the Prime Minister.

In evidence before the Commons Treasury and Civil Service Committee he spelt out in greater detail than ever before his concept for Britain becoming a full member of the European Monetary System.

If he is still living next door to Mrs Thatcher in a year's time it is almost certain that the frequently acrimonious row over the exchange rate, which has dogged their relationship since 1986, will resurface.

Britain's full membership of the European Monetary System seems sure to become an acute political issue from July 1990, when members of the European Community start abolishing their remaining exchange controls.

For the moment, however, in spite of all the talk of rifts between Numbers 11 and 10 Downing Street, the Chancellor and the Prime Minister — or First Lord of the Treasury, to give her her formal title — are probably more at one on economic policy than they have been for many months.

Combating inflation is their number one priorty. They both believe interest rates must be fixed at whatever level is necessary to control prices. Exchange rate stability has been pushed into the background. Both are even on record as agreeing that now is not the right time for Britain to join the EMS's exchange-rate mechanism.

But the present show of unity has failed to allay nervousness in the City and conviction in the media that wide differences exist. At a time when Britain's economy is looking more fragile than it has since the deep recession of the early 1980s, the knowledge that fundamental differences exist between the two politicians, whose job it is to safeguard the nation's economic welfare, is having a powerful, corrosive effect on confidence.

It is a testament to the pride and stubbornness of both the Prime Minister and her Chancellor that neither has bothered to hide their underlying differences about exchange-rate policy in recent weeks.

On Monday, Mr Lawson told the Commons committee that he supported Britain's entry into the EMS's exchange-rate mechanism — a currency grid which allows only small fluctuations in exchange rates between members — and suggested that not too long after July 1990 might be an appropriate time to join.

That is the closest any senior Government minister has gone in defining "when the time is ripe" — the anodyne form of words used since the creation of the EMS a decade ago to define Britain's intentions about joining the ERM.

Mr Lawson listed the key benefits of full membership — exchange-rate stability, lower interest rates and better control over inflation. He took on critics, such as Sir Alan Walters, the Prime Minister's personal economics adviser, who argue that the system is inherently unstable.

The Chancellor predicted that the EMS would survive the abolition of exchange controls in the European Community. In so doing, Mr Lawson answered the main objections to Britain's full membership made by the Prime Minister and her adviser.

A month ago, Mrs Thatcher, in a now notorious interview with the BBC World Service, blamed Britain's high inflation rate on the Chancellor's policy early last year of trying to hold the pound level with the D-Mark. She said of Britain's attempt to act as if in the exchange-rate mechanism that the "experience of artificially holding to an exchange rate has been such that it really makes it quite clear that you must take your own steps."

Those comments were a reminder of the very deep division that existed between the two a year ago, when relations were so strained that they barely talked to each other for weeks on end. In March last year, when Mrs Thatcher insisted that the pound should be allowed to rise above DM3, the immediate cause was her anger at what she saw as the Chancellor's attempt to take Britain into the EMS through the back door by his policy of shadowing the D-Mark.

Her violent reaction was a reflection of her visceral aversion towards fixing exchange rates. At the gut political level, Mrs Thatcher does not want to take orders from foreigners. Historically she has vivid memories of the humiliating attempt in 1972 to put the pound into the so-called European currency snake — the precursor to the EMS — when massive speculation against sterling forced Britain to quit weeks after joining.

In turning on the Chancellor a year ago Mrs Thatcher was influenced, at a distance, by Sir Alan Walters, who, having been the Prime Minister's economics adviser in the early 1980s, was then working in Washington for the World Bank. His return to Downing Street at the beginning of May has been a decisive factor in keeping alive the talk of a policy rift between Mr Lawson and his boss.

Sir Alan has been ultra-careful to keep his head down since his return. By all accounts an amiable man, he has, in his words, decided "simply to clam up," on the ground that he cannot be held responsible for any misrepresentations of his views in the press.

His deliberate aloofness has made his influence over the Prime Minister appear all the more potent. Her words have been analysed for traces of his ideas. It is clear, however, that he is influential: "He has a track record and so has to be taken seriously," said one Whitehall insider.

But to assume that Mrs Thatcher parrots his every word is to misunderstand the relationship between Prime Minister and adviser. It is well known that the Prime Minister delights in the cut and thrust of robust debate. So does her Chancellor.

Mr Lawson was probably being disingenuous when he told Mr Jonathan Dimbleby on BBC TV's On The Record last Sunday that his discussions with the Prime Minister were frequent and "very cordial." The view from Westminster is that relations between the two are quite strained.

But there is no denying that Mr Lawson has appeared ebullient in recent public appearances. The man who a year ago was unsackable because he had delivered the 1987 election victory and masterminded the 1988 tax-cutting Budget now probably is unsackable because he has to return the economy to stability.

Assuming he is not moved in the forthcoming Cabinet reshuffle, things might look different for Mr Lawson next year, especially if he succeeds in bringing down inflation without causing a recession.

The final abolition of exchange controls for Italy and France next July will bring the question of Britain's full membership of the EMS and the underlying differences between Chancellor and Prime Minister back in to sharp relief.

It may be that Mr Lawson has put a time bomb ticking not just under his relationship with Mrs Thatcher but under his own position as well.

PARTING OF THE WAYS OVER POLICY ON EXCHANGE RATES

LAWSON: I accept that in the right circumstances membership of a formal fixed exchange-rate system can itself provide a very effective framework for monetary policy ... over the medium term. Maintaining a fixed exchange rate against countries who share our resolve to reduce inflation is a pretty robust way of keeping domestic monetary policy on the rails.

But I see no role for an exchange rate target outside a formal exchange-rate system, shared by other countries, and supported by a co-ordinated approach to economic management and intervention. And that, for the UK, means outside the exchange-rate mechanism of the EMS. **Speech to the Lombard Association, April 16 1986.**

THATCHER: What it means is hitching your wagon to the D-Mark, doesn't it? That's what we are really talking about. Instead of a gold standard, or dollar standard, you have a D-Mark standard, and then you have all the problems that we used to have with devaluation, if it comes.

We are getting stronger and one day we will go in. I believe we will one day go in. **On EMS during an interview with the FT, November 17 1986.**

LAWSON: Nor, however, should there be any doubt of our commitment to maintain a stable exchange rate, with the rate against the D-Mark being of particular importance. It gives industry most of what it wants and provides a firm anchor against inflation. And we now have very substantial reserves with which to maintain that stability in the future. **Mansion House speech, November 4 1987.**

LAWSON: The EMS is an agreement between independent sovereign states whose economic policies remain distinct and different. By close co-operation, they can achieve greater stability of exchange rates, and — as we have seen — reinforce their efforts to bring down inflation. **Royal Institute of International Affairs speech, January 25 1989.**

THATCHER: We actually picked up our inflationary tendency during a time when we were trying to hold our pound level with D-Marks, and we had to do that because our pound tended to rise because people held sterling in high regard.

The pound tended to rise so we have to do it by piling in sterling, selling sterling to hold it down.

That is where we picked up the inflation, actually by trying to shadow the D-Mark. **Interview with the BBC World Service, May 19 1989.**

LAWSON: No. I think it was more related to the nature of the housing market in this country and the fact that we deregulated our financial sector far more than any other country, but what we have participated in is a worldwide resurgence of inflation. And I think if you are saying 'where did you go wrong', I think what it was, with the benefit of hindsight ... the loosening of monetary policy in the wake of the [October 1987 share price] crash." **Interview with the BBC's Jonathan Dimbleby, June 11 1989.**

THATCHER: The point I want to get over is please do not think of the exchange-rate mechanism as a magic wand to do things without effort.

It is not. Of course we have to look at it and we have a look at it from time to time and will continue to do so ... Our experience of artificially holding to an exchange rate has been such that it really makes it quite clear that you must take your own steps. **Interview with the BBC World Service, May 19 1989.**

Reprinted with permission from *Financial Times* 14 June 1989 © *Financial Times*.

In Extract 11.4, Nigel Lawson is credited with the view that the benefits would take the form of 'exchange rate stability, lower interest rates, and better control over inflation'. Let's explore these arguments in a little more depth.

The first clear benefit of full membership has always been that there would be a greater stability in our exchange rate; this would follow from the setting of an agreed central rate and the specification of the permitted margin of fluctuation around this. Membership of the EMS would then carry the obligation that national authorities would have to intervene to keep the nominal exchange rate within this permitted band of fluctuation. This does not differ greatly from our present dirty float system, but it would imply a more structured and predictable range within which the fluctuations would occur.

This greater stability of the nominal exchange rate would carry several important implications for domestic inflation. Firstly, it should impose a greater degree of discipline on both firms and workers by confronting them more directly (or 'transparently') with the consequences of their actions; wage, profit and pricing decisions could no longer shelter behind an anticipated fall in the nominal exchange rate, as has been the case all too often in the UK – although we know that it is the real exchange rate which matters in terms of international competitiveness.

Secondly, to conform to a stable central rate, domestic macroeconomic policy must be set to ensure that excessive (relative to other EMS members) inflationary pressure is minimized, if not completely avoided. There is an interesting and more sophisticated point to consider here in that inflation can be fuelled by domestic and international expectations; where a country is seen to align its currency with a 'hard' or strong currency, this is perceived as a serious statement of intent – so great is the necessary domestic discipline to maintain such an agreed parity. This could do much to modify both internal and external expectations, which should help the actual rate of inflation. Certainly, whatever the theory, EMS membership appears to have 'worked' for a number of other countries. Countries with an equal, if not worse inflation record than the UK have shown a remarkable improvement in domestic inflation rates during their recent membership of the EMS. What seems to have happened is that the West German economy has set its routine macroeconomic policy to ensure minimal domestic inflation; other member countries have then structured their own domestic policy actions to maintain nominal exchange rate parity with the central currency of the DM. The collective impact of the measures has been that the UK now lies above, and is drifting away from, the EMS 'average'. The low inflation DM has clearly provided a vital external anchor for other member countries.

Finally, and to complete our explanation of Nigel Lawson's views, with policies which provide a lower rate of inflation, and with a more stable nominal value for the exchange rate, there should be less pressure on domestic interest rates (either to control domestic demand levels, or to prevent movements of international capital). A final consequence of successful full membership of the EMS should, as Mr Lawson has argued, be that it helps to produce lower interest rates in the long run.

Despite this (by no means all-inclusive) list of advantages, Mrs Thatcher's implacable opposition to full membership indicates that there are counter-arguments and worries which must also be taken into account. One of her major concerns is that the necessary broad cooperation and harmonization of domestic macroeconomic policies (without which the stability of the EMS grid would be disrupted) would reduce the independence of action and control of the individual member states. Her suspicion that, ultimately, real control would lie in the hands of 'faceless bureaucrats' within the EC has not been helped either by the current strength of the West German central bank's influence on the domestic policy actions of member countries, or by the Delors' vision of a common unit of European currency and a strong European central bank to administer the final stages of the union. It is difficult to assess just how serious are the grounds for worry here. Certainly, no member state would be free to set its own target rate of inflation, where this diverged from the EMS pattern; but the current evidence appears to be that the benefits from this cooperation in the fight against inflation have far outweighed any perceived costs of diminished independence. At the same time, and on a sadly more cynical note, given the realities of the pursuit of personal interest and power by the average politician, it is difficult to envisage member states' governments drifting passively into a collectively dependent and minor role within the EC – certainly not over a relatively short period of time (defined as how long it takes to change human nature . . .).

A second worry is that the need to stabilize the nominal exchange rate would involve raising its status as a policy target – quite probably at the expense of the more normal range of domestic policy targets. The UK has followed the USA pattern of declaring its intention to use monetary policy to control domestic inflation, then to accept the exchange rate consequences of the necessary policy actions. For example, if domestic interest rates are raised significantly to curb domestic demand pressures, then this could well invite a major inflow of international capital, which would cause at least a short-term appreciation of the nominal exchange rate for sterling, or the dollar. But where exchange rate stability becomes the dominant policy target, then domestic interest rates must be set with an eye on their consequences for the foreign exchange market, which might well conflict with domestic policy responsibilities. A key Thatcher criticism has been that much of the UK inflationary pressure over 1988 and 1989 followed from Mr Lawson's attempts to hold down sterling's nominal exchange rate, while 'shadowing', or maintaining an informal parity with the DM. A little thought will tease out the main content of this criticism. While central bank intervention might well have played some part in holding down the nominal exchange rate for sterling at that time, by far the more powerful instrument was the Bank of England's ability to cut or to hold down domestic interest rates in the UK (which avoided unwanted capital movements in the balance of payments, and kept the UK exchange rate lower than it might otherwise have been). But a side-effect of these lower interest rates was that they also made domestic consumer credit cheaper, and might have played a crucial role in triggering and fuelling the consumer boom which sent the UK lurching into accelerating inflation again. In fairness to Mr Lawson, attractive though the logic of this argument might seem to the Prime Minister, it does present an oversimplified description of his policy intentions at that time. Part of his purpose in reducing interest rates was to counter the possibility of a major recession (following the Stock Market crash in the late autumn of 1987 and the then-current pessimistic macro-forecasts for the economy). Equally, much of our recent UK inflationary pressure has reflected events and price movements in the overheated property market of London and the South East – and has had little to do with any tentative rehearsal of possible EMS membership!

A third, and possibly more substantial worry of the Prime Minister is that the successful operation of the EMS might be seriously damaged when its member nations relax exchange and capital controls, as is intended in July 1990. Countries such as France and Italy have relied on capital controls to curb movements against their currencies, when realignment was seen to be imminent by financial markets. Equally, Italy and the new EMS member Spain have used these controls to keep capital out when domestic interest rates were particularly high (because of domestic demand and inflation problems). What will happen when capital markets are completely liberated? While capital outflows could help some realignment decisions (with capital flight preceding the anticipated cut in nominal exchange rates), consider the plight of high interest rate countries. They could be faced with the choice of fighting to hold their nominal exchange rates within the agreed upper margin of fluctuation from their central rate (with all the implications which this could carry for running down financial currency reserves and, probably, having to borrow) or, alternatively, they might have to reduce their domestic interest rates to take the pressure off their nominal exchange rate – and lose the use of the policy instrument of interest rates in their fight against domestic overheating. Can the EMS adapt to absorb the greater range of pressures on nominal rates as a result of liberalizing capital movements?[11]

Overall, it should be clear that there is no simple 'yes or no' answer for EMS membership – and we have only considered a selection of the main arguments. Some might even say that we have omitted the most important point of all. If the EMS is but the first stage in a series of developments which could take us towards a complete monetary union and a United States of Europe (and the Delors Committee Report has very much the flavour that this objective is no longer under debate, and that its real brief was to set out planning guidelines for the next few stages of that ambitious path), then it could be extremely dangerous *not* to be a member in this initial stage of the exercise. Protection, reassurance, genuine influence over current and future policy development can only be gained from within. If the UK continues to behave like Hamlet, after the audience has given up and caught the last bus (or started the last Porsche) home, and once the stage hands have switched out the final spotlight, then how can we provide any influence over events, how can we protect

---

11. It is important to recognize that *both* options could affect the EMS parity grid. As we have argued in the text, if countries focus on their appropriate domestic level of interest rate, then the exchange rate must find its own and higher level as international capital flows in to reap the benefits of the high interest rates. But also, if the domestic rate of interest is held down to stabilize the nominal exchange rate, *and* if there is no compensating deflationary fiscal policy action within the domestic economy, then excessive demand will spill over into both inflation and additional imports, either of which will ultimately attack the nominal exchange rate value.

our own interests? When joining finally becomes inevitable – for even the longest soliloquy must end (if only to the heavy silence of an empty theatre), then we will have no option but to accept what others have chosen to do in our absence . . .

SOME COMPLICATIONS OF THE OPEN ECONOMY

You might have realized that we have not really attempted to build the international trade sector into any of our models – apart from the introductory comments about the effect of the trade flows on our level of economic activity. The reason for this is that the interrelationship between the domestic and the world economy is very much an area of complex and specialist theory. We have therefore tried to deal with the subject by a discussion of particular topics rather than by rigorous modelling. Frankly, if we were to go into the business of model building, then we would need to use a much more advanced level of theory and analysis than would be appropriate for an introductory book such as this.

Having said this, it is still possible to explore – in a limited fashion – some of the main implications of the open economy for the operation of macroeconomic policy. Apart from the points which we have identified in earlier sections, it is interesting to see how fiscal and monetary policy, the two main management instruments of the closed economy, are affected by the more complex world of the full open economy.

Earlier sections have dealt with the role and the influence of the exchange rate (or, more exactly, the nominal rate of exchange); from them we know that the UK currently operates within a system of managed, or dirty floating exchange rates. To simplify matters, let's assume that it is, instead, a pure floating exchange rate system which is in operation. Even given the limitations of the depth and extent of our analysis, the results are interesting.

Within a floating exchange rate system, monetary policy emerges as a relatively powerful instrument, at least in the short term; in contrast, fiscal policy is substantially weakened by operating within this type of system. Why should this be so?

If monetary policy is used to *deflate* the domestic economy, then the government would raise domestic interest rates by reducing the supply of money, as shown in Figure 11.5(a); at the higher rate of interest r_2, interest sensitive expenditure elements such as C and I in Figure 11.5(b) would be cut back, reducing the level of aggregate expenditure to D_{A2} and setting off a contraction to the new and lower equilibrium level of GDP at Y_2. The different elements of this argument should be familiar from earlier chapters. However, in an open economy with freedom of international capital movement, the higher interest rate is likely to

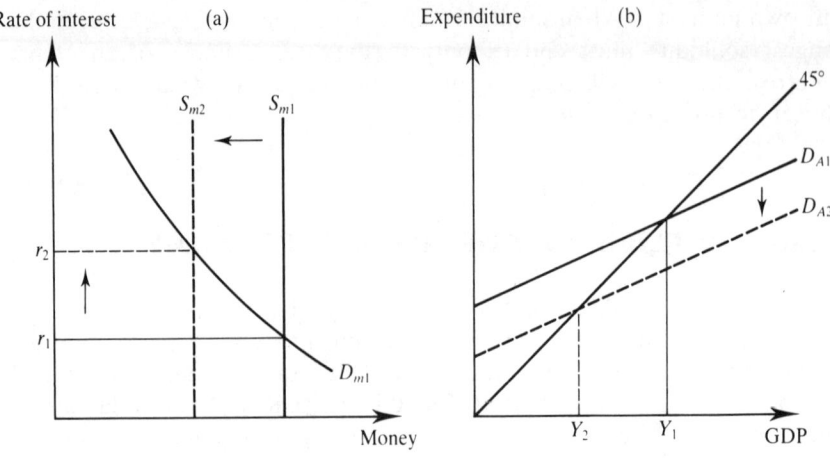

Figure 11.5 Floating exchange rates: deflation by monetary policy.

encourage an inflow of capital, which would increase the demand for sterling, and cause the nominal exchange rate for sterling to rise. This, in turn, would cause the price of UK exports to rise (which could cause the total of export sales to fall) and the price of imports to the UK economy to fall (which would cause an increase in the demand for imports). The current account would tend to move towards deficit to offset the surplus caused by the inflow of capital. But note how, if exports fall and imports rise, there are two more reasons why the aggregate demand function in Figure 11.5(b) should fall. And note particularly how all the effects on the real economy are moving in the same direction, which is towards the desired target of deflation.

Conversely, if monetary policy was used to *reflate* the domestic economy, the supply of money would be increased, to permit domestic interest rates to fall. Apart from its intended domestic effect, this could well trigger an outflow of international capital, which would tend to cause the nominal value of the exchange rate for sterling to fall. This would make UK exports cheaper in world markets, and imported goods and services more expensive in domestic markets. The combined effect of all of this would be for C and I to rise in response to the lower domestic rates of interest, while X would rise and M would fall in response to the lower UK exchange rate. In terms of Figure 11.5(b), the aggregate expenditure function would rise from D_{A2} to D_{A1}, allowing the economy to expand (always assuming that there was spare capacity to do so) to a higher equilibrium level of GDP. The model would run in reverse, but

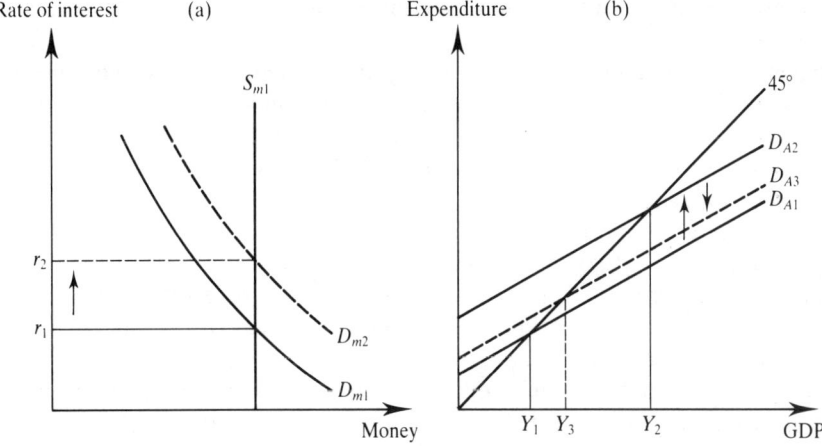

Figure 11.6 Floating exchange rates reflation by fiscal policy.

note again how all the effects are moving in the same, desired direction.[12]

So much for monetary policy; but what would happen if fiscal policy is used with the same intention of reflation? For fiscal reflation, the government could either raise government expenditure, or reduce taxation, or blend the two; the effect of the policy action initially would be to raise the aggregate demand function from D_{A1} to D_{A2}, as shown in Figure 11.6(b). However, as the economy begins to expand (again assuming that there is sufficient capacity for it to do so) from Y_1 to Y_2, we run into the familiar 'crowding out' effect, as the increase in the demand for money triggered by the expansion moves the demand for money function from D_{m1} to D_{m2}, forcing up the rate of interest to r_2 against an unchanged supply of money in Figure 11.6(a). As has been described in earlier chapters, this will trigger an adverse side-effect when the higher

---

12. We are faced with a difficult choice here. Strictly speaking, as the economy contracts in Figure 11.5(b) there will be a fall in the demand for money (since less will be needed for transactions and precautionary balances): if we showed the D_m function moving to the left against the new S_{m2} function, this would obviously reduce the interest rate from the illustrated level of r_2; this in turn would result in a lesser decrease in aggregate demand (if interest rates rise by a lesser amount, then there will be a lesser cutback in expenditure plans). There would be a similar offsetting adjustment to the D_m function in Figure 11.6. We have chosen *not* to illustrate this effect, partly because we feel that the diagrams are complicated enough – particularly Figure 11.6 – and partly because we believe that a monetarist government would change the supply of money by enough to neutralize this 'crowding out' type of effect. It does not affect the principle of the analysis, or the conclusions which are drawn on the relative power of fiscal and monetary policy under the two sets of exchange rate systems. But it is untidy – and well done if you spotted it without prompting!

interest rate affects interest sensitive investment expenditure. But we are still not finished in an open economy. The higher interest rate could trigger an inflow of international capital, which would drive up the nominal exchange rate. This in turn would make UK exports more expensive and could reduce export sales, so that exports as well as investment are crowded out in the intended expansion; at the same time the higher exchange rate would tend to reduce import prices, causing import purchases to rise. Note how, this time, all the side-effects are operating in the *opposite* direction to that which was intended by policy makers. It is difficult to predict where the combined result will leave the D_A function, as I and X fall, and as the propensity to import rises; we show it, tentatively, as resulting in the aggregate demand function D_{A3} in Figure 11.6(b), but so much depends on just how sensitive investment is to the higher interest rate, and on the extent of the exchange rate movement, and on the sensitivity of X and M to the change in the exchange rate. In terms of our illustration, the final equilibrium level of GDP shows only a marginal gain at Y_3 from its opening equilibrium position of Y_1.

Wherever the new equilibrium level of GDP lies, the model shows how fiscal policy is further weakened where it has to operate within floating exchange rates. A similar conclusion would have been reached where fiscal policy was used to bring about a deflation; the resultant fall in the demand for money would reduce interest rates, possibly causing an outflow of international capital and a decrease in the exchange rate. The lower rate of interest domestically would stimulate interest sensitive expenditure; the lower exchange rate internationally could stimulate exports and reduce imports through its price effect upon them. Once again, the side-effects would all move in the opposite direction to the intended effect on aggregate demand, leaving it difficult to predict the extent (and possibly even the direction) of the adjustment in GDP. And, as with monetary policy, note how the current account would tend to move in the opposite direction to the capital flow in each case, helping to secure a natural balance within the overall statement of the balance of payments.

At this late stage in the book, these complications may hurt a little; but the analysis does provide another insight into why Nigel Lawson opted to use monetary policy to raise interest rates, in his attempts to take the heat out of the UK economy. While we do not operate a pure system of floating exchange rates, intervention is still kept to a minimum and it is probable that fiscal policy is still relatively weak as a corrective instrument.

But, in marked contrast to these conclusions, where the economy operates within a fixed exchange rate system, the relative efficiency of the two policy instruments could be reversed! This time fiscal policy is strengthened and monetary policy weakened by operating in an open

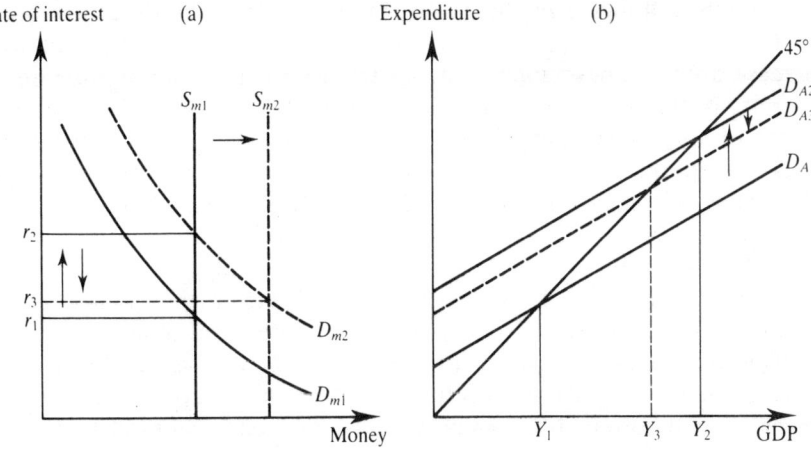

Figure 11.7 Fixed exchange rates: reflation by fiscal policy.

economy. This surprising result hinges on two new and critical factors. Firstly, under a system of fixed exchange rates the government would be obliged to intervene to maintain the agreed nominal exchange rate. Secondly, the process of intervention has repercussions on the domestic supply of money, as the government deals with the banking sector in the foreign exchange market.

Let's begin by tracing what might happen if the government decides to *reflate* the economy by the use of fiscal policy within a fixed exchange rate system. As before, the government could either raise its own expenditure or reduce taxation in an attempt to move the aggregate demand function to D_{A2} in Figure 11.7(b). When the economy expands to this new equilibrium, the demand for money will rise to D_{m2} in Figure 11.7(a), driving up the rate of interest to r_2. Once again this could trigger a capital inflow, if UK interest rates become relatively high in terms of world capital markets; *but this time the exchange rate cannot rise*, because it is fixed. And, if the nominal exchange rate is unchanged, then there will be no compensating price effect on the trade flows of exports and imports in the current account of the balance of payments. The surplus demand for sterling caused by the capital inflow will remain and, to protect its nominal exchange rate value, the government will have to intervene by selling sterling to counterbalance the demand pressure. It will do so by buying foreign currency from the banking sector, which will increase the deposits of the latter. You will remember from our 'money creation' example in Chapter 8 that, if bank deposits are increased by an action which is external to the banking system (we used central bank open market operations in that example), then this allows the banking sector to embark on a profitable multiple expansion of credit . . . which has the effect of increasing the supply of money. If you look at the money market model in Figure 11.7(a), you will see that the effect of this increase in the money supply to S_{m2} is to ease the pressure on the rate of interest. In the model, we show the interest rate as falling to r_3, but the extent of this movement will depend upon the size of the increase in banking deposits from the foreign exchange intervention activities of the authorities, and upon the response of the banking sector and the public to this opportunity to create credit.

Whatever the scale of the movement, it helps to minimize the crowding out effect in fiscal policy. The increase in the money supply damps down the increase in domestic interest rates, and should result in a smaller cutback in interest sensitive expenditure. At the same time, the fixed exchange rate prevents any crowding out of export sales (which might have followed if the exchange rate had been allowed to rise in response to the capital inflow). Therefore, overall, most of the reflationary intentions of fiscal policy are allowed to operate on the domestic economy; given that Figure 11.7(a) has retained a minor increase in interest rates from r_1 to r_3, we show in Figure 11.7(b) only a minor crowding out of investment, pulling aggregate demand down from the intended level of D_{A2} to D_{A3}. The economy should therefore expand, as intended, as it moves from Y_1 to its new equilibrium level of Y_3.

What would be the consequence of reflating through monetary policy, under a system of fixed exchange rates in an open economy? Figure 11.8 allows you to follow the sequence of events. Monetary policy would seek to reflate by increasing the supply of money, which would reduce the level of interest rates from r_1 to r_2 in Figure 11.8(a); this would stimulate interest sensitive expenditure (C as well as I, probably), which would raise the level of aggregate demand from D_{A1} to D_{A2} in Figure 11.8(b), permitting the economy to expand to the higher equilibrium level of GDP of Y_2.[12] But, in an open economy the fall in UK interest rates would probably result in an outflow of international capital; with fixed nominal rates of exchange there would be no compensating movement in the current account trade flows, so that an overall deficit could emerge in the balance of payments. Once again the central bank would have to intervene in the foreign exchange market to stabilize the UK exchange rate; since a deficit implies an excess supply of sterling, this intervention would take the form of buying sterling by selling from our reserves of foreign currency. The combination of the capital outflow and the central bank's intervention would *reduce* the supply of money in the UK.[13] In Figure 11.8(a) you can trace how this movement of the money

---

13. If the government does not wish the balance of payments surplus to increase the domestic supply of money, or the deficit to decrease the supply of money, then it could attempt to **sterilize** the domestic money supply. It would do so by using open market operations within the domestic economy to offset the money supply effects of the Balance of Payments (BOP): for example, to

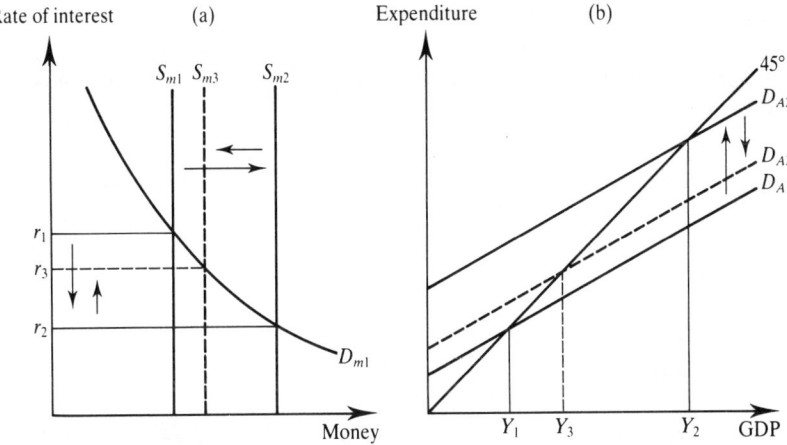

Figure 11.8 Fixed exchange rates: reflation by monetary policy.

supply from its intended position of S_{m2} to S_{m3} would weaken the intended cut in domestic interest rates, which would fall only from r_1 to r_3. This limited fall in domestic interest rates would also weaken the signal for expansion of the domestic economy (the smaller interest change would trigger a smaller response); in Figure 11.8(b) we show how aggregate demand might only rise from D_{A1} to D_{A3}, once the open economy effect is built into our more familiar analysis of the closed economy. This time it is monetary policy which has been weakened by the exchange rate regime.

We must stress that this is a very simplistic level of analysis of very complex internal/external relationships; but it does provide another possible insight into Mrs Thatcher's opposition towards genuine acceptance of a full membership role within the EMS. The EMS operates through relatively fixed nominal exchange rates; if there is an irreversible movement towards a common European currency, then these nominal rates will become even more fixed in the future, with the permissible margins of fluctuation either reduced or abolished. Within fixed exchange rates, the domestic adjustment power of monetary policy is substantially weakened. Fiscal policy becomes the more effective policy instrument, with domestic reflation and deflation achieved through variations in government expenditure or tax policy. Is this a palatable remedy for a government which has embraced both monetary policy and supply-side economics with such fervour? Particularly if we add the additional

---

sterilize a BOP surplus (which would increase the money supply) it would sell bonds on the open market; to sterilize a BOP deficit (which would reduce the money supply) it would purchase bonds in the open market. At this late stage in the game, it seemed to be kinder to introduce this new complication in a footnote, rather than the main text. Hang in there . . .

conviction in the efficiency of market force adjustment (that is, floating exchange rates) and the even greater conviction that any form of intervention will be riddled with bureaucratic inefficiencies? At least if we stay outside the EMS (and hope that it goes away) with a dirty float version of floating exchange rates, we can still continue to use monetary policy, and hold to these other cherished beliefs. Major decisions have often been taken by governments on the basis of preference rather than balanced logic. Our membership (or otherwise) of the EMS could be just another example, when history comes to be written.

CONCLUSIONS

1. Nations trade because, like individuals. they can draw benefits from specialization. If each nation devotes its limited resource endowment to the areas of economic activity in which it enjoys a comparative advantage then it will gain the maximum return from these resources; it can then trade output which is surplus to its own requirements for goods and services which are produced in a similar and efficient way by its international trading partners. All nations will benefit, and consumers will enjoy a wider range of choice at a lower cost than under any other system of production.

2. Study of the geographical pattern of the UK trade flows shows that the EC is by far our major partner for tradeable goods; member countries take up just under 50% of our total export sales and are the source of about 53% of our total import purchases. The USA is our second most important trading partner, accounting for about 16% of our total export sales and 12% of our total imports. Other countries such as Japan, Hong Kong and South Korea have grown rapidly in recent years as sources of imports, with lesser development being recorded in the sale of UK exports to their markets.

3. The balance of payments statement provides a comprehensive record of all international trading transactions, covering both the trade flows in goods and services in its current account, and the wide variety of banking and capital flows in its capital account.

4. A study of the current account shows that the normal UK pattern of trade has been to run a series of deficits in visible trade, which have been partly or even completely offset by the normal run of surplus balances in our invisible trade. However, there has been a steady worsening of the current account deficit position over the later years of the 1980s, as the overheated UK economy has sucked in additional imports to meet its level of demand, and as UK competitive advantage has been partially eroded by our higher rates of inflation over the last few years. When commentators have

become alarmed by the UK's 'balance of payments problem', they have normally been referring to the size and trend of the deficit balance on the current account, rather than the overall position of the complete balance of payments.

5. A study of the details of the capital account shows that there have been very substantial investment outflows from resident UK firms and households into foreign assets (which in the longer term will enhance our important invisible earnings in the current account). To some extent, this outflow has been offset by the counterflow of international capital into the UK economy. It is probable that, with the decline of the UK savings ratio, a sizeable proportion of UK investment expenditure has been funded from this international source. The capital account also shows the very considerable movements of money within the banking sector.

6. The transactions which are recorded in the current account and the capital account are carried out in a wide variety of currencies. The exchange rate is the mechanism whereby prices in one currency are converted into their equivalent value in terms of the other trading partner's currency. The exchange rate for any currency is set by the interaction of the demand for and the supply of that currency which, in turn, reflects the various debit and the credit items in the country's balance of payments. Where the exchange rate level is set purely by market forces, it is described as a floating exchange rate. Where it is set and held purely by an administrative decision (which might well reflect a judgement on the market forces for the currency) it is known as a fixed exchange rate.

7. While movements in the nominal exchange rate influence the world price of exports and the domestic price of imports, they do not contain sufficient information to permit an accurate judgement to be made of trends in a country's competitive position. This is revealed more clearly by movements in the real exchange rate, which takes the market or nominal exchange rate and adjusts this to reflect differential movements in the output prices of the two countries concerned. The purchasing power parity exchange rate provides an estimate of the appropriate level of the nominal exchange rate, if this is to compensate completely for the different rates of inflation in the two countries, and leave the real exchange rate at the same value as before.

8. Within a floating exchange rate system, it would appear that fiscal policy is substantially weakened by the influence of the open economy. In addition to the recognized domestic crowding out effect, whereby higher interest rates might result in reduced investment expenditure, the same higher interest rates might attract an inflow of international capital. If so, the resultant pressure on the

nominal exchange rate could make exports more expensive and imports cheaper, creating a second and international dimension to the crowding out effect. In contrast, monetary policy has an enhanced effect: the deliberate domestic interest rate changes not only affect their target domestic expenditure elements; the international capital flows which are triggered could move nominal exchange rates to nudge both exports and imports in the desired direction of deflation or reflation.

9. In contrast, within a fixed exchange rate system it is monetary policy which is weakened at least in the short term. This follows from the fact that the balance of payment surpluses or deficits affect the domestic supply of money. This could counteract the intended movement in domestic interest rates which would, in turn, weaken the response of expenditure elements within the domestic economy; and the fixed exchange rate blocks out any benefit from price adjustment in the current account. Fiscal policy, on the other hand benefits from the fixed exchange rate system, since the side-effect of money supply changes from the balance of payments position will normally help to neutralize the crowding out or offsetting side-effects on investment and exports.

10. The EMS provides a current example of a fixed exchange rate system; it involves the agreement and cooperation by a group of EC countries to operate within a parity grid, that is, to attempt to hold their nominal exchange rates as close as possible to the central values which have been established by the system. No nominal exchange rate is fixed at a rigid value; each is permitted to fluctuate within an agreed range of the central value. Member countries are expected to pursue policies which keep their nominal exchange rates within this margin of fluctuation although, where there is clearly a more permanent problem, a mechanism exists to permit the realignment of the currency within the grid (that is, at a revised central value for its nominal exchange rate).

11. The UK is not a full member of the EMS, although it cooperates on all other matters apart from placing sterling within the parity grid. There is considerable disagreement on the balance of advantage against disadvantage from becoming a full member and taking this final step. Full membership would confer a greater stability in the nominal exchange value for sterling; it should provide a greater degree of discipline to reduce the UK rate of inflation towards a level which is more consistent with that of other EMS members; the combination of these first two advantages should permit a lower level of domestic interest rates, which would benefit the domestic economy in the longer term. Against these points are the counter-arguments that the need to cooperate and coordinate domestic

macroeconomic policies to protect the parity grid reduces the scope for independent decision by member countries. The enhanced status of the central value for the nominal exchange rate could make domestic policy objectives subordinate to this EMS group objective. It is far from clear that the stability of the parity grid can be sustained if exchange and capital movement controls are abolished, as is intended for July 1990.

12. There must be a limit to the length of time during which the UK can view the EMS and its related developments with suspicion, and delay its final decision on entry. It would appear that the other EMS members no longer feel that UK membership is a critical condition. The Delors Report could be interpreted as a decision by the other member countries to prepare progress plans for later stages of greater integration and possibly, ultimately, a common currency – with or without the UK. While entry is by no means a clearcut decision the UK cannot, in its continuing absence, expect to influence and tailor both the current and the planned future developments of the EMS: the choice might well be to join within the fairly immediate future and have a voice in these developments, or to stay out and have little option but to accept what emerges. As late as June 1989 the UK government was still attempting to set (difficult) conditions for entry; it was far from clear how many of the other countries were still listening with more than half an ear . . .

SELF-ASSESSMENT QUESTION

Since this is the last chapter in the book, you deserve to have a break from the routine of slogging through the normal self-assessment questions and answers.

For a change, read your way through Extracts 11.4, 11.5, 11.6, 11.7 and 11.8. These all discuss various aspects of current developments in the EMS and the possible implications which they might have for the British decision on full membership.

Make up your own list of arguments for full membership. Make up a counter-list of arguments against membership, or points on which you would like more information. Then sit down and study your list.

What would *you* do?

No attempt has been made to provide you with a 'model solution'. In fact there may not be one for this most contentious of issues. You have covered all the basics which you need. You have more than enough relevant information on the topic (in the text as well as in these final extracts). You have been told often enough that there may not be a clearcut decision available on major debating issues – that's why there is a debate!

Get out there and try to swim on your own! Good luck – and remember, if you want to be an economist, you will have to develop as many hands as possible . . .

Extract 11.5 THE ECONOMIST 24 JUNE 1989.

EUROPEAN MONETARY UNION
From A to EMU

At their summit in Madrid on June 26th Europe's leaders will discuss the Delors report. Its vision of monetary union has been called both an unmissable opportunity and an accident waiting to happen. Which is it?

IN HIS excellent series of Reith lectures four years ago, Mr David Henderson, the chief economist at the OECD, decried an attitude of mind that blights many debates in economics. He called it Micawberism, after the celebrated dictum:

> Annual income twenty pounds, annual expenditure nineteen pounds nineteen and six, result happiness. Annual income twenty pounds, annual expenditure twenty pounds ought and six, result misery.

The habit of seeing issues as all or nothing is to blame for many of the mistakes that governments make in their economic policy. The present debate on European monetary union is already a classic case.

Many proponents of monetary union seem to think that a single European currency —the monnet, as this newspaper said it ought to be called —would by itself create a future of faster growth and lower inflation. Without it, they say, Europe will soon face more ups and downs in its interest rates and exchange rates, more stockmarket crashes, more recessions. Doubters talk of equal calamities if EMU happens. Governments would have to surrender monetary policy as a tool for managing their economies, condemning many parts of Europe to accelerating decline. The monnet would undermine the Community's political institutions, shifting sovereignty to a remote bureaucracy which lacks accountability.

The truth is much less stark. Monetary union in Europe is capable of being good, bad or indifferent. All depends on precisely how it is done. So far, one vision of what it must mean has dominated the discussion. This is the vision described in the recent report by the committee of central bankers and others chaired by Mr Jacques Delors, the president of the European Commission. The report will be debated by the Community's leaders at next week's European summit in Madrid. The questions it should have asked but didn't should be too.

The Delors vision, ultimately, is of a United States of Europe. Yet the committee's starting point was merely that the EEC aims to become a single market for goods and services by 1992 —that "in adopting the Single Act, the member states of the Community confirmed the objective of progressive realisation of economic and monetary union." The report did not bother to ask whether (its version of) monetary union was desirable. The committee has simply planned the transition. Governments would decide when, if ever, to go ahead.

Remarkably, those governments have produced no proper study of whether monetary union might actually be desirable—or, equally important, what form it might take. And for the moment they seem to have no intention of doing so. It seems odd to work out the details of a complicated journey without deciding whether or even where you want to go. It makes sense, in fact, only if you have no choice of destination, or if you expect the journey to prove so tiresome that you will be staying at home regardless. Roughly, these are indeed the views of the main pro- and anti-EMU camps. They are Micawberist in the extreme.

The refusal to tackle the first questions first—why is any sort of monetary reform needed, and what shape should it take? —has had one especially bad result. Enthusiasts for the Delors vision have formed an alliance with their enemies, the opponents of any sort of monetary union. Both argue that a single currency for Europe and a federal system of European government are necessary partners. The Delors lot thinks this proves the case for monetary union. The other lot thinks it refutes it. They are both ignoring a plausible vision of EMU that has nothing whatever to do with a United States of Europe.

The trouble with staying put

Why meddle with the European Monetary System at all? Mr Delors and many on his committee see reform less as a pressing need than as a matter of historical destiny. Their report looks back to an earlier plan for economic and monetary union (the Werner report of 1970), to the creation of the currency "snake" in 1972, the European Monetary Co-operation Fund in 1973, the EMS in 1979 and the signing of the Single Act in 1986; and then it gazes forwards, to 1992 and beyond. Europe's destiny is to move towards economic and monetary union. It is time to take another step.

Those unimpressed by irresistible historical forces might reply as follows. Yes, the EMS has worked well—better than many sceptics predicted in 1979. The system's full members have enjoyed greater exchange-rate stability than outsiders, and they have seen their inflation rates converge towards that of West Germany, whose low rate has acted as the anchor for the rest. It has all gone very well. So let's not press its luck.

One way for the system to press its luck is to admit new members. Just this week, Spain added the peseta to the eight currencies already there. Britain, Greece and Portugal are the three members of the EEC which are not yet full participants in the EMS. Broadening the membership, however, looks a small risk next to trying to peg the currencies more rigidly. Yet presumably that must be the next step if the system is to evolve towards EMU. A fully fixed system would eliminate the bands within which the currencies are allowed to fluctuate. Monetary union would then go one step further by adopting a single currency.

Greater fixity has drawbacks. It would put an added strain on traditional "weak-currency" countries such as France and Italy. They have used occasional realignments (that is, devaluations of the franc and lira against the D-mark) to maintain their international competitiveness. Without those realignments, they would have had to keep domestic costs and prices under tighter control to stay competitive at their EMS exchange rates. That would have been politically as well as economically difficult. This worry becomes all the greater if the three remaining outsiders, all high-inflation countries by EMS standards, are to be let in. A more rigid EMS might then simply snap. That is the case for leaving well alone.

When capital flows free

It would be a fair case—except for what happens in 1990. Most of Europe's governments have already committed themselves to removing their remaining controls on capital flows next summer. Hitherto, France and Italy have relied on capital controls as well as realignments to make life in the EMS tolerable. The controls matter most when an imminent realignment is expected by the financial markets. To persuade holders of a currency that might be devalued to hang on to it, a rise in interest rates is needed; sometimes this rise might have to be extremely steep. But if capital controls prevent holders switching out, a smaller rise will do.

Recently Italy and Spain (which had been shadowing the EMS for months) have used capital controls in the opposite way: to keep capital out. Their interest rates have been high for domestic reasons. Without controls their governments would have had to choose one of two courses. Either let their currencies appreciate, which would have broken the EMS-link that they were anxious to preserve; or cut interest rates, and see their domestic demand and their current-account deficits rise. Perhaps that sounds familiar. Britain, which has no capital controls, faced the same dilemma last year. To continue shadowing the D-mark the Treasury was forced to cut interest rates, with regrettable results.

Capital controls have been so important to the EMS that it is a mistake to assume that governments will, in the end, get rid of them—despite the undoubted microeconomic damage that they cause. (Sir Alan Walters, Mrs Thatcher's economic adviser, objects to the EMS partly because it makes capital controls harder to get rid of. He sees this as a high price to pay for the benefits—in any case dubious, he would say—of exchange-rate stability.) But suppose that governments keep their promise and abolish the remaining controls. Suppose too that they do not find subtle ways to sneak them back (eg, by tightening the "prudential" rules that many of them place on the foreign investments of their savings institutions). What then?

The answer is: substantially more volatility in interest rates than the EMS has been used to, and a greater risk of speculative runs on the weak currencies. Steps can be taken (and have been already) to lessen these dangers. Realignments can be managed, for example, so that the bands move without causing discrete jumps in exchange rates. This avoids the one-way bets that the markets love. And arrangements for better co-operation over foreign-currency reserves have given central banks a bigger gun to point at

The missing middle

If capital is going to flow more freely in Europe it seems likely that the EMS cannot stay where it is. Economics will nudge it forward or back. The Delors report should have stressed this, but didn't. Moving back would mean a less rigid system with broader currency bands. This would accommodate the new economic strains—in effect by sharing them between interest-rate volatility and somewhat greater exchange-rate flexibility. But that would also be the cost. The EMS would be less good at what it was set up for in the first place: keeping currencies stable.

The alternative is to move to a more rigid system. Instead of accommodating the strains, this approach aims to reduce them at source. Recall that capital controls tend to look necessary when interest rates are set to move sharply, and that happens when exchange rates are about to jump. In a flexible system, exchange rates move fairly freely to and fro. They rarely jump, because the stress caused by differences in inflation rates does not get bottled up. In a somewhat more rigid system like the EMS, stress does get bottled up but it can be released from time to time in a realignment. Currencies are therefore sometimes expected to jump. That is the source of the trouble.

In a fully rigid system currencies cannot jump. This solves the problem of financial-market volatility—but it leaves the question of how countries deal with persistent differences in inflation rates. The answer, or the hope, is that the stricter framework of exchange-rate discipline will itself eliminate these differences. A rigid exchange-rate system therefore has to do two things. First, the part that looks easy to begin with, peg exchange rates. Second, the hard part, achieve a more-or-less common inflation rate.

A fully-fixed exchange-rate system (such as the gold standard of the nineteenth century) is capable of doing both. It works because governments are forced, in effect, to make monetary policy the servant of an automatic mechanism for settling international payments. With exchange rates permanently fixed, international competition between producers should then bring the prices of traded goods into line. If, repeat if, this process of competition does its job, the loss of monetary policy in its usual role is of no concern.

If governments want to go in for stabilisation policy (or to assist their depressed regions) they still have taxes, spending and budget deficits. All they can no longer do is aim for an inflation rate different from their partners'. Provided the system as a whole is anchored to low inflation, with a peg to gold or to a low-inflation currency, monetary policy should not be missed.

A currency union has further advantages. The competition that is needed to bring prices into line—and without which exchange-rate changes might sometimes be useful as an economic lubricator—would work more powerfully. (Volkswagen would find it harder to charge different prices in its various European markets if they had to be quoted in the same currency.) The possibility of a currency realignment would be even more remote than under a gold or other standard, because it could be done only by creating a new currency to realign. This too would increase the power of competition to hold prices in line.

There would also be a big saving in transaction costs. The story goes that somebody setting out from Britain with £1,000 to visit each of the EEC countries, changing his money into local currency every time but buying nothing, would arrive back with only £500. Monetary union would be such a blessing to people like that. And to everybody else. To judge the microeconomic benefits, simply ask whether America would be better off with separate currencies for each of its states.

The rub

The analogy raises a bigger question than it answers. Does a monetary union have to be a political and economic union, too? The answer is no. A wider-ranging union might be desirable in its own right, as Mr Delors would argue, but a narrower union is perfectly feasible. There could be two main reasons to think otherwise. One is the need to make the central monetary authority politically accountable. The other is the need for a Community-wide tax-and-benefits policy (of the sort that channels resources automatically across America, from prosperous states to poor). Consider each in turn.

In a monetary union the design of the central authority is crucial. It must be the anchor against inflation that gold was in the gold standard and the D-mark is in the present EMS. An EMU under a badly run European central bank would be much worse than the EMS under the well-run Bundesbank. In setting up the new central bank a balance would have to be struck between accountability and independence.

The Delors report suggests a central-bank board (with members appointed by the European council of ministers) and a central-bank council (comprising governors of the existing central banks plus members of the board). The council would be responsible for the broad formulation of monetary policy, and the board (and its staff) for its execution. The council would submit annual reports to the European parliament and to the council of ministers, and its chairman could be "invited" to report at other times. The independence of the council would be bolstered by giving its members security of tenure.

All this seems workable. Fears that the European central bank would be too soft on inflation—ie, that it would not be the Bundesbank—are almost certainly overdone. Central bankers, given a measure of independence, are capable of being a lot tougher than the politicians who first appointed them might wish—as, from time to time, the Bundesbank and America's Federal Reserve have both shown.

Which leaves the trickier question of fiscal policy. Suppose a country in the union is hit by a temporary economic shock that makes its products less competitive, and that market forces are too weak to drive its prices quickly down in response. Demand will fall and the country may sink into a recession. It cannot use monetary policy to restore demand. It can, however, use fiscal policy. If the government spends more than it collects in taxes, borrowing the difference, it can cushion the fall in private demand.

The Delors report says that EMU members would have to set "binding limits" on each other's fiscal deficits. If that were true, a bigger Community-wide fiscal system such as Mr Delors wants anyway might indeed be necessary. But it is not true. The report offers no reason for limiting fiscal policies except "convergence" as an end in itself. The proper use of fiscal policy is as a shock absorber. A monetary union can be upset by economic shocks that affect its members to differing degrees. In just such circumstances it makes sense for national budget balances to differ, perhaps greatly. The only reason for wishing to tie them down would be to strengthen the case for a bigger Community budget.

Nationally determined budget deficits will have to be financed. But a monetary union, far from making that difficult, would facilitate it. In making their borrowing decisions, governments would see an advantage and a disadvantage as compared with now—but both factors would be working in the taxpayers' interest.

The advantage is that an increase in borrowing would drive interest rates up by less. That is because investors would incur no currency risk in lending the cash. Within a monetary union, differences in interest rates would reflect the market's view of the borrowers' creditworthiness—and nothing else. Unless a government borrowed recklessly, it could therefore expect to borrow comparatively cheaply. The disadvantage, as governments would see it, is that they could no longer fall back on inflation as the emergency cure for past overborrowing. For both reasons, they would be likely to approach their borrowing decisions more as private companies do.

The implication is that Mr Delors's "binding limits" on national fiscal policy are not just unnecessary but undesirable. A new and more elaborate Community-wide fiscal policy may still make sense, but this can be judged on its merits. There is no need for it—and its associated political difficulties—to veto the narrow vision of monetary union. The monnet can take it or leave it.

There are thus two visions of what EMU might mean. A broad economic and political union that would be a conscious stride towards a United States of Europe. Or a narrow currency union demanding the minimum transfer of sovereignty—a gold standard for the 1990s and beyond. The second ought to commend itself to the gritty realists who question the merits of European federalism, or fear Brussels the harmoniser, or have no time for the "social dimension". But it should also appeal to the idealists who want the EEC to expand as widely as possible—a genuinely single market ready to embrace any country willing to join on those terms. Reform of some sort is coming to Europe's monetary arrangements. It is high time that ministers on both sides of the present debate started taking this second course seriously.

Reprinted with permission from *The Economist* 24 June 1989 © *The Economist*.

Extract 11.6 FINANCIAL TIMES 20 APRIL 1989.

THE CASE FOR EMS DESPITE DELORS

The case for eventual European monetary union — and *a fortiori* British membership of the existing European Monetary System — is too strong to be put in jeopardy by the unholy mixture of central bankers' and central planners' ideas that make up the Delors Report. So if any reader is in the least bit of a hurry, may I beg him to jump straight to the political conclusions at the end of the article.

* * *

THE BEST parts of the Delors Report are, as one would expect, the setting out by the monetary experts of the three stages towards monetary union.

The first is the strengthening of the existing Central Bankers' Committee. This will involve an attempt to work out agreed, although not identical, monetary guidelines for member countries, all of whom would join the Exchange Rate Mechanism. The exchange rate bands would remain as they are, although there would be an attempt to minimise realignments.

The second and third stages lead on to the permanent fixing of EMS parities and the establishment of a European central banking institution. No timetable is even suggested for these later stages.

But one obvious mistake is the attempt to force governments into acceptance of all three stages now in principle, including the need to amend the Rome Treaty.

After the first stage two decisions will be required (not necessarily at the same time). They are:
- Whether to stay with an improved Bretton Woods type system, as the EMS is at present, or move to monetary union with permanently fixed exchange rates.
- If the latter, whether permanently fixed rates between national currencies — as occurred under the gold standard, and which Professor Ronald McKinnon advocates today — will do: or whether it really is necessary to move to a Federal Reserve type single currency and central bank. (The distinction is blurred by the Committee.)

The Delors mistake is to prejudge both issues now, when the answers, especially to the second question, are still genuinely uncertain.

The underlying error of principle in the report goes much deeper. It lies in its search for so-called economic policies, which it would like to co-ordinate. The Committee members are, however, looking in a dark room for a black cat which is not there.

Often in talking to Continental central bankers I have been told: "We have discussed monetary policy. Shouldn't we now move on to economic policy?"

It soon became clear that these distinguished gentlemen meant none of the mundane, but vital, aspects of micro-economic policy. What they mean by economic policy is fiscal policy. In other words they have rediscovered the most dubious aspects of Anglo-American economics of the 1960s and early 1970s: namely the upward or downward manipulation of budget surpluses in the supposed interest of demand management or fine tuning.

The report is full of these fossils. We are told that Community governments must agree on an overall budgetary stance, with specific objectives for each country and surveillance to make sure they do as they are told. And just to make doubly sure, governments are to be discouraged from borrowing not merely from central banks, which is reasonable enough, but in non-EC currencies at all. Some of the suggested restrictions could leave national governments with less fiscal discretion than regional authorities in the US or Germany.

Of course, these fiscal claims paper over huge chasms between the Keynesian expansionists who want to add to budget deficits and fiscal conservatives who want to reduce them. But central bankers fall for this bait because they are looking for something that will reduce to so-called "load on monetary policy." Like most humans they believe that they are being expected to do too much and that others should bear more of the burden.

It is not being asserted here that fiscal policy has no effect. Merely that there has never been less agreement than today on what that effect is or which rules should govern its application. It is only because of the lack of substantive economic discussion in the report — not even any charts or tables — that these divergences can be papered over.

The objections to the Delors line go further. There is a positive advantage in countries experimenting with different fiscal policies and leaving it to the financial markets (with the aid of credit rating agencies) to impose their own disciplines if anyone goes too far.

All that is desirable or feasible on the fiscal side is occasional consultation, if it is felt that the combined borrowing of Community countries is exerting too great an upward pressure on world or Community real interest rates. It scarcely needs a treaty amendment to do that.

The other supposed economic policy requiring parallelism is on the regional side. Here Delors is much vaguer and simply asserts without evidence that the removal of economic barriers is likely to hurt the peripheral regions, leaving the reader guilty, uncomfortable and in a mood to dip into his purse.

The time has arrived to call the regional bluff. It is individuals rather than regions who are poor, suffer or deserve help. There is no principle of human dignity that dictates equality of average living standards in geographical areas.

The processes by which regions flourish or decline are subtle ones. So are individual adaptations to them. All too often the effect of so-called regional policies is to establish cathedrals in the desert or to enable local politicians to reward supporters with succulent contracts.

* * *

The basic political economy of the EMS is easier to understand without Delors. It has been a semi-fixed exchange rate area based on the D-mark. The role of exchange controls in the arrangement has diminished, is diminishing and will diminish further. It will certainly survive without them.

Because some countries, historically prone to inflation, have been prepared to tie their currencies to the German one, their inflation has come down to a rate well below the British one. The most obvious of such countries is France, which has adopted a monetarist policy towards inflation (whatever the rhetoric), but a monetarism based on the exchange rate. A less well-known example is that of Ireland, which has been following a similar course since its 1986 realignment and now has an inflation rate down to 2½ per cent. (This has been pointed by Dr David Lomax in a trenchant but non-dogmatic article in the National Westminster International Review.)

Of course it would be possible to bring down the British inflation rate further with sufficiently draconian monetary policies even if the EMS had not been invented. The question is: at what price?

It just so happens that the credibility of a government's counter-inflationary resolve is much greater if it is seen to be linking its currency to a hard money country, than if it plays around with alternative monetary targets each of which has its fervent and mutually irreconcilable adherents. And when credibility is low, the cost in terms of lost output and employment is high. The fact that even under a leader with as strong an anti-inflationary persona as Mrs Thatcher the underlying British inflation rate is now 5½ to 6 per cent, should give one pause before expecting too much from the domestic route.

The UK faces two alternatives after Delors. It can join the Exchange Rate Mechanism of the EMS and accept stage one of the Committee's proposals, while reserving its position on all further stages and on treaty amendments. This would put Britain in the same position as other members, who are not about to abandon their own currencies or control over their own budgets. Britain would then have a very strong influence over future developments and would in practice be able to veto the common currency idea if it came onto the agenda this century. Such a course would be in keeping with the known convictions on monetary substance of the Chancellor, Foreign Secretary, Bank of England Governor and other British ministers and officials.

Alternatively Britain can stay out of the EMS and allow the first stage of Delors to go ahead without it. It will then lose all influence on further developments. Sterling would be quite likely to be thrown out of the Ecu basket; and in any case the two-speed Europe will be here. Domestically British policy will be left floundering without any external anchor for monetary policy; and if any country needs such an anchor it is surely the UK. There will be no more talk of a British supply-side miracle: and we will be back to recriminations over the trade figures and inflation rate.

One final point, British die-hard opponents of the development of the Community such as the Bruges group are just throwing in the towel. They are leaving the future of Europe — the birthplace of liberal economic as well as political thinking — to the corporatists and *dirigistes*, while basking in a self-righteousness unjustified by their own record. It is surely time to form a group of Free Marketeers for a United Europe.

Reprinted with permission from *Financial Times* 20 April 1989 © *Financial Times*.

Extract 11.7 THE INDEPENDENT 27 JUNE 1989.

EMS MEMBERSHIP COULD LEAD TO LOWER INTEREST RATES

LOWER interest rates and a reduced likelihood of surcharges on European holidays are two possible results of the UK joining the exchange rate mechanism of the EMS, *writes Peter Wilson-Smith*.

Interest rates could go down because, once fully part of the EMS, increased confidence in the pound would lead to an inflow of money from abroad and, in order to prevent sterling rising, UK interest rates would have to fall. This is much what has happened to the Spanish peseta since it recently went into the exchange rate mechanism.

The reason why EMS membership might affect holiday surcharges is that sterling should remain more stable against other European currencies.

There would still be the possibility of its rate changing against other European currencies but it would be less likely. The impact of European monetary union would be more far-reaching and permanent than EMS membership.

Monetary union would eventually involve the abolition of national currencies within the EC. There would then be no need to buy foreign currency for holidays within Europe.

Reprinted with permission from *The Independent* 27 June 1989 © *The Independent*.

Extract 11.8 FINANCIAL TIMES 19 JUNE 1989.

DISCIPLINE FOR AN OVER-STRONG PESETA

Peter Bruce on Spain's decision to plump for full membership of the EMS

When Mr Felipe Gonzalez, the Spanish Prime Minister, meets Mrs Margaret Thatcher, his British opposite number, in London today, the talks will take place a few hours after the peseta officially joins the exchange rate mechanism of the European Monetary System (EMS).

The snap decision to join — taken by the Spanish Cabinet on Friday — leaves sterling as the only major EC currency still not a full EMS member. (The Greek drachma and the Portuguese escudo are also outside the exchange rate mechanism.)

Within the Madrid EC summit that ends Spain's presidency of the Community just a week away, Mr Gonzalez's message to London could hardly be less subtle — Britain should drop its objections to the recent Delors report supporting European monetary union and join the exchange rate mechanism soon.

Mr Gonzalez is not a bombastic man, though, and he will not be pounding any tables. As much as he wants to end Spain's EC presidency with a flourish — unanimous agreement to enter phase one of the Delors recommendations on July 1 next year and an implied commitment to follow through to total monetary union — he is already partly resigned to the likelihood that Mrs Thatcher will refuse. (The Delors report says all EC currencies should be full EMS members before the start of phase one.)

But Mr Gonzalez and some other EC leaders are beginning not to care that much about what Mrs Thatcher does. At an informal EC Finance Ministers' meeting on the Costa Brava last month, it was being quietly suggested that, if the UK refused to start phase one next year, then ways would have to be found to proceed without it.

Spanish membership of the exchange rate mechanism — it joins at Pta 65 to the D-Mark, and, like the Italian lira, will be allowed to fluctuate in a generous 6 per cent band — has come remarkably quickly. Less than two weeks ago, Mr Carlos Solchaga, the Finance Minister, promised a gathering of bankers in Madrid Spain would join before July 1 next year, but hardly anyone expected a decision so soon. Even more striking was the Government's ability to keep its intentions secret.

The move, although it will strengthen Mr Gonzalez's case when he presses Mrs Thatcher to take the pound into the EMS today, was made primarily for domestic reasons:

• May inflation figures published just before Friday's Cabinet meeting were the best so far this year — 0.1 per cent — an enormous boost for a government which has been forced to abandon its ambitious 3 per cent inflation target for 1989 and which is now facing price rises of around 6 per cent for the year. Its efforts to stop runaway consumer spending have driven up interest rates and subsequent speculation has strengthened the peseta to an uncomfortable degree. In the past few weeks, however, the currency has begun a welcome decline and closed in Madrid at Pta 64.39 to the D-Mark before the EMS announcement.

• Mr Gonzalez, in his seventh year in power and facing a general election in June, 1990 at the latest, appears to have won a big vote of confidence in the European elections last Thursday. Normally reliable exit polls say his Socialist Party won 38 per cent of the votes, just one percentage point down on the last European poll in 1987. His two main right-wing opponents — Mr Manuel Fraga's Partido Popular, and the Centro Democratico y Social headed by the former Prime Minister Mr Adolfo Suarez — lost more and failed lamentably to capitalise on the Government's rift with Spain's trade unions and its troubles with inflation.

Now Mr Gonzalez is gambling his anti-inflation policies and Spain's economic growth by accepting full membership of the EMS. Reaction from Spanish business has been swift and enthusiastic, despite some carping by a wounded opposition.

"It was a very courageous decision," said Mr Manuel Soto of Arthur Andersen, who is a pillar of Spain's business establishment. "It is a reflection of the Government's commitment to fight inflation and to establish a new challenge for Spanish society, which will have to accept the discipline of the EMS."

"Although it might create some difficulty, EMS membership will remind us that we are not alone in Europe. We will have to abide by the rules."

No one, in all probability, was happier about the Government's move than Mr Mariano Rubio, the Governor of the Bank of Spain, who has been beating the EMS drum for nearly two years. With the Government hesitant about cutting its spending or raising taxes, he has had the thankless task of increasing interest rates every time Spain's economic boom has threatened to run out of control.

Two years ago, it was costing Spaniards more than 20 per cent to borrow money. The official rate fell to nearly 10 per cent last summer, but has since risen to almost 15 per cent again.

Taking the peseta fully into the EMS now — with prices rising, tourist receipts falling, and the trade balance so bad that the current account deficit will more than double this year to £8bn. or 2 per cent of Gross Domestic Product — is a risky business.

Trade union pressure for increased social spending will not go away, largely because union leaders know that the Government has a huge £42bn currency reserve cushion to fall back on.

By submitting to the discipline of full EMS membership now, the Prime Minister is betraying either a reckless Spanish machismo or another local trait which recently led one long-resident foreign banker to describe the Spaniards as the "Prussians of the Mediterranean."

The Government has not had an easy ride politically since the end of last summer. A one-day general strike on December 14 in protest at the conservative drift in economic policy brought the country to a standstill. Mr Gonzalez's refusal to meet subsequent union demands almost brought him to the brink of a panicky general election but his nerves have held.

In January, Mr Solchaga was forced to impose a fierce credit squeeze after it had become obvious that his 6 per cent inflation target for the year was implausible.

During the European election campaign, in which for the first time ever the Socialist trade union, the UGT, refused to support the Socialist Party, it looked as if Mr Gonzalez would shed votes quite heavily. But, apart from a tiny leakage to the Communists, nothing happened.

By placing the peseta in the EMS now, he is clearly signalling that Spain's period of complete reliance on monetary policy is at an end.

The 1990 budget will be tough. The Government has already shown some willingness to rein in its fiscal policies: last month it took Pta 250bn (£1.27bn) out of circulation by cutting ministerial budgets and raising and bringing forward corporate withholding taxes.

For a start, Mr Solchaga is going to have to find at least Pta 220bn to pay for a constitutional court ruling last December that has thrown Spanish tax collection into disarray this year. The court said married couples could no longer be forced to declare joint incomes. Because it has taken months to design a new tax regime, income tax declarations have been delayed six months until November, when married couples will be able to report separately, and, hence, move into lower tax brackets.

The affair will lose the Treasury about Pta 120bn in collectable taxes and at least another Pta 100bn in interest on revenues that have not yet been collected.

But Mr Gonzalez's political arithmetic will have told him that, if he was able to hold the Socialists' European vote last Thursday despite the bad political and economic omens, only a major blunder — and not mere belt-tightening — can stop him winning a third general election. He may even call one early, perhaps in November.

Spain's EC presidency has not been a glittering success, but the going gets tougher as 1992 approaches, and Madrid has brought the presidency's big issue — monetary union — to the point where only the obvious opponent, Britain, remains isolated.

No doubt, both that issue, and the equally contentious social charter, will come up in Mr Gonzalez's talks with Mrs Thatcher in London today. He is every bit as hard-working and energetic as she is, and he feeds off trouble. Picking his moment and then suddenly subjecting Spain's young and fragile economic success to the discipline of a body — the EMS — which he cannot fully control is typical of Mr Gonzalez. "It is better that everyone (business, unions, and foreign investors) knows the rules of the game," says Arthur Andersen's Mr Soto. And that is what Mr Gonzalez intends.

Reprinted with permission from *Financial Times* 19 June 1989 © *Financial Times*.

Solutions

CHAPTER 2

True/False

2.1. True; it can be measured either from final transactions or by computing the value added at each stage in the industries; the two totals should be equal.

2.2. True; they are included in gross domestic fixed capital formation, or investment, in the national accounts.

2.3. False; if it is a recognized form of economic activity, then its output or value added must be included.

Multiple choice

2.1. (d); if (a) did not exclude profit income, it would have provided an income based measure of GDP at factor cost.

2.2. (b); the calculation should include only transactions of final goods or alternatively the sum of the value added at each stage of the production process.

2.3. (b) and (f); in the national accounts the term investment covers fixed capital formation by public and private sectors; in the theoretical models used in the course, the analysis is simplified by relating the term solely to private section investment items.

2.4. (a); if prices have risen by 160%, then the price index would be 260 when GDP was £195.0 billion in 1980; 1980 GDP at 1975 prices would be approximately £195.0 billion × 100/260 = £75.0 billion; real output and income would have increased by approximately 9.6% over the period.

Exercises

2.1.

	(000 crowns)	
Consumers' expenditure		90
Gross fixed investment	32	
Stockbuilding	−5	27
General government consumption		29
Exports of goods and services	21	
Imports of goods and services	−18	3
GDP		149

2.2. Final goods transactions (000 doubloons)

Breadfruit	20
Timber exports	15
Houses	23
GDP	58

2.3. If income tax was raised, then this would increase the severity of the withdrawal from the income loop in Figure 2.2, and therefore reduce the income received by households. While this effect would probably be split between savings and consumption (that is, savings would also probably be reduced a little), it is probable that consumption expenditure would fall. At its simplest, this fall in expenditure would tend to cause GNP to fall a little (less income received by firms from their sale of output). At a more sophisticated level, the fall in consumption would also probably result in a drop in import purchases by consumers which should (if export sales remained at the same level) reduce the balance of trade deficit (exports less imports to the USA). This was one of the reasons behind the suggested change in taxation. At a still more sophisticated level, the overall increase in taxation receipts against unchanged government expenditure would also tend to reduce any fiscal deficit (government expenditure less government taxation receipts), which was another dimension of the suggestion.

. . . all of which goes to show that you don't need a degree in economics to make sense!

CHAPTER 3

True/False

3.1. True; while investment is assumed to have a constant level, the upward sloping consumption function will ensure this form of behaviour for imports.

3.2. False; the model is concerned with the generation of income from UK output; exports represent extra sales, or output, or income, and imports a loss of domestic output and income.

Multiple choice

3.1. (d); at equilibrium output is taken up by $C + I$: (b) and (f) apply to any income level, since income will either be consumed or saved.

3.2. (b); the consumption function will pivot downwards, likewise the $C^* + J$ function, forcing the income level to fall. This has been described as the 'paradox of thrift'; the paradox is that, as people attempt to save more, they will reduce consumption and, ultimately aggregate expenditure, which will reduce the equilibrium level of GDP, and therefore income, and therefore savings . . . despite the original intention to increase these!

3.3. (a); consumption will rise less than in proportion to the increase in income.

3.4. (a); it would fall less than in proportion.

3.5. (c); if $C = a + cY$ and $c = 0.6$, $a = 30$, then

$$C = 30 + 0.6(240)$$
$$= 174$$

3.6. (b); total savings will be the difference between income available and consumption, that is,

$$S = Y - C$$
$$= 240 - 174$$
$$= 66$$

Outline answer to exercise

Construct the complete model, and accompany the diagrams with a brief explanation of why the functions behave as shown, and how new equilibrium income emerges. This will improve your own understanding of the analysis. Only a brief outline of the main changes is given below; in most academic courses, you would be expected to illustrate each change in a separate model, and to expand a little on the brief answers given below; the latter are merely there to help you to check your own conclusions.

(a) Increase in business confidence will tend to raise investment; this would raise the J function to J_2; this would raise aggregate expenditure function to $C^*_1 + J_2$; this would increase equilibrium income to Y_2.

(b) If the proportion of new income allocated to import expenditure rises, this would reduce the slope of the C^* function to C^*_2, reducing aggregate expenditure function to $C^*_2 + J_1$ and equilibrium income to Y_2.
Note that, strictly the new C^* function should not be parallel to the old. This follows since:

$$M = mC = ma + mcY$$

If the value of m (the marginal propensity to import) rises, then both the intercept and the slope of the C^* function will be affected. At zero income $M = ma$ and with a larger value for m, consumption net of imports at zero income (i.e. the intercept for the C^* function) is reduced. Equally, at higher levels of Y, imports will be higher than before (via mcY), so that C net of imports will rise more slowly (that is, the slope of the C^* function will be reduced as will its position – reflecting the lower intercept).

(c) A decrease on G will reduce the total value of the J function to J_2. This will reduce the aggregate expenditure function to $C^*_1 + J_2$ and lower equilibrium income to Y_2.

CHAPTER 4

True/False

4.1. False: it is the sum of all the incomes received from all sources, less the taxation payments due on that.

4.2. False; they can change the time pattern of consumption and so raise or lower current consumption.

4.3. True; both expansion and contraction will be magnified by the multiplier process.

4.4. False (you should be shot if you got this one wrong!) The two-sector economy was used to simplify the example and the algebra; the principle is that any disturbance will trigger an adjustment process, which implies a whole new series of rounds of expenditure, during which a leakage steadily reduces the size of the flow. If you bring in the international trade sector, then X is an additional source of disturbance – and M an additional source of leakage. If you bring in the public sector, then G becomes another possible source of disturbance – and T an additional leakage. You simply wind up with more terms within your brackets (that is, the multiplicand), and more leakages within your multiplier formulation, which will reduce its size and strength.

Multiple choice

4.1. (c) and (e); to the extent that investment will reflect short-term credit rates for example, for stocks and inventories.

4.2. (e); the MPC affects the slope of the C function, which eliminates (a) and (b), that is, the functions will pivot upwards; this will move the intersection point to the right, eliminating (d). Draw the model and be certain that you agree.

4.3. (a) and (d); the value of the multiplier will be set, in a simple two-sector economy, by the value of the MPC (and therefore the slope of the consumption function), or the MPS (since $s = 1 - c$, then the multiplier formula can be restated as $1/s$). Draw the consumption and aggregate expenditure functions for large and small MPCs and observe the different effect of a given change in investment on the income level.

4.4. (c); if the *MPS* = 0.15, then the *MPC* = 0.85 (if 15% of additional income is saved then the balance of 85% must be available for consumption spending). This leaves the multiplier with a value of 6.67, and the increase in income is 6.67(100) = 667.

CHAPTER 5

True/False answers

5.1. False; even ignoring the effect of inflation, future sums are worth less than present sums given the normal pattern of time preference.

5.2. False; they must be discounted to the present values before being added.

5.3. True; their opportunity cost is what they could earn on the market.

5.4. False; that model only shows it to be constant and autonomous with respect to income, that is, influenced by factors other than income. If the interest rate rises, then the level of investment will fall in terms of the model shown in Figure 5.2; this will, in turn, cause a fall in the level of investment, as contained in the injection function of Figure 5.4.

'Fill in the blanks' answers

You should have something along the lines of the missing words as shown in the brackets below.

5.1. (The market rate of interest); this means that the funds allocated to the project will earn at least the market rate of return.

5.2. (Lower than); if the discount rate is reduced, it will raise the present values of the profit stream towards that of the capital outlay; the discount rate which equates the two is the IRR.

5.3. (The left, or downwards); (lower or reduce); this would follow from the downwards revision of the forecast profit stream for the projects available.

Exercise answer

See Table 5.9 on next page for the detailed calculations on the exercise.

(a) If cost of capital is 10%, both projects are viable, in the sense that they show a positive *NPV* at that rate of discount (X has a *NPV* of 60; Y a *NPV* of 41).

(b) Since capital costs differ between the two projects, the decision cannot be made from a straightforward comparison of *NPV* figures. You can answer by using either a profitability index, or IRR values.

The profitibility index approach:

Table 5.9 Estimation of internal rate of return for Project X and Project Y.

(a) Project X

Year	Profits	Discount factor 10%	PV profits	Discount factor 13%	PV profits	Discount factor 14%	PV profits
1	400	0.90909	364	0.88496	354	0.87719	351
2	300	0.82645	248	0.78315	235	0.76947	231
3	200	0.75131	150	0.69305	139	0.67497	135
4	100	0.68301	68	0.61332	61	0.59208	59
5	100	0.62092	62	0.54276	54	0.51937	52
6	50	0.56447	28	0.48032	24	0.45559	23
			920		867		851
	Capital outlay		860		860		860
	Net present value		60		7		−9

$$\text{IRR} = 13\% + \frac{7}{16} = 13.4\%$$

(b) Project Y

Year	Profits	Discount factor 10%	PV profits	Discount factor 12%	PV profits	Discount factor 11%	PV profits
1	200	0.90909	182	0.89286	179	0.90090	180
2	200	0.82645	165	0.79719	159	0.81162	162
3	200	0.75131	150	0.71178	142	0.73119	146
4	200	0.68301	137	0.63552	127	0.65873	132
5	200	0.62092	124	0.56743	113	0.59345	119
6	200	0.56447	113	0.50663	101	0.53464	107
			871		821		846
	Capital outlay		830		830		830
	Net present value		41		−9		16

$$\text{IRR} = 11\% + \frac{16}{25} = 11.6\%$$

$$X = \frac{PV \text{ profits}}{\text{capital outlay}} = \frac{920}{860} = 1.07$$

$$Y = \frac{PV \text{ profits}}{\text{capital outlay}} = \frac{871}{830} = 1.05$$

Thus, X is the better, or more profitable project. See below for the IRR values, which will confirm this result on relative profitability.

(c) The IRR values for the projects: these can be found by trial and error; Table 5.9 provides you with the necesary check for your calculations. From this, you will see that project X has an IRR value of 13.4% and project Y an IRR value of 11.6%. Both are viable at the 10% user cost of capital. The calculation confirms that project X is superior to project Y.

CHAPTER 6

True/false answers

6.1. False: but it is difficult to give a clearcut answer here. The demand for labour is a derived demand, so that it will reflect changes in the output level. However the link between output and any single input such as labour is not fixed (for example, it will be affected by changes in technology and in work practices), so that the level of employment does not reflect mechanically any fluctuations in output.

6.2. Broadly true: if output continues to become less labour intensive, for example as a result of technological change, then output must rise to support a given level of employment. However, in theory at least if labour becomes relatively less expensive than the input capital, this could result in a switch in production methods to substitute the relatively cheaper input of labour for capital.

6.3. False: the claim is based on a series of annual rates of change in GDP and is therefore also picking up the short-term influences of recovery from the severe depression phase of the business cycle. There are several reasons for believing that there has been a real improvement in our growth performance, but we need a longer series of GDP data to make any really convincing claim. After all, the figures for international rates of growth for the 1980s in Table 6.2 still show us to be the second weakest of the 11 countries in that table.

6.4. False (in the absence of an option which states 'partially true'!): it will also depend upon the quality of that investment and on the efficiency with which it has been used (both built into the term σ in the growth model in the text).

Multiple choice answers

6.1. (c) and (e); it is essential that distortions caused by changes in price and expenditure taxes are eliminated from the analysis so that only fluctuations in the real output level remain to be analysed.

6.2. Of the reasons stated, (b) will bring into effect the checks to growth in output posed by lead times and capacity constraints in the capital goods industry; (d) might cause a downward movement along the demand function for investment funds – but much would depend upon whether or not revisions upwards in business expectations might still move that function to the right. While (e) applies to any single disturbance, during the upswing there will be a whole series of these, for example, as investment (I) plans are revised upwards via the accelerator and/or growing business optimism.

6.3. (a) is not impossible, but loss of confidence is more likely to take place at a later stage in the recession; (b) will apply if accelerator type behaviour is reflected in the investment decision; (d) might also affect investment if it is felt to reduce the estimated present value of profits from potential investment projects, that is, again it could move the demand function for investment funds to the left. (c) and (e) are both nonsense suggestions – go back and revise the appropriate points if you have selected these!

Food for thought: points for consideration

Limitations of space have forced us to leave out a major section in the text which would have dealt with this topic. Obviously, economic growth does not only offer benefits; many senior and respected economists have drawn attention to a whole series of dubious, or simply worrying issues. Some of the main reservations are given below – and these by no means constitute an all-inclusive list.

Distribution of benefits
Growth need not imply prosperity for all; much will depend upon the pattern of distribution of the benefits among different groups in society. It is very possible that countries which have apparently successful records in terms of growth and prosperity, will still have the most appalling conditions for many subgroups within society, leaving them to live in abject poverty and squalor.

Finite resources
Growth implies a steady increase in the level of real output – which will also imply a steady increase in the demand for inputs to produce that output. But resources are finite in some cases; could we be ripping out scarce resources to provide inputs for our current selfish prosperity – then leaving depleted resources as the bill which must be paid by future generations?

Artificial demand
As we have argued several times in the text, growth in potential output is only possible if we can generate sufficient new sales to take up this output from the market. A massive marketing effort is therefore an essential element in any successful growth process. But how many of the goods which are produced are only trivial uses of our scarce resources? Do we really need to consume such high levels of particular products, or has our consumption been artificially stimulated, in order to generate sales?

Increase in demand
For sustained economic growth, demand as well as supply potential must grow. One of the main components in demand is replacement demand; if producers can speed up the replacement cycle, then they can increase total demand. For example, earlier 'white goods' such as electric cookers, refrigerators and washing machines were designed to have a life expectancy of between 10 and 12 years; 'technological improvements' have apparently resulted in a *shortening* of physical life

expectancy of such products – a five- to seven-year replacement cycle is now the norm. Whatever the reason, most of us have to buy two machines over 10 to 12 years when, previously, one old faithful was enough. 'Built-in obsolescence' has become a fact of life, and the whole replacement cycle is further speeded up by the increased importance of 'fashion' changes. It may increase demand, but how necessary is it, and what are its resource implications, as discussed earlier.

Pollution
Production involves not only output, but also pollution – whether in the form of noise, or dust, or occupational/industrial illness, or effluent, or waste products. Pollution costs are seen as 'external' to the business creating them, and are not included in the price of final output. Equally, the consumption of some products can itself create a major pollution hazard, for example, lead, noise, vibration damage and congestion time loss from the use of private cars. Once again, car users are not explicitly charged for any externalities which they impose on society. In effect, most goods are under-priced, and therefore demand is higher than it would be – if consumers had to pay for all the costs involved. But economic growth implies ever-increasing output levels which, in the present legislative environment, implies ever-increasing levels of pollution. Who carries these costs – and are they adequately compensated for doing so? Should we try to produce less (for example, cutting down on trivialities) and therefore pollute less? Should we impose a series of pollution taxes on polluters, increasing their costs, and their prices – and so damage their growth potential? There is a very major area of concern here.

Competition
Growth is competitive: you can only increase your sales of output if you either increase the size of the market (which would come under the artificial stimulation discussed above), or if you take customers from someone else's share of the market. In international trade terms, your export growth implies increasing import penetration of someone else's domestic markets, which could reduce the demand for their domestic output. If you are dealing with a developed economy, this could cause at least short-term stagnation and depression. If you are dealing with a developing country, you could damage its prospects for indigenous development; a common problem in such a country is that indigenous entrepreneurs tend to move into the easier and more lucrative opportunities offered by importing – which only increases the difficulties of developing a more balanced indigenous economic base. At best, economic growth can create fiercely competitive pressures; at worst, it can create real damage and intense hostility. In the real world, it is real blood which is spilled – and not just tomato ketchup . . .

An objective view
Before you think that we are arguing the case for retreating back into our caves as an economic society, our intention is simply to list the opposite views to the more normal enthusiasm for growth. It is not for nothing that economists are depicted as malformed, with not simply two but three or even four hands: on the one hand . . . and on the other . . . and still another . . . and even another. We try hard to be objective, and this forces us to be aware that there is seldom only a single point of view – and not even the luxury of a simple black and white case for and against. The real world is full of different shades of grey, and apologetic multi-handed economists – all to the intense irritation of politicians and any others who prefer to deal in simple black and white solutions.

Economic growth does offer the potential for real benefit. It also poses many problems, not all of which are open to compromise. All we ask is that you are aware of possible alternatives. With lots of training and clean living, you too could develop a third hand . . .

CHAPTER 7

True/false answers

7.1. True: there is a clear element of conflict between the two, since the higher the level of economic activity (and therefore employment) the greater are the inflationary pressures on prices. (See also Chapter 9, with particular reference to the Phillips relationship, and the NIARU.)

7.2. It was originally felt that the normal fluctuations in the cycle should result in an equal number of deficits and surpluses as depressions alternated with booms; thus the budget would balance over a series of years, although not necessarily in any single year of the period. In practice the statement has proved to be true: this reflects a series of problems discussed under the 'lessons of experience' heading in the chapter – not the least of which is the probability that policy makers will reflate more frequently and enthusiastically than they deflate; if so there will be a net deficit over time which must be financed from borrowing. The present 'neutral' fiscal stance of the government, allied to the benefits of the automatic stabilizers (as shown in Extract 7.3) would appear, from provisional figures, to have left the UK with a current fiscal surplus balance over 1987 and 1988 – an extremely rare occurrence in UK history!

7.3. False: consider your wrist smacked if you got this one wrong – but it is one of the most common theory errors in macroeconomics. A change in income (upwards or downwards) does *not* affect the position of the consumption function. It simply results in a movement along the existing consumption function (see Figure 7.2). If still unsure, revise Chapter 3 to see what factors do cause the position of the function to be revised.

7.4. False: because changes in taxation affect disposable income and, only through this, consumption expenditure, they will be subject to a savings leakage initially; this reduces their final multiplier effect relative to an increase in G (which goes directly into the multiplier process without any initial savings leakage). Government expenditure is therefore said to be more 'high powered', in the sense that it generates more income per pound than the 'weaker' taxation receipts.

Multiple choice answers

7.1. (b), (d) or (e), or some combination of these: if (b) is used it would lower both C and J functions; (d) would reduce the C function; (e) would reduce the J function.

7.2. (d): in contrast, any change in taxation can only affect expenditure through disposable income, so that it will involve a savings as well as a consumption decision. This leaves only a proportion of the initial change to go into the multiplier expansion process. You should recognize that (e) is quite wrong; after the initial round or disturbance, only income generated by ΔG during the expenditure rounds of the multiplier will be subject to savings and taxation leakages.

7.3. (c): in simple terms this follows from the different strengths or values of the respective multipliers; more formally, where k_g is the government expenditure and k_t the taxation multiplier, then

$$\Delta Y = k_g \times \Delta G - k_t \times \Delta T$$

Since $\Delta G = \Delta T$ can be rewritten as

$$\Delta Y = \Delta G(k_g - k_t)$$

$$= \Delta G \left(\frac{1}{1-c} - \frac{c}{1-c} \right)$$

$$= \Delta G \left(\frac{1-c}{1-c} \right)$$

$$= \Delta G$$

And, since G is a reduction, income will fall by this amount, not rise as stated in (e).

7.4. Not an easy one to think through, but (e) is the correct answer. If you introduce income tax, you add an extra leakage into the expenditure round by sucking back some of the increase in income. If you acknowledge that some people, in an expansion, will no longer collect unemployment benefit payments but will switch to earned income, then you must adjust the expansion in income by deducting these lost benefit payments from it (or, in a contraction, you must adjust the multiplier loss of income by adding the new income from those moving onto unemployment benefit); the effect, in either direction, is to reduce the size of the final change in income – it is an automatic stabilizer, remember. Therefore both adjustments will reduce the extent of multiplier impact, or the multiplier value. Since we are modifying the leakages during the expenditure rounds which are common to all multiplier adjustments, it does not matter whether the disturbance is triggered by changes in G, T or B, all multipliers will be equally affected . . . which rules out the various carrots dangled in (b), (c) and (d). (a) is only there to trap you if you have really fallen asleep; if you chose that one, stop, have a cup of coffee and take the dog for a walk. Alternatively, transfer from economics to marketing!

CHAPTER 8

True/false answers

8.1. True: really only notes and coins are under the direct control of the government through its central bank, the Bank of England. These items accounted for 14.1% of M1, 6.6% of M3, 4.1% of M4 and 4.0% of M5, as at September 1988 (the figures are drawn from Table 8.1, if you would like to check and work out the ratios for yourself).

8.2. True: since any cheques drawn in payment against agreed loan limits will be honoured by the banks, advances are one of the components of the money supply. If commercial banks (indeed if any financial intermediary) can create credit in this way they are also creating money.

8.3. False: it involves an adjustment within the items which make up the liquidity reserve and will have no significant net effect on the size of that reserve (since the net effect will reflect only any differences in the purchasing and selling prices of the bills concerned).

8.4. True: the exclusion from the text of the international trade sector (in fiscal as well as monetary policy) omits some important links between internal and external policy. Lower UK interest rates could cause international funds to move from sterling and lower the exchange value of sterling. This in turn will affect the prices of UK exports and imports and the effect on trade flows will depend upon how sensitive to relative prices are the demands for each of them. Therefore the government in its monetary policy must always consider the international repercussions of its policy intentions and actions.

Multiple choice answers

8.1. (c) and (d): the banks can only create credit – they cannot create reserves and, to do the former, people and firms must be willing to borrow: in terms of (a), only Scottish commercial banks have a traditional and limited right to issue their own notes – and these must be convertible, on demand, to legal tender. (e) would be valid if the approach was taken that the maintenance of adequate liquidity was needed to attract deposit and permit profit maximization.

8.2. (a), (c) and (d): (a) is true if the D_m function does not change its position; but if the decrease in the money supply reduces the level of economic activity, the transactions and precautionary demands for money will also fall, moving the D_m function to the left; then the effect on the rate of interest will depend upon the relative magnitude of the two changes in the positions of the functions. (c) will be true if the demand for transaction and precautionary balances, and therefore the demand for money, are revised upwards. (d) is also true, since both the movement to the left of the D_m function and to the right of the S_m function, will tend to depress interest levels.

8.3. (a): if the reserve ratio is 25%, the credit multiplier is $1/0.25 = 4$; total deposits will therefore rise by £160 million of which £40 million will be accounted for by the initial increase in deposits from the injection. The possible increase in advances is therefore £120 million.

8.4. (d): with a reserve ratio of 33% the credit multiplier value would be $1/0.33 = 3.03$. As a result of the initial contraction of £21 million, advances would have to be reduced by £42.6 million (that is, total deposits would fall by £63.6 million).

8.5. (c): the effect of Bank purchases, when its cheques are paid in by commercial banks' customers is to raise balances at the Bank and permit a multiple expansion of credit. If households and firms were not prepared to take up the new credit opportunities available, so that the commercial banks were left with excess liquidity, then (d) could also apply, allowing them to increase the profitability of their asset deployment.

8.6. (a) and (c): while the increase in expenditure would raise income levels and therefore the demand for money, the net effect on interest rates of an increase in the supply of money would still normally be a reduction, so that (b) would represent only a partial offset. In the case of (d), if market prices of securities rose, yields would fall, placing downwards pressure on the rate of interest and stimulating investment. An increase in speculative balances would normally result from a fall in the rate of interest, so that again investment should be encouraged.

CHAPTER 9

True/false answers

9.1. False: normal changes in demand and supply conditions over time will be reflected in the relative prices of the goods concerned; for example, when a particular good is scarce, then its price will tend to rise – and, conversely, when there is an unwanted surplus (excluding all EEC butter mountains and wine lakes . . .) the price will normally be reduced to make the good more attractive to consumers, and so to stimulate demand. Zero inflation would simply mean that the overall index of prices (which is based on a weighted average of a sample of selected goods) would show no change, but it docs not rule out the normal flow o price adjustments of individual items either within the sample, or in goods and services in general.

9.2. False: it takes the *rate* of unemployment and uses this as an indicator of the strength of the demand for labour, and correlates this with the *rate of increase* which would result in money wages. The lower is the rate of unemployment then the greater is the pressure of the demand for labour, and the higher is the rate of increase in money wages which will result.

9.3. False: input costs can rise for reasons not associated with domestic demand levels – for instance, if world prices are rising or, again, if the government's energy policy is to raise the cost of non-oil energy forms into line with oil prices; these cost increases are not induced. At the same time, institutional pressures (for example union or workshop militancy) can result in wage claims continuing to exert pressure on prices even after demand for labour has eased. However, it was tempting to say 'Yes' here; *most* of the increases which take place in input prices are simply reflecting the demand pressures placed on input markets by excessive demand in the market for final output. The key word was 'all' . . . Never trust an economist bearing gifts, in the form of a plausible statement!

9.4. True: Friedman has argued that this is the case; given a relatively stable value for $\dot{V}$, any change in $\dot{M}$ will affect both $\dot{P}$ and $\dot{Q}$ but not necessarily equally and at the same time. Normally, he has suggested, the initial impact will be on $\dot{Q}$, then through this on $\dot{P}$; in the long run, $\dot{Q}$ is determined by factors other than the rate of growth in the money supply, so that $\dot{M}$ will affect only $\dot{P}$; in the long run, the initial gains in output and employment will be eroded by inflation.

Multiple choice answers

9.1. (b) is a possibility: if productivity gains from technology are sufficiently strong to absorb the increase in money wages, this might leave the S_A function of Figure 9.6 at the same position; (c) is what Keynesian inspired governments have frequently done in the past, that is, attempted to offset S_A movements by raising D_A to compensate – at least in the short run; but in an open economy, none of the reasons put forward provide a guarantee that employment levels will be unaffected: (e) is not sustainable in an open market economy where the demand for labour is derived from the demand for output.

450 *Understanding the Economy*

9.2. (d) and possibly (e): the former is discussed in detail in the text; the latter is described as the 'Pigou effect', after the economist of that name; however the real wealth effect is likely to be limited in reality – although it will still provide some deflationary impulse; (a) would probably result in an increase in expenditure as people converted money balances into real goods.

9.3. (b) and (e): Friedman's research suggests that (given a reasonably stable value for $\dot{V}$) any excessive increase in $\dot{M}$ will tend to impact more on $\dot{Q}$ in the short run; it will ultimately cause $\dot{P}$ to rise for final goods and inputs, which will normally erode the initial benefits to output and employment (which would eliminate (c)). This does not deny that $\dot{P}$ will also be affected in the short run, but as argued above $\dot{Q}$ will also be affected, which eliminates (d). At the extreme, if confidence is lost in the monetary unit, $\dot{V} > 0$ is possible, so that (a) might also apply.

9.4. (a): technically monetarists are sceptical of the real-world response of investment to the rate of interest, so that (b) would be more in keeping with Keynesian views on the impact of an increase in the money supply on expenditure; monetarists would also see (c) as a symptom of an overheated labour market, responding to demand pressure and a falling standard of living, both caused by the excessive increase in the money supply.

9.5. (e) would probably represent the fairest statement of Keynesian views; (a) is more of an introductory teaching model than a genuine policy option; (c) is closer to the monetarist view that wage bargaining in the UK is distorted by institutional influences; Keynesians would tend to argue for incomes policy constraint here, with a longer term attempt to improve information flows to and involvement in economic planning for the institutions; (d) is very much an over-statement of the Keynesian view of the role of government in a mixed economy.

9.6. (d) is again the fairest statement of the monetarist position, both for gradually reducing the rate of growth of the money supply to more reasonable levels and for establishing the longer term context of monetary and price stability; (b), (c) and (e) all represent convictions of lesser importance in the broader monetarist view that market forces should be relied upon to a greater extent, with government intervention, public sector spending and activity, and unionized bargaining all reduced in emphasis. However control of monetary growth is their key policy ingredient for dealing with inflation.

CHAPTER 10

True/false answers

10.1. False: Keynesians were well aware that the position of the aggregate supply function could be varied; in particular, if economic growth could be achieved, then this would move the aggregate supply function to the right – exactly as is claimed by supply-siders. Probably the main point of distinction was that Keynesians believed that aggregate demand would be *more* responsive to policy, and therefore tended to concentrate on this in their attempts to influence and control the economy. They would also have argued that aggregate supply would probably respond indirectly to increases in aggregate demand, so that consistent demand management would create conditions of prosperity and business confidence, which would tend to stimulate investment, aggregate supply and economic growth. Their only attempts to devise policies which were more directly 'supply-side' in their nature would have been the various taxation incentives and grants which were used to encourage investment, and their tentative attempts to develop manpower forecasting and training programmes (to remove the constraint of labour skill shortages on economic growth).

10.2. True: supply-side economics is simply one of the themes which reflect a disillusionment with state interventionist policy, and a rekindling of interest in the classical economists' belief in the efficiency of market forces. Supply-siders would argue that markets should be left free to the discipline of competitive pressure and the incentive of self-interest, to ensure that appropriate new opportunities are exploited, and existing production is kept as efficient as possible.

10.3. False: in the sense that it is only partially true! The argument put forward in the question applies only to the backward sloping section of the Laffer Curve, that is, where the tax rates lie above the threshold rate t^*, in terms of Figure 10.2. The problem is that no one can say where this threshold rate lies – so that a cut in tax rates could also result in a fall in government revenue from taxation, if the economy is operating on the more orthodox upwards sloping section of the curve below t^* (and this could well be a partial explanation of the continuing USA fiscal deficit, following the tax rate cuts of the Reagan administration).

10.4. True: taxes are levied on money income, which will tend to rise alongside the rate of inflation; as money incomes rise, and as people drift into higher income bands and are subject to higher marginal rates of tax, then the amount of tax which has to be paid will increase. Where money incomes were rising by just enough to keep real incomes constant during the inflation, the effect of the increased bite from tax could be to reduce net of tax real income, and so to reduce the incentive for additional effort.

10.5. True, at least in theory: in terms of the Quantity Theory model, any increase in the value of $\dot{Q}$ will ease the pressure on $\dot{P}$ for any given $\dot{M}$. In terms of the more familiar model shown in Figure 10.1, the increase in potential output (or economic growth) will move the aggregate supply function to the right, which will also help to reduce inflationary pressure. The problem is that, in practice, the tax cuts will also affect aggregate demand; if aggregate demand rises by more than aggregate supply, if only in the short run, then this could *create* fresh inflationary pressure for the economy . . .

Multiple choice answers

10.1. This is where we run into difficulties as we try to disentangle political slogans and public prejudices from economic theory! Only (d) can be argued with any conviction; competition between organizations and with new entrants, possibly, will bring about the pressures which should improve efficiency. (a) is a possibility, if efficiency is measured in terms of costs and profits, and the state monopoly redrafts its corporate objectives to reflect a more narrow set of commercial criteria than that under which many nationalized industries have been asked to operate in the past; but the current debate on the government's proposals for the National Health Service shows that there is a widespread fear that, despite apparent improvements in commercial efficiency, the actual quality of the range of services which are currently provided could be adversely affected. (b) sounds plausible, yet there is reason to suspect that distant shareholders can be kept at arm's length rather more easily than politicians and civil servants, provided that a satisfactory rate of return is earned by the new business. There is, at best, conflicting evidence to support cases for either (c) or (e), however dear they might be to your heart . . .

10.2. Sometimes we can be distinctly evil, and make all the choices correct, to some degree! (a) and (c) are the most obvious elements in terms of supply-side thinking (although remember that the chain between households and investment will normally pass through the increase in savings, which will be used by financial institutions to provide funds for investment purposes to borrowers from the firms' sector); (b) is a possibility if there is a surge in growth and prosperity; if there has been an element of 'crowding out' from excessive government expenditure, then (d) is also possible; only (e) is a little far fetched – yet heavy taxation does tend to drive some areas of activity underground, so tax cuts might just conceivably bring some ventures back to the surface, or at least keep them there on a marginal decision.

10.3. (c) is the option which has been identified as providing a distinct 'crowding out' effect, although much depends upon how the deficit is funded in financial markets. If the market rate of return exceeded the forecast return on investment, than a rational firm might well take the option outlined in (b) – but this would not correspond to the normal usage of the crowding out term. So far as (e) is concerned, the savings from low income groups are likely to be limited in any case, so that at full macro level, this would be unlikely to have any effect on the rate of interest. If you voted for (d), you should feel thoroughly ashamed of yourself; savings balances are channelled by financial intermediaries into usage as investment funds!

Index

accelerator
  and business cycles 156, 161
    in recession phase 163–5
  principle of 138–40
aggregate demand
  in fiscal policy 205–6
  and inflation 307
  and quantity theory of money 326
  and supply-side economics 345–6, 367
aggregate expenditure: *see* expenditure
aggregate supply
  and consumption 72–4
  and inflation 306, 311
  and quantity theory of money 326
  and supply-side economics 344–6, 367
  and tax cuts 357–8
agriculture, expenditure on 196–7
Ando 94
assets
  reserve 273–4
  UK banks 256–7
average propensity to consume (APC)
  and income 80–2, 94
  and savings 83, 85

balance of payments
  forecasts 60
  and international trade 392–401
  and OPEC oil price increases 167–8
  United Kingdom 415
balance of trade
  in fiscal policy 201–2
  and inflation 324
  in international trade 379, 394–5
  and money supply 330–1

  see also exports
balanced budget theorem 214–15
Bank of England 234, 256–7, 258
  and commercial banks 264–5
  hire purchase credit 275–6
  and inflationary gap 303
  and international trade 401
  as lender of last resort 264
  minimum lending rate (MLR) 265
  monetary management 276
  and monetary policy 263–5
  open market operations 269–72
  reserve ratios 272–4
  special deposits 274–5
  supplementary 275
banking sector 235
banks
  balances (UK) 256
  central 234
    and monetary policy 263–5
  commercial 235
    and Bank of England 264–5
  equity of 256–7
  merchant 235
  and money creation 255–63
  reserve assets of 273–4
  reserve ratios of 273–4
barriers to entry in transport 353
Belgium, growth of GDP 166–7
benefit payments
  in fiscal policy 215–16
  as flexible control 221–2
  ratchet principle of 222
big bang (1987) 235
black economy 28–9
bonds
  and liquidity reserves in open market operations 271–2
  and speculative demand for money 243–5

boom phase of business cycle 160, 161
borrowing: *see* credit
Boskin, Michael 344
bracket creep in taxation 351
British Airports Authority, privatized 354
British Gas, privatized 354
British Steel, privatized 354
Brumberg 94
building societies 235
business confidence and expectations for investment 129–31
business cycles
  and accelerator principle 156, 161, 163–4
  causes of 156–64
  damped 156–7
  defined 143–5
  depression in 153, 157
  and economic growth 146–9
    in UK 149–56
  explosive 156, 158
  managed 203–4
  recession 147, 150, 163–4
  recovery 159
  regular duration of 150

Cairncross, Sir Alec 57
Cambridge Economic Policy Group (CEPG) 220
Canada
  GDP
    forecasted (1985–9) 59
    growth of 164–5, 169
  money aggregates 254
capital
  formation 196–7
  fixed, and GDP 18–19, 22
  gains and losses 243–4
  international, in UK 180
  transfers 197
  UK banks 256

453

454 *Index*

capital account in international trade 393–4, 397–400
capital consumption and gross national product 18, 23–4
capital controls and European Monetary System (EMS) 416
capital markets and deregulation 353
capital stock
 assumptions of in macroeconomic model 37
 and capital:output ratio 138–40
 changes in and recovery 158
 and depression in business cycles 157
 and investment 104, 113, 115, 116
 optimum and economic growth 171–2
 in recession phase 164
 and volatility of investment 114–15
capital:output ratio 138–40
 and economic growth 171
 incremental (ICOR) 173–5
 and investment in economic recovery 159–60
 and role of tax cuts in supply-side economics 358
central banks: see banks
certificates of deposit (CD) 235–6
circular flow model
 of income 9–11, 16
 and money 234
 and multiplier effect 97
Clark, Colin 350
coach travel and deregulation 353
Coe, D.T. 316
commercial banks: see banks
comparative advantage in international trade 381
competition
 enhancement of in monetarism 352–7
 role in supply-side economics 347–52
Confederation of British Industry (CBI) and business expectations 127–8
consumer
 prices and index of inflation 291
 sovereignty 364
 spending forecasts 60
consumption 69–103
 behaviour, 'ratchet effect' of 93–4

 and credit 89–90
 and disposable income 85
 expenditure
  in fiscal policy 207–8
  imports as in macroeconomic model 45–6
  in macroeconomic model 37–9, 43
 and national savings 71–6
 factors affecting 85–93
 goods in measurement of economic activity 12
 and government expenditure 72
 and household wealth 91–3
 and income 76–82
  which year 93–5
 and multiplier 95–101
 and savings 71–6, 82–5
 and unemployment 90
continuing inflation 299
cost-push inflation 304–6, 308–11
costs, external and deregulation 363
credit
 bank and reserve ratios 272–4
 and consumption 89–90
 expansion of, in open market operations 269–70
 and hire purchase 275–6
 and money supply 258–9
 multiplier 261–2
 in recession phase 164
creeping inflation 296
crowding out effect in fiscal policy 226–7
currency
 over- or under-valued 404–6
 value of 14–15
current account
 deflation and monetary policy 418
 in international trade 394–5, 397
Customs and Excise duties 13

debt interest 189
debt interest (UK) 190
defence, expenditure on 196–7
deflation
 and monetary policy with floating exchange rates 417–18
 policies for and aggregate expenditure 168
delay: see time lag
Delors, Jacques 409, 414, 416
demand
 aggregate: see aggregate demand

 domestic, forecasted (1985–9) 58
 excess 300–1
demand management
 in fiscal policy 204–5
 stages of in fiscal policy 217–20
demand-induced inflation 308
demand-pull inflation 304
Denmark, growth of GDP 166–7, 169
Department of Trade and Industry (DTI) and business expectations 127–9
deposits of UK banks 256
depression
 in business cycles 153, 157
 in UK 169–70
deregulation and enhancement of competition 353, 363
discount houses 235
 and Bank of England 264–5
discounting 121–3
 defined 134–8
 rate of and internal rate of return 126
disposable income 85, 364–5
 and consumption 85
 and fiscal multipliers 210, 213
 in fiscal policy 207–8
Duesenberry 93
dynamic path analysis of business cycles 145

economic activity
 defined 5–8
 measurement of 8–16
 over time 144–6
economic forecasts in fiscal policy 217–20
economic growth
 and business cycles 143–6
 equilibrium rate of 179
 in fiscal policy 201–2
 and international trade 179, 378–9
 measurement of 146–9
 rates, comparison of 165–70
 theory of 170–80
 in UK 149–64
education, expenditure on 196–7
efficiency and supply-side economics 347–52
eligible liabilities of banks 273–4
employment, full, in fiscal policy 201–2
equilibrium
 defined 42
 level of income in macroeconomic model 41–4

Index 455

price in macroeconomic model   42
equity of banks   256–7
Eurocurrency markets   236
European Community, trade balance with UK   389–92
European Monetary Co-operation Fund   410
European Monetary System (EMS)
  benefits   413
  and exchange rates   403–4, 407, 413
  and international trade   410–17
exchange controls and international trade   397–9
exchange rate mechanism and European Monetary System (EMS)   410, 413–14
exchange rates
  defined   401–2
  and international trade   382–3, 401–14
  nominal and real   406–7
  in United Kingdom   52–4
expectations
  in boom phase   161
  changes in and investment   127–31
  and consumption   90
  in recession phase of business cycle   163
  role of in inflation   311–23, 334
expenditure
  aggregate
    and deflationary policies   168
    and GDP   131
  of consumption: *see* consumption
  domestic, by category   19, 21
  investment   104–39
    and GDP   19
  in measurement of economic activity   9–11
  and national accounts in fiscal policy   187–99
  retained output as   12
  on social security   196–7
exports
  in economic recovery   159
  forecasts   58, 60
  and GDP   18, 22, 377
  and international trade in macroeconomic model   45–7
  in macroeconomic model   37, 45
  in measurement of economic activity   11, 12–13

and money supply   330–1
and recession in UK   154
see also balance of trade

family expenditure survey (FES)   290
Feldstein, Martin   344
financial institutions/houses   235–6
  banks as   255
financial intermediaries   235–6
financial securities and speculative demand for money   243
firm sector
  and changes in money supply   330–1, 333
  economic activity of   8–12
  in macroeconomic model   40–1
fiscal deficits   168
fiscal deflation   209
fiscal multipliers   209–16
  and disposable income   210, 213
  and government expenditure   211
fiscal policy   185–232
  aggregate demand in   205–6
  benefit payments   215–16
  contra-cyclical   203–4
  crowding out effect   228–9
  defined   185–6
  and deflation with floating exchange rates   419–20
  and delays in   225–6
  discretionary controls   223
  and economic growth   201–2
  and expenditure in national accounts   187–99
  experience of   216–30
  Keynesian context of   201–4
  and Keynesian principles   216–17
  monetary repercussions in   229–30
  passivity in   202–3
  and politicians   227–8
  and reflation with fixed exchange rates   421–2
  and role of tax cuts in supply-side economics   357–8
  side effects of   228
  and stabilizers   223, 226
  timing   227
Fisher, Irving   326
fixed capital formation in GDP   19, 22
fixed exchange rates   403–4, 409
  reflation
    and fiscal policy   421–2
    and monetary policy   422–3

flexible control
  benefit payments as   221–2
  and fiscal policy   220–3
  government expenditure as   220–1
  taxation system as   222
floating exchange rates   402–3
  deflation
    and fiscal policy   419–20
    and monetary policy   417–18
forecasting, macroeconomic   54–64
fractional banking   258
France
  GDP
    forecasted (1985–9)   59
    growth of   166–7, 169
  international trade and economic growth   179
  money aggregates   254
Friedman, Milton   94, 318–20, 325–31, 333
full employment level of output   301

Gagliardi, F.   316
Galbraith, J.K.   364
Girobank   235
Goodhart's Law   277
government
  capital expenditure   190
  capital receipts   190
  and circular flow of income   11
  competition, enhancement of   352–7
  consumption, forecasted (1985–9)   58
  expenditure   13–14, 190
    and consumption   72
    and GDP   187
    international comparisons   188–9
    and taxation   196–7
  gross domestic fixed capital formation   187–90
  and inflation, prolonging of   314–15
  and interest rates and monetary policy   280–2
  investment   108
    expectations for   130–1
    international comparisons   110
    United Kingdom   107
  in macroeconomic model   48–51
  and money supply growth (1979–81)   118–19
  as monopsonist   348–51
  official statistics and national accounts   17, 20

456 Index

receipts 190
and supply-side economics
 345–6
and taxation
 in measurement of economic
  activity 13–14
 and supply-side economics
  348–9
and unemployment, reduction
 of 319–20
see also United Kingdom
government expenditure
 as flexible control in fiscal
  policy 220–1
 increase in 205
 in macroeconomic model 37
 multiplier 211
 and taxation
  in balanced budget theorem
   214
  cuts 213
grants 190
and expectations for
 investment 131
gross domestic fixed capital
 formation (GDFCF) 113,
 173
government share of 187–90
gross domestic product (GDP) 6
 and aggregate expenditure
  131
 and black economy 28–9
 in business cycles (UK) 149,
  152
 changes over time 26–7
 and consumption 91
  expenditure 72–5
 cyclical path of in business
  cycle 164
 decline in UK 153
 and economic growth 146–7
 and exchange rates (UK)
  53–4
 by expenditure category 18
 and exports 18, 22, 377
 at factor cost 18–19, 21, 23–4
 and fiscal multipliers 207–8
 fixed capital formation in 19,
  22
 forecasts 58–60
 and formal open markets
  27–8
 and government expenditure
  187
 growth of 109, 112–13
  rates of 166–9
 and imports 18, 22, 377–8
 by income category 19
 and inflation 301
 and international trade 397

in macroeconomic model
 45–7
and investment
 international comparisons
  110
 over time 113
 United Kingdom 107
in macroeconomic model 44
at market prices 21
and quantity theory of money
 326
and role of tax cuts in supply-
 side economics 358
in UK (1986) 50
gross investment: see investment
gross national product (GNP) 6
and black economy 28–9
and capital consumption 18,
 23–4
by expenditure category 18
at factor cost 18–19, 21, 23–4
and formal open markets 28
growth
 economic, annual rate of
  165–7
 of GDP 109, 112–13
 rates of
  in consumption 72–4
  in GDP 72–4
  and investment
   international
    comparisons 110
   United Kingdom 107
 razor edge of 179

health, expenditure on 196–7
Heath, Edward 363
Hicks, J.R. 156
hire purchase credit 275–6
household expenditure: see
 consumption
households/household sector
 and changes in money supply
  330–1, 333
 and disposable income 85
 economic activity of 8–12
 in macroeconomic model 41
 wealth, and consumption
  91–3
housing, expenditure on 196–7
hyper-inflation 299–300

import penetration of United
 Kingdom 388–90
imports
 and consumption expenditure
  72
 forecasts 58, 60
 and GDP 18, 22, 377–8
 and international trade in

macroeconomic model 45–7
in macroeconomic model 37,
 45
in measurement of economic
 activity 11, 12
and money supply 330–1
and recession in UK 154
income
 circular flow of 9–11, 16
 and consumption 76–82
 equilibrium level of
  in boom phase 161
  and changes 51–2
  in macroeconomic model
   41–4
 velocity and quantity theory
  of 326–30, 361
see also disposable income
income effect of taxation 364–5
income flow and measurement of
 economic activity 24–5
incremental capital:output ratio
 (IOCR) 173–5
induced cost-push inflation 310
industrial production, forecasted
 (1985–9) 58–9
inflation 287–342
 and balance of trade 324
 in boom phase of business
  cycle 160–1
 definition 290
 and exchange rate mechanism
  415
 and expectations, role of
  311–23, 334
 index of and consumer prices
  291
 and interest rates 324
 Keynesian view of 300–11
 learning curve effect of 313
 lower and recovery 158
 measurement of 289–95
 momentum of 298–9
 monetarist's view of 322–31
 and money, Keynesian view
  of 323–5
 policy correction, need for
  296–300
 and purchasing power 296
 and retrospective compensation
  in wage demands 313
 and supply-side economics
  346, 360–1, 367
 and taxation in supply-side
  economics 351–2
 and trade balance (UK) 385
 in UK (mid-1970s) 153–4
 unanticipated 313
see also continuing; creeping;
 demand-pull; demand-

Index

induced; hyper-inflation;
  wage-push
inflationary gap 302
informal economy: *see* black
  economy
inputs in measurement of
  economic activity 9
interbank markets 236
interest rates
  in boom phase of business
    cycle 160–1
  domestic and international
    capital 414
  equilibrium and demand and
    supply of money 247, 280–2
  and expectations for
    investment 129
  forecasts 60
  and investment 116–19, 119,
    132
  UK 132, 143
  and Keynesian view of money
    323–5
  lower, and recovery 158
  medium-term 266
  and monetary policy 279,
    280–2
  oil price increases 292
  and recession in UK 154
  reduction of
    in business cycles 144–5
    in open market operations
      269–70
  short-term 265–9
    and monetary policy 265–6
  and speculative demand for
    money 244–6
internal rate of return (IRR)
  estimation of 125–7
  and expectations for
    investment 129–31
international capital, in UK 180
International Monetary Fund
  (IMF) 168, 399
international trade 376–437
  balance of 379, 394–5
  and balance of payments
    392–400
  and current account 394–5,
    397
  and economic growth 179,
    378–9
  and European Monetary
    System (EMS) 409–17
  and exchange rates 382–3,
    400–9
  and exports 45–7
  flows and monetary policy 279
  and inflation 297–8
  in macroeconomic model
    45–7
  and open economy 417–24
  rationale for 380–3
  of United Kingdom 383–92
  intervention failure and
    Keynesian policies 344
inventories
  cut in UK 175
  see also capital stock
investment 104–41
  appraisal 119–27
  of banks 256–7
  behaviour
    influences on 127–31
    theory of 115–19
  and business confidence
    129–31
  and capital stock 104, 113,
    115, 116
  constraint in boom phase of
    business cycle 160
  defined 104–6
  and economic growth 172–3
  in economic recovery 159
  and effect of multiplier on
    consumption 95–6
  equilibrium growth rate of
    179–80
  and expectations 127–31
  fixed, forecasts 60
  indices of 113–14
  influences on 116
  and interest rates 119, 132
  international comparisons of
    110
  low levels of and inflation 297
  in macroeconomic model
    51–2
  in measurement of economic
    activity 11
  and national accounts 107–15
  and opportunity costs 117
  paradox of 177–80
  and recession in UK 154
  and short-termism 110–12
  over time 113
  trusts 235
  under- 109
  in United Kingdom 107
  volatility and business cycles
    156
investment expenditure 12–13
  assumptions of in
    macroeconomic model 37
  in fiscal policy 206
  and international trade 378–9
  in macroeconomic model
    37–8, 40–1, 43
  quality of and tax cuts 359
  and role of tax cuts in supply-side economics 358–9
  invisible trade in international
    trade 393–6
Italy
  GDP
    forecasted (1985–9) 59
    growth of 166–7, 169
  international trade and
    economic growth 179
  money aggregates 254

Japan
  consumer prices, rise in 295
  consumption expenditure and
    GDP 73–4
  current account position 398
  GDP 22
    forecasted (1985–9) 59
    growth of 166–7, 169
    growth, rates of 112
  government expenditure and
    GDP 188–9
  incremental capital:output
    ratio 174
  international trade and
    economic growth 179
  investment 108–9, 110
  money aggregates 254
  receipts and expenditure
    193–5
  trade balance with UK 391–2

Keynes, John Maynard and
  Keynesianism 60, 106
  and demand for money
    241–2, 245
  and fiscal policy
    context of 201–4
    principles of 216–17
  and managed business cycles
    203

labour
  assumptions of in
    macroeconomic model 37
  input, in macroeconomic
    model 44
  market and inflation 296–7,
    304–5
labour force, and NAIRU
  315–18
Laffer, Arthur and curve 344,
  349–50, 365
Lawson, Nigel 16, 144, 379
  and European Monetary
    System (EMS) 410, 413–15
  and inflation 295
  and interest rates and monetary
    policy 420
Layard, R. 316

legal tender 263
liabilities, UK banks 256–7
life assurance 235
'Life Cycle Hypothesis' and
  consumption 94
liquidity 255, 257
  and open market operations
    269, 271–2
  reserves for 258
local authority markets 236

M0 supply of money 248–51,
  253–4
  and monetary policy 278
M1 supply of money 247–51,
  253–4
M2 supply of money 248–51,
  253–4
M3 supply of money 248–51,
  253–4, 258, 262
M4 supply of money 248–51,
  253–4
M5 supply of money 248–51,
  253–4, 258, 262
macroeconomics
  defined 5–8
  model of 34–67
    equilibrium income,
      changes 51–2
    and equilibrium level of
      income 41–4
    first stage 36–41
    forecasting 54–63
    and government sector
      48–51
    and international trade
      45–7
    testing 52–4
managed exchange rates 404
  in open economy 417
manufacturing output, forecasts
  60
marginal flow of expenditure, and
  multiplier effect 98
marginal propensity to consume
  (MPC)
  and benefit payments 215–16
  and fiscal multipliers 211–12
  and income 78–82, 94
  and multiplier effect 97–100
  and savings 81–5
marginal propensity to save
  (MPS)
  and fiscal multipliers 212–13
  and paradox of investment
    178, 180
  and role of tax cuts in supply-
    side economics 358
markets
  competition, and supply-side

economics 348, 363
deregulation of 345–6
failure of and Keynesian
  policies 343–4
formal open 27–8
loans by banks 256–7
measures of money 247–51
  relationships between 249
merchant banks: see banks
minimum lending rate (MLR)
  265
mining and manufacturing,
  expenditure on 196–7
model
  of business cycle 156–64
  circular flow, and multiplier
    effect 97
  of consumption and income
    77–9
  of economic activity 8–16
    over time 144–6
  of economic growth 170–80
  of excess demand 300–1
  fiscal 204–9
    multipliers 209–16
  of induced cost-push inflation
    310, 314, 318
  of inflationary gap 302–3
  of investment 117–19, 131
    and expectations 129–30
  macroeconomic 34–67
    basic assumptions 36–7
    equilibrium in 42–4
    forecasting 54–63
    and government sector
      48–51
    income, equilibrium,
      changes 51–2
    and international trade
      45–7
    testing 52–4
  of money creation 259–63
  multiplier, fiscal 209–16
  of paradox of investment
    177–80
  of quantity theory of money
    326–30
Modigliani 94
monetarism 154, 168
  and enhancement of
    competition 352–7
  and inflation 325–31
  and quantity theory of money
    339–40
  and supply-side economics
    344
monetary management 276
monetary policy 263–86
  and Bank of England 263–5
  and control 278–9

and deflation with floating
  exchange rates 417–18
and interest rates 280–2
and money supply 265
problems of 276–9
and reflation
  with fixed exchange rates
    422–3
  with floating exchange rates
    418–19
side effects of 277–9
monetary repercussions in fiscal
  policy 229–30
money 233–86
  bonds and speculative demand
    for 243–5
  creation of 255–63
  definition of 237
  demand for 241–6
  illusion 312–13
  Keynesian view of and
    inflation 323–5
  markets 234–6
    and deregulation 353
  as medium of exchange 237
  multiplier 261–2
  and open market
    operations 269–71
  nature of 237–41
  quantity theory of 326–30
    and monetarism 339–40
  as standard of deferred
    payment 238
  as store of value 238
  supply of 246–55
    and balance of trade 330–1
    and credit 258–9
    and exports 330–1
    growth (1979–81) 118–19
    and quantity theory of
      326–30
    and reflation under monetary
      policy 418–19
    in supply-side economics
      361
  transmission mechanism
    330–1, 332–3
  as unit of measurement
    237–8
mortgage interest rates 292
multiplier
  and acceleration principle 140
  and business cycles 156
  and consumption 95–101
  credit 261–2
  fiscal 210, 212–13
  and income 100
  and investment in economic
    recovery 160
  money 261–2

and open market
  operations 269–71
and recession phase of business
  cycle 163
savings, effect of 98
taxation 213–14
Mundell, Robert 344

national accounts 17–25
  accuracy of 25
  circular flow model of 37
  and consumption expenditure
    71–6
  data on expenditure and
    taxation 187–99
  and economic growth 146
  investment 107–15
  value of measures for 25–9
National Bus Company,
  privatized 354
National Debt 263
national income 6
  and gross national product
    23–4
  in national accounts 18
National Institute of Economic
  Research 220, 334
National Insurance,
  contributions 190, 192, 198
National Loans Fund 263
National Savings scheme 235
natural state of unemployment
  315
net economic welfare 29
net present value (NVP)
  and expectations for
    investment 131
  and profit streams 123–6
  and role of tax cuts in supply-
    side economics 359
Netherlands
  consumer prices, rise in 295
  consumption expenditure and
    GDP 73–5
  current account position 398
  GDP 22
    growth of 166–9
  government expenditure and
    GDP 188–9
  incremental capital:output
    ratio 174–5
  investment 108–9, 110
  receipts and expenditure
    193–5
Nickel, S. 316
nominal exchange rates 406–7,
  414–15
  deflation and monetary policy
    418
  in open economy 417

stability of in European
  Monetary System 413
non-accelerating inflation rate of
  unemployment (NAIRU)
    315–18
  estimates of in OECD 316,
    318
Nordhaus 29
Norway, growth of GDP 166–7,
  169

official financing in international
  trade 394, 400
oil
  North Sea 153–4
  and growth, rates of 75
  OPEC
    price increases 152–3, 167
    and inflation 291
open economy, complications of
  417–24
open market operations
  by Bank of England 269–72
  and expansion of credit
    269–70
  and liquidity reserves 269,
    271–2
  and money multiplier 269–71
opportunity costs and
  investment 117
Organisation of Economic
  Cooperation and
  Development (OECD)
    and comparison of growth
      rates 165–7, 169
    consumer prices, rise in 292,
      295
    forecasting 57, 59, 60
    and fiscal policy 220
    investment 108, 110
    and monetarist policy 334
    and non-accelerating inflation
      rate of unemployment
      (NAIRU) 316
    projections for UK 175 6
output
  in measurement of economic
    activity 9
  potential
    in business cycles 148
    and role of tax cuts in supply-
      side economics 358
    and quantity theory of 326–30

Paish, F.W. 57
Paymaster General Account 263
payments
  in measurement of economic
    activity 9
  system: see money

pension funds 235
'Permanent Income Hypothesis'
  and consumption 94
personal sector capital
  formation 197
Phillips, A.W., and curve
    304–5, 308
  long run 319–20
  short run, break down 312,
    318, 322
  and supply-side economics
    351
plastic money 258
policy objectives, conflict between
  in fiscal policy 202
politicians and fiscal policy
  226
precautionary demand for
  money 241–2, 246
Prest, A.R. 217
price levels
  assumptions of in
    macroeconomic model 36–7
  and consumption 90
  quantity theory of 326–30
  and supply-side economics
    361–2
prices
  changes and GDP 26
  consumer, forecasted
    (1985–9) 58
  stability in fiscal policy
    201–2
private consumption, forecasted
  (1985–9) 58
private investment
  international comparisons 110
  United Kingdom 107
private sector borrowing and
  monetarist policy 332–3
privatization and
  enhancement of
    competition 353–5
producers goods in measurement
  of economic activity 12
production costs and international
  trade 382–3
productivity per unit of capital
  171
profit margins and international
  trade 382–3
profit stream
  discounted 122–3
  forecasts 121–2
  from investment 120–1
profitability of banks 255, 257
protectionism in international
  trade 380
public corporations
  investment 108

international comparisons 110
United Kingdom 107
public finance, and supply-side economics 344
public order, expenditure on 196–7
public sector borrowing and monetarist policy 332–3
public sector borrowing requirement (PSBR), defined 48
public services, expenditure on 196–7
purchasing power parity exchange rate 409

quantity theory of money 326–30
and monetarism 339–40

ratchet effect of consumption behaviour 93–4
ratchet principle of benefit payments 222
Reagan, Ronald 7, 60, 350
real exchange rates 406–7
recession
in business cycles 147, 150, 163–4
in UK 153–4
recovery
in business cycles 147–8
and business optimism 159
generated 157–64
in UK 153, 155
recreation and cultural affairs, expenditure on 196–7
reflation
fiscal
direct 205
with fixed exchange rates 421–2
indirect 206–9
and monetary policy 277
with fixed exchange rates 422–3
with floating exchange rates 418–19
rent 190
reserve assets of banks 273–4
reserve ratios of banks 273–4
resource allocation and inflation 297
retail price
index (RPI) 290–2
inflation, forecasts 60
retained output 12
retained profits
and investment 116–17

in supply-side economics 365
retrospective compensation in wage demands under inflation 313
Rumsfield, Donald 349

salaries 13
Samuelson, Paul 156
savings
and average propensity to consume 83, 85
and consumption 71–6, 82–5
increases in supply-side economics 365
in macroeconomic model 39
and marginal propensity to consume 81–5
in measurement of economic activity 10–11
and money 234
and multiplier effect 98
ratios and household wealth 91
Schwartz, Anna 325
self-interest and supply-side economics 362–3
short-term factors and consumption 91
short-termism in investment 110–12
side effects
of fiscal policy 228
in supply-side economics 367
Single European Market and deregulation 353
small businesses, promotion of startup and enhancement of competition 355–7
Smith, Adam 347, 356
social security
benefits 194–5
contributions 190
expenditure on 196–7
as transfer payments 191, 193
special deposits 274–5
supplementary 275
specialization in international trade 380–1
speculative demand for money 242
stabilizers and fiscal policy 223, 226
Stein, Herbert 344
sterling
and business cycles 144–5
exchange rates of 401–9
index, forecasts 60
rise in value of 14–16
stocks: see capital stock
subsidies 189, 190, 194

and GDP 18
substitution effect of taxation 364–5
supply, aggregate: see aggregate supply
supply-side economics 192, 343–75
assessment of 360–71
and efficiency 347–52
and enhancement of competition 352–7
potential weaknesses 364–7
and role of tax cuts in aggregate supply 357–60
Switzerland, growth of GDP 167

taxation
bracket creep 351
on capital 197–8
corporation 196–7
cuts
and government expenditure 211
role of in supply-side economics 357–60
direct 193–4
and consumption 86–9
and equilibrium income 88
and expectations for investment 130–1
on expenditure 190, 192, 196–7
in fiscal policy 206, 208
as flexible control 222
and GDP 18
and government expenditure in balanced budget theorem 214
in measurement of economic activity 13–14
and incentives in supply-side economics 348–52
on income 190, 192, 196–8
income effect of 364–5
indirect 194
in macroeconomic model 37, 49–50
in measurement of economic activity 11
multiplier 212–14
and national accounts in fiscal policy 187–99
progressive 192
regressive 192–3
social security 196–8
substitution effect of 364–5
and supply-side economics 344, 362
as transfer of income 191

Index   461

wedge effect in supply-side economics   349–50
technology
  changes and expectations for investment   130
  and unemployment in business cycles   143
Thatcher, Margaret   16, 144, 352–3
  and European Monetary System (EMS)   410, 414, 423
time lag/delay
  GDP response to money supply   327–8, 333
  and inflation   303–4
timing in fiscal policy   225
Tobin   29
total domestic expenditure (TDE)
  and consumption   71–4
  and international trade   397
  and investment   108
    international comparisons   110
    United Kingdom   107
trade-offs between inflation and unemployment   311–13, 320
transaction costs of bonds   243
transaction demand for money   241, 246
transactions, flow of   9–10
transfer payments   189, 191
  as social security   191, 193
transmission mechanism in money supply   330–1, 332–3
transport
  barriers to entry   353
  and communications, expenditure on   196–7
Transport Act (1980)   353
treasury bills   256–7
  and Bank of England   264
  and commercial bills   235
Trustee Savings Banks   235

unemployment
  and consumption   90
  forecasted   58, 60
  and inflation   311–23
  natural state of   315
  and recovery in business cycles   148, 153
  and technology in business cycles   143
unit trusts   235
United Kingdom
  balance of payments   394–6

balance of trade and inflation   324
bank balances (1988)   256
business cycle   149–52
  analysis of   152–6
  causes of   156–64
consumer prices, rise in   295
consumption expenditure and GDP   72, 74–5
depression in   169–70
economic forecasts (1985–9) 58, 60
enhancement of competition   352–7
and European Monetary System (EMS)   409–17
exchange rates   52–4
exports   383–4
  components of   382–3
GDP
  in 1986   50
  forecasts (1985–9)   59
  growth, rates of   112
government expenditure
  and GDP   187
  and taxation   196–7
growth
  rates compared   165–70
  recent   169
imports   154, 384
  penetration   387–91
incremental capital:output ratio   173–4
  rise in   175
index of inflation and consumer prices   291
interest rates and investment (1988–9)   132, 143
investment expenditure (1976–86)   107, 109
measures of money supply   251, 254
monetarist policies   334–5
money supply growth (1979–81)   118–19
and non-accelerating inflation rate of unemployment (NAIRU)   316
private investment   107
public corporations
  investment   107
  receipts and expenditure   190
savings ratios   83–5
tax cuts (1980s)   358–9
trade balance   384–9
trade flows   383–92

and volatility of investment   114–15
United States of America
  consumer prices, rise in   295
  consumption expenditure and GDP   73–4
  current account position   398
  GDP   22
    forecasted (1985–9)   59
    growth of   112, 166–7, 169
  government expenditure and GDP   188–9
  incremental capital:output ratio   174
  investment   108–9, 110
  money aggregates   254
  receipts and expenditure   193–5
  trade balance with UK   391
user costs of capital and investment   116–19
  in economic recovery   159

value added, in measurement of economic activity   10
Value Added Tax (VAT)   13
visible trade, in international trade   393–5
volatility
  and expectations for investment   129
  of investment   113–15

wage-push inflation   319–20
wages   13
Wanniski, Jude   344, 349
West Germany
  consumer prices, rise in   295
  consumption expenditure and GDP   73–4
  current account position   398
  exchange rates   405–6
  GDP   22
    forecasted (1985–9) 59
    growth of   166–7, 169
    growth, rates of   112
  government expenditure, and GDP   188–9
  incremental capital:output ratio   174–5
  international trade and economic growth   179
  investment   108, 110
  money aggregates   254
  receipts and expenditure   193–5